BARTOLUS

Frontispiece

GREAT JURISTS OF THE WORLD

EDITED BY

SIR JOHN MACDONELL
FELLOW OF THE BRITISH ACADEMY

AND

EDWARD MANSON
SECRETARY OF THE SOCIETY OF COMPARATIVE LEGISLATION

WITH AN INTRODUCTION BY

VAN VECHTEN VEEDER
JUDGE OF THE UNITED STATES DISTRICT COURT, NEW YORK

WITH PORTRAITS

THE LAWBOOK EXCHANGE, LTD.
Clark, New Jersey

ISBN: 9781886363281 (hardcover)
ISBN: 9781616190767 (paperback)

Lawbook Exchange edition 1997, 2011

The quality of this reprint is equivalent to the quality of the original work.

THE LAWBOOK EXCHANGE, LTD.
33 Terminal Avenue
Clark, New Jersey 07066-1321

Please see our website for a selection of our other publications and fine facsimile reprints of classic works of legal history:
www.lawbookexchange.com

Library of Congress Cataloging-in-Publication Data

Great jurists of the world / edited by Sir John MacDonell and Edward Manson; with an introductory by Van Vechten Veeder.
    p. cm.
  Originally published: Boston: Little, Brown, and Co., 1914.
  Includes bibliographical references and index.
  ISBN 1-886363-28-5 (alk. paper)
    1. Lawyers—Biography. 2. Law—History. I. MacDonell, John, Sir, 1846-1921. II. Manson, Edward, 1849-1919.
K170.G73 1997
340' .092'2—dc21
  [B]   97-8298
                                                        CIP

Printed in the United States of America on acid-free paper

THE CONTINENTAL LEGAL HISTORY SERIES
Published under the auspices of the
ASSOCIATION OF AMERICAN LAW SCHOOLS

GREAT JURISTS OF THE WORLD

EDITED BY

SIR JOHN MACDONELL

FELLOW OF THE BRITISH ACADEMY

AND

EDWARD MANSON

SECRETARY OF THE SOCIETY OF COMPARATIVE LEGISLATION

WITH AN INTRODUCTION BY

VAN VECHTEN VEEDER

JUDGE OF THE UNITED STATES DISTRICT COURT, NEW YORK

WITH PORTRAITS

BOSTON
LITTLE, BROWN, AND COMPANY
1914

EDITORIAL COMMITTEE

OF THE

ASSOCIATION OF AMERICAN LAW SCHOOLS

ERNST FREUND, Professor of Law in the University of Chicago.

ERNEST G. LORENZEN, Professor of Law in the University of Wisconsin.

WM. E. MIKELL, Professor of Law in the University of Pennsylvania.

MUNROE SMITH, Professor of Jurisprudence in Columbia University.

JOHN H. WIGMORE, *Chairman*, Professor of Law in Northwestern University.

LIST OF TRANSLATORS

THOMAS S. BELL, of the Los Angeles Bar.

JAMES W. GARNER, Professor in the State University of Illinois.

RAPELJE HOWELL, of the New York Bar.

JOHN LISLE, of the Philadelphia Bar.

ERNEST G. LORENZEN, of the Editorial Committee.

ROBERT W. MILLAR, of the Chicago Bar, Lecturer in Northwestern University.

FRANCIS S. PHILBRICK, of the New York Bar.

JOHN SIMPSON, of New York.

JOHN WALGREN, of the Chicago Bar.

JOHN H. WIGMORE, of the Editorial Committee.

I might instance in other professions the obligation men lie under of applying themselves to certain parts of History; and I can hardly forbear doing it in that of the Law, — in its nature the noblest and most beneficial to mankind, in its abuse and debasement the most sordid and the most pernicious. A lawyer now is nothing more (I speak of ninety-nine in a hundred at least), to use some of Tully's words, "nisi leguleius quidem cautus, et acutus praeco actionum, cantor formularum, auceps syllabarum." But there have been lawyers that were orators, philosophers, historians: there have been Bacons and Clarendons. There will be none such any more, till in some better age true ambition, or the love of fame, prevails over avarice; and till men find leisure and encouragement to prepare themselves for the exercise of this profession, by climbing up to the vantage ground (so my Lord Bacon calls it) of Science, instead of grovelling all their lives below, in a mean but gainful application of all the little arts of chicane. Till this happen, the profession of the law will scarce deserve to be ranked among the learned professions. And whenever it happens, one of the vantage grounds to which men must climb, is Metaphysical, and the other, Historical Knowledge. — HENRY ST. JOHN, Viscount BOLINGBROKE, *Letters on the Study of History* (1739).

Whoever brings a fruitful idea to any branch of knowledge, or rends the veil that seems to sever one portion from another, his name is written in the Book among the builders of the Temple. For an English lawyer it is hardly too much to say that the methods which Oxford invited Sir Henry Maine to demonstrate, in this chair of Historical and Comparative Jurisprudence, have revolutionised our legal history and largely transformed our current text-books. — Sir FREDERICK POLLOCK, Bart., *The History of Comparative Jurisprudence* (Farewell Lecture at the University of Oxford, 1903).

No piece of History is true when set apart to itself, divorced and isolated. It is part of an intricately pieced whole, and must needs be put in its place in the netted scheme of events, to receive its true color and estimation. We are all partners in a common undertaking, — the illumination of the thoughts and actions of men as associated in society, the life of the human spirit in this familiar theatre of coöperative effort in which we play, so changed from age to age, and yet so much the same throughout the hurrying centuries. The day for synthesis has come. No one of us can safely go forward without it. — WOODROW WILSON, *The Variety and Unity of History* (Address at the World's Congress of Arts and Science, St. Louis, 1904).

CONTINENTAL LEGAL HISTORY SERIES

GENERAL INTRODUCTION TO THE SERIES

"ALL history," said the lamented master Maitland, in a memorable epigram, "is but a seamless web; and he who endeavors to tell but a piece of it must feel that his first sentence tears the fabric."

This seamless web of our own legal history unites us inseparably to the history of Western and Southern Europe. Our main interest must naturally center on deciphering the pattern which lies directly before us, — that of the Anglo-American law. But in tracing the warp and woof of its structure we are brought inevitably into a larger field of vision. The story of Western Continental Law is made up, in the last analysis, of two great movements, racial and intellectual. One is the Germanic migrations, planting a solid growth of Germanic custom everywhere, from Danzig to Sicily, from London to Vienna. The other is the posthumous power of Roman law, forever resisting, struggling, and coalescing with the other. A thousand detailed combinations, of varied types, are developed, and a dozen distinct systems now survive in independence. But the result is that no one of them can be fully understood without surveying and tracing the whole.

Even insular England cannot escape from the web. For, in the first place, all its racial threads — Saxons, Danes, Normans — were but extensions of the same Germanic warp and woof that was making the law in France, Germany, Scandinavia, Netherlands, Austria, Switzerland, Northern Italy, and Spain. And, in the next place, its legal culture was never without some of the same intellectual influence of Roman law which was so thoroughly overspreading the Continental peoples. There is thus, on the one hand, scarcely a doctrine or rule in our own system which cannot be definitely and profitably traced back, in comparison, till we come to the point of divergence, where we once shared it in common with them. And, on the other hand, there is, during all the intervening centuries, a more or less constant juristic sociability (if it may be so called) between Anglo-American and Continental Law; and its reciprocal influences make the story one and inseparable. In short, there is a tangled common ancestry, racial or intellectual, for the law of all Western Europe and ourselves.

For the sake of legal science, this story should now become a familiar one to all who are studious to know the history of our own law. The time is ripe. During the last thirty years European scholars have placed the history of their law on the footing of modern critical and philosophical research. And to-day, among ourselves, we find a marked widening of view and a vigorous interest in the comparison of other peoples' legal institutions. To the satisfying of that interest in the present field, the only obstacle is the lack of adequate materials in the English language.

That the spirit of the times encourages and demands the study of Continental Legal History and all useful aids to it was pointed out in a memorial presented at the annual meeting of the Association of American Law Schools in August, 1909:

"The recent spread of interest in Comparative Law in general is notable. The Comparative Law Bureau of the American Bar Association; the Pan-American Scientific Congress; the American Institute of Criminal Law and Criminology; the Civic Federation Conference on Uniform Legislation; the International Congress of History; the libraries' accessions in foreign law, — the work of these and other movements touches at various points the bodies of Continental law. Such activities serve to remind us constantly that we have in English no histories of Continental law. To pay any attention at all to Continental law means that its history must be more or less considered. Each of these countries has its own legal system and its own legal history. Yet the law of the Continent was never so foreign to English as the English law was foreign to Continental jurisprudence. It is merely maintaining the best traditions of our own legal literature if we plead for a continued study of Continental legal history.

"We believe that a better acquaintance with the results of modern scholarship in that field will bring out new points of contact and throw new light upon the development of our own law. Moreover, the present-day movements for codification, and for the reconstruction of many departments of the law, make it highly desirable that our profession should be well informed as to the history of the nineteenth century on the Continent in its great measures of law reform and codification.

"For these reasons we believe that the thoughtful American lawyers and students should have at their disposal translations of some of the best works in Continental legal history."

And the following resolution was then adopted unanimously by the Association:

"That a committee of five be appointed, on Translations of Continental Legal History, with authority to arrange for the translation and publication of suitable works."

The Editorial Committee, then appointed, spent two years in studying the field, making selections, and arranging for translations. It resolved to treat the undertaking as a whole; and to co-ordinate the series as to (1) periods, (2) countries, and (3) topics, so as to give the most adequate survey within the space-limits available.

(1) As to *periods*, the Committee resolved to include modern times, as well as early and medieval periods; for in usefulness and importance they were not less imperative in their claim upon our attention. Each volume, then, was not to be merely a valuable torso, lacking important epochs of development; but was to exhibit the history from early to modern times.

(2) As to *countries*, the Committee fixed upon France, Germany, and Italy as the central fields, leaving the history in other countries to be touched so far as might be incidentally possible. Spain would have been included as a fourth; but no suitable book was in existence; the unanimous opinion of competent scholars is that a suitable history of Spanish law has not yet been written.

(3) As to *topics*, the Committee accepted the usual Continental divisions of Civil (or Private), Commercial, Criminal, Procedural, and Public Law, and endeavored to include all five. But to represent these five fields under each principal country would not only exceed the inevitable space-limits, but would also duplicate much common ground. Hence, the grouping of the individual volumes was arranged partly by topics and partly by countries, as follows:

Commercial Law, Criminal Law, Civil Procedure, and Criminal Procedure, were allotted each a volume; in this volume the basis was to be the general European history of early and medieval times, with special reference to one chief country (France or Germany) for the later periods, and with an excursus on another chief country. Then the Civil (or Private) Law of France and of Germany was given a volume each. To Italy was then given a volume covering all five parts of the field. For Public Law (the subject least related in history to our own), a volume was given to France, where the common starting point with England, and the later divergences, have unusual importance for the history of our courts and legal methods. Finally, three volumes were allotted to general surveys indispensable for viewing the connection of parts. Of these, an introductory volume deals with Sources, Literature, and General Movements, — in short, the external history of the law, as the Continentals call it (corresponding to the aspects covered by Book I of Sir F. Pollock and Professor F. W. Maitland's "History of the English Law before Edward I"); another sets forth the historic parts played by the great jurists; and a final volume analyzes the specific features, in the evolution of doctrine, common to all the modern systems.

Needless to say, a Series thus co-ordinated, and precisely suited for our own needs, was not easy to construct out of materials written by Continental scholars for Continental needs. The Committee hopes that due allowance will be made for the difficulties here encountered. But it is convinced that the ideal of a co-ordinated Series, which should collate and fairly cover the various fields as a connected whole, is a correct one; and the endeavor to achieve it will sufficiently explain the choice of the particular materials that have been used.

It remains to acknowledge the Committee's indebtedness to all those who have made this Series possible.

To numerous scholarly advisers in many European universities the Committee is indebted for valuable suggestions towards choice of the works to be translated. Fortified by this advice, the Committee is confident that the authors of these volumes represent the highest scholarship, the latest research, and the widest repute, among European legal historians. And here the Committee desires also to express its indebtedness to Elbert H. Gary, Esq., of New York City, for his ample provision of materials for legal science in the Gary Library of Continental Law (in Northwestern University). In the researches of preparation for this Series, those materials were found indispensable.

To the authors the Committee is grateful for their willing co-operation in allowing this use of their works. Without exception, their consent has been cheerfully accorded in the interest of legal science.

To the publishers the Committee expresses its appreciation for the cordial interest shown in a class of literature so important to the higher interests of the profession.

To the translators, the Committee acknowledges a particular gratitude. The accomplishments, legal and linguistic, needed for a task of this sort are indeed exacting; and suitable translators are here no less needful and no more numerous than suitable authors. The Committee, on behalf of our profession, acknowledges to them a special debt for their cordial services on behalf of legal science, and commends them to the readers of these volumes with the reminder that without their labors this Series would have been a fruitless dream.

So the Committee, satisfied with the privilege of having introduced these authors and their translators to the public, retires from the scene, bespeaking for the Series the interest of lawyers and historians alike.

THE EDITORIAL COMMITTEE.

GREAT JURISTS OF THE WORLD

CONTENTS

	PAGE
EDITORIAL COMMITTEE AND LIST OF TRANSLATORS	v
GENERAL INTRODUCTION TO THE CONTINENTAL LEGAL HISTORY SERIES	ix
EDITORIAL PREFACE. BY SIR JOHN MACDONELL	xxi
INTRODUCTION. BY VAN VECHTEN VEEDER	xxvii

GAIUS. BY JAMES CRAWFORD LEDLIE	1
PAPINIAN. BY E. C. CLARK	17
DOMITIUS ULPIAN. BY JAMES CRAWFORD LEDLIE	32
BARTOLUS. BY THE LATE SIR WILLIAM RATTIGAN	45
ANDREA ALCIATI AND HIS PREDECESSORS. BY COLEMAN PHILLIPSON	58
JACQUES CUJAS. BY COLEMAN PHILLIPSON	83
ALBERICUS GENTILIS. BY COLEMAN PHILLIPSON	109
FRANCIS BACON, BARON VERULAM. BY JAMES E. G. DE MONTMORENCY	144
HUGO GROTIUS. BY THE LATE SIR WILLIAM RATTIGAN	169
JOHN SELDEN. BY EDWARD MANSON	185
THOMAS HOBBES. BY JAMES E. G. DE MONTMORENCY	195
RICHARD ZOUCHE. BY COLEMAN PHILLIPSON	220
JEAN BAPTISTE COLBERT. BY H. A. DE COLYAR	248
GOTTFRIED WILHELM VON LEIBNITZ. BY SIR JOHN MACDONELL	283
SAMUEL VON PUFENDORF. BY COLEMAN PHILLIPSON	305
GIOVANNI BATTISTA VICO. BY MICHAEL RAFFERTY	345

	PAGE
CORNELIUS VAN BYNKERSHOEK. By Coleman Phillipson	390
CHARLES LOUIS DE SECONDAT, Baron de la Brède et de MONTESQUIEU. By Sir Courtenay Ilbert	417
ROBERT JOSEPH POTHIER. By James E. G. de Montmorency	447
EMERICH DE VATTEL. By Coleman Phillipson	477
CÆSAR BONESANA, Marquis di BECCARIA. By T. Bridgwater	505
WILLIAM SCOTT, Lord STOWELL. By Norman Bentwick	517
JEREMY BENTHAM. By John Maxcy Zane	532
CARL JOSEPH ANTON MITTERMAIER. By Levin Goldschmidt	544
FRIEDRICH CARL von SAVIGNY. By James E. G. de Montmorency	561
RUDOLPH von IHERING. By Sir John Macdonell	590
INDEX	601

LIST OF ILLUSTRATIONS

BARTOLUS	*Frontispiece*
	TO FACE PAGE
ALCIATI	58
CUJAS	83
BACON	144
GROTIUS	169
SELDEN	185
HOBBES	195
COLBERT	248
LEIBNITZ	283
PUFENDORF	305
BYNKERSHOEK	390
MONTESQUIEU	416
POTHIER	447
BECCARIA	505
STOWELL	517
BENTHAM	532
MITTERMAIER	544
SAVIGNY	560
IHERING	590

EDITORIAL PREFACE

In his *Nova Methodus discendæ docendæque Jurisprudentiæ* Leibnitz describes a catalogue of *Desiderata*, and mentions among them the publication of lives of the great jurists.[1] More than two centuries have passed without the suggestion bearing fruit. Only Leibnitz, with his encyclopædic knowledge, could have adequately carried out his proposal; but it appeared to me that an attempt might be made by several writers to give effect in some form to the long-neglected suggestion. The result was this book, most of the contents of which appeared in a series of articles published in the *Journal of Comparative Legislation*.

I have been asked to add to this collection of lives of eminent jurists a brief introduction or prefatory note. Perhaps no preface is needed; the book explains and, I hope, justifies itself. I do not claim that it carries out strictly a precise plan. Each writer has been, within certain wide limits, free to deal with his subject as he deemed fit, and in his own way; each is, consequently, responsible for his own contribution. Complete unity in the mode of treatment there is not. Not only the lives of the jurists, but their chief works are described; and the book, though not a history of jurisprudence, may be a help to a description of the great movements of jurisprudence which form no small part of the life of every people.

Some of the biographies are based upon materials either new or little used; none of them are mere summaries of existing works. Not a few points of importance are for the first time elucidated. I might refer, for example, to the lives of Gaius, Papinian, Alciati, Cujas, Hobbes, and Bacon. It has been usual in writing the history of jurisprudence to omit the jurists. The book will have fulfilled one of its purposes if it helps somewhat to correct the habit of describing doctrines apart from their historical setting and the time in which their expounders lived. The *Zeitgeist* is

---

[1] Dutens, Opera, iv., 217. Leibnitz's *Desiderata* were to some extent suggested by Bacon's *Desiderata* mentioned in the *Increase of Learning*.

much; so also is the personality of jurists. We know how particular judges in our own times have influenced the development of certain branches of law. That is true of the past. The development of English law would not have been the same as it has been if there had been no Coke or Mansfield, or if Bacon instead of the former, Buller instead of the latter, had at momentous periods presided over the King's Bench. To know what manner of man was Cujas, or Grotius, or Ihering, is a help to understand his teaching.

The volume, beginning with Gaius and Papinian, and ending with Ihering, ranges over a period of nearly two thousand years, and the collection includes accounts of the representatives of four great periods of jurisprudence: (1) The period in which Roman law was fully developed; (2) that in which it was regarded as the common law of Continental countries; (3) the period of the supremacy of natural law in its many forms; (4) the age of codes and legislation.

The collection includes jurists who were innovators, such as Grotius; distinguished practising lawyers, such as Zouche and Bynkershoek; reformers, such as Mittermaier and Bentham; philosophic jurists, such as Leibnitz and Vico. Many jurists of influence and importance are necessarily omitted for lack of space; but the omissions may some day be supplied in an additional volume. My hope would be that, supplemented by a brief narrative connecting the various lives, this book would form the outlines of a history of jurisprudence. As it is, it attempts to do what has not been done before.

The volume tells of a score of men of different ages who looked at jurisprudence from different points of view, and had very different conceptions of its provisions. Some readers, noting these differences, and observing the contrast between the lofty pretensions of the earlier jurists and those of the modern, will perhaps ask the question: "Is the history of jurisprudence in substance a history of disillusion? Has it any lesson to communicate? Has it outlived its work? Have we got much beyond the opening words of the *Institutes:* 'Juris præcepta sunt hæc: honeste vivere, alterum non lædere, suum cuique tribuere'?" Compare the definition of Ulpian with that, say, of Austin, and we see a remarkable change. Perhaps the jurist who once held a place second only to that of the theologian must retire with the latter to a lower position. Jurisprudence cannot in a literal sense be "divinarum atque humanarum rerum notitia, justi atque injusti scientia." Some may think it merits the gibes of Mephistopheles in *Faust*.[1]

Jurists cannot again occupy the position enjoyed by Bartolus and Cujas, to the former of whom was given the privilege that he and his descendants who were professors of law should "have the power of legitimizing their pupils in case of bastardy or of relieving them from the disabilities of minority" (p. 50). Their teaching cannot, for many reasons, be what it once was. Their functions have changed and are changing, and in these ways among others: in the first place there is a division of matters once dealt with under jurisprudence.[2] It is no longer, after the manner of Leibnitz and Vico, inextricably mixed with ethics and philosophy. The latter taught *tutto scibile*, and called it jurisprudence. He made it a reproach that Grotius had severed jurisprudence from theology. Modern jurisprudence is secularized—*i.e.*, separated from theology, and to a certain extent from ethics. Then, too—and it is the second great change—the wide extent and activity of legislation have narrowed the field of the jurist. Where he was permitted to be a sub-legislator he is reduced to the position of an interpreter—often an interpreter working in fetters—subject always to this: that if the legislature has the power, the jurist has, as to much, the knowledge.

There is a further class of changes in operation. Jurisprudence has to adjust itself to psychology; by which I mean that all the roots of law have to be investigated, and not, as in the past, only a few; that its origin is not to be found solely or perhaps chiefly in the commands of a superior; that we must look to the motives which urge people without pressure to adopt certain rules and to carry them out, and note the impulse of the civilised man to conform to law and order. Further, jurisprudence must adjust itself to sociology; no purely legal analysis of social relations is complete; they are not wholly explicable by juristic methods or to be all included in juristic categories, such as contracts, express or implied.[3] Society consists of men living together and co-operating in many ways and from many motives, selfish and sympathetic, with ties ethical, economic, traditional; and sociology, not jurisprudence, must give the explanation of this

---

[1] See Kirchmann's *Kritik der Rechtswissenschaft*, 568.
[2] Wundt, *Logik*, iii. 1.   [3] Wundt, *Logik*, iii. 533.

consensus and harmony. The former science (if such it be at present) may help us to explain how all the social forces are connected and co-operate.

Jurisprudence has also to tell that which until lately, owing to the absence of the necessary data, was wrapt in obscurity—the process of evolution of law. It must explain the various stages through which law passes—*e.g.*, continue the work of Maine, Bastian, and Post; the stage in which symbolism is universal; that in which form and the letter are all powerful; the stage at which law is in the main customary.[1] It must explain the separation of jurisprudence from religion and ethics, and their true relation; it must show how international law was no happy accident or clever invention, but an inevitable growth.

A further difficult task awaits the jurist. Several legal categories and conceptions must be reshaped to meet new facts and new ideas. Thus, the conception of property is no longer what it was. It is subject to many new limitations—so many in the case of land that one may say that the rights of the first occupier and those acquired through him are now everywhere limited by the rights of the last-comer.[2] The jurist is called upon to define, if he can, "a fair rent," "a fair wage," "a minimum wage," and "a reasonable length of working day." Read the test of monopolies which, according to English common law, are lawful as distinguished from those which, being unreasonably in restraint of trade, are unlawful; then turn to an analysis in a modern book of political economy of the various forms of monopoly and their detrimental and beneficial effects, and it will be seen that the jurist is working with antiquated definitions. Jurisprudence has to find a firmer basis for criminal law, a more satisfactory theory of punishment, a better definition of such kinds of insanity as are incompatible with responsibility. Here, too, the jurist is working with obsolete or imperfect tools.

The latest form of social order is not necessarily the final or the best, and the jurist has to help in the process of transition and reconstruction. He has spoken much of the past; he is now called upon to solve problems hitherto unknown.

Even as to the humble function of interpretation of enactments a change seems imminent, and jurists must carry it out. The

---

[1] See as to the domination of forms, Ihering, *Geist des römischen, Rechts*, ii. 470.

[2] The expression is used by Fouillée, *La propriété sociale*, p. 15.

rules of construction employed by English lawyers and those of Continental lawyers for ascertaining the intention of the legislature—the former keeping to the letter of the statute, and applying certain technical rules; the latter seeking light in collateral documents or proceedings at which the former would not look—cannot both be right, and one day a choice must be made.[1]

Still the great task of jurists remains what it was — to help, with the assistance of ethics, to answer, when the law is silent or ambiguous, the question: "What is justice?" That answer cannot be expressed in terms of power or volition. The conscience of man, working in ever-changing circumstances, demands another solution—a demand which cannot be explained away.

At all times there exists a sense of justice which approves of some kinds of legislation and condemns others, which seeks to create a *Rechtsordnung*. In some societies and at certain times it is more exigent than at others. It does not always speak alike, but at all times it has to be reckoned with. A law which condemned the accused without hearing him, which took away property from one person and gave it to another selected capriciously, or which made laws retrospective—such a measure might conform to all statutory requirements; it would not seem the less unjust. Out of astrology grew astronomy; out of alchemy, chemistry; in the false conception of a universal immutable law may be the root of a new form of jurisprudence. There is a sense in which Ulpian's famous description of natural law may still be true.[2]

Regarding "the great jurists of the world" as all engaged, each in his own way and time, in one task, we see in the different persons whose lives are told in this volume a certain unity of purpose carried on for nearly two thousand years, to be continued while men distinguish between good and evil.

JOHN MACDONELL.

[1] There is said to be a tendency to adopt English methods (Gény, *Méthode d'interprétation*, p. 257).
[2] See Mr. Ledlie's *Life of Ulpian;* also Rümelin, *Reden*, Neue Folge, 337; Stammler, *Die Kultur der Gegenwart*, 2. viii., p. xliii.

INTRODUCTION

A SURVEY of the course of development of European jurisprudence necessarily presents methods and points of view somewhat remote from Anglo-American experience. This selection of great jurists of the world has been made with particular reference to international repute. But an international reputation as a jurist does not necessarily signify a conspicuous influence upon the actual development of any national system of law, and a selection made on such a basis passes over jurists who, upon all other grounds, are unquestionably pre-eminent. Lord Mansfield was one of the greatest jurists known to legal history, although his influence was exclusively national. The selection may also seem to lend undue prominence to doctrinal and institutional writers as compared with jurists whose distinction was attained in the practical administration of justice. In countries where the formulation of legal principles has been mainly the work of judges, and largely embodied in judicial opinions, the conspicuous type of jurist is the judge. On the continent of Europe, however, legal development took another course, and legal literature, systematically pursued as a branch of University study, obtained a direct and controlling influence upon the decisions of the courts.

In jurisprudence, as in theology, all roads lead to Rome. The imposing fabric of Roman law received the impress of those qualities which have given it such enduring vitality during the early period of the Empire, when the Roman jurists were at once the makers, the expounders, and the administrators of law for the civilized world. Roman civil law had already been liberalized and vitalized by the *jus gentium*. The appointment of a *prætor peregrinus* in 246 B.C. was designed to mitigate the exclusiveness of the *jus civile;* it established a law for the alien, as such. But in the course of time the prætorian edict changed the form and spirit of the *jus civile* itself. Being in fact only that part of the Roman law which was in accord with the private law of other peoples, the *jus gentium* came to be regarded as the universal law of mankind, resting upon the nature of things and the general sense of equity which obtains among all men. The jurists who carried on the development of Roman law in succession to the prætorian edict had always occupied a unique position. While they gave advice to those who chose to consult them, and delivered opinions on the issues involved in pending litigation, they neither prepared nor argued cases, and they served without compensation. Controversies were decided at Rome by private citizens called *judices*, who were instructed in the law by the jurists, as jurors are instructed by judges in our tribunals. When at length the Emperor conferred upon certain jurists the right of responding, these authorized jurists approached nearly to the functions of a modern judge. Still, although jurists occasionally acted as *judices*, their influence, prior to the second century, was indirect. With the establishment of a supreme court of appellate jurisdiction in the Imperial Auditory in the second century, jurists designated by the Emperor to act in his name performed the duties of a judge in the modern sense. The resulting juristic literature continued to exert a controlling influence upon the development of the law until the Emperors began to interfere with the general effect of rescripts issued in particular cases. The last vestige of respect for judicial precedent was destroyed by Justinian's enactment that no judge should consider himself bound to follow any decision which he believed to be erroneous, for, it was announced, justice must be administered according to law, not according to examples.

The final form of Roman legislation, which gave to the civil law the shape in which it descended to the modern world, was the imperial ordinance. The number of *leges* and *senatus consulta* was slight in comparison with the surviving body of law enacted by the Emperor as decisions or opinions in particular cases, as instructions to officials, and as public ordinances or proclamations. These vast legislative and judicial functions were discharged mainly by a council, called in Diocletian's time the *Consistorium*, composed largely of jurists, who acted as assessors to the Emperor in the hearing of causes and advised him in legislation.

For centuries after the death of Justinian the *Corpus Juris* was almost lost to sight. Of the Gothic codes, which borrowed much of Roman law, but neglected its real spirit as found in the *Digest*, Alaric's *Breviary* alone exerted wide influence. In the twelfth century the study of Roman law was revived by Irnerius. The Glossators aimed to explain difficult passages, and their work, as collected by Accursius in 1260, constituted the staple of legal learning for centuries. The Glossators were animated by the belief in authority characteristic of the Middle Ages, and their work is therefore without historical perspective; but they rendered a service of great value in collecting and preserving the text of the great monuments of Roman law.

The post-Glossators, or Bartolists, applied to the law the methods of the Schoolmen, developing the comparatively simple methods of their predecessors into a highly artificial system. While they contributed little of importance to the knowledge of Roman law, they undoubtedly aided in adapting it to a later age. To Alciati and Cujas we are indebted for the methodical presentation of Roman law as a portion of classical antiquity. By directing their attention to the sources, and studying them in their historical perspective, they contributed materially to a real understanding of the subject. The influence of Alciati and Cujas in the direction of historical and positive jurisprudence soon gave way, however, to the philosophical conception of natural law.

Natural law is the term applied to the Stoic conception of Nature as the embodiment of universal law. The development of the *jus gentium* brought Roman jurists in contact with Greek philosophy, and when at length, under Roman dominion, universal law and universal citizenship became established facts, there was a close approach in actual conditions to the Stoic theory. The conception of a law of Nature common to all men became a real influence in the hands of Papinian and Ulpian, whose opinions had the force of law throughout the civilized world. But in comparison with the practical aim of the Roman jurists the philosophical implication was vague. In the Institutes *jus naturale*, as used by Ulpian, means the elementary instincts common to man and animals; in another passage it is identified with the *jus gentium*, although elsewhere the two are contrasted. The jurists generally mean by *jus naturale*, not a positive law or custom, but a conception of ideal justice with which positive law should approximately harmonize. Its influence upon the civil law was, therefore, not so much in supplying specific principles of adjudication as in the direction of simplifying and harmonizing those principles. It was not regarded as something superior to the *jus civile*, for it was founded upon the *jus gentium* and became valid and effective only when adopted as part of the *jus civile*.

When, about the middle of the sixteenth century, the whole western part of continental Europe recognized Roman law, conditions were again favourable to the philosophical doctrine of natural law. The prevalence and power of Roman law was not derived from the sanction of any distinct authority. It was a common groundwork of ideas and method, standing towards the positive law of particular countries somewhat in the same relation as the Roman doctrine of *jus gentium* to *jus civile*; for, although Roman law was said to be the common law of the Empire, its actual application was subject to modification by the custom of the country. This supremacy of Roman law, not as a system actually in force, but as a type assumed by actual systems as their exemplar, although without correspondence in detail to any of them, inevitably led to reasoning from an ideal fitness of things and to the depreciation of positive authority. At length the distinction between positive law and theoretical rules evolved from assumed principles was almost lost to sight, and the idea, always latent in the theory, that human law which is not in harmony with natural law is of no authority was ultimately employed in support of revolution.

A positive conception of natural law, as distinguished from the purely negative conception of natural right, involves some demonstrable and authoritative source. The Stoics and the ancients generally derived natural law from the universal nature, Aquinas and the mediæval theologians from the Divine nature, Kant and other modern philosophers from human nature. Modern thought has rejected these bases, but the term survives. The fundamental idea which underlies the variety and apparent diversity of the applications of natural law is doubtless that of conformity with the nature of man as a rational and social being. This principle, which is the justification of every form of positive law, is fully recognized in English law under the name of reason.

The process of constructing a system of jurisprudence which ought to be in force everywhere, but was not necessarily so anywhere, was most fruitful when applied to a subject like international law, which had no existing positive law. Finding that large parts of the field of international relations were not covered by existing custom, Grotius and his successors, seeking a basis for a system of international law, recurred to the law of nature as a law grounded in reason and valid for all mankind.

Meanwhile, an entirely independent system of law had developed in England along lines which had nothing in common with Continental methods. In England, the early development of a strong central authority impressed the law with a distinctive form and character. From an early time a powerful legislature made statutes binding on the whole realm, and the judgments of the King's judges were accepted not only as a decision of the case in hand, but as a declaration of the law. Hence, English law was eminently national, positive, and practical. Juristic speculation hardly existed in England before Bentham. Such approaches to it as might be discovered in the earlier literature belong rather to political theory than to jurisprudence proper, and even in the domain of public law reliance was placed upon precedents rather than upon abstract principles. The practical maxim that the test of law is to be found in its recognition by the courts coloured English juristic philosophy, and limited the conception of law to a definite set of rules administered by tangible authorities. The English school of jurisprudence, as stated by Hobbes and applied by Bentham and Austin, is the direct descendant of the empiricism of Bacon.

The historical theory of law formulated by Savigny was one of the results of the reaction against the French Revolution. In opposition to the revolutionary tendencies of the natural law theory it set up, not the will of the sovereign, but the authority of the past. Law is not made consciously; it is a growth, a creation of the collective national mind, interwoven with the national life and character, and is no more the creation of an arbitrary will than language or religion. With the historical jurists the type of law is custom, and historical continuity is an essential condition of healthy growth. The historical theory also represents a reaction against the analytical school, which regards legislation as the normal source of law.

Later jurists, under the leadership of Ihering, have attempted a synthesis of the foregoing theories, at the same time pointing to the merits of a comparative method. Law is the product of conscious and increasingly determinate human will. While it is undoubtedly an historical phenomenon, it is by no means exclusively a national product. Its history, like that of civilization in general, is a history of borrowings and assimilation. The justification of law as a human institution is expediency. Law is made for society, and must meet its actual needs.

The prevalence at a given time of one or another school of jurisprudence is the outcome of historical conditions. But conditions change, and theories once regarded as final are found to be illusory or inadequate. Each of the theories of law—the philosophical, the analytical, the historical, the comparative—embodies a partial truth, and, as methods, each is in its place legitimate and necessary. All methods were used to some extent by the Romans without the formulation of any theory. Long ago Bacon pointed out the danger from merely scholastic conceptions of law. On the other hand, a merely practical attention degrades the science into a dry and unfruitful routine. The study of the philosophical and ethical foundations of law is of vital importance, but the ideal should be pursued, not as an abstraction leading to empty generalities, but for the purpose of realizing it in practice. The illuminating effect of the historical method is well shown in some of the judicial opinions of the late Lord Bowen, but in other hands it too often leads to mere antiquarianism. The analytical method is essential to all clear juristic thinking, yet, pursued to the exclusion of other points of view, it begets abstract and mechanical formalism. The maintenance of general principles is essential to the uniformity, certainty, and impartiality of the administration of justice, but logical deduction from established rules is not always adequate to meet changed conditions. The rigidity and formalism which constitute the greatest defects of a system of case law can only be overcome by constant reconsideration of principles with reference to the ends subserved. Legal conceptions should be regarded as working hypotheses rather than as final truths.

VAN VECHTEN VEEDER.

THE
GREAT JURISTS OF THE WORLD

GAIUS

IF the traveller in Northern Italy should feel a wish to escape for a moment from the atmosphere of ever-expectant attention that besets the eager sightseer on every side, he may, if he choose, have his way when he comes to Verona. Quitting the Cathedral by the west entrance, he may cross the little Piazza del Duomo to the Palazzo dei Canonici, the home of the Chapter library—a modest enough home, for all its grand name—and there, if he likes, he may leave the glare and noise of the streets, and the pushfulness of touts, behind him, and pass for a while into the dim, peaceful sanctum of scholarship. He will be received with kindly dignity by the courteous librarian—he will probably be the only visitor—and, on stating his wish to see the palimpsest of Gaius, he will be shown, without further ado—it lies ready to hand—a strange-looking, time-stained, much-mauled bit of parchment. This curious document, with its words (a great many of them contractions) all joined together and innocent of punctuation, will probably convey little meaning to him, unless he happens to be an expert palæographer. Nevertheless, it has a strange, eventful history to tell, and our traveller might do worse than listen for a few moments to its story in the peace of the old library, while without, on the one side, the sounds of the modern town's life pass muffled by, and on the other, not many yards away, the Adige—Virgil's "Athesis amœnus"—rushes joyously on its impetuous course, just as it did some 1,750 years ago, when Gaius wrote law-books and taught law (we know not where), and when, some 300 years later, an industrious scribe made (we know not where) this copy of Gaius's most widely known work.

Who, then, was Gaius? We know next to nothing about him personally. Where data are few, guesses are many. The very dearth of our information has produced an overwhelming volume of literature, a perfect riot of conjecture. We do not even know his name, or his birthplace, or where he lived. Was Gaius his nomen, or his cognomen, or merely his praenomen? The last is the most generally accepted view, but authorities have been found to champion each of the other alternatives. And if "Gaius" was a praenomen, what was his complete name, and how came he to be universally called by his praenomen only? Here, again, the guesses are numerous, and some of them utterly fantastic. Among the names proposed are Gaius Pomponius, Titus Gaius, Gaius Bassus, Gaius Noster (as though "noster" were a proper name), Gaius Laelius Felix. Another conjecture is that his full name was C. Cassius Longinus, and that he was identical with the famous lawyer of that name who was Consul in A.D. 30, and succeeded Masurius Sabinus in the leadership of the Sabinian, or Cassian, school. In support of this theory it is pointed out that Gaius was admittedly a prominent adherent of the school mentioned, and, further, that of the only four passages in the Digest in which an author is cited simply by the name of "Gaius," three—one (Dig. 24, 3, 59) from Julian, and two (Dig. 35, 1, 54, and 46, 3, 78) from Julian's "praeceptor," Javolenus—refer almost certainly to C. Cassius Longinus, while the fourth (from Pomponius, Dig. 45, 3, 39) probably does so too.[1] From this it is argued that Gaius must have been the short name by which C. Cassius Longinus was generally known in the profession. This theory, however, cannot be reconciled with the evidence furnished by Gaius's works as to the dates at which he lived. From that evidence it is abundantly clear that the author of the Institutes must have lived much later than A.D. 30. In order to get over this difficulty, it has been suggested that our Gaius, if not identical with the leader of the Cassiani, was, at any rate, a descendant and namesake of his. But this theory is little more than a random guess, and is merely an attempt to explain why Gaius was called by his praenomen only—the idea, apparently, being that he was

[1] There is still some doubt (assuming C. Cassius Longinus and our Gaius to be different persons) to which of the two writers Pomponius's "Gaius noster," in Dig. 45, 3, 39, refers (see Roby, *Introduction to the Study of Justinian's Digest*, p. clxxv; Muirhead, *Roman Law*, second edition, p. 301, note 6).

so called for short, in order to distinguish him from his supposed ancestor. Huschke has conjectured that Gaius may have been one of two jurists bearing the same nomen and cognomen, and differing only in their prænomen, and that, in order to differentiate them, it became customary to call our Gaius by his prænomen. He offers, however, no surmise as to who Gaius's mysterious namesake may have been. Dernburg has put forward a theory that Gaius was simply an affectionate nickname given by students to a popular lecturer, and that the name stuck to him ever after, both among members of the legal profession and in the book trade. Other writers, abandoning the search for the full name, have turned the single name to account in support of some theory concerning his personal history. Plain Gaius, it is said, must have been a man of humble position—a freedman, perhaps; certainly he could not have held any important office. Mommsen uses the single name as an argument for his view (below, p. 5) that Gaius was a Greek provincial, the practice of calling a man by his prænomen being peculiar to Greek districts. The mystery is still further deepened by the curious fact—one of the many curious facts in the story of Gaius—that (apart from the doubtful passage from Pomponius in Dig. 45, 3, 39, above referred to) not a single mention of his name occurs in any legal writer or historian, whether contemporary or other, during a period of some 250 years from his death—not even in Ulpian's *Liber singularis regularum*, where the resemblances with Gaius's works are numerous, and where one would naturally have expected some allusions to the earlier writer. And yet, during those 250 years, Gaius's literary reputation was steadily on the increase, and his name was becoming a household word wherever law was taught. Diomedes the grammarian, indeed, who lived towards the close of the fourth century, mentions him once; but, as far as the law is concerned, the earliest references to him occur in Valentinian III.'s *Law of Citations*, of A.D. 426 (see below, p. 8), and in the *Mosaicarum et Romanarum Legum Collatio*.[1] Nowhere, however, is he spoken of otherwise than as "Gaius," and the riddle of his full name (if he had one) remains unsolved.[2]

[1] The date of the *Collatio* is uncertain. Huschke assigns it to the end of the fourth century; others think that it was later than the Law of Citations. Tit. xvi. 2 of the *Collatio* contains an extract from Gaius's Institutes (book iii., 1-17).
[2] On the whole question, see Professor Goudy's Appendix to the second edition of Muirhead's *Roman Law*, pp. 431-3.

When we come to the question of Gaius's dates, we are on much firmer ground. The evidence on this point is almost entirely derived from his extant writings — his Institutes, and the excerpts from his other works in the Digest—but, such as it is, it is sufficient to produce substantial agreement among the authorities. We are able, for example, to infer from a passage in his book on Trusts, which is preserved to us in Dig. 34, 5, 7, pr.—"nostra quidem ætate Serapias, Alexandrina mulier, ad divum Hadrianum perducta est cum quinque liberis quos uno fetu enixa est"—that he lived in the reign of Hadrian, and that at the time when this passage was written Hadrian was probably no longer alive, it being the general, though not the invariable, practice of Gaius to prefix the word *divus* to the names of deceased Emperors only, and to describe a living ruler (if he gave him any adjective at all) by some such term as *optimus* or *sacratissimus*. We derive much assistance, again, from the various references in Gaius to contemporary senatusconsulta and Imperial laws, the dates of which we are able to determine from other sources. And whenever Gaius, in dealing *in extenso* with a particular subject, fails to mention a recent alteration in the law—*e.g.* in his discussion of the law of *cretio* in Institutes ii. 177, he makes no mention of the change by Marcus Aurelius referred to in Ulpian's *Fragmenta* (xxii. 34)—we have some reason for assuming that the alteration was made too late for him to take it into account. Of course, such facts as the absence of any reference in the Institutes to well-known enactments like the Senatusconsultum Tertullianum, Vellæanum, or Macedonianum, can be explained on other grounds, and, in any event, allowance has always to be made for the many lacunæ which still, unfortunately, mar the text of the Institutes. But, on the whole, the evidence for fixing Gaius's dates is fairly satisfactory, and, accordingly, it is generally held that he lived in the reigns of Hadrian (A.D. 117-138), Antoninus Pius (A.D. 138-161), and Marcus Aurelius (A.D. 161-180)[2];

---

[1] One of these lacunæ occurs in the very part of the manuscript where a discussion of the SC[um] Tertullianum might have been expected. The absence of any notice of these senatusconsulta and of other matters of importance to students, such as commodatum, depositum, pignus, dos, is pointed to by Dernburg as evidence in favour of his theory that the Institutes were not published as a complete book, but were merely a collection of notes for lectures (*Die Institutionen des Gaius ein Kollegienheft aus dem Jahre 161 nach Christi Geburt*).

[2] It is doubtful whether he survived into the reign of Commodus. A.D. 180 is the last date traceable in his life.

that is, in the Golden Age of the Roman Empire, the age when its material prosperity and the efficiency of its administration were at their highest, and when the rapid growth and spread of Greek influences—which, as Huschke says, borrowing a simile from Cicero, from a *tenuis rivulus* had become an *abundantissimus amnis*—had produced a remarkable rise in the level of general culture, and a keen interest in art, poetry, and philosophy. Within the domain of law, the age in question covers a period of the most brilliant and fruitful literary activity that the world has ever seen. Midway in this period stands Gaius. The great names of Celsus, Africanus, Pomponius, and, above all, Salvius Julianus (the last jurist cited by Gaius), already belong to the past. The bearers of still more illustrious names—Papinian, Ulpian, Paul—had yet to come.

The next question—the question where Gaius lived, and what his precise vocation was—raises difficulties of a formidable kind. There are two main theories in the field, associated with the honoured names of Theodor Mommsen and Eduard Huschke respectively,[1] and each of these theories has its variations in matters of detail. According to Mommsen, Gaius was by birth a Greek, and by profession a jurist, who wrote and lectured on law at Troas, an important town in the Province of Asia (though nothing is known of any law-school there), and one of the three places "iuris Italici" mentioned by Gaius himself in Dig. 50, 15, 7. The fact that he was called by his praenomen only is pointed to as evidence of his Greek origin (above, p. 3). He was, obviously, also familiar with the Greek language and with Greek literature and history, for he quotes Homer and Xenophon and the laws of Solon. He always shows a keen interest in the laws of foreigners—he wrote a commentary in thirty books on the Edictum Provinciale,[2] the only book of its kind that is known to us—and makes specific mention of the laws of the

---

[1] The arguments in favour of Mommsen's theory, and Huschke's grounds of objection, are conveniently summarized by Dr. Roby (*op. cit.*, p. clxxv *ff.*).

[2] What this Edictum Provinciale precisely was is a highly controversial question, as to which reference may be made to Dr. Roby (*op. cit.*, p. clxxviii *ff.*). Some hold that it was the traditional common part of the several provincial edicts. Mommsen, however, maintains that a general edict applicable to all the provinces was an impossibility, and that each provincial edict was only valid in the province for which it was promulgated, though he agrees that the substance of the various edicts may have been, to a large extent, the same. The edict commented on by Gaius must, he thinks, have been the Edictum Asiaticum. Huschke, however, points with much force to the great improbability of any jurist composing a work in thirty books on the edict of a single province.

Galatians (Inst. i. 55) and the Bithynians (i. 193), both of them peoples living in Asia Minor. He was not, according to this theory, a practising lawyer, but devoted himself entirely to literary work and lecturing. A large number of his works have undoubtedly a definitely educational aim. It is almost certain— and here Mommsen has the great weight of authority on his side— that he never had the *ius respondendi*, the right, that is, to pronounce binding legal opinions *ex auctoritate principis*. This explains why, among his numerous works, there is no trace of any collection of *responsa* (authoritative opinions) or of *quæstiones* (practical cases), the *liber de casibus* (from which there are seven extracts in the Digest) being apparently concerned, not with actual cases, but with hypothetical points and examples. If Gaius had ever enjoyed the *ius respondendi*, and the prestige which such a privilege would naturally have conferred upon him, the fact (already adverted to) that he is not mentioned by a single legal writer for some 250 years after his death would be simply unaccountable, especially if, as some think, he lived and practised at Rome. If, on the other hand, the true view is that he was a professor of law in a provincial town in Asia Minor, not possessing any recognized status among the law-making agencies of his time, and cut off from the main current of contemporary legal life, the fact in question—though still somewhat remarkable in view of the immense popularity that subsequently fell to his share—becomes, at any rate, explicable.[1] True, he took a vigorous part in the controversial warfare of the schools, and frequently, in the Institutes, ranges himself on the side of the Sabinians (*nostri præceptores*), in opposition to the Proculians, the *diversæ scholæ auctores*. But he was the last eminent jurist in whom this antagonism of the schools appears, and it is quite possible that the controversial spirit lingered for some time in the provincial law-schools long after it had become, in M. Girard's words, "une habitude démodée" in the capital.

As against Mommsen's theory, Huschke and others point out, with regard to Gaius's name, that there are many instances of undoubted Romans being called by their prænomen only—*e.g.*, Appius (Claudius), Servius (Sulpicius), and Sextus (Pomponius),

---

[1] The language used by Gaius in a passage from his commentaries on the Edictum Provinciale (Dig. xi., 7, 9)—"miror quare constare videatur, neque heredi neque in heredem dandam hanc actionem"—is certainly, as Puchta points out, suggestive of the attitude of a man who considers himself as standing outside a charmed circle, and ventures, "with deference," to criticize a ruling of the official authorities.

and some Emperors, such as Titus and Marcus—and, further, that there were other Greek writers who did not limit themselves to a Roman prænomen. And as for Gaius's references to the Greek language and Greek literature, Huschke, while not concerned to deny that Gaius may have been a Greek born in a Roman colony in the East, urges with some force that, in view of the very general spread of Greek culture at that time, it would be rash to draw any such conclusion from those references alone. Unlike Papinian and Modestinus in a later age, Gaius never wrote any of his works in Greek. The Greek quotations (*e.g.* the passage from the *Iliad* vii. 472-5, quoted in Inst. iii. 141) were, it is suggested, for the most part the merest commonplaces of the legal controversies of the time. As for foreign laws, they had received attention from other jurists besides Gaius, and the spread of Greek influences and the increased intercommunication between the different parts of the Empire—Hadrian, the "travelling Emperor," was nicknamed "Græculus" by his contemporaries—had produced a very widespread interest in what we should call comparative law. Up to this point the criticisms of Huschke are effective enough, but when he comes to the constructive part of his argument the result is less satisfactory. In two passages of the Digest Gaius gives as an example of a "condition" "si navis ex Asia venerit"; in another, "si ex Africa venerit." In Dig. 45, 1, 74, he mentions, by way of illustration, "fundus Tusculanus" and "vinum Campanum." In Dig. 45, 1, 141, 4, he has "si inter eos qui Romæ [not Troade] sunt, talis fiat stipulatio: hodie Carthagine dare spondes?" It is suggested that examples like these—and there are others—would never occur to a writer not living in Rome. Huschke is fain to admit that this is a somewhat frail argument. "These things," he says, "taken by themselves, prove little," though he ventures to think that, "taken together," the points urged by him "have great weight in refuting" the rival theory. His conclusion is that a lawyer so well abreast of the legal knowledge of his time, and so keenly interested in the controversies of the schools, could not possibly have lived "in aliquo provinciarum angulo abditus," but must have exercised his profession at the centre of the legal world.

Of the two theories, Mommsen's is perhaps the more plausible and ingenious, but, after hearing the advocates on each side, it is difficult to gainsay the conclusion of Mr. Roby (*op. cit.*,

p. clxxvii) that neither party has proved his case, and that the problem as to where Gaius lived and wrought still remains unsolved.

Gaius was a prolific writer. The Florentine Index (which will be found prefixed to Mommsen's edition of the Digest) enumerates thirteen works, but the list is not exhaustive. In the Digest he is represented by 535 excerpts, as compared with 601 from Papinian, 2,081 from Paul, and 2,464 from Ulpian. Only the most important of his works need be specifically mentioned here. Besides the commentary on the Edictum Provinciale already referred to (p. 5), Gaius wrote a commentary on the Edictum Urbicum (of which, according to the Index, only ten books were found); six books on the Twelve Tables (he was the only post-Augustan jurist who was sufficiently interested in this ancient statute to write a commentary on it); fifteen books on the Leges Julia et Papia (representing the modern *ius civile*); a book *de casibus* (above, p. 6); and several monographs. The most famous of his works was probably the *Rerum cottidianarum, sive aureorum, libri vii.*, in which he discussed—more fully than in the Institutes, but on similar lines—a number of "everyday" fundamental legal truths. The sub-title of the work—*aurea*, the golden book (which was no part of the name given by the author himself)—bears testimony to the admiration which subsequent generations felt for the book.

But of all Gaius's works, the one that possesses the greatest interest for us is, of course, the Institutes, or, to give it its full title, *Institutionum iuris civilis commentarii quatuor*, and it is with the romantic history of this work that the story of Gaius is, for us, inseparably bound up. Its success was remarkable. It gradually established itself as the standard textbook for students of Roman law, and maintained that position for upwards of 300 years. Other eminent jurists wrote *Institutiones*—Callistratus, Marcianus, Florentinus, even Paul and Ulpian—but none of them was able to dethrone Gaius's work from the proud place it had secured for itself. The Institutes and *Res cottidianœ* were perhaps the first of Gaius's writings to achieve definite recognition among lawyers; but as his reputation grew, his other works came to enjoy an equal authority. Accordingly, when Valentinian III., in A.D. 426, enacted his Law of Citations—thereby, most probably, giving effect to a recognized practice of the courts and the legal profession—he included Gaius among the five select jurists *all* of whose writings were to have binding authority (*universa scripta firmamus*), adding, in regard to Gaius (so as to remove any doubt that might arise from the fact of his never having had the *ius respondendi*), "ita ut Gaium quæ Paulum, Ulpianum, et cunctos comitetur auctoritas, lectionesque [= passages] ex omni eius opere recitentur." Thus it came to pass that Gaius, the unpatented jurist, the humble professor of law and writer of books, the theoretical lawyer—a mere provincial, maybe—whose works no contemporary or subsequent legal writer or historian deemed worthy of citation, was ranged side by side with the illustrious names of Papinian, Ulpian, and Paul, and firmly established among the coryphæi of the law. And when, about a century later, Justinian, a few years after his accession in A.D. 527, took his great work of codification in hand, and decided to preface his Code with an introductory treatise of an elementary character, it was to the Institutes and *Res cottidianæ* of Gaius that he looked for a model of what such a treatise ought to be. Justinian's Institutes, composed, as he tells us (Constitutio Imperatoriam), "ex omnibus antiquorum institutionibus et præcipue ex commentariis Gaii nostri tam institutionum quam rerum cottidianarum aliisque multis commentariis," follow very closely the order and arrangement of Gaius's work, and are, indeed, to a large extent a transcript of it, the obsolete and historical portions being omitted, and account being, of course, taken of the changes that had occurred in the law. A glance at Gneist's *Syntagma*, in which the two Institutes are printed in parallel columns, will satisfy anyone as to the heavy debt which Justinian's compilers owed to the older writer. The Institutes of Justinian—in other words, the revised Institutes of Gaius—were officially promulgated on November 21, A.D. 533, with statutory force for the Eastern Empire as from December 30 of that year.[1]

Meanwhile a different fate had befallen Gaius in the West. The Western Empire, shattered by the German tribes, had formally come to an end in A.D. 476. In the German kingdoms which were founded on its ruins the system of personal laws prevailed. The Roman section of the population thus continued to be governed by Roman law. But Roman law had become

---

[1] The Eastern Empire did not at that time include Italy itself. The Code was not introduced into Italy till after the reconquest of that country by Justinian in 553, but it maintained itself there even after the further separation from the Byzantine Empire which took place not long after Justinian's death.

obscured and corrupted during the turmoil of the preceding half-century, and some authoritative statement of its provisions was urgently called for. As in the East, so in the West, the spirit of codification was in the air; hence the various *Leges Romanæ Barbarorum* (*i.e.*, records of Roman law for the use of the Roman population in the German kingdoms) that came into being early in the sixth century, or, roughly, about a generation before Justinian's legislation. Of these by far the most important, both on its own account and by reason of its connexion with Gaius, is the *Lex Romana Visigothorum*, or *Breviarium Alarici*, compiled in A.D. 506 by order of Alaric II., King of the Visigoths, for the large Roman population of France and Spain. Like Justinian at a later date, the German King decided to introduce his code with a short elementary treatise; and, like Justinian again, he pressed Gaius's Institutes into his service. The first three books of Gaius were condensed into two, and the fourth (on actions) was omitted altogether. The historical and controversial parts were struck out. This is the so-called "West-Gothic Epitome of Gaius." As edited by Alaric's commissioners, it was thought intelligible enough without the aid of an *interpretatio* such as the other parts of the *Breviarium* were supposed to require. As a statement of Roman law, Alaric's code will not bear comparison with Justinian's. The Roman law there set forth is a rude, fragmentary, barbarized Roman law. The writings of the great jurists, out of which the Digest, the most valuable part of Justinian's Code, was composed, were beyond the comprehension of Alaric's compilers. Such as it was, however, it became the standard source of Roman law for Western Europe, and maintained that position all through the first half of the Middle Ages. In the East, during the same period, Justinian's Code, enacted twenty-seven years later, held undisputed sway.

During the twelve centuries and more that followed the reign of Justinian, the history of Gaius and his works is merely part of the history of Roman law in general. The first five centuries of this period were years of more or less complete legal stagnation. In the East an age of ste dy decay set in. Justinian's Code was continuously pruned down and attenuated into a series of "epitomes of epitomes." In the most successful work of this class —the *Hexabiblos* of Harmenopulus, of A.D. 1345—a queer jumble of a compilation that managed, somehow, to survive the wreck

of the Eastern Empire, and actually to obtain statutory force for
the kingdom of Greece in 1835—Gaius is jauntily referred to as
"the chief of the wise men who added other laws and actions [to
the laws of the Twelve Tables]." In the West the period in question was one of dire disorder and confusion. True, the study of
Roman law never completely died out, and in Italy itself the
traditions of Roman law showed a marked vitality. Nevertheless, for a long period Roman law, imperfectly apprehended as it
was, led a precarious existence, and was increasingly exposed to
the risks of corruption and mutilation.[1] When at last the clouds
lifted ; when Western Europe, confronted with the task of discovering afresh the very elements of law and political order, was
beginning to find herself again ; then it was that the immense
intellectual force of Roman law—the Roman law, however, of
Justinian's Code, not the barbarized versions of the *Leges
Romanæ*—asserted itself with such striking results During the
eleventh century the great revival of the study of Roman law
took place, and the fruitful epoch of the Glossators commenced.
Roman law was now launched on its triumphant career in Continental Europe, and in this triumph Gaius bore no inconsiderable
part—not, indeed, through the Institutes directly (for they, in
their original form, still lay buried in an obscure library), but, in
the main, through such parts of his works as Justinian's Code had
preserved. So far as any distinct influence can be assigned to
Gaius among all the great names that figure in the Digest, such
influence is all in favour of orderly classification and system. It
may, perhaps, be putting Gaius's claims a little too high to say
that he has "supplied the ground-plan for all modern European
codes" (Ilbert, *Legislative Methods*, p. 15); but it is quite true
that, thanks to his keen sense of order and method, he has exercised a very definite influence on the shape which some of the most
successful modern codes have assumed, notably the French Civil
Code of 1804, itself the model for a number of subsequent codes.
And it was just some twelve years after the enactment of the

---

[1] A striking illustration of the low intellectual capacities of the age is
furnished by the Lex Romana Curiensis, which at the same time affords
us a very quaint glimpse of our author. The Lex Curiensis was a statement
of legal custom drawn up by certain judges and ecclesiastics of the Grisons
for the Romance population of the district. In the course of their labours
the compilers were rash enough to attempt to quote Valentinian's Law of
Citations. The result was lamentable. The law itself was misunderstood,
and mutilated beyond recognition, and among the jurists named at the head
of the quotation Gaius figures as "Gagius," in company with Scævola
disguised as "Scifola" (Vinogradoff, *Roman Law in Mediæval Europe*, p. 13).

Napoleonic Code that the strangest of the many strange incidents in the story of Gaius occurred, and the original text of the Institutes came to light again.

Thus we come back to Verona, and the Palazzo dei Canonici, and the queer, tarnished document before us. Somewhere in the early Middle Ages a pious scribe, being minded to record the *epistulæ* of St. Jerome, and being unable or unwilling to purchase the necessary clean parchment for the purpose, succeeded in getting hold of a piece of parchment containing some writing which to him, if he could read it at all, seemed doubtless of trifling value compared with the epistles of his saint. Having procured his parchment, he set to work to prepare it for receiving the new writing. The first thing to do was to expunge the old writing, which happened to be the text of Gaius's Institutes. Our scribe seems to have tried washing and bleaching, and, where the old characters were too stubborn, pumice-stone, or a file, or a knife, was resorted to. Having cleared the ground satisfactorily to himself, he proceeded to superpose the new writing directly on the old, and so precious was the parchment that 60 out of a total of 251 pages had to be written over twice (*codex bis rescriptus*). By some accident one leaf—pp. 235 and 236, containing §§ 134-144 of the Institutes—became detached from the rest, and thus escaped the attentions of our scribe. This leaf was discovered at Verona by Scipio Maffei, the Italian author and scholar, who published its contents in his *Istoria teologica* in 1740. Maffei recognized the likeness of the fragment (which is mainly concerned with interdicts) to Justinian's Institutes iv. 15, but he thought it was merely a compendium of the latter work by some later jurist. He did not suspect its connexion with our palimpsest, though he had noticed that the manuscript of St. Jerome's letters was a *codex rescriptus*. The first to identify Gaius as the author of the writing on the stray leaf was Haubold, in his *Notitia Fragmenti Veronensis de Interdictis*, published in 1816. It so happened that in the very same year, but before the publication of Haubold's *Notitia*, Niebuhr, while on his way to Rome as Prussian Minister to the Apostolic See, spent a couple of days at the library in Verona, during which he examined some manuscripts, including our palimpsest. He evidently suspected that something of interest might be found under the letters of the saint. An infusion of nut-galls which he was allowed to apply to the ninety-seventh leaf of the obliterated writing enabled him to decipher the contents of that leaf, which he took to be part of a work of Ulpian's. He communicated the result of his examination to Savigny, who at once recognized the manuscript as a work of Gaius. The whole story was told by Savigny in the *Zeitschrift für geschichtliche Rechtswissenschaft*, vol. iii., p. 129 *ff*., where that learned writer put forward the conjecture, fully verified later on, that the text was that of Gaius's Institutes, and that the detached leaf had formerly been part of the manuscript. The subsequent story of the manuscript, which probably dates from the fifth century, will be found in Professor Muirhead's *Roman Law* (pp. 308-10), and in the Introduction to Mr. Poste's edition of the Institutes (fourth edition, pp. lii, liii), and it is not necessary to repeat it here. It may not, however, be out of place to pay a tribute of admiration, on the one hand, to the patience and single-minded devotion with which a number of learned men applied themselves to the infinitely laborious task of deciphering this obscure and mutilated text ;[1] and, on the other hand, to the public-spirited action of the Royal Prussian Academy of Sciences in first despatching its commissioners to prepare a transcript of the manuscript, and in publishing the first edition of the Institutes in 1820, and subsequently, after the appearance of many intervening editions,[2] in enabling Studemund to produce in 1874 his magnificent facsimile of the text (*Apographum*). If we can now pride ourselves on possessing a fairly complete text of the Institutes—a completer text, in fact, than that of any other work by an ancient legal writer [3]—it is to the efforts of these able scholars and to the enterprise of the Prussian Academy that we owe so splendid a result.[4]

The Institutes, as is well known, are an elementary textbook of Roman private law, dealing partly with legal doctrine and partly (and, fortunately for us, fairly liberally) with legal history.

---

[1] May an amnesty be accorded even to the over-zealous Blume, whose disastrous chemicals destroyed more than they saved ?

[2] See Muirhead (*op. cit.*, p. 310, note 6).

[3] About one-thirteenth still remains undeciphered, half of which belongs to book iv. In the original manuscript three leaves are missing in the middle. The first of these can be to some extent supplied from the West-Gothic Epitome. A kind fate has preserved the contents of the second in the *Collatio* (above, p. 3). The loss of the third is most regrettable, as it probably contained some much-needed additional information about *legis actiones*.

[4] A palimpsest discovered by M. Chatelain at Autun in 1898 (the so-called "Autun MS. of Gaius") was at first thought to be another copy of Gaius's Institutes, but proved, on closer examination, to be merely a paraphrase of that work (Girard, *Manuel élémentaire de Droit Romain*, third edition, p. 66, note 1).

The term *Institutio* was apparently borrowed from the writers on rhetoric, who used it to describe a book designed for the instruction of students (*cf.* Quintilian's *Institutio Oratoria*). Gaius's work was, so far as we know, the first to appear under this name, and, indeed the first of its kind generally, in the history of Roman legal literature. It exhibits very clearly our author's two most salient characteristics—lucidity of expression and orderliness of arrangement. The style throughout is neat, vigorous, precise. The points are stated tersely and accurately. There is no rhetoric, no redundancy. And the whole scheme of the work is carefully thought out and skilfully executed. With Gaius the love of systematic arrangement and definite classification was almost a passion. It seems to pervade the whole range of his work. He sought, as Cicero said of his friend S. Sulpicius Rufus, to treat law "with the hand and mind of an artist." It was his constant endeavour to reduce the whole domain of law and its several provinces to an orderly system. It was characteristic of him that, when he wanted to write on case law, he did not follow the prevailing habit of compiling an undigested collection of *quæstiones* (p. 6) of the type of the various books *Ad Sabinum* —*deliramenta Masuriana*, as Fronto, the orator, contemptuously called them—but elected to proceed by way of critical notes on Q. Mucius Scævola, the famous contemporary of Cicero, whose glory it was to be the first methodizer of Roman law, the man who "ius civile primus constituit generatim." It may well be that the main lines on which the Institutes were planned were not altogether of Gaius's invention, but rested largely on the traditions of the schools. That could hardly be otherwise. A treatise that holds its own as a standard legal textbook for several centuries does not spring complete from the brain of any one man: it necessarily presupposes a great deal of detailed preliminary work. But whatever the extent of Gaius's indebtedness to his predecessors may have been, to him belongs the credit of having, by a wise and discriminating use of his materials, and by a keen sense of proportion in the ordering of them, presented the world with a textbook of law to which, in the words of Mr. Bryce (*Studies in History and Jurisprudence*, vol. ii., p. 512), "we have nothing comparable."

The persistence with which the praises of Gaius have been sung, and the undiscriminating admiration with which his virtues have been extolled, have produced in recent years a certain amount of depreciatory reaction. It may be true, too, that the curious and dramatic circumstances in which the Institutes came to life again (at the very moment when the historical school of law was rising into prominence) have "led to Gaius's elevation to a higher pinnacle of fame than his actual merits altogether warrant" (Muirhead, p. 302). But there is no reason why his virtues should be exaggerated or his shortcomings denied. Gaius cannot be said to be a great creative lawyer of the type of Julian or Papinian, though it is only fair, in this connexion, to remember that we do not possess any large work of his in a complete form that would give him an opportunity of displaying wider constructive powers. It may be that he is not a profound or erudite writer. Some of his classifications may be open to objections. His historical statements may not always bear the test of modern scientific criticism, as Kuntze, his chief assailant, seems to think they ought to do. His etymologies are as naïve as most of those of his age. Even his lucidity may be an overrated quality; for has not lucidity been described as the negative virtue of mediocre minds? But all this means nothing more than that he had the defects of his qualities and some of the defects of his time. Even after every deduction has been made, there remains a solid residuum of sterling merit which entitles his Institutes to take rank as one of the most valuable and important works in the whole range of legal literature. The discovery of the Veronese palimpsest may not have opened "a new epoch in the study of Roman law," and the "revolutionary" effects of the discovery may not have been so far-reaching as some writers have alleged. Nevertheless, it would be churlish indeed to refuse our meed of gratitude to Gaius, both for what he has done for us, and for the way he has done it— that is to say, both for the wealth of legal and historical material he has opened up to us, and the flood of light he has thrown on so many dark places in the history, not only of Roman law, but of human institutions in general (and more particularly on the obscure early history of legal procedure); and also for the masterly simplicity, the deftness and finish, the "intellectual urbanity,"[1] with which he has accomplished his task.

Ihering tells us (*Scherz und Ernst in der Jurisprudenz*, ninth edition, p. 139 *ff.*) how once, when he was pondering the problem of *usucapio pro herede lucrativa*, it occurred to him that it might be useful if he could cross-examine Gaius on a few passages from

[1] Bryce, *op. cit.*, p. 198.

his Institutes bearing on the subject (ii. 52-58; iii. 201). He accordingly proceeded, there and then, to summon the ghost of Gaius from Orcus. In the midst of the clouds of cigar-smoke that enveloped the professor there appeared a strange figure of a man, tall, shrivelled, slightly bow-legged, with freckled brow, and the general air of a schoolmaster. This was Gaius. It may well be that many a student of Roman law, worried by what appears to him the author's inordinate delight in the antiquities of law, in the laws of Latins and foreigners, in subtle distinctions between different kinds of legacies, in the *cretionum scrupulosa solemnitas*, has, in his first struggle with the Institutes, unconsciously formed a similar image of Gaius in his own mind, just as many a student of English law, repelled in his first wrestlings with the *Lectures on Jurisprudence* by the merciless iteration and the hammer-like irresponsiveness of Austin's style, may have gleefully recognized the aptness of Carlyle's thumbnail sketch of the "lean, grey-headed, painful-looking man, with large, earnest, timid eyes, and a clanging, metallic voice" (Froude's *Life of Carlyle*, 1795-1835, vol. ii., p. 194). But in one case, as in the other, further study may lead to a revision of the first impression. The reader of Austin will come to recognize that there is more in the *Jurisprudence* than a tiresome dogmatism and a parched style of writing. In the same way, if the student of Roman law carries his labours a little farther, he may find that there is a good deal more in the Institutes of Gaius than a mere dryasdust antiquarianism. When he comes to the Digest, it may happen that, after a hard struggle with a passage from Julian or Africanus ("Africani lex, ergo difficilis") or Papinian, he will greet with no small pleasure the sight of the plain five-lettered name at the head of the next excerpt, well knowing that, whatever the point to be dealt with, he will be sure to find a model of terse and lucid exposition. He may then, perhaps, form a different picture of our author—the picture of a kindly, alert, keen-faced man, neat and tidy in his person (was it not he who condemned the practice of plunging into one's subject without orderly introduction, "illotis, ut ita dixerim, manibus"? Dig. 1, 2, 1), quickly responsive in his sympathies, readily appreciative of others' difficulties—the picture, in a word, of a born teacher. May it not perhaps be that this is a truer likeness of "Gaius noster" than the whimsical figure of Ihering's smoke-dimmed vision?

PAPINIAN

Connection with Septimius Severus.—The full name of this jurist appears in Justinian's Code, and in a quotation (from Paulus) in the same emperor's Digest, as Æmilius Papinianus. In the time to which he belonged no trustworthy inference as to ancestry can be drawn from these two words. There is sufficient evidence to show that he was a lifelong friend of the Emperor Septimius Severus, with whom, according to one story, he was connected by marriage, through Severus' second wife. An interesting connection, if true : for this was that famous Julia on whom Gibbon passes such a warm, and questionable, encomium at the beginning of his sixth chapter. For the scandalous part there seems to be little authority but a cock-and-bull story retailed by the omnivorous Dio ; of her strange half-Jewish beauty and imperious ambition we have some record, in the likeness on the empress's coins and the newly assumed title " Domna "—best explained, it would seem, by the literal " Lady."

Papinian, therefore, may quite possibly have been a native of Syria—the empress was from Emesa—and come as a provincial to the study of Roman law. To this effect his omission of the regular style—*divus*—for deceased emperors has been remarked, in his earlier *Quæstiones*. It has been suggested that he may have been at one time a lecturer at Berytus ; and on his whole career, Mommsen dubs him " in thought and speech the least Roman of the Roman jurists." Possibly we may credit his Syrian origin with the greater kindliness and the wider humanity which he certainly does seem to introduce into the strait-laced logic of his predecessors—such, for instance, as his " leader," the difficult Cervidius Scævola. Whether actually pupils of Scævola or not, Severus and Papinian are stated to have made their *début* as consulting counsel and teachers of law (*professio*) under the auspices of this jurist, who is a connecting-link between those of the Antonine period and the last great group—Papinian, Ulpian, and Paulus.

The above statement (of Spartianus) is the earliest historical notice of Papinian, whom we may infer, if contemporary with his friend the future emperor, to have been born about A.D. 146. For a late fabrication about his parentage see below (p. 21). He succeeded Severus, as we learn from the same authority, in the office of counsel to the Fiscus—sometimes, I think rather inaccurately, translated Privy Purse. It is not, however, my business here to investigate the constitutional position of the Fiscus and its gradual approximation to, or absorption of, the State Treasury. The specific office of *advocatus fisci*, which probably originated under Hadrian, must have had a large and increasing sphere of operation in the way of claims to *bona damnatorum, vacantia,* and *caduca.*

We next find Papinian appearing—probably, as Karlowa suggests, by appointment of his friend Severus, who became emperor in A.D. 193—in the position of *magister libellorum* or *a libellis*. This office had no doubt very largely to do, as Mommsen shows, with petitions for admission to equestrian or senatorial rank, and the investigation of sufficiency of means in the applicant. One is tempted to translate its style "Master of Petitions," and to think of our own old Court of Requests. But it must be remembered that the word *libellus* was one of very wide signification, covering, it would seem, almost any application to the emperor either from private persons or magistrates.

Drafting of the Imperial Rescripts: "Præfectus Prætorio."— Dr. Roby, who uses the style "Master of Petitions," indicates, however, the probable influence of this officer upon what was practically legislation, in adding that the Imperial rescripts were framed by him. The one which is actually stated to have been delivered "under Papinian's management of the *libelli*" (Dig. 20, 5, 12 *pr.*) is really an equitable decision, or rather rule, in contract law. And we should probably not be far out in attributing to the *magister libellorum* a considerable part of the functions of our early chancellors and keepers of the Privy Seal, with a practical power of direct legislation which those officers did not possess.

Finally—perhaps, to adopt another suggestion of Karlowa, upon the fall of Plautianus, A.D. 203—Papinian was raised to the position of *Præfectus Prætorio* (General of the Guard), which he retained till his death, or at least till the accession of Caracalla in 211. Whether his predecessor shared this office with colleagues or not, Papinian would seem to have held it alone. Its original military character, though still subsisting, had undoubtedly by this time become subordinate or overshadowed by a supreme civil and criminal jurisdiction, which its holder had acquired as the personal representative or delegate of the emperor.

With the criminal law of the Roman Empire I am not now so much concerned as with the civil law and its various methods of development. One of these is to be found in the *judicial decisions* of the emperor or his delegate, and the general rules often coupled with them. A good instance of this supreme jurisdiction —or practically of *legislation* (for the case seems to be a hypothetical one, of the John Doe and Richard Roe kind)—occurs in the interpretation of a draft bond brought before Papinian in his Court as Præfect of the Prætorium (Dig. 12, 1, 40).

The "Quæstiones" and "Responsa."—But a more remarkable feature in the development of Roman civil law, and one with which Papinian was particularly connected, consists of the *opinions* given by *licensed* or *patented* jurists, whether in the consulting-chamber, the lecture-room, or the textbook. It is of this mode of development that I propose to speak more especially in what follows.

The works of Papinian coming under this head are mainly his *Quæstiones* and *Responsa*. The *Quæstiones* show in the first book some sign of that early, perhaps provincial, style above referred to, and may have been written before Severus' accession; but the greater part of the work—*e.g.*, Books 17-37—obviously belongs to the sole reign of that emperor (A.D. 193-198). The *Responsa* possibly begin under the joint reign of Severus and Caracalla (198-211), but from Book 4 onward they are later than A.D. 206, a constitution of which year is therein discussed (Dig. 24, 1, 32 *pr.*, 16); and the last five books (15-19) may have been written in the period between the death of Severus (February 4th, 211) and that of Papinian himself in the early part of the following year.

Murder of Papinian by Caracalla.—A certain amount of somewhat contradictory legend seems to have collected round the execution, or rather murder, of Papinian by Caracalla, but the main facts are fairly established. He accompanied Severus to Britain, where he evidently became aware of an attempt made by Caracalla to murder the emperor his father, though the language used by the latter does not, as I agree with Dr. Roby, amount to any imputation on the loyalty of Papinian himself. I need not give Dio's story (l. 76, c. 14), in which the aged Severus is made to play the part of the Admirable Crichton to his unworthy son, who does *not*, however, copy or anticipate the young Mantuan prince. It is perhaps worth remarking, by the way, that Zonaras, in *his* version of the story of Dio (l. 12, c. 10), written in the twelfth century A.D., gives the name of the Præfect as *Papianus*, thus furnishing a confirmation, which I do not remember to have seen noticed before, of the view now generally taken, upon the *style* of the Burgundian law-book, *Papiani Liber Responsorum* (see Savigny, *Gesch.*, ii., chap. vii.; Brunner, *Deutsche Rechtsgesch.*, i. 356-357, etc.).

Severus died and was buried, as Yorkshiremen hold, at York, in that mound which I have had pointed out to me, when a boy, under the odd title of *Saint* Sevĕrus' (*sic*) hill. Then broke out at once the hatred of the brothers, or perhaps half-brothers (Spartianus, Severus, 20, 21; Geta, 1)—at any rate, the hatred of Caracalla for Geta—against which their father had uttered his last warning (Dio, l. 76, c. 21), and which had been suppressed or ignored under the wise management of the empress (see the interesting coins in Cohen's *Monnaies*, iv. 100). For the picturesque details of their return to Rome, I must refer again to the sixth chapter of Gibbon, who gives them in full from Herodianus. The end of the story is the murder of Geta in his mother Julia's arms (Dio, l. 77, cc. 1, 2), shortly followed by that of Papinian, who had been dismissed at the beginning of the reign, and was despatched by the blow of an axe. According to one account, after a hypocritical show of friendship towards him by Caracalla (Spartianus, Caracalla, c. 3), Papinian's son, a Quæstor, was put to death at the same time, a fact which may possibly have contributed some part of Pancirolli's story, given below.

Whether the great jurist was killed as an adherent of Geta, or because he refused to defend the fratricide; whether he met his fate as one would expect, in silence, or, as Spartianus says, forecasting a similar end to his murderer; what truth or point there is in Caracalla's reported speech that the *sword*, not the *axe*, had been the proper instrument of execution—all this is matter of little concern to the present inquiry (Spartianus, Severus, c. 21; Caracalla, cc. 4, 8; Dio, l. 77, c. 4). It may, however, be worth note to remark that the famous constitution of

Caracalla, by which all freeborn persons in the *orbis Romanus* were made Roman citizens (wrongly attributed in *Nov.* 78, 5, to Antoninus Pius), appears from Dio (1. 77, c. 9) to belong to this year, and not to be due to the foresight of any jurist or politician, but to the craft of a tyrant, wishful partly to palliate his evil deeds by an ostensibly popular measure, partly to increase his revenue by the subjection of a large number of people to taxation from which they were previously free.

Pancirolli (*De Claris Legum Interpretibus*, i. 55) gives a strange story of a silver urn found in the early part of the fifteenth century at Rome, purporting to contain the ashes of Papinian, and to have been dedicated to his memory by his father and mother, Papinianus Hostilius and Eugenia Gracilis—the old, contrary to the natural order, mourning for the young. Papinian is accordingly made to die at the age of thirty-six—an age absolutely irreconcilable with the facts of his life as preserved by contemporary, or almost contemporary, historians. The story, therefore, is not even *ben trovata*, and only shows the special interest felt at the Renaissance in this great jurist. A forged urn may quite possibly exist in some collection, but I have not had leisure to trace it. The names of the parents are most probably pure invention. For the possible suggestion of part of this story by the death of the *younger* Papinian, see above.

Papinian's Pre-eminence as a Jurist.—The encomiums passed on Papinian by historians of the time are very high, and not quite so vague as in other cases. He is the "*asylum* of right and treasury of legal learning" (Spartianus, Severus, c. 21); the one who "for knowledge and exposition of the laws surpassed all Roman legislators (*sic νομοθέτας*) before him or after him (Zosimus, 1, 9). The repeated recognitions of his superiority over his peers by Justinian are, no doubt, attributable partly to the pre-eminence accorded Papinian in the Law of Citations (see below) : this latter is, however, in itself the strongest testimony. Modern writers on jurisprudence and legal history echo his praises, from the early times of the Renaissance to the present day. But I only wish here to call attention to one particular characteristic of Papinian, which is especially remarked by some of the latest authorities (*e.g.* Karlowa, *Rechtsgesch.*, i. 736; Krüger, *Sources*, French translation, 265; Sohm, English translation, 2nd ed., p. 103).

Papinian's special greatness, it is observed, lies in his application of theory. He teaches largely by concrete cases, but he ever strives to view the individual case with reference to its governing principle. His conclusions are, comparatively, very little encumbered with particular circumstances, but are stated, as far as possible, in an abstract and general form, etc., etc.

Now, this characteristic, though pre-eminent in Papinian, is more or less shared by all the great jurists of the Digest. It has to do with a peculiar, and, to my mind, a very advantageous, mode of development in Roman civil law—a mode of development which, as it is distinctly connected with the authoritative *licensing* or *patenting* of certain jurists, is best considered by a brief view of that difficult and interesting subject. It is not impossible that a system to which the Roman law owed much of its merit might have some lesson for us even at the present day. And although many points in its earlier history are, and will probably continue to be, matter of dispute, that to which I particularly wish to draw attention is an ascertained fact, for at least as early as the time of Papinian.[1]

The "Prudentes" and their Hypothetical Cases.—The *prudens* of Roman law does not exactly correspond with any one of *our* recognized professional men. He was not a pleader, but rather combined the character of solicitor with that of equity draughtsman and conveyancing counsel, being consulted at his own house both by clients directly and by their *patroni*, or public pleaders. To these functions many, probably among the most active and able *prudentes*, added that of giving *public instruction* in law. They offered their services and leisure, to quote Pomponius' expression, as much to *learners* as to clients. Thus, although their *responsa* were no doubt originally delivered with regard to points actually in litigation, there naturally arose that framing or putting of *hypothetical* cases to which Sir Henry Maine justly attributed, as a consequence, a special development of *general rules or principles* (see the latter part of chap. ii. in *Ancient Law*).

This form of development may also be inferred on other grounds, partly philological, partly based on what we know of early practice, and partly on the sadly scanty accounts given by Pomponius

---

[1] On the authorities for much of the following matter I must refer to Part II. chap. ix. of my own work, *Practical Jurisprudence*, from which most of this matter is taken, with such revision as has been suggested by later reading. Reference is also made from time to time to the sections of Pomponius' Enchiridium, Digest, 1, 2, 2, which is our main authority on the subject.

and Gaius, writing under Hadrian or shortly after, of a very important accession of influence to some, at least, among the body of *prudentes*. During the republic the *prudentes* were simply teachers, textbook writers, or chamber counsel, without the necessity of any "call" or diploma. The profession was open to all who had confidence in their acquirements; they had no official position, and their opinions, in actual cases, were not binding on the judge, to whom they were communicated by the *prudens* or quoted by the litigant. These communications had the practical weight of their author's reputation—no more. Such, at least, was the state of things in the later republican Roman law. At an earlier time, it is held by some that the Pontiffs, or one of their number appointed for the year, *had* the power of delivering opinions which were binding on the *judex*. But this is extremely doubtful, and it is more in accordance, both with *a priori* probability and the general testimony of our only authority, Pomponius, to regard the measure of which I have next to speak as no revival of an old principle, but the introduction of a new one by Augustus.

The Emperor Augustus and Licensed "Prudentes."—It was by no means to the interest of that astute sovereign to leave entirely out of his own hands the influence exercised by leading *prudentes* upon the development of Roman civil law. Such influence was undoubtedly very great, operating through the current administration of justice, and its resultant rules of practice crystallized from time to time in the Prætor's edict; although, as has been said, the opinion of the *prudens* on an actual case was not binding on the *judex*. It was most probably with a view of exercising some control over this influence that Augustus, ostensibly "in order to enhance the influence of the unwritten law," directed "that *prudentes* should give *responsa* on his (the emperor's) authority or guarantee"—which naturally became a subject of petition, as matter of privilege (Pomponius, § 49). Much question has been raised as to whether the intention was henceforth to *prohibit* unofficial *responsa* (that is, in actual cases) or merely to give special weight—most probably a binding character on the *judex*—to official ones. The latter is my own view, which seems to me somewhat confirmed by the subsequently professed intention of the despot Caligula to prohibit *anyone* from giving a *responsum* but himself (see below. I have adopted what I believe to be the better reading, in

Suetonius, Cal. c. 34, "ne *qui* respondere possint præter eum").

After the institution of these licensed or patented jurists, their *responsa* were regularly delivered under their seal, not, of course, to conceal the opinion from their consulter—I avoid the word *client*, more properly expressing the relation to a *patronus*—but to accredit it as coming from the particular counsel. On the manner of quoting counsel's opinion which previously obtained there is some difficulty in the interpretation of Pomponius (§ 49). I still venture to hold, as against Dr. Roby (*Introduction to Digest*, 102), that the *ipsi* spoken of are the *consulters*, not the *prudentes;* but, whoever it was that originally communicated the opinion to the *judex*, it is clear that he received it from the patented counsel under the latter's official seal.

Whether, again, the celebrated Masurius Sabinus was the very first, or the first of equestrian rank, to receive the new distinction, and at what exact time he received it, are matters immaterial to the present subject. I retain my opinion, in spite of Mommsen's suggested emendation of Digest, 1, 2, 2, 48, that Sabinus was the actual first, and that the difficulties about his appointment by Tiberius may be solved by supposing the appointment to have taken place about A.D. 12-14 (see *Practical Jurisprudence*, p. 295).

For some time it would not appear that the privilege *respondendi ex auctoritate principis* was granted very widely. The threat of the Emperor Caligula seems to refer to a class, but the class is probably that of consulting counsel in general.

The Authority of the "Responsa": Hadrian's Rescript.— In the reign of Hadrian, however, the number of the licensed *prudentes* was most probably increased and the authority of their *responsa* more clearly defined. The former point seems to me fairly deducible from the somewhat obscure jocosity of the emperor's reply, to a request by men who had held the office of Prætor, that they might be allowed the right of response. This must clearly mean the licensed or patented position, whether that excluded the old practice or not. The reply, as reported by Pomponius (§ 49), was "that the position of adviser was not generally asked for, but volunteered, and that the emperor was only too well pleased if anyone had sufficient confidence in his own powers to train himself to advise the public."

Whatever may be the precise meaning of this speech, a plurality of licensed counsel is clearly postulated in an actual rescript of Hadrian cited by Gaius (i. 7) as to the juridical effect of opinions delivered by jurists to whom the emperor has granted the *jus respondendi*. If they all agree, such common opinion is to have the force of statute ; if they differ, the *judex* may follow which he pleases.

We have not, unfortunately, the *ipsissima verba* of this rescript, and it is quite allowable, on our information, to maintain that the powers which Hadrian originally intended to confer, or confirm, were simply judicative, or practically judicative, on actual cases for which the licensed jurists had been consulted.

The Testimony of Gaius.—On the other hand we have, in the first book of Gaius, written after the death (A.D. 138) of Hadrian (who is called *divus* in the passage referred to), and possibly, as some think, published after the death of Pius (A.D. 161), other testimony, of rather a significant character, as to the ultimate effect and the probable form of the *responsa* in question. Here we are told that they are among the permanent rules of law of the Roman people ; they are the *sententiæ et opiniones* of men who had a definite permission *jura condere* (Gaius, 1. 2, 7). This curious phrase is often explained with reference simply to the time of Hadrian (of whose rescript it probably formed no part) or that of Gaius. As a matter of fact it descended from republican times. We find it, for instance, in Plautus' *Epidicus* (3, 4, 89, 90), written shortly after 195 B.C. The second old man of the play—a wise-acre after the style of our own Polonius—has the name of being *omnium legum atque jurum fictor (et) conditor."* Condere " leges " is, of course, predicated only in joke, of a private individual ; *condere jura* was, as we shall see from another passage of Gaius (4, 30), a recognized function of the *prudens* in the system of the *legis actiones*. It is clear, not only from the natural meaning of the words, but from the manner in which they are used, by Plautus here and elsewhere, and by Gaius, that the phrase does *not* mean, as Austin and many later and better authorities take it to mean, *judicial decision*, but some work of non-judicial *prudentes*. It would also appear that *jura* must mean something more than an isolated *opinion* delivered on, and confined to, a particular case. I adhere, therefore, to my view, previously expressed in my *Practical Jurisprudence*, that the *prudens* spoken of as *jurum conditor* is so spoken of as *framing statements or maxims of non-statutory law*—law, that is, of custom or practice.

The stage of legal proceedings at which these *jura* were employed, and their authority when so employed, varied for the time of the *legis actiones*, for that of the formulary system, and for that of the later empire, but their matter and form were probably determined by their earliest usage.

The "Legis Actiones": Statement of General Principles.—There are, as is well known, such deplorable *lacunæ* in our fragmentary information as to the *legis actiones*, that some stages of the procedure must be matter of inference, to be based, of course, on common sense and what seems obvious necessity. As one of these inferences, I myself hold, with a fair number of good authorities, that under the old system, except in the *legis actio per condictionem*, there *may* have been in all, and *must* have been in some cases, a brief statement as to the specific kind or ground of claim, made *before the magistrate* (*in jure*), partly to enable him to decide broadly whether this claim came within the law or not, partly to constitute some degree of definiteness in the reference to the *judex*, *arbiter*, or *centumviri*. These statements I take to be the *jura*, or rather the *raison d'être* of the *jura*, spoken of by Gaius in 4, 30, where he speaks of the *nimia subtilitas eorum qui tunc jura condiderunt*. They were brief allegations of legal principle, based, no doubt, as far as possible upon a statutory text, but also often, no doubt, including statements of law never embodied in statute, and sometimes inferences or generalizations entirely new. These were the subject-matter of *legis actiones* meaning what Muirhead terms "specific actions," as distinguished from *legis actiones* meaning generic modes of pleading—those specific *actiones* which Sex. Ælius, in his *Tripertita* (Pomponius, § 38), and other *conditores jurum* endeavoured, by more and more ingenious refinements, to adapt to new requirements less and less capable of being brought under the rigid old law.

How hazardous became these subtle statements of law, as the opening claim, made orally and irrevocably by the party or his *patronus*, before the Magistrate ; how they came to be superseded by special statements of the case (*verba concepta*), capable of amendment and mutual settlement *in jure* in the Magistrates' Court before they were sent down to the *judex ;* how, in fine, the *legis actiones* were replaced by the formulary system, it is not my business here to tell. My object is simply to point out a natural meaning of *condere jura*, which is accountable for in the early system of procedure, and was presumably retained in the later. For there is no reason to believe that this "statement of general principles," which is properly indicated by the phrase, ceased to be employed by *prudentes* under the formulary system, whether in the building up of the reference to the *judex* or in the opinion read to him at the hearing; while it was equally or more applicable, as we see from the evidence of extant writings, to the practice of the legal teacher instructing his pupils.

Dual Capacity of the "Prudens": Counsel and Teacher.—In fact, when considering their answers or opinions, we must never lose sight of the double capacity filled by almost every *prudens* of eminence in the later republican and early imperial times. At first perhaps only a consulting counsel, he gradually became, almost more conspicuously, a teacher of law. His opinions were delivered, not only upon cases coming before the Courts, but upon questions raised in the Schools. And from this double position we find, as we might expect, in all his *dicta*, even where opinions are given on a case and in no way systematized into an educational work, a *generality* and an endeavour to lay down *principles* which is as far as possible removed from the guarded barrenness of some English judgments (of all good judgments as represented by Austin) or a modern counsel's opinion.

This characteristic has been specially remarked, as we saw above, in the instance of Papinian; but the same treatment, by other leading jurists, of cases whether actual or hypothetical, is very obvious in the numerous *Responsa, Opiniones, Disputationes, Quæstiones*, etc., of the Digest—where, of course, the fact that all were ultimately turned into so many *leges* by Justinian makes no difference in the original character of the extracts themselves.

Form of "Responsa" as General Maxims: Their Growing Authority.—With regard, then, to *form*, it is probable that the views even of contemporary jurists, consulted on an actual case *sub judice*, were stated rather in the shape of general maxims. With regard to ultimate *effect*, it seems likely that, even in Gaius's time, the conflict contemplated by him was possibly one between maxims delivered at different times and cited to the *judex* for some case to which they had no original reference. The *sententiæ et opiniones* had assumed, in practice if not by legislative sanction, a persistent authority, which in time communicated itself to other *sententiæ* and *opiniones*, never connected with actual cases at all. For, by the date of Constantine, it is certain that such authority was enjoyed, not only by *responsa* to consultations or inquiries, but by the works in general of some at least among the licensed jurists, that order having ceased to exist for nigh upon a hundred years. Hence it is that we find, in Justinian's Digest, so large an amount of matter quoted from treatises—dogmatical, institutional, or exegetical—which are pure text-book law: general propositions not in the least resembling individual precedents, whether actual or hypothetical, nor like answers to particular questions. I need not do more than refer to the unreasonable manner in which these general propositions are questioned or condemned by Austin (Lect. 37; see *Practical Jurisprudence*, p. 299), who forces them into his hidebound conception of case law.

It is not my purpose, either, to enter here into the subject of *precedents* proper, in Roman law—into the influence, that is, which a particular *judgment* has, as in our law, upon similar subsequent cases. In spite of the oft-quoted passage in Cicero's *Topica* (5, 28), I venture to question whether *res judicata* had ever the exact meaning of an individual precedent. In the case of decisions, indeed, by the emperor, or the person to whom his supreme jurisdiction was delegated, a special principle of precedents *was* recognized, but with considerable variation, during the legislative period from Hadrian—possibly from the beginning of the empire—to Justinian. It was distinctly abandoned in a constitution of Arcadius and Honorius, A.D. 398 (Cod. Theod. 1, 2, 11), but finally recognized by Justinian in his Code (1, 14, 12 *pr.*) A.D. 529.

Conflicts of Opinion and the "Lex Citationum" of Theodosius.—The remaining history of the *sententiæ et opiniones prudentium* is short and fairly clear: it contains, moreover, an interesting recognition of the superior merits of Papinian. The unanimity of opinions which had been required by Hadrian, for binding effect, naturally became more and more rare as the number of such opinions increased. Accordingly, we find Constantine (in A.D. 321, 327) complaining of the never-ending *contentiones prudentium*—the authors mentioned being long dead—abrogating the notes of Paulus and Ulpian upon Papinian, but subsequently confirming all the writings of Paulus. These constitutions of Constantine were followed a hundred years later by the so-called *Lex Citationum* (a late designation) of Theodosius II. and Valentinian III. (A.D. 426). I give the main upshot of this enactment, avoiding its special difficulties. It confirms the entire writings of Papinian, Paulus, Ulpian, Modestinus, and Gaius, expressly giving the last-named author equal authority with the others. Validity is, at the same time, conferred upon the writings of a number of authors habitually quoted by all the above-named five—among whom, we may remark, is included Sabinus, the first licensed *prudens*. In case of a divergency or conflict, Papinian's view is to prevail over that of any *one*, but not *two* of the other writers; the comments upon him being again formally deprived of weight, though an absolute authority is given to the "Sentences" of Paulus. Where two jurists equal in the scale conflict, the judge is, of course, to choose.

This law is specially valuable as explaining difficulties which arise out of the *list* of authors *quoted* in Justinian's Digest. The collection purports to be made from the books of those old *prudentes* to whom previous emperors had given authority for compiling and interpreting laws (*conscribendarum interpretandarumque legum*, Const. Deo Auctore, § 4).

Whatever *condere jura* originally meant, these words certainly indicate, for the subject-matter spoken of, generality of form and subsisting authority. The authors cited ought at first sight to be *confined* to the authorized or licensed *prudentes*. They are, in fact, quoted as early as Q. Mucius Scævola, who died 82 B.C., before Augustus was born. The presence, then, of this and other jurists who wrote before the licensing system is accounted for by their *quotation* in the writings of the five principal or, as they are sometimes called, *academic* authorities specified in the Laws of Citations. The same statute, it was remarked, expressly includes Sabinus, whom we should have expected to appear in his own right. This gives a strong reason for thinking that the opinions, even of the licensed jurists, were not intended to have a binding force as precedents or general rules before the time of Hadrian's rescript, if then.

We may also infer from the language of the *Lex Citationum* that Papinian, Paulus, Ulpian, and Modestinus most probably did, and Gaius did not, belong to the privileged class.

The "Digest" of Justinian.—The objections are obvious to such a mechanical or arithmetical estimate of opinions as that above described. Justinian accordingly converted all the passages which he embodied in his Digest into some many *leges*, and placed them on an indiscriminate level (Const. Deo Auctore, § 6). As this was to be henceforth the sole book of reference, contradictions were, of course, not to be admitted, nor obsolete matter (*ibid.*, §§ 8, 10)—a direction only imperfectly carried out. There are, it must be admitted, irreconcilable contradictions in the Digest, which can by no sophistry be explained away ; which, on the other hand, give us, as marshalled by the date of their cited authors, many interesting examples of the gradual development which takes place in principles of practical law.

The "Feast" of Papinian.—One last word as to Papinian. In the old course of legal study which obtained down to the time of Justinian, who remodelled it in accordance with his own codification, the students were first introduced to the special reading of Papinian's *Responsa* in their third year, whence these third-year men were called *Papinianistæ*, and kept a feast or high day in honour of their author (Const. Omnem, § 4). Justinian, in order to retain in part the old study of this year, and to keep alive the respect due to that great name, contrived a somewhat artificial order and composition of the Books 20, 21, and 22, with which the *Umbilicus*, or central part, of his Digest begins. These books are accordingly called by certain anonymous annotators of the twelfth and fourteenth centuries (as being *instead* of Papinian) *Antipapian* or *Antipapin*. The former curious corruption of the name has been mentioned above (p. 20). It is just conceivable that the further one, of *Papin*, may have given rise to an honoured name in French natural science. Of any *calembour* suggested by Denys Papin's best-known invention I am innocent.

The Work of the "Prudentes": Its Juristic Value.—The institution of licensed *prudentes* is often regarded as the mere establishment of a high court of civil justice, and their opinions as practically judgments on appeal or on reserved cases, which no doubt they often were. But, if I am right in the view here taken, the work of the *prudentes* from an earlier period than that of the imperial licence, and the work of the licensed *prudentes* afterwards, was something more. It habitually included—on principle, not as a mere *obiter dictum*—some amount of generalization, much wider than Austin's *ratio decidendi*, and, moreover, directly expressed by its author—not requiring to be inferred or extracted by the laborious processes described in Austin's thirty-seventh and thirty-ninth lectures.

The advantage, or rather the necessity, for generalization is only too apparent for ourselves, with our enormous and increasing mass of case law. This is no doubt done, and very ably done, to some extent in the headings of our yearly *Law Reports*, in reviews, and from time to time in textbooks—the increasing consideration for the last being a noticeable feature in our Courts. Nor are our judges now, I think, so averse from laying down general rules or delivering themselves of general maxims as they used to be, and as they are, according to Austin, in duty bound to be. But the reduction of that most important branch of law which is continually growing out of the practice of the Courts, to an amount *cognoscible*, to use Austin's expression, even by the profession, becomes daily farther off than ever.

With all due appreciation of the gradual building up of our legal principles and the historic value of the process, one cannot but look with envy, in the interest of general utility, on Justinian's heroic remedy—to secure once for all, at whatever cost, an authoritative Digest of our present case law and make a clean sweep of the past cases. Of course, case law must continue to go on, but it could be with ease subjected to a periodic authoritative revision and reduction to the form of general rules.

This, far more than the mere consolidation of Statutes, seems to me the one chance which has any hopefulness about it, of the much-talked-of Codification of English Law (see generally *Practical Jurisprudence*, Part II., chap. xvi.).

ULPIAN

Political Conditions of Ulpian's Age.—The social and political conditions of the age in which Ulpian lived seem ill adapted to the growth and development of a great legal talent. A period of stability and tranquillity, in which the supremacy of the law is secure and the search for truth undistracted by the play of violent, elemental passions, would appear indispensable for the fruitful pursuit of legal as of other kinds of knowledge. Concerned as he is at every point with questions of right and wrong in human conduct, the student of law is not unlikely, when passions run high, to swerve from the strait path of single-minded, unbiassed truth-seeking. It happens often enough, indeed—as our own history shows—that great lawyers rise to eminence in periods of storm and stress, when the reign of the law itself is imperilled. But the truth seems to be that the forces of human character which are evoked on such occasions as these are the forces of political rather than of specifically legal instinct.

The period covered by the last part of the second and the early years of the third century of our era was certainly not a period of tranquillity, though, on the other hand, it cannot be said that the supremacy of the law was seriously in danger. It is true there was a great deal of lawlessness "in high places," and within the sphere of high political intrigue human life was held very cheap, and the claims of justice and morality were frequently and flagrantly ignored. Nevertheless, as far as the great mass of mankind was concerned, the strong legal machinery of the Roman Empire worked, in all probability, smoothly and efficiently. Men bargained and sold, let and hired, managed their property and made their wills, under the full protection of the law, and of a law to the development and shaping of which some of the wisest minds of all ages had contributed, and were, at that very moment, still contributing.

On the other hand, no period ever had less claim to be ranked as tranquil. While Ulpian was growing to manhood (the exact year of his birth is uncertain, but we shall probably not be very wide of the mark if we assume it to have been about A.D. 180), Septimius Severus was Emperor of Rome (A.D. 193-211). He had "waded through slaughter to a throne," and for some twenty years he succeeded in maintaining his supremacy by that sinister combination of shrewdness and cruelty which, in such times as his, is apt to take the place of statesmanship. During all these years the law was inflexibly upheld, and justice was wisely and impartially administered. But when Severus died, the chaos which he had foreseen set in. The hatred which had smouldered for some years between his two sons Caracalla and Geta burst into full flame. In the short, fierce struggle which ensued, Caracalla is reported to have caused no less than twenty thousand persons to be put to death on the ground that they were partisans of Geta. Such was the reign of terror that no one (we are told by Dion Cassius) ventured to utter the hated name of Geta in the presence of the Emperor and his friends, and the very estates of those who introduced it into their wills were ordered to be confiscated. Nor did the murder of Geta and the extirpation of his adherents appease the fury of Caracalla. From the capital he turned his mad frenzy against the provinces. "Every province," Gibbon tells us (cap. 6), "was by turns the scene of his rapine and cruelty. The senators, compelled by fear to attend his capricious motions, were obliged to provide daily entertainments at an immense expense, which he abandoned with contempt to his guards. . . . The most wealthy families were ruined by partial fines and confiscations, and the great body of his subjects oppressed by ingenious and aggravated taxes. In the midst of peace, and upon the slightest provocation, he issued his commands at Alexandria in Egypt for a general massacre. From a secure post in the temple of Serapis he viewed and directed the slaughter of many thousand citizens, as well as strangers, without distinguishing either the number or the crime of the sufferers."

Ulpian's Literary Activity.—It was while events such as these were taking place, while "a monster whose life disgraced human nature" was at the head of the Roman Empire, that Ulpian composed the greater part of his legal works. Whether (as Mommsen thinks) the larger portion of his great treatise *Ad*

Edictum (in eighty-three books) was written before the reign of Caracalla, or whether the whole of it was written during that reign,[1] it is certain that his literary output during this period was enormous. Besides the treatise *Ad Edictum*, we should probably assign to this reign, not only the elaborate commentary on the *ius civile* (in fifty-one books) known as the *Libri ad Sabinum*,[2] but also a number of monographs on sundry statutes, treatises on the functions of the different magistrates,[3] two books of Institutes, and other works.[4]

Early Career.—There would be nothing very exceptional in the spectacle of Ulpian's quietly composing lengthy treatises on legal subjects while Rome was (figuratively speaking) burning, if he had been by temperament a student. But such was very far from being the case. Throughout his life he was in close touch with political affairs, either as an actual participator or, at any rate, as a keenly interested and vigilant observer. He appears for the first time in public life at a comparatively early age. In

---

[1] This is the work the excerpts from which in the Digest are stated to be more numerous than the excerpts from all the works of any other single jurist.

[2] The Sabinus referred to is, of course, the famous jurist Masurius Sabinus (the author of the *libri tres iuris civilis*), who lived in the reign of Tiberius. Lampridius, one of those "wretched, untrustworthy writers" (as Puchta calls them) on whom we have to fall back, for want of any better, for much of our information concerning this whole period, confuses him with a friend of Alexander Severus called Sabinus—a characteristic piece of ignorance and slipshodness.

[3] One of these, *De officio Proconsulis libri X*.—which was a treatise on the criminal law—dealt, amongst other things, with the penal laws then in force against the Christians. It is extremely unlikely that Ulpian, whose only business was to present a complete account of the existing criminal law, expressed either approval or disapproval of the penal statutes in question. Most probably he "cared for none of those things," apart from their legal aspect. Nevertheless he came to be regarded in the Middle Ages as a vehement enemy of the Christians. The charge probably originated in a passage in the *Institutiones Divinæ* of Lactantius (V. 11): "Domitius de officio Proconsulis libris VII. (*sic*) rescripta principum nefaria collegit, ut doceret quibus pœnis affici oporteret eos qui se cultores Dei confiterentur;" and elsewhere Lactantius speaks of the "constitutiones sacrilegæ et disputationes iurisperitorum iniustæ" directed "contra pios." To which statements an old commentator adds the quaint remark that he had hitherto borne a certain grudge against Justinian for abolishing the writings of the old jurists with a view to compiling his *Pandects*; "nunc vero præterea etiam hominem laudo qui incestas illas et, ut (Lactantius) noster vocat, sacrilegas (constitutiones) sustulit."

[4] A complete list of Ulpian's works will be found in Rudorff's *Römische Rechtsgeschichte*, vol. i., pp. 190, 191. See also Dr. Roby's *Introduction to the Study of Justinian's Digest*, pp. 199, 200. There is much uncertainty as to the dates when many of his books (*e.g.* the two books of *Responsa*, the *Liber singularis Regularum*) were composed. Much of his work was done in the reign of Heliogabalus. The treatise *De adulteriis* was certainly written after Caracalla's reign.

the reign of Septimius Severus he was an assessor in the auditorium of Papinian, and served as a member of the Imperial Council. There are some stories afloat as to the existence of a certain rivalry between him and Papinian, and, according to Rudorff (*Rechtsgeschichte*, i., p. 189), he was even implicated in the fall of his great predecessor. But the evidence for all such allegations is extremely untrustworthy. Under Caracalla he held the post of *scriniorum magister* (Master of the Records), Paul being at the same time *ad libellos* (Master of Petitions).

Heliogabalus: Ulpian's Tyrian Extraction.—Under Heliogabalus, the High Priest of the Syrian Sun-God, who succeeded Caracalla after the brief but sanguinary interlude of Macrinus' reign, Ulpian appears to have suffered a check in his career. He was deprived of all his dignities,[1] banished from Rome, and even threatened with execution. During the five years of Oriental effeminacy and despotism which marked the Syrian's reign (A.D. 218-222), Ulpian appears to have devoted himself, in the main, to literary work, though he doubtless kept a watchful eye on public affairs. There were indeed good reasons why Ulpian should feel a kind of special, personal interest in the politics of the Court at that time. Heliogabalus (whose mother, Soæmias, was a first cousin of Caracalla and Geta, and a sister of Julia Mamæa, the mother of the future Emperor Alexander Severus) was the first Roman Emperor of Asiatic extraction. Now, Ulpian —as he tells us himself in a passage which has been preserved to us in the Digest[2]—was of Tyrian origin. Strong as was the solidarity of the Roman Empire, and powerful as were the tendencies of the time towards an elimination of the smaller local

---

[1] According to some accounts these dignities included the highest post of all, that of *Præfectus Prætorio*, with which Heliogabalus had invested him. According to other accounts he did not become *Præfectus Prætorio* till the reign of Alexander Severus.

[2] 50, 15, 1 *pr*. "Sciendum est esse quasdam colonias iuris Italici, ut est in Syria Phœnice splendidissima Tyriorum colonia, unde mihi origo est, nobilis regionibus, serie seculorum antiquissima, armipotens, fœderis quod cum Romanis percussit tenacissima." The words "unde mihi origo est" seem to indicate that Tyre was not his actual birthplace. Bremer (*Rechtslehrer u. Rechtsschulen im römischen Kaiserreich*, p. 87) suggests that he may, at any rate, have resided at Tyre for some time, and may have been, temporarily, professor at the University of Berytus. It is remarkable how prominently Syria and Syrians figure in this period of Roman history. It is quite possible that Papinian was a Syrian (see p. 17 of this volume). Julia Domna, the wife of Severus, was a Syrian. Ulpian, the Emperor Heliogabalus, and Julia Mamæa (see the text above) were all Syrians. The Emperor Macrinus held a Court at Antioch, and a battle fought in Syria put an end to his short reign.

patriotisms in favour of a wider Imperial unity, nevertheless it is clear that Ulpian retained throughout his life a keen personal interest in Tyre and things Syrian.[1] The accession of the priest of Emesa as the first emperor of Asiatic extraction—Emesa was, like Tyre and Berytus, an important Syrian town—naturally, therefore, added a stimulus to Ulpian's interest in public affairs, and inspired him with the hope of rising to a still higher eminence than any to which he had previously attained.[2] Julia Mamæa, a clever and ambitious woman, had probably foreseen that the eccentric rule of Heliogabalus would inevitably be short-lived, and had been quietly preparing the way for the proclamation of her son Alexander as Emperor. Ulpian appears to have gained the full confidence of Mamæa, and may have assisted her with advice in carrying her designs into execution. About A.D. 222, at any rate, he held the post of *præfectus annonæ* (Commissioner of Corn Supply), and no sooner had the dagger put an end to the tragi-comedy of the Sun-Priest's rule, than we find Ulpian forthwith installed as the guide, philosopher, and friend of the sixteen-year-old Emperor.

Friendship of Alexander Severus.—For the rest of his life Ulpian retained the complete confidence of his Imperial master and (what was perhaps more important) his Imperial mistress. In one place Alexander speaks of him as "amicus meus," in another as "parens meus," and several passages in the historians bear testimony to the close personal relationship which existed between Emperor and jurist.[3] Ulpian was now, and remained for some six years, the virtual Regent of the Empire, " a partner " (to use

---

[1] Thus in the passage already quoted from the Digest in the last note, there is a pleasant ring of pride in the antiquity and natural beauty of Tyre, though at the same time its obligations as a city of no mean Empire are emphasized. In other passages Ulpian mentions Syria, and Asia, and the Punic language. Thus in Dig. 32, 11 *pr.*, after stating that *fideicommissa* could be expressed in any language, he adds, " non solum Latina vel Græca, *sed etiam Punica* vel Gallicana vel alterius cuiuscumque gentis." Again in Dig. 45, 1, 1, 6, after stating the rule that a *stipulatio* is valid, if the question is put in Latin and the answer given in Greek, or *vice versa,* " dummodo congruenter respondeatur," he proceeds to ask whether this rule is limited to Greek, or whether it is equally applicable to other languages, " Pœnum forte vel Assyrium vel cuius alterius linguæ," and he decides that any language will serve, " ita tamen ut uterque alterius linguam intelligat "—a characteristic piece of minute comment on a matter of growing practical importance.

[2] It is assumed here that Ulpian did not become *Præfectus Prætorio* till the reign of Alexander. But see p. 35, note 1.

[3] Thus we are told that Ulpian was one of the only two people whom Alexander would see alone, and was a constant guest at the Emperor's table.

the words of Zosimus) "in the Imperial power." His actual position is variously described. According to some reports the office of *Præfectus Prætorio*[1] was, so to speak, held in commission by Ulpian and two other persons, Flavianus and Chrestus, though it would seem that the latter were soon removed, Ulpian thus becoming sole *Præfect*. According to another account, Ulpian was President of a Council of sixteen Senators specially selected by the Emperor to discuss public matters of moment and to advise the Emperor thereon. Anyhow, his duties were of a most exacting character, and he found no leisure for literary activity. Alexander's attention to the judicial duties of the Emperor is stated to have been most assiduous, and it is probable that Ulpian bore the largest share in lightening the heavy burden of work which devolved on the Emperor as the supreme fountain of justice throughout the Empire. We are told that Alexander devoted the greater part of the mornings and a large part of the afternoons to the consideration of letters and petitions; and in exercising that "patience and discretion above his years" which, as Gibbon says, he showed in the determination of private causes, he was presumably largely guided by the wide knowledge, ripe experience, and shrewd wisdom of Ulpian.[2]

Military Opposition to Ulpian: his Death.—But the difficulties of Ulpian were not merely those of a very hard-worked official. Strong as he was in the favour of the Emperor and his mother, his position was far from secure. His promotion excited a considerable amount of jealousy which gradually developed into open hostility, and ultimately led to his destruction. It is not easy at the present day to determine the exact nature of the dispute between Ulpian and his foes. His steady opposition to the increasing influence of the military caste is probably rightly assigned as the main cause of the quarrel, though it is not unlikely that a certain amount of his unpopularity was due to personal reasons. Ulpian was not only a clever lawyer, but also an adroit courtier, and we are perhaps not doing him any in-

---

[1] The *Præfectus Prætorio*, who was originally merely the Captain of the Guards, had gradually become the first officer of the State, the direct representative of the Emperor not only in military, but also in legal and financial matters.

[2] "Wise" is the favourite adjective applied by Gibbon to Ulpian. In Novel 97, 6, Justinian calls him τὸν σοφώτατον; in Cod. 6, 51, 9, he is referred to as "summi ingenii vir," and elsewhere (by Diocletian, Cod. 9, 41, 11), as "vir prudentissimus." Such adjectives are bandied about pretty freely in connection with the great jurists, but they are certainly appropriate in the case of Ulpian.

justice if we assume that he was no more averse to intrigue than most of the Court officials of the time. By temperament he was probably out of sympathy with the military class, and indeed the influence and unbridled licence of the prætorian guards must have been wellnigh intolerable to any one to whom the supremacy of the law and orderly administration were matters of prime concern. The Emperor himself was, in a large measure, at the mercy of his soldiers. He could only maintain his authority by keeping the prætorian guards in a good humour. Firmness and discipline had to be tempered with a liberal admixture of flattery and indulgence. In Severus's time the prætorian guards—originally the flower of Italian youth ("Italiæ alumni et Romana vere iuventus": Tacitus, Hist. i. 84)—were largely recruited from other parts of the Empire, e.g. Macedonia and Spain. The bonds of discipline, which an honourable tradition of close association with the ancient centre of the Empire had helped to maintain, were thus gradually relaxed. The prætorians, having long enjoyed a virtual immunity for their excesses, had grown impatient of restraint. It is probable that Alexander's efforts to abridge the privileges of the prætorians were strongly backed by Ulpian, whose influence at Court since the removal of Flavianus and Chrestus[1] was almost unchallenged. After a lengthy period of plotting and counter-plotting and smouldering hatred, some accident precipitated the catastrophe in the year 228. A formidable riot broke out in Rome and lasted three days. Knowing his life to be in danger, Ulpian took refuge in the Imperial palace, but the angry soldiery forced their way in and slew him in the very presence of Alexander and Mamæa.[2] So powerful was the influence of Ulpian's enemies that Alexander did not venture openly to punish the ringleader of the riot, who was removed to a nominal post of honour in Egypt, and subsequently transferred to Crete. There he was quietly put out of the way some time afterwards, when the excitement caused by the riot had subsided.

Ulpian's Special Excellence as a Jurist.—Such was the life of this remarkable Roman, who, thanks to the liberal extent to

[1] See above, p. 37. It is probable that Flavianus and Chrestus were opposed to the influence of Mamæa and to the curtailment of the privileges of the prætorians. An epitomator of Dion Cassius says they were removed by foul means to which Ulpian was privy, but there is no evidence to support this allegation. Flavianus and Chrestus are sometimes spoken of as Ulpian's predecessors, elsewhere as holding office for a time jointly with him.

[2] The whole story of the death of Ulpian is passed over by the writer of the life of Alexander Severus in the Augustan Histories—another example of the untrustworthiness of much of our material for the history of this period.

which Justinian's compilers drew on his works in composing the Digest, has probably exercised a larger influence over European jurisprudence than any other jurist. To say this is not equivalent to saying that he was one of the very greatest jurists. Ulpian was not a lawyer of the strong, originative type like Labeo, Salvius Julianus, and Papinian, the type that may be said to create—or, rather, to discover—the law. Ulpian's powers did not lie in the direction of arduous pioneer-work. His was rather the faculty of lucid, orderly exposition. Having mastered the whole domain of law as it then existed, he proceeded to apply a mind of singular shrewdness and perspicacity to a restatement, in his own terms, of the rules of law on a large variety of topics. In his works the hard-won achievements of his great predecessors are set forth in a clear and agreeable style. Not that he was a mere compiler, a purveyor of other men's goods. It is true that the opinions of others figure rather prominently in his writings. But Ulpian did not simply reproduce other men's views. Whatever he took in was, so to speak, dissolved and recrystallized. He had a keen appreciation of what was of permanent value in the literature before him. This he subjected to a criticism at once acute and practical. Rejecting what he deemed unimportant, he tested what remained with minute care, and expounded it afresh in his own clear way, pointing out the qualifications and limitations which the practical requirements of the law seemed to him to impose on the legal propositions under review.

Lucidity of his Style.—As regards style, Ulpian is a consummate master of lucid expression—indeed, with Gaius, the greatest master of clear exposition among the Roman jurists.[1] In his writings there is no mannerism, no affectation, no turgid rhetoric.[2] The language, as Dr. Roby points out,[3] is "the ordinary language of daily life and business among educated persons" of the time. In other words, it is simple and straightforward.[4] Such a style

[1] We do not possess very much of Ulpian's work in its original form, but, such as it is, it amply justifies the praise that has been bestowed on it. Even as "edited" in the Digest, he exhibits a remarkable power of lucid exposition.

[2] As to this, see below, p. 43, the observations of Austin.

[3] *Introduction*, p. 209. Dr. Roby is speaking of the classical jurists generally, but his remarks are particularly applicable to Ulpian.

[4] Of course it was not the language of Cicero, the "Latin pure, discreet" demanded by the fastidious scholarship of Browning's Bishop when ordering an inscription for his "Tomb at St. Praxed's Church":

"Aha, 'elucescebat,' quoth our friend? No Tully, said I, Ulpian at the best!"

is not indeed without its drawbacks. True, we are spared the pedantries and artificialities of the lawyers of some other ages, but, on the other hand, there is an occasional looseness of expression, and in the flow of facile utterance[1] the real difficulties of legal problems are often in danger of being hidden out of sight. For us, however, the very faults of Ulpian's style have proved an almost unmixed advantage. The extraordinary readiness of his pen enabled him to enrich juristic literature with an astonishing abundance of legal matter of the utmost value. His very diffuseness has helped us—as it helped the generations which succeeded him in the Roman Empire—to understand much that is difficult and obscure in his predecessors. Accordingly, when Justinian's compilers came to compose the Digest, the writings of Ulpian were more liberally drawn upon than those of any other jurist. They supply, indeed, the groundwork of the Digest. The excerpts from Ulpian (2,462 in number, as compared with 2,080 from Paul and 595 from Papinian) form about one-third of the whole body of the Digest. Long as some of these excerpts are, they are very much shorter than the originals from which they were taken. For it was the business of the compilers "from vain excess to clear the encumber'd laws,"[2] and in performing their task they subjected Ulpian's writings to a very liberal process of pruning. A comparison of the Vatican Fragments 75 to 83 (containing the full text of Ulpian) with Digest 7, 2, 1, 2 to 4 and 7, 2, 2 and 3 (where the "vain excess" has disappeared) will illustrate the extent to which the process was carried.[3]

Alleged Decline of Roman Jurisprudence.—It is said that the decline of Roman jurisprudence commences with Ulpian and Paul.[4] It is true that neither Ulpian nor any of his successors ever attained to the same eminence as Julian or Papinian, and it

---

[1] In Cod. 6, 25, 10, the term "*disertissimus*" is applied both to Papinian and Ulpian. It seems far more appropriate to Ulpian than to Papinian.

[2] "Son Giustiniano
  Che . . .
  Dentro alle leggi trassi *il troppo e 'l vano*."
                      DANTE: *Paradiso* vi. 10-12.

[3] The two passages are set out, in a most instructive way, in parallel columns in Dr. Roby's *Introduction*, p. 73 ff. It is, however, hardly necessary to say that what the compilers rejected was not therefore necessarily "vain excess." The nature of their task compelled them to exclude all obsolete matter, and also much that was valuable, and even essential, from a literary point of view. It would be most unfair to appraise the literary quality of the jurists' writings by reference to the excerpts in the Digest alone.

[4] F. Hofman, *Kritische Studien zum römischen Rechte* (1885), p. 3 *ff.*

is further true that the work of his successors shows signs of failing power. Nevertheless, the theory is apt to do some injustice to Ulpian. It would be difficult to find any definite symptom of decadence in his writings, any relaxing of the intellectual grip, any blurring of the clear, legal vision, any idle circumlocution doing duty for thought. The mere fact that Ulpian's powers lay in the particular direction we have tried to indicate (p. 39) is not enough to stamp him as a "decadent." A man of his special type might just as well have flourished, and done useful work, before as after Papinian. Among his contemporaries and successors he enjoyed an immense prestige, and, indeed, it was largely due to the influence of Ulpian's writings that the great tradition of Roman jurisprudence was so successfully upheld during the following centuries, when the faculty for fully appreciating the grand achievements of the classical age was slowly but steadily dwindling. Ulpian's pupil Modestinus ("studiosus meus," Ulpian calls him in Dig. 47, 2, 52, 20), himself no mean judge of juristic capacity, ranks Ulpian with Scævola and Paul as one of the κορυφαῖοι τῶν νομικῶν, thus passing over Papinian altogether. And during the ensuing centuries the authority enjoyed by Ulpian in the Courts—especially in the Eastern half of the Empire—was second only to that of Papinian, a fact to which formal expression was given in Valentinian's Law of Citations, 426 A.D. (see Professor Clark's article, *loc. cit.*, p. 4, note 2).

Ulpian's Ius Naturale.—A brief reference may here be allowed to Ulpian's famous triple division of law into *ius civile*, *ius gentium*, and *ius naturale*, or law peculiar to the Romans, law common to all nations, and law common to human beings and animals. This division is not, as is sometimes suggested, peculiar to Ulpian. We cannot, of course, say how far it was adopted by the numerous other jurists whose writings have not been preserved to us. But as far as the Digest is concerned, it appears not only in the well-known passages from Ulpian in the first title of the first book, but also in two other passages, in one (from Tryphoninus, Dig. 12, 6, 64) explicitly, in the other (from Hermogenianus, Dig. 1, 1, 5) by necessary implication. Nevertheless, it is true (as Savigny has conclusively shown[1]) that the doctrine in question exercised no perceptible influence on the rules of Roman law, and cannot indeed be made to serve as a

[1] *System des heutigen römischen Rechts*, i., Beilage I.

basis of legal classification. To admit this is not, however, equivalent to saying that the whole doctrine is as meaningless and absurd as Austin's unfortunate strictures might lead one to suppose. Savigny himself—adopting in its essentials the defence of Ulpian by Donellus (I. 6)—points out the true significance and value of Ulpian's theory. He reminds us of the important consideration that in every relation we must distinguish the matter and the form, and that the matter of a legal relation can be conceived of apart from its form. In the great majority of legal relations, such as ownership or obligation, the matter is *arbitrary*, in the sense that the human race could conceivably continue to exist without it. But what differentiates the relations mentioned by Ulpian—" maris atque feminæ coniunctio, liberorum procreatio, educatio "—is just the fact that their matter is *not* arbitrary, consisting, as it does, of natural relations, common to human beings and animals, without which the human race could not continue to exist. Ulpian's reference to " ius " (" videmus etenim cetera quoque animalia, feras etiam, istius iuris peritia censeri ") is somewhat fanciful and bizarre, but it is ridiculous to suppose that he really imagined legal relations to subsist as between animals. All he wished to point out was that that which constitutes the matter (as distinct from the form) of certain fundamental legal relations between men, has its almost exact counterpart in the animal world. Nor is this a mere "foolish conceit " or " inept speculation " (Austin's *Jurisprudence*, 5th ed., pp. 209, 210, 552). Ulpian's view, understood in the sense indicated, is, as Savigny says (*loc. cit.*), " not only true, but important and deserving of consideration," and, though useless as a basis of legal classification, its influence on legal thought in other directions—not only in Ulpian's time, but also centuries afterwards—was considerable. Savigny's treatment of Ulpian's theory affords an admirable model of the temper and spirit in which such questions must be approached if the discussion is to yield fruitful results. For what is the position ? A lawyer of vast knowledge and experience, a man steeped in the traditions of a great legal and philosophical past, and working in an atmosphere of strenuous juristic endeavour, deliberately enunciates a particular theory. This theory is adjudged worthy of preservation three hundred years later by a body of lawyers of far more than average attainments. Centuries afterwards the theory is still found to exercise a strong influence over minds of the most different cast.[1] And, finally, in our own age, it is deemed worthy of patient examination by the greatest jurist of modern times. In face of such facts as these an attitude of half-petulant, half-supercilious contempt such as marks so much of Austin's criticism—an attitude which finds expression (unconscious expression, perhaps) in references to the "good" Ulpian and "this legal oracle"—is, we venture to submit, entirely futile and barren.

Ulpian's Idealism.—When Austin complained of Ulpian's Latin being "too declamatory" for his taste (*loc. cit.*, p. 563), he may have been thinking of such passages as the one just discussed, and those dealing with the nature of jurisprudence (Dig. 1, 1, 10, 2), and the functions of the jurist (1, 1, 1, 2). The term "declamatory" cannot, however (as we have endeavoured to show), be fitly applied to Ulpian's style, so that Austin's objection may have been intended for the matter rather than the form of Ulpian's statements. Of the passage on the *ius naturale* nothing more need be said. As to the other two passages, though they obviously have no claim to scientific precision, they are very far indeed from being mere "declamatory" rhetoric. They present, it is true, a somewhat exalted ideal of the nature of jurisprudence[2] and the functions of the true jurist.[3] But

[1] Austin himself mentions two—Hooker and Montesquieu. "A fustian description of law" is his urbane reference (*loc. cit.*, p. 211) to the definition of law in Hooker's *Ecclesiastical Polity* (I., c. 18). As for Montesquieu—whose robust sanity has earned for him the title of "the father of the modern historical method"—it is perhaps enough to say that it would be difficult to name a thinker less prone to "foolish conceits" and "inept speculations."

[2] We take Ulpian's meaning to be somewhat as follows: The business of the jurist is to ascertain the legal *truth*, either by testing existing rules of law, or by seeking to discover new rules. In doing this, he must keep two considerations—corresponding to two aspects of law—steadily in view. In the first place, he must consider the requirements of justice, which is the life-principle of law—*i.e.*, he must apply an *ideal* standard, a standard which, in its ultimate origin, passes beyond the limits of purely human things. This is the standard implied (though not always acknowledged) in the frequent appeals to a "higher justice," "equity," "the reason of mankind," and so forth. In the second place, he must consider the requirements of utility—*i.e.*, he must apply a *practical* standard, for the rules of positive law are intended to regulate human acts and human affairs. The greatest lawyer—be he judge or jurist—is he who combines a firm grasp of the material realities of life with a clear vision of the ideal beyond." Iurisprudentia est divinarum atque humanarum rerum notitia, iusti atque iniusti scientia."

[3] " Cuius (artis) merito quis nos sacerdotes appellet: iustitiam namque colimus et boni et æqui notitiam profitemur, æquum ab iniquo separantes, licitum ab illicito discernentes, bonos non solum metu poenarum, verum etiam præmiorum quoque exhortatione efficere cupientes; veram, nisi fallor, philosophiam, non simulatam affectantes." Ulpian is speaking, of course, of the jurists of his own time. The peculiar bent of the national genius of the Romans tended to make the jurists regard their science as the "true philosophy." But Ulpian's remarks are not without value even for us.

even if they did nothing more than that, the fault, if fault it be, is surely on the right side. The law is continually beset with temptations from outside which tend to lower it from the proud dignity of a free science to the level of a smart trade. Our thanks are due to those who keep the higher ideal steadily before our eyes. Within the sphere of jurisprudence, as elsewhere, there is much to learn from the man who, in Emerson's phrase, " hitches his waggon to a star."

BARTOLUS[1]

Bartolus compared with Ulpian.—In some respects the great jurist of the Middle Ages whose name stands at the head of this article bears a somewhat close resemblance to Ulpian, the most famous jurist of the decadent Roman Empire of the West, from which the animating health and vigour of the Augustan age had already fled[2] or was fast fleeing. Like Ulpian, Bartolus was not distinguished by originality of thought or exposition, but he had Ulpian's faculty of clearness and perspicacity of vision, to which he mainly owed the high reputation he acquired in the course of a comparatively brief career, and which his writings continued to maintain for at least two centuries after his death. He could also on occasion play the part of an adroit courtier, as we shall see in connection with his mission to the Emperor Charles IV.

Their Respective Periods contrasted.—It is interesting, moreover, to notice that while Ulpian flourished in a period which witnessed the grant of citizenship to all Roman subjects, involving, as Gibbon says,[3] the vain title and real obligations of Roman citizens, thereby proclaiming to the world the universality and unity of the Roman sovereignty, and elevating the Roman Law into a great system of territorial jurisprudence which displaced every other, Bartolus saw the light of day under very changed circumstances. Unity had then given place to diversity, the Empire of the Cæsars had long since ceased to represent a living political force in the west of Europe, and under

---

[1] The following authorities have been mostly consulted: Savigny's *Geschichte des Römischen Rechts im Mittelalter*, vol. vi., 122-163 ; *La Grande Encyclopédie*, vol. v., p. 524 *et seq.;* Lainé, *Introduction au droit International Privé*, tome i., 115-163 ; Weiss, *Traite théorique et pratique de droit International Privé*, vol. i., s. 2, p. 15 *et seq.;* Rivier, *Introduction Historique au Droit Romaine*, ss. 214-215, p. 568 *et seq.;* Laurent, *Le droit civil International* chap. iii., p. 273 *et seq.;* Fiore, *Diritto Internazionale Privato*, vol. i., cap. iv. p. 43 *et seq.;* Laghi, *Il diritto Internazionale Privato*, vol. i., bk. i., cap. i., p. 39 *et seq.;* Holtzendorff's *Encyklopädie der Rechtswissenschaft*, i., p. 155 *et seq.*

[2] Gibbon, *Decline and Fall of the Roman Empire*, vol. i., chap. vii., p. 194, Bury's edition.

[3] *Ibid.*, p. 164.

the influence of barbarian individualism man, and not the citizen, had become the true juridical being and the subject of rights. The invasions of the barbarian hordes, under Attila the Hun, Alaric the Goth, and Genseric the Vandal, had already broken to a large extent the spell of Roman universality. Even so early as A.D. 476 the greater part of the lands which had formerly composed the Roman Empire of the West, had been divided into six large Teutonic kingdoms. Italy and Noricum formed the kingdom of Odoacer; North Africa constituted the dominion of Genseric or Gaiseric the Vandal; from the Loire to the Straits of Gibraltar was ruled by Euric; the valleys of the Rhone and Saone belonged to Gungobad, the Burgundian; the Frankish princes reigned on the Meuse, Moselle, and Lower Rhine; and the Suevi carved out a kingdom which would correspond with North Portugal and Galicia. Under the influence of this general disruption and partition of the former Roman Empire, a new order of things now took the place of the older system, and henceforth we find that the independence of the individual, which, as Guizot rightly says, is the dominant character of barbarism, furnishes also the keynote for a right understanding of that march of progress in the history of the development of legal ideas which evolves gradually between the opposite poles of juridical thought, marked by the principle of Roman territoriality on the one hand, and by that of personality of the later European jurisprudence on the other. Each Hun, Goth, or Frank cherished his own free and independent personality, and acknowledged no law but that of the folk-right of his own tribe, which he had brought with him. Therefore, just as it is in the pristine forests of Germany that Montesquieu tells us we must seek to find the roots of liberty, so it is amongst the barbarian hordes who invaded Italy that we must look for the first germs of that fundamental notion which consecrated the supreme authority of personal laws, and which was destined to exercise so large and dominating an influence upon the development of Private International Law in Continental Europe.

Commerce of Free Burghal Cities in Italy favours Notion of Personality.—As we advance towards the twelfth and thirteenth centuries the growth of commerce in the free burghal cities of Italy had no small influence in confirming the notion that a man carried his personality with him, and did not lose it by mere temporary residence for the purposes of trade or the like in a city other than that in which he was born. Nay, even in the same city it was no uncommon experience to find conflicting laws prevailing in different quarters of it, much in the same way as local customs in India regulating the right of pre-emption are found to vary at the present day in different *muhallas* or subdivisions of the same city.

Study of Roman Law.—But although the Middle Ages as a period were distinguished by the growth of a vast body of personal laws, the study of the Roman Law had never actually ceased to attract the attention of the best intellects of each succeeding century. It may be, and is no doubt true, that Rome, which was the proper seat of legal education in Ulpian's time, ceased to be so some time (probably four centuries) after the reign of Justinian, who, himself, on his conquest of Italy, had confirmed the Roman School of Law in its privileges, and contributed to its upkeep by supplying funds for the payment of its teachers. But with the dismemberment of the Western Empire law-schools as public endowments were no longer maintained. The Roman Law was, nevertheless, taught in the ordinary secular schools as a branch of old literature, and an instance of this at Toul is quoted by Savigny from a contemporary account of Pope Leo IX., who died in A.D. 1054. About the same time we have undeniable traces of a school of law at Ravenna, and, according to Odofredus, who wrote in the thirteenth century, this was the same school which had formerly existed at Rome.

In Bartolus's time we know that law was taught in Italy, at Pisa, Perugia, Padua, and Bologna; so that while a new world of legal ideas had been called into existence, it was more by way of supplement (*in subsidium*) than in substitution of that system which the genius of Rome had established for the perpetual instruction and guidance of civilized humanity. And this tendency was materially strengthened by the attitude of the Roman Catholic Church. By its very constitution the Church of Rome stood forth as the embodiment of unity and universality; and while the priesthood represented the people in the abstract, the papacy was the symbol of the State and sovereignty. Accordingly, from the seventh century onwards, the principle *Ecclesia vivit lege romana* was one which was constantly recognized by ecclesiastical writers.

The School of Glossators.—But it is from the end of the eleventh century that a systematic study of the Roman Law can be said to have been revived. This was the work of the Jurist Irnerius, who was the founder of the School of Glossators which flourished down to the middle of the thirteenth century, but of whose personal history we know very little, except that he died about A.D. 1188, and, according to Odofredus, *studuit per se, sicut potuit*. It was this school which was the precursor of that of Bartolus, and which derived its name from the fact that its teaching consisted in brief glosses on the text of the original Roman law-books. Its chief ornament was Accursius (1182-1260), whose masterly *glossa ordinaria* fittingly closed this era. This work obtained such general repute that it practically superseded the original sources of the law, to such an extent, indeed, that it became a recognized rule *quod non agnoscit glossa, non agnoscit curia*.

Followed by that of the Commentators and Post-Glossators.—This era was followed by that of the Commentators and Post-Glossators, who abandoned the form of glosses upon texts, and adopted instead the more comprehensive and more scientific method of dealing separately with particular branches of law, and grouping together all the principles governing the same. These rules were, perhaps, not always very clearly expressed nor arranged in the most convenient order, while the Latin which the commentators employed was described, but perhaps by too captious a critic—Rabelais—as that of the *cuisinier et marmiteux, non de Jurisconsulte*. Among the earliest jurists of this school were Oldradus (1335), who was a professor of law at Padua, Siena, Montpellier, Perugia, and Bologna, and among his disciples were Bartolus and Alberic; Pierre de Belleperche or Petrus de Bellapertica, who died in 1308; Joannes Andreæ (Jean d'André), the most celebrated authority on procedure in the Middle Ages, who died in 1348; and Cinus, the pupil of Dinus, a Florentine and former professor at Bologna, who died in 1303, the friend of Dante and the master of Bartolus and Petrarch, a poet himself (whose sonnet in memory of Selvaggia and the canzone to Dante are fine examples of his style at best) as well as a jurist of considerable eminence, who *inter alia* is distinguished for having maintained, contrary to the then prevailing opinion in favour of the *lex rei sitæ*, that the form of a testament was to be regulated by the *lex loci actus*.

Bartolus: Personal History.—It was in this era in the history of jurisprudence, and in the midst of such surroundings, that we reach the name of Bartolus. Of his birth and early years we have little reliable knowledge. He was a native of Sassoferrato, a town in the province of Ancona, on the River Sentino, which was also the birthplace of Perroti (died 1480), a leading scholar of the fifteenth century, who was celebrated for his commentaries on Statius and Martial, and who also translated five books of Polybius into Latin. The year of Bartolus's birth is variously stated between 1309-14, but as he tells us himself (*Dig. Novum.* L. *quidam cum filium* 132, de V.O.) that he was promoted to the degree of Doctor of Laws at the age of twenty-one, and as this event occurred on November 10th, 1334, we may safely accept the suggestion of Savigny,[1] that Bartolus must have been born between November 10th, 1313, and November 10th, 1314. His father's name is given in his doctor's diploma (a copy of which is given by Lancellotus) as Franciscus, son of Bonaccursius, and his mother's name, we are told by his biographer Lancellotus, who published his Life in 1576, was *Sancta*, which seems to effectually dispose of the story that he was a foundling. He had two brothers, Bonaccursius (called after his grandfather) and Peter. His first tutor was the grammarian Peter of Assisi, a man of whom he speaks with earnest gratitude, as learned without hypocrisy, and of wonderful piety. At the age of fourteen he began the study of law at Perugia, and his principal tutor was the Cinus already mentioned, whose lectures, he told Baldus, had exercised most influence upon his legal training. He subsequently removed to Bologna, and there he studied under four distinguished jurists, Buttigarius, Rainerius, Oldradus, and Belvisio. He seems also to have applied himself to the study of geometry under Guido of Perugia, a *magnus Theologus*, as Bartolus calls him, and of the Hebrew language. He held the office of judicial assessor at Todi and Pisa, and it is said by Diplovataccius that he was banished for four years for an unjust sentence of death he had passed while exercising one of these offices. But the story is disbelieved by Savigny,[2] and there is no contemporary proof in support of it. In the autumn of 1339 we find him appointed as a colleague of his former master Rainerius at Pisa on a salary of one hundred and fifty florins, at which time he tells us he was twenty-six years of age, and the house in which he lived in Pisa was still preserved in Savigny's time with an

[1] *Geschichte des römischen Rechts im Mittelalter*, bd. vi., p. 125, *n.* 5.
[2] Vol. vi., p. 129.

inscription upon it commemorating the fact. In 1343 he removed to Perugia, where he soon established a widespread reputation as a law teacher, and pupils from all parts of Italy flocked to his lectures, two of the most famous being Baldus and his brother Angelus. Five years afterwards Perugia, in grateful remembrance of his eminent services, conferred upon him and his brother Bonaccursius the right of citizenship, and in 1355 this city had still greater cause to revere his memory, for, being sent on a mission to the Emperor Charles IV., who was then at Pisa, Bartolus obtained for it many privileges as well as a confirmatory charter for its University. Nor did he return without personal honours for himself, for the Emperor ennobled him, and appointed him a councillor, besides conferring upon him other marks of imperial favour. Among these was the singular privilege that he and all his descendants who should be professors of law should have the power of legitimizing their pupils in cases of bastardy, or of relieving them from the disadvantages of minority. Bartolus was twice married: his first wife was a native of Ancona, but beyond this fact and that the union did not last long, we know little else about her; his second wife was Pellina di Bovarello of Perugia, of the Alfani family, who survived him, and by whom he had a family of two sons and four daughters. He died at Perugia in July, 1357, at the age of forty-four, and was buried in the Church of St. Francesco, where a monument was erected to his memory with the inscription so eloquent in its brevity, *Ossa Bartoli*. By his will, executed on May 14th, 1356, Bartolus designated his two sons as his principal heirs, but he gave each of his daughters a legacy of four hundred and fifty florins, and he also made a suitable provision for his wife. He bequeathed his modest library, which consisted of thirty juristical and thirty-four theological volumes, indicating in which direction his tastes lay, to a monastery in Perugia, from whence it is said a monk stole the volumes and carried them to Naples. He belonged to the moderate clerical party more by reason that he lived, as he says, *in terris amicis ecclesiæ* than from strong conviction, and as a rule he avoided mixing himself up in the politics of the day arising out of the Guelf and Ghibelline feud.

His Great Authority.—Such are the few particulars of his private life which have come down to us; and considering that his public career was confined within the brief period of eighteen or twenty years, it is astonishing what a reputation he succeeded in building up for himself at an age when most men are only beginning to lay the foundations of their future fame. No jurist of the Middle Ages ever acquired such a reputation as was universally conceded to him. His authority as an expounder of the Roman Law was unquestioned in his lifetime, and revered for centuries after his death. He was called *lucerna* or *pater juris*[1] and *dux jurisconsultorum*, and he exercised for a long time in Italy, Spain, and Portugal the authority of a legislator. At Padua a Chair was even created for the exposition of the opinions of Bartolus. If his reputation was subsequently overshadowed in France and Italy by the historical school represented by Cujas, Alciati (*b.* 1492, *d.* 1550 A.D.), and others, it continued more or less unimpaired in Germany from the "reception" of the Roman Law as the "Common Law" in the fifteenth century down to modern times; and even at this date we must admit that there were solid grounds for the pre-eminent respect that was originally accorded to him. He was above all things a practical lawyer, and his strong practical common sense convinced him of the necessity of evolving from the chaos of conflicting Statutes, customs, and feudal laws which prevailed in his day some principles of general application which were suitable to the age in which he lived. This was the great aim of his life, unhappily cut short by an untimely death while he was still in the vigour of manhood. He wished to draw from the Roman Law, the Canon Law, the Feudal Law, and Customary Law, a sort of Common Law which would avoid the technicalities of the one, the narrowness of another, the harshness of a third, and the defects and deficiencies of a fourth; and if he had been spared to run the average age allotted to man, he would probably have left behind him more imperishable work as the fruit of his labours. But, as we shall see presently, there are still to be found in his works the materials for the construction of many of the leading doctrines of Private International Law.

His Distinctive Teaching.—In their original shape his writings for the most part took the form of lectures, which were delivered by him as part of his University courses; but these were subsequently amplified from notes and manuscript comments, and published in the collected edition of his works, which first appeared in Venice in 1475 in five volumes, and finally in eleven volumes in 1615. This circumstance, no doubt, accounts for the

[1] Laurent, *Le Droit Civil International*, i., p. 299.

fact that in their published form his writings do not reveal that strong personality of the man which was so impressed upon his students in the lecture-room. Many of his critics, therefore, have been unable to account for the superior reputation he enjoyed over his predecessors and contemporaries, and have attempted to account for it in various ways. But the truth is that his exegetical teaching of the law was carried out in a new spirit, with a freshness and energy, combined with a judicial calmness and soberness of judgment, which were wanting in others. So, again, if he employed the dialectical method which was so much in vogue in the previous century, and to an extent which rendered the works of his predecessors tiresome and unprofitable to read, he never abused it.

To us, however, he is chiefly interesting for the influence he exercised in developing the theory of Statutes, which can only be compared with that of d'Argentré at a much later period. That he was not the originator of this celebrated theory, as was once claimed for him, is now well established, for it is certain that both his own masters, Cinus and Oldrodus (to mention no others), directed their attention to the subject of the conflict of laws, and proposed certain rules for its solution. But if Bartolus cannot claim to have originated the above theory, it is certainly equally undeniable that he gave such an extended application to it, and so amplified the work of his predecessors that, while their names have more or less ceased to be connected with it, his own has been imperishably associated with its history. As Weiss says, if he was not the creator of this theory, he was at least one of its ancestors.[1] If, however, he has received in this connection more credit for originality than he deserved, he has, on the other hand, suffered from a want of true appreciation of his actual teaching. It has been said, for instance, that the fundamental notion underlying his theory was the general division of all laws into real and personal Statutes. But such a dual division is completely foreign to the whole school of Italian writers of the period and equally to his own,[2] and is really characteristic since the sixteenth century of the French school under the teaching of d'Argentré, who was responsible for

---

[1] *Traité théorique et pratique de droit International Privé*, i., p. 16, Paris, 1898.
[2] The modern Italian school regards all rules of law as being in principle personal Statutes, and holds that in territorial and international operation they have no other limit than the so-called laws of public order.—*Von Bar*, p 18 (c); Laurent, i., p. 307.

it.¹ It is true that Bartolus incidentally affirms that a disposition of the law is to be regarded as real or personal, according as its terms may relate to things or persons. But that is only in the nature of a passing observation by way of illustration, and by no means embodies what may be termed the kernel of his own teaching, as many writers have affected to believe.

In substance the doctrine of Statutes, as taught by the Post-Glossators, may be summarized in this way : (1) The Roman Law is universal, and therefore common to strangers also ; (2) the Statutory Law, as an exception to the former, is restricted to those persons and things which are subject to the sovereignty which enacted it. From these leading principles the following consequences resulted : (*a*) that a Statute which affected *persons* only did not operate against strangers (*Statuta in non subditos jurisdictioni statuentem disponere non possunt*) ; (*b*) that a Statute which referred to *things* operated against strangers as well as natives, because things were supposed to be under the power of the legislating authority (*Statuta quæ afficiunt res ligant forenses*) ; and (*c*) that a Statute which affected the person follows the citizen wherever he goes (*Civis ligatur etiam extra territorium statuto patriæ*).² As illustrating the application of these general principles, Bartolus taught that a Statute which either permitted a son of the family (*filius familias*) to execute a testament, or prohibited a husband from instituting his wife as his heir, did not affect strangers who were mere residents of the city where such a law prevailed. Conversely, a Statute which prohibited a husband from alienating his wife's estate without her consent is one that has an extra-territorial effect, and the like rule prevails, speaking generally, in dealing with other Statutes affecting the incapacity of a person. But Bartolus not unfrequently found himself confronted with complex cases (as in the matter of succession) which compelled him to devise special regulations and even to resort to ingenious constructions of a text to get over difficulties. It is here that the heel of Achilles is apparent in his armoury, and his vulnerable points were eagerly laid hold of by his later critics to subject him to merciless ridicule. Thus d'Argentré says, *ridere vulgo solent cum dicitur* JUS ATRUM *aut* ATRUM JUS *diversa dicere volenti*.

Dumoulin (1500-66) is equally severe upon him for deciding

---

[1] Lainé, *Introduction au droit International Privé*, i., p. 132, Paris, 1888.
[2] Laghi, *Il diritto Internazionale Privato*, i., p. 50, s. 46.

the controversy as to whether a Statute which provided that the eldest son should succeed to his father's whole estate applied to natives extra-territorially or was confined to persons within its own territory, by inquiring whether the law said *primogenitus succedat in omnibus bonis* or *bona decedentium veniant in primogenitum:* in the former case, according to Bartolus, the Statute was to be held to be one that dealt with persons; in the latter, one that dealt with things. Very naturally his critic says: *Tamen rejicitur hæc distinctio quæ verbalis est et communiter reprobatur.* But advocates of this distinction, puerile as it now seems to us, were nevertheless to be found as late as the eighteenth century, and it must not be forgotten that a very eminent French writer saw a distinction between *Jus vert* and *vert Jus*.[1] Bartolus was, in fact, trying to discover some way of distinguishing between Statutes which fell under one or the other of the above categories, and he begins the passage already quoted by saying: *Mihi videtur, quod verba statuti seu consuetudinis sunt diligenter intuenda,* an observation to which no possible objection could be taken. He then proceeds to say: *Aut illa disponunt circa res,* as, for instance, by the words, *Bona decedentis,* or that the *verba statuti seu consuetudinis disponunt circa personas;* and by way of illustration he adds: *ut per hæc verba: Primogenitus succedat.* It is clear, therefore, that the main object of Bartolus was to lay down the rule that the actual words of a Statute or custom must furnish the true key to its purport and intent, which is a rule well recognized at the present day. His particular illustration of that rule may have been well or ill chosen, but that is quite a secondary matter, and does not affect the soundness of the rule itself. Nor have his critics, d'Argentré and others, been any more successful in their own definitions, and they in turn have been criticized by later jurists. Besides, it must be remembered, in justice to Bartolus, that in the age in which he lived it was usual in the solution of every question to base one's opinions upon some definite text of the Roman Law, and as he had to deal with new conditions and necessities unknown to the Roman jurists, it is not surprising that his interpretations were occasionally of a forced and arbitrary character. As Contuzzi aptly says: *Il pensiero era dei Glossatori, la formola era del Diritto Romano.*[2] When due allowance is made for this

---

[1] Laurent, vol. i., p. 299.
[2] *Diritto Internazionale Privato,* Milan, 1890, p. 42.

circumstance, we need not dwell too much upon the more or less pardonable defects which are alleged against him. It is more generous to recognize that in him we have a jurist who, so early as the first half of the fourteenth century, was capable of laying down the principle, which has served as the foundation of all modern juristic science (*e forma e sempre formerà la base di ogni futuro sistema*, as Fusinato says), that there are certain laws which have an extra-territorial effect, and others which have not ;[1] and, in further illustrating this broad principle by establishing the following important rules : (1) that juridical Acts, such as contracts and testaments, are valid as to form if they comply with the extrinsic requirements of the law of the place where they are made (*ubi est celebratus contractus*) ; (2) that the natural and presumably intended consequences of a convention are to be judged according to the law of the place of contract (*locus contractus*) ; (3) that *accidental* consequences which arise *ex post facto* by reason of neglect or delay (*propter negligentiam vel moram*) are, on the contrary, to be judged by the law of the place of performance (*in illo loco, in quem est collata solutio*), or, if no such place is fixed, or an alternative of many places is provided involving an election, then in that place *ubi petitur;* and (4) that rules of procedure and everything relating *ad litis ordinationem* are to be regulated by the *lex fori*—that is to say, the law of the *locus judicii*. The legists of later centuries have done little more than to elaborate these rules by a further process of development, and posterity, as Laurent[2] rightly contends ought to be more indulgent and just to the memory of a man who, after all, has the glory of being a pioneer of the juristic science of to-day. It is easy to criticize the defects and errors of our predecessors, but if men like Bartolus had not paved the way for later writers, no science would ever be perfected.

His Principal Works.—Bartolus has left behind him a considerable literature on a variety of legal subjects. But amongst his principal works may be mentioned the following :

1. *Commentarius in tria Digesta,* first published in Venice in A.D. 1470.

2. *Commentarius in libros IX. Codices priores,* 1478.

3. *Commentarius Super libris III. posterioribus Codicis,* pub-

---

[1] *Cf.* Fiore, *Diritto Internazionale Privato,* 3rd ed., vol. i., p. 48, Torino, 1888 ; Guido Fusinato, *Il principio della Senola Italiana,* p. 23, Bologna, 1885.

[2] Vol. i., p. 301.

lished in Naples in 1470. In the preface to this work he tells us that he undertook it after a severe illness which prevented him from pursuing his ordinary avocations, in order to occupy his mind with a useful study

4. *Lectura Super Authenticis* (1477), which is an attempt to compile an additional (eleventh) book of novels from the ordinances of the Emperor Henry VII. from the year 1312.

5. *Processus Satanœ contra Divam Virginem Coram Judice Jesu*, a mock trial between the Devil and the Virgin Mother of our Lord, in which the former claims the human race as his property, invoking his long possession in support of his claim, to which the Virgin replies that his possession has been *mala fide*, and therefore of no avail. It is needless to add that the claim is eventually defeated. The treatise is intended as a practical lesson on judicial procedure, and has been frequently printed and translated from the Latin into other languages. It has also suggested many similar works by other writers, such as the *Liber Belial, s. processus Luciferi contra Christum*. Savigny calls it a pedantic and extravagant jest,[1] but Bartolus certainly did not mean it to be accepted otherwise than as a serious contribution to the practical study of the rules of procedure.

Their Value at the Present Day.—Except as a connecting-link between the older system of law prevailing in the period preceding the break-up of the Roman Empire of the West and that of the system adopted by the modern nations of Europe, the works of Bartolus offer little attraction to the ordinary student of the present day. They are now scarcely consulted, and lie neglected—at least in this country—on the shelves of public libraries. Nor is it likely that they will ever again regain much attention. But to those who are interested in discovering how the jurisprudence of modern times has arisen, by mere development and progressive change, from earlier systems, the influence which Bartolus exercised in the latter part of the Middle Ages is full of abiding interest. This period of history is particularly distinguished by examples of awakened energy and restless enterprise, and it is only by a knowledge of the part it played in the development of scientific law that we can hope to be able to appreciate the march of progress in subsequent centuries, or to understand the striking divergence of legal thought in different parts of Western Europe which even now distinguishes

[1] vi. 160.

the Italian, French, and German schools of jurisprudence. English law, of course, stands apart from the laws of the rest of the European nations in its relation to Roman Law, for here that law never acquired the same degree of influence which it naturally obtained on the continent of Europe. Insular isolation has here served to mould our laws, our constitution, and our customs according to ideals suitable to the peculiar conditions under which we live. But even here expansion of trade and increasing intercourse with foreign nations have brought us face to face with the intricate problems arising out of a conflict of laws with which foreign jurists of the thirteenth and later centuries had to deal. No one who is interested in the solution of these problems, which are constantly becoming more and more complex in character, can be indifferent to, or fail to derive advantage from, a study of the principal works of those earlier thinkers in this department of jurisprudence; and it is from this point of view that Bartolus still deserves attention in this country. There was a time when it was usual to brand the Middle Ages as a dark and barbarous period distinguished only by *Faustrecht* or *Kolbenrecht*. But an age that could produce a Dante and a Petrarch can never be said to be unilluminated by genius, and among the jurists of the same age Bartolus can never be denied a pre-eminent position. It has been said that there is even a poetry in law; but, as Von Ihering has eloquently observed, *die wahre Poesie des Rechts liegt in der Erhabenheit seines Problems und in seiner an Majestät und Gesetzmässigkeit dem Laufe der Gestirne vergleichbaren Bewegung.*[1] And a man like Bartolus, who took a leading part in this evolutionary movement, and initiated some of those lofty problems, deserves a niche in any gallery of great jurists of the world.

[1] *Geist des römischen Rechts*, i. 62.

ANDREA ALCIATI AND HIS PREDECESSORS

LAW may be investigated from various points of view—its historical evolution and its organic relation to its age, the synthesis of its dogmatic content, or the philosophical significance of its fundamental principles. Of the second and third categories there are several notable representatives in the present series of Great Jurists; the great importance and fruitfulness of the comparative and historic method will be exemplified in this and the following essays devoted to two jurists who were pre-eminent pioneers in the application of that method to the study of Romanistic jurisprudence. Alciati, kindled by the humanist movement in Italy, was the veritable inaugurator; then followed Cujas, his great disciple, who elaborated and perfected this method, and indeed surpassed his predecessor in many respects. To them is largely due the subsequent rational study of Roman law, the more accurate restoration and interpretation of its numerous texts, its scientific development generally, and its influence on national legislations.[1]

Roman Law before Alciati—In the East.—During the half-century following Justinian, in the Eastern Empire, there appeared, with his sanction, numerous Greek translations and epitomes of his legal compilations, and also—though prohibited by him—commentaries and interpretations. The century after was a period of stagnation and neglect; the public law school of Constantinople was closed in 717. Then came, between 740 and 911, a brief succession of Graeco-Roman codes or manuals issued by the authority of the Byzantine Emperors. Thus we find the *Ecloga Legum* (740), the *Prochiron* (c. 878), the *Epanagoge Legis* (884-6), and, most important of all, the *Basilica* (or *Basilicae*) (906-11). Ostensibly these works were based on the Justinian

---

[1] As the subjects of this essay and the following partly overlap, and the periods to some extent synchronize, the two studies are presented with the hope that they will be taken as supplementing each other; otherwise it would have been impossible to avoid a considerable amount of repetition.

ANDREA ALCIATI

codes; in reality they were drawn from translations, epitomes, and commentaries which ultimately superseded the original texts. Thus by the end of the eleventh century the great Roman jurisprudence fell into abeyance owing to the prevalence and usurped authority of these compilations, the substitution of the Greek language for the Latin, and the ever-growing influence of the canon law.

In the West.[1]—In order to appreciate duly the position and reformative influence of Alciati and the other humanists, it is essential to bear in mind the fortunes of Roman law in the West from the time of Justinian to the sixteenth century. This long period may be subdivided into more or less defined stages: Roman law to the middle of the eleventh century; revival in the second half of the eleventh century mainly connected with Irnerius at Bologna; the glossators; the Bartolists, or commentators; the fifteenth-century preparation for humanist jurisprudence, and the sixteenth-century humanism. An adequate treatment of this evolution would obviously demand many volumes; but for the purposes of the present study, its characteristic features may be very concisely indicated, so as to enable us to discern in truer perspective the bearing and significance of the main subject under consideration.

(a) **Roman Law to the Middle of the Eleventh Century.**—The epoch of the last struggle between the Western Empire and the barbarians was marked by "the romanization of the provinces and the barbarization of Rome."[2] The imperial courts and the Roman law exercised supreme authority; but the principle of personality, in view of racial differences and conflicting legal systems, had already begun to assert itself. In the provinces, Roman law assumed, in the hands of the barbarians, a debased and distorted form. Before the publication of the *Corpus Iuris* we find various complications, *e.g.* the edicts of the Ostgothic Kings, the *Lex Romana Burgundionum*, the *Lex Romana Visigothorum* (the *Breviarium Alaricianum*, drawn up in 506, as an

---

[1] *Cf.* for the history of Roman law in the Middle Ages, P. Vinogradoff, *Roman Law in Mediaeval Europe* (London, 1909), where the chief authorities are conveniently given. Special reference may be made to the various works of H. Fitting, and to that of M. Conrat (*Geschichte der Quellen und Literatur des römischen Rechts im früheren Mittelalter*, Leipzig, 1889-91). For the entire subject, however, previous to Alciati, the great work of Savigny (*Geschichte des römischen Rechts im Mittelalter*) still remains unsurpassed, though later contributions have in many respects amended some of his views.

[2] Vinogradoff, *op. cit.*, p. 4.

abridgment of the Theodosian Code, by Alaric II.), the last of which, serving as a whole body of law for the Roman population of France and Spain, long exercised a great influence in Western Europe. The compilation of Justinian, some three decades later, was accepted only in the East, and in those parts of Italy which that legislator had retaken, and for several centuries was practically dead in the West. Further decay is shown in the barbarous *Lex Romana Curiensis* (end of the eighth century), a statement of legal custom based on an imperfect abstract of Alaric's Breviary, which was used in East Switzerland, North Italy, and the Tyrol; and again in the Romano-Germanic *Lex legum*, which embodies a miscellany of rules taken from the Edict of Theodoric, the law of the Visigoths, the Justinian Code, and barbarian law.

In the early Middle Ages, the barbarian governments could not avoid the various inconsistent mixtures in their legal systems; and even under the Carolingian sovereigns, who effected therein some harmony and unity, racial differences were emphasized, the application of law became personal and local, and legislative conflicts hence obtained. Nor was the principle of personality entirely eradicated by the rise and operation of local customs, which naturally assumed a Roman, Lombard, or Frankish character, according as one or other race predominated in the region concerned. And Roman law supplied the basis of such customs in several districts, *e.g.* in Central Italy the Justinian Code prevailed, in South Italy the *Corpus Iuris* as well as the law of Justinian's successors, in South France and North Spain Alaric's Breviary applied; further Roman influence was clearly manifested also in Germany, in North France, and in England. Moreover, the compilations that were drawn up for ecclesiastical use show a great indebtedness to Roman jurisprudence: thus the *Lex romana canonice compta*, a Lombard work of the ninth century, is a collection of Roman rules for the use of the clergy, the *Collectio Anselmo dictata* is a mixture of Roman and canon law. The popes and the pontifical courts consistently maintained the authority of a good deal of the Roman civil law, and esteemed it only a little lower than the canon law. In the meantime other classes of works helped to preserve the life of Roman law; amongst these are productions like the *Etymologies* or *Origins* of Isidore of Seville, which contains extracts from classical literature, enactments, and from the writings of jurisconsults; and—what is much more important—the numerous

Epitomes, *Summae* (*e.g.* the Perugian *Summa* of the Code), and Glosses[1]—which were often less juridical than grammatical—on the Code and the Institutes (*e.g.* the Pistoian Gloss on the Code, the Turin Gloss on the Institutes).

Thus it is seen that Roman law, though here and there in a more or less debased, adulterated, or garbled form, persisted in practice throughout the momentous vicissitudes of the five centuries after Justinian; neither territorial conquests nor the development and supremacy of the feudal system could entirely crush it. As a science it preserved less vitality; the earlier example of the law schools of Rome, Constantinople, and Berytus proved then of no avail; such theoretical teaching and systematic study of Roman law as obtained were mainly confined to the schools of the clerical and monastic orders, and even then commonly regarded as supplementary to the study of rhetoric and preparatory to that of canon law.

(*b*) **A Revival in the Second Half of the Eleventh Century.**—The eleventh century was a period of transition. The religious, social, and political organization of Europe underwent considerable change. The papacy had made continual encroachments on the hierarchy and on civil governments, and now in Gregory VII. we see the great representative of its temporal claims, and the opponent of the secularization of the Church. The feudal system was perfected. Scholastic philosophy, with its dialectics, its theological and metaphysical speculations, was established in the age of Lanfranc and Anselm, and further developed by Abelard and Peter Lombard. A juridical renaissance—preceding the revival of letters—was witnessed, and bore lasting fruit in certain localities—in South France, Lombardy, Ravenna, and Bologna. About the middle of the eleventh century a knowledge of the Pandects spread in France; and by the side of Glosses and abstracts appeared more systematic treatises, *e.g. Petri exceptiones legum Romanorum* ("Excerpts by Peter"), a manual designed for the use of magistrates, which is drawn from the *Corpus Iuris* and refers also to the laws and customs of the barbarians; the *Brachylogus iuris civilis*, a compendium of the

---

[1] A gloss (*glossa*, γλῶσσα) meant originally (for example, in Greek and Latin writers) an archaic, or poetical, or foreign word requiring interpretation. Later it was referred to the explanation itself; thus Isidore of Seville uses the word in this sense, and Alcuin defines it accordingly: "unius verbi vel nominis interpretatio." With the glossators the gloss was extended from single words to entire sentences and passages, and sometimes became a running commentary.

Justinian law made on the model of the Institutes, and taken from the Code, Julian's Epitome (middle of sixth century), and Alaric's Breviary; and the recently discovered *Lo Codi* (c. 1149), a summary of the Code, for the use of magistrates, written in the Provençal language, is mainly remarkable as being the first work on Roman law in a vernacular tongue.[1] As to the Lombard cities, they had grown in population, power, and wealth; the organization of their communes, their love of liberty and independence gave to civil and political life a new activity and new needs; increasing commercial and private relationships demanded a civil law much more developed and consistent than that which was supplied by the various Germanic tribes. Glosses on Germanic law made more and more reference to Roman law; and about 1070 appeared the *Liber Papiensis*, a compilation of edicts and capitularies passed by the magistrates of Pavia, which presents a mixture of Roman and Lombard law. The law school of Ravenna became conspicuous for its support of Henry IV. and Clement III. against Gregory VII., but it was soon transcended by the school of Bologna, founded by the Marchioness Matilda in order to counteract the influence of Ravenna. Pepo lectured in Bologna about 1076; but the most illustrious professor of the time was Irnerius,[2] who was designated by the subsequent glossators the "lucerna iuris." His lectures on the Code and the Institutes were a great stimulus to the study of Roman jurisprudence. His works embrace numerous glosses, *summae* (summaries, compendiums) of Lombard law and the Code, treatises on legal formulæ and interpretation. He was in some respects a creator; he was the first systematically to collate and compare texts, and establish consistent conclusions therefrom. Under him Bologna became supreme in law studies; and thence began a continual flow of distinguished Romanists to the universities of Italy, France, and other parts of Europe; thus Placentinus did pioneer work at Montpellier, Vacarius at Oxford.

(c) **The Glossators (about 1100 to 1250).**—The immediate successors of Irnerius were the "four doctors," Bulgarus, Martinus, Jacobus, and Ugo, who made the famous declaration at

---

[1] See Vinogradoff, *op. cit.*, pp. 60 *seq.*

[2] Irnerius (Guarnerius or Warnerius) first taught the "artes liberales," and probably began teaching law about 1088. He died after 1125.—On this part of the subject, the chief authority is H. Fitting, *Die Anfänge der Rechtsschule zu Bologna* (Leipzig, 1888). *Cf.* also G. Pescatore, *Die Glossen des Irnerius* (Greifswald, 1888).

the Roncaglia Diet (1158) in favour of the Emperor Frederick Barbarossa's right to tax the Lombard cities. Though their leaning was to monarchical centralization as against feudal disintegration, yet their decision was due to the way they interpreted certain texts of Roman law rather than to any spirit of political partisanship. They regarded feudal law as a development of the doctrine of *emphyteusis*.[1] A distinguished pupil of Martinus was Placentinus, who taught at Mantua, Bologna, and then at Montpellier, where he died in 1192. The teaching of Bulgarus, the Chrysostom of jurisprudence, was transmitted by disciples like Rogerius and Bassianus to Hugolinus and Azo, and by these to Accursius, the head of the Bolognese glossators. Azo (died c. 1230) lectured at Bologna and Montpellier; and his gloss and *Summa* of the Institutes and Code enjoyed such great authority, especially in the Courts, that a knowledge of these works was considered indispensable to those who aspired to sit on the bench —"chi non ha Azzo, non vada a palazzo." In England he was followed by Bracton, whose work *De legibus et consuetudinibus Angliae* is the most important British contribution to Romanistic jurisprudence. It was intended for practitioners, and was based largely on the case law of Henry III.'s age and on Roman materials derived from Azo. Similarly, in Germany appeared manuals of customary law, *e.g.* Eike von Repgow's *Sachsenspiegel* (Saxon Mirror), a compilation of the law of the Saxons; this was soon followed by kindred productions, showing the rising influence of Roman conceptions. The *Glossa Ordinaria* of Accursius (c. 1182—1260) is a comprehensive collection of many previous glosses and extracts from numerous manuscripts, most of which are no longer extant; it is thus an epitome of the entire school, and as such it brings together and compares diverse scattered texts and opinions, and endeavours skilfully and acutely to reconcile seeming inconsistencies.

In general the work of the glossators was of a practical character, designed mainly for consultative and magisterial purposes. In some quarters the Courts attached thereto such high authority that it became a current maxim that the bench recognized only what the gloss laid down: "Quod non agnoscit glossa non agnoscit curia." The *Glossae* offered elucidations and interpretations of individual texts, and were at first interlinear, then marginal: sometimes they even amounted to a running commentary (*ap-*

[1] *Cf.* Vinogradoff, *op. cit.*, p. 51.

paratus) on an entire book. They dealt with various matters, from mere grammatical notes to important juridical theories. The *Summae* attempted a more systematic treatment of particular titles or whole books of the Justinian compilation. In the earlier legal writings the scholastic method with its dialectical argumentation is in the ascendancy; but afterwards in the more characteristic work of this school, a more or less literal interpretation, couched in concise terms, and a marshalling of texts and opinions constitute the general mode of treatment, though the formal method is still applied in the developing of conclusions. How could it well be otherwise in an age which produced such pre-eminent masters of scholastic philosophy as Albertus Magnus, Thomas Aquinas, and Duns Scotus? However, Justinian gradually became to the new order of lawyers what Aristotle was to the old. Jurisprudence did not become, like philosophy, the servile handmaid of theology. Further, the law of procedure (*ordo iudicarius*) was set forth, and collections of controversies (*dissensiones*) and investigations (*quaestiones*) on this and other subjects were produced. All these works show their authors' knowledge of the whole Justinian body of law, except the Novels in Greek. But the writings of Gaius, the fragments of the classical jurisconsults like Ulpian, and the *Basilica* seem to have been unknown to them, nor did they take account of the Theodosian Code or Alaric's Breviary; they made use, however, of the Lombard canon, and feudal law, and of the statutes of the Italian cities. To them is due that strange division of the Digest which is usually adopted in the sixteenth-century editions—*Digestum vetus* (Bk. I.—Bk. XXIV. t. 2), *Infortiatum* (Bk. XXIV. t. 3—Bk. XXXVIII.), *Digestum novum* (Bk. XXXIX.—Bk. L.). They were not infrequently on the right line in comparing and critically examining (as Accursius in particular does) various texts, in order to arrive at the correct source. But their glaring defects, in spite of much good and useful work, were soon to bring the whole school into discredit. In the first place, trivial verbal meanings were too commonly offered, *e.g. quamvis* as an equivalent for *etsi*, absurd explanations were sometimes propounded, as in deriving the *lex Furia Caninia* from *canis*, Tiber from Tiberius, and in interpreting *pontifex* simply by *episcopus* or *papa;* secondly, superabundant exegesis tended to overwhelm the intrinsic content of the text; finally, historic perspective was wanting, alike in numerous details as in attributing to Ulpian and even Justinian a date prior to the Christian era, confusing Caracalla (Antoninus) with Marcus Antonius, and in more fundamental assumptions, *e.g.* that the Empire under the German rulers was a regular continuation of the Roman, and therefore subject to similar law and polity. A good many of the erroneous interpretations advanced are due to a failure to realize the historical relationships of the constituent parts of the Corpus Iuris.

(*d*) **The Commentators, or Post-Glossators.**—The glossators had done much to restore the Justinian law, but with the condensation of their work by Accursius and the almost exclusive attention paid to the latter by courts and schools, the progressive movement was checked. Texts and sources were disregarded in favour of the gloss. It was said that some even went to the length of glossing the gloss of the gloss. The school of the fourteenth and fifteenth centuries—variously designated the post-glossators, the commentators, the *Scribentes*, or Bartolists—rose against the tyranny of the gloss. Some of the earliest representatives were found in France, *e.g.* Jacques de Revigny (Jacobus a Ravanis, *d.* 1296), who proved himself a formidable opponent and skilful dialectician, and his pupil, Pierre de Belleperche (Petrus a Bellapertica, d. 1308), who became Chancellor of France; in Italy we find the jurist-poet Cinus a Pistoia, friend of Dante, model of Petrarch, and master of Bartolus. Cinus severely condemned the blind devotees of the gloss, and declared that " glossa illa est diabolica et non vera."[1] The Italian Bartolus[2] (1314-1357), who taught at Pisa and Perugia, was the acknowledged head of this school; the reactionaries regarded his authority with the utmost veneration, styled him the " monarcha iuris," and some, like Jason, spoke of him as a terrestrial deity. Even Alciati considered him in some respects the first of jurisconsults; but Cujas had a higher opinion of Accursius. The works of Bartolus include commentaries (or *lecturae*) on the Digest and Code, treatises on public law, private law, and on procedure (*e.g. Ordo iudicii, De testibus*), some controversial writings (*quaestiones*), and professional consultations (*consilia*). In many quarters these writings enjoyed the force of law. At Padua a chair was established to expound the law, the gloss, and Bartolus ("lectura

---

[1] *Comment in Cod.*, viii. 45. *Cf. ibid.*, vi. 15: " Ita dixerunt doctores et glossa ... et quotquot fuerint etiamsi mille hoc dixissent, omnes erraverunt."
[2] See the preceding essay.

textus, glossae, et Bartoli ")[1]; as a French writer remarks, one had almost said the law and the prophets.[2] Other prominent members of the school were—in Italy, Baldus (1327-1406), who taught at Perugia and Pavia, and often acted in a judicial and diplomatic capacity, P. de Castro (*d.* 1438), P. de Imola, Jason de Mayno, B. Caepolla, P. Decius (1454-1535); in France, G. de Cuneo, who became a bishop, J. Faber (*d.* 1340), a seigniorial judge who was, through his practical works, called "pater practicae." Their juristic productions, like those of Bartolus, include exegetical works, manuals of practice and procedure, casuist works consisting of *casus, quaestiones, consilia,* and systematic treatises.[3]

The aim of the Bartolists was to unite practical applications with theoretical disquisitions, to draw from Roman jurisprudence a law that would meet the needs of their time. The original sense of texts was thus often perverted; Roman elements were made to serve in the construction of doctrines which in their entirety were foreign to ancient civil law. And in this process the dialectic method of the scholastic philosophy was adopted, not indeed for the first time, but with greater thoroughness and subtlety. Paris had become, through the influence of Abelard, the leading centre of scholasticism; and, as Savigny has shown,[4] this method was first consistently applied to law by French legists in the second half of the thirteenth century, and soon after Cinus introduced into Italy the doctrine of these "moderni" (as they were called, in contradistinction to the earlier glossators, the "doctores antiqui"). Thus, while the attitude of the glossators was to some extent "humanistic" and their Roman law was more or less divorced from actual life, in the hands of the commentators there was usually a co-ordination of life and law, together with scholasticism. They correlated Roman law, though in isolated texts, with canon law and the ordinances and statutes of the Lombard cities, and in such correlation they were always mindful of actual forensic causes. The glossators had deemed the Corpus Iuris an embodiment of the *ius commune,* the universal law of civilized mankind; but this was so on theoretical grounds. Their

---

[1] *Cf.* Savigny, *op. cit.*, vol. vi., p. 154.
[2] J. Flach, *Cujas, les Glossateurs et les Bartolistes,* in *Nouv. Rev. Hist. de dr. fran. et étranger* (Paris, 1883), vol. vii., pp. 205-27, at p. 217.
[3] *Cf.* J. Brissaud, *Cours d'histoire générale de droit français,* 2 vols. (Paris, 1904), vol. i., pp. 219-20.
[4] *Op. cit.,* v., pp. 603 *seq.*

successors went further and imported it, in an adulterated form, in to the actual legislative construction and the practical administration of justice; and so they established, as it were, a "usus modernus Pandectarum." Practitioners paid more heed to the "communis opinio" than to theory and cogent reasoning from first principles; thus the citation of authorities was preferred to the propounding of reasons. Subtle distinctions, however, as well as arguments *pro* and *contra* abound. Though the Bartolists were contemporaries of, sometimes intimate with, some of the greatest literary masters the world has ever seen, as, for example, Dante, Petrarch, Boccaccio, yet their style is marked by tedious diffuseness, prolixity, commonplace; the observation of Cujas is fully merited—"verbosi in re facili, in difficili muti, in angusta diffusi."

In Italy and France their influence remained till the coming of men like Alciati and Cujas, and here and there persisted even for some time after; in Germany it lasted much longer, indeed till the time of Savigny. In the latter country the definitive "reception" of Roman law took place in the fifteenth century; but it was an impure, glossed, Bartolized Roman law; the "heutiges römisches Recht" was more Roman in name than in substance.

(*e*) **The Renaissance of Roman Jurisprudence.**—The fifteenth century brought forth no predominating jurist like Irnerius, or Accursius, or Bartolus of the preceding centuries. Circumstances were at first not favourable to legists. Intestine dissensions and the strife of political parties were frequent. The excesses of unrestrained democratic power accelerated the downfall of the Italian republics. Professors of law were not always honoured in their own countries; and so they were obliged to adopt the wandering life of peripatetic teachers, now appearing in one university, now in another. Their method of holding "disputationes," substantially borrowed from their predecessors, saved professorial activity from absolute barrenness. They combined practice with teaching; and in their consultations they largely used principles of Roman law. Roman law had come to be regarded as a kind of "common" law, or as a subsidiary law useful for filling up gaps in local legislations. Amidst the multiplicity of customs and statutes, varying from place to place, producing, through their frequent incompatibility, conflicts and confusion, the Roman body of law offered principles that might be universally recognized and adapted to promote greater unity and harmony. Moreover, it was looked upon with favour by the clergy, to whose interests it was not antagonistic, and also by sovereigns, whose aggrandizement it did not oppose. Further, the century was fruitful in momentous events, which prepared the way for a vigorous revival of Roman jurisprudence. Constantinople fell. Printing was invented, and great improvements in paper-making were effected. Libraries, manuscripts, and books multiplied. Exploration of new lands was undertaken. A deep interest in ancient civilization was aroused; the study of classical history, literature, antiquities, institutions was more thoroughly cultivated. In Italy the literary renaissance had already established itself in the previous century. And now we find not so much jurists proper, but humanists like Ambrogio Traversari (d. 1439), who translated many Greek manuscripts into Latin, and recommended the study of the laws in their original sources and not in the compilations of the commentators; Laurentius Valla (1405-1457), who, in the course of his classical and philological studies, sometimes threw light on the language and phraseology of the ancient jurisconsults; and Angelo Politian (1454-1494), poet and scholar, who regarded the texts of Roman law as an invaluable product of antiquity—not only intrinsically, but also as an aid to solve problems of Latin philology—and who was one of the very earliest to apply the results of scholarship to juridical investigations, in his comparison of an edition of the Digest printed at Venice, 1485, with the famous Florentine manuscript. And now with the approach of the sixteenth century and the ever-increasing humanistic fermentation manifested in all branches of intellectual activity, and fast spreading from Italy to other countries, there appeared three men—Alciati in Italy, Ulrich Zasius (d. 1535) in Germany, and Budé[1] (Budaeus, 1467-1540) in France—who showed the world the grave defects of the glossators, the commentators and their legal predecessors in general, and inaugurated with greater thoroughness, consistency, and systematic application a more rational and scientific method for the study and true comprehension of Roman law. And of these men, Alciati was the greatest.

Estienne Pasquier, who commenced in 1561 the publication of his *Recherches de la France*, classified the jurists from the twelfth to the sixteenth century into three schools, viz. the

[1] His work relating to law is *Annotationes ad Pandectas*.

Glossators, the *Scribentes* (so called, as he says, by scholars, and whom he terms "Docteurs de droict "), and the "Humanistes," so called "pour avoir meslé en beau langage latin les Lettres Humaines avec le Droict." He goes on to say that the sixteenth century brought forth "une nouvelle estude de Loix, qui fut de faire un mariage de l'estude du Droict avecques les Lettres Humaines, par un langage latin net et poly."[1]

Life of Alciati.[2]—Andrea Alciati or Alciato (Andreas Alciatus) was born May 8, 1492, in Alzate near Como in the Milanese. He was an only son, and his father, Ambrogio, a wealthy merchant, was a decurion (municipal magistrate or councillor) in Milan, and had acted as envoy to Venice; his mother, Margherita, was a woman of high nobility. Among his ancestors were men distinguished in Church and State and in learning. From his early youth he was devoted to studies. He received his first education in Milan, an important centre of the Hellenic renaissance. One of his masters there was Janus Parrhasius, a Neapolitan, to whom he was largely indebted for his knowledge of the classical languages, especially Latin; and among his school friends was Franciscus Calvus. About 1508 Alciati proceeded, with a view to study law, to the university of Pavia, where he attended the lectures of professors like Jason Maynus (de Mayno), who adhered for the most part to the traditional method of exposition by dealing with the "communis opinio" rather than with the legal text itself, but whose taste for ancient literature greatly influenced Alciati; Philippus Decius, who showed great skill in his vigorous disputations with Maynus; and Paulus Picus a Monte Pico, whose discourse, as Alciati wrote in 1522, was marked by labyrinthine confusedness and obscurity.[3] It appears, from an observation made at Basel University by his friend, Bonifacius Amerbach, in 1526, that Alciati recognized the futility of his three years' legal course as soon as he directed his attention to Justinian's Institutes, instead of glosses and com-

---

[1] Liv. ix. c. 39.—The term "humanitas" as applied to the classical culture of the Renaissance is found much earlier. Thus in a medallion (made by Pisano before 1450) of Pier Candido Decembrio (1399-1477), the latter is described as "studiorum humanitatis decus." *Cf.* L. Geiger, *Renaissance und Humanismus in Italien und Deutschland* (1882), p. 167.

[2] This section of the paper is much indebted to E. von Moeller, *Andreas Alciat* (Breslau, 1907).

[3] *Emblemata*, ed. 1599, p. 115, No. 96:

" Obscurus et confusus, ut Picus fuit,
Labyrinthus appellabitur."

mentaries.[1] In 1511, owing perhaps to war disturbances, Alciati removed to Bologna, and became a pupil of Carolus Ruinus. Two years afterwards, whilst still a student, he published his first work—written, as he himself says, in a fortnight—a commentary (*Annotationes*) *in tres libros Codicis* (the last three books of the Justinian Code), which filled a gap. The first nine books were well known in the Middle Ages, and were often referred to as the *Codex*; but the remaining portion, dealing mainly with public law and possessing greater historical than practical interest, was much neglected. This work not only showed the young author's knowledge of ancient literature, but—what was of more vital importance—contained, in brilliant style, definitely formulated demands for a new method of jurisprudence, in harmony with humanist conceptions.[2] The following year the doctor's degree was conferred on him.

Alciati now returned to Milan, and became a member of the College of Jurists ("Collegium iurisconsultorum") with a view to practising at the bar. He was mindful of the proverbial saying— "Esto advocatus iuvenis et medicus senex"—that whereas long experience is necessary in a doctor, energy, ardour, ambition, untiring handling of authorities would stand a young advocate in good stead; moreover, as Accursius had said, "Quanto iuniores tanto perspicaciores."[3] The first case in which his opinion was asked was one of witchcraft. The accusation had first been brought before the Ecclesiastical Court, and the presiding bishop before delivering judgment submitted the question to Alciati. The inquisitor's allegations were parried by Alciati with urbane good-humour; yet the young lawyer does not appear to have differed fundamentally on this matter from his contemporaries.[4]

In 1518 he was appointed professor extraordinary ("regens extraordinarius") at Avignon, for a period of two years, at a stipend of 300 ducats (about £105). At the same time Franciscus a Ripa entered the law faculty, and both of them obtained the ight to confer certain degrees. Henceforth began Alciati's series of writings—his *Dispunctiones*, *Praetermissa* and *Paradoxa* —and his great influence on the new movement in France. On

---

[1] *Cf.* T. Burckhardt-Biedermann, *Bonifacius Amerbach und die Reformation* Basel, 1894), pp. 193 *seq.* (cited by Moeller, p. 17, n. 1).

[2] On this see further *infra*.

[3] *Cf.* what Alciati says in his *Parerga*, x. c. 21; in *Opera*, 4 vols., folio, ed. F. Alciatus (Francofurti, 1617), in vol. iv. col. 465.

[4] *Parerga*, viii. c. 22 (*Opera*, iv. col. 424).

the completion of his term, he was about to return to Italy owing mainly to the inadequacy of his salary; but the authorities secured a renewal of the engagement for two years more at an increase of a hundred ducats. His fame now spread rapidly throughout Europe. At this time he had an audience of some 700, including old as well as young students, lay and ecclesiastical, noblemen, abbots, and other dignitaries of Church and State.[1] In the winter term, 1520-1, he lectured on the title "De verborum significatione," and by his learning and style roused universal admiration. Sympathetic hearers realized that Alciati invested with flesh and blood what had really been dry bones, and imparted to it fresh life and sprit. From many countries scholars sent him warm greetings and commendatory epistles. Ulrich Zasius,[2] struck by the brilliance, erudition, and penetration of the *Paradoxa*, which seemed to the eminent German jurist literally true rather than presumedly paradoxical, wrote to Bonifacius Amerbach[3] that a mighty reformer of the study of Roman law had arisen, and expressed his readiness to fight under Alciati's flag. Amerbach at once went to Avignon to continue his legal studies. At this time (1520) Alciati also met Budaeus, and soon after began to correspond with Zasius. Thus was established that remarkable triumvirate—already designated "triumviratus constituendae rei pandectariae," and so recognized by Erasmus, the very prince of humanists—which exercised such a profound influence on the subsequent development of scholarship and jurisprudence. "Zasius, Budaeus, and Alciat sind das Dreigestirn das damals am Himmel der Jurisprudenz leuchtete."[4] Shortly afterwards Amerbach introduced Erasmus and Alciati to each other, and many letters thereafter passed between them. Nevertheless the Italian jurist was not without opponents both in France and Italy. In 1521, owing to an outbreak of plague, the university of Avignon was closed, and Alciati returned to

---

[1] Moeller, p. 34.
[2] Zasius was born in Constance, 1461, and died in 1534; he was thus much older than Alciati. He was appointed a notary of the episcopal Court in his native town and the highest functions were afterwards entrusted to him. In 1500 he became a professor in the university of Friburg. He agreed with Alciati, as he himself avowed, on the main points, and differed only on minor details. In one respect, however, he was quite unlike his Italian friend—he was not a migratory, wandering professor, but adhered to his own university.—*Cf.* R. von Stintzing, *Ulrich Zasius. Ein Beitrag zur Geschichte der Rechtswissenschaft im Zeitalter der Reformation* (Basel, 1857).
[3] U. Zasii *Epistolae*, ed. J. A. S. von Riegger (1774), ii., pp. 12 *seq*.
[4] Moeller, p. 38.

Milan, where he resumed his practice; but learning that the danger in Avignon was over, he went back in November. In the following spring the plague reappeared; but meanwhile his engagement terminated. A renewal was proposed to him, with the condition that his stipend should be proportionately reduced if the plague again suspended teaching. He rejected this offer and left for Milan, where he published the first edition of his celebrated book of Emblems (*Emblematum libellus*).

His practice grew fast; but his restless disposition got the better of him, and he became anxious to obtain a professorship in an Italian university, preferably in Padua. In 1523 he suffered great loss through the prevailing wars and tumults; his house was burnt down, and everything in it destroyed. In spite of his increasing *clientela* (which in a letter he jestingly describes as "clitellae," a pack-saddle for beasts of burden), he found time for pursuing his literary activities, and for cultivating various branches of knowledge—philology as well as jurisprudence, theology, and history, cookery by the side of medicine, and several other subjects. As a humanist he loved the "bonae literae" as much as the Corpus Iuris; he translated into Latin plays from the Greek (for example, the *Clouds* of Aristophanes) wrote epigrams, completed his *Emblemata*, and even produced a comedy (entitled "Philargyrus," *i.e.* the lover of money). He followed with keen interest the momentous events of the time, and especially those relating to the kindred movements, the Renaissance and the Reformation. His German friends kept him in touch with the happenings in Germany; in his correspondence we find frequent references to Luther's burning of the papal bull (1520), and to the burning of his own writings; and he states that Luther's personality made a deep impression on him, though he did not admire the great reformer's invective and rough manners. Alciati never abandoned Catholicism (in which respect he was unlike a good many of the humanists and legists of the time); nevertheless he was adverse to the licence of the papal court, as well as to any belief of a superstitious character and to violent assertion of authority wherever found. But knowledge, not religion, was his element.[1] Early in 1528, fresh war disorders breaking out suddenly in Milan, he went back to Avignon.

His succeeding professorship in Bourges (1529-1533) marks an important period in his career, and in the development of human-

---

[1] Moeller, p. 48.

ist jurisprudence, particularly in France. In the Renaissance movement the decline of Italy was followed by the ascendancy of France. At the beginning of the sixteenth century Italian culture was fast passing over to the latter country; and this transference was accelerated by the intercourse and circumstances incidental to the French wars in Italy. Francis I. was a great admirer and patron of Italian art and learning; Italian artists, linguists, and scholars found a ready welcome in his court. Thus Alciati, feeling that he was already highly appreciated in France, that his new doctrines might meet there with wider sympathy and acceptance, and that the sovereign's protection might further his cause, therefore assented to the offer of a two years' engagement (the usual period) in Bourges—in succession to the Portuguese Salvator de Ferrandina—at a salary of 600 ducats, together with travelling allowance, etc. Here Alciati soon took part in numerous controversies with eminent men, for example, with Pierre de l'Estoile (Petrus Stella), a famous professor of law in the university of Orleans, and with Budaeus, particularly in regard to ancient weights and measures (on which subject Alciati had already produced his treatise, *De ponderibus et mensuris*). His lectures, inaugurated by a public *disputatio*, "De quinque pedum praescriptione" (which was afterwards published together with the replies of his six opponents),[1] consisted of expositions and interpretations of certain titles of the Digest and Code, *e.g.* "De verborum obligationibus" and "De pactis." Alciati now added to the number of his distinguished friends some of the leading lights of the French Renaissance, such as Montaigne; and he met with a great reception from his students, who flocked to him from all parts of Europe, especially France, Italy, and Germany, and many of whom were already distinguished, or were destined to become so. The mere mention of the names of some of them show what a remarkable concourse of men of intellect, energy, and genius listened to his lectures. There were John Calvin, Viglius von Zuichem, Karl Sucquet (the latter two having been recommended to Alciati by Erasmus, who urged them to combine literature with jurisprudence). François Connan, a friend of Calvin, Theodore Beza, J. Amyot, M. Wolmar, C. Gessner, J. Cañaye, Ausonius Hoxvir, and others.[2] Other notable personages came occasionally to hear his discourses, *e.g.* the Dauphin, and even Francis I. himself. On the occasion

[1] *Opera*, iii. col. 339 *seq*. [2] Moeller, p. 59.

of the latter's visit Alciati adorned his introductory address with apt citations ;[1] he emphasized the greatness and magnificence of Roman jurisprudence, the high respect due to it, and pointed out that even the peoples who demolished the Roman Empire gladly preserved the Roman law ("libentissime ius Romanum servaverunt"), and by way of an elegant compliment to the king ended with the lines of Ausonius addressed to the Emperor Theodosius.[2]

Alciati's fame continued to extend ; the number of his hearers increased from term to term. So he applied for an increase in his stipend. At the same time, however, he was thinking of Italian universities like Padua and Siena, and was negotiating with the secretary to the Duke of Milan. To the latter he wrote that teaching was more agreeable in France than in Italy, where there were among the students hostile cliques who turned up their noses at humanistic culture.[3] In March, 1531, his appointment at Bourges was extended for two years more at double the previous stipend. (His negotiations with the Italian authorities had had the desired effect.) Now publications—lectures, dissertations, translations, poems—appeared in rapid succession. The climate of the locality, however, proved uncongenial to him, and in 1532 he suffered several months' illness. This circumstance, together with disputes which arose between him and the university as well as with the municipal authorities, induced him to leave Bourges. He was urged by Bembo (then secretary to Leo X., afterwards cardinal) to go to Padua, but was not satisfied as to the amount and security of the stipend. Aurelius Albucius, a delegate from Pavia, came to him from Francis Sforza, Duke of Milan, with promises of dignities and honours (*e.g.* that of senator) and an offer of 1,500 ducats. On the conclusion of his engagement, Alciati left for Pavia.

At the Italian university his expectations were not fully realized. Thus in his letters to Bembo he complained of the effrontery of the "scholastici," and regretted that, whereas the French and the Germans accepted his ideas with favour, the Italians received them with mockery and derision. The year 1535 is described as a most brilliant one for the university of

---

[1] *Cf. Opera*, iv. col. 870 *seq.*

[2] " Non habeo ingenium ; Princeps sed iussit : habeo.
    Cur me posse negem, posse quod ille putat."

[3] Hoynck van Papendrecht, *Analecta Belgica*, i. 1 (1743), pp. 73 *seq.* (Cited Moeller, p. 61, n. 2).

Pavia, both as regards the lustre of the professorial chairs and the numbers of students. At this time Alciati suffered great loss through the death of illustrious friends. Zasius died in 1535. Sir Thomas More, who, like many other great humanists of the Renaissance, had exchanged letters with the Italian juristic pioneeer, was executed in the same year. And in 1536 Erasmus died, of whom Alciati wrote, "cuius fama frequens totum circumvolat orbem." In the latter year appeared the first part of the *Parerga;* and also *Processus iudicarius*, a work which the publisher falsely ascribed to Alciati, as he knew too well the value of the name when placed on the title-page. Owing to the outbreak of war between the Emperor Charles V. and Francis I., Alciati's activity in Pavia was interrupted ; many students left the town ; and Alciati wrote to Amerbach that only his solicitude for his mother prevented his abandoning professorship, clients and property. At the end of 1537, however, he accepted for three years a chair at Bologna ; the reduced sum of 1,200 ducats shows that on this occasion his bargaining capacity failed him. Here the unruly students, by their tricks played on him as well as on other professors, caused him much annoyance. Alciati discerned in this academic hostility or indifference a certain sign of the lamentable decline of Italian humanism. As Paolo Giovio (Paulus Jovius) said,[1] almost in Alciati's words, the flame of knowledge was extinguished in Italy about the middle of the sixteenth century, and passed over to France and Germany. In 1538, in consequence of a rumour that Alciati was thinking of leaving Bologna before the due expiration of his engagement, the Bolognese threatened to confiscate his property, and also made an appeal to the pope. However, he made new friendships, like that of Vasari (then a young painter), and so agreed to remain a fourth year at the university. At the instance of Charles V. he was then recalled to Pavia ; but hostilities having arisen again (1542) between the Emperor and Francis (notwithstanding the ten years' truce agreed upon in 1538 between them and the pope), he migrated to Ferrara at the invitation of Hercules d'Este, and was there treated with great liberality and consideration. The pope, Paul III., conferred on him the title of apostolic protonotary, though it appears that Alciati had expected a cardinalate. In a letter to a friend written at this time he offers an apology for his wandering life : what with the commands

[1] In his *Historiae sui temporis* (Florence, 1550-1552).

of sovereigns and the tumults of war he is, he says, driven about hither and thither, and is deprived of rest and tranquillity; he thinks a book might some day be written on the peregrinations of jurisconsults and especially of himself.[1] In spite of his feeling unsettled he continued with his *Parerga*, and in 1543 added eight new books. Three years later he was back again in Pavia. For some time he suffered great physical pain; and his restless career was brought to an end on January 12, 1550. He was buried in the church of S. Epifanio.

His death was universally lamented. Alessandro Grimaldi expressed the feeling of all when he said at the funeral oration that the passing away of their eminent jurist laid a great sorrow on Pavia, on Italy, on France, on the whole world. It was said that with his death law itself was dead, that the muses perished. His epitaph, more modest, shows the great esteem in which he was held and the recognition of his pioneer services in restoring the study of jurisprudence to its ancient glory: "Qui omnium doctrinarum orbem absolvit, primus legum studia antiquo restituit decori."[2]

Alciati was a man of vigorous constitution, of over medium height, broad-chested, inclined somewhat to corpulence; his complexion was swarthy brown, and he had big, wide-open prominent eyes,[3] thick lips, a long nose, and large ears. All these characteristics gave him a striking appearance, which could not fail to attract notice; and his speech, accompanied (as Cardano says) by a smile which ever played about his lips, commanded the attention of his hearers.

Alciati's Writings and their Character.—Alciati's writings do not present a dogmatic or systematic treatment of law or of any other subject. They are more or less—and necessarily so, having regard to the time and circumstances of their production—of a fragmentary character, and as such they represent the life-long strivings of an ardent explorer, and the results attained by him. His aim was to demonstrate the intrinsic significance of the Roman law, to clear it from the spurious additions made by alien hands, to set it forth in the condition in which it left the classical jurisconsults, and interpret its meaning and application not through the vision of subsequent glossators and commentators, but from the point of view of the time and place of its elaboration.

---

[1] *Opera*, iv. col. 861 *seq.*
[2] F. Argellati, *Bibliotheca scriptorum Mediolanensium* (Mediolani, 1745), vol. i. col. 23.   [3] *Ibid.*, i. col. 24.

For this purpose Alciati did not adopt a regular, definite method either in his professorial lectures or in his literary productions. This is seen in the very titles of his writings—"Paradoxa" (paradoxes, seemingly incredible views), "Praetermissa" (things overlooked or omitted), "Parerga" (*obiter dicta*, appendices), "Dispunctiones" (examinations, investigations, revisions), "Annotationes" (annotations, remarks), and so on. Besides his voluminous commentaries on various titles of the Digest and the Code, he wrote miscellaneous treatises and contributions, such as *De magistratibus, De praesumptionibus, De ponderibus et mensuris, De verborum significatione*, etc. His legal opinions (*Responsa*), comprised in a posthumous publication the fourth edition of which, issued at Basel in 1582, contains some eight hundred decisions, relate to municipal law, canon law, feudal law, criminal law, wills, contracts, *privilegia*, and civil procedure. Some of these opinions throw light on important controversies of contemporary history, as, for example, the conflict between Duke Ulrich of Würtemberg and Ferdinand of Austria,[1] and that between Duke Henry the younger of Brunswick and Goslar.[2] Alciati's interest in history is shown apart from his devotion to ancient life and institutions, by his *Encomium historiae* (1530), though already in 1519, in his dedicatory epistle to his Notes on Tacitus, he emphasized the value and importance of historical science. In the latter work he skilfully compares and contrasts Livy and Tacitus, and, being the sound judge that he is, he has no hesitation in awarding to the latter a much higher rank.[3] He began also a history of Milan, which reaches to the fifteenth century; in this work, however, he does not manifest a very great critical power in the handling of the sources, but shows too strong a leaning to roam in curious interesting by-paths. "Er besass in hohem Masse . . . den Sinn für das Interessante."[4] But his collection of inscriptions has a much greater value, and has been utilized by later researchers. No less a writer than Mommsen, whose authority in this category of historical documents is supreme, has declared that not only did Alciati reform jurisprudence, but he also laid the foundations of the science of epigraphy.[5] As a humanist he had a deep love for classical litera-

[1] *Responsa*, col. 354 seq.   [2] *Ibid.*, col. 694 seq.
[3] *Opera*, iv. col. 876.   [4] Moeller, p. 125.
[5] *Corpus Inscriptionum Latinarum*, vol. v. pt. 2 (Berlin, 1877), pp. 624 *seq.*; at p. 624, col. 2: ". . . Non solum iuris prudentiam reformavit, sed etiam epigraphiam ita fundavit, ut primus corpus conderet inscriptionum patriarum itaque viam aperiret."

ture; he issued several Latin translations from the Greek, *e.g.* a version of Aristophanes' *Clouds*, and also a compilation of epigrams (*Selecta epigrammata graeca latine versa*, 1529). He wrote also an original comedy which has already been mentioned, and a number of Latin poems, the most important of which are his *Emblems*, which were widely appreciated: indeed numerous editions were published in many countries, and translations into most European languages were made in course of time. Finally he wrote a treatise on duelling (*De singulari certamine*), and the various questions arising he discusses not merely as a skilful lawyer, but as a luminous writer possessing both classical and modern culture.

His works are written in a clear fluent style, free from tedious circumlocutions, pedantic heaviness, and pompous display of scholarship. This is all the more noteworthy as he wrote in an age not yet liberated from the influence of the scholastics and their overloaded citations. His object is to give pleasure to his readers as well as to impart instruction. As his recent biographer says: "Er will seine Leser nicht nur belehren, er will sie zugleich unterhalten."[1] He mingles illustrations taken from the Middle Ages and from contemporary history with those culled from antiquity; and here and there he relieves the seriousness of his disquisitions by interspersing personal anecdotes and autobiographical reflections. Thus he was perhaps the first of lawyers in whose writings we find purity and elegance of diction, and that marked personal note, that indefinable charm which characterizes the cultured humanist and the true artist.

Alciati as Reformer.—Alciati took a keen interest in all branches of learning, and notably in such as were ancillary to law, *e.g.* history, philology. He followed with delight the new discoveries of ancient writings, whether of a purely literary or technical character, as, for example, those relating to medical questions. To the literature of his age as well as to that of the Middle Ages, he was a zealous adherent. He had a wide knowledge of Roman authors in general, and was especially attached to Cicero, whom he regarded as the very begetter of eloquence, "parens eloquentiae"; like Erasmus he cultivated a pure, terse, flexible Latin style, and, like Erasmus—though unlike so many other writers of the time—he refused to pay homage to the prevailing fetish of factitious Ciceronianism. What was a rarer acquisition,

[1] Moeller, p. 111.

especially so in the case of the majority of preceding and contemporary jurists, he possessed an excellent knowledge of Greek, though he was not, of course, a consummate Hellenist like Budaeus ; in any case he made fruitful use of his acquaintance with Greek authors and texts of Romanistic jurisprudence.

He was one of the leaders of the humanist movement, and he cherished all the aspirations and made all the high claims of his illustrious fellow-workers. To these high claims regarding the many-sided knowledge and accomplishments necessary to the making of a sound lawyer, there were not wanting replies and reproaches of opponents, who restricted their attention to the subject-matter of jurisprudence proper and had little time or aptitude for cultivating classical literature. Thus Albericus Gentilis maintained that the presumptuous humanists or "Alciatists" ("Alciatei," as he called them) were scarcely entitled to the name of jurists at all, and that jurists could get on well enough without devoting themselves to Greek and Latin letters.[1] However, Alciati throughout insisted on independence and culture as against the shackles of blind faith and tyrannous authority. He emphasized that conviction based on right and adequate knowledge, and sound judgment founded on the actual materials concerned (as the ultimate data from which valid conclusions may be drawn), are of greater import than a passive acceptance of the conclusions of scholastic exegesis, and still more so than acquiescence in the accumulated opinions of commentators merely repeating each other.[2] Truth, inviolable, immutable, is alone the all-compelling authority. Though he was near to becoming a cardinal, yet he denied the large claims of the pope, and even refused to accept the Bible as finally decisive.

The new method introduced in the sixteenth century into the science of Roman law is not the result of an isolated manifestation, but is at one with the general revolt of the human mind against the burdens of tradition and its accompanying abuses ; it is part of the gradual efflorescence of the human intellect in all the regions of thought and belief. Thus it has a close affinity with the religious insurrection of Luther and Calvin, with the philosophic doubt of Descartes, with the scepticism of Rabelais and Montaigne, with the pioneer work of scholars like Scaliger and Lipsius, with the general literary revolt in Europe, with the

[1] A. Gentilis, *De iuris interpretibus dialogi sex* (Londini, 1582)
[2] *Cf. Opera*, iv. col. 860.

efforts to reintroduce classical types of architecture, and with many other phenomena of a like tendency. In a word, it indicates the passing away from medievalism with its dogma and authority and stifled individuality, to modernism with its freedom, expansion of personality, and demand for the actual and real.

Already in the first of his published writings, the Commentary on the last three books of the Code, Alciati proclaims defiantly in his prefatory dedication the demands of the new method in jurisprudence, and the necessity to bring it into line with humanism. He realizes that before him some effort had here or there been made to bring about an emancipation from the old incubus by appealing to the Corpus Iuris and taking refuge in it. But no one had as yet clearly indicated the desired goal and cleared the way thereto. And so Alciati, though scarcely more than a youth, comes with his call to arms; he exclaims that the old traditions are going and must go, and he will show the world how to establish a new condition of things; he expects opposition, he imagines the subtle retorts of the old doctors and the noise of those who would demolish with their invective what they are too stupid to understand; he will not, however, turn from his purpose, he is courageous and hopeful in his enterprise.[1] In this undertaking Alciati was supported by Zasius in Germany, and Budaeus in France; and Erasmus declares (in a letter to Karl Sucquet) that they were the three who were instrumental in remedying the lamentable conditions of the hitherto existing jurisprudence, by pointing out the corrupt and mutilated character of the texts and restoring to them their original form and meaning.[2]

Alciati did not eliminate from his consideration canon law, customary and local law, German, Lombard, French, or Italian; as an advocate he had frequent occasion to refer thereto. But when he speaks of jurisprudence he means, of course, Roman law; and in his view it would be the highest glory of a modern jurist to grasp it and expound it as forcibly and acutely as a Papinian or a Scaevola. Times and seasons, he says, come and go; but the Roman system remains in all its splendour and greatness,— as the ancients said, it is a work of the eternal gods.[3] A great jurist is only a priest in the service of Justice. The theoretical

---

[1] *Cf. Opera*, iii. col. 479-80.
[2] Erasmus, *Epistolae* (Lond. 1642), col. 1262-63.
[3] *Opera*, iv. col. 849.

work of explanation and construction is in many respects of greater importance than the practical work of the advocate; theory represents the captain, practice the men. And to do that work efficiently it is indispensable to go to the sources, and not to the glosses and labyrinthine commentaries of the glossators and the Bartolists (though sometimes to consult Bartolus himself might prove profitable) ;[1] in order rightly to interpret a *lex* it is fatal both to one's own understanding and to that of others to offer the inextricable maze of opinions on opinions and explanations of explanations.[2] At best the system of exegesis may succeed in elaborating some rules and formulas, but a harmonious unified system can never result therefrom.[3] One perusal of the Corpus Iuris itself is far more profitable than a whole life given to *interpretationes, repetitiones,* and *disputationes*. What would Justinian have said of the dialectical proceedings concerned, as they were, more with words than with things, more with dogmatic asseverations than with unprejudiced searching for truth?[4] Return, then, to the method of Justinian if you would find your way out of the existing confusion. And again, besides going to the veritable sources, we must effect a constant alliance of the study of law with that of other relative subjects, so that the results of the latter will help to explain or reinforce, or if need be modify, the conclusions of the former. On account of the unity of knowledge and essential correlation of its branches, the subsidiary subjects in question will be numerous; but some are of especial importance, *e.g.* history, philology, literature ("bonae literae"). And, reciprocally, sound conceptions of law will prove an invaluable aid to the attaining of a fuller and more rational understanding of each of these subjects. Hence the philologists, the "grammatici" who confine themselves to verbal constructions, very rarely discern the right meaning of legal passages, and the fundamental import of the law set forth ;[5] thus Angelus Politianus was once laughed at by Socinus for not knowing the real meaning of "suus heres."[6] As to the glossators and commentators, Accursius, Bartolus, and their associates, not once did they even sip of non-juristic knowledge.[7] True jurisprudence, indeed, necessarily embraces, or is closely related to, all other sciences: "Haec ars ceteras omnes in se continet,"[8] and so

[1] *Opera*, col. 868.
[2] *Ibid.*, col. 73 (*Paradoxa*, iv. *prooemium*).
[3] *Ibid.*, col. 866.
[4] *Ibid.*, col. 860.
[5] *Ibid.*, col. 275.
[6] *Ibid.*, col. 191.
[7] *Ibid.*, col. 753.
[8] *Ibid.*, col. 852.

is, in a sense, pre-eminent. The comparative method, therefore, of Alciati aims at revealing the indissoluble connection of the Corpus Iuris with the entire ancient culture, by making systematic use of mutual illustration and exemplification; and the sound application of this method consequently demands many-sided knowledge. The exaction of such high qualifications is perhaps not so unreasonable in an age which produced men of universal genius like Leonardo da Vinci, Leo Baptista Alberti, Michaelangelo. As to the history of Roman law, however, Alciati thought there was then little prospect of successful results; in the earlier period more particularly only suppositions and conjectures are possible; for that part of the subject is clouded in obscurity, and what there is of it is but a feeble shadow.[1] He was but little concerned with pre-Justinian sources, and scarcely realized how much early Roman law is embodied in the Corpus Iuris.

In conclusion it may be said that Alciati certainly did not accomplish as much as his methods and projects promised. He was one of those—like our own Coleridge, for example—who design much, but leave only a few fragments—fragments, however, destined to prove of the greatest influence and a vital inspiration to his contemporaries and successors. He restored texts, showed how they were to be interpreted, from what point of view they were to be regarded, how they were to be related to the life and thought of the time which brought them into being. No doubt he committed mistakes, some of them the errors of an explorer, others inherited from inveterate tradition; but his fundamental intention, namely, the establishment of a rational scientific method, was fulfilled. He more than any other jurist has a right to the title of founder of the humanist method; to him is due the rise of the great French school of jurisprudence in the sixteenth century, with, on the one hand, systematizers like the eminent Doneau, and, on the other, humanist investigators and restorers like Cujas, the real juristic coryphaeus of the century.

[1] *Opera,* col. 443 *seq.*

JACQUES CUJAS

JACQUES CUJAS

Law in France before Cujas.—Already in the eleventh century the wave of learning and culture was felt in France as well as in Italy. The curriculum of the university of Paris included legal instruction (that is, canon law which however contained Roman elements), as well as theology and the arts. With the influence of men like Abelard, as was pointed out in the preceding essay, Paris became the leading centre of scholasticism; and the scholastic method and spirit at once had a great effect both on the study of jurisprudence and on legal practice. Various compilations were made of the usages and customs of France; thus we find at the very beginning of the eleventh century a collection entitled *Assises de Jérusalem*. Numerous manuals and epitomes were also composed, incorporating a large body of Roman law; such were the *Decretum* and *Panormita* of Ivo of Chartres, the *Exceptiones Petri*, the *Brachylogus iuris civilis*, and *Lo Codi*, all of which have previously been mentioned.[1] Two rival schools of law contributed much to the advance of jurisprudence, both native and Roman: one was that of Montpellier, which was greatly indebted to Placentinus, and established itself as the leading representative of law teaching in the "pays de droit écrit," the other was that of Orléans, which was organized by Philip the Fair, and became the authoritative guide for legal exposition in the "pays de droit coutumier." Besides, under the French monarchy jurisprudence was from early times applied to the affairs of government and the State. Philip Augustus (who in 1190 established royal courts of justice presided over by officers designated bailiffs or seneschals), St. Louis (who extended the organization of parlements in the French provinces),

---

[1] Many observations which would have been necessary are omitted in the present essay, because its subject-matter is meant to be supplementary to, and not a repetition of, that set forth in the study of Alciati. The reader is once and for all referred thereto.

and Philip the Fair gathered legists round them. With the gradual development of Roman doctrines, the influence of these lawyers rapidly increased; and they were entrusted by their sovereigns to draw up collections of ordinances—those "Établissements" which were destined to undermine the feudal régime, and to restrain the advancing power of the papacy. The enlargement of the royal power and the spread of law teaching gave greater importance to the parlements, whose magistrates, being able jurisconsults, decided cases in accordance with the evidence brought, instead of by the obsolescent trial by battle. The *Établissements de Saint Louis* (about 1270), drawn from that monarch's ordinances, from the customs of Touraine-Anjou and of the Orléanais, and also from the Corpus Iuris of Justinian, established a great code of rules of civil and criminal procedure, and principles formulated from a large variety of legal decisions. In 1283 appeared the *Coutume de Beauvosisis*, compiled by Philippe de Rémi, sire de Beaumanoir. This work shows what a great influence Roman law exercised on the usages of Northern France, and how in the hands of the judge the rules of the ancient jurisprudence often triumphed when brought into conflict with Germanic conceptions. At about the same time were produced Durand's *Speculum iuris* and Foucaud's two works on Roman law, viz. *Quaestiones iuris* and *Recipiendarum actionum rationes*.

At the beginning of the fourteenth century, France possessed an original school of Romanistic legists, of whom the most prominent were Jacques de Revigny, Pierre de Belleperche, Guillaume de Cunéo, Petrus Jacobi, and Johannes Faber. They were professors and advocates at Orléans, Montpellier, or Toulouse, and became distinguished in Church and State. Their writings have an eminently practical character, and endeavoured to impart to the customary institutions and political organization of their time a new vigour and vitality by ingrafting therein principles of Roman law. This aim is shown more particularly in the works of Faber—*Breviarium in Codicem* and *Commentarius ad Instituta*. Other practical manuals were issued, like G. du Breuil's *Stylus parlamenti*, which set forth the usages and formulæ incidental to the procedure of the Royal Court of Justice. In the fifteenth century various projects were set on foot by Charles VII., Louis XI., and Charles VIII. Thus Charles VII. devoted himself to the reorganization of French government, issued an ordinance (1453) for the reform of justice, and ordered the preparation of materials for a code. Similarly Charles VIII.'s ordinance (1493) provided for the amendment of judicial administration ; and in his reign also compilations of local customs were made. In the meantime the Bartolist current was gaining ground in France, though it never penetrated as deeply as it had done in Italy. The French doctors were never addicted to the scholastic subtleties and vagaries as much as the Italians were. As a recent writer says : " L'esprit français est trop logique pour accepter sans résistance une création aussi bâtarde que celle des Bartolistes."[1] Nevertheless, in the decline of the study of jurisprudence during the fifteenth century, the influence of the Bartolists reached several schools in France, and predominated till the following century. Thus Forcadel, the rival of Cujas, owed to this circumstance his favour at Toulouse.[2]

The Sixteenth-Century Movement.—No century was more blemished than the sixteenth ; but no century achieved a more glorious distinction. At its opening, it found in the West (excluding Italy—as was shown in the previous essay) practically a medieval world ; at its close it witnessed a definitive transfiguration. Modernism, heralded by Renaissance and Reformation, came to displace once and for all old beliefs, old institutions, the old attitude to life and thought. The universal, more or less homogeneous consciousness of the West developed into the particular, individual consciousness of States—each working out, on its own lines, its own polity, its vernacular literature, its national religion, its native art. The Teutonic Renaissance was inaugurated, like the Latin, by an insurrection against the supremacy of scholastic Aristotelianism ; but its spirit was more democratic, more religious, more theological ; its bulwarks were St. Paul, representing Biblical authority, and St. Augustine, conducing to neo-Platonism, mystic philosophy. As to the Latin movement, the French Renaissance was distinguished from its progenitor, the Italian, in that it was more specifically educational, literary, and juristic, whilst the latter was more philosophical.[3] For a short time, however, the French Renaissance had assumed a distinctively Italian colour ; this was specially

---

[1] J. Flach, *Cujas, les Glossateurs et les Bartolistes*, in *Nouvelle revue historique de droit français et étranger* (Paris, 1883), vii., pp. 205-27, at p. 224.
[2] See further *infra*.
[3] *Cf.* Rev. A. M. Fairbairn, *Tendencies of European Thought in the Age of the Reformation*, in *Cambridge Modern History*, ii. ch. xix.

marked in the second quarter of the century, when there was so great an influx of Italians into France after the fall of Florence (1530), and the marriage of Francis I.'s second son to Catharine de' Medici. There was not always a clear line of demarcation between the Renaissance and the Reformation; though on the whole it may be said that the first was of a more secular, the second of a more religious character. But in France the Reformation never became an entirely national movement. The Catholics constituted the great majority of the population, and detested the Protestants more for their schismatic and separatist attitude than for their heretical beliefs. This antagonism brought about over thirty years of religious wars, culminating in the massacre of St. Bartholomew—wars which had an injurious effect on the free intellectual work of scholars and jurists (most of whom were amongst the Reformers), and on French humanism in general.[1] France had just before then contributed a great deal to the classical and legal erudition of Europe. The Collège de France was supreme in classical philology, the university of Bourges was unrivalled in jurisprudence. French literature had received a great impulse and a fecundating force from humanism. There were eminent professors of Greek and masters of Latin who continued the great work of Budaeus; *e.g.* Jacques Toussain (Tusanus), a favourite pupil of the latter, and Adrien Turnébe (Turnebus), who issued Greek editions, translations, and commentaries on Latin authors; Denys Lambin (Lambinus), whose Latin editions enjoyed great fame; Jean Dorat (Auratus), the Aeschylean critic and inspirer of the Pléiade; Marc Antoine Muret (Muretus), that master of Latinity who struggled against the superstition of Ciceronianism; Henri Estienne (Stephanus), who issued from his press a large number of Greek and Latin editions nearly all edited by him, and in his *Thesaurus Graecae Linguae* (1572) bequeathed a rich legacy to scholarship; Jacques Amyot, one of the few translators of genius, and an inspirer of the French spirit; Pierre Pithou, a man of versatile activity; Joseph Scaliger, the greatest name in the history of French classical learning; and finally Isaac Casaubon, whose aim was "to revive the picture of the ancient world." To these names may be added that of Pierre de la Ramée (Ramus), whose famous treatise on logic (*Dialecticae Institutiones*, Paris, 1543, translated into French 1555) was a reaction against Aristotelian authority,

[1] See *infra*, under life of Cujas.

and was welcomed in Protestant universities (with the notable exception of Oxford).

As to humanist jurisprudence, though the real founder was Alciati, we may regard as a pioneer Pierre de l'Estoile (Stella), who began to lecture at Orléans in 1512. In France more than elsewhere was systematic opposition manifested to the subtleties and dogmatic methods of the Bartolists, and to the bewildering accumulation of glosses of their predecessors. Though the glossators merited, in some respects, more indulgence than their scholastic successors, men of the Renaissance like Rabelais treated them all alike with contempt. Thus Pantagruel says to the doctors of Paris : " Au cas que leur controverse était patente et facile à juger, vous l'avez obscurcie par sottes et déraisonnables raisons et ineptes opinions de Accurse, Balde, Bartole, de Castro . . . et ces aultres vieulx mastins qui jamais n'entendirent la moindre loy des Pandectes, et n'estoyent que gros veaulx de disme, ignorans de tout ce qui est nécessaire à l'intelligence des loix ; car (comme il est tout certain), ils n'avoyent cognoissance de langue ny grecque, ny latine. . . ."[1] And comparing the glosses of the Accursians with the text of the Digest itself, he observes : " Au monde n'y a livres tant beaux, tant ornés, tant élégants comme sont les textes des Pandectes, mais la brodure d'iceux, c'est assavoir la glose d'Accurse est tant infâme, tant sale, tant punaise, que ce n'est qu'ordure et vilenie."[2] Rabelais demanded that jurisprudence should be reinforced by humanist culture ; he, like the others of the new school, maintained that philology, history, science in general are indispensable to a true jurisconsult. Similarly, Douaren, one of the most eminent of the humanist jurists, derided the Bartolists for their barbarous language, absence of method, and scholastic procedure ; he complained that they gave themselves entirely to logic, chopping and attacking the opinions of others rather than to seeking the truth in the sources themselves. Without devotion to letters, claimed he, no one could become either a jurist or a statesman, but only a cavilling pettifogger.[3] The bad Latin and wretched style of the post-glossators were attacked by formidable critics and consummate masters like Muret, who said their compositions were a hotchpotch ("farrago"), a confused mass ("acervus perturbatus"), a vile medley of barbarous, foreign, unheard-of

[1] *Pantagruel* (1533), ii. c. 10.   [2] *Ibid.*, ii. c. 5.
[3] *Cf.* his letter to André Gaillard, in his *Opera* (Francofurti, 1592), p. 1100.

expressions ("foedissima barbararum, peregrinarum, inauditarum vocum colluvio ").[1] Other notable assailants of the "mos italicus " of the Bartolists were, besides Cujas himself, E. Baron,[2] F. Hotman,[3] and Baudouin.[4]

The aim of the new French school of Romanists was, in the first place, to restore, by means of every collateral aid furnished by a thorough and comprehensive humanist culture, the true sources and texts of Roman jurisprudence, to indicate the original significance and applicability of its laws; secondly, to effect a synthesis and a coherent systematic structure of these re-established elements, and make manifest the spirit and philosophy of the entire body. This aim was not only part of the general revolt implied in the Renaissance, the revival of classical antiquity, but was also stimulated by the widely felt desire to remedy the abuses of judicial administration;[5] for it was felt that a more rational knowledge of Roman law would conduce to the amelioration of existing practice by introducing classical conceptions and principles. Noteworthy appeals on this ground were made in France by Hotman (*Antitribonianus*, 1567), and in Germany by that great reformer and accomplished humanist, Melanchthon (*Oratio de legibus*, Haguenau, 1530), and by Oldendorp (*Disputatio forensis de iure et aequitate*, Cologne, 1541). The latter emphatically insists that the reform of the administration of justice must begin by reforming the teaching of law.

The chief French representatives of the humanist method of jurisprudence issued critical editions of old or newly discovered texts; *e.g.* D. Godefroy (Gothofredus, 1549-1622), *Corpus iuris civilis;* J. Godefroy (1582-1652), belongs to the sixteenth-century school more by the nature of his work than by date, *Quatuor fontes iuris civilis* (ante-Justinian texts); J. du Tillet (*d.* 1570) and Cujas (1522-1590), *Theodosian Code;* P. Pithou (1539-1596), *Lex Dei*, and the post-Theodosian *novellae;* F. Pithou (1544-1621), Julian's *Epitome* and the laws of the Visigoths; J. du Tillet,

---

[1] *Oratio de doctoris officio deque modo iurisprudentiam studendi.* His orations were published in 1576.

[2] *De ratione dicendi discendique iuris civilis ad studiosam legum iuventutem commonefactio* (1546).

[3] *Iurisconsultus sive de optimo genere iuris interpretandi.*

[4] *De optima iuris docendi discendique ratione.*

[5] *Cf.* Flach, *loc. cit.*, p. 221, n. (1) : " La procédure était devenue en beaucoup de pays un vain simulacre qui ne servait qu'a éterniser les procès, à en rendre la solution arbitraire ou aléatoire, et le juge même instruit, laborieux et intègre, ne pouvait se reconnaître au milieu des commentaires amoncelés depuis des siècles."

Ulpian's *Regulae;* A. Bouchard, *Institutes* of Gaius and the *Sententiae* of Paul; E. Bonnefoi (Bonefidius, *d.* 1574), *Juris orientalis l. iii;* Cujas and A. Augustin, the *Basilica;* other sources of Graeco-Roman law were issued by Baudouin, Labbé, Bosquet, and others.[1] Then there were other eminent French jurists of the century who did not devote themselves entirely to Roman law ; *e.g.* Charles Dumoulin (1500-1566), surnamed by some of his contemporaries the " French Papinian " ; F. Hotman (1524-1590); Douaren (1509-1559); Doneau (1527-1591), the great systematizer; Baudouin (1520-1573), eminent theologian as well as jurist; Ranconnet (*d.* 1559); Govéa (1505-1566); Connan (1508-1551), who began the general classification continued afterwards by Domat and other systematizers ; B. Brisson (1531-1591), A. Le Conte (*d.* 1586), P. Faber (1540-1600), and others.[2] This assembly of names certainly gives France, with regard to sixteenth-century jurisprudence, the foremost place in the world ;[3] and in this magnificent concourse Cujas stands out supreme.

Life of Cujas.[4]—Jacques Cujas (Jacobus Cujacius)—whose real name was Cujaus, which was changed for reasons of euphony—was born, the son of a fuller, in Toulouse, 1522. He first studied law in his native town under Arnaud Ferrier, who was a disciple of Alciati, and who subsequently attained high distinction as president of the Parlement of Paris, then French ambassador to the Council of Trent and to Venice, and afterwards as chancellor to the King of Navarre. Cujas, unlike Alciati, was fortunate in his first instructor ; indeed, he ever after regarded him as the ablest professor he had known. At Toulouse he read all the known expounders of law, and frequently took part in public disputations with his fellow-pupils. But he applied himself also

[1] *Cf.* Brissaud, *op. cit.*, vol. i., p. 357 ; A. Tardif, *Histoire des sources du droit français : Origines romaines* (Paris, 1890), p. 467.
[2] *Cf. infra*, on the relation between Cujas and his chief contemporaries.
[3] *Cf.* the opinion of the English civilian, Sir Arthur Duck, *De usu et authoritate iuris civilis Romanorum* (London, 1653), l. ii. c. 5 : " Iurisprudentia romana, si apud alias gentes extincta esset, apud solos Gallos repiriri posset."
[4] An adequate life of Cujas is greatly to be desired. The best account, short as it is, is still that of Berriat Saint-Prix, *Histoire du droit romain, suivie de l'histoire de Cujas* (1821), pp. 373-454, and notes, pp. 455-611.—The German translation of E. Spangenberg, *Jacob Cujas und seine Zeitgenossen* (Leipzig, 1822), contains a few additions and notes of not very great consequence ; it is mainly useful for the convenient chronological list of Cujas' works.—Savigny's brief article in *Themis*, iv. (1822), pp. 194-207, gives a little supplementary matter.

to the ancient languages, especially Greek, to history, rhetoric, philosophy, ethics, philology, and poetry. In 1547 he began a private course of lectures on the *Institutes*; and this venture was so successful that soon the sons of eminent men were sent to him from distant regions. Some seven years later he left Toulouse never to return, because, as it is averred, he failed in his application for a chair of Roman law. It is certain that he was a candidate, and that Forcadel, his Bartolist opponent, obtained the professorship in 1556. But it is doubtful whether Cujas took part in the actual test proposed by the authorities, as the records of the university for this epoch no longer exist.[1] In any case Forcadel's selection was influenced by the fact that Toulouse was still a stronghold of Bartolism, and that the majority of the students—who had a voice in the appointment—voted for him, owing to the persuasions of Jean Bodin (an adversary of Cujas), and to the long experience, good presence, and witty, rhetorical speech of Forcadel. Gravina observes that in preferring the latter to Cujas the university preferred an ape to a man. After the departure of Cujas, one of his pupils, Jean Amariton, published the former's notes on Ulpian, and dedicated the work to him.

In November, 1554, Cujas received a chair at the neighbouring town, Cahors, in succession to the Portuguese professor, Antoine de Govéa, who had spent nearly all his life in France, and established his position as a distinguished Romanist. About six months afterwards, however, Cujas was called to the university of Bourges (then pre-eminent for civil law—in Hotman's phrase, " le grand marché de la science ") to fill the chair of Baudouin, who left for Germany owing to his religious opinions. This invitation was made by the Duchess of Berry, Marguerite of France, daughter of Francis I., on the advice of her chancellor, Michel de l'Hospital. She was, like her father, a patron of art and learning. Bourges then possessed several distinguished professors, *e.g.* Le Conte, a pupil of Alciati and editor of the Corpus Iuris, Douaren, and Doneau, a great representative of the historical school. The two latter, seeing in Cujas a formidable rival, created all kinds of difficulties for him, and in his absence

[1] Papyre Masson in his *Vie de Cujas*, written in the year of Cujas' death (1590), asserts that he really suffered defeat in the competition, and many others repeated this statement. This was denied in 1671 by Bernard Médon, in his *Histoire de Maran*, who maintained that the report was not in accordance with the university records, which, however, he did not quote. Berriat Saint-Prix accepts the traditional opinion.—For other references to this controversy, see Brissaud, *op. cit.*, i., p. 350, n. 2.

instigated the students against him; at their instance also Pulvaeus afterwards published a violent satire against him, to which his pupil Antoine Foquelin of Orléans replied. In spite of the support of Le Conte and the sympathy of his auditors (amongst whom were pupils like Pierre du Faur de Saint-Jory (P. Faber), Loysel, Pierre Ayrault, François Ragueau, Nicolas Cisner, and Pierre Pithou), he left Bourges in August, 1557, and in November was called to Valence. During his stay at Bourges he had begun the publication of the great works—Notes on the Institutes and on Paul's *Sententiae*, Commentaries on certain titles of the Digest, and the *Observationes*,—which assured him the position of the leading jurist of the day, and procured him the friendship of eminent men like Etienne Pasquier. Several pupils accompanied him to Valence. At this time he married the daughter of a doctor of Avignon. He soon published a second edition of the above works, and issued a further portion of the Commentaries and the *Observationes*, of which the former was dedicated to Jean de Montluc, Bishop of Valence, whose friendship he enjoyed. His reputation was now so great that a legist, M. Vertranius Maurus, stated[1] that there was no need to quote passages from the writings of Cujas, as they were in everybody's hands.

In June, 1559, Douaren died, and the Duchess of Berry recalled Cujas to Bourges, where he was generous enough to pronounce a eulogy on his late opponent. During the next few years further publications appeared, *e.g.* his commentaries on the last three books of the Code, on the title "De verborum obligationibus" which he dedicated to Marguerite and to l'Hospital. When the former became Duchess of Savoy, she and her husband were desirous of restoring to the university of Turin its former renown; and so, on the death of Antoine de Govéa (whom they had brought from Grenoble), they persuaded Cujas to accept the vacant chair (September, 1566). During his residence in Italy, he paid visits to various universities to see the methods of teaching and to examine manuscripts; he tried unsuccessfully to obtain the loan of the famous Florentine manuscript of the Digest. It appears that Cujas was not able to habituate himself to the climate of Turin or to Italian manners; hence in August, 1567, he returned to Valence university, which had greatly increased in importance by its union with the university of Grenoble. Very soon took

[1] *De jure liberorum* (Ludguni, 1558), c. 27.

place a general rising of Protestants, and Valence was seized ; teaching was in consequence suspended until the conclusion of peace in the following year. On the resumption of his professional work, his fame was at its height, and his lectures were attended by large numbers of pupils, many of whom came from distant places abroad, notwithstanding the political and religious disturbances in France. Again in 1570 he was compelled to withdraw to Lyons, where he wrote new works and revised some of the old ones for new editions. He now received invitations from several other universities, *e.g.* Avignon, Besançon and Bourges, but after the peace of St. Germain (in July) he was back in Valence. His students continued to increase in numbers, and amongst them were the prince of scholars, Joseph Scaliger, and one of the greatest of French historians, Jacques Auguste de Thou. In the autumn of 1571 he fell ill, but none the less continued his lectures, and begged the indulgence of his audience when he was carried into the lecture-room. On the fateful day of St. Bartholomew (August 24, 1572) he saved the life of Scaliger, and of his colleague, E. Bonnefoi. Later Charles IX. recognized the high position of Cujas by making him honorary councillor of the Parlement of Grenoble (May, 1573).

In June, 1575, hoping to obtain more tranquillity, he proceeded to Bourges, which was then almost entirely Catholic and was situated in a peaceful province. But he was not more fortunate there, and the civil dissension compelled him to remove to Paris. At the instance of the procureur-général of the King, the parlement, by a decree of April 2, 1576, suspended in Cujas' favour the ordinances prohibiting the public teaching of civil law in the university, and even authorized him to confer degrees—" d'autant que le dit Cujas est, comme la cour sçait, personnage de grande et singulière doctrine et condition."[1] Some three months later, on the restoration of peace, he went back to Bourges, and never left it again. He was granted a pension by the Duc d'Alençon.

The greater part of the rest of his life was embittered by civil and religious disturbances, as well as by grief and sadness from other causes. In 1581 he lost his wife and only son, and for a time was overwhelmed with grief. He said in a letter that the friendship of Scaliger stayed his tears and saved him from a

[1] *Cf.* G. Périès, *La faculté de droit dans l'université de Paris*, p. 173. (Referred to by Brissaud, *op. cit.*, i., p. 354.)

wretched grave. To another friend he wrote that he was pining to see him, that the sight of him would help to remove the sadness which was bearing him down in his loneliness. At this time offers reached him from Italy. Gregory XIII. himself wrote to him offering a large stipend and high honours if he accepted a professorship at Bologna ; but various circumstances induced him to remain in Bourges. He deeply felt the need of domestic companionship and of an heir ; and so, though over sixty years old, he married a young wife. But the only issue was a daughter (born in 1587). The following year he went to Paris to ask leave to retire, but Henry III. refused. The last two years of his life were still more troubled. After the assassination of the King (August 1, 1589), the leaguers proclaimed King, under the title of Charles X., the Cardinal de Bourbon, uncle of Henry IV. Cujas was asked, with promises of magnificent rewards, to write in favour of the Cardinal ; the promises were followed by threats, and fanatics in Bourges were roused against him. But nothing, not even a riot in which he nearly lost his life, could shake his refusal. Civil war continued, especially in Berry, and affected him deeply till his death, which took place on October 4, 1590, and was followed by a public funeral.

Like Alciati, Cujas led a restless, wandering life : the incessant disturbances and menacing circumstances of the time, together with the intriguing hostility of rival professors and of those adhering to the older schools, made it impossible for him to enjoy peace and tranquillity. This kind of life was then shared by many ardent spirits who ventured to strike out new paths for themselves. Amongst these we find—to mention only legists or publicists—men like Dumoulin, Baudouin, Doneau, and Hotman. After the massacre of St. Bartholomew, the position of professors in France who were suspected of heresy or of sympathy with the reform movement became still more intolerable. Ramus, assailed by the doctors of the Sorbonne, by the scholastic controversialists, and, after he turned Protestant, by the orthodox avengers, perished in the massacre. The classical critic and scholar, Lambinus, died of shock almost immediately after. Scaliger, like Doneau and Hotman, was compelled to seek a temporary refuge in Geneva. Cujas, however, did not assume such an uncompromising or decisive attitude towards religion. He perhaps belonged, with Erasmus and Montaigne, to that party which was characterized by a mild scepticism or by the broadest toleration, and detested fanaticism of any kind. This point of view was not due to lack of courage or vacillation ; when necessity arose, he was ready to risk his life rather than surrender his convictions to the seditious clamours of a threatening crowd of leaguers. He practised Catholicism, but it is significant that in his will he made no declaration in its favour, forbade the sale of his books to the Jesuits, and recommended his wife and daughter simply to abide by the precepts of the Holy Scripture. It was thought that he had openly embraced the reformed faith, for we find Hotman accusing him of deserting it again. However, in his discussions, whenever legal matters were confronted by religious arguments, he was wont to observe : "Nihil hoc ad edictum praetoris," and thus constantly emphasized that the spheres of law and religion were separate, affirmed the secular character of jurisprudence, and declared that it could no longer be the humble servant of theology.

Cujas does not appear to have possessed a marked professorial aptitude, in so far as secondary accomplishments are concerned. It is said that in his lectures his exordium was too precipitate, his general delivery rather rapid, his voice unequal ; that he did not answer immediately ("ex abrupto," as Alexander Scot, one of his pupils, says) the difficult questions put to him. He invariably avoided talking law at table or when he was in the society of his friends ; and when they suggested problems to him he referred them to his lectures. There is no doubt that he lacked readiness of retort and rhetorical flourish, and other controversial attributes which were then so much appreciated ; indeed, he seems to have had a deep contempt for the art of declamation, and forensic eloquence without true insight and deep knowledge he disdained above all. He carefully prepared his public discourses, which were always characterized by lucid expression, exact and pentrating analysis. Under his scrutiny, backed up as it was by scientific method, immense erudition, and new suggestive ideas, the most obscure passages yielded their meaning. He always took a personal interest in his students, and they were attached to him. He admitted them to his table and to his library, and often helped them pecuniarily. Before and after lectures they formed a procession and escorted him to and from his house. Many accompanied him in his frequent peregrinations, and when they left him still kept up the most friendly relations.

Works[1] and their Character.—The works of Cujas, like those of Alciati, do not set forth an elaborate, systematic account of Roman jurisprudence as a whole. The time was not yet ripe for such an undertaking. But Cujas, more than any other single investigator, contributed to the realization of this object. His voluminous publications—a magnificent array of mighty tomes—were nearly all devoted to the exegetic study of the sources. The most important of these writings are the Commentaries on Papinian (issued after his death), and above all the *Observationum et emendationum libri XXVIII.*, which, originally designed to extend to forty books, appeared at intervals from 1556 to his death, except the last four books posthumously published by Pithou. The latter work, described by eminent Romanists like Heineccius as an "opus incomparable," and "opus divinum," presents with but little order a rich harvest of restorations of texts or suggestive conjectures, of corrections and interpretations. Other writings, representing for the most part the substance of his lectures, like the *Tractatus ad Africanum*, and the *Recitationes sollemnes* on Paul, Ulpian, Modestinus, Marcellus, Julian, Scaevola, and others, seek to re-establish in their original form and restore to their original meaning the contributions of the classical jurisconsults comprised in the Justinian compilations. His *Paratitla* on the Digest—a small book which his opponent Hotman advised his son always to carry about with him—offers a concise exposition of the titles of that collection. He also issued learned and considerably amended editions of texts which had before been published with greater or lesser defects, and, what is much more noteworthy, he gave to the world for the first time numerous texts based on collated manuscripts, which he searched out in every promising quarter. In addition to these writings on Roman law, we find in his volumes a few inaugural discourses, which academic duties demanded of him, two polemical compositions (the *Notata Antonii Mercatoris, i.e.* written under the pseudonym of "Antonius Mercator," and the defence of Bishop Montluc against the attack of Doneau), also a work relating to

---

[1] The collected works were edited by C. A. Fabrot—*Opera Omnia*, 10 vols., folio (Paris, 1658). There is also an eleventh volume under the title of Appendix, which contains, besides other matter, his *Notata Antonii Mercatoris*.—The editions of Naples (1722-27) and Venice (1758-83) in 11 vols. are practically mere reprints; but they are more convenient as there is an index to them, entitled *Promptuarium operum Jac. Cujacii*, 2 vols., 1763 (2nd ed. 1795).

feudal law (Treatise on Fiefs), and one on ecclesiastical law (a commentary on three books of the Decretals of Pope Gregory IX.). As for the important constituents of French national law, viz. customs, royal ordinances, judgments and orders of the parlements, he did not make any of them the subject of a separate work, but he utilized his knowledge of them in the illustrations and comparisons which enrich his works, and necessarily so in his professional consultations.

In consideration of the manuscripts discovered or published by Cujas, he occupies the foremost place in the history of Roman law. His zeal in the search of these documents was inexhaustible. To procure them he spared no toil, no expense. One of the chief reasons for his going to Italy was to examine manuscripts. In 1571 he made a journey to Provence for the same purpose. In the preceding year he kept several persons occupied in the like quest; in 1572 he obtained the services of a friend in Italy to make investigations; in 1575 a nobleman came expressly from Padua to Bourges with a collection of *Sententiae* of the ancient jurisconsults. All this indefatigable enthusiasm was not that of a bibliomaniac, but that of a true explorer and scholar; he was indeed ever ready to lend his precious acquisitions to students who might desire to consult them, and gave some to friends and publishers, and lost many which had been temporarily borrowed and never returned.[1] It appears from a catalogue drawn up by one of his pupils, about 1574, that there were some two hundred manuscripts in his library; and according to a later list, copied from an inventory made after his death and published quite recently,[2] there were actually about four hundred. And these numerous documents of his own were but a small part of those he consulted during his literary labours. The greater portion of his correspondence is concerned with this subject. The manuscripts of which he took cognizance and of which many are no longer extant related to the three periods of Roman jurisprudence —ante-Justinian, Justinian, and post-Justinian. For example, he published in 1566 the *Lex Romana Burgundionum*, probably after a manuscript belonging to Pierre Pithou, but he was mistaken in considering it the work of a jurist named Papian.[3] He

---

[1] *Cf.* B. Saint-Prix, *op. cit.*, pp. 421-22.
[2] *Cf.* M. Omont, in *Nouvelle revue historique de droit*, 1885, pp. 233-7; and 1888, pp. 632-41.
[3] See the title of his edition of 1586: *Burgundionis iurisconsulti, qui Papiani responsorum titulum praefert, liber.*

also issued for the first time the *Consultatio veteris iurisconsulti*, after a manuscript now lost, of which fragments appeared in 1564 and 1566, then the text itself in 1577, and more completely in 1586. This was prefixed to his collection of sixty consultations; and in his dedicatory epistle he says he did not himself discover the manuscript, but that his knowledge of it was due to Antoine Loysel. The book *De asse et ponderibus*, attributed generally to Volusius Moecianus, a jurisconsult of the time of Antoninus Pius, though held by others to have been written after the Theodosian Code (438), was published for the first time by Cujas in 1586, together with various other texts of ante-Justinian law. He was the first to issue Books VI. to VIII. of the Theodosian Code, after the Charpin manuscript; and this work, incomplete though it was, proved of great assistance to Jacques Godefroy in the preparation of his superior edition which appeared, several years after his death, in 1665. Modern students are indebted to him for numerous portions of Paul's *Sententiae* presented (1585) in Book XXI. of his *Observationes*, and taken from the Besançon manuscript. Of the post-Justinian collections, he was the first to bring to light many books of the *Basilica*, for which he consulted more complete manuscripts than those now in existence, *e.g.* those which were in the library of Catharine de' Medici, and others acquired by himself during his stay in Italy.[1] His labours were afterwards utilized for the great edition of the *Basilica* published by Fabrot. As for the Justinian compilations themselves, he did much towards the restoration of the Code; and nearly all the Greek constitutions were re-established by him and by Antonius Augustinius. He also revised, by collating old manuscripts, the text of the Institutes, and brought out an edition in 1585. Further, in many cases Cujas offered encouragement and counsel to other researchers in their handling of juristic documents: thus Julian's *Epitome* (already published several times in the sixteenth century) was issued by the brothers Pithou, by his advice and under his patronage; and Le Conte's edition of the *Novellae* was revised by him. Finally, he sometimes supplied valuable materials even for non-legal publications: thus to him was mainly due the Latin translation of the letters of the ancient Greeks found in the library of Pierre Pithou, and published at Geneva, 1606.

The style of Cujas is marked by extreme conciseness, which

---

[1] *Cf.* the letter of Cujas, dated August 7, 1567, to be found in *Themis*, i., p. 94.

makes the reading of his works difficult to all but students of experience; apart from this striking quality we find an elegance of language, a clearness of expression, and rational sequence in the argument, backed up by apt citations, comparisons, and a controlled erudition, all of which combine to distinguish his diction and his whole manner from the dull, heavy, un-Roman Latin of the majority of his contemporaries, especially of the jurists. He does not possess the power of felicitous construction and classical propriety of a Muret; but his prose is certainly a very effective medium for conducting critical investigation with force, directness, and precision.

Method of Cujas.—Alciati was the principal founder of the humanist school of jurisprudence; but in his time his ideas and methods were accepted by a very small minority, and opposed by a multitude of formidable adversaries attached to old ways and conceptions. With the coming of Cujas the new method was once and for all established, opposition was gradually overcome, and unanimity secured amongst most of the enlightened and unprejudiced students. The course of the new school, more or less undecided before, was now definitively determined; its aim was marked out with greater precision. Before, the Bartolist adherents might well have maintained their authority, perhaps they might with some success have re-asserted their pre-eminence; now, their methods were shown to be hopelessly bad and their point of view fallacious. The work of Cujas, more than that of any other jurist of the time, conduced to the repudiation of the earlier juristic heritage, and brought about the triumphant victory of the historical school. As a humanist he was well versed in the classical literature, and used this knowledge with remarkable efficacy in the comparison of legal and historical texts with the purely literary. He laicized the study of law. He liberated it from the custom of heaping up commentaries on isolated enactments, and from that of spinning out scholastic subtleties and endless artificial distinctions. Accursius and the glossators, however, he held in far less disesteem than Bartolus and the commentators with their futile "fictions and ill imaginings."[1] Of the latter he tersely—and truly—observes: "Verbosi in re facili, in difficili muti, in angusta diffusi"[2] whilst Accursius

---

[1] *Observationum*, xii. c. 16: "... Accursium longe magis corona donaverim, a quo quidquid aberrat Bartolus, vanae fictiones et aegri somnia videntur."
[2] *Respons. Papin.*, lib. v. leg. 17 (*De iniusto rupto*).

he places high amongst juristic interpreters.[1] His main reason for holding the glossators in higher favour is that they had made an effort to examine the texts. He incessantly urged his students to study the sources, rather than the verbose and obscure commentaries of the doctors.[2] Similarly, in his endeavours to make of law a rational science, he assailed the ignorant practitioners and their accredited decisions in the courts—decisions based on prejudice, personal considerations, narrow views, erroneous conceptions, shifting fundamentals. No doubt he held theory in higher regard than practice—and necessarily so, in view of the nature of his work and the circumstances of the time; but he by no means despised practice, as his consultations show.[3] As to his immediate predecessor Alciati, whilst recognizing the indisputable merit of the Italian jurist in having been the first to apply systematically the historical and comparative method to juristic investigations, Cujas none the less holds that he was only a mediocre interpreter, inexact in his citations, incomplete and superficial in his exegetic expositions.[4]

The method of Cujas, then, is comparative, critical, historical. The constituent elements of Roman jurisprudence—as represented, for example, in the Justinian compilation—are derived from various sources which were afterwards lost; and the only guidance we have as to its intrinsic composition is solely an indication of the place those elements occupied in the original works. Hence the study of the ancient civil law may be approached in three ways: firstly, by accepting the classification so found, making the best of it, and pointing out how discovered defects might have been avoided by a prior modification of the plan; or secondly, by disregarding the original sequence of the subject-matter, and substituting therefor an arbitrary order, more general, coherent, and logical; or thirdly, by restoring, as far as is possible, the indicated sources in the light of every suggestion obtained from the original materials, and by the aid of conceptions and results furnished by cognate subjects. The first method of procedure would give best the legislation of Justinian in its purely juridical aspect; the second is more in accordance with the exigencies of universal reason, and would

[1] *Observat.* iii. c. 11: "Accursius noster, quem ego et Latinis et Graecis omnibus interpretibus iuris facile antepono. . . ."
[2] *Oratio de ratione docendi iuris.*
[3] See, for example, his 23rd consultation.
[4] *Cf. Notata Antonii Mercatoris,* ii. c. 29.

present the legislative product in its philosophical significance; the third is the historic method, and would set forth, with regard to time, place, and circumstance, the intrinsic sense and relative force of the respective elements composing the whole. This latter method was that of Cujas and the new school.[1] In his hands, therefore, the *Corpus Iuris* was not treated as a homogeneous body of laws (for such it had been frequently assumed before him), but a complex mass which could not well be understood without decomposing it again and examining all its parts. It was his bold design to re-create what Tribonian, that versatile and remarkable minister of Justinian, had altered or consigned to oblivion, to restore the purity of Roman traditions which had been adulterated by the pretentious barbarism of Byzantium, to resuscitate the work of the classical jurisconsults by uniting scattered fragments, to set forth the very principles of Roman jurisprudence as they had been in the minds of those who conceived them, to show the magnificent Roman heritage in its most favourable, that is, in its true, light. Cujas brought to bear on his work the disinterested judicial view of an historian, the imagination of a creative artist, and the exact learning of a scholar. Whenever he proposed a new interpretation he did not fail to refute or criticize the one previously accepted; and he showed that his method, applied by one who possessed a mastery over details and a dispassionate judgment, would demolish the false and confirm the true. In pursuance of his design he inquired into and annotated the *Regulae* of Ulpian, the *Sententiae* of Paul; he wrote a commentary on Africanus; and restored the work of Papinian, that profound legal genius and victim of Caracalla. This supreme jurist's works had reached us only in mutilated fragments; but Cujas applied himself to these sacred remains, and with diligence and penetration brought them to life, and extracted their secret, hitherto unascertained. In the fragments of the contributors to the Justinian compilation, he saw more than groups of legal dispositions conceived in a restricted sense and adopted fortuitously; he recognized that these colourless fragments represented a certain crystallization of the past, and in his handling of them the past was made to live again. He took the isolated texts, restored them with felicitous effect, replaced them in the work of the respective jurisconsults, set the

---

[1] *Cf.* L. Cabantous, in *Revue de législation et de jurisprudence* (Paris), x., (1839), pp. 32 *seq.*

latter in their respective schools, and the schools in their particular epochs. It is noteworthy that the great Romanists of the seventeenth and even of the eighteenth century did not adopt this exacting method; thus jurists like Vinnius, Voet, Heineccius, Pothier generally adhered to the defective order of the various compilations of Justinian, and others like Domat adopted, in conformity with the project of Leibnitz, a somewhat arbitrary classification based on ideas foreign to the classical jurisconsults.

Before the sixteenth century attempts were made to explain texts, but legal interpretation, ill-proportioned, unsystematic as it was, had not yet risen to the dignity of a science, which necessarily implies a complete methodical body of doctrines embracing facts classified according to certain determinate principles, which are controlled by constant reference to these facts, and which govern the doctrines set forth. By consistently applying philology, history, antiquarian lore to the examination of texts, Cujas founded a method which proved an instrument of the greatest efficiency, and from which posterity has derived the most fruitful results. It was not his aim, however, to create a general systematic structure of the entire body of Roman jurisprudence; such exposition was reserved for successors, who were able to benefit by his pioneer work. His genius was essentially critical, analytic; he did not possess in an equal degree that philosophical power which enables one to generalize on broad lines, and coordinate separate parts—the results of analytic investigation—into an all-comprehensive unity.

To conclude this brief statement of Cujas' method and point of view, it will perhaps be of interest to give one or two of his specific opinions on the different parts of Justinian's compilation, and on various legal manuscripts and editions. He appears to have approved of the general plan and structure of the Institutes; he thought it was unnecessary to make long commentaries on the work, that it was best to confine oneself to such brief notes as would effect a restoration of the passages altered by time or by the carelessness of the copyists and publishers, and that the best way to study it is by a comparison with the paraphrase of Theophilus.[1] With regard to the relation of the Institutes to the other portions of the Justinian law, he observes that many passages of the Digest and the Code can be cleared up by the application of facts, dispositions, and principles enunciated in

[1] *Observat.* xi. c. 34.

the former, and supports his contention by giving a large number of examples.[1] He prefers the Greek text of the *Novels* to the Latin translation known as *Vulgata* or *Authentica*, but favours this translation more than those published in his day by G. Meltzer (Haloander, 1501-31) and others—perhaps because the earlier version is more literal and was the one used by the glossators and accepted in the courts.[2] The Novels of Leo he refers to merely to throw light on the obscure passages of the Digest, Code, or Institutes. In the fine edition of the Florentine Pandects by Taurellus (1553), Cujas detected various matters which needed emendation, though he recognized the high merit of the work; he was anxious to make good the defects, but he failed to obtain the loan of the jealously guarded manuscripts. He maintained —and his view is shared by Savigny—that amongst the existing manuscripts of the Digest several are copies of earlier manuscripts other than the Florentine, and that all ought to be collated and examined with a view to establishing the best text;[3] and in conformity with this opinion he effected large restorations, especially in the last ten laws of the title "De interdictis et relegatis" which were wanting in the Florentine manuscript.[4]

Relation of Cujas to his Contemporaries.—Some of the distinguished pupils and contemporaries of Cujas have already been mentioned above; and some of the Romanists and other jurists belonging to his school have been indicated. To the latter may be added the German legist and philologist, Hubertus Giphanius (Giffen, 1534-1616), and, in the Netherlands, Viglius Zuichemus (1507-1577), the first editor of the paraphrase of Theophilus. In some quarters the methods of Cujas met with strong opposition—for it is to be remembered that the Roman law found a hardy opponent in the customary law, which had powerful adherents and advocates. The old maxim, "coutume passe droit" (*i.e.* Roman law), was often emphasized. Indeed, in the university of Paris the teaching of the civil law had by ordinance been for a considerable time forbidden, and, as we have seen, it was partially revived by way of a special favour to Cujas. Among his notable adversaries were his own countrymen, Douaren and Doneau, Dumoulin and Hotman. The vigorous controversies that took place show the novelty of Cujas' doctrine and their historical significance.

[1] *Observat.* xi. c. 38.
[2] *Ibid.*, viii. c. 40.
[3] *Ibid.*, i. c. 1; ii. c. 1.
[4] *Opera*, vol. x., p. 286.

François Douaren (Duarenus), a pupil of Alciati, was born in 1509 and died in 1559 at Bourges, where he had been a professor, after having practised at the bar and manifested much hostility to Cujas. He had also conflicts with Baudouin and Baron. Like his master Alciati, he united the study of letters to that of law. His works, the chief of which is the Commentary on the Digest, are written in an elegant classical style, and were highly esteemed by his great rival. He attached greater importance, than Cujas did, to forensic practice : his poignant criticism of the Bartolists and their methods has already been referred to. He was among the first to purge legal science from the barbarous importations of predecessors. He had associated himself to Calvin, and his *De sacris ministeriis* breathes a spirit of religious liberty.

Hugues Doneau (Donellus, 1527-1591), a pupil of the preceding, was first a professor at Bourges, then, on account of his religious opinions, fled from France in disguise, and resided successively at Geneva, Heidelberg, Leyden, and finally at Altdorf, where he died. He was the most eminent constructive jurist of the century. Unlike Cujas, he did not inquire into the historical connection of laws, and search out what the Roman jurisconsults and legislators meant when the laws were first propounded ; for him the question was the actual significance of the texts, and what they implied when they were incorporated into the compilation of Justinian. Thus Doneau was more strictly a lawyer, whereas Cujas was also, and deliberately so, a historian. For Doneau Roman law was only law, a constant guide in civil and political society ; for Cujas it was also a precious fragment of antiquity. For Doneau it was to be handled systematically, geometrically, as a finished product; for Cujas it was to be treated comparatively, as a changing organism. And so Doneau presented a dogmatic treatise, Cujas produced commentaries, annotations, purged texts. Doneau rehandled the subject-matter of this or that title, set it forth in a new order, and bound together the diverse elements. He systematically advanced definitions, laid down principles, and logically deduced conclusions. In this syllogistic procedure he sometimes resorted to the dialectic artifices and scholastic distinctions, and was particularly fond of using the dilemma. He was, however, a humanist and not a Bartolist. In his style, markedly inferior to that of Cujas, he preferred simplicity to elegance ; and he condemned that excessive conciseness of some jurists which was often productive of obscurity. In Germany above all his methodical exposition of Roman law, the *Commentarii iuris civilis*, acquired a great reputation, and became the model for numerous treatises of the same character.

François Hotman (Hotomannus, born in Paris, 1524, died in Basle, 1590), whose father, Pierre, was councillor in the Parlement of Paris, studied law in Orléans, then practised at the bar, and afterwards lectured in Paris. He became a Protestant, fled to Switzerland, taught at Lausanne, then (1555) at Strasburg, where he found Baudouin exiled also for religious reasons. He soon acquired a great reputation, obtained help from Germany for his French co-religionists, returned to his country, taught at Valence (1563-6), then replaced Cujas at Bourges. The massacre of St. Bartholomew finally drove him (like Doneau) from his country. Henceforth he remained in Switzerland, and died at Basle, overwhelmed with sickness and misery, but to the last full of fortitude. Hotman applied to the study of law not so much history proper as archæology and philosophy.[1] He was mainly concerned with interpretation, and adduced examples from classical authors. He made no attempt at generalization, or at constructing a systematic treatise. Apart from works on Roman jurisprudence, he wrote on feudal law, and on the public law of France, *e.g. De iure regni Franciae*, and *Franco-Gallia*, in the latter of which he discussed the ancient constitution of France, and was among the first to insist on the idea of the sovereignty of nations. In his *Antitribonian*, published in French (1567), he pleaded for unity of legislation and for a union of practice—which had been to some extent hindered by the antagonism between the Bartolists and the humanists[2]—with the historical and synthetic treatment of law. He showed that the new direction taken by the study of Roman law must result in the revision of French national law. He demanded a code, which was to embody the most valuable portions of the Roman jurisprudence, and whatever was found good in other sources; and he insisted on the claims of the vernacular language as a medium for legal publication. Unlike Cujas, he was not an ardent worshipper of the ancient legal system; he even doubted if its study in France would be productive of good.

François Baudouin (Balduinus, born at Arras, 1520, died 1573),

---

[1] *Cf.* his *Institutiones dialecticae ex fontibus philosophorum*.
[2] *Antitribonian*, c. xv.

after studying at Louvain, became secretary to Doumoulin, gave a free course of lectures in Paris (1546), and then was professor successively at Bourges, Strasburg, Heidelberg, Paris, Angers. He was a friend of Calvin and Bucer ; but he does not seem to have definitely embraced Protestantism. He practised Catholicism in France, Lutheranism in Germany, and Calvinism in Switzerland, and finally retracted his heterodox opinions. Just as Cujas refused to defend the conduct of the leaguers, so Baudouin refused to justify the French Court for the massacre of St. Bartholomew. Like Cujas, he was for tolerance and individual liberty of conscience as against outward form and symbol, and repudiated extreme violence and schism. He belongs to the historical school of law, and emphasized the importance of history as vigorously as Cujas did: jurisprudence, he said, is blind without history ("Sine historia caecam esse iurisprudentiam"). Unlike Cujas, however, he often concerned himself with historical disquisition as an end, and not as ancillary to the development of legal doctrine. Thus, he usually chose such subjects as lent themselves best to historical treatment. He tried to trace the orgin of Roman law. In his account of the Twelve Tables he constantly asked himself why the provisions were conceived in this sense rather than in that. When he took up the Novels of Justinian it was only to discuss the modifications therein introduced by the legislator, and how these were demanded by the changing circumstances of the time.[1]

Charles Dumoulin (born in Paris, 1500, died there 1566) studied law at Orléans and Poitiers, then went to the bar in Paris, but was not successful. He embraced Calvinism ; and owing to civil dissensions was obliged to leave Paris, and then taught law at Strasburg and Besançon. He returned to his native town in 1557. Like most of the jurists, he proved himself an able religious controversialist. He published violent treatises against papal authority. He appealed to jurisprudence as a palliation in the incessant theological and political disputes of the time. He insisted on a combination of law with public affairs and forensic practice. He had a leaning towards the Bartolist methods, and seems to have had some esteem for Forcadel, the inept rival of Cujas and facetious adorer of Bartolus. Besides his notable

[1] *Cf.* his *Scaevola seu Iurisprudentia Muciana ; De institutione historiae universalis et eius cum iurisprudentia coniunctione,* etc. (These and others are to be found in the collection of Heineccius, *Iurisprudentia romana et attica,* vol. i., Leyden, 1738.)

work on the customary law of Paris, he wrote on feudal law (*De feudis*) and on other subjects. His works show ample learning and dialectic subtlety, but are written in a difficult and unpleasant style. He brought together and investigated a large body of French customs and usages, indicated a basis for more unified and consistent French legislation, and declared himself an enemy of feudalism. He did for French law what Cujas did for Roman law. In his commentary on the custom of Paris, he disengaged the fundamental principles of French law; and by his systematization of the customary law he in a large measure prepared the way for the work of Pothier and for the Civil Code. Some of his contemporaries called him the prince of jurisconsults, to which he all too readily subscribed; it was his proud boast that he yielded to no one and could be taught by no one.

In the polemical discussions in which Cujas and the foregoing jurists were involved, a good deal of bitterness, invective, satire, gross insult was imported. "Les grands jurisconsultes de cette époque," says M. Brissaud, "s'injuriaient à la façon des héros d'Homère."[1] In this age personal abuse accompanied, and often replaced, argument. Thus Hotman, in his attack on Cujas, reproached him for returning to Catholicism after having joined the reformers, said that he would blot out from all his books the name of the apostate, and calumniously described him as "temulentus," "lutulentus," "turbulentus" (drunk, dirty, turbulent). He was even more severe with Baudouin. Similarly Doneau made use of ridiculous vituperation and false charges. Lesser men like Fournier and Jean Robert, professor at Orléans, likewise wrote insultingly of Cujas' person, and made captious and malignant attacks on his method and doctrines. On the other hand, Cujas did not disdain to reply—and with no great moderation—to such pamphleteering abuse, and even descends to making trivial anagrams[2] from the names of opponents unworthy of his steel. But in all these conflicts he was rarely the aggressor. He appears to have been extremely sensitive to criticism, and never forgave Mérille for compiling a list of his inconsistent statements. (It were a miracle indeed to find none in work—and mostly pioneer work—covering such an immense ground, and necessarily demanding self-correction in the light of subsequent conclusions.)

[1] *Op. cit.*, i., p. 354.
[2] *Cf. Observat.*, ix. c. 37; *ibid.*, xv.-xvii. passim; *Notata Antonii Mercatoris*.

Result of his Work. Conclusion.—Both in his lifetime and after his death Cujas was esteemed abroad as much as in his own country. It is related that the professors in Germany were accustomed to raise their hats when they mentioned his name.[1] Le Conte (Contius), one of the most learned of his contemporaries, described him as "vir doctissimus et iurisconsultorum nostri temporis princeps";[2] and it was said that he was the man born to restore jurisprudence to its ancient dignity ("vir iurisprudentiae in antiquam dignitatem restituendae natus"). Pasquier, referring to the different schools of jurisprudence, mentions the last as that of the humanists, and awards the palm to Cujas, who, he says, never had and perhaps never will have his equal.[3]

Posterity has justified the work of Cujas, the great humanist jurisconsult, and the greatest of his time, as against feudal traditions, scholastic procedure, and the practice of accumulating opinions. He showed how it was possible to transform the indiscriminate and irrational treatment of Roman law into a sound investigation, by which a veritable science of jurisprudence might be established. Literature, history, and philology were henceforth to be brought into the service of legal research. Scholars as well as practitioners interested themselves in Roman law, which came to be recognized as an instrument of general culture, as well as a rich pasture for the practical needs of the advocate and the legislator. The work of the jurist was regarded by Cujas not as a thing apart, but as a part of the life and wellbeing of the community. With regard to the restoration of texts and the interpretative exposition thereof, the works of Cujas proved a fruitful field for the unsparing gleanings of successors. The editions of the *Corpus Iuris Civilis* by Charondas (1575), Pacius (1580), and Godefroy (1583) were greatly indebted to Cujas for textual improvements, as well as for exegetical annotations. Godefroy's edition had authoritative force in the courts throughout the seventeenth and eighteenth centuries; and the parlements were frequently guided in their decisions by the opinions and results of Cujas. Even much earlier, according to J. A. de Thou, the distinguished historian of the time, he was frequently referred to in the tribunals and at the bar as "le

---

[1] *Cf.* Pasquier, *Recherches de la France*, vii. 8; ix. 29.
[2] See the preface to his edition of the *Corpus Iuris Civilis*.
[3] *Op. cit.*, ix. 39: "... Je donne le premier lieu à nostre Cujas, qui n'eut, selon mon jugement, n'a et n'aura jamais par aventure son pareil."

jurisconsulte."[1] Towards the end of the eighteenth century the judicial practice of the "pays de droit écrit" was profoundly influenced by his work; and Pothier accepted him as a guide in his *Pandectae Justinianae*, and in those parts of his treatises on contracts relating to Roman law. And so the work of Cujas served as an authoritative appeal and powerful inspiration to successive ages, until it was in a large measure finally embodied in the French Civil Code, which has still more assured it perennial vitality.

[1] *Histoire*, liv. 99, an. 1590.

ALBERICUS GENTILIS[1]

It has too long been the custom to consider Grotius as the father of modern international law,[2] as a resplendent luminary in a seemingly dark age, and accompanied, at a distance, by certain minor satellites barely worthy of mention. The influence of Grotius has undoubtedly been great; but it is usually forgotten that the way was prepared for him by others, and notably by Gentilis. The achievement of the Dutch jurist could not possibly have been what it was in the absence of the forcible, reasoned, and — comparatively speaking — pioneer work of the Italian lawyer. A study of the work of Gentilis—and to appreciate it duly, it must ever be borne in mind that he was Grotius' predecessor—will show what a high place he takes in the history of modern international law, and particularly in regard to its development on the positive side; and it will be seen that because of the greater affinity between his point of view and that of modern States he is, in that respect, more truly than is Grotius, the progenitor of the existing law of nations.

Life.—Albericus Gentilis (Alberico or Alberigo Gentili) was born on January 14, 1552, at San Ginesio, a small town in the mark of Ancona. It is commonly held that he was the eldest of seven, though some reports state that he was the second son. His father, Matthaeus (Matteo), was a physician. After receiving a thorough home education, Albericus was sent to the University of Perugia, then one of the most famous in Italy, and particularly noteworthy as a school of law, where distinguished men like

[1] The available bibliographical materials are given by Professor Holland in his article on Gentilis in the recent edition of the *Encyclopædia Britannica*; and by H. Nézard in *Les Fondateurs du droit international* (Paris, 1904).

[2] In the recently published work, *The International Law and Custom of Ancient Greece and Rome*, 2 vols. (Macmillan and Co.), the present writer has shown that modern international law is by no means a creation, but partly a restoration, partly a continuation of ancient institutions and customs. Indeed, Gentilis and Grotius and all the early writers on the law of nations constantly appeal to the classical times for authority, for rules, for practices, for analogies, for all kinds of illustrations.

Baldus and Bartolus had been professors. Soon after reaching his twentieth year he graduated as Doctor of Civil Law. For some time afterwards he held the office of "proctor" or judge at Ascoli; then took up the work of advocacy in his native town, and was often consulted in matters relating to its municipal statutes and institutions.

His father having embraced Protestantism, he was obliged, through the oppressive exertions of the Inquisition, to leave home, and, together with Albericus, he proceeded to Laybach in Carniola. There they were soon joined by the youngest son, whom Albericus took to Tübingen. The latter then went to Heidelberg, and some months after came to England (August, 1580). Here he was welcomed by a group of Italian Protestant refugees, amongst whom were men like Contio, a theological writer, Borgarucci, physician to the Earl of Leicester, and Castiglione, Italian tutor to Elizabeth. Through this circle Albericus soon became acquainted with Sir Philip Sidney, Leicester, then Chancellor of Oxford University, Robert Dudley, Vice-Chancellor, and Tobie Mathew. In January, 1581, he was admitted, through the Earl's letters of commendation, into the University as Doctor of Civil Law, and a little later was appointed reader. He was delighted with his work, and expressed great admiration and enthusiasm for Oxford—for its studious colleges as well as for its beautiful situation.[1] In the meantime his fame as a civilian spread rapidly through his lectures, disputations, and writings.

In 1584 the English Government consulted Gentilis, together with Jean Hotoman (who had been received into the University at the same time as the former), on the Mendoza affair; and in spite of deep feeling aroused by the treacherous conduct of the Spanish ambassador, the opinion of Gentilis was followed.[2] The next year he developed the doctrine of the rights and duties of ambassadors, first in a University *disputatio*, then in a published work, *De legationibus*, dedicated to Sir P. Sidney.[3] In 1586, by

---

[1] *Cf.* the preface to his *Dialogi Sex*, which was dedicated to Leicester: "Qui Oxoniam norint et ii norint necesse est ut mecum agatur qui Oxoniae vivo, in ea scilicet civitate quae, situs amoenitate felicissima magnificentissimis studiosorum collegiis, proculdubio augustissima in toto orbe."

[2] See *infra*, on Ambassadors.

[3] Wheaton, *History of the Law of Nations*, pp. 232-233 (following Ward), states that the famous consultation took place the year after the publication of the *De legationibus*. This is not correct. Besides, Wheaton appears to have misunderstood the purport of Gentilis' opinion on the question.

the influence of Walsingham, Albericus accompanied Horatio Pallavicino, who was despatched on an embassy to the Elector of Saxony; and on his return to Oxford the next year he was appointed to the Regius Professorship of Civil Law.

Various publications were issued by him on a large number of questions of the day; besides treatises on civil law and on ancient war practices, there were the more famous *Prima commentatio de iure belli*, published in London, 1588, the second and third parts 1589. The three books were issued together in 1598 at Hanau as a practically new work, *De iure belli libri tres*. Notwithstanding his academic and literary activities, he became a member of Gray's Inn, August, 1600, and found time for forensic engagements. In 1605 he was appointed, with King James's permission, advocate to the Spanish embassy; and in that capacity appeared on behalf of the King of Spain before the English Court of Admiralty which tried certain prize cases that had arisen in the war between Spain and the Netherlands. (The notes of the cases in which he took part were published after his death under the title of *Advocationis Hispanicae libri duo*, Hanoviae, 1613.) Gentilis died in London on June 19, 1608, and was buried in St. Helen's Church, Bishopsgate.

The importance of his writings, and the great services he rendered to international law, have only recently been fully realized. For a long time writers had looked to Grotius as the founder of the modern law of nations, and had neglected to take account of his forerunners. But the great work of Gentilis was bound to be sooner or later recognized. It may be said that his resuscitation was due to men like Emerico Amari, W. A. Reiger of Groningen, Mancini, and most of all to Professor Holland. In November, 1874, Professor Holland delivered an inaugural lecture on the life and writings of Albericus Gentilis, whose contribution to international law was pointed out and whose claims were duly emphasized. A published copy of this lecture came to the notice of Professor Mancini of Rome; and in March, 1875, an influential Italian committee was formed under the chairmanship of Mancini and the honorary presidency of Prince Humbert. In the following September it issued a manifesto, which spoke of Gentilis as "the prophet of God, the inspired apostle of peace," as an illustrious advocate of liberty of conscience, as an initiator of a new epoch. Festivities were in many quarters held in his honour. But the movement was not without opposition. On the one hand, in Italy the ultra-Catholic press condemned the "impious" project to do honour to an "apostate" and an "enemy of the Church." On the other hand, in Holland the worshippers of Grotius manifested overmuch anxiety as to the threatened supremacy of their countryman, and even accused Professor Asser of treachery to his country for identifying himself with the Italian movement—the outcome of which was the unveiling in 1886 of a statue of Grotius at Delft. It was not till 1908, the tercentenary of the death of Albericus, that the Italian authorities succeeded in erecting a monument to him in his native town. In England, a committee under the honorary presidency of Prince Leopold set up, in 1877, a memorial to the Italian jurist in St. Helen's Church, and—what was of more practical importance—caused a new edition of his greatest work, the *De iure belli*, to be published under the editorship of Professor Holland.

Works.—The works of Gentilis show a very wide range of subjects; and, apart from a quantity of existing manuscripts and some writings no longer extant, they comprise some thirty publications.[1] His attention was constantly occupied with the various legal, political, and moral controversies of the time, including questions relative to the law of nations, the union of England and Scotland, the limits of sovereign power, the application of certain old rules of civil and canon law and the conflicts thereof, the problem of remarriage, the legal and moral position of stage plays, the justifiableness of lying, etc. Of all his works those of most lasting importance are the three dealing with matters of international law—namely, first and foremost *De iure belli*, secondly *De legationibus*, and *Advocatio Hispanica*. These three works deal more or less systematically with the principal portions of the entire subject, and, on the one hand, contain vigorous arguments on new and doubtful questions, on the other, emphasize previously established rules which from time to time had been broken. Gentilis is far from attempting the detailed elaboration of a complete code; but in each of his contributions to the subject he has made his mark.[2]

The *De iure belli* probably owes its origin to a series of in-

---

[1] For a detailed list of his writings see *Alberico Gentili*, by Professor Holland—a reprint of the inaugural lecture of 1875—in *Studies in International Law* (Oxford, 1898); and the same writer's article in the *Encyclopædia Britannica*, as already mentioned.

[2] The editions referred to in the present essay are *De iure belli* (ed. Holland); *De legationibus* (Londini, 1585); *Advocatio Hispanica* (Hanoviae 13).

augural "disputationes," though the work betrays few signs of the usual character of academic disputations. The subject of the law of war is at once liberated from the archaic point of view which confounded it with the regulations of military discipline, and is definitively placed on firm foundations, supported by legal as well as moral sanctions. It is divided into three parts. Book I. deals with war in general—who may make it, and what motives or causes justify it. Book II. lays down the lawful mode of conducting belligerent operations—declaration, acts permitted and forbidden after open hostilities have commenced, use of spies, poison, and stratagems, treatment of the person of the enemy (non-combatants, prisoners, hostages), and of the different kinds of enemy property, pacts and truces of the commanders. Book III. discusses the conclusion of war, rights of occupation, and of the victor as to the persons and property of the conquered, establishment of peace. Thus the question which the *De iure belli* undertakes to answer is: Under what circumstances is war justly undertaken, conducted, and terminated?

The *De legationibus* presents perhaps less a development of principles of the law relating to ambassadors than an historical account of legations. It is similarly divided into three books—the first dealing with the historical origin of different kinds of embassies, the ceremonies and solemnities of the Roman fetial envoys, the place, time, and mode of reception of foreign ambassadors coming to Rome and the *munera* bestowed upon them; the second book with the privileges and immunities of accredited envoys generally; and the third with the qualifications which an ambassador ought to possess.

The *Advocatio Hispanica* is, as has already been pointed out, a collection of interesting notes on cases in which the author was engaged as counsel for Spain against the Netherlands. In the war between these two countries the latter had claimed the right to capture Spanish prizes in English waters. Besides the appeal to historic precedents and the application of rules of Roman jurisprudence, there is a precise and vigorous statement of the doctrine of territorial sovereignty (including exclusive jurisdiction in adjacent seas) as the fundamental principle underlying the mutual rights and obligations of belligerents and neutrals. In reference to this great question Gentilis makes a decided advance, and we find that his conclusions forestall, for the most part, those of modern international law.

These works are, on the whole, written in a style characterized by energy, directness, and clearness; though at times, indeed, passages are found which betray a certain scholastic pedantry, with the usually accompanying faults of prolixity and ambiguity. Gentilis does not, it is true, write Latin with the facility and classical grace of an Erasmus, or some of the other practised Ciceronians of the time; but in comparison with most of his contemporaries, especially those who wrote juristic or theological treatises, he is at advantage through his ease, vivacity, variety, conversational tone, freedom from elaborate rhetorical flourishes. Moreover, by virtue of his shrewd humour and his concentration on the particular matter before him, his style is invariably saved from dryness and tedious irrelevancies.

Position and Method.—What position does Gentilis occupy in the history of international law, what is his point of view, and what is his method of dealing with the subject? Gentilis is the first great writer of *modern* international law, the first clearly to define its subject-matter, and to treat it in the way which is fundamentally in harmony with the conception and practice of our own time.[1] For this reason it may justifiably be claimed that—as the precursor of Grotius, and as the one who substantially prepared the way for him and greatly influenced his and all succeeding work—Gentilis is the real "father" of the modern law of nations (that is, if it is at all proper to confer such a title on any particular jurist).[2] Amongst the pre-Grotians he is the illustrious representative of the historical school; his insistence on the positive aspect of international law is almost as emphatic as in the work of Bynkershoek.[3] On Zouche,[4] the earliest English exponent of the same general view, the Italian writer's influence was unmistakable. Notwithstanding various shortcomings—indeed, inevitable at the time he wrote—the entire work of Gentilis is manifestly superior to all previous productions, such as, for example, those of Ayala, Victoria, Soto, Belli,

---

[1] *Cf.* D. H. L. von Ompteda, *Literatur des gesammten sowohl natürlichen als positiven Völkerrechts* (Regensburg, 1785), § 49, p. 168: "Dieser ist der erste Gelehrte, der sich einige wahre Verdienste um die Völkerrechtswissenschaft erworben hat ... der solche als einen Gegenstand des Völkerrechts abhandelte."

[2] *Cf.* Lampredi, *Del commercio dei popoli neutrali*, in the preface; C. von Kaltenborn, *Die Vorläufer des Hugo Grotius* (Leipzig, 1848), p. 228: "Er ist der erste wichtigere Autor des modernen Völkerrechts und in dieser Beziehung als der eigentliche und unmittelbare Vorläufer des Grotius zu betrachten. Ja ich halte ihn für die unmittelbare Grundlage des Grotius."

[3] See the present writer's article on Bynkershoek, *infra*.

[4] See the present writer's article on Zouche, *infra*.

or Suarez, who either confused civil law with rules regulating international relations or failed to grasp the difference between philosophical or theological principles and juridical rules, or, again, confounded the rules of interstatal war with the municipal prescriptions of military discipline,[1] or identified the "societas gentium" with an exclusive Christian commonwealth. The theological basis of the whole subject, which was generally affirmed or assumed by his predecessors, was once and for all undermined. The dogmatic procedure of the theologians was unreservedly impugned; they were roundly advised not to meddle with matters which did not concern them, "silete theologi in munere alieno."[2] Similarly, the *a priori* methods of the philosophers were rejected. The abstract principles and metaphysical assumptions associated with the investigations into the intrinsic nature of God, mankind, and the State he disregarded as necessarily leading to the establishment of an ideal system which could not meet the demands nor guide the growth of an actual society of nations which possesses an essentially organic and dynamic character. What Bacon insisted on as the true method of science, Gentilis had already maintained to be the method of international law: the examination of actual phenomena, of concrete facts, and then by a process of induction the inferring therefrom of general rules, which, however, are still subject to subsequent modification or even cancellation, in accordance with newly discovered facts.

The apprehension of the various issues arising out of this conception was facilitated by his restricting the field of juristic inquiry, and eliminating such matters as were not clearly germane thereto. In contradistinction to the "Humanists," the "Alciatists," a school founded by Alciati,[3] and including men like Cujas and Hotman, Albericus associated himself to the old school of civilians, the "Bartolists,"[4] who confined themselves more to the subject-matter of jurisprudence proper, and devoted themselves but little to the assimilation of classical culture and

[1] *Cf.* the early but influential example of Isidore of Seville (beginning of seventh century), who, after enumerating the various subjects comprised in *ius gentium*, admits a further division, *ius militare*, including a large variety of heterogeneous matters, such as the mode of commencing hostilities, breaches of military discipline, desertion, military dignities and awards, sharing of booty, etc. (*Originum sive Etymologiarum lib. v.*, especially Book V., cc. 4-7). We see here considerable borrowings from Ulpian.
[2] *De iure belli*, I. 12.
[3] See the present writer's article on Alciati, *supra*.
[4] On Bartolus and his school, see *supra*.

wide literary learning. To the rebuke of Cujas that the Bartolists, through neglecting the "humanities," were foolish and shameless babblers and a sordid crew—"blaterones, insipientes, improbi, avari "—Gentilis retorted that the pretentious Alciatists hardly deserved the name of jurists at all, and that jurists might manage well enough without giving themselves to Greek and Latin letters.[1] Nevertheless, Albericus, though not possessing the great erudition of Grotius, had wide learning, and, in order to support or illustrate his facts and conclusions, he quotes or refers to a great number of writers, classical and modern, including contemporary authorities ; e.g. Herodotus, Thucydides, Aristotle, Polybius, Livy, Plutarch, Cicero, Dio Cassius, Diodorus Siculus, Dionysius of Halicarnassus, Philo, the Bible, the Digest, Corpus Iuris Canonici, Tertullian, St. Augustine, Zonaras, Baldus, Alciati, Bodin, Hotman, Polydore Vergil, Machiavelli, Guicciardini, Covarruvias, Belli, and others.

Whilst Gentilis belonged to the Bartolists, so far as municipal jurisprudence was concerned, he adopted an independent and what was then a revolutionary attitude with regard to the law of nations. We may well believe him when he states that he has read nothing good on the law of war ;[2] though we must admit that he was to some extent indebted to writers like Franciscus a Victoria (1480-1546),[3] and to Pierino Belli (Bello, or Bellinus) (1502-1575).[4] He at once rejected the methods of the civilians, especially those of the school of Bologna, who considered international law as a mere application or extension of the civil law : his disquisition and development of principles in general do not take the form—so common before him—of an elaborate and indiscriminate commentary on the Roman codes. And this careful discrimination on his part is the more remarkable in view of the fact that he was devoted to Roman law and had contributed much to its revival at Oxford, as has been testified by a contemporary English writer.[5] Gentilis adopts the convenient expression "societas gentium," but is at pains to insist that a "societas" of this character is not analogous to a "civitas" under one sovereign authority, and that therefore its rights and

---

[1] *Dialogi Sex* (1582). *Cf.* T. E. Holland, *Studies in International Law.*
[2] *De iure Belli*, I. 1.
[3] *Relectiones theologicae* (Lyons, 1557), especially V. and VI.
[4] *De re militari et de bello*, written in 1558, published in Venice 1563.
[5] W. Fulbecke, *Direction or Preparation to the Study of the Law* (1599), c. iii., where he remarks that Gentilis " who by his great industrie hath quickened the dead bodie o the civill law written by the aunceint civilians."

obligations cannot be determined by provisions of the civil law. Occasionally he introduces principles and conceptions of Roman law, as in his application of the *lex Iulia maiestatis* in discussing the question of the exterritoriality of ambassadors,[1] in his inquiry whether military pacts are contracts *stricti iuris* or *bonae fidei*, in his treatment of the doctrine of prescription. But these considerations of Roman jurisprudence are not advanced in the manner of preceding writers for the purpose of indicating any ultimate legal sanction or furnishing final solutions, but mainly with a view to illustrate his argument. Thus Gentilis broke with the tradition which had lasted for several centuries—from the time of Accursius and Bartolus (who, as Grotius says, might perhaps be excused on account of the "temporum suorum infelicitas ")[2] down even to the authorities of his own age, such as Covarruvias and Vasques. Of course, neither Gentilis nor any one else could entirely eliminate the principles of the civil law from a system of international law. There are, on the one hand, fundamental matters which are of necessity common to the two, and, on the other, various doctrines in the *Digest* "to facilitate the solution of differences arising between States." Thus, James I. in a speech in Parliament, March 20, 1609, expressed his great appreciation of the Roman law which he regarded as, in a sense, a *lex gentium*.

Again, Gentilis is an innovator in that he considers recent and contemporary events, and invokes testimony drawn from the practice of the time, in support of his conclusions. It is true he constantly refers also to ancient authorities, but in doing so he never forgets he is dealing with modern questions; and, therefore, such references are not a mere array of scholastic erudition. His conception of the position and conventional nature of international law is emphasized throughout by his discussion of the events of the time, which—whether in the form of express treaties or customary acts pointing to implied rules—he holds to be of preponderating importance, especially so as law is made for nations and is, therefore, necessarily subject to organic development and adaptation to circumstances. Whereas Grotius deliberately avows that he prefers examples from ancient Greece and Rome on the ground that proceeding from such sources they will have most weight, Gentilis occupies himself largely with the political affairs and problems of the sixteenth century—with the

---

[1] *De legationibus*, II. 7-8. [2] *Proleg.* 54.

conflicts between Charles V. and Francis I., between Spain and the Netherlands, between England and Spain, between Italy and her oppressors, with the wars of conquest in America, and also with many matters other than warlike, such as the question of papal prerogative, the alliance with non-Christian nations, the conflicting claims of neutral merchants and belligerents, the freedom of the sea. In the treatment of all these controversies, Gentilis, if somewhat chary of detaching himself from the facts and launching forth into wide generalizations, imported vigour, freshness, and common sense, and suggested acceptable solutions in accordance with the criterion of utility and necessity, and with the idea of justice and equity of a prudent impartial man of affairs. And these solutions, in the form of determined principles, were advanced, it must be remembered, at a time when States and sovereigns were too prone to practise bigotry and dissimulation, deceit, and evasion, to resort to excessive rigour and cruelty, to consult considerations marked by caprice or inordinate self-interest.[1]

1. **Conception of the Law of Nations; Community of States; Civil Basis.**[2]—The law of nations, designated by Gentilis *ius gentium*[3] is that law which all nations or at least the greater part of them, "maior pars orbis," agree upon. It is the law of the society or community of States.[4] The fundamental notion is thus clearly defined, although he does not use the more precise expression "ius inter gentes" consistently adopted by Zouche[5] and even foreshadowed by Franciscus a Victoria.[6] Such law regulating the relationships between independent sovereigns or peoples is the result either of express conventions or of tacit compacts inferred from long-established customs generally acquiesced in. The members of the "societas gentium" are interdependent as well as independent; hence as human beings are in question who have interests and needs in common, mutual relationships are inevitable, association, understanding, and

[1] *Cf.* R. Ward, *An Inquiry into the Foundation, and History of the Law of Nations in Europe*, 2 vols. (London, 1795), vol. ii., p. 612.
[2] For the sake of clearness and convenience, and to obviate repetition, I have considered Gentilis' work as a whole under the classification here adopted and have avoided separate analyses of his three principal writings.
[3] On the conception of *ius gentium*, see *International Law and Custom of Ancient Greece and Rome*, vol. i., pp. 70 *et seq.*, 89 *et seq.*, and *passim.*
[4] *De iure belli*, I. 1.
[5] See the article on Zouche, *infra.*
[6] Thus in his *Relectiones theologicae*, V. 1, we find this definition: "Quod naturalis ratio inter omnes gentes constituit vocatur ius gentium."

governing laws are necessary.[1] These laws have, on the one hand, a positive basis—the "usus gentium"—and, on the other, are due to the exigence of natural reason.[2] The authority of the *ius naturae* or *ius naturale* or *ratio naturalis* was invoked by all writers, earlier[3] and later, including Grotius, and even such positivists as Bynkershoek and De Martens. But unlike the sixteenth-century writers, especially the Jesuits, with their revived scholasticism and their *a priori* procedure, Gentilis was not given to the indiscriminate adoration of this "natural" principle, and to the elaboration of a multiplicity of theses largely irrelevant and extraneous to the main subject. In the sixteenth century, indeed, investigations into the *ius naturae* began to be made by writers like Oldendorp,[4] Hemming,[5] and others, who treated the subject from a wider point of view than the Jesuit or Franciscan theologians had done or were doing. Albericus introduced the principle of natural reason partly to explain the origin of international law, and partly to fortify the positive sanction; and, in so doing, he adopted the Protestant conception as against the Catholic notion—in accordance with the canon law—of a universal hierarchy under the papal headship, or, in matters temporal, the idea of an empire under the Emperor as a continuation of the "imperium romanum," in accordance with the views of the civilians.[6] Very frequently we find that Gentilis appeals to the *ius naturae* in order to test the validity of any doctrine or the legitimacy of any practice, and usually disregards the current vague metaphysico-legal significance of that

[1] As to the reason for the establishment by mankind of laws in general, he says: "Ut haec duo sunt, fragilitatis conscientia et poenae timor, ex quibus omnia fere iura humanitatis oriuntur" (*De iure belli*, III. 13; Holland's edition, p. 344).

[2] *De iure belli*, III. 9; p. 316: "... Naturalis ratio, quae auctor est iuris gentium..."; p. 319 (referring to the authority of Aristotle): "... rem naturalem esse, quae semper fieri et ubique solet." Cf. the similar point of view of Suarez, *Tractatus de legibus* (1612), II. 19, 9.

[3] *E.g.* Victoria; Bracton, *De legibus ac consuetudinibus Angliae* (written in the middle of the thirteenth century), defines *ius gentium* as the law which nations use, and which is derived from natural law. Also in the *Siete Partidas* (finished in 1265 under the direction of Alfonso X. of Castile) frequent reference is made to natural law, which is defined as the law of all animate beings.

[4] J. Oldendorp (d. 1561), *Isagoge seu elementaria introductio iuris naturae gentium et civilis* (Coloniae, 1539).

[5] N. Hemming (1513-1600), *De lege naturae apodictica methodus* ... (Witebergae, 1562).

[6] Victoria likewise denied the Pope's claim to be "dominus orbis" in things temporal, and rejected the alleged world lordship of the Emperor as being contrary to the *ius naturale, divinum*, or *humanum* (*Relectiones theologicae*, I. 6; V.).

term, and interprets it in the sense of humanity, justice, the highest common sense of mankind.¹ And throughout his argument he insists on the positive juridical sanction quite as much as on the considerations of ethics or on the behests of divine law, and he is careful to discriminate between the work and objects of theologians and the sphere and functions of jurists.²

The pioneer work of Gentilis was in harmony with the larger movement of the sixteenth century, which witnessed a transformation of society, the establishment of a new spirit and wider outlook, the decline of theocracy, the rise of the modern State. The political conceptions of the Middle Ages, which identified civil and ecclesiastical authority, were derived on the one hand from Greek and Roman doctrines, on the other from Hebrew and Christian. Towards the end of the thirteenth century the papal temporal supremacy began to be seriously opposed, especially in France, and its decline was further hastened on by the great schism. The conciliar movement of the fifteenth century spread the theory that sovereign power was of the nature of a trust. The Renaissance and the Reformation revived "humanism," scientific curiosity, established a spirit of independence, political as well as spiritual, and a desire to find a more rational basis for human society than the theocratic, and substituted civil for clerical authority, a society of territorial States resting on a lay and juridical foundation for a theocratic confederation subject to canon law. And at the head of such States are monarchs who, in the view of Gentilis, are in the position of guardians or "administrators" of their respective countries, and not absolute rulers independent of law. Grotius approves St. Thomas's interpretation of the fifty-first Psalm as to the irresponsibility of princes and their superiority to law; Gentilis, though writing earlier, shows himself to be more in harmony with modern views when he asserts that it is a hallucination of theologians, mere adulation of lawyers to represent to kings that they are permitted to do everything, and that their sovereignty is absolute.³

---

¹ *Cf. De legationibus*, II. 18 : " Habet ius gentium rationes naturales quae, insitae omnibus a natura, sic notae sunt ut argumento nullo indigeant, nullaque, quibus adprobentur, arte."

² *Cf. De iure belli*, I. 3 ; p. 16.

³ *Ibid.*, III. 15 ; p. 357 : " Hallucinantur theologi, adulantur iurisconsulti, qui persuadent omnia principibus licere, summamque eorum et liberam esse potestatem."

Finally, having conceived of a "societas gentium" on a civil basis, a system of rules freed from the bonds of theological casuistry, Gentilis took a further step—a remarkable one, though a corollary flowing from his general thesis—and included in this society of States infidel and even barbarian communities.[1] The common opinion of writers was that only Catholic, or, at most, Christian, princes could be vested with *dominium;* but Gentilis held that heretics and infidels could legitimately enjoy the right of sovereignty in their own domains. Heresy or infidelity or even idolatry is not intrinsically a just cause of war.[2] Treaty relationships may be established with peoples of this character,[3] who possess also the right of legation.[4] On the other hand, those who have no religion at all are in the position of pirates,[5] as the natural enemies of mankind, and are therefore outside the pale of the society of States; they are on the level of the lowest brutes and are in a sense opposed to God and to nature, and consequently ought to be warred upon and compelled to follow the ways of the rest of mankind.[6] As to brigands and other marauders, it was also a universally established rule that they, like pirates, could not take advantage of the law of nations, "neque praedones eo iure gentium fruuntur aut piratae";[7] and Gentilis expresses astonishment at the contrary assertion of Hotman: "Ergo miror Hotmannum adfirmare voluisse ius gentium imo et cum fugitivis et cum praedonibus esse."[8]

2. **International Relations: Freedom of Intercourse; Freedom of the Sea.**—From the conception of the world as a community of States, autonomous and independent, whose relationships are regularized, whose transactions depend upon the principle of *societas*, which is itself of the essence of natural law, it follows that, subject to the exercise of territorial sovereignty, both the earth and the sea belong to all. Hence innocent passage over a

---

[1] Victoria had already in a modified form advanced this view, in his discussion of the rights of the Spaniards in the Indies (*Relectiones theologicae*, V.).
[2] *De iure belli*, I. 25. *Cf.* Victoria, *Relectiones theologicae*, V. 10. (See further, *infra*, on grounds of war.)
[3] *De iure belli*, III. 19.   [4] *De legationibus*, II. 11.
[5] *De iure belli*, I. 4; p. 21: "Piratæ omnium mortalium hostes sunt communes."
[6] *Ibid.*, I. 9; p. 39: "At neque nos nunc de his qui, ferarum modo magis quam hominum viventes, sine ulla omnino religione sunt; hos enim quasi piratas, communes hostes omnium, bello persequendos, et cogendos in mores hominum arbitrarer. Hi enim vere videntur iniurii omnibus hominibus, qui in specie hominum agunt brutorum brutissimorum.... Hi sunt, qui gigantum more bellum gerunt cum Deo."
[7] *De legationibus*, II. 8.   [8] *De iure belli*, I. 4; p. 21.

nation's territory cannot legitimately be refused, and all have the right to undisturbed maritime navigation, to carry on commercial intercourse in general, to secure shelter in foreign ports, to enjoy the right of market. To deny such natural rights without good and sufficient cause is a violation of the fundamental principles of *societas*, and consequently is not only an unlawful injury to the party directly involved, but an offence against human society in general.[1] And for the purpose of vindicating such rights war may be justly declared—"si iter negetur, si portubus, si commeatu, si mercatura, si commercio excludimur."[2] That is why, says Gentilis, war was made on the Turks: their attempt to refuse passage to the Christians, who were proceeding against the Saracens, was unjustifiable.[3]

The question of the right of passage was long one of the great controversies in which opinions were sharply divided and recorded practices opposed to each other. Gentilis, following the view of St. Augustine, decides in the affirmative,[4] on the ground firstly that it is a right conferred by nature, and secondly, that the normal condition of mankind is peace and amity, not war and enmity. The right, however, is not an unrestricted one. Freedom to traverse another's field does not imply freedom to hunt there without the owner's permission;[5] much less does it imply any liberty to commit acts of war there without the licence of the sovereign of the territory. It is customary, however, and in better order to obtain a safe-conduct; so that having become general, the practice may be considered to have been incorporated into the law of nations.

The right of navigation follows from the principle that the sea, like the air, is naturally free to all, and is the exclusive property of no one.[6] Similarly, shores,[7] banks, international rivers,[8] ports,

[1] *De iure belli*, I. 19; p. 84: "Sane qui ista tollit, societatem humanam lædit."
[2] *Ibid.*, I. 19, pp. 81, 82.   [3] *Cf. Advocatio Hispanica*, I.
[4] Similarly Bonet, *L'arbre des batailles*, held that a sovereign has a right of passage and provisioning, if he undertakes to cross peacefully, to pay any expenses involved, and make good any damages inflicted.
[5] *De iure belli*, I. 19; p. 83: "Transire per agrum alienum fas est. Ingredi fundum alienum venandi caussa, licet item per gentium ius, et ergo nec fuerint iniusti, si qui transeunt venia non petita, nec prohibiti. . . . Venatio incommoda est agro. Transitus non est incommodus."
[6] *Ibid.*, I. 19; p. 86: "Hoc natura omnibus patet; et communis eius usus omnibus est, ut aëris. Non igitur prohiberi a quoquam potest."
[7] *Advocatio Hispanica*, I. 6: "Mare etiam est commune omnibus, et littus maris."
[8] *De iure belli*, I. 19; p. 86: "Littora item a natura omnibus vacant; item ripae; item flumina."

harbours, are open to all for the purpose of obtaining shelter and provisions, and assuring the various reciprocal rights and duties of hospitality. The local sovereign has only the right of supervision and jurisdiction.[1] Hence the claim of peoples to the exclusive sovereignty over adjacent or even territorial seas is invalid—as, for example, in the case of Venetian pretensions as to the Adriatic. Any attempt on the part of the people of Venice to close that sea on the ground of their being "possessores" (as was alleged), or "domini maris" (an obviously indefensible contention), is nothing more than a deliberate usurpation. Similarly (it may be recalled), in the conflict between England and Spain in 1580, when the Spanish ambassador, Mendoza, laid before Elizabeth complaints as to certain acts of Drake, the Queen strongly contended that all were at liberty to navigate the ocean, as the use of the sea, like that of the air, is common to all; that neither a sovereign nor a nation could claim exclusive right thereto, since its occupation is contrary both to the course of nature and to public usage.[2] A like argument was used in 1602, against the Danish king's claim to dominion in the northern seas, and his attempt to prohibit fishing without a licence from him.[3]

Finally, as to the right of commerce, intercourse, etc., Gentilis points out that the Spaniards rightly made war on the people of the New World for refusing to trade with them.[4] In the Anglo-Spanish dispute, above referred to, the Queen reminded the ambassador that his countrymen had brought upon themselves the injuries complained of through their excluding the English, "contra ius gentium," from commercial intercourse with the West Indies; and she did not recognize the power of the Pope to bestow these territories on the Spanish king.[5] To constitute such refusal a ground for war, says Gentilis, the prohibition must be a general one. It is not unlawful to forbid the importation of certain goods deemed to be injurious, or the exportation of certain precious products like gold and silver. To deny to foreigners

[1] *De iure belli*, p. 88.
[2] Camden's *Annals*, sub ann. 1580, p. 309, ed. 1605.
[3] See further on the subject the article on Bynkershoek, *infra*.
[4] Similarly Victoria (*Relectiones theologicae*, V.) maintained that the Spaniards had the right of journeying to and remaining in Indian territory, and trading with the natives, provided no injury was done. In case of opposition, the Spaniards were entitled to make war in self-defence, and occupy the territory of the conquered people.
[5] Camden, *ibid*.

internal trade, whilst allowing them access to the coasts or frontiers, does not necessarily amount to a breach of the *ius commercii*.

3. **International Relations: Ambassadors.**[1]—After defining ambassadors and pointing out their public and sacred nature,[2] Gentilis distinguishes legations according to the character of the one who despatches and the one who receives them; and also according to the object in view, *e.g.* free embassy ("libera legatio"),[3] where a person bearing the title of ambassador goes to treat of his own affairs; public embassy, including "legatio negotii," extraordinary, as for declaring war or peace, and "legatio officiosa," as for offering compliments, condolences, etc.; temporary missions, in which case the "legati temporarii" are called "residentes."[4]

The reception of public envoys may not be refused, except for a just and good cause; but a sovereign is entitled to refuse at any time titular, "officious," and temporary embassies.[5] Thus Henry VII. of England rightly refused to receive "residents." The right of legation is suspended at the commencement of hostilities; the ambassadors of the respective belligerents are not to be treated as enemies, but are to be sent back in safety to their sovereigns.[6] As pirates and brigands are outside the law of nations, they do not enjoy the *ius legationis*;[7] nor do rebels as against their ruler.[8] But heretics and excommunicated sovereigns and peoples cannot merely as such be deprived of the right, for they still belong to the society of States, which is based on political and not on religious considerations.[9] Thus when Pope Julius II. laid Venice under an interdict, she none the less retained the right, as guaranteed by the law of nations. Similarly, embassies of Protestant, Mahometan, and Jewish peoples were always admissible, in accordance with the demands of natural reason.[10] In the case of a civil war, if the contending factions

[1] *Cf.* the article on Bynkershoek, and that on Zouche.
[2] *De legationibus*, I. 2: ". . . qui publico, aut sacratiori nomine ad rempublicam personamve aliam sacratiorem ob rem publicam, aut sacratiori missus sine imperio est rei dicendae, agendae caussa."
[3] *Cf.* the Roman practice, *International Law and Custom of Ancient Greece and Rome*, I., p. 308.
[4] *De legationibus*, I. 5.
[5] *Ibid.*, II. 12: "Puto autem liberas, legationes officiosas, temporarias tales esse."
[6] *Ibid.*, II. 13: "Legati abire iubentur, si eo tempore eos in regno suo degere princeps nolit."
[7] *Ibid.*, II. 8. [8] II. 7. [9] II. 11. [10] II. 11.

are approximately equal in power so that they regard each other as "iusti hostes" and not as mere rebels,[1] they may justifiably despatch ambassadors to one another and to other States.[2]

The most important matters relating to ambassadors are the closely connected questions of inviolability and exterritoriality. On this portion of international law Gentilis exerted a profound influence both by his personal counsel and by his writings. He holds that ambassadors are not necessarily everywhere inviolable, but only within the territories of the State to which they are accredited.[3] Nevertheless they ought in all cases in every quarter to be courteously treated, as they are promoters of peace and good understanding, and represent the *persona* of the sovereign or the commonwealth.[4] Legates sent on a purely sacred mission are always and everywhere inviolable. All alike are entitled to undisturbed passage over any intermediate territory.[5] An envoy who is discovered to be really a spy,[6] or to be engaged in other treacherous conduct towards a sovereign or nation, or who has committed any other criminal offence, ought to be sent back to his country, and not subjected to any harsher personal treatment.[7] If, however, the ambassador inflict a personal injury on the sovereign, he is liable even to the capital penalty; and his own prince ought in such a case to surrender him to the jurisdiction of the offended State.[8] The general privilege of security extends also to the suite, their goods, and their residence.[9]

As to the civil local jurisdiction, Gentilis lays down certain restrictions on the ambassador's immunity. In questions arising out of contracts entered into on foreign territory during his official residence there, he is to be subject, like any other domiciled alien, to the local tribunals;[10] for, otherwise, he might be able to take advantage of his position and unjustly deprive a subject of his

---

[1] *De legationibus*, II. 10 (title): "Nec a subditis nec ad subditos recte mittuntur legati.—Non esse ius legationis cum suo domino subditis, hinc patet, quod potentioribus et dominis pares esse non possumus."
[2] II. 9.
[3] II. 3: "Legati ex ipso nomine ad alios non sunt [tuti], nisi ad quos legantur. Cum aliis ergo iura legationis non obtinent."
[4] II. 3.   [5] *Ibid.*
[6] II. 4: "Ceterum cum legato speculatore non arbitror agi durius posse, quam ut non admittatur, vel expellatur admissus."
[7] II. 18: ". . . quia legatus quoque principis personam gerit."
[8] II. 19.   [9] II. 15.
[10] II. 16: "De omni autem contractu, quem tempore legationis iniit, subire eum iudicium volo."

property, and hence no one would be willing to make any engagement with him.[1]

The view of Gentilis expressed here respecting the ambassador's exemption from the territorial criminal law had already been advanced by him in 1584, when he, together with Hotman, was consulted on the Mendoza affair. The Spanish ambassador was, on Throckmorton's confession, charged with complicity in the plot to liberate Mary Stuart and depose Elizabeth. The English Government was at first inclined to adopt stringent measures against Mendoza, some of the members of the Council arguing that "in vaine he putteth himselfe under the safeguard of nations which violateth the lawe of nations." However, the opinion of Gentilis prevailed, in spite of the contrary precedent of Leslie, Bishop of Ross; and the Government ordered the expulsion of the offending envoy, and the despatch of one of the Secretaries to the Privy Council to explain to the Spanish sovereign the reason for this action.[2]

4. **International Relations: Treaties.**—Gentilis emphasizes the doctrine that a king exists for his State, and not the State for the king—"non regna esse propter reges, sed reges propter regna factos esse."[3] Hence certain duties are imposed upon him, and certain restrictions on his conduct are laid down. The monarch has always to consider the good of his country, and not merely his own personal advantage. He is not the absolute proprietor of his dominions, but only the administrator thereof, the "tutor," the "curator," the "usufructuary."[4] He cannot enter into any engagement to the palpable detriment of his kingdom.[5] He cannot by treaty alienate his kingdom, and no authority, papal or even that of his people, can confer such power on him.[6] If

---

[1] *De legationibus*, II. 16. In regard to this provision, Gentilis refers to the statements of Julian and Paulus in the *Digest*, and was perhaps unduly influenced by certain rules of Roman law.

[2] *Calendar of State Papers, Spanish*, 1580-1586, pp. 513-515; Birch, *Memoirs of the Reign of Queen Elizabeth*, I. 458; Hotman, *The Ambassador* (1603), pp. 103-106. Opinions on the extent of the ambassador's privilege varied considerably; but it may be pointed out that even before 1584 certain writers had advocated total immunity; *e.g.* Ottaviano Maggi, *De legato* (1566), Pierre Ayrault, *L'ordre, formalité et instruction judiciaire* . . . (1576). [The present writer may say that, in common with all students of the earlier history of international law, he is much indebted to the writings of Professor Nys.]

[3] *De iure belli*, I. 16; p. 73.

[4] *Ibid.*, III. 22; p. 395.   [5] *Ibid.*

[6] *Ibid.*, III. 15; p. 357: "Omne dedit populus imperium et potestatem sane: sed ad regendum quasi homines, non ad alienandum quasi pecudes. . . . Aut num plus dederit populus, quam ipse habuit? Ipse populus non id poterat."

such a convention is concluded, the successors of the sovereign who has thus acted *ultra vires* are not bound thereby. A prince is entitled, however, to dispose of tribute and other such sources of profit.[1] Only despotic rulers like the Sultan, whose subjects are no better than slaves, can consent to such alienations. Further, a ruler can make no stipulation for single combat instead of regular war when the latter has become necessary and is legitimate.[2] A treaty concluded by the sovereign in person has binding force as soon as he has signed it, but if entered into by his representative it is not binding until due ratification.[3]

Are sovereigns and peoples bound by the legitimate conventions of their predecessors? Gentilis says that the common opinion is that treaties of peace are in general binding on successors, in the same manner as pecuniary obligations; but not necessarily so pacts of friendship and alliance—on the ground that the nature of *societas* implies only personal relationships, wherefore a contracting party cannot stipulate for the continuation of the engagement after his death. But such a distinction, urges Gentilis, is to be rejected, for the question of personal relationships enters into private undertakings but not in a *societas* of a public character. In actual practice, however, it is better for successors formally to renew alliances;[4] but renewal may be inferred from a variety of acts or words or even from acquiescence.[5]

Treaties of peace must be so clearly and definitely drawn up as to make subsequent controversies thereon impossible;[6] and in this connection Gentilis devotes two chapters to consider how certain clauses, stipulations, and terms (*e.g.* army, fleet, arms, fortification, etc.) ought to be construed.[7] Like all engagements of sovereigns, they are contracts of good faith, and not *stricti*

---

[1] *De iure belli*, III. 22; p. 395: "Potest princeps vectigalia et alia emolumenta alienare."
[2] *Ibid.*, III. 15.
[3] *Ibid.*, III. 23; p. 403: "Nec satis est stipulatio notarii pro absentibus; non eos enim tenet, nisi secuta ratificatione."
[4] *Ibid.*, III. 22; pp. 400, 401: "Successores tenentur, si contractus sint ex natura et consuetudine principatus; ut isti quidem sunt pacis et foederum. . . . At probandum est maxime, quod et fieri consuevit, ut foedera cum successoribus renoventur."
[5] *Ibid.*, pp. 401, 402: "Renovatur porro his actis, gestis, quae admitti citra nomen et ius societatis non valent. . . . Ut adfirmata et renovata censeatur. si reliqui in foedere pergant tacite."
[6] III. 14; p. 347.
[7] III. 20, 21.

iuris, as Baldus claims.¹ Before the time of Gentilis it was generally held—and the doctrine was by no means obsolete in his day—that the binding force of treaties depended on the oath, that the Pope could compel a refractory signatory to respect his pledged word, and that infringements were ecclesiastical offences.² Thus in the Treaty of Arras (1435) Charles VII. specifically recognized such papal sanction; Edward IV. begged the Pope to cancel his oath; and again in the treaty of 1514 Henry VIII. and Francis I. admitted the power of the Pope's Bull to enforce agreements under pain of excommunication. Treaties of peace are not vitiated through fear—for this is an essential concomitant of war.³ The engagements of captive princes are binding on them, if their capture has been legitimately effected; but their subjects are not obliged to obey them.⁴

As to pacts of friendship (*amicitia*) and alliance (*societas*), the first imply only general obligations of a moral character, as, for example, the furnishing of assistance, whilst the second are of two kinds, ἐπιμαχία, defensive, and συμμαχία, both defensive and offensive. But a pact or an alliance ceases to be valid if an illicit object be involved, or if illegitimate or irregular hostilities are to be made.⁵ Should war break out between two States, to both of which a third is bound by treaties of friendship, the latter ought to be guided, where conflicting duties appear, by certain general considerations. Aid should be offered in order to equalize as nearly as possible the condition of the contending parties,⁶ or given to the State having greater justice on its side,⁷ but if there be doubt on the point, then the prior alliance might decide.⁸ The defending State has, other things being equal, a better claim than the offending.⁹ Both may receive aid in money, provisions,

---

¹ *De iure belli*, III. 14; p. 347: "Stricti autem iuris contractum, ut transactionis, dicit Baldus. At ego contrarium docui. . . . Contractus [principum] omnes sunt bonae fidei. Est omnis principalis tractatio ex bono et aequo; omnis consuetudinum et institutorum gentium."

² *Cf.* Martinus Laudensis, *De confoederationibus, pace et conventionibus principum*, Quaest. 19 and 22.

³ *De iure belli*, III. 14; p. 349: "Metus est de natura victoriae . . . et ergo servanda pacta ab eo, qui sub duello vincitur et paciscitur; et idem de pactis dedititiorum belli."

⁴ III. 14; p. 351: "In principe captivo hoc putem, non esse necesse ut ei obtemperent subditi."

⁵ III. 18; p. 372: "Neque enim rei turpis societas intelligitur, neque confoederati intelliguntur ad bellum illicitum."

⁶ III. 18, p. 374: "Ut uni auxiliemur, quum nec est aliter condicio par sociorum." ⁷ III. 18; p. 375: "Ut causae iustiori auxiliemur."

⁸ *Ibid.*: "Inque pari causa is sit potior qui est tempore prior."

⁹ *Ibid.*, p. 376: "Ut utrique foederato, bellum gerenti invicem, non sit auxilium ferendum."

etc.¹ If it is doubtful which of the belligerents acts more in accordance with the treaty, each appealing to it in support of its claim, no aid ought to be offered to either ;² and similarly, if neither side can be satisfied and there is no valid reason for assisting one rather than the other.³

Is it legitimate to conclude pacts with infidel peoples ? Treaties of commerce are allowable, for such depend on the law of nature, the fundamental law of men at large.⁴ As to other contractual relationships, it is lawful to hold people of a different religion in an unequal league, *e.g.* as tributaries ;⁵ and, inversely, a league of this nature is legitimate when a Christian nation is forcibly subjected to infidels.⁶ Under no circumstances may an alliance be made with infidels as against believers ;⁷ hence the league of Francis I. with the Turks must be condemned.

With regard to facts vitiating conventions, and to circumstances in which treaties may be renounced, Gentilis says that, as in the case of private contracts, fraudulent misrepresentation and substantial error avoid treaties.⁸ Otherwise the public compacts of sovereigns are to be interpreted by the law of nations and not by the civil law. Thus the fact that one of the signatories is a minor is not a valid reason for renouncing the treaty ; so that the claim of the young King Edward III. respecting his treaty with the Scots was invalid. In international compacts the question in such cases is not minority, but actual exercise of sovereignty.⁹ The clause "rebus sic stantibus" is always understood ;¹⁰ a radical change of circumstances or the occurrence of new disputes may excuse the performance of one or other of the conditions previously laid down.

---

¹ *De iure belli*, III. 18; p. 377 : " Quod si tamen auxilia essent alterius generis, ut commeatuum, pecuniarum ; tum afferri utrique possent et vero deberent."
² P. 376 : " Quum et est dubium, quis duorum pluriumve petitorum agat pro iure foederis, quod quisque pro se citant . . . ut nemini auxilium praestetur."
³ P. 378 : " Si foederatus nequit utrique satisfacere : et causa non est cur uni magis quam alteri satisfiat : ut neutri auxilia ferantur."
⁴ III. 19 ; p. 384 : " Commercium non interdicitur cum infidelibus . . . et lex omnibus humana iubet commercium cum hominibus omnibus. . . . Dico licitum foedus universale commerciorum."
⁵ III. 19 ; p. 384. ⁶ P. 385.
⁷ P. 385. ⁸ III. 14 ; p. 351.
⁹ III. 14 ; p. 351 : " Sed quid si foedus percussum est cum minore ? Et Edvardus tertius Angliae negabat se foedere teneri, quod se minore cum Scotis ictum erat. Atque hic tenendum sic est, non eum esse minorem, qui iure regnandi aptus regno est et muneribus regni." ¹⁰ *Ibid.*

A treaty is violated if the State, and not merely private subjects, deliberately acts in contravention of any clause. If one party conducts an expedition against piratical subjects of the other,[1] or offers asylum to its exiles when not specifically prohibited in the convention, there will be no breach. It is otherwise if enemies are knowingly harboured, or the surrender of deserters and other fugitives is refused on demand being made.[2] As every treaty is one and indivisible, it may be repudiated *in toto* when any one of the conditions is not fulfilled by the other side, or when its execution becomes impossible. Necessity and *vis maior* are sufficient grounds for non-performance; but in every such case the alleged cause must be just, and not an excuse for evasion.[3] Wilful renunciation exposes the offending party to the vengeance of the other: though it does not entitle that other to resort to acts of perfidy in subsequent negotiations with the treaty-breaking State.

1. **Character and Aim of War; Conditions of Just War.**—Gentilis points out that the regulation of war depends on practices definitely agreed upon, on general customs tacitly followed, and on natural law; but not, as was the case in earlier times, on Roman and ecclesiastical law. War is not the normal condition of peoples; it behoves all to try always pacific settlement by means of diplomatic negotiation and conference, "disceptatio," by submission to arbitration (of which mode of settling conflicts various examples are cited), or by other peaceful means indicated by natural reason, rather than by rushing to arms, or resorting to other violent remedies.[4]

His definition of war is the briefest and most precise that has ever been enunciated: "Bellum est publicorum armorum iusta contentio."[5] This includes the three essential elements: (1) a public contest between sovereigns (hence excluding private differences, "rixa, pugna, inimicitia privatorum")[6]—war being justified only by the absence of a superior tribunal competent to settle the dispute and able to enforce its judg-

---

[1] *De iure belli*, III. 23; p. 406.
[2] P. 407.
[3] III. 24; p. 410: "Foedus non violatur, si ab eo disceditur per rationem iustam"; p. 414: "... Qui promittit non offendere, is subintelligit exceptionem, ' Nisi causa superveniat : Nisi culpa accesserit eius cui promissio ista fit et pactio foederis : Rebus sic stantibus.' "
[4] I. 3; p. 19: " Voluntario compromisso antea est disceptandum, et ratione naturali."
[5] I. 2; p. 10.   [6] I. 2; p. 11.

ment;[1] (2) by force of arms ; (3) begun and conducted in a just and regular manner, in conformity with the law generally established and adopted by both belligerents[2] (hence excluding irregular hostilities, like "excursiones," "populationes," "praedationes," "latrocinia,"[3] which are the acts of brigands and freebooters—"latrunculi," "praedones"—and not of regular enemies, "iusti hostes ").[4] The definition of Grotius, who speaks of the condition of parties maintaining a contest by force,[5] is too wide and indefinite, and may also imply conflicts like private war or single combats.

A *iustum bellum* is not required as against pirates and brigands or rebels,[6] who, wilfully withdrawing from the human community and from the institutions of human law, have forfeited all rights guaranteed thereby. Even formal promises made to them need not be kept.

The justice of a war depends on the legitimacy and sufficiency of the alleged cause. A war is justifiable if made on the grounds of necessity,[7] *e.g.* self-defence, public safety, and sometimes on the grounds of "utility" and "honour." Justice may exist on both sides, if it is doubtful which has the superior right, as Victoria and others held.[8] Several writers before Gentilis, *e.g.* Baldus, Joannes Lupus, Arias, Victoria, Wilhelmus Mathiae,[9] had laid down the conditions of a just war, and had invariably insisted on the criterion of necessity, apart from just and sufficient causes and regular proceedings. In some cases difference of religion as an alleged ground was condemned, in others pursuit of self-aggrandisement and vainglory, in others, again, slight injury. From time to time the conditions of lawful war were in a more or less fragmentary manner investigated, and usually from the point of view of war against Christian nations. But no one before Gentilis or at the time he wrote examined all these

---

[1] *De iure belli*, I. 3 ; p. 13 : " . . . quoniam inter summos principes populosve liberos fori disceptationes esse nequeunt, nisi inter volentes . . . non est principi in terris iudex." (This point had been emphasized by Franciscus Arias, *De bello et eius iustitia tractatus*, in the first half of the sixteenth century.)

[2] I. 2 ; p. 12 : " Sic iustum, non solum quod a iure est, sed et quod est ex omni parte perfectum, significat."   [3] I. 2 ; p. 13.

[4] I. 3 ; p. 13 : (In this connection Gentilis accepts the definitions and distinctions laid down by Pomponius and Ulpian.)

[5] *De iure belli et pacis*, I., i. 2.

[6] *De iure belli*, I. 4 ; p. 20 : " Cum piratis et latrunculis bellum non est "; p. 21 : " . . . ius belli a gentium iure est ; et tales non fruuntur illo iure, cui hostes sunt."

[7] I. 3 ; p. 19 : " Itaque concludo quod si necessitas non subsit, bellum esse iustum nec possit."

[8] I. 6 ; p. 28.   [9] *Libellus de bello iusto et licito* . . . (Antwerp, 1514).

questions as fully, as logically, as rationally, and as impartially as he did.

2. **Grounds for War.**—Religious difference, as in the case of heretic or infidel nations, is not a ground for war; for no one should be compelled to accept another faith unwillingly.[1] Moral persuasion and intellectual argument are justifiable for bringing others over to our faith, but not so physical force—as religion has to do with the mind and the free will.[2] Religion is, as it were, a union of God and man;[3] and God alone has dominion over the soul. Hence hostilities against heretics and infidels, simply because they do not share our faith, are unjust, as Victoria maintained.[4] Gentilis criticizes Baldus in that he confused the spiritual motive of the Church with the temporal objects in her wars against infidels, and confutes his assertion that infidel kings cannot exercise legal sovereignty over their territories. "Sacred" wars are justifiable only on the ground of urgent necessity; though an exception might perhaps be made in the case of wars against people without religion altogether, who are thus practically on a level—so far as an ordered "societas gentium" is concerned—with pirates and other enemies of mankind at large.[5] Further, a sovereign cannot by war compel his subjects to adopt his religion;[6] they may lawfully change their faith if the State does not thereby suffer any real injury—"nisi quod detrimenti illinc respublica capiat."[7] And the sovereign enjoys a similar liberty.[8]

Just as in private transactions the right of action may be barred by lapse of time, so in international affairs the principle of prescription may operate to extinguish old causes of war and other claims.[9] Thus the Emperor is not entitled to regain possession by force of arms of the territories which were formerly part of the Roman Empire. The frequently advanced theory of the Holy Roman Empire is absurd; the "imperium romanum," says Gentilis, is no more, and a new order of things now exists.[10] The decease of a prince does not necessarily cause the rule as to

---

[1] *De iure belli*, I. 9.
[2] I. 9; p. 36: "Religio autem ab animo est, et voluntate." (This question may be of no account nowadays, but it was of supreme importance when Gentilis wrote his work.)
[3] I. 9; p. 37: "Coniugium quoddam Dei et hominis est religio"; p. 39: "Religio erga Deum est."
[4] *Relectiones theologicae*, V. 10.
[5] *De iure belli*, I. 9; p. 39. [6] I. 10. [7] *Ibid.* [8] I. 11.
[9] I. 22; p. 99: ". . . Si vetustae causae afferri possunt ad bellum faciendum. In qua ego sane arbitror, non afferri posse." [10] I. 23.

prescription to operate; his successors may justly be liable to be warred upon if he refuses to make reparation for an unatoned offence on the part of the predecessor.[1]

As to the legitimate causes of war, that is, those which "materiam belli praebent,"[2] they may be divided into three main classes: divine, natural, human.[3] Under the first head may be mentioned the express command of God,[4] as in the case of the divine injunctions to the Israelites, the utterances of the oracles and soothsayers in Greece and Rome. "Natural" causes[5] have sometimes been urged (*e.g.* by the Jews against the Canaanites, by the Greeks and Romans against the "barbarians," by the Christians against the Saracens, etc.), on the ground of some alleged innate hostility between certain classes of men. But, says Gentilis, this is a false assumption; all men belong to one class—the human species; there is no fundamental antagonism between them; rather their natural kinship is self-evident and predominant.[6] The Christian wars against the Turks were lawful, not for religious reasons, or for reasons of natural enmity, but because of their perfidious, harassing, hostile conduct; whereas had they remained peaceful any attack on them would have been illegitimate.[7]

Self-defence is an instinct implanted in all living beings, and is a "natural" reason for taking up arms.[8] Self-defence may be immediate, "necessaria defensio." It may be anticipatory, "utilis defensio," against an attack prepared or meditated,[9] or even when it is probable; in other words, when balance of power is to be maintained. To render anticipatory steps lawful, however, there must be reasonable cause for apprehension. Hence, resistance may be justly offered to the Turks and to the Spaniards, as it is manifest they are aiming at universal dominion.[10] Further, there is "honesta defensio,"[11] which permits help to be given to a

---

[1] *De iure belli*, I. 24.   [2] I. 7; p. 33.
[3] *Ibid.*; just as law was commonly divided into "divinum," "naturale," and "humanum"; *cf.* Victoria, *Relectiones theologicae*, V. 1.
[4] I 8.   [5] I. 12.
[6] I. 12; pp. 52, 53: "Et itaque hominibus cum hominibus non est repugnantia per naturam. Sed neque antipathia est inter animalia eiusdem speciei."
[7] I. 12; p. 55: "Non inferendum bellum quiescentibus, pacem colentibus, in nos nihil molientibus."
[8] I. 13; p. 56: "Vim vi repellere, omnes leges, et omnia iura permittunt. Lex una, et perpetua, salutem omni ratione defendere."
[9] I. 14; p. 57: 'Utilem dico defensionem, quum movemus nos bellum, verentes, in ipsi bello petamur."
[10] I. 14.   [11] I. 15.

nation against its unjust aggressors :[1] for the "generis humani societas" is a unity, the world is one body, "mundus unum est corpus."[2] Gentilis quotes with approbation the statement of Ambrose[3] as a principle of canon law : "Plena est iustitia quae defendit infirmos."[4] May we defend the subjects of another State as against their sovereign ?[5] If the dispute between them is a private one, it is a question for their own tribunals; but in a public conflict, in which a great number of subjects rebel against their ruler, we may intervene if it is clear that he is grossly unjust or cruel; hence the justifiable intervention of England in the Netherlands, especially so in view of the ties of old friendship and consanguinity. Gentilis heartily approves of the Earl of Leicester's policy in favour of the Belgians, and agrees with Justus Lipsius that Spanish violence would be left unrestrained if that part of the continent fell.[6]

Apart from the law of defence in general, which concerns rather the warding off of war than the making of it, there are "natural" causes for declaring hostilities.[7] These grounds refer to motives of necessity, utility, and honour.[8] Examples of necessity are—when foreigners are refused civil rights, or if the immigration to and occupation of vacant territory be interfered with; of utility —avenging injuries received and so making it impossible for others to be committed,[9] vindicating violated natural rights, such as the rights of intercourse, passage, navigation, shelter,[10] in the absence of good reasons for refusal; of honour—making war not merely on one's own account, but "communi ratione et pro aliis," e.g. against cannibals, people who practise immolation, or indulge in bestial vice.[11]

Finally, "human" causes of war appear when an offended State proceeds to exact reparation for violated positive rights.[12] The alleged reason must not, however, be a trifling one, "levis causa"; one must not rush to arms on the least provocation, but only when war is really necessary. Moreover, the violation of these rights must be the work of sovereigns or peoples; for the acts of private subjects are not necessarily the acts of their

---

[1] *De iure belli*, I. 15 ; p. 66 : " Non aliena homini res est hominum tueri rem et salutem."   [2] *Ibid.*, p. 64.   [3] *De off.*, I. 27.
[4] I. 15 ; p. 68.   [5] I. 16.   [6] *Ibid.*   [7] I. 17.
[8] I. 17 ; p. 75 : " Atque bellum quidem infertur eodem modo, aut necessarie, aut utiliter, aut honeste."
[9] I. 18 ; p. 79.   [10] I. 19 ; pp. 81, 82.   [11] I. 25.
[12] I. 20 ; p. 89 : " Quum violato aliquo iure hominum ad bellum descenditur."

State, unless it acquiesces when several offences have been committed.[1]

3. **Conduct of War.**—Not only must the cause of war be just, but the war must be begun and conducted justly; otherwise it would be as wrongful and odious as murder.[2] Public declaration is necessary, and a certain delay is to be thereafter made, as in the Roman *rerum repetitio*, in order to give an opportunity for peaceful settlement.[3] Proclamation may, of course, be omitted in the case of a sovereign as against his rebel subjects, or in that of a suzerain as against his subordinate rulers.[4] An immediate effect of declared war is the cessation of commercial relationships.[5]

The employment of assassins is unlawful;[6] of spies lawful, but at the risk of their lives; similarly of traitors as against traitors.[7] The use of poison,[8] magic arts, serpents, savage beasts, is forbidden; of elephants, horses, dogs, allowed.[9] Stratagems are permissible,[10] but these do not include perfidious conduct; both acts and pledged words must be *bonae fidei*;[11] apart from this there may be cases in which it would be justifiable to deceive the enemy by a lie, *e.g.* as Themistocles did.[12]

Gentilis approves of the opinion of Polybius[13] that the laws of war permit the destruction of fortresses, towns,[14] villas, gardens, ships, productions, in order to weaken the enemy and bring the conflict to a speedy conclusion; but all useless destruction, *e.g.*, of temples, porticos, statues, fruit-bearing trees, and other "res innoxiae," and all violation of sacred objects, *e.g.* altars, sepulchres, must be condemned.[15] He differs from Polybius

[1] *De iure belli*, I. 21; p. 94: "Non imputatur universitati delictum singulorum"; p. 96, ". . . civitatem teneri pro delictis civium non momentaneis, sed successivis, continuatis."

[2] II. 2; p. 133: "Et iniustum, et detestabile, et internecinum bellum est: id est, quod nulla lege belli, sed pro libidine geritur; et in quo omnia iura belli merito cessare videntur." [3] II. 1; p. 124.

[4] II. 2. [5] I. 21; p. 97. [6] II. 8. [7] II. 9.

[8] Other writers were in this respect less humane, *e.g.*, Michel d'Amboise, *Le guidon des gens de guerre* (1543), who says one may "gaster, infester, intoxiquer et empoisonner les eaues des ennemys."

[9] *De iure belli*, II. 6, 7. [10] II. 3. [11] II. 4.

[12] II. 5 (in accordance with the doctrines of Gratian, *Decretum*, II. 23. 11. 2, and Thomas Aquinas, *Summa Theologiae*, II. 40. 3).

[13] *Cf. International Law and Custom of Ancient Greece and Rome*, II., pp. 248 et seq.

[14] Belli, writing in 1558, was against the destruction of towns, in the absence of serious offence on the part of the enemy: "Non deberent urbes diripi, nisi pro magno flagitio . . ." (*De re militari*, IV. 8).

[15] *De iure belli*, II. 23; p. 261: "Bellum certe neque adversus Deum, neque adversus res sacras, sed est adversus armatos." Thus, in the instructions given to the Earl of Essex, June, 1597 (the work of Gentilis had already been published in London by 1589), the violation of hospitals and all sacred places was forbidden.

however, in allowing temples to be destroyed in certain circumstances : by way of retaliation, if the enemy does not respect them or has not done so in a previous war ; if the enemy has already profaned them ; and if they are an impediment to victory.[1] As against barbarians, and in cases of exceptional urgency, such usually forbidden acts may be lawful.[2]

With regard to the person of the enemy, it is laid down that non-combatants, including women, children, harmless and undefended persons, peaceful peasants[3] (who are held to be in the same position as foreign merchants),[4] are exempt from the ordinary hostile treatment. Suppliants seeking refuge in sacred places are by the unanimous opinion of the world considered inviolable.[5] Hostages are not in the position of prisoners of war, though they are debarred from making a will. They are not to suffer for the breach of faith of their countrymen.[6] Fugitive hostages may be put to death ; to receive them is an offence against the law of nations.[7] Both natural and divine law command that prisoners are not to be put to death ; the practice has sometimes been otherwise, but not everything so permitted is to be approved.[8] Rigorous treatment, however, may be resorted to in exceptional cases, *e.g.* by way of reprisal, where captives had inflicted injury on their captors, or had used treachery and violated the laws of war, where released prisoners have been taken a second time.[9] A man is not a prisoner until led " intra praesidia," but one who has surrendered before being brought there is not to be slain if he lays down his arms and does not attempt to escape. Voluntary surrender is a protection, and

---

[1] *De iure belli*, II. 23 ; p. 264.
[2] *Cf.* Victoria (*Relectiones theologicae*, VI. 52), who emphasizes that excesses are to be avoided, unless absolutely demanded by " necessitas."
[3] *De iure belli*, II. 21. Similarly, Victoria (*Relectiones theologicae*, VI. 36) insists on the protection of "innocentes," including "innoxii agricolae, gens togata et pacifica." Belli does not except women and children. It may be recalled that when Leicester took command of the forces in the Netherlands, 1584, it was laid down in the *Laws and Ordinances* : " That no man ... shal lay violent handes upon any woman with childe, or lying in childebed, olde persons, widowes, yong virgines, or babes, without especiall order from the magistrate, upon paine of death " (*State Papers, Domestic, Elizabeth*, cclxiii. 102).
[4] II. 22. See *infra* as to the position of foreign merchants within the territory of the belligerents.
[5] II. 20. The directions to the Earl of Essex were more stringent : those seeking asylum in hospitals or churches could be captured, if they were " worthy to be taken as a prisoner " (*State Papers, loc. cit.*).
[6] To the same effect writes Victoria. [7] *De iure belli*, II. 19.
[8] II. 16, where he quotes Paulus (*Digest*, L. 17, 144 : " Non omne, quod licet, honestum est "). [9] II. 18.

should always be accepted, unless there are urgent reasons to the contrary. Capitulation by the commander, or by the majority of the forces, protects those who were opposed to submission.[1] Exchange of prisoners must be made equitably and *bona fide*. Ransom ought not to be excessive. If a liberated prisoner die before his ransom is paid, it is due from his heir.[2] When a prisoner is released on his promising not to take part in that war against his captors, such promise is binding; but not necessarily so, if his undertaking is prejudicial to his State or contrary to military law. In the latter case jurists commonly hold that the liberated prisoner ought to return to captivity.[3] A captive who regains his liberty has the right of *postliminium*.

Commanders-in-Chief (or, in their absence, inferior officers) may enter into military conventions, which are binding if they are within the limits of their powers and are ratified. Such powers are in general restricted to matters relating to military operations, and do not include that of establishing a definitive peace.[4] Truces may be made for the burial of the dead, which is demanded by natural and divine law and the universal consensus of humanity,[5] and for the exchange and liberation of prisoners. The unauthorized act of an individual does not amount to a breach of truce; but the offender ought to be surrendered for punishment. During a truce forces are not to be surreptitiously advanced or withdrawn. Safe-conducts are based on good faith; violation by one side permits of similar retaliation by the other.[6] All these agreements and guarantees must be free from evasive intentions, verbal subtlety, captious interpretation, and everything else which is inconsistent with true *bona fides*.[7]

4. **Conclusion of War.**—The obligation imposed on belligerents to avoid excesses and observe "honestas" (honour, justice, humanity) is likewise applicable to the victor, when he has the conquered in his power. Generally the victor's conduct will depend on the seriousness of the injury received, the amount of damages suffered, the necessity of insuring ultimate security. To go beyond such limits is unjust; for war is made not for its

---

[1] *De iure belli*, II. 17.   [2] II. 15.   [3] II. 11.
[4] II. 10; p. 172: "Quod igitur bellicum est, id duces tractent belli, non aliud."
[5] II. 24; p. 268: "Hoc est gentium et humanitatis ius."   [6] II. 12-14.
[7] II. 4; pp. 136, 137: "... Et valde respuunt scrupulosas interpretationes, disputationes de apicibus iuris, id est, de subtilitatibus; et ab omni malitia longe esse debent; et solam veritatem intueri, quam colit ius gentium, et post quam vadit, non autem post subtilitatem bona fides."

own sake, but with a view to attain peace—which may be defined as "concordia ordinata";[1] and peace will be more likely to be durable if the conqueror acts in harmony with the law of nature, and observes the *ius gentium*, rather than merely relying on oaths and undertakings exacted from the conquered.[2] To inflict monstrous or cruel punishments, even under great provocation, is barbarism. Jurists have differed considerably as to the guiding principles to be observed; but Gentilis unhesitatingly affirms that *aequitas* is to be preferred to *ius strictum*, and *honestas* to *utilitas*.[3]

The vanquished party may be deprived of all weapons of war,[4] as well as of their standards, insignia, etc.[5] Their fortifications and, if necessity demand, their towns taken by storm may be destroyed,[6] and harbours "filled up."[7] Their temples and sacred objects must be spared, even though their religion is deemed false.[8] Works of art, libraries, manuscripts are inviolable.[9] If the various proceedings from the commencement to the termination of hostilities have been in conformity with law and justice, then the victor may enter into occupation of his opponent's territory.[10] But such occupation is in general to be effected only to the extent of the territory occupied by the forces, as the right is "particular" and not "universal" (which Hotman also holds); it is a case of "adquisitio universalis" only when a State is entirely absorbed by another, and its territory passes along with its rights and burdens.[11] The test of occupation is effective possession, complete control.[12] If not otherwise laid down by a treaty of peace, the lands, places, buildings, etc., as well as ships, arms, and other booty are in the power of the occupier, and do

---

[1] *De iure belli*, III. 1.   [2] III. 13.
[3] III. 12; pp. 335-337; p. 338: "Integra iustitia est quae honestatem rebus omnibus anteponit" (according to the opinion of Aristotle).
[4] III. 11; p. 334.   [5] III. 6; p. 296.
[6] III. 7; pp. 301, 302.   [7] III. 7.
[8] III. 6; p. 298: "Neque enim licet victoribus, perdere victis iura Dei aut naturae. Etiam et quum est ea religio victi falsa, ut sic putet oxymore, parcere victo decet."
[9] In this respect, as in so many other questions, Gentilis is in advance of his time. Thus, in 1623, when Heidelberg was taken, its famous library was pillaged, and valuable manuscripts were carried off to the Vatican. Later it became the practice to stipulate that if a town capitulated, its charters, public documents, etc., were to be spared by the conqueror—as was the case in 1678 when Louis XIV. took Ghent.   [10] *De iure belli*, III. 4; p. 292.
[11] III. 5; p. 296: "Et civitas quae de principe in principem transierit, censetur cum omnibus suis qualitatibus transiisse."
[12] III. 17; p. 370: "Is dicitur occupare, qui sic incipit occupare ut possit conservare et possidere; qui autem nequit tenere, nisi capiat aliquem locum principalem, is occupasse non dicitur."

not revert to the original owners if the enemy is not expelled from the country.¹

As to the person of the vanquished, Gentilis emphasizes that it is unlawful to slay the prisoners or the heads of the army or of the defeated State, in the absence of urgent reasons,² or retain them in captivity after peace is concluded. Certain rigours might perhaps be excused in the heat of a battle, but not so when the war is over.³ Further, prisoners of war may not be reduced to slavery, at least as between Christians.⁴

Other rights of the conqueror are—to change the form of the government of the conquered country, if demanded by reasons of general security,⁵ to impose his religion (but only in the absence of any other)⁶ and the language of his country.⁷ Finally, he may justly exact a war indemnity,⁸ impose a tribute and other pecuniary obligations, and demand such cessions of territory as he deems "pro arbitrio boni viri" indispensable to the security of his State.⁹

5. **Maritime War.**—Apart from the rights and duties of belligerents in general warfare, a few questions are raised by Gentilis in regard to naval war. The granting of letters of marque—the recognized and usual practice of the age—is emphatically condemned by him as amounting to a deliberate sanction of robbery of unarmed and harmless merchants and others: "Dico esse odiosissimum hoc ius litterarum markae quod merito divinissimus noster rex abominatur ; per quod geretur latrocinium verius quam bellum contra inermes et innoxios mercatores et alios ab aciebus longe positos."¹⁰ Jurists like Covarruvias and Ayala¹¹ had admitted the legitimacy of reprisals ; and even Grotius held that the goods of subjects may be seized in respect of any debt or unfulfilled obligation of their sovereign or State.¹²

---

¹ *De iure belli*, III. 17 ; pp. 364, 367.
² III. 8 ; p. 313. Gentilis refers to the famous case of Conradin, who was defeated in 1268 by Charles of Anjou, and, with Pope Clement's consent, was executed. Gentilis says it was wrong to treat Conradin like a criminal when he was taken prisoner, but his death was demanded by supreme necessity. This precedent was cited by Elizabeth when Mary's complicity in Babington's plot was detected in 1586.
³ III. 8 ; p. 311 : "Sed in bello licuit eos occidere inter iram vindictam et arma, non in pace."
⁴ III. 9.   ⁵ III. 10.
⁶ III. 11.   ⁷ III. 11 ; p. 331.
⁸ III. 3.   ⁹ III. 4.
¹⁰ His opinion given in a consultation, and to be found in *Lansdowne Manuscripts*, vol. cxxxix.
¹¹ *De iure et officiis bellicis et de disciplina militari* (1582), I. 4. 3.
¹² *De iure belli et pacis*, III. 2. 2.

As to maritime capture, various doctrines were advanced by writers and different practices adopted by States. Some held that the property in a prize vested in the captor the moment it was taken; others insisted that in order that the property might pass, the prize must have remained in his hands for twenty-four hours;[1] others, again, amongst whom was Gentilis, argued that acquisition of property can follow only after "deductio intra praesidia."[2] The rule of twenty-four hours prevailed.[3]

6. **Neutrality.**[4]—In his treatment of the rights and duties of neutrals Gentilis lays down, as the indispensable criterion, the territorial principle. A belligerent has not, as was often claimed, an unrestricted and absolute right to pass over a neutral's territory. Innocent passage, however, is lawful; and it is the better practice to obtain permission from the State or sovereign in question, who is entitled to prohibit within his dominions any military operations whatever.[5] Foreign merchants remaining temporarily within the territory of a belligerent State cannot be treated as enemies by the other adversary, if they take no part in the war and faithfully observe the obligations imposed on neutrals. Hence they are free from all acts of war, including reprisals.[6] But if such merchants or other aliens have established a permanent residence there, and have taken over their fortunes, or the greater part thereof, with the intention of settling, then they may be justly identified with the enemy as occupying the position of subjects of their new country, even though they had not acquired the full rights of citizenship.[7] The test, then, is not origin or naturalization—for one may be a citizen of various places—but domicile;[8] and this depends not only on the *factum*, but also, and more particularly, on the *animus manendi*[9]—though

---

[1] *Cf.* Grotius, III. 6. 3. n. 2.

[2] *Advocatio Hispanica*, I. 2; p. 4: ". . . quod res hosti capta non prius ei quaereretur, quam et intra eiusdem praesidia perducta esset, quamvis ea diu possessa esset, per duos amplius menses in mari habita." The *Siete Partidas* had admitted this principle, as well as that of *pernoctatio*.

[3] *Cf.* the article on Zouche, and that on Bynkershoek.

[4] See the article on Bynkershoek.

[5] *De iure belli*, I. 19; p. 83.—Bonet, *L'arbre des batailles*, had written to the same effect; but there were then no fixed rules on the subject.

[6] II. 22; p. 252: "Mercatoribus neque nocendum est; qui apud hostes deprehenduntur, etenim nec hostes isti sunt; ut nec alii peregrini. . . . Peregrinos neque represaliae afflictant."

[7] *Ibid.*, p. 253.

[8] *Ibid.*, p. 258: "Subditi dicuntur non respectu originis, vel allectionis, sed domicilii."

[9] *Ibid.*, p. 255.

in a doubtful case domicile may be presumed from ten years' residence. Moreover, it is possible to have several domiciles.¹ From these considerations it follows that though the goods of domiciled persons may be taken, those of aliens proper must be respected (as was the case in the recent war between England and Spain), unless they actively assist the enemy.

In pursuance of the principle of territoriality, goods or prisoners taken within neutral territory do not pass to the captor, but must be delivered up on the demand of the sovereign of that territory.² The same rule applies even if flight began where capture was lawful: for change of territory implies another sovereignty and another jurisdiction.³ Hence in the war between France and Spain, Spanish fugitives pursued to England by the French were held to be protected; and similarly in 1588 when the Spaniards fled before the English fleet to the French coast.⁴

All neutrals who supply munitions of war and provisions to the enemy, and instigate or encourage him in any way, are deemed to have taken up his cause and to be therefore invested with hostile character. In general terms it may be stated that he is an enemy who does what pleases the enemy. There are no positive rules of *ius gentium* expressly forbidding the commercial relationship of neutral States with belligerents; but a general proclamation⁵ or a special demand for the cessation thereof may be made by either adversary, in accordance with the principles of *aequitas* and *natura*. Freedom of trade and the rights of merchants are undoubtedly to be respected; but where there is a conflict between the interests of neutral traders and the supreme interests of a belligerent State, the latter must predominate.⁶ Thus, recalls Gentilis, Elizabeth in 1589 rightly claimed that the English fleet lawfully despoiled the ships of the Hanseatic States for sending victuals, naval stores, and vessels to Spain.⁷ (On

---

¹ *De iure belli*, II. 22; p. 258.
² *Advocatio Hispanica*, I. 5.
³ *Ibid.*, I. 5; p. 16: "Alienum territorium securitatem praestat. Et mutato territorio mutatur potestas."
⁴ *Cf. ibid.*, I. 8, where he approves of the wide English claim to maritime jurisdiction.
⁵ It had become customary as early as the thirteenth century to issue proclamations against the supply of munitions and provisions to the enemy.
⁶ *De iure belli*, I. 21; p. 97: "Ius commerciorum aequum est; at hoc aequius tuendae salutis. Est illud gentium ius; hoc naturae est. Est illud privatorum; est hoc regnorum. Cedat igitur regno mercatura, homo naturae, pecunia vitae."
⁷ *Cf. State Papers, Domestic, Elizabeth*, ccxxii. 86, 89; ccxxiii. 64; ccxxv. 43.

this occasion, and again in 1597 at the request of Danish ambassadors, the English government drew up a list of contraband goods;[1] and in 1604 prohibited articles were enumerated in the treaty between James I. and Philip III. of Spain, and, again, later in the treaty between Sweden and the United Provinces.) Accordingly, the action of the English and others was illegitimate, says Gentilis, when they supplied munitions of war ("commoda bello") to the Turks, who were at war with the Emperor. For like reasons Charles of Burgundy adopted severe measures against foreign traders for attempting to carry provisions to his besieged enemy. The guiding rule in all these questions may be expressed in the form of the universal imperative: "Quod tibi fieri non vis, alteri ne feceris."

Conclusion.—The work of Gentilis is of enduring value in the history of the law of nations. He did more than any other writer to free international law from the besetting theological importations and the incubus of scholastic casuistry. In his clear recognition of and constant insistence on the predominant positive aspects of the subject, he foreshadowed the modern prevailing view, which emphasizes that the regulation of interstatal relationships is based on law and not merely on courtesy. He frequently appeals to divine law; he is always ready to invoke the authority of "natural reason," of the law of nature, but in doing so his aim is to apply additional sanctions to matters which are universally affirmed by the intuitive consciousness of mankind. Metaphysical abstractions and dialectic subtleties he avoided as being a menace to the stability of the very foundations of the subject. His aim is a thoroughly practical one; he considers with the mind of an impartial judge—a mind swayed by common sense rather than by ancient authority—the great controversies of the time; and, in default of prior agreement or consistent practice, he suggests brief definite solutions in accordance with the behests of justice and humanity. In comparison with the comprehensive work of Grotius, the work of Gentilis may seem

[1] It may be interesting to refer to Burleigh's proclamation, where justification is sought on the grounds of civil law, the law of nations, natural and divine law: "Her Majesty thynketh and knoweth it by the rules of the law as well of nature as of men, and specially by the law civil, that whenever any doth directly help her enemy with succours of eny victell, armor, or any kynd of munition to enhable his shippes to maintain themselves, she may lawfully interrupt the same; and this agreeth with the law of God, the law of nature, the law of nations, and hath been in all tymes practised and in all countries betwyxt prynce and prynce, and country and country" (*Lansdowne Manuscripts*, civ. 30, f. 70).

more or less fragmentary ; but it is important to remember that the work of the former was a later publication and had the great advantage of being modelled on that of the latter. No doubt Grotius is superior in philosophic grasp ; by virtue of this capacity he elaborated a magnificent system, parts of which, however, were in some respects retrograde, in others alien to the requirements and circumstances of the age. Hence at times his work presents the appearance of an abstract *a priori* treatise. Gentilis, on the contrary, always considered actual conditions and possibilities, and never forgot that a body of rules governing the relationships between men or between States is necessarily of an organic nature ; hence he avoids all arbitrary dogmatic methods. He clearly marked out the respective spheres of the international jurist and the theologian ; he carefully differentiated between the work of the international lawyer and that of the civilian. He is not given to fallacious presumptions of analogy between the civil law and the law of nations—presumptions which govern the fundamental classification of the work of Grotius.

When we carefully weigh all these considerations, and bear in mind the differences of the epochs of these two jurists, the greater difficulties attending the pioneer work of the earlier writer, the remarkable systematic powers and enormous European influence of the later, we can readily conclude that Gentilis and Grotius are the two greatest contributors to international law ; but, notwithstanding the glorification of the one by the Italian school and the apotheosis of the other by the Dutch, we cannot finally decide which of them really occupies the foremost place.

FRANCIS BACON

THE world of thought is apt to forget that Francis Bacon, the Master of Laws, was a lawyer. There were many tent-makers before the days of Saul of Tarsus and after, and lawyers were not wanting in England before the days of Lord Verulam of York House, nor have been since. But Paul we remember as an Apostle to the Gentiles, and Bacon as an Apostle to the Schoolmen. Their trades concern us not. Indeed, the fact that Bacon traded in law is one of the tragedies of history. Yet to forget that he was a lawyer is to forget that he was a jurist—a very different matter ; and is to overlook the fact that the laws which control the relationships of men are not less fundamental than the laws that express the interaction of particles or the flux of energy. To Bacon, as to another apostle, nothing was unclean or common, except perhaps municipal law, and all that appertained either to things or men were the subject of legitimate curiosity and ordered speculation. But the law of his nation claimed him as her own by hereditary right, and trained him to expound not only the laws of men, but the laws of Nature.

Sir Nicholas Bacon.—Francis Bacon belonged to a distinguished legal family closely associated with Gray's Inn. His example and that of his famous father, Sir Nicholas Bacon, no doubt in part accounts for the not unremarkable fact that in the sixteenth and subsequent centuries there were in all forty members of the Inn bearing the family name, of whom eight had the prænomen of Francis. Sir Nicholas Bacon was the first professional lawyer who ruled the Court of Chancery. He was perhaps Queen Elizabeth's first legal appointment. In 1558 she made him Lord Keeper of the Great Seal of England, an office that he held until 1578. During his time it was declared by Royal Warrant and Statute that this office was indistinguishable in operation from that of Lord Chancellor. Nicholas Bacon was

FRANCIS BACON

a great Elizabethan, and his greater son reaped the sterling benefit of his legal prestige. He was a man of honest, humorous, and humble heart, and he abhorred the dishonesties of his age and his profession. He spoke plainly to the Queen on the scandalous matter of the monopoly licences. "Will you have me speak truth, Madam? *Licentiâ omnes deteriores sumus.* We are all the worse for licence." Despite the greatness of his position, he kept, unlike his less wise son, no state. "My Lord, what a little house have you gotten!" said the Queen to him at Gorhambury. "Madam," he replied, "my house is well, but it is you that have made me too great for my house." A blunt, stern judge, he had little sympathy with the delays and garrulity of his profession. "There is a great difference betwixt you and me," he once said to a verbose pleader: "a pain to me to speak, and a pain to you to hold your peace."

Nicholas Bacon had been Lord Keeper three years when Francis was born in the legal purple on January 22, 1561. He was destined, as the Queen prophesied, to achieve the unique distinction of succeeding to the great office that his father held at his birth. At the early age of twelve years he was entered at Trinity College, Cambridge, but he came down in March, 1575-6, having but just completed his fourteenth year. He joined Gray's Inn on June 27, 1576, and on November 21 of the same year he was given, with his four brothers, out of compliment to his father's office, a position among the Grand Company of the Ancients. He was shortly afterwards sent to Paris to learn diplomacy in its subtlest school, and he remained in France for three years. During this period his father retired, and shortly afterwards, in February, 1578-9, died suddenly. Francis returned at once to England, and resumed his legal studies, taking up his residence in chambers at Gray's Inn that had been granted in 1579 to him and his brother Antony jointly for a term of years which was renewed in 1588. It is evident that the Lord Keeper had made arrangements for his son's return, and had probably designed in his retirement to watch over the student's progress in laws and manners. Bacon's greatest loss in life was the death of his wise father at this critical period. The lessons of the Continental school of diplomacy, with its fluent sophistries, needed to be modified by the slow wisdom of the man to whom it was "a pain to speak."

Gray's Inn: Bacon's Readings.—Bacon never gave up the chambers in Gray's Inn. At a pension of November 8, 1622, after the Lord Chancellor's fall, they were re-granted to him for a term of forty years. He had then retired to this "cell." "Myself for quiet and the better to hold out, am retired to Gray's Inn." In that faithful stronghold disgrace could not touch him, and he could look freely forth upon the walks that he had made and write about the gardens that he loved. These chambers that he occupied for five and forty years were by his will devoted to a pathetic use. He directed them to be sold, and the proceeds, to the extent of £300, to be applied "for some little present relief" of fifteen Cambridge and ten Oxenford scholars. His own bounteous nature looked back with pain on the narrow means that warped his own professional life. He took up residence in Gray's Inn in 1580, under a "special admittance," that excused him from keeping commons. Late hours, as his mother plaintively pointed out, had rendered his digestion incapable of student's fare. On June 27, 1582, he was called to the Bar, and two years later he entered the Parliament that met on November 23, 1584, as member for Melcombe Regis. He at once plunged into public affairs, and his letter of advice to the Queen of the same year on the treatment of Romanists and ultra-Protestants savoured of wisdom as unerring as it was precocious. In 1586, though he had not yet read, he was made an honorary member of the Reader's Table at Gray's Inn, and in the following year[1] he was elected as one of the Assistant Readers to the Reader Anthony St. Leger. In these two events there is evidence of the mark that he had already made as a studious lawyer. His first Reading dealt with the subject of Advowsons, the text being the fifth chapter of the second Statute of Westminster.[2] The Reading is extant in manuscript, but has not, so far as I am aware, yet been published.

The Stowe Collection was unfortunately closed to Mr. Spedding

---

[1] 1587, according to Mr. Heath; but 1588, according to the Gray's Inn Pension Book.

[2] 13 Edw. I. c. 5 (1285) (see *Co. Litt.* 17b, 119b, 344b). This section was enacted to provide a remedy for usurpations of the advowsons of churches. By Chapter I. of the Constitutions of Clarendon (1164) all questions relating to advowsons had been removed into the King's Court; but nevertheless the writs available were of little use to reversioners. It was found that heirs under age, reversioners, married women, and religious persons during the vacancies of their holdings frequently suffered the loss of their advowsons through fraudulent presentations to benefices by life tenants and other persons. There were three original writs—one writ of Right (*de recto advo-*

and Mr. Heath, with the result that it was not possible to obtain a transcript of the unique manuscript of the Reading for the purposes of Mr. Spedding's final edition of Bacon's works. This was a serious loss, for the Reading is the earliest extant of Bacon's legal writings, with the possible exception of *The Discourse upon the Commission of Bridewell*, which was written in 1587, and to which I shall have occasion to refer later as giving a clear view of his early constitutional ideas. It is plain that by this date Bacon had become a deeply read lawyer. Indeed, before this date, in 1586, his merit had been recognized, for in that year he was made a Bencher of his Inn, and thus, in pursuance of a resolution of the Privy Council of February 8, 1584, became qualified to sign pleadings and to plead at Westminster. In the normal course he could not have done so until five years from his call to the Bar. It would appear, then, that Bacon had begun seriously to practise in 1586. In the same year he was elected member for Taunton. In 1589 he sat for Liverpool, and was made Dean of Gray's Inn. A year later he was created Queen's Counsel Extraordinary. In the Parliament of 1593 he sat for Middlesex, and in the following year he was appointed as acting Treasurer of his Inn. All the evidence seems to point towards an active professional and political life. It is said, however, that it was not until 1594 that he first argued in Court. All the evidence is against this suggestion, for not only had he been a Bencher at this date for eight years, and a Queen's Counsel for four, but the class of cases he appeared in were of the first magnitude. It is probable, however, that it was on January 25, 1594, that he made his first striking success in Court—a success sufficient to call forth the approval of Burghley. He increased his reputation as an advocate, we are told, by further arguments on February 5 and 6, 1594. These successes were followed in the Easter Term by the great argument—still elaborately extant—in *Chudleigh's Case*, a cause in which he appeared with Coke. Bacon said of himself,

---

cationis), and two of Possession (*darrien presentment* and *quare impedit*)—but as they provided no sufficient remedy the statute gave the reversioners " such action by writ of Advowson Possessory as the last ancestor of such an heir should have had at the last avoidance happening in his time, being of full age before his death, or before the demise was made for term of life or in fee-tail." Bacon's view on this intricate subject must be valuable. The opinion expressed by Sir Edward Coke, that an infant could present, whatever his age might be—a view also taken by Lord Chancellor King (see 3 *Inst.*, 156 ; *Co. Litt.*, 89*a*, note 1)—could have found little favour in Bacon's eyes, save in so far as it negatives the idea of lapse.

"In weighty causes I always used extraordinary diligence"; and this is certainly confirmed by the arguments extant, all of which show profound learning in case law and immense elaboration. It is absurd to suppose that the author of the argument in *Chudleigh's Case* was unfamiliar with Court work. He, indeed, at this date considered himself entitled to a Crown officership, and when, despite the influence of Essex, he failed to obtain recognition, he felt that he had received a professional rebuff. Writing to Essex in 1595, he expressed a wish to retire from the legal profession. The want of money was, we may believe, at this time a serious matter. Naturally lavish in his expenditure, and with but small private means, some certainty of income had become a necessity. An application for the Mastership of the Wards failed. In May, 1596, he attempted, without success, to secure the Mastership of the Rolls. A corrupt competitor was appointed. Bacon himself was gradually drawn into the network of corruption that surrounded the whole judicial system. He secured, instead of the Rolls, the reversion of the Clerkship of the Star Chamber, and in 1597 he actually offered this post to the Lord Keeper, Sir Thomas Egerton, for his son, in consideration of the grant of the again vacant Mastership of the Rolls. This singularly unhappy proposal was repeated on November 12, 1597, at the very time that Egerton was acting as a member of a commission appointed to inquire into the corrupt practices of the Master who had secured the office in the place of Bacon in May, 1596.

The Judicial Sale of Offices in the Sixteenth Century.—This affair is important, though it is not mentioned by Lord Macaulay. It throws a vivid light upon the judiciary system of the period, and if we are to be just, as Mr. Macaulay expressed a desire to be in his unjust and melodramatic essay, it is necessary to realize what that system was. The Chancery Court in the late sixteenth century had become independent of the Privy Council, and the Lord Chancellor was its judge. There had been from early times twelve Masters in Chancery who at this date issued writs of grace, and assisted the chancellor in the hearing of causes and interlocutory motions. This assistance was necessary in the case of unprofessional chancellors such as Sir Christopher Hatton, who was appointed in 1589. Much work then, as now, was delegated to the Masters,—the taking of accounts and more serious matters. Bacon in his Chancery Orders greatly limited the system of delegation. It was absurd for a demurrer to be argued before a clerk. These Masters were paid, not by salary, but by fees, and were appointed at a price by the Lord Chancellor. Nominally the Crown appointed the chief of the Masters, who was known as the Master of the Rolls; but in practice this office was largely in the gift of the Chancellor. The fact that in the reigns of Elizabeth and James I. these offices were deliberately priced does not perhaps necessarily prove that the officials were corrupt, for the sale appears to have been quite open. But it is beyond doubt that the Masters were subjected to influences that involved corruption. They had to repay themselves out of fees for the price paid, and to increase legal business was to them a necessity of life. The Master of the Rolls had under him the notorious body known as the Six Clerks. These clerks were nominally the solicitors of the parties in every cause, and they in fact kept the records of the causes, and they compelled suitors to have useless copies of the proceedings at huge fees. It was to their interest to encourage litigation and the multiplication of formal documents. It was necessary for the fees to be large, since each of the Six Clerks had eight sworn clerks (which formed the body, known later, when the number in 1668 was increased to ten, as the Sixty Clerks), who were "paid a fixed percentage of the fees paid by suitors to the Six Clerks."[1] In Bacon's time, and before he attained judicial office, the Court of Chancery was not only necessarily corrupt, but also almost irreformable. "The fees were excessive, and the officials who received them were the most determined opponents to effective reform. . . . These officials did their work by deputies, whom they generally underpaid. Their deputies naturally tried to recoup themselves by questionable practices. Sometimes they concealed business from their superiors and kept the fees. . . . Thus, while the actual work was badly done by underpaid deputies, the suitor paid enormous fees to sinecure officials. These officials naturally regarded their offices merely as property. They were sold by the Chancellor or given to his relations. . . . From the Lord Chancellor, who sold the higher offices, to the under-clerk, who did the work of the higher official, all had an interest in maintaining the system. The Court, it was said with some truth, was 'a mere monopolie to cozen the subjects of their monies.'" There was nothing corrupt, as things were then understood, in Bacon's scandalous

[1] W. S. Holdsworth, *History of English Law*, p. 217.

offer to Sir Thomas Egerton. The Lord Keeper had something to sell and Bacon had something to buy with. The legal atmosphere where such a proposal could be made is the thing that makes one wonder. Bacon's conviction in 1622 did nothing to clear the atmosphere, which grew worse and worse. The price of the Mastership went up. In 1688 it was worth a thousand pounds ; and when Lord Macclesfield was impeached in 1725 it was worth six times that sum. This scandal was ended with the impeachment ; but the Chancery did not improve, and yet in 1816 Lord Eldon saw little that needed change. The best of men in the atmosphere of the Court of Chancery, up till comparatively recent times, had their whole moral nature perverted. It is still possible for a solicitor-trustee to involve an estate in an action against the wish of his clients, and for the sole purpose of incurring costs ; but such cases are rare. Yet it is not so long ago since the initiation of such actions by solicitors on the advice of counsel was regarded as legitimate professional enterprise and part of the daily task of otherwise quite blameless men. If Bacon was regarded as an honest man when he made his unsavoury offer in 1597, it is difficult to see why he was other than honest in 1622. The taking of large "expedition fees" and gifts from suitors after the conclusion of suits was not one iota more corrupt than the sale of judicial offices to notoriously unfit persons. It would be absurd to charge Lord Eldon with corruption, but his official life was lived in the midst of abuses which he never lifted a hand to reform. There was hardly a Chancellor from Bacon to Eldon who was not, in a court of conscience, as guilty as Bacon. Indeed, in the mid-eighteenth century "expedition fees" were so well recognized that in 1740 a committee of the House of Commons recommended their abolition. "Hardwicke signed the report. But he introduced no measure of reform. During the latter part of the eighteenth century all projects of reform seem to have been abandoned. No general orders were made by any Chancellor from Hardwicke (1737-57) to Loughborough (1793-1801)." As we shall see, Bacon did attempt to cleanse these Augean stables. That he was abominably soiled in the attempt, no one, and himself the least, denies. But he was, in the eyes of his own age, a political and not a criminal offender. He received his deserts, but not at the hands of justice. In the pathetic "Epistle Dedicatory" to "an advertisement touching an holy war," written after his fall in the year 1622, he compares himself to Demosthenes, Cicero, and Seneca : " all three ruined, not by war, or by any other disaster, but by justice and sentence, as delinquents and criminals ; all three famous writers, insomuch as the remembrance of their calamity is now, as to posterity, but as a little picture of night-work, remaining amongst the fair and excellent tables of their acts and works." This—and indeed the whole epistle, with its reference to " mine own country which I have ever loved," fails to strike the note of conscious guilt. Bacon knew perfectly well that Chancery was pitch, and that it was impossible to touch it without defilement. Again and again he would gladly have given up the law. The opportunity never offered. A man with a profession and nothing else must live by it. He had to reconcile himself to live by the law in the way that the men of his times and for more than two centuries after did live by it—a way certainly not honest, but a way that seemed honester to them than to us who have not their temptations.

The Maxims and the Digest.—It has been necessary to refer somewhat at large to the question of legal corruption at this stage, for it enables us to realize a little more clearly the manner of man that Bacon was and the difficulties of his path. We can now rapidly survey the remainder of his life as a lawyer. Immediately before his second application to Lord Ellesmere, Bacon had taken his seat as member for Southampton in the Parliament that met on October 24, 1597. He did not obtain the Rolls, and pursued his practice at the Bar. But legal projects more important even than practice were at this very period in his mind. The valuable work on the *Maxims of the Law* was composed in 1596-7. It must be read in connection with the principles of a Digest of English Law laid down in the 82nd and subsequent aphorisms in the 8th Book *De Augmentis* (published in 1623), and in the *Proposal for Amending the Laws of England*, and with other attempts to deal with the subject, such as the treatise *De Diversis Regulis Juris*, which he made from time to time henceforth almost to the close of his life. On May 2nd, 1614, Bacon introduced a bill " giving authority to certain commissioners to review the state of the penal laws, to the end that such as are obsolete and snaring may be repealed ; and such as are fit to continue, and concern one matter, may be reduced respectively into one clear form of law." This was followed, about June, 1614, by a memorial to the King, asking him to appoint a Commission on the Penal Laws and to codify the Reports that embodied the Common Law, and to restore the system of Official Reporters in order to create an authoritative body of Case Law. The attempts were never perfected. In the Epistle Dedicatory of 1622 he refers to the *De Augmentis Scientiarum:* " I have also entered into a work touching Laws, propounding a character of Justice, in a middle term, between the speculative and reverend discourses of philosophers, and the writings of lawyers which are tied and obnoxious to their particular laws. And although it be true that I had a purpose to make a particular digest or recompilement of the laws of mine own nation; yet because it is a work of assistance, and that I cannot master by mine own forces and pen, I have laid it aside." The *Maxims of the Law* is all that we have in a finished form of this designed Digest. We may well believe that he had no heart for it after the disastrous events of March, 1522. He preferred to revise his published writings and put into form some of his scientific work. The law was a broken bank. He preferred to invest his " poor talent, or half-talent " in " banks or mounts of perpetuity which will not break." The *Instauration* was not burdened with recollections of the Chancery.

As the century drew towards its close, Bacon's reputation as a practical lawyer and as an authority on great legal questions drew him into the important causes of the day (such as *Slade's Case* in 1596 and *The Lord Cromwell's Case* in 1601, reported by Coke), and placed him in the front rank of the profession. It is difficult to compare him with his only serious rival, Sir Edward Coke; but there can be little doubt that Bacon welcomed comparison. The *Statute of Uses* provided the most acute legal controversy of the age. Coke, as Reader at the Inner Temple in 1592, had dealt most successfully with this subject, and he appeared with Bacon in the great *Chudleigh Case* in 1594, when the functions of uses were analyzed with all the most refined reasoning that decadent Aristotelianism could provide. Bacon did not hesitate as to his theme when, on November 9, 1599, he was offered the Double Readership at Gray's Inn. He accepted the offer on November 14, and in the Lent Vacation of 1600 he gave his famous *Reading on the Statute of Uses*, which extended over six or possibly nine days. He was certainly not afraid of the precedent set by Coke. He deliberately challenged comparison. In this elaborate study, as in the *Maxims of the Law*, he wished to appear as a lawyer who not only rivalled but outshone the only man, with the possible exception of Croke, who stood in his rank.

On the Coronation Day of James I., Bacon was knighted, and shortly afterwards he married a daughter of Alderman Barnham, who presumably brought money as well as beauty to the now famous lawyer. In 1607 he obtained the long-desired Solicitor-Generalship.

The Case of the Post-Nati and Others.—There are extant certain arguments of law delivered by Bacon whilst Solicitor or Attorney, some corrected by his hand. There were the case of the Post-Nati of Scotland,[1] argued in 1607 in the Exchequer Chamber before the Lord Chancellor and all the judges; the case of the jurisdiction of the Marches, argued in 1604 by Bacon and Sir John Croke on behalf of the Council of the Marches against Coke, who appeared for the King's Bench, and again argued, this time before Coke, in 1608; *Lowe's Case of Tenures* (argued before 1616, in the King's Bench, see 9 Co. 23); *Lady Stanhope's Case of Revocation of Uses* (argued before 1616); the *Case of Impeachment of Waste* (*Lewis Bowle's Case*, 11 Co. 79), decided in 1615; and the *Case de Rege in consulto* (*Brownlow* v. *Michell*), argued in 1615-6.[2] In 1608 Bacon produced the legal compositions which were published in 1641, under the title of *Cases of Treason*. These writings include the papers known as the *Preparation of the Union of Laws* and the *Answers to the Questions of Sir A. Hay*. In 1614 was published his charge as Attorney-General "touching Duells, upon an information in the Starchamber against Priest and Wright. With the decree of the Star Chamber in the same cause."[3] In 1609 the Solicitor-General was elected Treasurer of Gray's Inn, a position which he held until he became Lord Chancellor in 1617. As Treasurer he laid out the walks and gardens of Gray's Inn, and induced the Bench to

---

[1] Bacon's speeches in this case, and his speech or papers on *The Union of the Lawes of the Kingdomes of England and Scotland*, were "published by the author's copy and licensed by authority" by Richard Badger in 1641. The *Cases of Treason*, published in the same year, also contained the essay on *The Union of Laws*, though probably a variant in form. The interest taken in the subject at this date was natural.

[2] We may also mention the interesting argument on the subject of Royal Forests in a deer-stealing case before the Star Chamber on October 23rd, 1614. The official charges against Oliver St. John, Owen, Sir John Wentworth, and the Earl and Countess of Somerset in 1615-6 hardly come within the scope of this paper.

[3] This appears to be a very scarce volume. Mr. Spedding reprints it. The copies were "printed for Robert Wilson, and are to be sold at Graies Inn Gate, and in Paules Churchyard at the signe of the Bible, 1614."

spend much money on this laudable object. The Pension Book tells us of the planting of many red roses and of much sweet-briar, while possibly some of the beeches and elms that he planted (at eightpence and tenpence each) survive even to this day. In 1613 Bacon became at last Attorney-General, and on March 11, 1616-7, he received the Great Seal that his father had laid down thirty-eight years before. A little later (1618) he became Lord Chancellor, with the title of Lord Verulam, to which was subsequently added, in 1621, the peerage of St. Albans.

Tothill's Reports.—The only law reports that cover this period are Tothill's. There are sixty-nine decisions in Chancery reported in Tothill between March 11, 1616-7, and May 3, 1621. This would seem a really rich source from which to derive some adequate knowledge of the work of Bacon as a judge. In fact, however, Tothill is a mine of disappointments. There are few of the cases that are at all intelligible as reported, and those that are intelligible often enough suggest erroneous reporting.[1]

---

[1] It will be convenient, however, to give a list of these cases. The page in Tothill is given after the regnal year. Curious persons may think it worth while to search the Chancery records for further particulars as to these cases. The list is as follows :

Gardiani de Eltham (15 Jac. 7), *Hunt* v. *Bancroft* (14 Jac. & 15 Jac. 146), *Mudget* v. *Davies* (15 Jac. 20), *Middleton's Case* (15 Jac. 32), *B's Case* (Hil. 15 Jac. 47-8), *Stafford* v. *Pasch* (15 Jac. 49), *Watson* v. *Maihne* (*Mich.* 15 Jac. 101), *Tirwhit's Case* (15 Jac. 110), *Dean and Chapter of Westminster* v. *Eldridge* (15 Jac. 110), *Simeon* v. *Dean of Windsor* (Trin. 15 Jac. 123), *Bayliff* v. *Longworth* (15 Jac. 140), *Holmes* v. *Conway* (15 Jac. 143), *Warcroft* v. *Lord Culpepper* (Mich. 15 Jac. 159), *Pistle* v. *Hardie* (Mich. 15 Jac. 180), *Middleton* v. *Lort* (Mich. 15 Jac. 180), *Wilson* v. *Dunstar* (Mich. 15 Jac. 181), *Garford* v. *Humble* (Mich. 16 Jac. 26), *Moreton* v. *Briggs* (Hil. 16 Jac. 43), *Denis* v. *Carew* (16 Jac. 63), *Wiat* v. *Wiat* (Mich. 16 Jac 93), *Goodfellow* v. *Morris* (Mich. 16 Jac. 131), *Price* v. *Lloyd* (circa 16 Jac. 137), *Austen* v. *Cheney* (Trin. 16 Jac. 138), *Lupton* v. *Harman* vel *Harmon* (Pasche Trin. and Mich. 16 Jac. 139 & 176), *Rowswell* v. *English* (Trin. 16 Jac. 147), *Starkey* v. *Starkey* (Mich. or Hil. 16 Jac. 149), *Harrington* v. *Horton & Cox* (circa 16 Jac. 156). *Dimmock* v. *Williams* (Mich. 16 Jac. 159), *Garfield* [vel *Garford ?*] v. *Humble* (16 Jac. 159), *Tooker* v. *Mayor of Exeter* (Mich. 16 Jac. 165), *Waller* v. *Waller* (16 Jac. 168), *Freeman* v. *Hugget* (Hil. 16 Jac. 168), *Ancher* v. *Frith* (16 Jac. 176), *Frith* v. *Trion* (16 Jac. 176), *Little* v. *Good* (Trin. 16 Jac. 181), *Arleston* v. *Kent* (Feb. 17 Jac. 27), *Hansly* v. *Hansly* (Trin. 17 Jac. 93), *Anon : Case* (17 Jac. 94), *Cartwright* v. *Drope* (Mich. 17 Jac. 110), *Barkley* v. *Pierson* (Trin. 17 Jac. 113), *Tiffin* v. *Tiffin* (Hill 17 Jac. 113), *Finch* v. *Hicks* (Hil. or Pasch. 17 Jac. 113), *Shapcot* v. *Dowrish* (Trin. 17 Jac. 138), *Hooe* v. *Arnold* (circa 17 Jac. 146), *Morgan* v. *Richardson* (Hil. 17 (?) 18 Jac. 154), *Banister* v. *Brooke* (Mich. 17 Jac. 158), *Lord Pembroke* v. *Eyre* (17 Jac. 158), *Thornburgh* v. *Grobdam* (circa 17 Jac. 161), *Huet* v. *Hurston* (17 Jac. 168), *Hoskets* v. *Hillier* (Pasche 17 Jac. 169), *Roane* v. *Stepney* (17 or 18 Jac. 176), *Prentice* v. *Roupe* (17 Jac. 176), *Eardley* v. *Eltonhead* (17 (? 15) Jac. 177), *Overmann* v. *Wright* (Hil. 17 Jac. 177) *Newton* v. *Price* (Pasche 17 Jac. 180), *Bourne* v. *Ironmonger* (Mich. 17 Jac. 181), *Peacock* v. *Reynell* (June 17 Jac. 186), *Hunt* v. *Youngman* (17 Jac. 187), *Long* v. *Long* (Hil. 17 (?) Jac. 190), *Posthumus Hobbie* v. *Smith* (18 Jac. 11), *Sacheverell* v. *Sacheverell* (18 Jac. 38), *Nelson* v. *Yelverton* (18 Jac.

The only further legal works with which Bacon was connected that need be referred to here[1] are the *Ordinances in Chancery.* It is certain that a considerable number, and it is probable that a good many, of these Ordinances were his own, were his attempt to cleanse the Chancery.

Bacon as a Jurist: an Appreciation.—We have now named in chronological order the various legal works that Bacon left to the world, and have indicated so far as was necessary the main facts of his life as a lawyer. The general impression left upon the mind by a perusal of the disordered fragments and arguments that constitute his contribution to the history of law and by an observation of his legal career is one of disappointment. His massive intellect and subtle mind appear at first never to have been persistently applied to, though they often approached and dallied with, the great problems of jurisprudence. One is tempted to imagine that he never repaid to the law of England the debt which he owed to it. He was a great advocate and a great pleader, we say, "great, even as a lawyer," to use Lord Coleridge's critical phrase, but there is no evidence to show that he was a great judge, and little evidence to prove that he was a great jurist. That is the way in which a perusal of the professional works inevitably at first strikes the reader. He lived by the law, but the law did not live by him. A second and third reading leave a different impresion. We realize that it is greatly due to the fragmentary character of the legal remains that this somewhat sordid impression arises. Bacon did in fact live by the law, and was on the whole careless as to the literary merit of his legal writings. When he thought that such writings were likely to advance him, he was at times, as in the case of the Four Arguments of Law, more careful. But not always. We have but a disordered fragment of his famous Double Reading on the Statute of Uses. We ought, if Bacon is a great jurist, to be able to disregard the disordered condition of his legal writings, and to find therein an essential orderliness and dry luminosity of thought calculated to give life to the law he lived by. The more closely Bacon's legal works are studied the more certain it becomes that this is the case, and the reader is more and more tempted to regret that his

---

39-40), *Grant* v. *Edes* (18 Jac. 42), *Harris* v. *Beadle* (Hil. 18 Jac. 73), *Dom Crispe* (Pasche or Trin. 18 Jac. 94), *Long* v. *Long* (18 Jac. 169), *Cottle* v. *Brooke* (Pasche 18 Jac. 176), *Underhill* v. *Joyner* (18 Jac. 184-5).

[1] The *Use of the Law* attributed to him is certainly an apocryphal treatise.

legal conceptions have been so rarely pursued and so generally disregarded. It will be useful briefly to consider the works in their chronological order.

The Commission of Bridewell.—The *Brief Discourse upon the Commission of Bridewell* was written in 1587, when Bacon was twenty-six years of age. It is in many ways a remarkable paper, showing an extraordinary knowledge of Statute and Case Law bearing upon constitutional questions. It is an argument against the legality of a charter granted to the city of London by the Crown, empowering the Governor of Bridewell to arrest, imprison, and punish evil characters in the city at his discretion. Bacon lays down the proposition that "a King's grant either repugnant to law, custom, or statute is not good nor pleadable in the law," and establishes it with abundant reference to the Statute Book and the Year Books. He then goes on to say, "Yet do not we see daily in experience that whatsoever can be procured under the Great Seal of England is taken *quasi sanctum;* and although it be merely against the laws, customs, and statutes of this realm, yet it is defended in such sort, that some have been called rebellious for not allowing such void and unlawful grants." Here, in no mincing language, was laid down the constitutional position that it was to be the special privilege of the seventeenth century to redeem. Bacon from first to last had no doubt of the limitations of the Crown, though when he held the Seal he dared not rebuke licence in high places, as his father had done. The weakness of the mother who excused Francis from the frugal commons of Gray's Inn played its fatal part in his character. But Bacon, if we may believe Tothill's report in *Sir Thomas Middleton's Case*,[1] was no favourer of corruption on the part of Crown officials. In that case the master and mariners of a government vessel agreed that a rateable proportion should be deducted from their wages for the relief of such of the crew as should be maimed at sea. Sir Thomas Middleton, the Treasurer for the Navy in 1590, at the end of the voyage paid the wages, but detained the rateable proportion that had been agreed to be deducted for the relief of the maimed seafaring men. The detention was made despite the fact that there were no members of the crew who had a right to claim the deduction. Bacon held that the Treasurer for the Navy must account to the crew for this money. He refused, in fact, to recognise that a Government department was above the

[1] P. 32, 15 Jac.

law or could override either a contract or the ordinary principles of equity. The case is both interesting and important, and apparently shows that Bacon was entirely proof against the influence that would naturally at that date have been brought to bear upon him in such a case. The cause, moreover, proves that throughout his career he refused to recognize any unconstitutional claims of the Crown. It is also an instance of the delay of justice that blotted the Chancery of England. Bacon's decision was given about thirty years after the cause of action arose.

The King's Prerogative.—*The Cases of the King's Prerogative* which Bacon adopted, if he did not actually compile, in 1608, admirably summarizes the prerogatival power, in matters relating to Parliament, to the persons of the King's subjects, to war and peace, money, trade, and traffic. There is no word in this terse code that clashes with Bacon's views expressed in the matter of the Bridewell Charter, in 1587, or in the Seafarer's Wages' Case in 1618. The *Preparation for the Union of Laws*, which was for the most part printed in *Cases of Treason* in 1641, and also in a volume of speeches published in the same year, is undoubtedly from Bacon's hand, and belongs, with its remarkable preface, to the year 1608. No word in this criminal code or its preface modifies the constitutional position that Bacon from the first held. In the preface he specially points out that the King has of himself no power of codifying existing laws, or of bringing the laws of England and Scotland into conformity, but that he can deal with administrative questions, such as the rearrangement of circuits and of the method of issuing commissions of peace.

The next work that requires some notice is the *Maxims of the Law*, composed when Bacon was thirty-five years of age.[1] It was dedicated to " Her Most Sacred Majesty "; to the Queen who never forgave his early protest in Parliament against illegal and unconstitutional subsidies, a protest the spirit of which (despite Macaulay's view) never fails in all Bacon's constitutional writings. The dedication, if stripped of its fine flowers of bitterness— " for if your government be considered in all the parts it is incomparable "—is an unflinching indictment of the evils of a system that Bacon himself was destined to administer, and a passionate plea for reform. He says :

---

[1] The argument in *Chudleigh's Case* was composed two years earlier, but that should be read with the Reading of 1600.

"Your Majesty's reign having been blest from the Highest with inward peace, and falling into an age wherein, if science be increased, conscience is rather decayed ; and if men's wits be great, their wills be more great ; and wherein also laws are multiplied in number, and slackened in vigour and execution ; it was not possible but that not only suits in law should multiply and increase, whereof always a great part are unjust, but also that all the indirect and sinister courses and practices to abuse law and justice should have been much attempted and put in use : which no doubt had bred greater enormities, had they not, by the royal policy of your Majesty, by the censure and foresight of your Council table and Star-Chamber, and by the gravity and integrity of your Benches, been repressed and refrained : for it may be freely observed, that, as concerning frauds in contracts, bargains, and assurances, and abuses of laws by delays, covins, vexations, and corruptions in informers, jurors, ministers of justice, and the like, there have been sundry excellent statutes made in your Majesty's time, more in number, and more politic in provision, than in any of your Majesty's predecessors' times."

The Plea for Codification.—Codification of the laws, he feels, is the only remedy for the many evils, and draws hope from the Queen's speech of 1593 of "a general amendment of the state of your laws, and to reduce them to more brevity and certainty ; that the great hollowness and unsafety in assurances of lands and goods may be strengthened ; the snaring penalties that lie upon many subjects removed ; the execution of many profitable laws revived ; the judge better directed in his sentence ; the counsellor better warranted in his counsel ; the student eased in his reading ; the contentious suitor that seeketh but vexation disarmed ; and the honest suitor that seeketh but to obtain his right relieved."

Perhaps the need for codification and the results springing from it have never been put so forcibly and happily before or since. Bacon, indeed, hoped much from the personal influence of the Queen, and believed, too, in the strengthening of the Crown that would result from a strengthening of the laws. The relationship of the Crown and the laws, not in their creation, but in their operation, was a note that he never tired of striking. In his pamphlet[1]

---

[1] As to authorship see *Acta Canellaiæ*, pp. 236-8, and *Lord Bacon's Works*, xiii., pp. 106, 115.

on the murder of Sir John Tyndale by Bertram — not printed by Spedding—he says: "The law is a dumb king, the King a speaking law. All subordinate judges are but organ-pipes, to sound forth such notes of concord as the King sets to keep his kingdoms in tune; so that if any one jar, no subject is to take upon him to mend or correct, but to tell the fault to him, who is the chief master of that music, and to let his ears distinguish the tunes." Beside this statement should be placed the picture of a perfect judge as drawn by Bacon in his famous essay on *Judicature*. He could not do the things that he would.

The Maxims of the Law.—The *Maxims of the Law* are Bacon's contribution to the perfect organ of law upon which he wished the King to play and produce perfect harmony. The Epistle Dedicatory and the Preface throw no mean light on the question of codification. He recalled Elizabeth's mind to the triumphs of Augustus Cæsar:

"*Pace data terris, animum ad civilia vertit
Jura suum; legesque tulet justissimus auctor.*"

He reminded her of Justinian, whose pride it was "to revisit the Roman laws, and to reduce them from infinite volumes and much repugnancy into one competent and uniform corps of law." He pointed out that the time of peace is the time of reform, since peace produces "abundance of wealth and fineness of cunning . . . multitude of suits and controversies, and abuses of laws by evasions and devices." He felt called to aid in the work of reform, for "I hold every man a debtor to his profession; from the which, as men of course do seek to receive countenance and profit, so ought they of duty to endeavour themselves, by way of amends, to be a help and ornament thereunto. This is performed in some degree by the honest and liberal practice of a profession, when men shall carry a respect not to descend into any course that is corrupt and unworthy thereof, and preserve themselves free from the abuses wherewith the same profession is noted to be infected; but much more is this performed if a man be able to visit and strengthen the roots and foundations of the science itself; thereby not only gracing it in reputation and dignity, but also amplifying it in perfection and substance." It is a pathetic statement of an ideal, a confession of a high faith, that Bacon, if history be true, deliberately abandoned. It tempts the reader to believe that there is some mystery yet unsolved behind the corruption of Lord St. Albans. In face of the evidence it seems, however, impossible to suggest that that corruption was the work of his clerks by which he never benefited, but for which he was morally and legally responsible.

In his preface he goes on to declare that from the first his object had been that the laws should be the better by his industry, and that that object would be best attained " by collecting the rules and grounds dispersed throughout the body of the same laws," and so abolish the great evil of English law—its uncertainty— and correct its " unprofitable subtlety." He felt it would have been possible to have digested " these rules into a certain method, or order, which, I know, would have been more admired, as that which would have made every particular rule, through his coherence and relation into other rules, seem more cunning and more deep." This suggestion is in itself one that is of immense value. He conceived the upbuilding of a coherent organic code of law out of the heterogeneous materials that lay to hand on every side. He specifically affirms the possibility of creating such a code, and the conception was one that could only spring from a great jurist. He apologizes for not undertaking the work. He desired merely to produce a code of immediate usefulness. He aimed at " a work without any glory of affected novelty, or of method, or of language, or of quotations and authorities, dedicated on to use, and submitted only to the censure of the learned, and chiefly of time." Bacon never produced the work that he designed. The *Maxims of the Law* are, so to speak, a sample of the work. When he became Attorney-General he was again labouring at it, and he actually issued his *Proposal for Amending the Laws of England*. Later still, in the *De Augmentis Scientiarum*, he is still thinking the work out. But it never attained form. We have fragments and suggestions all of great worth, and teeming with the wealth of ideas. But we have no code that could be submitted to "the censure of time." He realized that the actual working out of a digest of the laws of England could not be undertaken by one hand. The lapse of three centuries leaves his conception still in the main unrealized. In 1605 it could easily have been realized, but in 1905 we have the Justinianean task many times magnified before us. Bacon's fragment, the *Maxims of the Law*, does not call for analysis here. No one but a profound lawyer could have produced it, and it may be read with profit by the practising lawyer at the present hour.[1] However, this is not the place in which to deal with the *Maxims* in detail. The point of value is that Bacon, in an age of subtle prolixity, advocated the codification of the law, and demonstrated by experiment its possibility.

Chudleigh's Case : The Statute of Uses. — Some further reference must be made to *Chudleigh's Case* of 1594 and the Reading on the *Statute of Uses* of 1600. *Chudleigh's Case* raised the following point : A infeoffed certain persons of the land in question to the use of A and the heirs of his body, with remainder to the use of the feoffees and their heirs during the life of A's eldest son B, with remainder in tail to B's male issue, with remainder to A's other sons then living *nominatim* in succession, with remainder to A's right heirs in fee. A died in the lifetime of the feoffees, who infeoffed B in fee to the exclusion of the subsequent remaindermen. B had issue two sons, S and John, who possessed contingent uses so excluded. B infeoffed a stranger C, who infeoffed another stranger D ; S died without issue, and after B's death, his younger son John entered and granted a lease to Freine, the plaintiff in the action. Dillon, the representative of D, re-entered on Freine, who thereupon brought an action of trespass. Bacon and Coke were instructed to argue that as there was no estate left on the feoffees at the time when John's estate would have fallen into possession, his interest had gone. The action for trespass was dismissed by the majority of the judges in the Exchequer Chamber on the ground that where future uses are not vested they can only be executed when they arise if the feoffees possess a right to enter in pursuance of a *scintilla juris et tituli* or vestige of estate remaining in them. Chudleigh's feoffees had parted with their *scintilla*, and therefore John Chudleigh had no estate. Bacon, in his elaborate and weighty argument, urged the doctrine of the *scintilla juris*, as in duty bound ; but he lost no opportunity to scoff at the argument of Coke, the prime supporter of the doctrine. On the subject of this doctrine he says : " And

---

[1] The modern lawyer will, however, refuse to concede some of the propositions. The fifth maxim, *Necessitas inducit privilegium quoad jura privata*, carries the doctrine of necessity beyond our present limits. " First of conservation of life : If a man steal viands to satisfy his present hunger, this is no felony nor larceny." Staundford is quoted in support of this proposition. Bacon, under the same heading, deals with the question to which Sir James Stephen refers of two men clinging to a plank capable of supporting only one. Bacon declares that it is lawful for one to thrust the other away. Stephen declares the act not punishable (but see *R. v. Dudley and Stephens*, 14 Q.B.D. at pp. 285-6).

for that which has been objected, that the use is in the keeping of the law, and that nothing is in the feoffees; it is true that the use is preserved by the law, but not executed by the statute before the time. And therefore it appears, by evident demonstration, that an interest remains in the feoffees. A fee simple absolute is passed to the feoffees in possession, only a fee simple defeasible is executed by the statute, as is proved: if then the lesser estate be subtracted and deducted out of the greater, it is of necessity that a surplusage remains.[1] . . . This is the medium between the two estates; and if the first *cestui que use* be disseised and continued disseised, and the limitation comes in use, the first use ceases, and the second cannot rise by reason of the removing of the possession out of privity. And so the feoffees come to have right, and can enter or bring their writ of right; but after they have re-entered or recovered, the use now takes the possession from them. But in our case the feoffees are disabled by their own feoffment." The doctrine of the *scintilla juris et tituli* could hardly be put higher. Bacon was quite capable of playing the Neo-Aristotelians with their own weapons. But he did not for a moment accept his own argument. He was personally satisfied to establish what *Chudleigh's Case* in the long run only did establish, the common law control over statutory uses that could take effect as common law uses. In his arguments in this case and *Lady Stanhope's Case* on the revocation of uses, it is clear that he did not recognize the existence of statutory uses rendered indefeasible by that very fact of their independence of the common law. To him the statute of Henry VIII. " alters not the law as to raising of uses, but only to draw the possession after them. Wherefore if a contingent use could not rise at common law if the possession of the feoffees was estranged without regress, so no more can it at this day: for the statute leaves all questions of rising of an use merely to the common law, and makes no alteration." The statute must not be bent to meet the equity of the case. In *Chudleigh's Case* he told the Court bluntly: "For, as you, my lords judges, better know, so, with modesty, I may put it in your remembrance, that your authority over the

[1] He previously quotes Dyer on the point, " Adhuc remanet quaedam scintilla juris et tituli, quasi medium quid inter utrosque status. Which words are very significant. For the most proper sense is that, if two uses be limited, one to determine and the other to commence, between the cesser of the one and the rising of the other, the foeffees (who are vessels, as Mr Atkinson terms them) receive the land from the one *cestui que use* and deliver it to the other, and have a right, in the sight of the law, between the two."

laws and statutes of this realm is not such as the Papists affirm the Church to have over the Scriptures, to make them a shipman's hose or nose of wax; but such as we say the Church has over them, *scil*, to expound them faithfully and apply them properly."[1] His argument may well be memorable for such a pronouncement as this, which illustrates his entire position as a constitutional jurist. But the Reading seems to show his recognition of the fact that the statute did create a new type of use that could take effect without the aid of the common law, though he does not analyze the distinction between the two types of limitations. His main point is that a use is a species of property moulded by its creator, and not a mere metaphysical imitation of a real possession. "A conveyance in use is nothing but a publication of the trust." He will have no metaphysical imagining in an operative law. Realities are the only things that matter. "The conceit of *scintilla juris*" must disappear with the Lincoln's Inn subtlety of "imitation of possession." "The statute . . . succeeds in office to the feoffees," and it is the illogical will of Parliament, and not a logical spark of title dwelling *in gremio legis* or in the heavens, that keeps intact each tenuous remainder. Coke and Bacon both argued in *Chudleigh's Case*, and both read on the Statute of Uses; but it was Bacon only who realized that it was necessary finally to abolish the relationship of scholasticism and law. Bacon declines in his Reading "to stir conceits and subtle doubts, or to contrive a multitude of tedious and intricate cases, whereof all, saving one, are buried, and the greater part of that one case which is taken is commonly nothing to the matter in hand. But my labour shall be in the ancient course, to open the law upon doubts, and not to open doubts upon the law." It was his function, in fact, finally to extinguish the *scintilla juris* in the grave that he digged for the Schoolmen.[2]

Some space must be devoted—much ought to be devoted—to other great arguments. The case of the Post-Nati of Scotland (*Calvin's Case*) was, as Bacon told the Court, "of exceeding great consequence." The question was whether natives of England or Scotland were or were not naturalized in both kingdoms after

[1] See also the Essay on Judicature.
[2] In fact, the *scintilla juris* flickered up and down Lincoln's Inn until the passing of Lord St. Leonard's Act, 1860 (23 & 24 Vict., c. 38, s. 7), which specifically declared that no "*seisin to uses* or *scintilla juris*" should "be deemed necessary for the support of or to give effect to future or contingent or executory uses."

the accession of James. The Commissioners of Union in 1605 had advised in favour of the double naturalization; and in view of the attitude of the Commons, the matter was fully discussed by a hybrid committee of the two Houses on February 25, 1606-7. The next day ten judges against one advised the Lords in favour of the Post-Nati, thus confirming the view indicated before the committee by Lord Ellesmere. The Commons, however, refused to pass a declaratory Act, and consequently the Crown arranged the hearing of a specific case dealing with the question before the Easter term of the following year. Bacon argued for the Post-Nati, and his view was adopted by the Lord Chancellor and thirteen judges. Foster and Walmsley were the sole dissentients. Bacon's argument is very elaborate, and is professedly based upon "the foundations and fountains of reason." Was naturalization accessory to sovereignty, which in this case was joint, or to the legislature, which was several, was "the depth of this question." He appealed to a Schoolman's edition of Aristotle to prove that a monarchy is the natural state of government—"from the Monarch of heaven and earth to the king, if you will, in an hive of bees": "other states are the creatures of law." This appeal to the law of nature, which had long unconsciously been moulding the juristic systems of Europe, in such a case is as remarkable as it was ingenious. But it required immediate modification. Bracton is quoted: *Lex facit quod ipse est Rex.* Moreover, "his acts and grants are limited by law, and we argue them every day. But I demand, Do these offices or operations of law evacuate or frustrate the original submission, which was natural? Or shall it be said that all allegiance is by law?" In a fine passage he declares that this is not so. "No man will affirm that the obedience of the child is by law, though laws in some points do make it more positive: and even so it is of allegiance of subjects to hereditary monarchs, which is corroborated and confirmed by law, but is the work of the law of nature." Then in a fine legal frenzy he confirmed his argument by adducing the parliamentary title, Our *natural* sovereign and liege lord, flung in the face of the judges the saying of one of them that he would never allow that Elizabeth "should be a statute Queen, but a common-law Queen," and concluded with a further reference to "*Our natural liege sovereign;* as Acts of Parliament speak: for as the common law is more worthy than the statute law; so the law of nature is more worthy than them both."

Some such speech as this it must have been to which Ben Jonson listened : " The fear of every man that heard him was lest he should make an end."

The Law of Nature.—The value that Bacon attached to the law of nature, to " Natural equity," is significant of his position as a jurist and of the general tendency of legal thought. " Our law is grounded upon the law of nature," he declares in a later part of the argument. " For, my lords, by the law of nature all men in the world are naturalized one towards another. They were all made of one lump of earth, one breath of God. . . . It was civil and national laws that brought in these words, and differences, of *civis* and *exterus*, alien and native. And therefore because they tend to abridge the law of nature, the law favoureth not them, but takes them strictly. . . . All national laws whatsoever are to be taken strictly and hardly in any point wherein they abridge and derogate from the law of nature. . . . Furthermore, as the law of England must favour naturalization as a branch of the law of nature, so it appears manifestly, that it doth favour it accordingly. . . . In such sort doth the law of England open her lap to receive in people to be naturalized ; which indeed showeth the wisdom and excellent composition of our law, and that it is the law of a warlike and a magnanimous nation fit for empire."

In this argument Bacon achieved a remarkable feat—the reconciliation to his own satisfaction of the allegiance of the subject to the King with the allegiance of the King to the law. The right divine of kings to govern right was really the conclusion achieved. So long as the King governed according to law, no one would question the divinity of his origin or the Trinitarian metaphysic of Plowden (borrowed, one would think, at the same time as the Schoolman's Aristotle, with a gleam of humour by the author of the *Novum Organum*), with respect to the dual personality of the King. This part of the argument was of great importance in the history of the development of English law, for it shows how the doctrine of natural law had developed since the date when the *Doctor and Student* had been written a century before. But the sting of the great argument was in its tail. The union of the two kingdoms was a necessity : *si inseparabiles insuperabiles*. The law of nature admits no competitors when it becomes the law of necessity. Francis Bacon was born a generation too soon. His force as a constitutional thinker, combined with his great powers in debate, would have gone far to solve problems already in his time ripening in the sunlight of public opinion. Common law monarchy might still be with us had Bacon and not Strafford advised Charles Stuart.

Bacon's influence as a constitutional lawyer did not abate. His famous argument on the writ *de non precedendo rege inconsulto* (*Brownlow* v. *Michell*), delivered immediately before he received the Great Seal, was a forensic triumph. He spoke for two hours and a half, and "lost not one auditor that was present at the beginning." Queen Elizabeth had attempted to create a new office in connection with the grant of patents. The judges refused to admit the nominee on the ground that it infringed Magna Charta, and the Queen yielded. James renewed the attempt, and appointed one Michel to the office. Brownlow, the Prothonotary, claimed the fees under an assize, and thereby questioned the right of the Crown to create the office. Bacon appeared for the Crown, and Coke, his ancient adversary, declared that he presented "a famous argument." The wisdom of the speech is undeniable. The old constitutional position is maintained. The advocate laughs to scorn the suggestion that the writ *de non precedendo* which he had presented is "a work of absolute power, or a strain of the prerogative, or shocking of justice, or infinite delay." The only question for the judges is a question of procedure; to wit, whether the King's constitutional right is to be tested in the King's Bench or in Chancery. The King has a right to be a party when his prerogative is questioned, and none can doubt that it is questioned here. "The King shall have choice of his Courts upon his demand; much more shall he have it upon his defence." The Court must know "how sharp-sighted the law of England is on the King's behalf to preserve his right from loss." All loss to the King is fetched in by this writ. "Now, to say that the King cannot grant or erect any office *de novo*, no man, I think, will be such a plebeian (I mean both in science and honour) as so to affirm; I will cite no books for it; you have the book of time, which is the best book, and perpetual practice." The holder of the office will have by this writ the protection of the King. "Therefore I will end with this to your lordship and the rest, that *obedience is better than sacrifice;* that is a voluntary thing, and it is many times a glory or fame; but obedience is ever acceptable." With which half-threat the Attorney-General hies him away to the King, to induce him, "because the times were as they were," to command the Chief Justice to suspend the proceedings. This was done. Had Charles possessed such an adviser, he too might have learnt that "the times were as they were," and have kept within those constitutional limits of the Crown that Bacon in his most strenuous and brilliant advocacy was always careful never to overstep. This fact, did space permit, might further be illustrated by the famous and elaborate argument in the case of *The Jurisdiction of the Marches*. Bacon's cautious constitutional position may be also observed by his attitude in the proceedings that led up to this case. The King would not extend or withdraw the Royal Prerogative as an object of legal attack save "by the advice of the three estates in Parliament."

Bacon and the Court of Chancery.—The work of Bacon as a judge forms a chapter of the history of law as yet unwritten in detail or indeed at all adequately. That he made his mark in the Court of Chancery is, however, not to be doubted, brief though his rule was and disastrous its end. It is almost impossible to deal with the decisions as set out in Tothill, but some references must be made to some of them. In *Arleston* v. *Kent* bonds entered into for procuring a marriage were cancelled. In *Sir Thomas Middleton's Case* a Government department was compelled to account. In *Sacheverell* v. *Sacheverell* a member of a Commission of Rebellion who had allowed a prisoner to escape was committed to prison until such time as the prisoner was brought in. In *Grant* v. *Edes* the plaintiff made a conveyance to feoffees in trust to the use of his infant sons, with several remainders over. The Court enabled him to sell the settled lands to pay debts contracted after the date of the settlement. In *Moreton* v. *Briggs* it was held that want of livery could not avoid a conveyance. In *Goodfellow* v. *Morris* the mistake of a name in a conveyance was rectified, and the lands assured accord- to the intention of the conveying party. In *Morgan* v. *Richardson* the plaintiff, although protected by a writ of privilege, had been arrested. He was freed by *Habeas Corpus*, and his arrestor committed. In *Huet* v. *Hurston* it was held that there was no relief after judgment. In *Long* v. *Long* (C. Hill 17 Tac.) it was held that a witness once examined may be recalled. Lord Ellesmere had decided the other way.

When we turn to the *Ordinances in Chancery* issued by Bacon, we find that his Hundred Rules of Court finally fixed practice in

Chancery, and made the Court of Chancery a definite court of justice under ordered governance, and not a mere court of conscience dealing out an erratic measure of equity in graciously disordered fashion. To what extent the Hundred Rules were from Bacon's hand it is perhaps not altogether easy to tell. It is probable that he codified the existing practice, which had been reduced to order by Lord Ellesmere, and brought into an organic form by the aid of many additions the scattered orders that existed before his time. It is natural to suppose that this would be done by a man so imbued with the idea of codification as was Bacon. The Rules as we have them show the stamp of a mind that could store great matter in a little room, and could provide future ages with a pattern of practice which, as laid up in the Lord Chancellor's mind, and as exhibited in his Hundred Ordinances, was the direct ancestor of those Rules of the Supreme Court that to-day are hidden in the arid wastes of the Annual Practice. It is no mean title to juridical fame finally to have settled the procedure in equity for the Anglo-Saxon race.[1] In this alone we see a feat that would justify a claim to greatness. But when we regard his Century of Orders, as we must regard them, merely as crumbs from the feast of law and reason which Francis Bacon offered to the world, we can to some extent realize how great a jurist was this great Englishman. He regarded human law as the sister of physical law. In studying the latter he had in contemplation "the general good of men in their very being, and the dowries of nature," and in the former "the general good of men likewise in society, and the dowries of Government." The two were related by that Law of Nature which he expounded in *Calvin's Case*. A universal rule of law for men and things was the ultimate concept of the man who took all law for his province, and believed in the natural equity that pervades creation.

[1] *Cf. Ordines Cancellariæ* (London, 1698) with the *Ordinances in Chancery*.

HUGO GROTIUS

HUGO GROTIUS

It was in the declining years of the second epoch into which the history of Jurisprudence is usually divided — namely, from the Fall of the Western Empire in A.D. 476 to the Peace of Westphalia in A.D. 1648 — that the great Dutch jurist whose name stands at the head of this paper lived and flourished. It was an epoch which embraced the Middle Ages and reached the threshold of modern times—a period marked by much stress and storm, but gradually chastened towards its close by a new spirit of humanitarianism, which, however dimly at first, began to create fresh ideals and to establish new principles of statecraft. And among the jurists whose names are associated with this new movement there is none in whom it finds a more precise and abiding expression than the scholar, the philosopher, the statesman, the poet, the historian, and the eminent jurist whose surname, first given to his grandfather, was Groot, or Greut, afterwards latinized into Grotius. Judged from every standpoint of human greatness, no surname could have been more appropriate or more worthily borne; and his portrait, painted by his contemporary Rubens, now in the Dresden Gallery, shows him to have been a man of noble bearing, handsome features, and benevolent expression, while all accounts agree in bearing testimony to his piety, probity, and profound learning. Dr. Johnson, referring to him in a letter he wrote to Dr. Vyse on behalf of a nephew of Grotius, speaks of him as one " of whom every learned man has perhaps learned something."

Family Origin.—Born at Delft on Easter Sunday, April 10th, 1583, four years after the seven northern provinces had constituted themselves into a separate political union known as the Utrecht Union, Hugo Grotius was descended on the paternal side from an aristocratic French family named Carnet. His great-grandfather was Cornelius Carnet, who married Ermingarde, the daughter and sole heiress of Diederic de Groot, Burgomaster of

Delft, who stipulated that the issue of the marriage should assume his own surname, which had been conferred upon one of his ancestors for eminent services to the State. It was in accordance with this stipulation that the son Hugo took the name of Groot, which thereafter became the family surname, and descended through John (or Jan), his father, to the subject of the present article. Learning appears to have been hereditary in the family, and John himself was a Doctor of Laws and Rector of the Leyden High School, and was distinguished as an eminent scholar and a lawyer of considerable repute. But Hugo, his son, soon eclipsed all the other members of the family by the extraordinary precocity of his intellect.

Early Precocity.—At the early age of nine he was an accomplished versifier of Latin elegiacs, and at twelve he had entered the University of Leyden, where he became the pupil of the celebrated scholar Joseph Scaliger, having already had his praises sung by Douza, who was said to be one of the princes of the republic of letters, and who announced that "Grotius would soon excel all his contemporaries and bear a comparison with the most learned of the ancients." Two years later the youthful prodigy produced an annotated edition of the abstruse work of Martiänus Mineus Felix Capella on *The Marriage of Mercury and Philology, or of Speech and Learning*, in which he displayed such learning and critical acumen as to astonish the literary world of his day. His own account of the preparation required for the production of this work shows the extent and varied character of his reading. "We have collated," he says, "Capella with the several authors who have investigated the same subjects. In the two first books, we have consulted those whose writings contain the sentiments of the ancient philosophers, as Apuleius, Albericus, and others too tedious to name; on grammar, we have compared Capella with the ancient grammarians; in what he has said on rhetoric, with Cicero and Aquila; on logic, with Porphyry, Aristotle, Cassiodorus, and Apuleius; on geography, with Strabo, Mela, Solinus, and Ptolemy, but chiefly Pliny; on arithmetic, with Euclid; on astronomy, with Hyginus, and others who have treated on this subject; on music, with Cleonides, Vitruvius, and Boëthius." Nor is this a mere vain or boastful enumeration by a boy of fourteen of the authorities he professed to have consulted, for his notes contain internal evidence of his close acquaintance with these ancient writers. In the same year he published a translation of a work upon navigation by Simon Steven in 1586, in which he displayed a vast knowledge of mathematics; and in the following year he completed the translation of the *Phenomena of Aratus*, a poetical treatise upon astronomy, which Cicero had previously translated, but which had come down to modern times in an incomplete form. In the opinion of a competent critic, the Abbé d'Olivet, the editor of Cicero's works, "the Muse of Cicero did not throw the Muse of Grotius into the shade," and Grotius was complimented on his elegant latinity by some of the greatest scholars of the time. So great was the reputation he had already acquired that in A.D. 1598 he was asked by the Dutch Ambassador to France, the illustrious but unfortunate Barneveldt, to accompany him, and on his arrival at the court of Henri IV. he was received by that monarch with many marks of personal favour. It was during this visit that he took the degree of Doctor of Laws at Orleans. On his return to his native country he devoted himself to the practice of the Bar, and conducted his first case before he had reached the age of seventeen. He succeeded at the Bar beyond all expectation, and was appointed Advocate-General of Holland, Zealand, and West Friesland when he was only twenty-four. He was indeed well described as an *adolescentem sine exemplo; juvenem portentosi ingenii;* and he was gifted with an extraordinary memory, of which many striking instances are recorded.

His Marriage.—In July, 1608, Grotius married a lady of Veere, in Zealand, of good family, named Mary Reigersberg, with whom he lived for the rest of his life in perfect harmony. She proved a devoted wife, and is said to have been an ornament to him in prosperity, and his comfort and aid in adversity. By her he had three sons and a daughter who survived him. It is asserted by some that George Grote, the historian of Greece, was connected with the family of Hugo Grotius, though the evidence is wanting to prove this. But the distinguished Netherlands statesman, Count Van Zuzlen van Nierseld, a former Ambassador of his country at Vienna, was certainly descended in direct line from the daughter of the celebrated jurist, who was married to a Frenchman named Mombas. His eldest and youngest son died without being married; but his second son, named Peter de Groot, became Pensionary of Amsterdam, and died at the age of seventy.

His Religious Tendencies.—The son of parents who were both imbued with a deep sense of piety, it was only natural that a youth of such marvellous talents and cosmopolitan sympathies as Grotius should have imbibed at an early age the religious tendencies of the period, under the guidance of a tutor such as Uitenbogaard, who was destined to play an important *rôle* in the subsequent religious controversies which distracted the Dutch Church. There were about this time two schools of religious thought in the Netherlands, which were violently divided on the dogmas of Free Will and Predestination, represented by two professors of the University of Leyden—namely, Jacob Arminius, Rector of the University, and Franciscus Gomarus, one of the professors. The former taught a modified form of Pelagianism, which sought to modify the extreme harshness of the doctrine of Predestination which had been adopted by Luther, Calvin, and Beza, and of which Gomarus, on the other hand, was an ardent and uncompromising supporter. The latter school being the more orthodox, as its followers were then considered, had the largest number of adherents, and its bitter hatred towards the Arminians subjected the latter to many cruel persecutions, which led to a formal Remonstrance, which was drawn up by the old tutor of Grotius, Uitenbogaard, and submitted to the States-General. Although it is probable that the sympathies of Grotius were all along on the side of the Remonstrants, it was not until the death of Arminius, in 1608, that he really showed his own religious tendencies. He then published a poem entitled *In mortem Arminii*, which at once identified him with the school of which Arminius had been the guiding spirit.

His mission to England as Ambassador to the Court of James I. in 1613 removed him for a time from the sphere of religious controversies, and in the same year he was made Pensionary of Rotterdam, which he only accepted on condition that he should not be deprived of it against his will. That he was able to impose such a condition shows the respect in which he was still held by his countrymen, and it would seem that he abstained at first from openly participating in the religious quarrels which were then becoming more acute. His natural desire was for peace, and he strove to bring about conciliation and a larger spirit of toleration. With this view he allowed himself to be nominated head of a mission to the city of Amsterdam, and he addressed the assembled burgomasters in a speech in the Dutch language, in which he pleaded eloquently for the necessity and advantage of religious toleration, especially upon points of theoretical doctrine, which he maintained would restore tranquillity and peace to the Church. But his eloquence produced no effect, and he was so affected by the bad success of his mission, that he was seized with a fever, which nearly proved fatal to him. By degrees his alienation from the Lutheran Reformed Church became more and more evident, and involved him in the persecution which overtook his old friend Barneveldt. Finally he was arrested on August 29th, 1618, with the latter and another fellow-thinker named Hogerbrets, the Pensionary of Leyden, at the instance of Prince Maurice of Nassau, and brought to trial upon charges of high treason and of disturbing the established religion of the United Provinces, and also of being the authors of the Insurrection of Utrecht. The arrest was surreptitiously effected, and a special tribunal of twenty-four (some authorities say twenty-six) commissioners was appointed to conduct the trial. The prisoners objected to the constitution of the tribunal, urging that the States of Holland were their only competent judges, and they also pointed out that many of the commissioners were their accusers and notoriously prejudiced against the Arminians. But these objections were all overruled ; the prisoners were condemned. The aged Barneveldt, then in his seventy-second year, was sentenced to death, which was duly carried out, and Hogerbrets and Grotius to perpetual imprisonment, the former in his own house, and the latter in the Castle of Louvestein, in South Holland, at the point of the island formed by the Vaal and the Meuse. Grotius reached the castle on June 6th, 1619, and for a time his imprisonment was of a very rigid character ; but by degrees this severity was to some extent relaxed, and his wife was allowed to see him twice a week, and he was also permitted to receive books from his friends and to correspond with them except on politics. This indulgence furnished an opportunity for escape, which was quickly seized and carried out by his resolute and devoted wife.

It had become customary for Grotius to receive a chest of books and linen for his use at regular intervals, and although this chest was at first rigorously examined by his guards, their vigilance was gradually relaxed, and the chest was allowed to enter his apartment without suspicion. His wife had observed this laxity, and accordingly devised a plan by which Grotius was to escape in one of these chests. As a preliminary move she represented that

Grotius was becoming ill through over-study, and expressed her intention of taking all his books away from him and restoring them to their owners. The next step was to introduce a sufficiently large chest, ostensibly for the purpose of removing the books, but really with the object of secreting her husband inside of it, and thus effecting his escape. Holes were bored into the box to let in air, and when everything was ready, Grotius was placed in the box, while his wife got into his bed, having previously informed his guards that her husband was ill and was not to be disturbed. The device was well carried out, and the box, with Grotius inside, was safely conveyed to Gorcum, where an Arminian friend received it and released Grotius from his peril. The wife remained behind and fearlessly informed the guards, when a sufficient time had elapsed to insure her husband's safety, that their prisoner had escaped. The governor of the prison at once ordered her into close confinement; but to the honour of the States-General be it added that she was released after a few days, and allowed to take with her everything that belonged to her in the Castle. Thus after twenty months of unjust incarceration, during which he produced the treatise in Dutch verse on the *Truth of the Christian Religion,* which he afterwards translated into Latin prose, and which was much admired for its terseness, just reasoning, accuracy, and power, Grotius became an exile from his native country, which he did not cease to love with the devotion of the true patriot he was. It cannot be denied, however, that his Protestantism was of a very mild character, and his epistles contain very strong evidence of a decided leaning towards the Roman Catholic Church, which appealed to him (apart from all questions of dogmatic theology, which had little influence with him) on the ground of a venerable and unbroken authority. At the same time many other sects claimed him as an adherent, and this circumstance furnished Menâge with the matter for the following epigram:

> "Smyrna, Rhodos, Colophon, Salamis, Chios, Argos, Athenæ,
>   Siderei certant vatis de patriâ Homeri;
> Grotiadæ certant de religione, Socinus,
>   Arrius, Arminius, Calvinus, Roma, Lutherus."

His Exile and Residence in France.—With his exile Grotius may be said to have entered upon the second stage of his public life, which was destined to be even more distinguished and more fruitful in literary labours than his earlier years, and it was during this period that he produced the monumental work *De Jure Belli et Pacis*, which alone was sufficient to immortalize his name. He found an asylum in France, where he had many admirers, and where he was graciously received by the king (Louis XIII.), who settled a pension of 3,000 livres upon him. But this pension was very irregularly paid, as Cardinal Richelieu, who was then all-powerful, required such absolute and unqualified devotion as a *quid pro quo*, that Grotius was unwilling to barter his independence, and incurred the displeasure of the Cardinal, who made him soon feel that he was master of the situation. Grotius now applied himself to the writing of his *Apology*, which he dedicated to the people of Holland and West Friesland, and in which he ably defended himself against the charges upon which he had been unjustly condemned. This work, which he originally composed in the Dutch language, but afterwards translated into Latin, caused a great sensation in his own country, but it incensed the States-General more than ever against him, and they issued an edict, in which they proscribed it, and forbade all persons to have it in their possession under the penalty of death. This ungenerous edict shattered the lingering hopes he may have entertained of returning to the land of his birth, and made him even anxious for his personal safety. Acting upon the advice of his friends, he applied for and obtained, on February 26th, 1623, letters of naturalization from the French king, who professed to take him under his special protection. Some years later, in 1631, Grotius was induced by some protestations of friendship from Prince Frederick of Orange, and relying on the general good effect his *Apology* had created in Holland, to return there, and once more claim the hospitality of his countrymen. But he was doomed to disappointment. Bigotry still prevailed, and he was banished a second time. Grotius now quitted Holland, never to see it again. He first went to Hamburgh, and two years later (in 1634) he entered the diplomatic service of Sweden, and in the following year was appointed Swedish Ambassador at the French Court, a position which was held with honour and distinction for ten years, and proved himself in more than one difficult diplomatic negotiation more than a match for the crafty Richelieu. It was during this eventful period that he completed his *History of the Netherlands* and translated the *History of the Goths and Vandals*, by Procopius. He also wrote a work on *The Origin of the American Nations*.

His Death.—The conduct of the Swedish Embassy by Grotius won the warm approval of his staunch friend the Chancellor Oxenstiern, and Queen Christina, the only child of the great Gustavus, was also very favourable to him. But Grotius took umbrage at the Queen sending a favourite of hers in an ambiguous character to Paris, and, urging his age and increasing infirmities as an excuse, he applied for his recall, which was reluctantly granted, accompanied with most appreciative acknowledgments of his eminent services, which the Queen declared she would never forget. Grotius accordingly left Paris, and arrived at Hamburgh on May 16th, 1645, and from thence he travelled to Lübec and Wismar, receiving everywhere the most honourable reception. At Wismar the Admiral of the Swedish fleet placed a man-of-war at his disposal to transport him to Colmar, from whence he proceeded by land to Stockholm. The Queen was then at Upsal, but on being told that Grotius had arrived at the capital, she at once returned to meet him, and gave him a long audience on the following day, when she again assured him of her royal favour, and begged him to continue in her service as a Councillor of State. For some reason which is not known to his biographers Grotius had resolved to leave Sweden, and when the Queen discovered that he was determined to go, she presented him with a handsome present in money and appointed a vessel to convey him to Lübec. Grotius embarked on August 12th, 1645, but was overtaken by a violent storm, was shipwrecked, and was obliged to take shelter in a port fourteen miles distant from Dantzic. Thence he travelled by land in an open waggon; but his health had been fast failing, and when he reached Rostock (on August 26th, 1645) he was too ill to proceed farther. A physician was called in to attend him, but it was soon evident that recovery was hopeless. Grotius, conscious that his end was near, asked to see a clergyman, and John Quistorpius, a Professor of Divinity at Rostock, attended him in his last earthly moments. Quistorpius found him at the point of death, but still conscious and able to speak, and it is from the hands of the professor that we have a pathetic account of the dying words of the phœnix of Literature, as he calls Grotius. "I found him," he says, "almost at the point of death. . . . I went on and told him that he must have recourse to Jesus Christ, without Whom there is no salvation. He replied: 'I place all my hope in Jesus Christ.' I began to repeat aloud, in German, the prayer which begins 'Herr Jesu'; he followed me in a very low voice, with his hands clasped. When I had done, I asked him if he understood me. He answered, 'I understand you very well.' I continued to repeat to him those passages of the word of God which are commonly offered to the remembrance of dying persons, and asking him if he understood me, he answered : 'I heard your voice, but did not understand what you said.'" These were the last words of a fleeting spirit whose earthly course had been run, and which then ceased to animate the body of the great Dutchman, just as midnight tolled the close of one and the beginning of a new day. His body received temporary sepulture in the principal church of the city, but was afterwards exhumed and finally deposited in the mausoleum of his ancestors at Delft. His epitaph, written by himself, is mournfully reminiscent in its allusion to his exile, and runs with characteristic brevity as follows :—

> GROTIUS HIC HUGO EST, BATAVUM
> CAPTIVUS ET EXSUL,
> LEGATUS REGNI, SUECIA MAGNI, TUI.

His wife survived him, and is said to have died at The Hague in the communion of the Remonstrants.

His Character.—There is no better means of judging the character of this great man and of forming a correct estimate of the manysidedness of his richly endowed genius than by studying his collection of letters published in Amsterdam in the year 1687. His large sympathies, his freedom from all bigotry yet deep religious sentiment, his abiding interest in all current topics, his profound and almost universal knowledge, and above all his earnest desire to promote peace and union amongst the Christian Churches, are here all brought before us in the familiar style of confidential correspondence with his intimate friends. A spirit of candour and truthfulness pervades all his letters : not a trace of bitterness or ungenerous criticism is anywhere to be found in them. They are essentially the letters of a pious, learned, and thoughtful man who is keenly interested in the political, literary, and religious questions of the day, which he approaches from the standpoint of a cultured intellect, devoid of bias or prejudice, and with no other aim or desire than to reach a just conclusion. Even his enemies recognized his worth, and Salmasius declared that he had "rather resemble Grotius than enjoy the wealth, the purple, and grandeur of the Sacred College." As an instance of his impartiality as an historian, it is pointed out that in his *History of the Netherlands* he does full justice to the merits of Prince Maurice of Nassau, although he had much ground for personal resentment for the injustice he suffered at the hands of that prince. It thus appears that unmerited exile did not warp his judgment or stifle his patriotism, just as religious controversies did not affect his charity, or the contests of a political career cause him to deviate a hair's breadth from the path of honour and rectitude. His name has been carried down the stream of time untarnished, while his fame as a scholar and jurist seems to increase rather than diminish.

His Magnum Opus.—Of all his numerous works, the one upon which his reputation most solidly rests is his celebrated treatise *De Jure Belli et Pacis*, which has secured for him the lasting reverence of posterity. In an age which produced as his contemporaries a Scaliger, a Bellarmin, a Mariana, a Sarpi, a Bacon, a Pascal, and a Hobbes it is an epoch-making work of this kind which, as Calvo justly says, distinguishes the true man of genius from the ordinary publicist. No work, according to general testimony, has ever received more universal approbation or has maintained its reputation to so high a degree as this treatise of Grotius. He began it in the country house of Balagni, near Senlis, placed at the author's disposal by his friend Jean Jacques de Mesmes, in the month of June, 1623, and practically completed it in June of the following year; a remarkable performance even when we bear in mind that the discovery of a manuscript in 1868 entitled *De Jure Prædæ*, shows that the subject of the treatise had already occupied his attention so early as 1604, and that he was led to its investigation in the active pursuit of his professional vocation, as advocate for the Dutch East India Company, which was formed, it is true, for the peaceful purposes of commerce, but had been compelled, like the English company, to repel force by force. The question submitted to Grotius was as to the legality of a capture made by one of the Company's captains named Heemskirk, a claim which was contested in Holland on the ground that a private company had no right to make prize captures. Grotius undertook to prove that the capture was lawful, and the manuscript treatise discovered by Professor Fruin was the outcome of this effort. It is probable that Grotius was induced by his friend Peiresc to recast the work with the light of his additional experience during the first years of his exile as a mental diversion, calculated to engross his thoughts and lighten the sorrow and burden of banishment. The circumstances of the time also supplied an additional motive for such a literary undertaking. The Thirty Years' War, in the midst of which he wrote, had been waged with such relentless fury, and the miseries of such a protracted and unregulated war had pressed so heavily upon a sensitive nature like his, that he sought to discover some rules by which its horrors and atrocities should be mitigated in the future. "I saw prevailing," he tells us in his Prolegomena (Art. 28), "throughout the Christian world a licence in making war of which even barbarous nations would have been ashamed ; recourse being had to arms for slight reasons or no reason ; and when arms were once taken up, all reverence for divine and human law was thrown away, just as if men were thenceforth authorized to commit all crimes without restraint." The sight of these atrocities, as he tells us, had led many estimable men to declare arms forbidden to Christians ; but for his own part he took the more practical and moderate view to provide a remedy for both disorders, "both for thinking that nothing [relating to war] is allowable, and that everything is." He felt to some extent prepared for such a task as he conceived by having previously practised jurisprudence in his own country, from which he had been "unworthily ejected " ; and he hoped now in exile to promote the same science by further diligent effort. He claims that none of his precursors had treated the subject scientifically, and contends that the only way to do so successfully is by separating Instituted Law from Natural Law. "For Natural Law," he observes, " as being always the same, can be easily collected into an Art ; but that which depends upon institution, since it is often changed, and is different in different places, is out of the domain of Art." Special books had indeed been previously written concerning the laws of war, but their authors, he complains, had mingled and confounded natural law, divine law, law of nations, civil law, and canon law. He acknowledges, however, his indebtedness to Balthazar Ayala (who wrote a treatise, *De Jure et Officiis*, which was printed in Amsterdam in 1597), and Albericus Gentilis, who also wrote a treatise, *De Jure Belli*. The titles of the chapters of the latter work run almost parallel to those of the first and third books of Grotius, and some of the historical examples cited in the work of Gentilis are also mentioned by Grotius.

But here the extent of borrowing by the Dutch jurist from the earlier author seems to end, for, as Hallam points out, Grotius deals with the subject of each chapter with much greater fulness, and is throughout a philosopher, while Gentilis is a mere compiler. What dominates the treatise of Gentilis is the absolute authority of the texts and precedents which he quotes, and to which he slavishly adheres. Grotius, on the other hand, though he ransacks the whole of ancient and later literature, only cites texts and precedents to support his own independent judgment, for which he gives his own reasons. No one, in fact, as Pradier-Fodéré observes, prior to Grotius knew how to unite to the same extent the authority of reason combined with that of experience; his is the fruitful alliance of philosophy and history, which has so profoundly impressed the modern political world. The method which our author adopts is the inductive one. The individual man and his social instinct is the factor producing law and the State; but this *appetitis socialis* is not the mere need for a life spent somehow (*non qualiscunque*) in community with his fellow-men, but tranquilly and as a reasonable being (*sed tranquillæ, et pro sui intellectus modo ordinatæ*), for the welfare of others in contrast to mere utility irrespective of all ethical motives. It is this tendency to the conservation of society, which is in agreement with the nature of the human intellect, that forms the source of Jus or Natural Law, properly so called. To this Jus belongs the rule of abstaining from that which belongs to other persons; and if we have in our possession anything of another's, the restitution of it, or of any gain which we have made from it; the fulfilling of promises, and the reparation of damage done by fault. In short, the special office of Jus properly so called is "to leave to another what is his, to give to him what we owe." In a general sense Jus is divided into Natural Law and Voluntary or Positive or Instituted Law. The former is the dictate of right reason, indicating what is in agreement or disagreement with the rational and social nature of man, and therefore either commanded or forbidden by the Author of Nature; the latter is subdivided into *divinum* or *humanum*, according as it is ordained by God or prescribed by man, either as a rule of the Jus Civile or of the Jus Gentium. In this way he leads up to the humane principle which pervades his whole treatise, that between individuals, as between nations, it is not Utility but a common law of Rights which is of force in governing their mutual relations. To have established this principle and to have extended its operation to the conduct of war was to have justified his claim to be regarded as the founder, or, as Marten calls him, the father, of the science of International Law, and to be called, as Vico suggests, "the juristconsult of the human race." That his work is not perfect, that he does not conceive as clearly as some later jurists—like Christian Thomasius, for instance—have done the distinction between religion on the one hand, and law and morality on the other, and that he has not completely succeeded in disentangling himself from the bewildering maze of incoherent and arbitrary notions of ethical philosophy which prevailed in his time, may be conceded without detracting from his general merits, as one who, in the midst of a cruel and desolating war, was the first to discover a principle of right and a basis of society which was not derived from the Church or the Bible, nor in the insulated existence of the individual, but in the social relations of men, and to make it thus easy for those who followed him to broaden the pathway he had broken, and to elaborate his science. Thus it was through the treatise of Grotius that the idea of a law of nature came to influence the ethical and political speculations of Locke, Rousseau, and a host of later writers. So that, whatever defects and confusion there may be in the theory of Grotius, his great work still commands respect throughout Europe, and the opinion of Mackintosh no doubt expresses the prevailing view of the learned world of the present day. "It is perhaps," he says, "the most complete [work] that the world has yet owed, at so early a stage in the progress of any science, to the genius and learning of one man." Hallam has also vigorously defended Grotius against the criticisms of Dugald Stewart, which were not characterized by much acumen or sobriety of judgment, and every sentence of which, it is no exaggeration, in the opinion of Hallam to say, would lie open to counter and destructive criticism. Stahl again,[1] is another severe critic, who sees in the doctrine of Grotius an attempt to make the whole scheme of Natural Law in its final analysis rest on the obligation of compacts,[2] which is likewise the Mother of Civil Rights, and which only needed the further development it received at the hands of Kant and Rousseau to lead directly to the French Revolution. Grotius, in fact, makes *obligation* the dividing-line between a rule of moral right *obligans ad id quod rectum est* and *consilia honesta*, a sort of counsel of perfection

[1] *Philosophie des Rechtes*, vol. i., pp. 158-170.
[2] See Prolegomena, s. 15, 16.

which is not included in *Jus* or Law (*legis aut juris nomine non Veniunt*, 1. 1. 9). It was Grotius, Stahl contends, who first gave expression to the notion that the State has no authority in itself over men otherwise than by virtue of a compact, and it has no other purpose to serve but that of individual men. It is thus the germ of that theory which a century later was to overwhelm the political order of Europe; like a mere snowflake, it is true, at first, but which, set loose from the crest of a mountain, gains increasing volume in its whirling descent, until it falls at length with the accumulated force of an avalanche into the depths of the valley below. But despite all adverse criticism, we cannot forget that it was Grotius who gave, by this treatise, the death-blow to the Machiavellian policy *des Lugs und Trugs*, as Ahrens calls it,[2] and rendered possible the Peace of Westphalia, which marked the commencement of a new era proclaiming the legitimacy of reform, and consecrated the complete equality before the law of all religions. So large was the demand for this work that it passed through no less than forty-five editions up to A.D. 1758, and became a textbook in all European universities. But the author himself derived little pecuniary profit from it, his honorarium consisting of two hundred free copies, of which he had to give away a large number to friends, to the French King, and to the principal courtiers at the court of France, the remaining copies being sold at a crown apiece, which did not even recoup him his actual outlay. The great Gustavus Adolphus of Sweden so highly prized the work that he carried it with him in his wars, and a copy was found under his pillow after the battle of Lützen. On the other hand, it was condemned by the Papacy and entered in the *Index Expurgatorius*, a condemnation which Barbeyrac quietly observes, was really the highest honour, for otherwise one might have erroneously believed that the author favoured the principles and interests of a monarchy destructive of all the laws of nature and of nations.[3]

His Remaining Works.—Besides those already mentioned, Grotius was also the author of the following works:

(1) *The Comparative Merits of the Athenian, Roman, and Batavian Nations* (1602).

(2) *Mare Liberum* (*de Jure quod Batavis competit ad Indica*

---

[1] *Philosophie des Rechtes*, p. 169, 2nd edition.
[2] *Naturrecht*, s. 16, p. 93.
[3] P. 7, Preface to Translation.

commercia), a notable treatise in which he maintained, against the pretensions of the Portuguese that the Eastern Seas were their private property, that all oceans are free and cannot be appropriated by any one nation. This essay, which is really a chapter of the *De Jure Prædæ*, was printed separately in 1609, without, as Grotius tells us, his permission, and appears to have aroused little attention at first. But in 1632 the doctrine laid down by Grotius was vigorously assailed by Selden in his *Mare Clausum*, in which the right of England to exclude the fishermen of Holland from seas which she then claimed as her own was sustained with a profusion of learning which Grotius was the first to acknowledge. But while Selden was fitly honoured by his own king and country for his patriotic effort to maintain a doctrine which coincided with the insular position as well as with the national pride in the maritime supremacy of England, the countrymen of Grotius reserved nothing better for him than imprisonment and exile. The lapse of three centuries has, however, vindicated the freedom of navigation on the open seas claimed by Grotius. And modern international jurisprudence has since adopted the theory propounded by Bynkershoek in his *De Dominio Maris* of the cannon-shot limit. Russia indeed endeavoured in the last century to revive the old controversy in connection with Behring's Sea and Alaska, and still more recently the United States claimed, as successors to Russian dominion over Alaska, beyond the Bynkershoek limit, but ineffectually.[1]

(3) *Hugonis Grotii Poemata Omnia*, first published in 1616, containing a collection of his patriotic poems, epigrammata, elegies, marriage songs, silvæ, and three dramas, which, if they do not entitle him to be ranked as a poet of genius, are at all events compositions of considerable merit in point of scholarship and elegance of diction.

(4) *Excerpta ex Tragediis et Comediis Græcis, emendata ex Manuscriptis et hatinis Versibus reddita* (1626).

(5) *Euripidis Traged. Phenissæ, emendata ex Manuscriptis, et Latina Facta ab Hugone Grotio* (1630).

(6) *Lucani Pharsalia, sive de Bello Civili inter Cæsarem et Pompejum, libri X.* (1609), a valuable edition with a carefully revised text and critical notes.

(7) *Florilegium Stobœi* (1622), the Greek text with the Latin translation of the poetical passages from the ancient poets ; and

---

[1] Trendelenburg, *Naturrecht*, s. 220, p. 573.

it was in the spirit of the collection of Stobæus, which embraced several hundred excerpts, that Grotius a few years afterwards (1626) published a continuation of the same in his own excerpta from the Greek tragedians and comedians referred to above under (4).

Finally, at the age of sixty, we still find the indefatigable scholar preparing a learned and metrical Latin translation of the Greek Anthology, according to a Greek manuscript text which Salmasius had discovered in the year 1606 in the celebrated *Bibliotheca Palatina* at Heidelberg, which he did not live to see published, but which was afterwards edited by a countryman of his own and printed with the Greek text in the year 1795. In this, as in all his works, he displays the same desire after thoroughness, elegance, and accuracy, looking, as he tells us in his own graceful verse, merely for the gratification of his peaceful desires and expecting his reward from a grateful posterity :

> " Accipe, sed placidé, quæ, si non optima, certé
> Expressit nobis non mala pacis amor.
> Et tibi dic, nostro labor hic si displicet ævo,
> A gratâ pretium posteritate feret."

Such, briefly told, was the life and work of one of the most remarkable prodigies of the human intellect which the world perhaps has ever produced—a veritable giant among intellectual giants, as to whom posterity has long confirmed the prophetic words of Henri IV. of France, pronounced when Grotius was still in his early teens—*Voilà, le miracle de la Hollande!*

The following are the principal authorities consulted: Jean Barbeyrac's French translation of the *De Jure Belli et Pacis* (Amsterdam, 1724); M. P. Pradier-Fodéré's French translation of same (3 vols., Paris, 1867); Whewell's edition of same work (3 vols., Cambridge University Press); same work done into English by several hands, with Life of author (London, 1715); *Life of Grotius*, by Charles Butler (London, 1826); *Hugo Grotius*, by. L. Neumann (Berlin, 1884); *Opinions of Grotius*, by D. P. de Bruyn (London, 1894); Hallam's *Introduction to the Literature of Europe* (4 vols., 1864); *Geschichte der Rechtsphilosophie*. by Friedrich Julius Stahl (Heidelberg, 1847); Calvo, *Le Droit International* (vol. i., Paris, 1887); Ahren's *Naturrecht oder Philosophie des Rechtes* (Wien, 1870); *Elements du Droit International*, par Henry Wheaton (Leipzig, 1858); *Encyclopœdia Britannica*, tit. Grotius.

JOHN SELDEN

JOHN SELDEN [1]

THE stone which Ajax or Hector hurls with ease in the Iliad—ἀμαξοπλήθη—" scarce," says Homer, " could two degenerate mortals of to-day lift it " ; and when we contemplate the achievements of a man like Selden—scholar, lawyer, historian, statesman, antiquarian—the massy folios in which his learning is enshrined : his *Titles of Honour*, his *Jews in England*, his *Syrian Gods*, his *History of Tithes*, to say nothing of his lesser works—his *Jewish Calendar*, his *Arundel Marbles*, or the *Table Talk*, in which wisdom and wit sparkle in liveliest sallies—we feel that here is a true Homeric hero of the seventeenth century—" one of the giant races before the flood"—from whom we moderns have sadly degenerated.

Birthplace and Early Years.—Selden's father was a yeoman farmer with a small estate of about £40 a year at Salvington, a little hamlet half a mile north of West Tarring, near Worthing, Sussex ; but there ran, in his veins, as in Shakespeare's, a strain of noble blood, derived through his mother, Margaret, daughter and sole heiress of Sir Thomas Baker, of Rusington. Here, at Salvington, Selden was born in 1584. Sussex wit, by the way, is not famous ; but had not Bœotia its Hesiod ! The cottage where he first saw the light still stands, and is known as " Lacies." It bears on the lintel of its door the inscription, said to have been written by Selden before he was ten years old :

" Gratus, honeste, mihi, non claudar; in ito sed tu
Fue abeas ! non sum facta soluta tibi."

Which may be rendered thus :

" Welcome, thou honest man ; for such I ne'er will closed be ;
Enter and sit. Thou, thief, begone ! I open not for thee."

Selden's father, Aubrey tells us, took great delight in music, and played well on the violin ; " and at Christmas time, to please himself and his neighbours, he would play to them as they

[1] With the permission of the proprietors of the *Law Times* newspaper.

danced "—quite a Vicar of Wakefield idyll. At one of these Christmas entertainments, Aubrey goes on to say, Selden, then a young student, was pointed out to a visitor—Lady Cotton, the wife of the antiquary—as a youth of " parts extraordinary."

We talk glibly, in these days of education, of "the schoolmaster being abroad," and if " instruction ladled out in a hurry," as Lord Bowen expressed it, is education, no doubt we have it. But do we really treat the matter as seriously as our ancestors ? Take Selden's case. He began at the Free Grammar School of Chichester, founded in 1497 by Bishop Storry. From there, at the age of sixteen, he went to Hart Hall, Oxford, familiar to the older generation of living Oxford men as Magdalen Hall, and to the younger generation as Hertford College. Four years were spent at the University, and he then commenced his legal career at Clifford's Inn, and proceeded in due course to an Inn of Court—the Inner Temple—where he spent eight years more before he was called to the Bar—a period from matriculation to call of twelve years. And now we are contented with—what ? A third of that time.

Selden's chambers were at Paper Buildings, overlooking the gardens, "the uppermost story, where he had a little gallery to walk in." At the Bar he enjoyed a high reputation as a giver of opinions, and was called in in cases requiring special learning. But a large legal practice was not the sum of his ambition, nor was he contented to be a mere lawyer. " The proverbial assertion that Lady Common Law must lye alone never wrought with me," he says. Law must be liberalized by literature.

The Society of Antiquaries—Ben Jonson.—Cotton, the famous antiquary, was at this time living in a house in Westminster near Old Palace Yard, with a garden leading down to the river— the present House of Lords stands on a part of it—and had brought together there a magnificent collection of manuscripts, coins, marbles, and other antiquities. His library was the chosen meeting-place of all the scholars of the country. Cotton recognized in Selden a kindred spirit, and not only made him free of his fine library, but offered him the hospitality of his house, and he was thus introduced to the society of a choice circle of scholars, antiquaries, and poets—Camden and Spelman, Sir John Davies, Michael Drayton, and Ben Jonson.

Ben Jonson—himself one of the most learned men in an age of learned men—was a great admirer of Selden, and a cordial friendship subsisted between the two. Soon after James's accession, Ben Jonson and Chapman, of Homeric fame, had got themselves into trouble with King and Court by some satirical jests at the expense of the Scots in the play of "Eastward Hoe." For this the unlucky dramatists were sent to prison, and a report was propagated that their ears and noses were to be slit. They were released, however, without being subject to this indignity, and to celebrate their deliverance they gave an entertainment to Selden. Jonson's mother was present on the occasion, and at the feast this fine old lady drank to her son, and showed him a paper which she designed, she said, if the sentence had taken effect, to have mixed with his drink, and it was a strong and lusty poison. To show that she was no churl, Jonson adds, she meant to have first drunk of it herself.

Living Laborious Days.—Under the stimulating influence of this society at Cotton's house, Selden was soon himself an author, and bringing forth things new and old out of the treasury of his unrivalled erudition: now a controversy with Grotius on the *Mare Clausum* (see p. 183); now a history of the early inhabitants of Britain, now commendatory verses to Ben Jonson's play of "Volone," now a study of the Duello, or trial by combat, notes on Michael Drayton's wonderful poetical itinerary of England and Wales, known as the "Polyolbion," a discourse touching the office of Lord Chancellor, or an Introduction to Brown's Pastorals. Whatever the topic, his versatile pen was equally ready to enrich it out of all the stores of his multifarious learning. And these were but πάρεργα—in comparison of his more solid performances. The most interesting of them, perhaps, to the lawyer is his monograph on the Judicial Combat. Here he describes with much learning and particularity of detail how the combatants stood opposed to one another in the lists in the presence of the judges, each armed with a horn-tipped bastion and a quadrangular shield; how each in turn takes the other by the hand and delivers his challenge, and how they fight till one cries craven or a star comes out. Selden was far from superstitious; yet it is curious to remark how the old idea of the propriety of an appeal to Heaven clings to him—the idea that God will defend the right. "War is lawful," he says in his *Table Talk*, "because God is the only judge between two that are supreme. Now, if a difference happen between two subjects, and it canno t be decided by human testimony, why may they not put it to God to judge between them, by the permission of the Prince ?"

"**Titles of Honour**," "**Tithes**."—In 1614 appeared his *Titles of Honour*, the book with which—next to his *Table Talk*—his name is most associated. The history of titles, like those of King and Cardinal, Cæsar and Cham, Duke and Count, Landgrave and Margrave, Baron and Knight; of the rotes and insignia appropriate to each, of the ceremonies of investiture, and so on, gave unlimited scope to his learning, and have made the book ever since a quarry for the antiquarian and student of heraldry. His friend Ben Jonson, saluting the author on its appearance, thus apostrophizes him in a poetical epistle:

> " You that have been
> Ever at home, yet have all countries seen:
> Which grace shall I make love to first ? Your skill,
> Or faith in things ? Or is 't your wealth and will
> T' inform and teach ? Or your unwearied pain
> Of gathering ? Bounty in pouring out again ?
> What fables have you vexed ? What truth redeemed ?
> Antiquities searched, opinions disesteemed,
> Impostures branded, and authorities urged ?"

In 1616 came his valuable *Commentary on Chief Justice Fortescue's Leges Angliæ*; the following year his *De Déis Syriæ*—the *Golden Calf, Apis, Baal, Moloch, Astarte, Astaroth*—and his *Marriage and Divorce among the Jews—Uxor Ebraica*—both full of Oriental learning, and that not borrowed, but the fruit of original research. Then came his *History of Tithes*, in which he maintained that tithes were not *jure divino*, and so brought himself into great odium with the clergy. King James sent for him to bring his book to Theobalds, and Archbishop Laud forced him to write a sort of recantation of his opinions—a recantation which reminds us of Galileo's abjuration of his heresy that the earth goes round the sun.

Never in the whole history of letters was such prodigious literary activity crowded into so brief a span as into the ten years of Selden's life from his twenty-sixth to his thirty-sixth year. The contemplation of it in the great folios of Wilkin's edition simply staggers the beholder. How he accomplished it is a mystery. Partly, no doubt, by economy of time. He would have said, with the founders of the Middle Temple Library, "Nulla jactura gravior temporis." Even when under the hands of the barber, if a notion came into his head he would write it down to preserve it. Once, when Isaac Vossius, the great scholar of Leyden, came to see him while he was busy, he called out from the top of the staircase that he had no time to waste in idle talk.

"Above all things Freedom"—Political Life.—An interesting article might be written on the keynotes of great lives. The keynote of Selden's was his love of freedom. His chosen motto, repeated in all his books, is περὶ πάντων τὴν ἐλευθέριαι. But it was a—

> "Love of freedom rarely felt;
> Of Freedom in her regal seat,
> Of England—not the schoolboy heat,
> The wild hysterics of the Kelt."

It was this which drew him — by nature a student and a recluse—into the arena of political strife, and which made him a foe to tyranny in any form, whether it was the tyranny of the King or of the Parliamentary party. It was a stirring time—perhaps the most stirring in all our constitutional annals. The theories of prerogative and of divine right, which with King James had been speculative political tenets, had with Charles become active principles of government. In the struggle that ensued Selden was one of the protagonists of the Parliamentary party. It was he who, with Coke, drafted in 1628 the Petition of Right, the new charter of our national liberties. It was he, too, who figured most conspicuously in the memorable scene which took place a year later in the debate on tonnage and poundage. The goods of a member—one Rolle—had been seized for non-payment of the tax, and the House protested against the seizure not only as illegal but a breach of privilege. The Speaker tried to evade the situation by refusing to put the question. Then said Mr. Selden: "Dare not you, Mr. Speaker, put the question when we command you? If you will not put it, we must sit still; thus we shall never be able to do anything. They that come after you may say: 'They have the King's commandment not to do it.' We sit here by the command of the King under the Great Seal, and you are by His Majesty sitting in this royal chair before both Houses, appointed for our Speaker, and now you refuse to perform your office." The Speaker replied, "I have a command from the King to adjourn till March 10, and put no question," and endeavoured to go out of the chair, but was held there by two strong young members, Holles and Valentine, till a protestation had been published in the House (1) against Popery and Arminianism, and

(2) against Tonnage and Poundage. For his share in this "notable contempt," as Charles called it, "against ourself and our Government, and for stirring up sedition against us," Selden, with some others, was sent to the Tower, thence to the Marshalsea, and finally to the Gatehouse, Westminster. He was not liberated until May, 1631.

"**Not Leaning to this Faction or to that.**"—Such treatment might have bred lasting resentment in a mind less well balanced than that of Selden, but, so far from its doing so, we find him two years later one of the Committee of the Inner Temple for organizing a grand masque given by the Four Inns of Court to testify their loyalty to the King and their disgust at the virulence and indecency of Prynne's *Histriomastix*, and the same year he is dedicating his *Mare Clausum on the Rules of the Sea* to Charles ("regi serenissimo et potentissimo"), subscribing himself as his "humble and most devoted subject." But let no one suppose that Selden was a time-server because he steered a middle course between the contending factions. Like a wise man, he hated the "falsehood of extremes," whether in State or Church. Since Laud's treatment of him for his *Tithes* he was no friend to the Bishops, but he liked as little the fanaticism of the Presbyterian party. He was a member of the Assembly of Divines at Westminster in 1643, and utterly routed them with his Hebrew, Greek, and antiquities. When they cited their texts, he would say: "Perhaps in your little pocket Bibles with gilt leaves" (which they would often pull out and read) "it may be thus, but the Greek or the Hebrew signifies thus and thus," and he would totally silence them. There could be no better testimony to his moderation than the fact that Charles thought of making him his Chancellor, and would have done so had he not been persuaded by Lord Falkland, who knew that Selden would not for personal reasons accept the office. "He was in years," says Clarendon, "and of a tender constitution. He had for many years enjoyed his ease which he loved; was rich, and would not have made a journey to York or have lain out of his own bed for any preferment." "In person Selden was," says Aubrey, "very tall—I guess about six feet high; long nose inclining to one side; full grey eye."

He had for a long time been steward to the Earl of Kent, and after the Earl's death he continued to reside with the

Countess in her noble mansion at Whitefriars. "He never kept any servant peculiar, but my ladie's were all at his command." Aubrey says he was privately married to the Countess, but this is doubtful. If he were, it would be only a *mariage de convenance*, for Selden was no friend to the fair sex. He calls marriage a "desperate thing." "The frogs in Æsop," he says, "were extreme wise. They had a great mind to some water, but they would not leap into the well because they could not get out again." With a blooming and ardent young wife Selden would probably have been as uncomfortable as the learned Mr. Casaubon was with Dorothea in *Middlemarch*.

But Selden was no killjoy. "He kept a plentiful table, and was never without learned company." He died—of a dropsy—in 1654, and was magnificently buried in the Temple Church. At his death he left a very valuable library, and his executors—of whom Sir Matthew Hale was one—offered it to the Society of Lincoln's Inn. The Society, on its part, was very anxious to acquire it (see 2 *Black Books*, 407-410). But a difficulty arose about the terms—making the library a "publick library for the other Inns of Court"—and in the end the library went, much to the disappointment of the Bench, to the Bodleian.

Lord Clarendon's Sketch.—Selden's portrait has been drawn for us by a master hand—that of Lord Clarendon. "He was a person," says the historian of the Civil War, "whom no character can flatter or transmit any expressions equal to his merit and virtue. He was of so stupendous a learning in all kinds and in all languages—as may appear in his excellent writings—that a man would have thought he had been entirely conversant among books, and had never spent an hour but in reading and writing; yet his humanity, affability, and courtesy were such that he would have been thought to have been bred in the best Courts, but that his good-nature, charity, and delight in doing good exceeded that breeding. His style in all his writings seems harsh and sometimes obscure, which is not wholly to be imputed to the abstruse subjects of which he commonly treated out of the paths trod by other men, but to a little undervaluing the beauty of style and too much propensity to the language of antiquity; but in his conversation he was the most clear discourser, and had the best faculty of making hard things easy, and presenting them to the understanding that hath been known." Milton calls him the "chief of learned men and glory of our nation."

The "Table Talk."—It is often the light trifles which float down the stream of time, while the more solid things disappear. It has been so with Selden. The memory of his antiquarian and legal researches—preluding the historic method—has been perpetuated and honoured in the name of the Selden Society, but the works themselves—those vast tomes of obscure learning which would have called forth many a "Prodigious!" from Dominie Sampson—finds few readers. The *Table Talk* still lives and is popular. The very title *Table Talk* has a charm, whether it is the table talk of a Luther, a Rogers, a Coleridge, a Johnson, or a Selden. Here we have the saint, the sage, or the scholar expanding under the genial influences of the table, mingling wit with wisdom, and descending for a time from the heights to illuminate for an "ordinary apprehension"—as R. Milward, Selden's Boswell, expresses it—"the highest points of religion and the most important affairs of State." For the reader must not look to find in Selden "an agreeable rattle." It was still the custom in colleges and monasteries—dreadful as it may seem to a dyspeptic generation—to propound after dinner some deep and difficult thesis for debate, and in Selden's age many such grave problems were pressing for solution. Hence his *Table Talk*, though quite free from pedantry, consists rather "weighty bullion sense"—to use Coleridge's phrase—than of smart epigram or racy anecdote. One would say that the great lawyer was shrewd rather than witty. Yet there is at times a flavour of humour about him, as, for instance, in the "logic" which the boy who would have married his grandmother used to his father: "You married my mother. Why should I not marry yours?" Or, again, in this:—

Becking to the De'il.—"Speak not ill of a great enemy, but rather give him good words, that he may use you the better if you chance to fall into his hands." The Spaniard did this when he was dying. His confessor told him, to work him to repentance, how the Devil tormented the wicked that went to Hell. The Spaniard replying called the Devil "My Lord"—"I hope my Lord the Devil is not so cruel." His confessor reproved him. "Excuse me," said the Don, "for calling him so; I know not into what hands I may fall, and if I happen into his, I hope he will use me the better for giving him good words." It was much the same feeling as inspired the auld wife when she "beckit" (curtsied) to the Deevil. "It's aye gude to be ceevil," she said.

We are much struck by the boldness of many of his remarks,

especially in the matter of religion—a boldness exemplifying his favourite motto—περὶ πάντων τήν ἐλευθέριαν. "It is a vain thing," he says, "to talk of a heretic, for a man from his heart can think no otherwise than he does think"—a sentiment which reminds us of Sir Thomas More's reason for one of the oldest laws of the Utopians—that no man ought to be punished for his religion—"Because a man cannot make himself believe anything he pleases." "Religion," he goes on, "is like the fashion : one man wears his doublet slashed, another laced, another plain, but every man has a doublet. So every man has his religion. We differ about trimming." Selden's age, it must be remembered, was fertile of "fancy religions." Conduct—the influence of religion on the life—was what reckoned with him. "What care I," says he, "to see a man run after a sermon if he cozens and cheats as soon as he comes home ?" How true it is, as he says, that "Humility is a virtue which all preach and none practise"! "Equity" Selden calls "a roguish thing." "For law," he says, "we have a measure, and know what we have to trust to. Equity is according to the conscience of him that is Chancellor, and as that is larger or narrower, so is equity." In weighing this dictum we must remember that at the time it was uttered equity had not been reduced to a system—a "laboured connected system governed by fixed rules, and bound down by precedent"—such as it became under the moulding genius of Lord Hardwicke and Lord Eldon. Here, as elsewhere, the advice of his Boswell is good. "Be pleased," he says, "in reading to distinguish times, and in your fancy carry along with you the when and the why many of these things were spoken. This will give them the more life and the smarter relish."

"**Salus Populi.**" **Is it a Shoe ?**—Apropos of the maxim *Salus populi suprema lex,* Selden makes an acute observation. The true reading is *Suprema lex esto,* not *est.* In other words, the Twelve Tables mean, not that the *salus populi* is to overrule existing law, but that it is to be the spirit or principle animating all law and legislation. In the maxim *Ignorantia juris neminem excusat* he sensibly remarks that its justification is, "not that all men know the law, but because 'tis an excuse every man will plead, and no man can tell how to confute him." Charles II. once puzzled the wiseacres of the Royal Society by propounding to them the question why a bowl with goldfish in it was lighter than one without ; for which they adduced many excellent reasons, till told that the fact was not so. "We commonly," says Selden, "are at what is the reason before we are sure of the real thing. 'Twas an excellent question of my lady Cotton, when Sir Robert Cotton was magnifying of a shoe, which was Moses' or Noah's, and wondering at the strange shape and fashion of it. 'But, Mr. Cotton,' says she, 'are you sure it is a shoe?'"

THOMAS HOBBES

THOMAS HOBBES

THOMAS HOBBES was born in 1588, the second son of the Vicar of Charlton and Westport in Wiltshire. He was sent to school in Westport Church at the age of four, and "at the age of six was learning Latin and Greek." This stern beginning was not relaxed, and early in 1602-3 the boy was entered at Magdalen Hall, Oxford. To some extent certainly he was influenced by the Puritanism of his college, and we know that he was repelled by the medieval scholasticism that still permeated the atmosphere of Oxford. He took his bachelor's degree at the end of 1607 and became the tutor and friend of William Cavendish, afterwards second Earl of Devonshire. For twenty years he remained with his patron, and in 1631 he became tutor to the eldest son of his first pupil. This involved a further foreign tour, from which he returned in 1637. In the course of his long Continental journeys he had become acquainted with many of the thinkers of that age, including Galileo and Descartes. At some time he was on intimate terms with Francis Bacon, though at what date before 1626 is not clear. "Hobbes," says Mr. Leslie Stephen, "according to Aubrey, wrote from Bacon's dictation, showing, as may be believed, more intelligence than other amanuenses, and helped in turning some of the essays into Latin. Hobbes, however, makes very slight reference to Bacon, and does not seem to have been directly influenced by his philosophy."[1] It is, however, most probable that his legal ideas were affected by the views of the great Chancellor, and it may be possible to trace some juridical unity of thought.

Social Philosophy.—It was not until after 1637 that Hobbes began to produce in systematic fashion his scheme of philosophy, though he had for some years been gradually developing his philosophic position. In 1640 he completed his treatise on *The Elements of Law, Natural and Politique,* published some ten years later in

---

[1] He certainly inherited Bacon's contempt for Coke.

two parts, "Human Nature, or The Fundamental Elements of Policy," and "*De Corpore Politico*, or Elements of Law, Moral and Politic." In 1641 he finished his treatise *De Cive* containing his theories on politics and religion. This was published in 1642 and again in 1647, and an English version was issued some years later. Meantime Hobbes was out of England. He had fled in November, 1640, from what seemed to be the wrath to come and settled in Paris. Here he remained eleven years and here he composed his immortal work the *Leviathan*. This was sent to London for publication and appeared in 1651. Hobbes was accused of supporting in this work Cromwell and the results of the Great Revolution, but of this charge he is wholly free.[1] It is true that he compounded with the Republic in 1651, but so did far more eminent cavaliers. In 1655 he was at last able to publish his preliminary philosophical work the *De Corpore*, a volume "containing his first principles, as well as his mathematical and physical doctrines." The complete volume, *De Homine*, on psychology, never appeared, though a work with that title of little original value appeared in 1658. At this time Hobbes was largely wasting his time in fruitless, and indeed disastrous, conflicts with the Royal Society group of thinkers. He was not a mathematician, and in his former conflicts with Descartes had been as little successful as he was between 1660 and 1666 in his ridiculous battles with John Wallis, the Savilian professor of geometry. He lived on, working to the last, under the protection of the Cavendish family until his death on December 4, 1679, in his ninety-second year. In his later period his fame had increased and he was both idolized and attacked at home and abroad. To certain classes Hobbism became a species of sin, and as late as 1734 "he was reviled on all sides as the typical atheist, materialist, political absolutist, and preacher of ethical selfishness." But his acuteness and his pungency of mind and the brilliancy of his philosophic thought could no longer be in doubt when the peculiar bitterness aroused by his controversial manner and the novelty of his attack had died away. He set England thinking.

"Hobbes [says Mr. Stephen in his valuable biographical notice[2] already referred to] produced a fermentation in English thought not surpassed until the advent of Darwinism. . . . Hobbes was

[1] There is evidence enough of this in *The Dialogue of the Common Laws*.
[2] *Dictionary of National Biography*, vol. xxvii.

in truth a product of the great intellectual movement distinguished by such names as Bacon (1561-1629), Galileo (1564-1642), Kepler (1571-1630), Harvey (1578-1657), and Descartes (1596-1650). . . . He shared in the general repudiation of scholasticism. In his so-called *Philosophia Prima* he touched hastily upon first principles, but failed to recognize the significance of the ultimate problems the answer to which by Descartes founded modern philosophy. His thorough-going nominalism is his most remarkable characteristic. At the same time he was scarcely influenced by Bacon's theory of the importance of systematic induction and experiment. He conceived of a general scientific scheme of universal knowledge, deducible by geometrical methods from the motions of matter which he assumed to be the ultimate fact. The conception recalls in some respects that of Mr. Herbert Spencer. . . . His great achievement, however, is his political philosophy, especially as given in the *Leviathan*. It was the edifice under which he endeavoured afterwards to introduce the foundation of philosophy, doubtless congenial, but not the real groundwork of his doctrine. Like all the great thinkers of his time, he had been profoundly impressed by the evils caused by the sectarian animosities of the time. His remedy was the entire subordination of the ecclesiastical to the secular authority—a theory which made the religion of a state dependent upon its secular sovereign, and therefore not derivable either from churches or philosophers, and shocked equally the rationalists and the orthodox. . . . In support of his absolutism he interprets the doctrine of the social contract (which had been recently expounded by Hooker and Grotius) not as a compact between the sovereign and his subjects, but as between the subjects to obey the sovereign. Virtually he argues that states have been formed as the only alternative to the state of nature, or, on his showing, to anarchy and barbarism. The supremacy and unity of the sovereign power is therefore an expression of the essential condition of civilized life. To this, though with some reserves, he subordinates even the moral law; and his characteristic theory of human selfishness reduces the only sanction to fear of force or each man's hopes of personal advantage."

This last statement is somewhat misleading, as Hobbes includes under the idea of force the control exercised by the Supreme Being, and reduces all authority to a Divine source.

The Laws of Nature.—The laws of nature according to Hobbes are precepts or general rules "found out by reason, by which a man is forbidden to do that, which is destructive of his life, or taketh away the means of preserving the same; and to omit that, by which he thinketh it may be preserved." This is not, he tells us, to be confused with " the right of nature " (*jus naturale*) which is "the liberty each man hath, to use his own power, as he will himself, for the preservation of his own nature ; that is to say, of his own life ; and consequently of doing anything, which in his own judgment, and reason, he shall conceive to be the aptest means thereunto."[1] These laws and rights are not to be confused with the laws and rights arising therefrom which have what I may call a municipal origin. Hobbes forestalled Austin in defining law as " the command of him or them that have coercive power."[2] It is in reference to law so defined that we are told that " The desires, and other passions of man, are in themselves no sin. No more are the actions, that proceed from those passions, till they know a law that forbids them : which till laws be made they cannot know, nor can any law be made, till they have agreed upon the person that shall make it."[3] In this passage Hobbes seems to take from his own conception of natural law and natural rights all sanction, but he probably, or indeed certainly, does not intend this. His doctrine of an original or primeval " state of war " among men no doubt implies an irresponsible sinlessness before the advent of municipal authority. Moreover, since the laws of nature are " found out by reason," Hobbes probably assumed that these laws were still *in nubibus* during the period of primeval human chaos. Unwitting neglect of the laws of nature may be taken, as a result of the consequences of neglect, to have led to their instinctive appreciation and their ultimate formulation. This becomes clear—of course I am assuming for the moment the Hobbesian process of evolution—when we consider the laws that Hobbes enunciates. The " first, and fundamental law of Nature " is "to seek peace, and follow it." This is supplemented by what he calls "the sum of the right of nature "—namely, "by all means we can, to defend ourselves."

The original "state of war" gave to every one the right to everything. The first law of nature modifies that right by implication. The exact modification is contained in the second law, which runs as follows : " That a man be willing, when others

---

[1] *Leviathan*, Part I., cap. xiv.

[2] *Computation or Logic*, cap. v. (Sir William Molesworth's edition of the works, vol. i., p. 74. This edition is quoted throughout this article). See also *De Corpore Politico* and *A Dialogue of the Common Laws*.

[3] *Leviathan*, Part I., cap. xiii. (vol. iii., p. 114).

are so too, as far-forth, as for peace, and defence of himself he shall think it necessary, to lay down this right to all things; and be contented with so much liberty against other men, as he would allow other men against himself." The right given up is the right of hindering another's natural rights.[1] This is done in consideration of some right reciprocally transferred to the man who has transferred his right. "The mutual transferring of right, is that which men call CONTRACT." Where there is no mutuality the transfer of a right is a gift. When we reach this stage of "natural law" the existence of some definite coercive force becomes necessary, for where any part of a contract remains to be performed, there remains what Hobbes calls a "pact" or "covenant," and this has no reality unless it is enforceable.

"If a covenant be made, wherein neither of the parties perform presently, but trust one another; in the condition of mere nature, which is a condition of war of every man against every man upon any reasonable suspicion, it is void: but if there be a common power set over them both, with right and force sufficient to compel performance, it is not void."

The coercive force, however, need not necessarily be a municipal force. All that is necessary is a force that will bind men to the performance of their covenants. "The passion to be reckoned upon is fear; whereof there be two very general objects: one, the power of spirits invisible; the other, the power of those men they shall therein offend. Of these two, though the former be the greater power, yet the fear of the latter is commonly the greater fear. The fear of the former is in every man, his own religion: which hath place in the nature of man before civil society."

This last is a very significant sentence, for it refers back the true binding powers of the "laws of nature" to a religious and external power. Hobbes declares that a covenant between two men not subject to civil power is concluded by each party swearing by the God that he feareth; but adds: "it appears also, that the oath adds nothing to the obligation. For a covenant, if lawful, binds in the sight of God, without the oath."

If we turn to the essay on *Liberty*[2] we find the laws of nature

---

[1] We may compare this statement with the definition of right in Dante's *De Monarchia*. "The real and personal proportion of man to man, which, when preserved, preserves human society, and when infringed, infringes it" (Mr. Wicksteed's translation). Dante refers to the Digests: *Jus est ars boni et æqui*. [2] Vol. ii., p. 16.

there described as the "dictate of right reason." Hobbes warns the reader that "all authors agree not concerning the definition of *the natural law*, who notwithstanding, do very often make use of this term in their writings." This want of unanimity has not disappeared in the two centuries and more that have passed since the death of the philosopher.

Hobbes was sufficiently frugal in his output of juridical thought. This essay on *Liberty* contains in the second and third chapters practically a transcript of the chapters in the *Leviathan*, dealing with the laws of nature.[1] The law of nature is defined as "the dictate of right reason" and then the first and fundamental law of nature is stated as follows: "That peace is to be sought after, where it may be found; and where not, there to provide ourselves for helps of war." From this is derived "the first special law" corresponding to the second law of nature given above. Thus the "first special" law runs as follows: "That the right of all men to all things ought not to be retained; but that some certain rights ought to be transferred or relinquished."

The third chapter of the essay on *Liberty*, entitled "Of the other Laws of Nature," follows the fifteenth chapter of the first part of the *Leviathan*. The second special law is "to perform contracts, or to keep trust." This, we are told in the essay on *Liberty*, "is a precept of the natural law," since it is "a thing necessary for the obtaining of peace." In the *Leviathan* we are told that "in this law of nature, consisteth the fountain and original of JUSTICE." It is interesting to compare this with Plato's definition of justice[2] as a kind of natural harmony and healthy habit of mind. Justice, says Dante in the *De Monarchia*, is a certain straightness or rule, rejecting the oblique on either side. Bentham varies the conception: "Of two opposite methods of action do you desire to know which should have the preference? Calculate their effect in good and evil, and prefer that which promises the greater sum of good." Hobbes is really, however, as utilitarian as Bentham, as equity-loving as Dante. "The greater sum of good" is always the end aimed at. "Justice ... is a rule of reason, by which we are forbidden to do anything destructive to our life; and consequently a law of

---

[1] The first part of the treatise *De Corpore Politico* (Molesworth, vol. iv.) also deals fully with the laws of nature following the division into a primary law and secondary law. See also the *Answer to Bishop Bramhall* (Molesworth, vol. iv.) and *A Dialogue of the Common Laws* (Molesworth, vol. vi.).
[2] *Republic*, Book IV.

nature." This utilitarian conception is brought out in his seventh law, which declares that the degree of punishment must depend on the good that punishment produces. "Men look not at the greatness of the evil past, but the greatness of the good to follow." The ninth law anticipates the doctrine of Rousseau: "that every man acknowledge another for his equal by nature."

Both in the essay on *Liberty* and in the *Leviathan* we have the same high view of the laws of nature set forth. In the first we read that "the laws of nature are immutable and eternal: what they forbid can never be lawful; what they command, can never be unlawful," and in the latter "the laws of nature are immutable and eternal; for injustice, ingratitude, arrogance, pride, iniquity, acception of persons, and the rest, can never be made lawful. For it can never be that war shall preserve life, and peace destroy it. The same laws, because they oblige only to a desire and endeavour, I mean an unfeigned and constant endeavour, are to be observed. For in that they require nothing but endeavour, he that endeavoureth their performance, fulfilleth them; and he that fulfilleth the law, is just."

Hobbes in the next development of his doctrine of natural law is brought face to face with the difficulties that belong to the conception. He is logically led to declare that since the man who fulfils the natural laws is just, "the science of them is the true and only moral philosophy. For moral philosophy is nothing else but the science of what is *good* and *evil* in the conversation of society and mankind. . . . Now the science of virtue and vice, is moral philosophy; and therefore the true doctrine of the laws of nature, is the true moral philosophy."[1] He adds in the essay on *Liberty* that "all writers do agree, that the natural law is the same with the moral." Are then these statements in fact laws? Hobbes of course feels the difficulty: "Those dictates of reason, men used to call by the name of laws, but improperly: for they are but conclusions, or theorems concerning what conduceth to the conservation and defence of themselves; whereas law, properly, is the word of him that by right hath command over others. But yet if we consider the same theorems, as delivered in the word of God, that by right commandeth all things; then they are properly called laws.'[2] Here

[1] *Leviathan*, vol. iii., p. 147.
[2] *Ibid.*, Part I., cap. xv.; see also the essay on *Liberty*, cap. iii., and *De Corpore Politico*. Compare Dante's affirmation in the *De Monarchia* that "Right, since it is a good, exists primarily in the mind of God."

then we are again thrown back on a supernatural power from whom law issues as "the command of him or them that have coercive power." The apparently automatic punishment involved in the breach of natural laws led, empirically, to the recognition of those laws; led to their formulation as laws obedience to which is an antecedent condition to life itself; led to the recognition of the creative force behind nature, as the Law-giver from whom proceed the laws or conditions obedience to which will secure the safety of the creature. He who creates a living thing must create a cage for it to dwell in; must in fact formulate the conditions that will enable the creature to live and prosper. Those conditions are contained in the so-called laws of nature. That appears to be the position adopted by Hobbes. It is the argument from design inverted. In that argument from the laws of nature we infer God. Here we refer the laws of nature to God as an intuitive conception.

Kant and the Laws of Nature.—Immanuel Kant has something of Hobbes's idea in his *Metaphysic of Morals*. There he treats of obligatory laws for which an external legislation is possible. These he calls external laws: "Those External Laws, the obligatoriness of which can be recognized by reason *a priori* even without an External Legislation, are called Natural Laws. Those laws again, which are not obligatory without Actual External Legislation, are called Positive Laws. An External Legislation, containing pure Natural Laws, is therefore conceivable; but in that case a previous Natural Law must be pre-supposed to establish the authority of the Law-giver by the right to subject others to obligation through his own act of Will."[1] Hobbes had no difficulty in pre-supposing this previous natural law. The relationship of Creator and created gives birth to such a law. When Kant declares that "the Law which is imposed upon us *a priori* and unconditionally by our own Reason may also be expressed as proceeding from the Will of a Supreme Law-giver or the Divine Will," his position is practically identical with that of Hobbes. Nor would Hobbes have quarrelled with the conclusion that "such a Will as Supreme can consequently have only Rights and not Duties; it only indicates the idea of a moral Being whose Will is Law for all, without conceiving of Him as the Author of that Will." The laws of nature, said Lord Verulam in his *Confession of Faith*, are "nothing but the laws of the creation," "they began

---

[1] Kant's *Philosophy of Law* (W. Hastie), p. 33.

to be in force when God first rested from His works and ceased to create." In his famous argument in the *Case of the Post-Nati of Scotland* he declared that the law of nature underlay municipal law, since from that law flow preservation of life, liberty, and the society of man and wife—in fact, the elements of human society. Hobbes perhaps adopted from Bacon, with whom at one time he had close intercourse,[1] this conception of natural law—a noble conception, for it enables us to see the basis of natural law upon which the palace of municipal law must be built. Natural law in the Baconian or Hobbesian or Kantian sense must precede in the natural evolution of society not only the artifices of the political law-giver, but even the iron rule of custom. These thinkers are concerned with the beginnings of law in human society, with something that lies behind even the earliest customary forms. This something is not natural law in the sense of natural sequence, "the *will* or *ought* of natural sequence," to use Sir Frederick Pollock's phrase,[2] but is akin to "the *ought* of rational conduct and ethical duty" which the early mind confounded with the inevitableness of sequence in nature.

Hobbes the Lawyer.—Whence did Hobbes derives his doctrine of the law of nature ? Possibly through Bacon, but more probably through Bacon's law-books. Hobbes in *A Dialogue of the Common Law* tells us directly or by implication of the law-books that he had read and studied. Now he was no professional lawyer.[3] The civil law at Oxford never captured him, nor did he haunt the Inns of Court or Chancery in London save as the friend of Bacon and Selden. He was not, nor did he ever purpose to become, a professional lawyer. But at some time or another he had a perfect banquet of law. He tells us[4] that he had "looked over the titles of the statutes from Magna Charta downward to

[1] Hobbes is said to have been one of the hands that translated *The Life of Henry VII*.
[2] *Laws of Nature and Laws of Men*.
[3] One is almost forced to believe that Hobbes had a legal training, but a search has proved fruitless. There was a Thomas Hobbes called to the Bar at Lincoln's Inn in 1505, another called at Gray's Inn 1592. The first date is a century, the second a few years too early. A Thomas Hobbes of the Middle Temple was practising as a common attorney after 1635, and had been a gentleman of the House since 1620. But he is not the philosopher. Yet the statement "I meant not to plead for any but myself," suggests entrance at an Inn of Court or Chancery. It may well be that Hobbes was entered at an Inn of Chancery. Unfortunately the records of the Inns of Chancery are scattered among private hands, and for the most part are probably destroyed. If any are in existence they should be deposited at the British Museum.
[4] *A Dialogue of the Common Law*, vol. vi., p. 3.

this present time. I left not one unread, which I thought might concern myself; which was enough for me, that meant not to plead for any but myself. . . . I have also diligently read over Littleton's book of *Tenures*, with the commentaries thereupon of the renowned lawyer Sir Edward Coke." He goes on to praise Coke for declaring "that reason is the soul of the law," and expanding the expression "Nihil, quod est contra rationem, est licitum" into a complete scheme of law. He gives us Bracton's definition of law : " Lex est sanctio justa, jubens honesta, et prohibens contraria." He calls Bracton "the most authentic author of the common law," and quotes freely from him, in addition to Fleta, and Fitzherbert. He exhibits a full knowledge of the history of procedure in England. He uses Coke's *Institutes* with ease and judgment. He quotes Christopher St. German's *Doctor and Student*—a most significant fact. He was closely familiar with Roman law and Roman legal procedure ; his knowledge of the statute and common law was intimate ; while some of the obscurer legal problems are dealt with in professional manner. He must have read the reports available in his day, and did not restrict himself to the more notable, for in dealing with "Crimes Capital" he says : "Also I find in the reports of Sir John Davis, Attorney-General for Ireland, that in the time of King Henry VI. a man was condemned for treason for saying the King was a natural fool, and unfit to govern."

Hobbes does not spare his criticism of Coke. He declares : "Truly I never read weaker reasoning in any author of the law of England, than in Sir Edward Coke's *Institutes*, how well soever he could plead." The lawyer with whom the philosopher holds this dialogue replies : " Though I have heard him much reprehended by others as well as by you, yet there be many excellent things, both for subtilty and for truth, in these his *Institutes*." Hobbes answers with cunning contempt : " No better things than other lawyers have, that write of the law as of a science. His citing of Aristotle, and of Homer, and of other books which are commonly read by gownmen, do, in my opinion, but weaken his authority ; for any man may do it by a servant."

Edmund Plowden.—Hobbes's knowledge of law-books must have extended to those mines of legal learning and metaphysical thought, Plowden's *Reports* and *Quæries*. Edmund Plowden, who was born in 1518 and died in 1585, is reputed to have been the most learned lawyer of the Tudor period, and his published works certainly sustain his reputation. He was a man whose intellectual attainments were both feared and respected in his own time. As an unflinching Roman Catholic he was prepared, if necessary, to defend his position against both Crown and Parliament, relying upon the weight and reasonableness of the common law. In the very year (1554) that he was acting as a justice of gaol delivery in the county of Salop, he withdrew from Parliament as a protest against their proceedings, and in answer to a charge of contempt he "took a traverse full of pregnancy" so effectively that the Attorney-General in post-haste dropped the matter. Famous in the history of the Middle Temple as Treasurer when the great Hall was a-building, he was at the time regarded with suspicion as the shelterer within the precincts of the Inn of many papists. He worshipped openly as a Roman Catholic and defied all legal proceedings. His one act of abnegation for the faith was a tribute to his brilliancy and independence. Queen Elizabeth offered him the woolsack. Acceptance would have involved a repudiation of Rome, and he refused the honour with simple dignity. A great figure in a great age, he left behind him a reputation that has become almost legendary. In him were enshrined all the wisdom and all the principles of that common law which the Middle Ages, ending at about the date of his birth, had compiled for the use of Englishmen. Three years after Plowden's death Hobbes was born, and when some thirty years later he turned to the study of English law, Plowden's reputation as an authority had reached its height. Hobbes must therefore of necessity have used the *Reports* and *Quæries*, and in fact we find that from those sources he drew some of his most original thoughts about law and government.

In certain cases recorded in *The Reports* we get the laws of nature and of reason explained and examined with elaboration and force. Serjeant Morgan in the case of *Colthirst* v. *Bejushin*[1] speaks of "Reason, which is the Mother of all Laws." The case which deals most elaborately with the law of nature is, however, *Sharington* v. *Strotton*[2]—the report of which deserves the most careful attention from students of the history of law. In this case we find Aristotle and *The Politics* quoted freely, while the Law of Nature is treated in precisely the manner that it was subsequently

---

[1] Common Bench, 4th ed., vi. *The Reports*, London, 1779, at p. 27. See also 1 Finch 4 ; 2 Finch 4 ; *Doct. and Stud.*, lib. i., cap. ii.

[2] 7 & 8 Eliz. *The Reports*, at p. 303.

treated by Hobbes. We read in the argument of the common law pursuing the dictates of nature ; of "the Law of Nature, the Law of Reason, and the Law of God " ; that " there is nothing ordained in our law contrary to Nature or Reason, or the Law of God " ; that " the elder brother is bound by the Law of Nature to aid and comfort his younger brother, as the father is the son." In the argument, again, Bromley and his Apprentice allege that " things proceeding from nature are respected not only in philosophy, but also in our law, and are of great force and operation in our law, and therefore are esteemed to be good and sufficient considerations. From whence it follows that the consideration of Andrew Baynton here expressed for the provision of his heirs males is a sufficient consideration to raise a use in the land." " Every man has a natural desire to leave the substance which he has gotten by toil and labour to one of his own blood." Catline, C. J., upheld this position. "And the Apprentice said, May it please your lordship to show us, for our learning, the causes of your judgment. And Catline said, It seems to us that the affection of the said Andrew for the provision of the heirs males which he should beget, and his desire that the land should continue in the blood and name of Baynton, and the brotherly love which he bore to his brothers, are sufficient considerations to raise the uses in the land. And where you said in your argument 'Naturæ vis maxima,' I say 'Natura bis maxima,' and it is the greatest consideration that can be to raise a use."

In the *Case of Mines*[1] we read of "the common law, which is no other than pure and tried reason " ; " the common law, which is grounded upon reason." In this case we also find embedded Hobbes's doctrine of sovereignty, and on this account the case must take an important place in the history of politics. The following sentence exactly summarizes one aspect of the position Hobbes adopted : " The office of the king, to which the law has appointed him, is to preserve his subjects ; and their preservation consists in two things, viz. in an army to defend them against hostilities, and in good laws." Reference, in this matter, must also be made to the *Case of the Dutchy of Lancaster*,[2] in which the metaphysics of the dual personality resident in kingship are duly elaborated by Plowden. The king is "a body politic and a body natural together indivisible." Hobbes's views on statute law may be compared with some of the statements on the same

[1] 9 & 10 Eliz., *The Reports*, p. 316.   [2] 4 Eliz., *Reports*, p. 213.

subject, contained in various cases reported by Plowden. In the *Earl of Leicester* v. *Heydon*[1] we read that "every subject is party and privy to an Act of Parliament." In the very important case of *Partridge* v. *Sharpe and Croker*[2] we are given an interesting doctrine of interpretation: "Words which are no other than the verberations of the air, do not constitute the statute, but are only the image of it, and the life of the statute rests in the minds of the expositors of the words, that is the makers of the statutes. And if they are dispersed, so that their minds cannot be known, then those who may approach nearest to their minds shall construe the words, and these are the sages of the law, whose talents are exercised in the study of such matters." Again, in the same case (p. 88) we are told "that, which law and reason allows, shall be taken to be in force against the words of statutes. . . . So that there they would not expound the statute contrary to what the common law and common reason allowed, notwithstanding the words were against it." Again, in the case of *Fulmerston* v. *Steward*[3] we are told that "the judges have expounded the text which is general to be but particular, which exposition is contrary of the text, because the text is contrary to reason." In the case to *Stowel* v. *Lord Zouch*[4] the weight of the common law is more openly magnified: "The way to apprehend the sense [of an Act] is to consider the common law, which is the ancient of every positive law." Indeed the judges are "to approach as near as they can to the reason of the common law." The same case gives us that end of all law upon which Hobbes dwells. "Peace and concord is the end of all laws, and . . . the law was ordained for the sake of peace." "The law hath no other end but repose, and the law was ordained to put a stop to contention, and to make peace." The law of nature, the necessity of things, moreover lies behind everything else. "Where the words of a law are broken to avoid a greater inconvenience, or by necessity, or compulsion, or involuntary ignorance, in all these cases the law itself is not broken."[5] This position recalls Bacon's doctrine (in his *Maxims of the Law*), "Necessitas inducit privilegium quoad jura privata."

It would be possible greatly to multiply the instances where Hobbes is indebted to the common law and common sense of Plowden. That he studied his works there can be no manner of

[1] 13 Eliz., *Reports*, p. 396.   [2] 6 & 7 Ed. VI., *Reports*, 83.
[3] 1 & 2 P. & M. *Reports*, 109; see also *Stradley* v. *Steward*, 2 Eliz., pp. 804-5.
[4] 4 Eliz., pp. 363-5.   [5] *Reniger* v. *Fogosse*, 4 Ed. VI., *Reports*, p. 18.

doubt. The great Selden was also drawn upon, and last but not least Christopher St. German.

John Selden.—" Our learned Selden " (1584-1654) was on terms of intimacy with Hobbes, and many and fierce were the battles that they fought on fundamental issues. Richard Baxter tells us, quoting Sir Matthew Hale, that Selden "was a great adversary to Hobbs his errors; and that he had seen him openly oppose him so earnestly, as either to depart from him, or drive him out of the room." One must grieve that no Boswell has recorded these conversations between two of the greatest intellects that England has produced. That they modified each other's outlook there can be no doubt. We may compare the following passage from Selden's *Table-Talk* with the general position adopted by Hobbes with respect to the sanction attaching to the Law of Nature :

" I cannot fancy to myself what the Law of Nature means but the Law of God. How should I know I ought not to steal, I ought not to commit adultery, unless somebody had told me so ? Surely 'tis because I have been told so ? 'Tis not because I think I ought not to do them, nor because you think I ought not ; if so, our minds might change. Whence then comes the restraint ? From a higher Power, nothing else can bind. I cannot bind myself, for I may untye (*sic*) myself again ; nor an equal cannot bind me, for we may untie one another. It must be a superior Power, even God Almighty. If two of us make a bargain, why should either of us stand to it ? What need you care what you say, or what need I care what I say ? Certainly because there is something about me that tells me *Fides est servanda*, and if we alter our minds and make a new bargain, there's *Fides servanda* there too."[1]

Again, the definition of King is not far from the fundamental ideas of Hobbes : " A King is a thing men have made for their own sakes, for quietness' sake." On the other hand, essential differences appear when Selden declares that " Every law is a contract between the King and the People, and therefore to be kept." Many other passages, however, show that this was not Selden's true position.

Christopher St. German.—*The Dialogue of the Common Laws* amply proves that Hobbes knew all that was to be known in

[1] *Table-Talk, being the Discourses of John Selden, Esq. : or his Sence of various matters of Weight and High Consequence relating especially to Religion and State* (1689). Reprinted by Edward Arber, 1868.

the way of the theory, philosophy, and history of law in his day. It is indeed impossible to resent the conclusion that he was a pupil, a very apt pupil, of Francis Bacon and absorbed all that that master-mind had to teach in the way of law. Probably they both obtained their theory of the law of nature from Christopher St. German (1460 ?-1540), the author of *Doctor and Student* and *A Treatise concernynge the Power of the Clergye and the Lawes of the Realme*, and famous for his controversies with Sir Thomas More. The Dialogue between a Doctor of Divinity and a Student of the laws of England first appeared in 1518,[1] and it at once became a textbook which was not displaced by Blackstone. An eighteenth edition of an English version appeared in 1815, dedicated " to the young students and professors of law in the general Inns of Court." It is still apparently in practical use in America. In the first Dialogue we are told that there is a law eternal, itself unknowable, but which may be revealed to man either by the light of the natural understanding which gives us the law of reason, or by heavenly revelation which gives us the law of God, or by the order of a prince " that hath a power to set a law upon his subjects," which gives us the law of man.

" The law of reason is written in the heart of every man . . . teaching him what is to be done, and what is to be fled . . . the law of reason ordereth a man to the felicity of this life . . . the law of reason teacheth, that good is to be loved, and evil is to be fled : also that thou shalt do to another, that thou wouldest another should do unto thee ; and that we may do nothing against truth ; and that a man must live peacefully with others ; that justice is to be done to every man ; and also that wrong is not to be done to any man ; and that also a trespasser is worthy to be punished ; and such other. Of the which follow divers other secondary commandments, the which be as necessary conclusions derived of the first. As of that commandment, that good is to be beloved ; it followeth, that a man should love his benefactor ; for a benefactor, in that he is a benefactor, includeth in him a reason of goodness, for else he ought not to be called a benefactor ; that is to say, a good doer, but an evil doer : [Cic. l. 2, *De Legibus*] and so in that he is a benefactor, he is to be beloved in all times and in all places. And this law also suffereth many things to be done : as that it is lawful to put away force with force : and that it is lawful for every man to defend himself and his goods against an unlawful power. And this law runneth

---

[1] So it is stated in the 1815 edition, but the *Dictionary of National Biography* says 1523.

with every man's law, and also with the law of God, as to the deeds of man, and must be always kept and observed, and shall always declare what ought to follow upon the general rules of the law of man, and shall restrain them if they be anything contrary to it."[1]

It is clear enough that Hobbes's laws of nature are derived direct from Christopher St. German, though no doubt they are modified by some knowledge of the *De Monarchia* of Dante, of, possibly, the works of Marsilio, and of the classical sources from which the pre-Reformation lawyer derived his conceptions. Sir Frederick Pollock in his volume on *The Expansion of the Common Law*, p. 109, dealing with the fifth chapter of the first Dialogue notes that—

"The Student of the laws of England, being asked by the Doctor of Divinity what he had to say of the law of nature, makes answer that among common lawyers the term is not in use, but they speak of reason where a canonist or civilian would speak of the law of nature. 'It is not used among them that be learned in the laws of England, to reason what thing is commanded or prohibited by the law of nature, and what not, but all the reasoning in that behalf is under this manner. As when anything is grounded upon the law of nature, they say, that reason will that such a thing be done; and if it be prohibited by the law of nature, they say it is against reason, or that reason will not suffer that to be done.' It is curious that this passage should have been so far as I know, completely overlooked; but the mediæval tradition of the law of nature was broken up by the controversies of the Reformation, and seventeenth-century writers are quite confused about it."

This, however, hardly applies to Thomas Hobbes. He almost certainly knew the passage here quoted. Sir Frederick Pollock points out that, directly or indirectly, "the law of nature, as accepted throughout the Middle Ages, was derived from Greek theories of ethics." Hobbes carried on the mediæval doctrine, and in a new and non-scholastic guise handed it down to the jurists and philosophers of the eighteenth and nineteenth centuries. If Hobbes had no other claim as a jurist, he could claim that he revived for the purposes of social philosophy and juridical thought the whole mediæval conception of the law of nature. The *Leviathan* carried Hobbes's ideas far and wide, and Christopher

---

[1] *Doctor and Student,* Dialogue I., cap. ii.

St. German became the unconscious cause of a great new development of a conception that had suffered many things from many thinkers, on its way from Greece to Western Europe through Rome.

Hobbes probably took the dialogue form for his work on the common law from St. German's treatise, but the *Dialogue of the Common Laws* has brilliant literary qualities not altogether shared by the fine translation of the *Dialogus de Fundamentis Legum et de Conscientia*. If Hobbes developed in the *Leviathan* for future use the idea of natural law, in his Dialogue he attempted to add a new sanctity to the idea of the common law.[1] It is natural reason, natural equity, philosophy itself. The philosopher defines a law as "the command of him or them that have the sovereign power, given to those that be his or their subjects, declaring publicly and plainly what every of them may do, and what they must forbear to do." The distinction between *law* and right is next attempted, and with bitter jibes at Coke for his ignorance in the matter. "Law obligeth me to do, or forbear the doing of something; and therefore it lays upon me an obligation. But my right is a liberty left me by the law to do anything which the law forbids me not, and to leave undone anything which the law commands me not. Did Sir Edward Coke see no difference between being bound and being free?" Hobbes goes on to show that Bracton's doctrine concerning the rights of sovereignty "is the ancient common law, and that the only bridle of the kings of England ought to be the fear of God."[2] The supreme power of the king leads to an elaborate discussion "Of Courts." Hobbes proves that "the jurisdiction of Courts cannot easily be distinguished, but by the king himself in his Parliament. The lawyers themselves cannot do it; for you see what contention there is between Courts, as well as between particular men." In the course of this and other discussions, the unhappy Sir Edward Coke is trampled under foot with a vigour peculiar to Hobbes. There is a certain ingratitude in the insults that are levelled at him, for Hobbes learnt much of his law from the *Institutes*. However, the reason for the attacks is plain enough. He is accused of quoting an expired statute "on purpose to diminish, as he endeavours to do throughout his *Institutes*, the King's authority,

[1] Derived from Plowden's *Reports*.
[2] Compare the statement in the *De Monarchia*: "It is plain that the authority of the temporal monarch descends upon him without any mean from the fountain of universal authority."

or to insinuate his own opinions among the people for the law of the land." An even more serious charge follows : " He endeavours by inserting Latin sentences, both in his text and in the margin, as if they were the principles of the law of reason, without any authority of ancient lawyers, or any certainty of reason in themselves, to make men believe they are the very ground of the law of England." It was in much the same spirit that he attacked Wallis of the Royal Society in later years. Hobbes could not be moderate in controversy : he must needs slay, even if he has to do it with the jawbone of an ass.

Hobbes and the Law.—A perusal of the *Dialogue* exhibits not only Hobbes's fine knowledge of English law, not only his dialectical power by which he squares the common law with his doctrine of kingship, but a keen insight into the abuses of the legal system in vogue in his day, and for more than two centuries after his day. Some brief extracts will show his general attitude and his reforming policy towards the law. "That the reason which is the life of the law should be not natural, but artificial, I cannot conceive. . . . Obscure also are the words *legal reason*. There is no reason in earthly creatures, but human reason." Now declaring that "reason is the common law," he asks, "To what end were statute laws ordained, seeing the law of reason ought to be applied to every controversy that can arise ?" The answer is, "That the scope of all human law is peace,[1] and justice in every nation amongst themselves and defence against foreign enemies." " But what is justice ?" " Justice is giving to every man his own." " The definition is good, and yet it is Aristotle's. What is the definition agreed upon as a principle in the science of the common law ?" " The same with that of Aristotle." " See, you lawyers, how much you are beholden to the philosopher ;[2] and it is but reason ; for the more general and noble science and law of all the world is true philosophy, of which the common law of England is a very little part." The argument then proceeds that it is " a dictate of the law of reason, that statute laws are a necessary means of the safety and well-being of man in the present world, and are to be obeyed by all subjects, as the law of reason ought to be obeyed, both by King and subjects, because it is the law of God." But statute laws must be " laws living and armed." The laws are made by the king and he must have an army to

---

[1] See Plowden's *Report, Stowell* v. *Lord Zouch*, p. 365.
[2] See *Sharington* v. *Strotton*, Plowden's *Reports*, p. 303.

enforce them. Moreover, the king's reason, when it is publicly upon advice and upon deliberation declared as that *anima legis*; and that *summa ratio* and that equity, which all agree to be the law of reason, or all that is or ever was law in England, since it became Christian, besides the Bible." The king, Hobbes declares, has an unlimited right to levy soldiers and money for the defence of his people. Did not Oliver "when their new republic returned into monarchy" do so ? The king moreover is "the legislator both of statute law and of common law," since the king's reason supplies the place of the universal reason which gives the common law. The king, being the sole legislator, is also the sole judge. This leads to a consideration of the Courts of justice and equity— the former dealing with "the positive laws of the land," the latter with causes that are determined by the law of reason. The elaborate description of the Courts, of the various types of suits, and of the relation of pleas and suits to the theory of law and morals, is valuable reading, and shows the legal training that Hobbes passed through at some time or another. He is often enough dogmatic. He declares that "it is very plain by these letters-patent, that all causes temporal within the kingdom, except the pleas that belong to the exchequer, should be decidable by this Lord Chief Justice." The abuses of legal processes and of the Courts are frankly pointed out. "A pleader commonly thinks he ought to say all he can for the benefit of his client, and therefore has need of a faculty to wrest the sense of words from their true meaning, and the faculty of *rhetoric* to seduce the jury, and sometimes the judge also, and many other arts which I neither have, nor intend to study." "For my own part, I believe that men at this day have better learned the art of cavilling against the words of a statute, than theretofore they had, and thereby encourage themselves and others to undertake suits upon little reason. Also the variety and repugnancy of judgments of common law, do oftentimes put men to hope for victory in causes whereof in reason they had no ground at all : also the ignorance of what is equity in their own causes, which equity not one man in a thousand ever studied. And the lawyers themselves seek not for their judgments in their own breasts, but in the precedents of former judges : as the ancient judges sought the same, not in their own reason, but in the laws of the empire. Another, and perhaps the greatest cause of multitude of suits, is this, that for want of registering of conveyances of land, which might easily be done in the townships where the lands lay, a purchase cannot easily be had which will not be litigious. Lastly, I believe the covetousness of lawyers was not so great in ancient time, which was full of trouble, as they have been since in time of peace, wherein men have leisure to study fraud, and get employment from such men as can encourage to contention. And how ample a field they have to exercise this mystery in, is manifest from this, that they have a power to scan and construe every word in a statute, charter, feoffment, lease, or other deed, evidence or testimony."

A little before he has commented on the number of statutory informers, of concealers ("a number of cozeners, which the law may easily correct"), and attorneys. He felt with Bacon that the law was a miserable trade. Happily for him, unlike Bacon he had no need to live by it and could smoke his pipe and criticize in peace. He pleads for an extension of the power of the Court of Chancery, giving it the right to review the judgments of the Court of Common Pleas. The ideal he aimed at was the fusion of law and equity; to make all Courts Courts of Equity. Common law, he declares, *is* in its nature equity. "I would fain know to what end there should be any other Court of Equity at all, either before the Chancellor or any other person, besides the judges of the Civil or Common Pleas? . . . Besides seeing all Courts are bound to judge according to equity, and that all judges in a case of equity may sometimes be deceived, what harm is there to any man, or to the State, if there be a subordination of judges in equity, as well as of judges in common law?" The judicial business of construing written laws is put with remarkable force.

"It cannot be that a written law should be against reason; for nothing is more reasonable than that every man should obey the law which he hath himself assented to. But that is not always the law, which is signified by *grammatical* construction of the letter, but that which the legislature thereby intended should be in force; which intention, I confess, is a very hard matter many times to pick out of the words of the statute, and requires great ability of understanding, and greater meditations and consideration of such conjuncture of occasions and incommodities, as needed a new law for a remedy. For there is scarcely anything so clearly written, that when the cause thereof is forgotten, may not be wrested by an ignorant grammarian, or a cavilling logician, to the injury, oppression, or perhaps destruction of an honest man. And for this reason the judges deserve that honour and profit they enjoy."

The whole of this discussion is intended to demonstrate the essential relationship of justice and equity. The final conclusion is that "justice fulfils the law, and equity interprets the law, and amends the judgments given upon the same law. Wherein I depart not much from the definition of equity cited in Sir Edward Coke (Inst., see xxi.); viz. equity is a certain perfect reason, that interpreteth and amendeth the law written; though I construe it a little otherwise than he would have done; for no one can mend a law but he that can make it, and therefore I say it amends not the law, but the judgments only when they are erroneous."

At this point the interlocutors turn to the subject of crimes and punishment. His doctrine of government ever in view—the development of that doctrine is the ultimate object of the entire Dialogue—Hobbes proceeds to define treason from the first principles of "mere natural reason." Treason involves "a designing of a civil war and the destruction of the people." And, since the safety of the people is the highest law, the doing of any act that endangers it is the highest crime, namely high treason. After discussing treason at length, he turns to felony, and there he amuses himself by attacking with vigour and brilliancy the views of Sir Edward Coke. The Lord Chief Justice is pursued with an animosity that is hardly conceivable to a modern mind. He deals in this spirit with the doctrine of constructive murder. "Sir Edward Coke says (3 Inst., p. 56) that if the act that a man is doing, when he kills another man, be unlawful, then it is murder."

"This is not so distinguished by any statute," replies the philosopher, "but is the *common law* only of Sir Edward Coke. I believe not a word of it. If a boy be robbing an apple-tree, and falleth thence upon a man that stands under it and breaks his neck, but by the same chance saveth his own life, Sir Edward Coke, it seems, will have him hanged for it, as if he had fallen of prepensed malice. All that can be called crime in this business is but simple trespass, to the damage perhaps of sixpence or a shilling. I confess the trespass was an offence against the law, but the falling was none, nor was it by the trespass but by the falling that the man was slain; and as he ought to be quit of the killing, so he ought to make restitution for the trespass. But I believe the cause of Sir Edward Coke's mistake was his not well understanding of Bracton, whom he cites in the margin."

Hobbes goes on to show that where the act is in itself evidence of a felonious purpose, the death would be murder. Certainly modern practice is nearer the view of Hobbes than that of Coke. He has not done with Coke yet. On another matter the philosopher angrily cries out, "If his definitions must be the rule of law, what is there that he may not make felony or not felony at his pleasure? But seeing that it is not statute law that he says, it must be very perfect reason or else no law at all; and to me it seems so far from reason, as I think it ridiculous." This is the attack on the doctrine that there can be no larceny of growing crops or fruits since they concern the realty.

The question of heresy fills much space. He raises the question as to the right to burn heretics. It is forbidden by statute and could not have been a custom incorporated in the common law. Sir Edward Coke is therefore again punished with sufficient severity. On the question of præmunire he has no peace, while Coke's statement that the general power of pardoning resides in Parliament and not in the king (except in the case of high treason, which is a crime against the king) is met with the retort that all crime is an offence against the king.

The Dialogue turns finally to the "laws of *meum* and *tuum*." Here we have much said concerning the origin and growth both of prosperity and sovereignty and Parliament. The note as to the origin of the English Parliament is of value, and with it the *Dialogue of the Common Laws* abruptly ends.

"The law is the public conscience"[1] is the note that rings through the *Dialogue*. Hobbes desired to make the civil law nearer to the natural law—to the law that has governed the wills of men, the law that deals with the inner man. We know what is right, but cannot do the things that we would. Hobbes desired the civil law to carry the natural law into action and to become perfect equity. Hobbes had in mind a perfect commonwealth and deliberately claimed that if the opinions of law and policy expressed in his *Human Nature* and *De Corpore Politico* were held by men the kingdom of peace would be at hand: "it would be an incomparable benefit to the commonwealth, that every one held the opinions concerning *law* and policy here delivered."[2]

---

[1] *Leviathan*, Part III., 29.
[2] Dedication to William, Earl of Newcastle.

All perfect laws, he held, sprang direct from God. "The law of nature, which is also the moral law, is the law of the Author of Nature, God Almighty; and the law of God taught by our Saviour Christ is the moral law."

To Hobbes law and policy form a consistent whole: and if considered as a whole, as a system for producing a stable human society, and not merely in its religious aspect, it would not seem so vulnerable as it apparently seemed to the Bramhalls of the eighteenth century.

Hobbes as a Jurist.—It is impossible to deny that Thomas Hobbes was a great jurist in the deepest sense of that term. He was not, as he sat in his study and smoked his famous pipe, merely weaving the sand of words and ideas. Despite his jest that if he read as much as other men he would be as ignorant as they, he was a great student of books and records. His knowledge of English law is evidence enough of that. He went to the realm of fact and practice for his ideas. He worshipped the common law because it was a fact and not a theory, because it represented the law evolved from the experience during long ages of the relationship of man to man. He was a modern thinker in the best sense: he worked from fact to theory, worked perhaps imperfectly enough, but raised up his doctrines of law and government upon the ancient and current experiences of the English nation. It is in this fact that his work and thought are likely to outlive in philosophic influence the work and thought of Locke and Rousseau,—in so far as those thinkers did not base themselves on the far-reaching speculations of Hobbes himself. The influence of Hobbes as a thinker, indeed as a prophet, is likely to increase rather than diminish, for he preached a doctrine of governmental despotism that modern nations are rapidly realizing. Mr. Jethro Brown in his recent book on *The Austinian Theory of Law* says that "it may be noted, however, that the theory of Hobbes finds expression for government but not for the State, while that of Rousseau finds an expression for the State but none that is adequate for the government. The path taken by Hobbes leads on to governmental despotism; that taken by Rousseau to the despotism of majorities. While Locke may be said to have apprehended the existence both of the State and the government, his doctrine surely lends itself to an individualism of which the final outcome must be anarchy." Hobbes may not have chosen the better path, but he certainly chose the path indicated by the experience of his own day, by the manner in which the laws of England developed, and by the conception of natural law which he derived from mediæval jurists, thinkers, and lawyers. He chose the only possible method that would in a measure reconcile individualism and despotism. The despotism of majorities, he knew well enough, was bound to deteriorate into that "rule or the usurping of the popular or rascall and viler sort" called the Δημοκρατίαν ἁπαντῶν "because they be moe in number," of which Sir Thomas Smith writes in his *De Republica Anglorum*.[1] He looked forward instead to a system of governmental despotism, and who shall say that we have not attained to his grim ideal ? It is true that those who "be moe in number" make and unmake governments, and in some appreciable measure modify this or that political outlook, this grievance or some other, the tax or rate of last year or the year before. But the great governmental machine grinds on independent of majorities and of the political sky. Hobbes knew this as well as we do. He knew that Cromwell, successful in all else, failed hopelessly when he touched the governmental machine. The history of national finance in the later years of the Commonwealth shows that it is one thing to substitute one ruler for another, and quite another thing to interfere with the machinery of government. Hobbes was far too acute an observer not to realize that the end of government is social equilibrium, and that social equilibrium is impossible under the fluctuating despotism of majorities or the unordered despotism of the individual.

The fact that perhaps most strikes the imagination of the lawyer in regarding the social philosophy put forward by Thomas Hobbes is the remarkable fashion in which he gathered and dealt with his legal material. No source was too obscure, no legal record too dusty for him to use. From the dryasdust sources of mediæval philosophy, from the scattered mines of the common law he drew material that enabled him to restate as part of an ordered theory of government the law of nature, and the application of that law to the community (then in a state of flux) amidst which he lived. He was a jurist of the profoundest type, for he formulated laws relating to society that have had an abiding effect on society throughout Europe ever since his time. His laws and conceptions were not those vivid imaginations of pure thought that charm the philosophic mind, and leave the world where they

---

[1] Lib. i., cap. iii.

found it. They were conceptions founded upon the closest observation of the nature of the society amid which he dwelt, and of the evolution of a practical legal system through long ages in that society. He approached the problem of social government in the same scientific spirit as that in which Newton approached the problem of the laws governing the material universe, and it is probable that his influence on human thought in the region of sociology has not been less than the influence of Newton in the realm of applied science. In a very real sense Rousseau, Bentham, and Austin are descendants of Hobbes, while his methods are still the methods of those who are dealing with his problems to-day. Nor has his influence been evanescent in the obscure region of the philosophy of law. Kant directly or indirectly owes to him a debt not less great than the debt that he owes in another realm of thought to David Hume.

RICHARD ZOUCHE

RICHARD ZOUCHE, born at Ansty, Wiltshire, in 1590, was the son of Francis Zouche, lord of the manor of Ansty. In 1609 he became a Fellow of New College, Oxford, in 1617 was admitted an advocate of Doctors' Commons, in 1619 proceeded to the degree of D.C.L., and in the following year succeeded John Budden, the successor of Albericus Gentilis, as Regius Professor of Civil Law at Oxford. Soon afterwards he married, and resigned his fellowship. In 1623 he entered himself as a fellow-commoner at Wadham College, and two years later was appointed Principal of St. Alban Hall. He was twice elected a member of Parliament for Hythe (1621 and 1624), and in 1632 became Chancellor of the Diocese of Oxford.

From that date his activities were shared between legal practice in London and academic engagements at his University, where he also took a prominent part in the codification of its statutes (1629-1633). Finally, in 1641, he was appointed to a judgeship of the High Court of Admiralty.

At the time of the Civil War his sympathies were with the Royalists, and after some opposition he was obliged to submit to the parliamentary visitors, who sought to effect a reformation of the University. Zouche was removed from his judgeship when Cromwell came to power, though he was a little later appointed one of the judges to decide the famous case of Don Pantaleon Sa. The remainder of his life was spent mostly at Oxford, and during this time he does not appear to have gained the favour of either of the political parties. On the accession of Charles II. he was restored to the judgeship of the Court of Admiralty, but died about a month later.

His contemporaries undoubtedly appreciated his excellent qualities as a man, his high distinction as a scholar, and his learning and authority as a writer. Of his *Elementa Jurisprudentiæ*, Bishop Sanderson said that " no man could read it too often or commend it too much." Anthony Wood[1] gives a delightful portrait of him : "He was an exact artist, a subtile logician, expert historian ; and for the knowledge in, and practice of, the civil law, the chief person of his time, as his works, much esteemed beyond the seas (where several of them are reprinted), partly testify. . . . As his birth was noble, so was his behaviour and discourse ; and as personable and handsome, so naturally sweet, pleasant and affable. The truth is, there was nothing wanting but a forward spirit for his advancement, but the interruption of the times, which silenced his profession, would have given a stop to his rise had he been of another disposition."

The Writings of Zouche.—The books Zouche published indicate a remarkable versatility in range of subjects, as well as a considerable volume of work. Like his countrymen Selden and Bacon, to name no others, he was in some respects a product of the Renaissance, an age in which writers and thinkers were loth to limit their activity to work of specialization, but whose thirst for knowledge led them to wider fields, and to seemingly recondite or strange subjects. The publications of Zouche comprise a poem, a play, a book of miscellaneous maxims, handbooks for university disputations, and works of a more polemical nature ;[2] but his most important production is a systematic survey of the whole field of jurisprudence, followed by a more detailed examination of its various branches. Thus the basis of his writings on law is the *Elementa Jurisprudentiæ*, largely founded on Roman Law both in method and subject-matter. He introduces the twofold division of Rights (*Jus*) and Remedies (*Judicium*), and adopts this method systematically and logically—if somewhat automatically—in his subsequent exposition of the various departments of law, dealt with in a regular series of treatises (*descriptiones*)—"feudal," "sacred," "maritime," "military," and "fecial" law. Of all these dissertations, those dealing with questions of international law are the most important—indeed, his standing as an eminent jurist is mainly due to them : *Juris et judicii fecialis sive juris inter gentes et quæstionum de eodem explicatio* (Oxford, 1650), being a concise outline of a large body of international law, and *Solutio quæstionis veteris et novæ, sive de legati delinquentis judice competente dissertatio*[3] (Oxford, 1657),

---

[1] *Athenæ Oxonienses.*
[2] For a complete list of his works see Professor Holland's article on Zouche in the *Dictionary of National Biography.*
[3] These two works will henceforth be referred to, respectively, as *De jure inter gentes* and *Solutio quæstionis.*

which is a fuller treatment of one of the special matters of the preceding work, viz. the position of ambassadors in the law of nations. The present essay is concerned almost exclusively with Zouche as an international jurist.

To obtain a juster and more accurate appreciation of Zouche's position it will be well to consider briefly the work of his English predecessors in the field of international law, and the nature of interstatal relationships at the time he wrote.

Relation of Zouche to his English Predecessors.—The early development of international law was a laborious process, the main counteracting agencies to its quicker advancement being the practices of feudalism and the dominating influence of the Church. Towards the close of the fifteenth century, and in the early part of the sixteenth, we see the rise of great States, and, generally, more distinct lines of demarcation between them. The Pope's political power was largely overthrown; and the internal organization and external relationships of States are to some extent systematized under the guidance of the principles of sovereignty and autonomy. Thus the practices of war became somewhat regularized, and with the establishment and maintenance of standing armies a body of rules relating to military discipline grew up; further, through the increased interstatal communication many usages concerning ambassadors and envoys came to have legal force. At the head of this movement are to be found Spain, France, and England. In Spain, Alfonso IX. drew up the *Siete Partidas*, a manual of military laws, to which Zouche occasionally refers; in Italy, various treatises are produced—*e.g.*, by Gratian (the *Decretum*), Thomas Aquinas, Bartolus, Baldus, and others; in France we find already, at the end of the fourteenth century, *L'Arbre des Batailles* of Honoré Bonet; in Germany early attempts at similar disquisitions are made by Gabriel Biel in his *Collectarium*.[1]

In England the unification of the country began with the Norman Conquest; some two centuries later the principle of Parliamentary representation was firmly established; administration of justice was organized; to Henry VII. is due the innovation of permanent embassies; under Henry VIII. foreign politics occupied much attention, canon and Roman law were the predominant systems. Before this, Oxford had had a school

[1] *Cf.* E. Nys, *Notes pour servir a l'Histoire littéraire et dogmatique du Droit International en Angleterre* (Bruxelles, 1888).

of law ; and with the decline of canon law at the Reformation, Henry VIII. founded chairs of Roman law both at Oxford and Cambridge ; and at the time of Elizabeth the institution of Doctors' Commons was often consulted in regard to international affairs. Already in the fifteenth century in England writers issued important original monographs, or adaptations and translations. Nicholas Upton[1] followed Bartolus[2] in his discussions on knighthood, and on matters of war refers to Gratian and Johannes de Legnano ;[3] he deals with duels and reprisals, on which latter question he cites the authority of Bartolus, Guy de Baiso, Baldus, and others ; and finally as to prisoners adopts the severe measures in the doctrine of Baldus. In 1475 appeared anonymously *The Boke of Noblesse*, which inquires "whether for to make werre uppon christen bloode is lawfulle," and follows the authority of Honoré Bonet's work *L'Arbre des Batailles*, which was afterwards translated by Sir Gilbert Hay. Bonet held that war is primarily a relation between State and State. In the next century we get the great work of Albericus Gentilis.[4] A new phase of literary activity was manifested in the dissertations contained in the general memoirs of Government officers, and embodied as answers to particular questions proposed to them in their official capacity—*e.g.*, Valentine Dale's answer as to wars which have commenced illegally and without sufficient cause ;[5] again, his opinion of a book in which Don Antonio defended his claim to the Portuguese throne ; and other matters relating to piracy. The case of Leslie, Bishop of Ross, was referred to David Lewis, Valentine Dale, William Drury, William Aubrey, and Henry Jones, who were all advocates of Doctors' Commons ; and in the case of Mary Stuart, Dale was consulted, and drew up a written opinion.[6] There were besides, before Zouche, a large number of English writers who contributed fuller treatises on special subjects—*e.g.* Matthew Sutcliffe, William Fulbecke, William Welwood, John Selden, Richard Bernard, and Sir John Boroughs, who will be referred to below in connection with the different divisions of Zouche's work.

Zouche has been claimed by some writers to be the second founder of the law of nations, mainly, it may be, by virtue of his

[1] *De studio militari libri quatuor.*   [2] *De insignis et armis.*
[3] *De bello, de represaliis, et de duello.*
[4] *De legationibus libri tres* (London, 1585); *De jure belli* (London, 1588-89).
[5] *Calendar of State Papers : Domestic Series of the Reign of Elizabeth*, 1581-1590.
[6] *Cf.* Strype, *Annals of the Reformation*, iii., pt. i., p. 530 ; pt. ii., p. 398.

great terminological innovation—*jus inter gentes*—to replace the older, more ambiguous, though universally employed expression, *jus gentium*. Hence he is often referred to in writings on international law in connection with his new formula, which seemingly indicates a new point of departure, and a new, a more modern conception of fundamental doctrine. But of his views in general little has been said by writers. By adopting the positive method he at once shows himself to be in affinity with the English school. He is largely concerned with the citation of examples and precedents;[1] he does not undertake a scientific development of doctrine. Perhaps, having regard to the nature of the time in which he lived, the unsettled affairs, the contentious international politics, and more or less precarious interstatal relationships, he was too wise to develop doctrine, to rush to abstract generalizations, and to theorize in *a priori* principles which could not be made to fit the actual conditions, especially so in a strikingly transitional epoch. The English school is eminently practical; it considers policy and rules of law in relation to the particular environment and to the demands of necessity. Thus, Selden's *Mare clausum*, a reply to Grotius' *Mare liberum*, and his *De jure naturali*, adopt the positive method almost entirely. Selden's method is characterized by M. Scelle as an "aboutissement brutal de la doctrine positive."[2] The same positive tendency is likewise manifested in the great philosophical writers, Bacon, Locke, and Hobbes, though in other respects there are profound differences between them. There had for some time been at Oxford an influential juristic school; apart from foreigners, like Gentilis, who from time to time taught there, there was a considerable group of writers, of whom may be mentioned Valentine Dale, Sir Julius Cæsar, William Fulbecke, William Welwood; and after these came Zouche, to sum up, as it were, the whole school. A more or less similar spirit pervaded the work of all of them; all emphasized the importance of usages and practices, of treaties, conventions, and of the diverse phenomena consequent on political development. In the more theoretical portion of their work, whenever they attempted such treatment, the Roman law was called in to provide authority and furnish analogies; but recent events were at no time disregarded.

[1] "On reconnaît à ce signe l'un des représentants de la doctrine positive," *Fondateurs du droit international* (Paris, 1904); article on Zouche by G. Scelle, p. 325.
[2] *Ibid.*, p. 326.

Zouche and the Roman Law.—The Roman law has ever been an invaluable aid in the development of international jurisprudence, not to mention the municipal law of modern States. Indeed, it is in many respects the very foundation of the law of nations. There are very few writers and lawyers who have not been profoundly influenced by it.[1] The Church had promoted the study and application of the Justinian jurisprudence. It was ranked with the canon law by the Popes and the pontifical Courts. In Italy the study of Roman law had long been maintained; the school of Bologna and the Glossators (1100-1260) had European fame; and there was further a great revival during the Italian Renaissance, which soon extended to other countries. In France rules of Roman law had predominated over Germanic laws and customs, and early in the twelfth century the Justinian Code was there translated. The manual of Alfonso IX. of Spain—the *Siete Partidas*—was to a large extent founded on the Roman law. German students attended the schools of Italy as early as the twelfth and thirteenth centuries, and in the sixteenth century there were many famous foreign teachers in Germany. In Holland a school of jurists arose with the foundation of the university of Leyden in 1575; and in the following century flourished men like Grotius, Vinnius, Huber, and Van Leuwen. As for England, Selden states that the Justinian law was introduced from Bologna in the twelfth century. From the arrival of Vacarius, invited by Archbishop Theobald in the reign of Stephen to teach Roman law at Oxford, down to the death of Edward I., the civil law exerted much influence in England. Bracton's direct indebtedness to it is as great as his esteem of it.[2] In Fleta a good deal of the substance of the Institutes is adopted. Similarly, Coke's recognition of Bracton at the same time implies an acceptance of the Roman law. Various causes operated to extend the application of this foreign law, such as the influence of the universities, notably the Oxford school of civil law; the recognition of Roman law in ecclesiastical Courts; the growth of commercial intercourse and acquisition of property, through which the defects and omissions in the common law had to be remedied; and finally the intrinsic nature of the Justinian legislation itself,

---
[1] *Cf.* the observations of Bodin: *De la République* (Paris, 1577), l. v., c. vi.; Leibnitz, *Opera*, t. iv., p. 254; Sir Robert Wiseman, *The Law of Laws, or Excellency of the Civil Law above all other Human Laws Whatsoever* (London, 1686), p. 110.

[2] *Cf.* C. Güterbock: *Henricus de Bracton und sein Verhältniss zum Römischen Rechte* (Berlin, 1862); translated by B. Coxe (Philadelphia, 1866).

the comprehensiveness of its subject-matter, the universal applicability of its principles and generalization.

The influence of the Roman law on Zouche is manifested throughout his work. His standpoint, his divisions, his classifications, his conceptions, are greatly affected thereby. Thus he divides the law of peace and of war each into four categories—*status, dominium, debitum, delictum*. The Justinian rights and obligations of citizens are transferred to the case of States, and immediate application and inference of principles are made just as though the conditions were alike in the two cases. Zouche was not, of course, alone in such somewhat undiscriminating imitation ; his masters Gentilis and Grotius had done the same. Thus, in the *Mare liberum*, Grotius speaks of persons and goods, contracts and actions, possession and transference of property, as though he were dealing with a house or a horse.[1] But in Zouche a certain self-emancipation from the tradition is manifested, inasmuch as he gives many recent or contemporary examples of practice— and this Grotius does not do.

Relation to His Age.—Bynkershoek has often been greatly praised for his use of more modern instances ; but Zouche adopted this practice long before ; indeed, the subsequent growth of international law is greatly indebted to his bold innovation—a feature which cannot be too much emphasized. It is true that this practice is already found in Gentilis ; but Zouche was the first to adopt it systematically and persistently in the entire range of his work. Henceforth the law of nations acquires a vitality and elasticity which are absent in the earlier scholastic methods with their undiscriminated accumulations of learning. Zouche, however, unlike Bynkershoek, failed to draw definite inferences from his modern examples. He analyzes them, states the issue clearly, gives arguments for and against (much in the same way as disputations were conducted in his university), but usually avoids giving his own opinion in favour of the one side or the other, or suggesting any other course. It cannot be said that this attitude was due to judicial incapacity ; it was rather due to his aversion to dogmatic finality in view of the stirring flux of events in Europe at the time he wrote, his recognition of the then transitory

[1] Nowadays, a similarly false analogy is sometimes made by writers (seduced by certain superficial likenesses and indifferent to fundamental differences) in considering the evolution of a State or a nation in the same way as they would consider the organic development of an individual, and the economic and intellectual organization of his life.

character of international relationships, the reconstruction of national polity, and the inevitable transformation of rules of practice pertaining thereto.

The Thirty Years' War, beginning as a strife of Bohemian rebels against Ferdinand the Hapsburger, grew into the great conflict between Roman Catholicism and Protestantism, between imperialism and territorial sovereignty. In the sphere of international law the consequences were far-reaching. From the fifteenth century to the middle of the seventeenth, the worst features of a Machiavellian diplomacy prevailed, and almost shattered the very foundations of international law. The interests of monarchs were then by no means identified with those of their countries; treaties were violated or modified at the pleasure and for the convenience of the signatory States. But with the decline of feudalism in the sixteenth century, the gradual overthrowing of spiritual authority, the unification of States, their assertion of autonomy, the increasing body of writings by jurists and publicists, the way was prepared for the establishment of the principles of the Peace of Westphalia, which procured an international system of independent States, with an exclusive territorial jurisdiction for each, and by a recognition of the principle of equilibrium of the greater States laid the very basis of modern international law. During and after the Thirty Years' War certain Powers had been quickly developing their maritime resources, which were further promoted by colonial expansion. Questions of neutrality and of the freedom of the seas were raised; the exact status of ambassadors and envoys was examined; matters of military discipline and of naval warfare were discussed; and generally the eminently practical and universally utilitarian character of international law was grasped once for all. The affinity of Zouche to this movement will be seen when we consider more closely the various departments of his work; and in this connection it will be well to note that the Peace of Westphalia was signed in 1648, and that in 1650 appeared the first edition of his principal work, the *De jure inter gentes*.

Zouche's Method and General Treatment.—Just as all his works adopt one method of exposition and arrangement, so the whole of his system is based on one central principle, one originating factor—the rationale of human relationship, the *ratio communionis humanæ*.[1] This is the root idea of his *Elementa*

[1] See preface to *De jure inter gentes*.

Jurisprudentiæ, and his subsequent writings are further developments and extended applications of this. First he deals with the general principles of law (*juris et judicii principia generalia*) appertaining to the *communio in genere*, then with the relationships between private persons (*communio quæ inter personas privatas intercedit*), between the sovereign and his subjects (*communio quæ privatis cum principibus intercedit*); after these he devotes treatises to *communiones speciales*—e.g. *sacra*,[1] *militaris*,[2] *maritima*,[3] *feudalis*;[4] and finally he takes up in his most considerable work[5] the relationships subsisting between nations, *eorum quæ ad communionem, quæ inter diversos principes aut populos intercedit, conducunt*. In all these dissertations he considers first the *Jus* (rights), the propositions of law generally accepted, *quæ sunt minus dubitati juris*, then the *Judicium* (remedies), comprising questions which give rise to controversy, *ea quæ videntur juris controversi*.[6] In conformity with this plan, he takes up, in his work on the law of nations, first the *Jus*, under the twofold aspects of peace and war. After a preliminary consideration of the definition and principal sources, he subdivides questions of peace into those relating to (1) *status*, relation of sovereign and subjects, relative position of states; (2) *dominium*, possession and how acquired; (3) *debitum*, envoys, ambassadors, treaties, alliances; (4) *delictum*; and, again, having examined the kinds of war and whether declaration is necessary, he classifies questions of war likewise under (1) *status*, kinds of military power, kinds of enemies; (2) *dominium*, capture, postliminium; (3) *debitum*, military conventions, access, truce, treaty of peace, hostages; (4) *delictum*, breaking military conventions, irregularities in warfare, etc. Then comes the second portion of the book, the *Judicium*. After touching on the settlement of disputes, and on questions of jurisdiction, he again deals first with peace: (1) *status*, sovereignty, relation of sovereign to subjects, nationality; (2) *dominium*, theory of occupation, territorial seas; (3) *debitum*, precedence of princes, ambassadors, promises of a sovereign, whether a successor is bound by previous treaties; (4) *delictum*, whether an offence against a subject is an offence against his sovereign, extradition, intervention, requisition of foreign vessels, violation of treaties. Lastly comes war, with introductory con-

---

[1] *Descriptio juris et judicii sacri.*
[2] *Descriptio juris et judicii militaris.*
[3] *Descriptio juris et judicii maritimi.*
[4] *Descriptio juris et judicii feudalis.*
[5] *Descriptio juris et judicii inter gentes.*
[6] See preface to *De jure inter gentes.*

sideration as to its legitimacy, who may undertake it, urgency of pacific settlement; then, as before : (1) *status*, who may be considered an enemy, domicile ; (2) *dominium*, how property is acquired, maritime captures, neutral goods on enemy vessels, contraband, right of visit ; (3) *debitum*, single combats, prisoners, ransoms, pursuing the enemy on neutral territory, when an ambassador may be arrested, conditions of capitulation by generals, treaty of peace made by them, treaty made in captivity, hostages, truce, safe-conduct ; (4) *delictum*, whether declaration is necessary, hostages, whether *lex talionis* is justifiable, offensive practices in war as to prisoners, women, sacred places.

The various matters under *Jus* he considers more or less categorically, those under *Judicium* he puts in the form of questions. He offers no explicit solutions to these, claiming only to set side by side diverse opinions and many examples of fact and precedent, from which he hopes the reader will be able, by a process of inductive or Socratic reasoning, to form his own conclusions.[1] His citation of authorities is extensive and systematic, and in every case he gives the exact reference. Above all publicists and jurists, " auctores historico jure periti," his guides are Gentilis and Grotius ; but apart from ancient writers and the Digest, he frequently refers to Bodin, Conradus Brunus, Paschalius, Besoldus, Ayala, Bartolus, Hotman, Camden, Selden, Welwood, and many others, and mentions also the laws of Rhodes, the *Siete Partidas* of Alfonso IX., and the *Consolato del Mare*. He is not, however, a servile follower of Grotius : in the first place, as has been already pointed out, he deals with peace before war, emphasizing the prior interests of peace ; and, secondly, he attaches great importance to contemporary facts and events.

Definition and Source of International Law.—He defines international law as that which controls the relationships between heads of States or sovereign peoples, either in peace or in war. The adoption of this law is due to the force of custom operating in conformity with reason, and it is in accordance with its principles and behests that nations are distinguished, kingdoms founded, commerce established, and war intro-

[1] As he says in his preface, *loc. cit.*, " A statuendo quicquam pro sua sententia abstinuit, consultius Academiæ Socraticæ institutam imitari ratus, quæ post causas et rationes allatas et quid in unaquaque parte dici possit expositum, audentium judicium integrum atque liberum reliquit."

duced.¹ This definition and the fundamental notions underlying it constitute an advance of the greatest importance. He contrasts with it the Roman conception of the *jus gentium*, and the definition of Gaius.² Tracing the sources, he briefly refers to the Roman fecial law as having been based on the *jus naturale*, then adds to this two other sources—the law arising from customs, and that arising from consent, as evidenced in treaties, pacts, alliances, leagues, conventions, etc.³

In his *Solutio quæstionis*, the later work on the legal position of the ambassador and his suite, he states that the privileges of ambassadors are based not on the law of nature but on the consent of nations—i.e., on the *jus gentium voluntarium*, arbitrary law built up as occasion and circumstance demand ("usu exigente et humanis necessitatibus").⁴ Natural law and arbitrary law may agree or may conflict ; where there is a conflict, universal abstract principles may have to yield to narrower practical interests. Similarly, Selden, in his *Mare clausum* (1635), and in his *De jure naturali et gentium* (1650) (the latter published in the same year as Zouche's *De jure inter gentes*), distinguishes between natural law and voluntary law ; the latter he terms *jus gentium interveniens*, and also *jus gentium secundarium*.⁵ " Interveniens autem jus gentium dicimus quod non ex communi pluribus imperio sed interveniente sive pacto sive morum usu natum est, et jus gentium secundarium fere solet indigetari."⁶

(a) **International Law in Time of Peace.**⁷—Zouche first discussed certain general questions (with numerous references to Aristotle, Pomponius, St. Augustine) : whether it is possible and desirable to be at peace with everybody, for example with barbarians ; whether greater advantages are produced by peace or war ; whether we ought to prefer an unjust peace to a just war,

---

¹ " Jus inter gentes est, quod in communione inter diversos principes, vel populos penes quos est imperium, usurpatur. Quod scilicet, moribus rationi congruis inter gentes plerasque receptum est, et id in quod gentes singulæ inter se consentiunt, et observatur inter eas quibuscum pax est et inter eas quibuscum bellum " (Part I., s. 1).
² Part I., s. 1, pp. 1, 2.
³ " Deinde præter mores communes pro jure etiam inter gentes habendum est, in quod gentes singulæ cum singulis inter se consentiunt, utpote per pacta, conventiones et fœdera, cum communis reipublicæ sponsio legem constituat, et populi universi, non minus quam singuli suo consensu obligentur " (Part I., s. 1, p. 2). ⁴ C. i.
⁵ This expression he borrowed from Vasquez.
⁶ *Mare clausum*, lib. i., c. 3.
⁷ It is not intended to follow here Zouche's order and arrangement of subject-matter, but it will be more profitable to treat it under the two heads of Peace and War.

etc. Peace, defined as ordered concord (the " ordinata concordia" of St. Augustine), is the normal condition of nations, and its interests predominate. It is of two kinds : *pax moralis*, between superiors and inferiors—*e.g.*, between the head of a family and the other members ; *pax civilis*, between equals—*e.g.*, between cities or States. He admits, however, an inequality *de facto* between the existing States, and this condition points to the urgent necessity of maintaining peace, for the purpose of general intercourse, hospitality, and, above all, commerce. Bodin had indicated a certain precedence amongst sovereigns ; thus, after the Pope he placed the Emperor, and then the French sovereign, who had recently defeated the claims of Spain.[1]

Territorial Sovereignty, and State Policy.—Does the fact of contracting an unequal treaty or accepting protection modify the status of a prince or State ? According to Proculus, Zouche points out, protection does not mean dependence, and the liberty of the *de facto* subordinate State must be respected. Sylla is quoted to the same effect : " clientes sunt sub patrocinio, non sub ditione." The case of Mary Stuart suggested the question whether a sovereign on his own territory had power over another. For the negative he points out that Mary was a free and independent princess, and could not be guilty of lèse-majesté (" in majestatem peccare non posset "),[2] since she was the equal of Elizabeth ; for the affirmative, that there cannot be in one kingdom two independent princes, and, besides, the equal may submit to the judgment of his equal either by express or by tacit consent, or through delictual obligation. By modern practice those who have not supreme power cannot send ambassadors ; thus, Elizabeth refused to receive an ambassador sent by the Duke of Alba, as he was not accredited by the Spanish sovereign. The criterion of sovereignty is not merely the possession of territory, but the government of subjects. Territory may be acquired (1) by occupation, if it never belonged to any one, (2) by prescription, if previously abandoned, (3) by donation, (4) by succession. Under the last head he examines different modes of the devolution of the Crown. These matters were " burning questions " in his time, in view of the accession of William of Orange, and the Spanish Succession.

With regard to sovereignty over the sea,[3] Zouche quotes Ulpian

---
[1] *De la République*, lib. i., c. ix.   [2] Part II., s. 2.
[3] *Cf.* the present writer's essay on Bynkershoek in the *Journal of Comparative Legislation*, August, 1908, pp. 34 *et seq.*

and Paulus as being mutually contradictory in their conception of occupation, and follows Grotius in admitting the right of exclusive jurisdiction of a State over its territorial seas. This subject is not considered by him to any large extent, as it had been fully treated before by Grotius, Selden, and others.

If a State inordinately augments its military or naval forces, and its warlike equipment generally, such a proceeding, whilst not necessarily implying a violation of any specific law of nations, may nevertheless amount in reality to a molestation of, or a hostile or unfriendly act to, a neighbouring State; in which case it is contended,[1] with Grotius, that the latter State has the right of intervention. The passage in Bacon's *Essays*[2] on this point may be recalled: "For there is no question but a just fear of an imminent danger, though there be no blow given, is a lawful cause of war."

Each State has the right of self-preservation, and therefore the right to prevent such practices on the part of others as may tend directly or indirectly to injure it. The question is asked:[3] May one prohibit the passage over one's territory of troops of neutrals or forbid the commerce of their subjects? He answers that such prohibition may be exercised in three cases: "(1) Si cum armatis transitus requiratur. . . . (2) Juste negatur transitus iis qui hostes adducunt. . . . (3) Si non a principe territorii petatur transitus. . . ."[4] As to commerce, Zouche accepts the rigorous doctrine of his contemporaries. It may be prohibited if it is calculated to debilitate or impoverish the State in any way; thus anything tending to weaken morals or religious faith may be forbidden, as also the exportation of gold and silver.

If disputes should arise between sovereigns or between their respective subjects, they may be settled pacifically by permanent judges, or by reference to arbitrators, or by acceptance of the existing *lex loci*, or by following the opinion of learned men.[5] He adds, moreover, that citizens may *prima facie* be under the jurisdiction of foreign courts, by reason of their committing a crime in a foreign country. These propositions, set forth at a time when

---

[1] Part I., s. 5. [2] The whole series published in 1625.
[3] "An iis quibuscum est amicitia transitus sit denegandus?" (Part II., s. 5, p. 112).
[4] Part II., s. 5, p. 112.
[5] "Judicium inter gentes est quo de controversiis inter ipsas earumve subditos statuitur, utpote (1) cum certos judices habent; (2) cum in arbitros compromittunt, (3) cum ratione loci judicium subeunt, (4) cum prudentes de iis censura ferunt" (Part II., s. 1, p. 54).

nations were only too ready to rush to arms, have received high commendation from later writers.[1]

Nationality and Domicile.—The doctrine of nationality was very ill-defined and obscure in the time of Zouche. He refers to the policy of ancient Rome,[2] where it was a constitutional maxim that acceptance of foreign citizenship by a Roman citizen operated *ipso facto* as a disfranchisement of his former rights.[3] In Greece and in other ancient States a different custom prevailed. With reference to modern times, it has in some quarters been maintained that an individual can enjoy concurrently the rights of citizenship of two States. Thus Heffter[4] says that to be a subject of several States may be tolerated : " Unterthan mehrerer Staaten zugleich kann man persönlich nur durch Duldung sein." Though special exceptions may be made for urgent reasons, the general rule is now admitted that " a man can have only one allegiance " ; and this law is laid down by Zouche with precision and clearness. Referring to the propriety of a decision in the French Courts on a question of domicile, he observes : " Fortassis vero id respexerunt, quod quamvis incolatus et domicilium in externo regno sufficiunt ad constituendum aliquem subditum jurisdictioni et præstandis muneribus obnoxium non tamen sit satis ad constituendum civem, ut eorum privilegiorum civilium sit particeps quae in regno natis competunt, nisi specialis allectio supervenerit."[5] Heffter remarks that Zouche goes too far in denying outright the possibility of more than one allegiance ;[6] and also refers to the practice of various ancient States (though not Rome), and to more recent admissions.[7] But modern views follow Zouche's doctrine. In 1848, for example, when Lord Brougham was desirous of naturalizing himself as a Frenchman, the French Minister of Justice, M. Crémieux, informed him that to do so would necessarily entail a renunciation of his rights as a British subject.[8]

Other kindred questions are discussed by Zouche, in addition to matters which now belong to the domain of private inter-

---

[1] *Cf.* for example, E. Cauchy : *Le Droit maritime international* (Paris, 1862).   [2] Part II., ss. 2, 13.

[3] *Cf.* Cicero, *Pro Balbo :* " Sed nos (Romani) non possumus et hujus esse civitatis et cujusvis præterea. . . ." (c. 12).

[4] *Das europäische Völkerrecht* (Berlin, 1867), p. 114.   [5] Part II., s. 2.

[6] " Jedoch ist dies zu weit gegangen. Alles hängt von dem Willen der Einzelstaaten ab " (*Ibid.*).

[7] Referring, for example, to Moser, vers. vi., 52, and to Günther, ii. 326.

[8] " La France n'admet pas de partage : pour devenir Français il faut cesser d'être Anglais. Si la France vous adopte pour l'un de ses enfants, vous n'êtes plus Lord Brougham, vous devenez le citoyen Brougham."

national law. He distinguishes emigration induced by want or oppression, from the deliberate founding of colonies, by which, according to Thucydides, a new people is formed not subject to the mother-country but her equal. If one sovereign is at the head of two different countries, does an individual born in one of them enjoy full rights of citizenship in the other ? He reports an affirmative answer in the case of Robert Calvin, a Scotch subject, and John Bingley, an English subject, with regard to succession to some property in London at the accession of James of Scotland to the English throne.[1] May a citizen renounce his allegiance and leave his country without permission ? With Cicero and Tryphonius, he appears to hold the affirmative, unless it is to avoid payment of debts or military service; but, with Grotius, he says it is otherwise in the case of collective desertion.[2] A person having lived a long time in a foreign country and established a family there is not to be necessarily considered as having renounced his country of origin, unless he formally naturalize himself; a decree of the Parliament of Paris is cited to this effect. An honour conferred on a subject by a foreign sovereign need not of necessity be recognized in his own country. With regard to national jurisdiction, Zouche refers to the important question of extradition. He points out that this is not a matter of established law, but that special treaties are often entered into on the subject by the States concerned.[3]

Ambassadors and Diplomacy.—Respect and good feeling ought to exist between the heads of friendly States and between the nations themselves. Courteous relations may be established either by the sovereign in person or by means of ambassadors and envoys, so that the interests of the respective States may be adjusted pacifically. Envoys charged with a special mission by virtue of the principle of *Jus congressus sive colloquii civilis* must be persons of rank or distinction.[4]

Before and at the time Zouche wrote, there were really no fixed rules as to the rights of ambassadors and their suites. Divers doctrines had been advanced. It was contended by some writers and publicists that ambassadors alone enjoyed absolute immunity,

---

[1] Part II., s. 2, p. 65.   [2] Grotius, l. ii., c. 5, § 24.
[3] " Et proinde in fœderibus sæpe cautum est ut subditi delinquentes, si petantur remittantur " (Part II., s. 5).
[4] " Debitum, sive officium, inter eos quibuscum pax est, est quod præstandum est, inter diversos principes, vel populos quibuscum pax intercedit, veluti jus congressus, legationis, conventionis, et fœderis civilis, cui fides interponitur, vel jusjurandum solenne adhibetur " (Part I., s. 3, p. 10).

by others that their suites must be placed in the same category, and again by others that under certain circumstances the local jurisdiction may be lawfully exercised.[1] Grotius insisted on the principle of exterritoriality, with its necessary implications. This legal fiction had many adherents, but was not by any means generally accepted. The opinion of Gentilis[2] was not quite decisive, but he inclined to the view that an ambassador is amenable to the territorial law, though in the special case of conspiracy he may be sent back to his sovereign. This procedure was adopted in the case of Mendoza (1584). Soon after this date an anonymous pamphlet[3] was issued in England, urging that an ambassador or even his sovereign, if found guilty of conspiring against a foreign State on the latter's territory, may be put to death. Later, under James I., Sir Robert Cotton denied total exemption; and similarly William Welwood held that respect is due to ambassadors so long as they respect the laws of the sovereign to whom they are accredited.

Zouche, following Grotius, maintains that the privileges of ambassadors rest on the consent of nations, that is, on the *jus gentium voluntarium*. He distinguishes between the various kinds of ambassadors—*e.g.*, religious, permanent, extraordinary. Strictly speaking, an ambassador is a representative sent only by a supreme Power, and not by a colony, or province, or municipality. He may take with him his suite (*familia*)—wife, children, servants; and also auxiliaries (*comites*). His letter of credit is the manifest of his authority. His sovereign's mandate is sometimes open (*apertum*), sometimes secret (*arcanum*). Certain honours due to him in receptions and audiences, and other rules of courtesy, are considered in detail.[4] A few questions are raised, but not answered: *e.g.*, How far is an ambassador bound by his instructions? Does he bind his sovereign if he acts contrary to his mandate, and if so, to what extent? Is he entitled to intervene in private affairs concerning his countrymen? Is he to be respected by others besides the sovereign to whom he is sent—*e.g.*, by princes whose territories he traverses? Does security extend to an exile sent as ambassador to his own country by a foreign prince? As for the last question, Gentilis had decided in the negative, Sir Edward Coke in the affirmative.[5]

[1] *Cf. Journal of Comparative Legislation*, August, 1908, pp. 36, 37.
[2] *De legationibus libri tres* (1585).
[3] *De legato et absoluto principe perduellionis reo* (1587).
[4] Part I., s. 4.   [5] *Ibid.*

In case of offences against an ambassador, it is pointed out that they are offences against the State to which he is sent, as well as against the State sending him.

As to civil actions, Zouche follows Grotius in opposition to Gentilis, in denying liability of the ambassador and suite to the local jurisdiction, but in any case his house may not be made a place of refuge for malefactors, as was also the opinion of Paschalius. In the case of criminal offences, if they are not serious they may be overlooked, but if grave, he admits, with Grotius, that the offending ambassador must be conducted back to his sovereign with a demand for his punishment or surrender.[1] To prevent imminent danger he may be arrested and examined. Should he, however, be guilty of armed violence, he may lawfully be put to death, not under pretext of trying or judging him, but as a legitimate self-defence, "per modum naturalis defensionis, non per modum pœnæ."

In Zouche's special work on the whole subject, his *Solutio quæstionis*, published in 1657 after the famous case of Don Pantaleon Sa (1653), he considers the conflicting arguments and examples, ancient and modern, for and against the exemption of ambassadors and their suites. He justifies the condemnation of Don Pantaleon Sa[2] on the ground that, being in the suite of his brother, the Portuguese ambassador, he was not exempt from the English jurisdiction.[3] He refers to Henry IV., King of France, who imprisoned the Spanish ambassador's secretary for attempting to corrupt a servant of the King, and, the ambassador complaining, the King replied: "Where have you learnt that ambassadors and their servants are at liberty to plot against the State and dignity of the prince with whom they reside ?"[4] Finally four reasons are stated why members of the suite are not independent of the local tribunals :[5] (1) they are more of the nature

---

[1] ". . . Eum remittendum ad principem qui eum misit cum postulato ut eum puniat aut dedat" (*Solutio quæstionis*, c. i.).

[2] *Cf. Journal of Comparative Legislation*, loc. cit., p. 37.

[3] Leibnitz condemned the conduct of Cromwell in this case as an infraction of the law of nations (*De jure suprematus ac legationis principum Germaniæ*, c. vi.).

Similarly, Bynkershoek stated (*De foro legatorum*, 1721, c. xviii.) that he had found very few cases of such punishment, and that such rare exceptions ought not to be held as invalidating the general rule of immunity. (*Cf. Journal of Comparative Legislation*, loc. cit., pp. 36 et seq.).

[4] "Ubinam gentium didicistis legatos et eorum ministros potestatem habere machinandi contra Statum et dignitatem principis apud quem legationem obeunt ?" (*Solutio quæstionis*).

[5] *Ibid.*, c. xiv.

of the appurtenances of the ambassador (" comites vero facti sunt accessorie tantum "), and do not possess the same qualifications; (2) letters of credit are not given to them; (3) the ambassador alone is the representative of his prince, and this fact is the main basis of immunity ("legatus solus personam principis sustinet, quod est præcipuum immunitatis fundamentum "); and lastly (4) more credit and confidence are given to ambassadors by the sovereigns to whom they are accredited (" quod plus legatis quam comitibus eorum ab eo quo admittit credi oporteat ") because they are generally men of approved reputation, few in number, and easy to be watched and prevented in any mischievous design.

A few matters remain to be mentioned under the head of peace. The contractual transactions of a sovereign carry with them the same rights and obligations as they would in the case of a private citizen. Agreements made by a sovereign without any stipulation as to duration—for example, for the delivery of towns or other places, and sums of money—descend to his successors, when they have been concluded under considerations of public utility.[1] More solemn engagements, such as formal treaties, define clearly certain reciprocal rights and obligations, and have as an additional sanction the oath of fidelity, the *suprema religio*.[2]

May we conclude treaties with people of a different religion ?[3] This question points to the fact that, though the *De jure inter gentes* had been published two years after the Peace of Westphalia, it must have been written some time before; otherwise he would surely have taken cognizance of its new provisions indicating greater breadth of view and toleration. In the consideration of various other matters, it appears that Zouche does not hesitate to declare that where the undertakings or promises of a sovereign conflict with public policy or national interest of vital importance, the latter should predominate. For example: Is a sovereign who has promised help to another State bound to furnish it should there be afterwards serious difficulties in his way ?[4] Zouche adopts a stringent interpretation of the clause *rebus sic stantibus*. In 1585 Queen Elizabeth had promised the United Provinces men and money, but new circumstances having arisen, she referred the matter to certain jurists, who declared that every convention

---

[1] Part I., s. 4, and Part II., s. 4.   [2] Part I., s. 4.
[3] " An fœdus inire liceat cum iis qui alieni sunt a religione ?" (Part II., s. 4). [By *religio* he means the Christian religion.]
[4] " An princeps qui promisit auxilia cum commode non possit, præstare teneatur ?" (*ibid*).

must be understood *rebus sic stantibus*, and that hence she was relieved of her engagement. May we revoke privileges of commerce granted in an agreement with foreigners ?[1] Zouche does not admit that privileges may be so far exercised by foreigners as to inflict injury on our own subjects, and that therefore in such a case they may be revoked ; in support of which opinion he recalls a certain negotiation between Elizabeth and the Hanseatic towns. A solemn oath exacted through fear may not on that account be repudiated, though it may be otherwise in the case of an informal promise ; but an oath taken under a mistaken notion of material and relevant facts, or through fraudulent representations, cannot be considered as binding.[2] If one of the parties to a treaty violates a single condition, then the other contracting party may repudiate the whole.[3]

(*b*) **International Law in Time of War. Writings before Zouche.**—The chapters of Zouche's treatise which are devoted to war, like those dealing with peace, are more thorough and comprehensive, more systematic, and authoritative than any of the contributions by his English predecessors. The publication, indeed, of Gentilis' *De jure belli* (1589) marks an important date in the history of international law,[4] and Zouche alone of all the writers in England for a century subsequent to Gentilis recognized fully the importance of this work, and took an account of its doctrines, many of which are accepted by him unhesitatingly. Soon after the *De jure belli* there appeared in England several works—translations, adaptations, or more or less original contributions—*e.g.*, Eliot's *Discourse of War and Single Combat ;* and *Instructions for the Warres*, a translation from the French. Much more considerable than these is the original work, published in 1593 by Matthew Sutcliffe : *The Practice, Proceedings and Lawes of Armes*, the indebtedness of which to Gentilis is apparent. He deals with the various causes of war, ridicules the idea of war being illegitimate when there is a just cause (in opposition to earlier objections on the ground of its being contrary to religion), insists on the right of sovereigns to prevent the large increase of

[1] " An commercii sive negotiationis privilegia, de quibus cum exteris convenit, revocare liceat ?" (*ibid.*).
[2] " Si certum est eum qui juravit aliquod factum supposuisse quod revera ita se non habeat ac nisi id credidisset, non fuisse juraturum, non obligabit juramentum " (*ibid.*).
[3] " Si pars altera in fœdere fefellerit, potest altera discedere " (Part II., s. 5).
[4] *Cf.* E. Nys, *op. cit.*

forces by their neighbours, denounces the Spanish encroachments, points approvingly to the action of Louis XI., Lorenzo de' Medici preserving the balance of Italian States, and Elizabeth's policy with regard to the Low Countries, holds that declaration of war is not necessary when one is attacked (as in the case of the war with Philip II.), and emphasizes that in the sacking of towns mercy must be shown to women, children, the old and feeble. Questions relating to prisoners and prizes are also considered. The aim and nature of war are thus summarized : " Those warres are just and lawful which are made by the souveraigne magistrate, for lawful and just causes, being both orderly denounced in cases requisite and moderately prosecuted, to the end that justice may be done and an assured peace obteined." Some ten years later William Fulbecke issued *The Pandectes of the Law of Nations* ... (1602), of which the seventh chapter treats of war, based on the authority of Gentilis and Ayala. A solemn declaration is demanded, and prisoners are not to be put to death. Similarly, Richard Bernard, writing in 1629, urges moderation and mercy, and affirms the legitimacy of war, allows right of conquest and right of booty, and like Gentilis and Sutcliffe, admits the right of intervention with a view to self-preservation.

Zouche on the Law of Nations in time of War.—Though Zouche exhibits a greater grasp and breadth of treatment, his kinship to these earlier writers is obvious. He defines war as a struggle undertaken by the sovereign power for a just cause.[1] As a rule a formal declaration is necessary. Under such circumstances it would be *bellum solenne*, in contradistinction to *bellum minus solenne*—private war, as family against family, admitted by the ancients,[2] or as in the case of reprisals. Measures of reprisal are not permissible in private law, as it is contrary to natural equity to inflict an injury on one person on account of the liability of another. But it is otherwise in the law of nations ; in which case each individual is considered as forming a constituent part of the State, and therefore liable for its default.[3]

[1] " . . . Justa contentio quæ scilicet authoritate legitima et ex justa causa movetur " (Part I., s. 6). *Cf.* the statement of Suarez.
[2] ἀνδροληψία, literally "seizure of men" (λαμβάνω, λήψομαι) : an Athenian law, which, in case a citizen's murder abroad remained unpunished, authorized the seizure of three citizens of the offending State. (*Cf. Lex ap. Dem.* 647, 24 *seq.* : 1232, 4).
[3] " Jure tamen gentium introductum apparet, ut pro eo quod præstare debet civilis societas, aut ejus caput, sive per se primo sive quod alieno debito jus non reddendo, se obstrinxerint, obligata sint bona omnium subditorum " (Part II., s. 6).

It is the duty of States to try by every means to obtain satisfaction before resorting to warlike measures.

Declaration, however, may be legitimately dispensed with in certain cases : (1) when a war is begun for purposes of necessary self-defence ; (2) against those who are already considered as enemies (*hostes*) ; (3) against rebels or traitors to whom the law of nations does not apply ; and (4) when ambassadors are sent to demand satisfaction, and do not obtain it.[1]

He examines the different kinds of military power in war, and distinguishes classes of enemies : " Status inter eos quibuscum bellum est, est conditio inter ipsos quæ ad imperium militare refertur, quod est dominationis, præpotentiæ, et patrocinii militaris, vel conditio cum aliis ex qua alii inimici, alii hostes habentur."[2] Thus, military power is of three kinds : *dominatio*, acquired by force of arms ; *præpotentia*, authority of conqueror over the conquered ; *patrocinium*, military rights of the sovereign as to vassals. As to enemies, they may be *inimici, adversarii, hostes*—e.g., brigands, rebels, traitors, pirates (" quos offendere et perdere omnino licet "), and *justi hostes* (" quibus omnia belli jura debentur "). A few relative questions are next raised :[3] Can we consider as enemies those who violate natural law, or the law of nations, those of another religion [meaning probably those not of the Christian religion], subjects of a friendly State living in enemy territory ? Is an enemy subject living in neutral territory to be considered enemy or neutral ? Zouche gives many conflicting examples and opinions, but his own conclusion does not clearly appear.

Property may be acquired in two ways : *acquisitio particularis*, by individuals ; *acquisitio universalis*, by the State, when territories are invaded or surrendered. Are those things which are taken by the enemy and carried off to neutral territory to be restored to the original owners ? He inclines to the affirmative, and mentions a case in support : thus, when Spanish ships were

---

[1] " . . . (1) Cum suscipitur bellum ex causa necessariæ defensionis, (2) cum his bellum infertur, qui jam hostes habentur, (3) cum contra rebelles et defectores arma sumuntur, quia cum illis jus gentium non observatur . . . (4) . . . cum legatis res repetentibus eæ nec redditæ sunt, nec sit aliter satisfactum " (Part II., s. 10).

M. Scelle observes somewhat sarcastically on this statement and in reference to British practice : " On sait que les jurisconsultes anglais ont toujours admis que parfois la déclaration peut être omise, et que la pratique anglaise en a souvent sur ce point pris à son aise avec le droit des gens " (*op. cit.*, p. 313).

[2] Part I., s. 7.   [3] Part II., s. 7.

captured by the Dutch and carried to an English port, the Court of Admiralty ordered their restitution. Does a thing taken from the enemy become the property of the captors before it is carried by them to a safe place ? Can a thing be considered as captured when it can no longer escape from its pursuers ? Zouche defines *postliminium* in the terms of Paulus : " . . . Jus amissæ rei recipiendæ ab extraneo et in statum pristinum restituendæ . . .," and the different rules laid down are taken substantially from the Roman jurisprudence. May we plunder the property of those whose forts and fields are occupied by the enemy ? Yes, in the case of property previously belonging to the enemies themselves, or afterwards lawfully acquired by them.[1]

A large number of questions are suggested relating to military discipline and to the organization of military justice. Many of these matters had been more or less regulated in England from early times, rules for each war having been drawn up by the king or by the commander-in-chief. Thus, regulations and ordinances were issued by John, Richard I., Richard II., Henry V. (the latter of whom ordered the protection of women and children, priests and sacred objects, and men at the plough) ; further regulations were made by Henry VII., Henry VIII., and Elizabeth ; and in the Civil War rules were drawn up for the Royal forces by the Duke of Northumberland (1640), and the *Laws and Ordinances of War* (1643), by Essex, or the Parliamentary forces. Zouche, following this tradition, discusses divers matters arising in the conduct of warfare, and various reciprocal obligations of the belligerents. He deals with the *congressus militaris*, when sovereigns or commanders come to a conference or single combat ; military envoys ; ambassadors extraordinary to negotiate truces and conditions of peace. Military arrangements between the respective heads relate to (1) free access (*de commeatu*), (2) truces (*de induciis*), (3) exchange and ransom of prisoners (*de captivis permutandis et redimendis*), (4) surrender of places (*de conditionibus iis qui loca obsessa dedunt*). Military treaties are concluded by the sovereign power when armistices and final peace are concerned. Do treaties of peace concluded by generals bind the sovereign or State ? Zouche refers to the insistence of the Roman Senate as to the necessity of its sanction. But when the sovereign power has had cognizance of such treaty and has acquiesced, ratification is to be presumed where such circumstances exist as imply con-

[1] Part II., s. 8.

currence with the conditions; though mere silence in itself does not warrant this inference.¹ If an engagement entered into by a general is repudiated by the sovereign, ought the other party to be restored to its *status quo ante?*

Then follow some questions relating to hostages : Can they be restored after the death of the one for whom they had been given ? Can fugitive hostages be received by those who had given them ?² To the latter question Gentilis and Grotius gave a negative reply which, Zouche points out, is in conformity with the contention of Edward III. of England. May we put to death hostages for an offence of the one who has given them ? Gentilis says yes, Grotius no, but Zouche does not decide. Does the *lex talionis* exist between enemies ? Gentilis seems to defend it, and Grotius is against it. To kill prisoners taken by us when we have no means of securely maintaining them in our power is condemned by Gentilis. Illegitimate practices are pointed out— though rather suggested in the form of questions—*e.g.*, ill-treatment of prisoners, women and children, women who take up arms, profanation of sacred places, use of guile, lying, or ambush in military conferences, poison, assassination, refusal of burial to enemies, ill-treatment of envoys and of those who surrender, and various other practices of a like nature.

Maritime Law and Naval War.—English writings on maritime law before Zouche are not of great consequence. The rules of the *Consolato del Mare*, embodying customs many of which date from very early times, for a long time regulated the law as to prizes in England, as in many other States. Edward III., Richard II., and Henry VII. largely prohibited the importation of goods except on English vessels; Elizabeth excluded foreign boats from the fisheries in the adjacent seas, and also from the coasting-trade. In the sixteenth century England energetically opposed the rule "robe d'ennemi confisque celle d'ami," which France claimed to have established. In the middle of the next century, important legislative measures were passed—*e.g.*, the Long Parliament prohibited (1650) foreign vessels from trading with the American colonies, except by special licence; and in the following year Cromwell passed the *Act of Navigation.*

---

[1] Part II., s. 9.
[2] " Gentilis vero et Grotius ambo concludunt civitatem quæ dedit obsidem recipere et retinere non debere, non magis quam recipere rem datam pignori citra furti crimen ; et proinde Edvardus tertius Rex Angliæ uste accusabat quod contra jus obsidem fugientem recepisset " (Part II., s. 9).

William Welwood's *Abridgement of all Sea-lawes* (1613) touches on the jurisdiction of the judges of the High Court of Admiralty, and on the controversy as to fishing. He maintains that there is not necessarily a universal liberty to fish in any sea whatever, and protests against Grotius' confusing liberty of navigation with liberty of fishing. Gentilis, in his *Advocatio Hispanica* (1613), deals with the various disputes which had arisen between England and Spain and other Powers, and considers certain matters relating to contraband, prizes, and pirates.

The little that Zouche has to say on the law of naval war is concerned with the requisition of foreign vessels, maritime captures, and right of visit. He maintains that requisition for war of foreign vessels touching our ports may be quite legitimate.[1] Is it permissible to confiscate neutral property on an enemy vessel? In the time of Zouche the prevailing maxim was that if the vessel could be legally confiscated, then its cargo could also be seized.[2] In the opinion of Grotius this is only a presumption as to the enemy character of the cargo, and could be rebutted by evidence to the contrary. With regard to enemy goods on a neutral vessel, Zouche states that the English Court of Admiralty had decided that they may be lawfully captured. Right of visit is regarded by him from the point of view of a maritime ceremonial, which depends on the mutual agreement or comity of nations. A merchant-vessel which fails to salute a foreign man-of-war cannot merely on that account be taken as a lawful prize. A vessel is considered captured if it is brought to the captor's port, or to a station where his fleet lies, *intra præsidia*, in such a way that possibility of recapture is minimized;[3] but to make the rule more precise, safe detention during twenty-four hours, as Grotius stated, was recognized by European nations as the criterion.[4]

Neutrality, Contraband, etc.—Little is said by Zouche about the rights and duties of neutrals and the correlative rights and obligations of belligerents. He uses the terms *amicus* and *amicitia* instead of the more expressive *neutral* and *neutrality*, which had already been used before him, though by no means generally.[5]

---

[1] Part II., s. 5.

[2] "... Si navis sit obnoxia, bona etiam obnoxia haberi" (Part II., s. 8).

[3] "Placuit vero gentibus ut rem cepisse is intelligatur quia ita detinet ut recuperandi spem probabilem alter amiserit; ut, cum res mobiles intra fines, id est, intra præsidia perductæ fuerint" (Part II., s. 8).

[4] "Sed recentiori jure gentium inter Europæos, inquit Grotius, introductum videtur, ut talia capta censeantur, ubi per horas viginti quatuor in potestate hostium fuerint" (*ibid.*).

[5] *Cf. Journal of Comparative Legislation, loc. cit.*, pp. 42 seq.

Is it permissible to pursue an enemy on neutral territory ? He inclines to the opinion that an enemy, by the law of nations, may be pursued everywhere.[1] May we carry over neutral territory a prisoner captured on enemy territory ? His opinion appears to be in the negative, provided he has not yet been carried *intra præsidia*.[2] He recalls an instance in the war between Geneva and Milan ; the latter caused prisoners to pass over the territory of Bologna ; and John of Immola, a celebrated jurist, having been consulted by the pontifical legate, decided that it was an infraction of the law of nations.

The subject of contraband[3] has been one of the most disputed questions in the whole range of international law, from the earliest to the most recent times. In the time of Zouche, usage and practice were changeable and capricious, and adopted by each State as it thought fit and convenient in view of its own interests. It was only after his time that a distinct international effort was made—*e.g.*, in the Treaty of the Pyrenees (1659) and in the Treaty of Utrecht (1713), to indicate more clearly the nature of contraband goods, and to enumerate certain specific articles. Zouche follows Grotius' view that only such things ought to be considered contraband as directly serve for war, or can be so utilized— *e.g.*, arms, money, provisions. He admits that this is a logical inference from the fact that the institution of contraband is a penal measure. But he goes further than Grotius and Bynkershoek in regarding also as contraband, in certain cases, those things of which admittedly contraband goods can be made— *e.g.*, iron (for arms), wood (for ships), etc. In this respect, he takes into account the nature of the surrounding circumstances in each particular case, and urgent national necessity.[4] Sometimes, indeed, the more stringent measures will be necessary to prevent fraud. He is no doubt guided in this attitude by the provisions of the Roman law—*e.g.*, the *senatus consultum Macedonianum*—which prohibited not only loans of money to a minor, but also those things for which money could be procured, " cum contractus fraudem sapit."

Again, are accessories of prohibited articles—*e.g.*, sheaths for

---

[1] " Hostis qui est ubique secundum jus gentium impeti potest " (Part II., s. 9).

[2] " . . . Alibi captus, nondum intra præsidia deductus, in alieno territorio detineri, vel coerceri non debet " (Part II., s. 9).

[3] *Cf. Journal of Comparative Legislation, loc. cit.*, pp. 44 *seq.*

[4] "Ubi est eadem ratio prohibitionis, materiæ et speciei, item jus in utraque consendum est " (Part II., s. 8).

swords—to be themselves prohibited ? Many ancient examples are cited, but no opinion is expressed. Similarly, no solution is given to the further problems suggested : May we intercept those things returning from the enemy, as well as those going to him ? Is tobacco to be considered as contraband [on the supposition that it may be used for preserving provisions !] ? Finally, what is the position in the case of a mixture of contraband goods and lawful goods found on a vessel ? Zouche insists, and quotes an ancient author[1] in support, that it is essential to discriminate between the case where both kinds of goods belong to the same owner, and the case where they belong to different owners. In the event of the former, both may be lawfully confiscated,—at least if the owner was aware of the fraudulent shipment. There is no reference in Zouche's work to English contemporary practice, but it appears that the earlier custom of the Admiralty Courts was to condemn both ship and cargo irrespective of ownership ; afterwards the rule was relaxed, so that confiscation applied to the vessel and the innocent portion of the cargo only when they were the property of the owners of the contraband, or where there was fraudulent conduct.[2]

Value of Zouche's Work.—The substance of Zouche's work on international law has now been considered, his doctrines have been briefly set forth, and his relationship to his predecessors and contemporaries has been indicated. His wide learning, and great ability—judicial as well as literary—were recognized in his own time ; and his opinions, both in his lifetime and after his death, were regarded as possessing high authority. His versatility was remarkable. As M. Rivier[3] remarks : " Er war berühmt als scharfer, gelehrter, vielseitiger Jurist, 'living Pandect of the Law,' Civilist, Canonist, Feudist, Publicist, auch als Dichter ; vorzüglich bedeutend ist er aber als einer von den Begründern der Wissenschaft des Völkerrechts." His fame spread on the Continent, several editions of his work were reprinted, and translations were made.[4]

---

[1] Petrinus Bellus, *De re militari*.
[2] *Cf.* Robinson's *Admiralty Reports*, vol. iii., p. 221, note (*a*), (cited by Wheaton *History of the Law of Nations*, p. 134).
[3] In F. von Holtzendorff : *Handbuch des Völkerrechts* (Berlin, 1885), vol. i., p. 417.
[4] His *De jure inter gentes*, Oxford, 1650; Leyden, 1651; The Hague, 1659 ; Mayence, 1661 ; last Latin edition, 1759.
A German translation, or rather adaptation, in which Zouche's name is not mentioned, was published by Gottfried Vogel, Frankfort, 1666, under the

Varying estimates of his work, however, have been made in more modern times. Wheaton,[1] for example, regards the *De jure inter gentes* as a mere abridgment of Grotius, with illustrations for the most part drawn from Roman law and Roman history, and asserts that its title to fame rests merely on the happy terminological innovation—" jus inter gentes." On the other hand, M. Rivier, as above, terms him one of the founders of the science of international law; Kaltenborn[2] speaks of his principal book as the first real treatise on international law; Ompteda[3] uses similar expressions, and holds that Zouche occupies an important place in the history of the law of nations. The true estimate is nearer to the latter than to that of Wheaton, who cannot, surely, have read the work he so unjustifiably disparages.

It is true that Zouche is more of a systematizer of doctrines than an innovator; but then the same remark largely applies to such a great writer as Grotius. Indeed, it would have been impossible then to be otherwise, considering the epoch in which he wrote, the nature of contemporary events, the unsettled relationship between States, the clash of international politics, the conflict of religions—in a word, the rapidly changing character of the age. To write abstract, theoretically complete, and, as it were, final treatises—seemingly adapted more for a Utopia than for an imperfect world—is to do much towards instigating nations to discredit the whole fabric of international law; and Zouche was far too wise to attempt such a task.

The more certain subject-matter of the law of nations he

---

title of *Allgemeines Volkerrecht, wie auch allgemeines Urtheil und Ansprüche aller Völker*.

His other important work, dealing with the legal position of ambassadors, and forming a supplement to and expansion of his treatment of the same subject in the earlier work is the *Solutio quæstionis* . . . . first published at Oxford, 1657; Cologne, 1662; Berlin, 1669 (with notes by Hennelius).

A German translation was issued at Jena, 1717, by J. J. Lehmann, under the title of *Eines vornehmen englischen Jureconsulti Gedanken von dem Traktement eines Ministers;* an English translation by D. J., London, 1717; and another in the same year by an unknown translator, giving the Latin text also.

(The latter three translations were published in connection with the affair of Gyllenburg, the Swedish ambassador.)

[1] *Op. cit.*, p. 101.
[2] *Kritik des Volkerrechts* (1847): " Das erste eigentliche Lehrbuch des Völkerrechts."
[3] " Dieses ist als das erste Lehrbuch des gesammten Völkerrechts anzusehen, und verdienst daher vorzügliche Aufmerksamkeit. . . . Kann man sagen dass Zouchäus der erste ist, der das Völkerrecht in seinem ganzen theoretischen sowohl also practischen Umfange erkannt und abgezeichnet hat, und daher in dieser Wissenschaft eine wichtige Stelle einnimmt" (*Litteratur des Volkerrechts*, Regensburg, 1785, pp. 252, 253).

arranged consistently and logically, and set forth in a style marked by precision and conciseness. The more doubtful matter he incorporated in its proper place, but in the form of questions, many of which he leaves unsolved, and many, if not receiving a categorical answer, are impliedly answered—even then only tentatively—by means of examples and analogies. He does not attempt profound analysis, and carefully avoids metaphysical disquisitions; he is content to be guided by practical common-sense and the necessity of time and place.

His manner is characterized by modesty and reserve, being a marked contrast to the vigorous self-assertiveness and dogmatic insistence of Bynkershoek. The work of Zouche is of comparatively modest compass; it does not perhaps occupy as high a position in the evolution of international law as the treatise of Grotius; but the English writer made a distinct advance on his predecessor in many respects—*e.g.*, the use of the expressive "jus inter gentes," and its underlying conception, the recognition of the supremacy of conventional law over "natural," the use of recent examples of custom and practice, the constant implication of the relativity of legal development to political evolution. Zouche is the greatest of the earlier English school of international jurists and publicists; and the subsequent traditions of this school of writers—not to mention many Continental writers of the positive school—owe much to his influence and example.

JEAN BAPTISTE COLBERT

JEAN BAPTISTE COLBERT,[1] the famous Minister of Louis XIV.,[2] during the middle, and best, period of the latter's reign,[3] is

[1] At the time of his death Colbert was Marquis de Seigneley et de Chateauneuf sur Cher, Baron de Sceaux, Lumieres, and other places (see Jal's *Dictionnaire de Biographie et d'Histoire*, tit. Colbert, p. 399).

[2] Louis XIV.'s principal merit is said to have consisted in his allowing himself to be guided by such a mind as Colbert's, which was so vastly superior to his own (Bonnechose's *History of France*, 1862, English edition, p. 399). It should, however, be remembered that Louis XIV. himself was a man of strong character and great ability, in whom there was, according to Cardinal Mazarin, the wherewithal to make four good kings and one honest man (Martin's *History of France*, 4th ed., vol. xiii., p. 4), while, in the opinion of Lord Acton, he was by far the ablest man, born in modern times, on the steps of a throne (*Lectures on Modern History*, by Lord Acton, p. 234), and his reign, if Voltaire is to be believed, of greater value to France than twenty ordinary reigns (*Siècle de Louis XIV.*, vol. 18 of Voltaire's collected works, published in 1819, p. 206).

[3] That is to say, from 1661 to 1683. Cardinal Mazarin died on March 6, 1661, and, on the following day, Louis XIV. summoned to the Louvre the Chancellor Segnier and the three Secretaries of State—namely, Nicholas Fouquet (Superintendent of the Finances), Michael le Tellier (Minister of War), and Hugues de Lionne *or* Lyonne (Minister of Foreign Affairs), to whom he intimated, in the course of an address, that though, till then, he had allowed the late Cardinal to govern the country, in future he would be his own prime minister (" Je serai, à l'avenir, mon premier ministre "), to whom ministers could, when invited to do so, give advice. The Chancellor was, accordingly, forbidden to seal any document without the King's command, while the Secretaries of State were directed not to sign anything without the King's permission (Martin's *History of France*, 4th ed., vol. xiii., pp. 549, 550). Many doubted (and notably Fouquet) whether the young King, then only twenty-two and a half years of age, would persevere in his resolution henceforward to govern in person. How completely this doubt was falsified is proved by the fact that Louis XIV. held the reins of power in his own hands for fifty-four years (*i.e.*, till his death on September 1, 1715), and never once relaxed his hold of them (Martin's *History of France*, 4th ed., vol. xiii., p. 4). During this long period, Louis XIV., who possessed an excellent memory and immense fertility of resource, devoted nine hours a day to public business (*Lectures on Modern History*, by Lord Acton, p. 234). The first eleven years, however, of the young King's personal government (*i.e.*, from 1661 to 1672) were so much influenced by the ideas of Colbert that the reign of Louis XIV. and the biography of his great minister are almost identical (*Cambridge Modern History*, vol. v., p. 15 ; and see Martin's *History of France*, 4th ed., vol. xiii., p. 35). It was not, however, until 1669 that Colbert attained the full rank of Secretary of State, though for some years previously he had

JEAN BAPTISTE COLBERT

identified with so many splendid achievements [1] that his claim to recognition, as a jurist and law reformer is apt to be somewhat overlooked. To the ordinary student of French history, Colbert figures as an able and successful financier,[2] as the founder of the

---

really conducted most of the affairs of State (*post;* Martin's *History of France*, 4th ed., vol. xiii., pp. 23, 33, 34 ; *Colbert, Promoteur des Grands Ordonnances de Louis XIV.*, by Alfred Aymé, p. 11). In view of these circumstances, it is a little difficult to understand why Lord Acton should refer to Colbert as though the latter had been already, at the date of Mazarin's death, in 1661, a departmental minister (*Lectures on Modern History*, by Lord Acton, p. 234), though, undoubtedly, for some little time previously to the death of Cardinal Mazarin, Colbert had *secretly* and unofficially assisted Louis XIV. in overhauling Fouquet's financial budgets (see *post*), and, moreover, as far back as 1649, had been appointed a *Conseiller d'État*, at the instance of Michael le Tellier, with whom Colbert was connected by marriage.

[1] See *Lettres, Instructions, et Mémoires de Colbert*, by Pierre Clement, vol. i., p. 1. When, in 1669, Colbert was appointed Secretary of State, he was also given the control of the navy, commerce, the colonies, the King's household, Paris, ecclesiastical matters, and the government of L'Ile de France, and of L'Orleannais (Martin's *History of France*, 4th ed., vol. xiii., pp. 33, 34). He then only became the equal, in official rank, of obscure ministers whose names history has scarcely preserved (*ibid.*). It was, however, primarily as a great financier that he obtained recognition as a first-class statesman. But "les finances n'étaient pour Colbert, qu'un point d'appui, d'ou il allait saisir toutes les branches de la puissance publique." Il était prêt pour tout, et propre à tout" (Martin's *History of France*, 4th ed., vol. xiii., p. 32), and eventually obtained the control of nearly all the departments of government (*Colbert, Promoteur des Grands Ordonnances de Louis XIV.*, by Alfred Aymé, p. 11).

[2] When still working behind the scenes and unknown to fame, Colbert, on August 31, 1659, wrote to Cardinal Mazarin that "Les finances avaient grand besoin d'une chambre de justice, sévère et rigoureuse" (*Lettres, Instructions, et Mémoires de Colbert*, by Pierre Clement, vol. ii., part i., p. xiv) and that he could not conscientiously associate any longer with Fouquet, the Superintendent of Finance, who had ceased to be honest and devoted to the State (*ibid.*, p. v ; and see Martin's *History of France*, 4th ed., vol. xiii., p. 24). The Cardinal accordingly, shortly before his own death, advised the King to employ Colbert to help him secretly to discover Fouquet's financial delinquencies, a work which Colbert continued to discharge down to September 15, 1661, when Fouquet's arrest, which had been decided upon some months previously, took place (see Martin's *History of France*, 4th ed., vol. xiii., pp. 26, 27, 28 ; *Lettres, Instructions, et Mémoires de Colbert*, by Pierre Clement, vol. ii., part i., p. xiv ; *Life and Times of Louis XIV.*, by G. P. R. James, vol. iii., pp. 101, 122). After a trial, which lasted practically for four years, and in which all forms of law are said to have been violated in order to secure a conviction, Fouquet was, on December 20, 1664, condemned to perpetual banishment, a sentence which was immediately, and somewhat harshly, altered by the King to one of imprisonment for life (see *Lettres, Instructions, et Mémoires de Colbert*, by Pierre Clement, vol. ii., part i., pp. 1 *et seq.* ; *Life and Times of Louis XIV.*, by G. P. R. James, vol. iii., pp. 141, 142), being, *semble*, the only instance in the history of modern Europe of a monarch commuting a gentler for a severer punishment (*Life and Times of Louis XIV.*, by G. P. R. James, vol. iii., p. 142). Colbert and Le Tellier, who are accused of having entertained towards Fouquet a vindictive hatred (*Mazarin et Colbert*, by the Comte de Cosnac, vol. i., p. 80), and who certainly

French Navy,[1] as the reviver of the Commerce of France,[2] as the

worked together for his destruction, had hoped for Fouquet's condemnation to death (*ibid.*, pp. 141 *et seq.*; *Lettres, Instructions, et Mémoires de Colbert*, by Pierre Clement, vol. i., p. xxvii) for high treason, a sentence which, in view of the evidence produced at the trial, would not, it seems, have been altogether illegal and unwarrantable (*Lettres, Instructions, et Mémoires de Colbert*, by Pierre Clement, vol. ii., part i., p. ii). Marshall Turenne, in reference to the part taken by Colbert and Le Tellier in the Fouquet trial, said : "Je crois que M. Colbert à plus d'envie qu'il soit pendu, et que M. Le Tellier à plus de peur qu'il ne le soit pas" (*ibid.*, p. xxvii). Colbert's uncle by marriage, Henri Pussort, seems to have shared his nephew's dislike of Fouquet. At all events he spoke for four hours, with great vehemence and passion, against Fouquet at the latter's trial (*Lettres de Madame de Sévigné*, 1862 ed., vol. i., p. 469). Immediately after Fouquet's disgrace, Colbert, first in March, 1661, as Intendant of Finance, and eventually, in December, 1665, as Comptroller-General of Finance, proceeded to realize his projects of financial reform (Martin's *History of France*, 4th ed., vol. xiii., p. 39), introduced into the public accounts order, regularity, and simplicity, and adopted a new system of collecting revenue. He paid off, at the price of their original purchase, the Rentes which had been acquired by public moneylenders, at sums far below their face value, and endeavoured to put the State on the footing of a great mercantile community (see, generally, *Lettres, Instructions, et Mémoires de Colbert*, by Pierre Clement, vol. ii., part i., pp. xiv *et seq.*; *Life and Times of Louis XIV.*, by G. P. R. James, vol. iii., pp. 168 *et seq.*). Moreover, he made Fouquet's partizans, as they were called, disgorge the public monies they had appropriated (*ibid.*). By these means Colbert was enabled to remit some taxation and replenish the exhausted exchequer; and he eventually trebled the public revenue, but did not make it depend on the growth of private incomes or the execution of useful public works (*Lectures on Modern History*, by Lord Acton, p. 244). Owing, however, to the great wars carried on by Louis XIV. during Colbert's administration, the financial condition of France gradually degenerated, until national insolvency was again almost reached, and Colbert, much against his will, was obliged to revert to measures for raising money, which he had himself condemned when adopted by Fouquet (Voltaire's *Collected Works*, published in 1819, vol. xviii., pp. 220, 221).

[1] In lieu of the thirty old ships, left by Cardinal Mazarin at the time of his death, in 1661, ten years later—*i.e.*, in 1671—France possessed, thanks to Colbert, 270 battleships of all kinds, besides 30 galleys, and 52,000 sailors (*Lettres, Instructions, et Mémoires de Colbert*, by Pierre Clement, vol. iii., part i., p. iv), while the sum annually spent on the navy, which, in Mazarin's time, never exceeded two millions of livres, under Colbert was seldom less than six times that amount (*ibid.*). Colbert also established ports and arsenals, where the fleet could repair any damage (*ibid.*, p. viii); and likewise promoted l'Ordonnance pour La Marine, which was a sort of Marine Code (see *post*). His efforts on the part of the navy were, after his death, maintained by his eldest son, the Marquis de Seigneley, who succeeded to his father's post as Minister of Marine, in which he displayed marked ability (Martin's *History of France*, 4th ed., vol. xiv., p. 2), and during his brief career considerably increased the strength and power of the navy (*Lettres, Instructions, et Mémoires de Colbert*, by Pierre Clement, vol. ii., part i., p. iv). Colbert also provided for the land defences of his country, and, in doing so, caused to be erected a triple line of fortresses, on the north and east of France, for the protection of the frontiers (*Biographie Universelle, Ancienne et Moderne*, vol. ix., tit. Colbert, p. 224; *Lettres, Instructions, et Mémoires de Colbert*, by Pierre Clement, vol. v., *passim*).

[2] Commerce did not thrive under Richelieu or Mazarin. It was, however, greatly encouraged by Colbert, who caused trading companies to be estab-

developer of the French Colonial possessions,[1] as the encourager and protector of agriculture,[2] as the creator and restorer of great public buildings,[3] and as the patron of literature, science, and art.[4] And yet, though Colbert united in his person all these

lished, which it was declared all persons might join without compromising their nobility (Martin's *History of France*, 4th ed., vol. xiii., p. 117). French manufactures, and notably those of Lyons silk, and also for the making of the lace known as Point de France, or Point d'Alençon, near which town Colbert possessed a chateau (Voltaire's collected *Works*, published in 1819, vol. 18, p. 190), and the tapestries Gobelins and Beauvais (*ibid.*) were encouraged by Colbert, who was also largely instrumental in founding the manufacture of Sèvres porcelain and plate glass (*The Monarchy of France, its Rise, Progress, and Fall*, by William Tooke, F.R.S., p. 456). He also made several commercial treaties. Moreover, besides opening up for navigation rivers which, according to Pascal, are "les chemins qui marche" (*Lettres, Instructions, et Mémoires de Colbert*, by Pierre Clement, vol. iv., pp. cxii *et seq.*), he promoted the construction, by De Riquet, of the Canal Languedoc, which connects the Bay of Biscay with the Gulf of Lyons (*ibid.*, p. lxxix) and purchased from Charles II. of England the port of Dunkirk, in order to receive the commerce of the North (Martin's *History of France*, 4th ed., vol. xiii., p. 286). The economic precept, *laissez-faire*, was, it has been stated, borrowed by the eighteenth century (*Lectures on Modern History*, by Lord Action, p. 12) from Colbert, according to whom: "La liberté est l'âme du commerce. Il faut *laissez-faire* les hommes qui s'appliquant sans peine à ce qui convient le mieux ; c'est ce qui apporte le plus d'avantage" (Colbert in *Comptes Rendus de l'Institut*, xxxix., p. 93). L'Ordonnance du Commerce of 1673 was mainly the work of Colbert (*post*).

[1] Colbert reorganized the French colonies in Canada, Martinique, and St. Domingo, besides founding others at Cayenne and Madagascar and Pondicherry (*The Monarchy of France, its Rise, Progress, and Fall*, by William Tooke, F.R.S., p. 456 ; Martin's *History of France*, 4th ed., vol. xiii., pp. 113 *et seq.* ; *Chambers's Encyclopedia*, vol. iii., p. 337). The Code Noir (L'Ordonnance Coloniale), though issued after Colbert's death, was due to his inspiration (*post*).

[2] See Martin's *History of France*, 4th ed., vol. xiii., pp. 34, 35 ; *Lettres, Instructions, et Mémoires de Colbert*, by Pierre Clement, vol. iv., *passim*, pp. xl *et seq.* Colbert stimulated, as far as possible, the multiplication of cattle and the acclimatization of foreign animals, and renewed the exemption from seizure for taxes, etc., of cattle and beasts of burden (*Lettres, Instructions, et Mémoires de Colbert*, by Pierre Clement, vol. iv., pp. xlviii, lxvii), which exemption was first established by Sully in the time of Henri IV. (Bachelet's *Les Grands Ministres Français*, pp. 329 *et seq.*).

[3] In 1664 Colbert became, by purchase, Superintendent of Buildings. Besides (sorely against his inclination) transforming Versailles from a shooting lodge into a palace, enlarging and adorning Les Tuileries, the Louvre, Fontainebleau, St. Germain, and Chambord, he greatly beautified Paris (*Lettres, Instructions, et Mémoires de Colbert*, by Pierre Clement, vol. v., p. xli), entrusting this work mainly to the architects Perrault and Blondel (*ibid.*, p. xlix).

[4] The creation of the Academy of Inscriptions and Medals, of the Academy of Sciences, of the Academy of France in Rome, of the Academy of Architecture, and of that of Music, are due to Colbert (*Lettres, Instructions, et Mémoires de Colbert*, by Pierre Clement, vol. v., p. liii). He also founded a Professorship of Civil Law in 1679 (*The Monarchy of France, its Rise, Progress, and Fall*, by William Tooke, F.R.S., p. 456), while, during his administration, the Royal Library was removed to a more suitable place, and the books were increased in number from 16,000 to 40,000 (Bonnechose's *History of*

different titles to historic fame, which some consider entitle him to be regarded as the greatest Minister in the annals of mankind,[1] without excepting even Sully and Richelieu, not to mention Mazarin,[2] he was also the promoter of the great codifying ordinances of Louis XIV.,[3] in which character it is proposed mainly to consider him in this brief essay.

Before, however, concentrating attention on this aspect of Colbert's public career, it is desirable to give a few particulars of his life and origin. Jean Baptiste Colbert was born at Rheims on August 29, 1619,[4] and his parents were Nicholas Colbert and Marie Pussort. His father, who, in the early part of his career, does not appear to have been always solvent,[5] was engaged in

---

France, 1862 ed., translated by William Robson, p. 397). On May 21, 1667, Colbert was made a member of the Academy of France, and pronounced the customary oration (*Lettres, Instructions, et Mémoires*, by Pierre Clement, vol. v., pp. lvii, lviii).

[1] Bonnechose's *History of France*, 1862 ed., note by translator, William Robson, p. 399, where it is stated that the real glory of the reign of Louis XIV. begins and ends with Colbert, as the glory of Thebes rose and fell with Epaminondas. If Louis XIV. obtained the title of Great, it was mainly due to Colbert (*Biographie Universelle, Ancienne et Moderne*, vol. ix., M. Colbert, p. 223), after whose death the monarchy declined in power and importance.

[2] Mazarin has been termed "the ablest and most successful of Ministers" (*Lectures on Modern History*, by Lord Acton, p. 235) and "a statesman of the highest rank" (*ibid.*, p. 236).

[3] *Recueil Général des Anciennes Lois Françaises*, by Isambert and others, vol. xviii., p. 103. According to the President Hénault, "Colbert qui à rétabli les finances porta ses vues plus loin ; justice, commerce, marine, police, tout se ressentit de l'esprit d'ordre qui a fait le principal caractère de ce ministre et des vues supérieure dont il envisagesit chaque parte du gouvernement" (*ibid.*).

[4] Bachelet's *Les Grands Ministres Français*, tit. Colbert, p. 368 ; *Lettres Instructions, et Mémoires de Colbert*, by Pierre Clement, vol. i., p. xxiii. The baptismal certificate for the parish of St. Hilaire, Rheims, leaves no doubt as to the date and place of Colbert's birth. Nevertheless, it has been stated that the date of his birth was August 22, 1619 (Martin's *History of France*, 4th ed., vol. xiii., p. 21), that he was born in Paris in 1619 (Chalmers' *General Biographical Dictionary*, vol. x., p. 15), and that the event took place at Rheims, but not until 1625 (*Life of Famous John Baptist Colbert*, done into English in 1695, p. 3). In 1825, on the occasion of the coronation of Charles X., there was placed, in a house in the Rue de Cérès, near to the Place Royale at Rheims, a tablet on which was engraved, in letters of gold, the following inscription—namely : " Jean Baptiste Colbert, Ministre d'État sous Louis XIV. est né dans cette maison le 29 Août, 1619 " (*Lettres, Instructions, et Mémoires de Colbert*, by Pierre Clement, vol. i., pp. 473, 474).

[5] *Lettres, Instructions, et Mémoires de Colbert*, by Pierre Clement, vol. i., p. xxiii. Colbert's father is sometimes referred to as Nicolas Colbert de Vandière (*ibid.*). He eventually became Seigneur de Vandiére, Governor of Fimes, Maître d'Hotel in Ordinary to the King (*Biographie Universelle, Ancienne et Moderne*, vol. ix., tit. Colbert, pp. 208 *et seq.*), and Trésorier de l'Extraordinaire des Guerres (Bachelet's *Les Grands Ministres Français*, pp. 329, 403).

some commercial pursuits at Rheims, and was probably a cloth, wool, or silk merchant,[1] though it has been stated that he was first a wine merchant, and then a clerk to a notary.[2] Colbert's mother was the sister of Henri Pussort, who eventually became a distinguished councillor of the Parliament of Paris, and one of the two selected by the King to be "au conseil royal des finances."[3] His association with Colbert in notable projects of law reform will presently be noticed.[4] Colbert was, moreover, connected with Michael le Tellier,[5] whose sister was the wife of Colbert's uncle, Jean Baptiste Colbert de Saint Pouange,[6] a man of considerable commercial and financial repute, who ultimately attained to high official rank.[7]

Events of Life.—As regards Colbert's remote ancestry little need be said. When, indeed, he became famous as a statesman, efforts were made to trace his descent from a younger branch of a noble, if not royal, Scotch family, supposed to have settled in France in the latter part of the thirteenth century.[8] This origin Colbert

---

[1] See *Biographie Universelle, Ancienne et Moderne*, vol. ix., tit. Colbert, pp. 208 et seq. ; *Life of Famous John Baptist Colbert*, done into English, published 1695, p. 3; A. Jal's *Dictionnaire de Biographie et d'Histoire;* Colbert's *Life*, by Clement, 2 vols.
[2] *Ibid.* The author of *Les Soupirs de la France esclave*, published in Colbert's lifetime, refers to him, contemptuously, as "fils d'un marchand de Reims" (*Lettres, Instructions, et Mémoires de Colbert, supra*, vol. i., p. 467).
[3] See Martin's *History of France*, vol. xiii., p. 77; *Mémoires du Duc de Saint-Simon*, vol. i., p. 411.
[4] *Post ;* and see Clement's *Histoire de Colbert*, vol. ii., pp. 291 et seq. ; *Précis de l'Histoire du Droit Français*, by Paul Viollet, p. 186.
[5] Le Tellier ultimately became Chancelier, and was Secretary of State down to 1666 (Voltaire's *Works*, published in 1819, vol. xviii., p. 36). His son, Francis Michael le Tellier, Marquis de Louvois, one of the greatest of French War Ministers, became Colbert's great rival towards the end of the latter's public career. Louvois was the evil and Colbert the good genius of Louis XIV. (*The Life and Times of Louis XIV.*, by G. P. R. James, vol. iv , p. 60 ; and see also *Lectures on Modern History*, by Lord Acton, p. 239).
[6] *Lettres, Instructions, and Mémoires de Colbert*, by Pierre Clement, vol. i., p. xxiv.
[7] See *Nouvelle Biographie Générale*, vol. xii., pp. 101, 102 ; *Mazarin et Colbert*, by the Comte de Cosnac, vol. i., p. 81.
[8] Giles Ménage, a genealogist who was, it may be mentioned, eventually deprived by Colbert of a pension (*Life of Famous John Baptist Colbert*, done into English in 1695, p. 228), pretended to have traced Colbert's descent from the Kings of Scotland (*ibid.*), while Colbert himself claimed to belong to an ancient and noble Scottish family named Cuthbert (Clement's *Life of Colbert*, vol. i., p. 519 ; Chalmers' *General Biographical Dictionary*, vol. x., tit. Colbert), a younger branch of which was alleged to have settled in Scotland in 1281 (*Biographie Universelle, Ancienne et Moderne*, vol. ix., pp. 208, 225). Letters Patent of James II. of England, registered in Parliament May 21, 1687, attest that Colbert was descended from noble and illustrious Scotch parents, on both the paternal and maternal side (see Clement's *Histoire de*

by no means repudiated, but, on the contrary, is suspected of having endeavoured to uphold, by somewhat unworthy means.[1] It is, however, more than probable that Colbert's family was, in fact, of respectable, but thoroughly bourgeois, origin,[2] and it is certain that one branch of it settled at Troyes and the other at Rheims,[3] in both of which cities, and also in Paris, members of the Colbert family were engaged in commerce, and held in honourable repute, in the sixteenth and seventeenth centuries.[4]

It should, however, in fairness be stated that, in 1667, Colbert

---

Colbert, vol. i., Appendix, pp. 519-532, where the ancestry of Colbert is fully discussed). Colbert bore on his coat of arms a snake (Latin, *Coluber*; French, *Couleuvre*) impaled, in allusion to his name, and the whole Colbert family adopted the same device (Jal's *Dictionnaire de Biographie et d'Histoire*, p. 399). The Barons of Castelhill have been cited as common ancestors of the Colberts of Scotland and France, and as having the same coat of arms (*Biographie Universelle, Ancienne et Moderne*, vol. ix., tit. Colbert, pp. 208 *et seq.*). For further information as to pedigree of the Colbert family see *Lettres, Instructions, et Mémoires de Colbert*, by Pierre Clement, vol. i., Appendix, pp. 467 *et seq.*

[1] It has been stated on good authority that, by Colbert's orders, a stone slab placed over the tomb of his grandfather (a wool merchant), in the Church of des Cordeliers at Rheims, was secretly removed and another substituted for it, on which Colbert had had engraved, in old characters and language, an account of the supposed chivalrous exploits of a Scottish knight (one Richard Colbert), together with the legend, " En Ecosse je eus le berceau, et Rheims m'a donne le Tombeau " (Bachelet's *Les Grands Ministres Français*, tit. Colbert, pp. 329-403 ; *Nouvelle Biographie Générale*, vol. xii., pp. 100, 101 ; *Life of Famous John Baptist Colbert*, done into English in 1695, p. 228 ; *Mazarin et Colbert*, by the Comte de Cosnac, vol. i., p. 78 ; *Lettres, Instructions, et Mémoires de Colbert*, by Pierre Clement, vol. i., Appendix, p. 471).

[2] Martin's *History of France*, 4th ed., vol. xiii., p. 21 ; *Mazarin et Colbert*, by the Comte de Cosnac, vol. i., p. 81 ; *Lettres, Instructions, et Mémoires de Colbert*, by Pierre Clement, vol. i., pp. xxii. According to the Abbé Choisy, Colbert had great pride in ancestry (Bachelet's *Les Grands Ministres Français*, tit. Colbert, pp. 329 *et seq.*), but, nevertheless, was honest enough to tell his eldest son the truth about his origin in these words—viz.: " Coquin, tu n'es qu'un petit bourgeois, et, si nous trompons le public, je veux au moins que tu sachés qui tu es " (*Mazarin et Colbert*, by the Comte de Cosnac, vol. i., p. 79 ; *Mémoires de l'Abbé de Choisy*). Moreover, in writing to his son, he (Colbert) truthfully stated: " Mon fils doit bien penser et faire souvent réflexion sur ce que sa naissance l'aurait fait être, si Dieu n'avait pas beni mon travail et si ce travail n'avait pas été extrême " (*Lettres, Instructions, et Mémoires de Colbert*, by Pierre Clement, vol. i., Appendix, p. 468).

[3] *Mazarin et Colbert*, by the Comte de Cosnac, vol. i., p. 81.

[4] *Nouvelle Biographie Générale*, tit. Colbert, vol. xii., pp. 100, 101 ; Jal's *Dictionnaire de Biographie et d'Histoire*, tit. Colbert. Colbert's great-uncle, Odoart Colbert, who was born in the sixteenth and died in the seventeenth century, was originally a merchant of Troyes, who eventually extended his business operations to Antwerp, Frankfort, Lyons, Venice, and Florence, where he established branch houses for the distribution of the products of Champagne (see Martin's *History of France*, 4th ed., vol. xiii., pp. 21, 22 ; *Mazarin et Colbert*, by the Comte de Cosnac, vol. i., p. 79 ; *Nouvelle Biographie Générale*, *supra*).

was, it appears, able to furnish proofs of nobility, which had to be produced to enable one of his sons to obtain admission into l'Ordre de Malte.[1] Probably such proofs were not too critically examined by officials only too anxious to gain the thanks and approval of a powerful Minister.

Of Colbert's childhood no reliable details are forthcoming, though it has been affirmed that a profound reserve and impenetrable discretion distinguished even his earliest years.[2] His personal appearance can hardly have been attractive,[3] if, as stated by some of his contemporaries, his mien was low, dejected, and stern, not to say forbidding.[4] In spite, however, of this unprepossessing external appearance, he was, as has been remarked, of the race of lions and not of foxes,[5] though his extreme caution and discretion may, in the opinion of some, somewhat belie this description of his character. Certainly, if his contemporaries are to be believed, he was a man of few words, who regarded long conversations as so much time lost, and seldom returned a verbal answer to a question of any importance until the proposition put before him had been first reduced into writing for his more careful consideration.[6] His industry and attention to business were such, and his complete mastery of details so exceptionally complete and accurate,[7] that it has been stated

[1] *Lettres, Instructions, et Mémoires de Colbert*, by Pierre Clement, vol. i., p. xxiii.

[2] *Eloge de Jean Baptiste Colbert* (1783), p. 3. The following anecdote of Colbert's early manhood is worth repeating: When in the service of Michael le Tellier (see *post*), and by his order, Colbert delivered to Mazarin, then at Sedan, a letter from the Queen Mother (Anne of Austria). Colbert had strict instructions not to leave the letter in the Cardinal's possession, but to return with it, after His Eminence had read it. Mazarin, wishing to retain the letter, had recourse to various stratagems to enable him to do so, which, however, entirely failed, owing to Colbert's firmness and fidelity to his trust. When, in subsequent years, Colbert, on Le Tellier's recommendation, entered the service of Mazarin, the latter remembered the incident just described, but as one wholly to Colbert's credit (Chalmers' *Biographical Dictionary*, tit. Colbert, vol x., pp. 15 *et seq.*; *Life of Famous John Baptist Colbert*, done into English in 1695, p. 4; Jal's *Dictionnaire Biographie et d'Histoire*, tit. Colbert).

[3] See *Mazarin et Colbert*, by the Comte de Cosnac, vol. i., p. 80. The best portrait of Colbert, which hardly seems to justify written descriptions of his personal appearance, was by Nanteuil (Martin's *History of France*, 4th ed., vol. xiii., p. 23).

[4] *Life of Famous John Baptist Colbert*, done into English in 1695, p. 3; Jal's *Dictionnaire de Biographie et d'Histoire*, tit. Colbert.

[5] Martin's *History of France*, 4th ed., vol. xiii., p. 23.

[6] *Life of Famous John Baptist Colbert*, done into English in 1695, p. 3; *Eloge de Jean Baptiste Colbert* (1783), p. 3.

[7] *Lettres, Instructions, et Mémoires de Colbert*, by Pierre Clement, vol. i., p. xxi.

of him that no man was ever more laborious and diligent.[1] Whether his apprehension was as quick as that of Cardinal Mazarin may perhaps be doubted,[2] though it must certainly have been far above the average. He slept but little, and was most temperate in his diet, and knew only one sort of repose—namely, that experienced by change of work, or by passing from one difficult task to one less difficult.[3] As a man's nickname sometimes affords a clue to his character, it is perhaps worth mentioning that Colbert was called by some "*Vir marmoreus*,"[4] and that Madame de Sévigné dubbed him "*Le Nord*," and trembled at the very idea of seeking an audience of him.[5]

Though Colbert was undoubtedly, in the main, the architect of his own fortunes, and obtained his ultimate promotion to the highest ministerial rank in France by his own personal merits and exertions,[6] he did, nevertheless, owe his first introduction to public life to his Uncle Jean Baptiste Colbert de Saint Pouange (already mentioned),[7] who rescued Colbert from the commercial career for which he was originally destined,[8] and, in 1648,[9] pro-

---

[1] *Lettres, Instructions, et Mémoires de Colbert*, by Pierre Clement, vol. v., p. lviii; *Dictionnaire de l'Academie*, ed. of 1694, Preface. Like Napoleon I. (see Sloane's *Life of Napoleon*, vol. iii., p. 163), Colbert never seems to have found the limit of his capacity for work.

[2] Martin's *History of France*, 4th ed., vol. xiii., p. 22.

[3] *Mémoires de Charles Perrault*, p. 34.

[4] Bachelet's *Les Grands Ministres Français*, tit. Colbert, pp. 329 *et seq*.

[5] *Ibid.*; and see *Lettres de Madame de Sévigné* (annotated edition, 1862), vol. iii., p. 33.

[6] *Lettres, Instructions, et Mémoires de Colbert*, by Pierre Clement, vol. i., p. xxxi. Colbert might truly have exclaimed with Corneille, "Je ne dois qu'a mois seule, toute ma renommée" (*Biographie Universelle, Ancienne et Moderne*, vol. ix., tit. Colbert, pp. 208 *et seq.*).   [7] *Ante*, p. 253.

[8] *Mazarin et Colbert*, by the Comte de Cosnac, vol. i., p. 81; Martin's *History of France*, 4th ed., vol. xiii., p. 22. In his early youth, Colbert was sent to Paris, and then to Lyons, to learn commerce, returning eventually to Paris, where he passed from the office of a notary (said to have been the father of the poet Chapelain) into that of a procurator (*procureur*), and then became a clerk " Chez un trésorier des parties casuelles" (Martin's *History of France*, 4th ed., vol. xiii., p. 22; *Mazarin et Colbert*, by the Comte de Cosnac, vol. i., pp. 79 *et seq.*). Whether Colbert was ever in the service of Mazarin's bankers, Cesanni and Maserani, appears to be doubtful (*Mazarin et Colbert*, by the Comte de Cosnac, vol. i., p. 81; *Biographie Universelle, Ancienne et Moderne*, vol. ix., tit. Colbert, pp. 208 *et seq.*).

[9] This was also the year of Colbert's marriage to the wealthy Marie Charon, the child of James Charon (Sieur de Minars, and a native of Blois) and of Marie Begon (*Life of Famous John Baptist Colbert*, done into English in 1695, p. 6; Martin's *History of France*, 4th ed, vol. xiii., p. 22). By her he had nine children, who all achieved distinction, in the Government, Church, or Army (Bachelet's *Les Grands Ministres Français*, tit. Colbert). One of his daughters married the Duc de Chevreuse, and the other the Duc de Beauvilliers. Colbert's eldest son, better known as the Marquis de Seignelay,

cured for him employment under Michael le Tellier, at that time either Comptroller-General of Finance or Minister of War.¹ Under this distinguished statesman, Colbert, thanks, in no small measure, to the commercial, legal, and financial training he had already received,² exhibited great aptitude for business and those eminent qualities of head and heart which determined Le Tellier to introduce and recommend for office his protégé to Mazarin,³ who soon gauged Colbert's worth,⁴ and, besides entrusting him with several delicate diplomatic missions,⁵ eventually appointed him his *intendant*, and finally made him one of the executors of his will⁶—so well satisfied indeed was Mazarin with Colbert's supreme gifts in administrative and financial matters,⁷

---

who by some is said to have owed his success in life to propitious circumstances rather than to individual merit (*Lettres, Instructions, et Mémoires de Colbert*, by Pierre Clement, vol. iii., part 2, pp. ii and xli), while others assert that he was at least as able a man as his father (Voltaire's collected *Works*, published in 1819, vol. xvii., p. 35; *Lettres de Madame de Sévigné*, annotated ed., 1862, vol. ix., pp. 582, 583), hoped, according to a published letter of Madame de Maintenon, to succeed to *all* his father's various posts (*Lettres, Instructions, et Mémoires de Colbert*, by Pierre Clement, vol. iii., part 2, p. xv; Martin's *History of France*, 4th ed., vol. xiv., p. 2), and did, in fact, become Minister of Marine, in which office he rendered good service to his country (*ibid.*, vol. iii., part i., p. iv; Voltaire's collected *Works*, published in 1819, vol. xvii., p. 35). He only survived his father seven years, dying November 3, 1690, aged thirty-nine (*Lettres de Madame de Sévigné*, annotated ed., 1862, vol. ix., pp. 582, 583). Another son of Colbert was Marquis de Blainville et d'Amory, who held certain Court appointments, of which he was deprived in favour of Michael le Tellier's son, Louvois (*Lettres, Instructions, et Mémoires de Colbert*, by Pierre Clement, vol. iii., part 2, p. xvi). One of Colbert's sons became Archbishop of Rouen.

¹ Jal's *Dictionnaire de Biographie et d'Histoire*, tit. Colbert.
² Martin's *History of France*, 4th ed., vol. xiii., p. 22.
³ *Ibid. Mazarin et Colbert*, by the Comte de Cosnac, vol. i., p. 81.
⁴ Colbert did not at first appreciate Mazarin's greatness of intellect, though he eventually estimated the Cardinal's qualities at their true worth (Martin's *History of France*, 4th ed., vol. xiii., pp. 22, 23).
⁵ These missions comprised one to Rome to Pope Alexander VII., to induce the latter to restore to the Duchy of Parma the Duchy of De Castro, and to help the Venetians (*Biographie Universelle, Ancienne et Moderne*, vol. ix., tit. Colbert, p. 210). Prior to this mission Colbert was created Marquis de Croissi (*ibid.*), and he eventually became Marquis de Seignelay, a title subsequently borne, after Colbert's death, by his eldest son.
⁶ *Mazarin et Colbert*, by the Comte de Cosnac, vol. i., pp. iii *et seq.*; *The General Biographical Dictionary*, new edition by Alexander Chalmers, F.S.A., vol. x., tit. Colbert, pp. 10 *et seq.*; Jal's *Dictionnaire de Biographie et d'Histoire* p. 395; *Lettres, Instructions, et Mémoires de Colbert*, by Pierre Clement, vol. i., p. ci.
⁷ As Richelieu and Mazarin may be said to have been the founders of *political* despotism, so Colbert may be regarded as the founder of *administrative* despotism (*Mazarin et Colbert*, by the Comte de Cosnac, vol. i., p. v).

both in public and private life, that, when dying,[1] he recommended Colbert to Louis XIV. in the following words, namely: "Je vous dois tout, Sire, mais je crois m'acquitter en quelque sorte avec votre majesté en vous donnant Colbert."[2] The King, however, scarcely needed this recommendation from his dying Minister, as, for some time before Cardinal Mazarin's death, Colbert had secretly helped Louis XIV. to investigate and criticize Fouquet's daily statements of account, and in so doing had revealed to the King talents which were not unmixed with genius.[3] Still, it was not until some months after Mazarin's death that Colbert was, upon Fouquet's disgrace, made *intendant* of the finances, while his appointment as Comptroller General of Finance was deferred until 1665.[4] Colbert's subsequent career was one of rapid advancement in the public service, to which the age in which he lived was undoubtedly favourable, for the constitution of France then consisted in its being a Government through Councils, to which, with few exceptions, neither birth nor rank gave any right of admission.[5] Hence it was that bourgeois like Colbert, Bossuet, and Louvois were employed by, and in high favour with, the Grand Monarque, who became *par excellence* the King of the Merchant Classes,[6] and was quite content that his nobles should remain courtiers rather than statesmen. This policy may have been, in part, dictated by

[1] Mazarin's recommendations of Colbert to Louis XIV. are said to have been almost his last words.

[2] *Eloge de Jean Baptiste Colbert*, p. 4; *Biographie Universelle, Ancienne et Moderne*, vol. ix., tit. Colbert, p. 211; Martin's *History of France*, 4th ed., vol. xiii., p. 26; *Mémoires de Choisy*, p. 579. Though Colbert did not at first esteem Cardinal Mazarin, he did at last thoroughly appreciate his talents and many good qualities (see Martin's *History of France*, 4th ed., vol. xiii., pp. 22, 23).

[3] Martin's *History of France*, 4th ed., vol. xiii., pp. 26, 27; *Biographie Universelle et Moderne*, vol. ix., tit. Colbert, pp. 210, 211. Louis XIV. recognized in Colbert "l'homme solide, l'homme des choses sérieuses; le serviteur devoué; le merveilleux instrument du pouvoir royal, le génie qui créait et avait l'habilité, de faire croire à son maître qu'il ne faisait qu'obéir aux pensées du souverain" (Jal's *Dictionnaire Critique de Biographie et d'Histoire*, p. 395).

[4] *Lettres, Instructions, et Mémoires de Colbert*, by Pierre Clement, vol. ii., part i., p. xlix.

[5] *Cambridge Modern History*, vol. v., p. 3; *Lettres, Instructions, et Mémoires de Colbert*, by Pierre Clement, vol. i., Appendix, pp. 467 *et seq.*

[6] *Social France in the Seventeenth Century*, by Cecile Hugon, p. 147; and see *Lettres, Instructions, et Mémoires de Colbert*, by Pierre Clement, vol. i., p. 467, where a passage is cited from a work, published in Colbert's lifetime, called *Les Soupirs de la France des Esclave qui aspire après sa liberté*, complaining of the admission into the Government of bourgeois like Louvois and Colbert.

dread lest those who were born in the purple should in time, if promoted to fill high offices of State, become powerful enough to attack and limit the rights and prerogatives of the Crown itself.[1] At all events, it is certain that, after Colbert's death, and when his eldest son, the Marquis de Seignely, and Louvois were no more, Louis XIV., with no one of sufficient intellect and strength of character to thwart him, reigned supreme over a Ministry composed of persons who may fitly be described as "titled clerks."[2]

It is not proposed to trace at greater length Colbert's general career as a Minister, especially as its principal achievements have already been briefly recorded on an earlier page;[3] and, moreover, form the subject of detailed notice in the volumes of French history and works of general biography. Attention must, however, now be called to Colbert's position as a jurist and law reformer.

Colbert as Law Reformer.—That Colbert should, amidst his many other absorbing occupations, covering at one time, as has been seen, the whole field of departmental administration,[4] have had time and courage to initiate and superintend the Herculean task of consolidating and amending the laws of his country, may well amaze the most strenuous statesman of modern times. He possessed, however, a powerful incentive to action in the knowledge that in an age which, in its ideals and efforts, both political and literary, typified order and authority,[5] the administration of justice throughout France, but especially in the provinces, was both irregular and corrupt.[6] This was partly due to the rival claims of innumerable feudal Courts, as against Royal Magistrates and one another,[7] for, notwithstanding the encroachments of the Crown on its

---

[1] Introduction by Charles Sarolea to Nelson's abridged edition in French of the *Mémoires du Duc de Saint-Simon*.
[2] *François de Fénelon*, by Viscount St. Cyres, p. 45.
[3] *Ante*, p. 248.
[4] Martin's *History of France*, 4th ed., vol. xiii., pp. 33, 34; *Lettres, Instructions et Mémoires de Colbert*, by P. Clement, vol. i., p. 1; *Colbert, Promoteur des Grands Ordonnances de Louis XIV.*, by Alfred Aymé, p. 11. From 1661 to 1672 were the most glorious years for Colbert, and when his ideas reigned supreme (Martin's *History of France*, 4th ed., vol. xiii., p. 35).
[5] *Cambridge Modern History*, vol. v., p. 15.
[6] *Ibid*. The extraordinary assizes held at Clermont Ferrand, called "Les Grands Jours d'Auvergne," must have revealed the existence of many abuses calling for reform (Martin's *History of France*, 4th ed., vol. xiii., pp. 69 *et seq.*).
[7] *Ibid*.

independence, feudal justice still subsisted, though in a confused, arbitrary, and corrupt form.¹ Moreover, both Civil and Criminal Procedure were in a more or less imperfect condition, and, in the interest of humanity and the speedy administration of justice, demanded simplification and reorganization, while the brutality of the punishments attached to crimes sorely needed mitigation, seeing that, instead of reforming the criminal himself, or acting as deterrents, they seemed calculated to have, and in fact had, a precisely opposite effect.

It was, then, in such conditions as these that Colbert, actuated by noble and sincere motives, urged Louis XIV. to signalize, if not immortalize, his reign, then already becoming famous on other grounds, by giving his sanction and an impulse to a great scheme of legislation, designed to reduce into one body all the existing ordinances,² thereby rendering jurisprudence fixed and certain throughout the entire kingdom, and also destined to bring about a necessary reduction in the number of persons invested with judicial power.³ That Colbert did not fully achieve all that he hoped to accomplish as a law reformer was certainly not his fault.⁴ He did, however, initiate that codifying process which eventually produced the Codes Napoleon, and thereby aided the work of bringing the customary law of France again into harmony with the Roman law.⁵

From an undated paper in Colbert's handwriting, which reveals his idea of codification, it is evident that he was well aware that such idea was by no means original, though he seems to have considered that Henry III. alone, amongst previous French

¹ *Cambridge Modern History* vol. v., p. 15, In the reign of Philip II. of France (called Philip Augustus) the administration of justice by feudal lords was curtailed, and they were no longer allowed to decide cases according to their mere caprice, while, at the same time, judges were appointed to try and determine causes in accordance with settled law.
² *Colbert, Promoteur des Grands Ordonnances de Louis XIV.*, by Alfred Aymé, pp. 15, 16, 17; *Précis de l'Histoire du Droit Français*, etc., by Paul Viollet, p. 185; *Cours Elémentaire d'Histoire du Droit Français*, 2nd ed., by Adhémar Esmein, p. 785.
³ *Précis de l'Histoire du Droit Français*, etc., by Paul Viollet, p. 185; *Biographie Universelle, Ancienne et Moderne*, vol. ix., tit. Colbert, p. 216.
⁴ See *Colbert, Promoteur des Grands Ordonnances de Louis XIV.*, by Alfred Aymé, p. 17.
⁵ *Studies in History and Jurisprudence*, by James Bryce, pp. 107, 376, 377; *Manuel du Droit Français*, 9th ed., by Judge Pailliet, p. viii. Ever since the discovery, in the reign of Louis VII. (Le Jeune), in the twelfth century, of a copy of the Institutes of Justinian, the Roman civil law had, in the greater part of Europe, and notably in France, become the absorbing study of the learned.

Kings, had planned to reduce the whole of the ordinances of the country into a single body,[1] assigning the execution of this task to the President Brisson, who did indeed compile what is termed the "Code Henry," which, however, never came into actual operation.[2]

In Colbert's time, and indeed before the great Revolution, the civil legislation of France was divided into two general systems, namely, the customary and the written law, each of which branched into a multitude of subdivisions.[3] There were upwards of 180 customs, extending more or less over the various provinces of France.[4] In many parts of the country, though less in Provence and Languedoc, the Roman law had gone back into that shape of a body of customs from which it had emerged a thousand years before, while in Northern and Middle France some customs, and especially those relating to land, were not Roman at all.[5] Independently of customary law and written law, considered as local law, France was also governed by Roman law, the laws of the Prince, and the decisions of the local Parliaments.[6]

---

[1] *Histoire de la Procédure Criminelle in France*, by Adhéman Esmein, p. 173; Clement's *Histoire de Colbert*, vol. ii., p. 297; *Manuel du Droit Français*, 9th ed., by Judge Pailliet, p. xiv. Ideas of codification have been attributed to earlier French Kings than Henry III.—namely, to Charles VII., Louis XI., and Henry II. (see *The Civil Laws of France*, by D. M. Aird, p. 19), not to mention Henry IV. (*Colbert, Promoteur des Grands Ordonnances de Louis XIV.*, by Alfred Aymé, p. 14). Moreover, these royal projects of codification were seconded by many eminent jurists of the sixteenth century in their writings (*ibid.*), while Colbert himself resumed the work at an auspicious moment, seeing that Domat was then composing his treatise on civil law (*ibid.*) and Lamoignon, first President of the Parlement de Paris, was contemplating and evolving a scheme of unified and general legislation for the whole Kingdom of France (*ibid.*), in which work there was eventually associated with him the learned jurisconsult Barthélimi Auzanet (*Précis de l'Histoire du Droit Français*, etc., by Paul Viollet, p. 184).

[2] See authorities in preceding note. La Garde des Seaux Marillac had, in a measure, the same fate as the Code Henry (*Histoire de la Code Criminelle en France*, by Adhémar Esmein, p. 178).

[3] *The Civil Laws of France*, by D. M. Aird, p. 20.

[4] *Ibid.* According to one authority, before the Revolution, French legislation comprised not less than fifty general customs and 225 local customs, without taking into account those provinces which were under the written law (*Dictionnaire Usuel de Droit*, by Max Legrand, avocat, tit. Code, p. 189).

[5] *Studies in History and Jurisprudence*, by James Bryce, p. 107.

[6] *The Civil Law of France*, by D. M. Aird, p. 19. The "Parlements" must not be confounded with Les États Généraux (National Assemblies), which were summoned at uncertain intervals by the King, and in some reigns not at all, though they alone were supposed to grant subsidies to the Crown and sanction the levying of contributions from the people (see Judge Pailliet's *Manuel du Droit Français*, vol. i., p. x). Les Parlements were Courts of Justice, and the first of these to be established was the Parlement de Paris, in the year 1302, by Philip IV. (Le Bel), down to which time a Court of Justice

Having once secured the King's sanction and approval of his scheme for the amendment and codification of the law,[1] Colbert lost no time in carrying it into execution, and at once proceeded to settle the essential preliminaries.[2] Accordingly, a Council was created to make all needful preparations, to discover and discuss existing defects and abuses, and to devise remedies for them.[3] Two classes of persons only were, in the first instance, employed as members of this Council—namely, eminent jurisconsults and members "du Conseil du Roi," to the exclusion of such members of the Parlement de Paris[4] as were not ministers, and also to the exclusion of the judicial body (Les Corps Judiciaires).[5] This Council, termed the Conseil de Justice, was subdivided into three sections.[6] Of these, the first had assigned to it ecclesiastical

from the earliest period followed the person of the King, a practice which was found to be irksome, and led to the gradual establishment of eleven Sovereign Courts or Parlements, in various parts of France (*The Monarchy of France, its Rise, Progress, and Fall*, by William Tooke, F.R.S., p. 208). In 1674, Louis XIV. himself gave Parlements, or Sovereign Courts, to Franché Comté at Dol, and afterwards at Besançon (*ibid.*). For a very interesting account of "Le Parlement de Paris et les autres sur son modèle," see *Mémoires du Duc de Saint-Simon*, 1857 ed., vol. xi., chap. 17, pp. 306 *et seq.*

[1] Colbert communicated his plan to Louis XIV. about the year 1664 or 1665 (*Histoire de la Procédure Criminelle en France*, by Adhémar Esmein, p. 180). Louis XIV. was in the habit of attributing to himself the primary idea of Codifying Ordinances (*ibid.*, p. 177).

[2] *Ibid.*; and see *Colbert, Promoteur des Grand Ordonnances de Louis XIV.*, by Alfred Aymé, pp. 15 *et seq.* The Ordonnance Civile was prepared with the greatest solemnity (*Recueil Général des Anciennes Lois Françaises*, vol. xviii., p. 103). These preliminaries about to be described were prior to the issue of the Ordonnance Civile, but the history of this Ordinance may be regarded as the history of all the ordinances, and especially of the Ordonnance Criminelle of 1670 (*Histoire de la Procédure Criminelle en France*, by Adhémar Esmein, p. 206).

[3] *Colbert, Promoteur des Grands Ordonnances de Louis XIV.*, by Alfred Aymé, p. 17; and see Martin's *History of France*, 4th ed., vol. xiii., pp. 67 *et seq.*

[4] *Précis de l'Histoire du Droit Français*, by Paul Viollet, p. 186; *Cours Elémentaire d'Histoire du Droit Français*, by Adhémar Esmein, 2nd ed., pp. 785 *et seq.* The dislike conceived by Louis XIV. and Colbert to the Parlement de Paris, and to some of the Provincial Parlements, dated from the troublous times of the Fronde, when grave excesses were committed which were connived at if not inspired by les Parlements (*Lettres, Instructions, et Mémoires de Colbert*, by Pierre Clement, vol. i., p. xx). Colbert is supposed to have meditated fatal designs against the Parlement de Paris, and partly on this account had no wish to associate any of its members in his proposed legislative reforms (*Précis de l'Histoire du Droit Français*, by Paul Viollet, p. 186; *Histoire de la Procédure Criminelle en France*, by Adhémar Esmein, p. 179).

[5] *Cours Elémentaire d'Histoire du Droit Français*, by Ahhémar Esmein, 2nd ed., pp. 785 *et seq.*

[6] *Colbert, Promoteur des Grands Ordonnances de Louis XIV.*, by Alfred Aymé, p. 17; *Histoire de la Procédure Criminelle en France*, by Adhémar Esmein, p. 179.

affairs, the second matters concerning the nobility, while to the third section was relegated, in a special manner, all that related to civil and criminal justice and police.[1] Colbert was himself a member of the last-named section, at the sittings of which, in his absence, his ideas and wishes were ably represented and expounded by his uncle, Henri Pussort,[2] in whom he had complete confidence.[3]

To aid the Council in its work, and to enable it to fulfil its duties effectually, by Colbert's advice, given to the King, memoranda were obtained from legal experts in various parts of the country detailing the abuses to be remedied and suggesting remedies.[4] Moreover, also by Colbert's advice and direction, inquiries were set on foot among recognized and effective bodies (Corps Competents) with a view to obtaining valuable and reliable information, and, further, while the Council was maturing its projects, eight able and trustworthy Maîtres des Requêtes[5] were despatched to do duty in all the "Parlements du Royaume,"[6] to ascertain and receive complaints and criticisms, and to forward same to the Conseil de Justice, certain members of which were specially deputed to receive all reports and communications from the Maîtres des Requêtes, and to maintain a regular correspondence with them.[7]

The first sitting of the Conseil de Justice is said to have taken place after Mass on September 25, 1665,[8] at the Louvre, in the

[1] *Colbert, Promoteur des Grands Ordonnances de Louis XIV.*, p. 17.
[2] *Ibid.;* and see *Précis de l'Histoire du Droit Français*, by Paul Viollet, p. 186.
[3] Martin's *History of France*, 4th ed., vol. xiii., p. 77.
[4] *Colbert, Promoteur des Grands Ordonnances de Louis XIV.*, p. 17 ; *Précis de l'Histoire du Droit Français*, by Paul Viollet, p. 186. These memoranda still exist in the Bibliothèque Nationale (*Histoire de la Procédure Criminelle en France*, by Adhémar Esmein, p. 180). Of these memoranda Henri Pussort's was the only one to which Colbert attached real importance and which he analyzed (*ibid.*).
[5] They received special instructions from Colbert himself (*Colbert, Promoteur des Grandes Ordonnances de Louis XIV.*, by Alfred Aymé, p. 17). A Maître des Requêtes was a member of the Council of State, next in rank to a counsellor.
[6] *Histoire de la Procédure Criminelle en France*, by Adhémar Esmein, p. 194.
[7] *Ibid.;* and see *Colbert, Promoteur des Grands Ordonnances de Louis XIV.*, by Alfred Aymé, p. 17.
[8] There appears to be some difference of opinion in regard to the date of the first sitting. Thus, while the date given in the text is vouched for by one authority (*Histoire de la Procédure Criminelle en France*, by Adhémar Esmein, p. 194), according to another authority the first sitting took place on October 10, 1665 (Martin's *History of France*, 4th ed., vol. xiii., p. 77, note 1), while October 28, 1666, has also been mentioned as the correct date (*ibid.;* Isambert's *Recueil Général des Anciennes Lois Françaises*, vol. xviii., p. 104).

King's study, and in the presence of Louis XIV., who presided over it in person, and delivered an allocution.[1] From that moment the great work may be said to have commenced, and it was continued, without interruption, to its conclusion and achievement.[2] The Conseil used to assemble at least every fifteen days (and generally under the presidency of the King himself), when the articles adopted by the Commission de Justice[3] were submitted for deliberation.[4]

The second sitting, which was also held at the Louvre in the King's presence, took place, it is believed, on October 11, 1665,[5] and seems to have been a notable one.[6] It was at this sitting that Louis XIV. interrogated the different members of the Conseil de Justice, asked each of them his advice, and decided to divide the matters in hand into principal heads, confiding each of these to two or more members, who, after discussing them with some famous advocates, were required to report their views thereon to the King, to whom the final decision was, however, reserved.[7] Colbert himself also spoke at great length on the same occasion, praising the King and expounding in detail the scheme recommended for adoption.[8]

It is quite unnecessary to refer to each of the several sittings held by the Conseil de Justice, but it should be noted that it was not until January 26, 1667, that, by the King's express

---

[1] *Histoire de la Procédure Criminelle en France*, by Adhémar Esmein, p. 194. At this first sitting, besides the Chancellor Seguier, who knew so little of the project in hand that he appears to have blundered somewhat (*Histoire de la Procédure Criminelle en France*, by Adhémar Esmein, p. 194), there were present MM. Voisin, Hotman, de Villeroy, d'Aligre, le Tellier, de Lyonne, de Verthamon, Poucet, Boucherat, et Henri Pussort (*Précis de l'Histoire du Droit Français*, by Paul Viollet, p. 186 ; *Histoire de la Procédure Criminelle en France*, by Adhémar Esmein, p. 195).

[2] *Histoire de la Procédure Criminelle en France*, by Adhémar Esmein, pp. 194, 198.

[3] See *Colbert, Promoteur des Grands Ordonnances de Louis XIV.*, by Alfred Aymé, p. 19.

[4] It has been stated that the sittings of the Conseil de Justice commenced October 28, 1666, and continued every week, and sometimes lasted for many days, down to February 10, 1667 (Isambert's *Recueil Général des Anciennes Lois Françaises*, vol. xviii., p. 104).

[5] *Histoire de la Procédure Criminelle en France*, by Adhémar Esmein, p. 196. Those who differ as to the date of the first sitting of the Conseil de Justice must obviously also be taken as disputing the dates of the second and some of the subsequent sittings.

[6] *Ibid.* MM. d'Estampes, de Morangis, and de Sève figure, for the first time, at this second sitting of the Conseil de Justice, while M. Poucet's name disappears (*ibid.*).

[7] *Précis de l'Histoire du Droit Français*, by Paul Viollet, p. 186.

[8] *Histoire de la Procédure Criminelle en France*, by Adhémar Esmein, p. 198.

command, Lamoignon, the First President of the Parlement de Paris, who had previously explained to Louis XIV. his own ideas on codification,[1] appeared at the Conseil de Justice, accompanied by an imposing deputation of Presidents of Courts of Justice in their robes of office, and wearing their judicial caps.[2] From this period the Conseil de Justice represented both the Parlement de Paris and the Conseil, and continued its work, mainly, if not invariably, in the house, and largely under the direction, of the Chancellor Seguier.[3] The Members of the Parlement de Paris were, however, not permitted to take part in the preparatory labours undertaken in respect of all the codifying ordinances promoted by Colbert, but only in respect of those relating to the Civil and Criminal Ordinances.[4] The other ordinances were, it appears, framed in strict accordance with Colbert's original plan, which completely ignored, for purposes of consultation, the members of the Parlement de Paris.[5]

It was during the sittings of the Conseil de Justice, and while the Civil and Criminal Ordinances were under discussion, that the ancient independence of the Parlement de Paris, admirably defended by its First President, Lamoignon, seemingly against Henri Pussort, but, in fact, against Colbert and Louis XIV.,[6]

---

[1] *Précis de l'Histoire du Droit Français*, by Paul Viollet, pp. 185, 186, 187.
[2] Isambert's *Recueil Général des Anciennes Lois Françaises*, vol. xviii., p. 104, note 1 ; *Colbert, Promoteur des Grands Ordonnances de Louis XIV.*, by Alfred Aymé, p. 19 ; *Précis de l'Histoire du Droit Français*, by Paul Viollet, p. 187 ; These Presidents of Courts of Justice were, on account of their headgear, termed " Presidents à Mortier " (*ibid.*).
[3] *Précis de l'Histoire du Droit Français*, by Paul Viollet, pp. 186, 187. The first of these sittings in Chancellor Seguier's house was held on January 26, 1667, and the last on March 17 of same year ; there were altogether fifteen of these sittings (Isambert's *Recueil Général des Anciennes Lois Françaises*, vol. xviii., p. 104, note 1). While the sittings of the Conseil de Justice were being held, six advocates, designated by the King for the purpose, prepared " les éléments," and, together with the First President and members of the Parlement de Paris, discussed the titles and articles of the proposed ordinance (Clement's *Histoire de Colbert*, vol. ii., pp. 304 *et seq.* ; *Histoire de la Procédure Criminelle en France*, by Adhémar Esmein, p. 192 ; *Lettres, Instructions, et Mémoires de Colbert*, by Pierre Clement, vol. vi., p. 21).
[4] *Cours Elémentaire d'Histoire du Droit Française*, 2nd ed., by Adhémar Esmein, p. 788.
[5] *Ibid.* ; and see Martin's *History of France*, 4th ed., vol. xiii., p. 77.
[6] Louis XIV.'s recollection of the excesses committed during the Fronde, which obliged him to quit his capital and go from province to province in order to assist at the siege of the revolted towns, caused him, when he became his own master, to punish " les Parlements," and especially " le Parlement de Paris," as the inciters, if not the authors, of the riots and insurrections ; in thus acting he was supported by Colbert (*Lettres, Instructions, et Mémoires de Colbert*, by Pierre Clement, vol. i., p. xx).

expired.¹ Nevertheless, the Parlement itself emerged from this ordeal, stricken indeed, but still alive, while Lamoignon, its discreet First President, on the day that the first of the Ordinances (L'Ordonnance Civile) was registered, was still able to reserve to the Parlement de Paris the right of remonstrance, but veiled indeed by such necessary and delicate flatteries as were exacted by the presence of an autocratic sovereign² who, in 1673, completely abrogated such rights.³

The history of the discussions which took place at all the different sittings of the Conseil de Justice is not fully known, though the subsequent conferences between the members of such Conseil and the delegates of the Parlement de Paris were eventually published, and afforded means for the correct interpretations of the Ordinances themselves when issued.⁴

The Ordinances.—It was on April 20, 1667, that the first of the Codifying Ordinances—that is to say, L'Ordonnance Civile, sometimes called the Code Louis[5] — was registered,[6] and without the necessity of any *lit de justice* being held by the King to compel its registration.[7] This Ordinance, which was in itself a veritable Code of Procedure,[8] contained thirty-

---

[1] *Histoire de la Procédure Criminelle en France*, by Adhémar Esmein, p. 187.
[2] *Précis de l'Histoire du Droit Français*, by Paul Viollet, p. 187.
[3] *Ibid.*, p. 189.
[4] *Histoire de la Procédure Criminelle en France*, by Adhémar Esmein, p. 194.
[5] Martin's *History of France*, 4th ed., vol. xiii., p. 78.
[6] *Ibid.*, p. 186; *Colbert, Promoteur des Grands Ordonnances de Louis XIV.*, by Alfred Aymé, pp. 19, 20.
[7] When a Parlement refused to register an Ordinance, Edict, or Declaration, a *lit de justice*, or séance royale, was held, at which the King, by his own absolute authority, compelled the registration, in his presence, of any such Ordinance, Declaration, or Edict (*Manuel de Droit Français*, 9th ed., by Judge Pailliet, p. x). Ordinances and Edicts came into operation on the day of their registration (*ibid.*, p. ix). From the time of Louis IX. (Saint Louis), the laws which previously had been called Capitularies and Etablissements were termed Ordinances or Edicts (*ibid.*), and these were addressed to the Parlements and Sovereign Councils to publish and transcribe on their Registers (*ibid.*). Declarations were letters patent, issued by the King, which applied, reformed, or revoked Edicts or Ordinances, and, like them, had to be registered (*ibid.*). Les Arrêts du Conseil, which were issued by the King, *mero motu*, interpreted Edicts, Ordinances, and Declarations (*ibid.*). Often the Parlements and Sovereign Councils addressed remonstrances to the King on particular Edicts, Ordinances, and Declarations before registering them, or only registered them with certain restrictions and modifications, so that an article rejected by one Parlement or Sovereign Council was sometimes accepted by another (*ibid.*, p. x). Thus L'Ordonnance Civile of 1667 and L'Ordonnance Criminelle of 1670 were not received in Lorraine (*ibid.*). The right of remonstrance was abolished, in the case of the Parlement de Paris at all events, in 1673 (*supra*).
[8] Martin's *History of France*, 4th ed., vol. xiii., p. 178.

five articles. The Preamble[1] and first eight Titles were, at the time, considered to be of the highest legal and political importance,[2] while the entire Ordinance, which it is not, however, proposed to examine in detail, aimed, like those which were subsequently issued, at producing a complete, systematic, and detailed codification of a branch of law of wide and general importance.[3] According to the intentions of its framers and editors, this particular Ordinance was principally designed to diminish the length of lawsuits, to reduce their cost, and also to simplify procedure.[4] Its very first article was styled "de l'observation des ordonnances," and provided that all Ordinances, Edicts, and Declarations are to be "gardées et observées par toutes nos cours de parlement, grand conseil, chambres des comtes, cours des aides et autres nos cours, juges, magistrats, officiers, tant de nous que des seigneurs, et par tout nos autres sujets, même dans les officialités,"[5] and further declares "tous arrêts et jugements, qui seront donnés contre le disposition de nos ordonnances, edits, et déclarations, nuls et de nul effet et valeur ; et les juges qui les auront rendus, responsables des

[1] The Preamble was, in substance, as follows: "*Louis, &c. . . .* Comme la justice est la plus solide fondement de la durée des états, qu'elle assure le repos des familles et le bonheur des peuples, nous avons employé tous nos soins pour la rétablir par l'autorité des lois au—dedans de notre royaume après lui avoir donné la paix par la force de nos armes—c'est pourquoi, ayant reconnu, par le rapport de personnes de grande expérience, que les ordonnances sagement établies par les rois nos prédécesseurs pour terminer les procès étaient observées differemment en plusieurs de nos cours, ce qui causait la ruine des familles par la multiplicité des procédures, les frais des poursuites, et la variété des jugements ; et qu'il était nécessaire d'y pourvoir, et rendre l'expédition des affaires plus prompte, plus facile, et plus sure, par le retranchant de plusieurs délais et actes inutiles, et par l'établissement d'un style uniforme dans toutes nos cours et siéges. A ces causes de l'avis de notre conseil et de notre certaine science, pleine puissance, et autorité royale, nous avons dit declaré, et ordonné, disons, declarons, et ordonnons, et nous plait ce qui ensuit " (*Recueil Général des Anciennes Lois Françaises*, by Isambert and others, 1829, vol. xviii., pp. 103, 104, 105).
[2] *Précis de l'Histoire du Droit Français*, by Paul Viollet, p. 186. The following are the headings of the eight Articles referred to in the text—namely: I. De l'observation des ordonnances ; II. Des ajournements ; III. Des délais sur les assignations et ajournements ; IV. Des présentations ; V. Des Congés et défauts en matière civile ; VI. Des fins de non-procéder ; VII. Des délais pour délibérer ; VIII. Des garans (Isambert's *Recueil Général d'Anciennes Lois Françaises*, vol. xviii., pp. 105 *et seq.*).
[3] *Cours Elémentaire du Histoire du Droit Française*, 2nd ed., by Adhémar Esmein, p. 785. This method of Codification introduced by Colbert was afterwards continued in the reign of Louis XV. (*ibid.*).
[4] *Colbert, Promoteur des Grands Ordonnances de Louis XIV.*, by Alfred Aymé, p. 22.
[5] Title I., art. 1 (Isambert's *Recueil Général des Anciennes Lois Françaises*, vol. xviii., p. 106).

dommages et interêts des parties, ainsi qu'il sera par nous avisé.[1] The length in point of time of adjournments before the various civil tribunals was likewise prescribed by this Ordinance,[2] which also forbad the use of certain dilatory pleas, which experience had proved to result in the needless prolongation of trials and increase of costs.[3] Moreover, in order to stifle at an early stage of a lawsuit useless and unfounded litigation, litigants were, by the same Ordinance, obliged to supply copies of the proofs on which they relied in support of their cases.[4] L'Ordonnance Civile also carefully regulated and defined the right and limits of appeal from one court to another, reduced the time for the exercise of such right from thirty years to three years and six months,[5] and prescribed the cases in which judges might be challenged.[6] By the same Ordinance, a distinction was established between commercial debts and civil debts, and the enforcing of the latter, by means of corporal restraints, regulated and restricted.[7]

With regard to the holding of inquiries by witnesses (Enquêtes),[8]

[1] Title I., art. 8 (Isambert's *Recueil Général des Anciennes Lois Françaises*, vol. xviii., pp. 106, 107). This particular article was stoutly resisted by Lamoignon, First President of the Parlement de Paris, and other Parliamentary deputies, as being derogatory of the dignity and honour of the judicial Bench (*Colbert, Promoteur des Grands Ordonnances de Louis XIV.*, by Alfred Aymé, pp. 20, 21). This want of confidence in the Judges is also indicated by an Edict of 1673, prohibiting Judges from taking fees or salaries in excess of the sum prescribed by law, and which the First President of the Parlement was required to fix, until the financial condition of the State could permit of gratuitous administration of Justice (*Anciennes Lois Françaises*, Tit. XIX. p. 86). By Title II., art. 14 of the Ordonnance Civile, Ushers and Bailiffs were required to be able to read and write.

[2] Ord. Civ., Tit. II. ; and see *Colbert, Promoteur des Grands Ordonnances de Louis XIV.*, by Alfred Aymé, pp. 22, 23.

[3] Ord. Civ., Tit. VI., IX., and XIV. ; and see *Colbert, Promoteur de Grands Ordonnances de Louis XIV.*, by Alfred Aymé, p. 25.

[4] Ord. Civ., Tit. II., art. 6 ; Tit. III., art. 5. These proofs were termed *pièces justificatives*.

[5] Ord. Civ., Tit. XXVII., art. 12.

[6] *Ibid.*, Tit. XXIV.   [7] *Ibid.*, Tit. XXXIV.

[8] Ord. Civ., Tit. XXII. In the early history of the French Courts the maxim, "*Témoins passent lettres*," prevailed (Boddington's *French Law of Evidence*, p. 92), but, gradually, by various causes, including the spread of printing and writing, the rule contained in this maxim was, in February, 1566, reversed by Article 54 of L'Ordonnance sur la reforme de la justice (commonly called L'Ordonnance de Moulin de 1566). Accordingly, even at the present day, in Civil (as distinguished from Criminal) Causes in France witnesses give their testimony in chambers, not in open Court, under a special procedure known as "Enquête," conducted before a judge specially appointed for the purpose, sitting in chambers (Boddington's *French Law of Evidence*, pp. 2, 92, 93 ; Code Civil, Book III., Tit. III., arts. 1341 *et seq.*). This testimony, when given, comes before the Court in written form only,

L'Ordonnance Civile contained various provisions, and prohibited their being held by deputies,[1] while "les enquêtes par turbes" et "celles d'examen" were abolished.[2]

On the subject of registration of births, deaths, and marriages the Ordinance under consideration contained various provisions and, as some previous ordinances had also done,[3] placed these "Actes de l'État Civil," as they are termed, almost entirely in lay hands,[4] whereby they forfeited their exclusively religious character and significance.[5] Nevertheless, the French Revolution, when it took place, still found the Register Books in the hands of the curés.[6]

Owing to difficulties having arisen in the execution of the Ordonnance Civile, another, supplemental thereto, "pour la réformation de la justice, faisant la continuation de celle du mois d'Avril, 1667," was issued.[7] Moreover, several Edicts were also, at various times, registered, which form, as it were, appendices to the original Ordonnance Civile.[8] Thus, by an Edict of August, 1669, a new court, called la Tournelle Civile, was attached to the Parlement de Paris, for the adjudication of cases in which the amount in dispute did not exceed a thousand écus,[9] while another Edict, issued in 1673, not only reduced the fees payable to the judges, and curtailed

---

and the judges composing such Court have to sort out the wheat from the chaff, and form their opinion upon the facts which they consider relevant and proved (*ibid.*). In short, it is true to say in France that "le principe qui domine notre droit civil, relativement à la preuve testimoniale, est que celle—si n'est admissible, que dans des cas exceptionnels permettement visés par la loi; il n'est pas permis d'appliquer ce mode de preuve par analogie" (*Code-Civil Annoté*, by Fuzier-Herman, vol. 3, p. 450).

[1] Ord. Civ., Tit. XXII., art. 12.

[2] Ord. Civ., Tit. XXXV.; and see *Colbert, Promoteur des Grands Ordonnances de Louis XIV.*, by Alfred Aymé, p. 26.

[3] *I.e.*, the Ordinances of August, 1539, and May, 1579.

[4] Title XX. of L'Ordonnance Civile (Des faits qui gisent en preuve vocale ou littérale), Articles 7 to 18 (inclusive). Subsequent Ordinances on the same subject were issued in the reign of Louis XIV.—namely, in August, 1683, in October, 1691, in June, 1705, in October, 1706, and in July, 1710.

[5] *Colbert, Promoteur des Grands Ordonnances de Louis XIV.*, by Alfred Aymé, p. 25; Martin's *History of France*, 4th ed., vol. xiii., p. 80, note 1.

[6] Laurent's *Principes du Droit Civil Français*, 2nd ed., vol. ii., pp. 6 *et seq.*

[7] Isambert's *Recueil Général des Anciennes Lois Françaises*, vol. xviii., pp. 341 *et seq.* The Ordinance referred to in the text contained the following articles—namely: I. Des Evocations; II. De règlements de juges en matière civile; III. De règlements de juges en matière criminelle; IV. Des committimus et gardes gardiennes; V. Des lettres d'Etat; and VI. Des Répits.

[8] Martin's *History of France*, 4th ed., vol. xiii., pp. 79 *et seq.*

[9] Martin's *History of France*, 4th ed., vol. xiii., pp. 79, 80. An écu, or crown, was worth about 4s. of our money.

the length of their vacations, but it also contained provisions for promoting and securing uniformity throughout France in certain legal forms then in use.[1] Moreover, by an Edict of March, 1673, the publicity of Mortgages was prescribed, a measure which has been regarded as one of the wisest and most important introduced by Colbert in that which touches and concerns civil rights.[2]

In honour of the passing of L'Ordonnance Civile, several medals were struck, one of which represents Louis XIV. holding the scales of justice, in presence of a figure of Justice, and bears the legend "*Justitia judicanti.*"[3] Moreover, many learned works, by eminent jurists, were written to explain and interpret the Ordinance.[4]

Reference must now be made to another of the great codifying ordinances promoted by Colbert—namely, L'Ordonnance Criminelle of August, 1670, which, when issued, became the French Code d'Instruction Criminelle[5] for 120 years,[6] and, together with L'Ordonnance Civile, which preceded it, forms part of one and the same design,[7] and was subjected to very similar preliminary labours and ordeals.[7] The Ordinance in question exhibits the same meritorious features as l'Ordonnance Civile, viz., order, clearness, uniformity, and simplicity.[8] Unfortunately, however, it left untouched those baleful provisions of the Ordonnance de Villers Cotterets of 1539, in regard to secret legal procedure,[9] and to the withholding from accused persons, in the

---

[1] Martin's *History of France*, 4th ed., vol. xiii., pp. 79, 80. This useful measure, owing to the difficulties experienced in putting it into practice, was revoked in 1674 (*ibid.*).   [2] *Ibid.*, p. 80.

[3] *Ibid.*, p. 79.

[4] *Recueil Général des Anciennes Lois Françaises*, by Isambert and others, vol. xviii., p. 104.

[5] *Histoire de la Procédure Criminelle en France*, by Adhémar Esmein, p. vj.   [6] *Ibid.*

[7] *Ibid.*, p. 206; and see *Les Anciennes Lois Françaises*, t. xviii., p. 371.

[8] Martin's *History of France*, 4th ed. vol. xiii., p. 82. The Preamble of L'Ordonnance Criminelle is, in substance, as follows : " Les grands avantages que nos sujets ont reçus des soins que nous avons employés à reformer la procédure civile par nos ordonnances d'Avril, 1667, et d'Août, 1669, nous ont porté à donner une pareille application au réglement de l'instruction criminelle qui est d'autant plus importante, que non seulement ille conserve les particuliers dans la possession paisible de leurs biens, ainsi que la civile, mais encore elle assure le repos public, et contient, par la crainte des châtiments, ceux qui ne sont pas retenus par la considération de leur devoir. A ces causis, &c, &c." Isambert, *Recueil General des Anciennes Lois Françaises*, vol. xviii., pp. 371, 372).

[9] *Ibid.* The secret procedure referred to in the text existed in France long before 1539, when, however, resort thereto became general (*ibid.*).

majority of cases at least, of the professional aid afforded by trained advocates.[1] Moreover, it also retained the barbarous practice (termed *la question*) for procuring confessions of guilt, and the disclosure of accomplices' names, from accused persons by the use of torture, where other measures failed.[2] The retention of such objectionable provisions[3] was in no small measure due to the arguments and influence of Colbert's uncle, Henri Pussort, which seem to have prevailed over the wiser and more humane arguments urged with great force and eloquence by Lamoignon, the First President of the Parlement de Paris,[4] who, however, did succeed in introducing into the Ordinance many amendments and corrections,[5] while, on the other hand, he seems to have resisted some useful reforms, and is known to have protested against any attempts to curtail judicial privileges and profits.[6]

In a memorandum, addressed by Colbert to Louis XIV., he defined, in the following words, the task of the Conseil de Justice in the sphere of penal legislation:

"Examiner tout ce qui concerne la justice criminelle du royaume, comme la plus importante, en retrancher toute la chicane, et prendre garde d'établir des moyens assurés pour, en conservant et assurant les innocents, parvenir promptement à la punition des criminels."[7]

This was to be the aim of the Ordonnance Criminelle of 1670,

---

[1] Martin's *History of France*, 4th ed., vol. xiii., p. 82. *Semble*, prisoners were allowed to have counsel only in non-capital cases (*Colbert, Promoteur des Grands Ordonnances de Louis XIV.*, by Alfred Aymé, p. 33).

[2] Tit. XIX. (Des jugements et Procès-verbaux, de Question et Tortures) (*Colbert, Promoteur des Grands Ordonnances de Louis XIV.*, by Alfred Aymé, p. 33). This, and certain other objectionable, not to say barbarous, features of the Ordonnance Criminelle caused Voltaire to express the opinion that "Le Code Criminelle est une preuve du mépris que des hommes qui se croient au-dessus des lois osent quelquefois montrer pour le peuple" (Voltaire's collected *Works*, published in 1819, vol. xviii., p. 197, note 1). It is only fair to state that Art. 12 of Title XIX. of L'Ordonnance Criminelle provided that "Quelque nouvelle preuve qui survienne, l'accusé ne pourra être appliqué deux fois à la question pour un même fait."

[3] The original author of these provisions is said to have been De Paget, the Chancelier of 1539.

[4] Martin's *History of France*, 4th ed., vol. xiii., p. 83; *Précis de l'Histoire du Droit Français*, by Paul Viollet, p. 188; *Histoire de la Procédure Criminelle en France*, by Adhémar Esmein, p. 193.

[5] *Précis de l'Histoire du Droit Français*, by Paul Viollet, p. 187.

[6] *Ibid.*; and see *Histoire de la Procédure Criminelle en France*, by Adhémar Esmein, pp. 209, 210.

[7] *Colbert, Promoteur des Grand Ordonnances de Louis XIV.*, p. 30; *Revue Rétrospective*, 2d série, t. iv., p. 257.

which, however, it must be confessed, was not fully achieved, so that, of all the codifying Ordinances issued in the reign of Louis XIV. and promoted by Colbert, this particular one has remained, upon the whole, the least bold, the least innovating, and the least praiseworthy.[1]

It is not proposed to discuss or examine in detail the provisions of the Ordonnance Criminelle, which, it may be mentioned, comprised twenty-eight Titles,[2] and, without introducing a new procedure, regulated a system which had been gradually formed in France, and had also developed in neighbouring countries.[3] The Ordonnance did, however, reduce to precision the anterior law,[4] and, in the conferences which took place while the Ordinance was still being discussed, care was taken by its framers, when a particular article, suggested for adoption, contained new matter, to direct special attention thereto.[5] Nevertheless, the Ordonnance Criminelle was by no means a mere reproduction of a picture somewhat tarnished by age, for it did renovate the law in certain respects, and unfortunately added some new rigours to ancient severities,[6] though it did likewise somewhat modify the brutal scale of punishments, till then in force, and also introduced some much-needed prison reforms.[7] Moreover, while it adhered to fundamental principles, fixed by previous ordinances, it settled the details thereof, and, for the first time, presented a systematic exposition of criminal procedure,[8] even condescending to the most minute particulars of the inquisitorial, written, and secret methods of such procedure.[9] The Ordinance likewise sought to prevent future conflicts of the different magistrates amongst themselves, in regard to their respective jurisdictions over crimes and minor offences, by determining and defining, as far as possible, their respective spheres and powers.[10] Indeed, according to memoranda supplied

---

[1] Martin's *History of France*, 4th ed., vol. xiii., p. 83.
[2] *Ibid.*, p. 81.
[3] *Histoire de la Procédure Criminelle en France*, by Adhémar Esmein, pp. vj, vij. [4] *Ibid.*
[5] *Histoire de la Procédure Criminelle en France*, by Adhémar Esmein, p. vij. [6] *Ibid.*
[7] *Cambridge Modern History*, vol. v., p. 15.
[8] *Histoire de la Procédure Criminelle en France*, by Adhémar Esmein, p. vij.
[9] *Ibid.* The oral and public accusatory inquisition of the Middle Ages gradually became secret and inquisitorial (*ibid.*).
[10] *Colbert, Promoteur des Grands Ordonnances de Louis XIV.*, by Alfred Aymé, p. 30.

by members of the Conseil d'État, prior to the drafting of the Ordinance under consideration, the reform of the magistracy, rather than of the law itself, was recommended, though the remodelling and modernizing of the existing Ordinances was also suggested as being desirable.[1] This can hardly be wondered at, having regard to the scandalous appointments to the Magisterial Bench which, in the time of Colbert, were often made, vacancies thereon being sometimes filled by mere boys, fresh from college, who were invested with powers of life and death.[2]

In forming a critical judgment upon the Ordonnance Criminelle of 1670, it would be most unfair to compare it with modern criminal codes, or with existing penal legislation. It was the product of an age in which public opinion sanctioned what would now be regarded as cruel, not to say barbarous, methods of dealing with crimes and criminals. Draconian severity was then considered to be justifiable, in order to enforce obedience to the law. Whether Colbert himself was in favour of such a system may well be doubted. Probably he was far in advance of his time, and was content therefore to regard the Ordonnance Criminelle, not as a perfect code, but as a mere step in the right direction.

Though the two Ordinances already referred to were the principal ones registered during the reign of Louis XIV. and in the lifetime of Colbert, they are by no means the only important ones attributable to the latter's initiative and genius. Thus, even while the Civil and Criminal Ordinances, already examined, were in process of incubation, Colbert, surrounded by some twenty-one Commissioners, who, by diligent and searching investigations, extending over eight years, had made themselves acquainted with the necessary particulars and details, was preparing his magnificent scheme of legislative reform in the department of Waters, Woods, and Forests,[3] which eventually took shape as "L'Ordonnance des Eaux et Forêts" of August, 1669,[4] has been designated a monument of legislative wisdom,[5] and sub-

---

[1] *Histoire de la Procédure Criminelle en France*, by Adhémar Esmein, p. 185.   [2] *Ibid.*, p. 182.
[3] *Colbert, Promoteur des Grands Ordonnances de Louis XIV.*, by Alfred Aymé, p. 37; Martin's *History of France*, 4th ed., vol. xiii., p. 90; Bachelet's *Les Grands Ministres Français*, tit. Colbert, p. 369; Isambert's *Recueil Général des Anciennes Lois Françaises*, xviii., p. 219.
[4] Martin's *History of France*, 4th ed., xiii., p. 90.
[5] *Colbert, Promoteur des Grands Ordonnances de Louis XIV.*, by Alfred Aymé, p. 37.

sisted, almost intact, down to 1827.[1] This Ordinance, by itself, would have sufficed to render any Minister producing it illustrious.[2] It codified and produced a multitude of confused and contradictory laws, which had survived from the remote times of Charlemagne, who himself attempted to organize the service of "les eaux et forêts,"[3] in the hope of being able to check numerous invasions of, and encroachments upon, water and forest rights. Certainly there was ample justification for the issue of the new Ordinance, mainly in order to preserve and protect forest rights, both public and private, and to prevent, in the interest of private individuals, commerce, and maritime requirements, the wanton destruction of timber trees.[4] Without attempting to reproduce the provisions of this Ordinance, which was of wide scope and vast importance to France, suffice it to to state that it introduced uniformity of jurisprudence for all offences within its purview,[5] and that, besides legislating for woods and forests, properly so called, it also contained elaborate police regulations in regard to fishing in rivers, suppressed alleged rights of toll having no legal origin, controlled the exercise of sporting rights by various prescriptions, prohibited hunting in vineyards and in lands under cultivation, and abolished the death penalty for acts of poaching committed by peasants.[6] That the Ordinance was largely intended to safeguard the interests of sea and river navigation is clearly indicated by its Preamble and by many of its articles.[7] It has been said of this great Ordinance that it is one of those monuments of human skill and forethought in which order and reason are combined, and which, once overturned, cannot readily be replaced.[8] Certainly the Code Forestière of 1827 does not seem to have been regarded as an improvement upon the Ordinance of 1669.[9]

[1] *Colbert, Promoteur des Grands Ordonnances de Louis XIV.*, by Alfred Aymé, p. 37; and see *Lettres, Instructions, et Mémoires de Colbert*, by Pierre Clement, iv., p. lxii.
[2] Martin's *History of France*, 4th ed., xiii., p. 90.
[3] *Ibid.*; and see, generally, *Lettres, Instructions, et Mémoires de Colbert*, by Pierre Clement, iv.
[4] *Colbert, Promoteur des Grands Ordonnances de Louis XIV.*, by Alfred Aymé, pp. 37 *et seq.*; and see Martin's *History of France*, 4th ed., xiii., pp. 90 *et seq.* [5] *Ibid.*
[6] *Colbert, Promoteur des Grands Ordonnances de Louis XIV.*, *supra*, p. 39.
[7] Martin's *History of France*, 4th ed., xiii., p. 91. In 1681 Colbert wrote to the Intendant de Tours et Limoges: "Que rien n'est d'une plus grande utilité et n'apporte plus d'avantages aux peuples que la navigation des rivières" (*Lettres, Instructions, et Mémoires de Colbert*, by Pierre Clement, vol. iv., p. cxv).
[8] Martin's *History of France*, 4th ed., xiii., p. 92. [9] *Ibid.*

Passing over certain Ordinances of minor importance, including one of August, 1871, establishing uniformity of weights and measures in all the ports and arsenals of France, we come to another great Ordinance, namely, L'Ordonnance pour le Commerce of 1673.[1] The object of this Ordinance is indicated by its Preamble in the following words : "Comme le Commerce est la source de l'abondance publique, et la richesse des particuliers, nous avons depuis plusieurs années appliqué nos soins pour le rendre florissant dans notre royaume. C'est ce qui nous a porté premierement à eriger parmi nos sujets plusieurs compagnies, par le moyen desquelles ils tirent présentement des pays les plus eloignés, ce qu'ils n'avaient auparavant que par l'entremise des autres nations. C'est ce qui nous à engagé ensuite à faire construire et armer grand nombre de vaisseaux pour l'avancement de la navigation, et à employer la force de nos armes par mer et par terre pour en maintenir la sureté. Ces etablissements ayant en tout le succés que nous en attendions nous avons cru être obligé de pourvoir à leur durée, par des reglements capables d'assurer parmi les négocians la bonne foi contre la grande, et de prévenir les obstacles qui les détournent de leur emploi, par la longueur des procès, et consommant en frais le plus liquide de ce qu'ils ont acquis."[2] This Ordinance, which embraces all that concerns commerce,[3] is believed to have been Colbert's favourite piece of legislation.[4] It contains twelve Titles, and was considered to be, in all respects, worthy of the pains bestowed upon it by Colbert himself and by Savari, the great commercial specialist, author of a work once considered famous, called, *Le Parfait Negociant*,[5] published in 1675,[6] who is said to have prepared the first draft of the Commercial Ordinance, which has, on this account, sometimes been called, after him, the Code Savari.[7] Colbert was not, however, content to consult only one commercial

[1] In connection with this Ordinance, reference should be made to the Edict of August, 1669: "Portant que les gentilshommes, pourront faire le commerce de mer sans deroger" (Isambert's *Recueil Général des Anciennes Lois Françaises*, vol. xviii., pp. 217 *et seq.*).
[2] Isambert's *Recueil Général des Anciennes Lois Françaises*, xix., pp. 92, 93.
[3] *Biographie Ancienne et Moderne*, ix., tit. Colbert, p. 216.
[4] *Précis de l'Histoire du Droit Françaises*, by Paul Viollet, p. 189.
[5] Martin's *History of France*, 4th ed., vol. xiii., p. 152. He also wrote *Les Paréres*, which was published in 1688 (*Précis de l'Histoire du Droit Français*, by Paul Viollet, p. 189).
[6] *Précis de l'Histoire du Droit Français*, by Paul Viollet, p. 189.
[7] *Ibid.*

specialist. On the contrary, he enlisted the services of the best-known French merchants of the day, and invited them to visit him, so that they might afford him trustworthy information and discuss amongst themselves, and with him, mercantile usages and law.[1] He even lodged some of them under his own roof, and presented them to the King.[2] The Ordinance under consideration was designed to free commercial men from needless anxiety in their profession, engendered by a variety of customs, to protect good faith from fraud, to establish uniform legislation in commercial cases, and to diminish the length and cost of litigation.[3] It rendered interest upon interest illegal,[4] and contained elaborate and minute provisions in regard to the conduct of mercantile affairs, and regulated the conduct of business by merchants, obliging them to practise book-keeping, to ascertain from day to day the state of their accounts, and also to make and preserve copies of all letters despatched, and to file those received.[5] Moreover, it likewise regulated the conditions of age and apprenticeship for those wishing to become merchants, providing that, for commercial purposes, minors should be regarded as of full age.[6] The same Ordinance also contained various provisions as to Companies or Partnerships,[7] which do not call for notice, and required that disputes amongst members thereof should be submitted to compulsory arbitration.[8] Finally, in order to secure obedience to its provisions, the Ordinance rendered merchants failing to observe its more important provisions at least liable, in case of insolvency, to be declared fraudulent bankrupts and sentenced to death.[9]

[1] *Précis de l'Histoire du Droit Français*, by Paul Viollet, p. 189.
[2] *Ibid.*
[3] Martin's *History of France*, 4th ed., xiii., p. 153; *Colbert, Promoteur des Grands Ordonnances de Louis XIV.*, p. 40. The twelve Titles into which the Ordinance is divided are as follows: I. Des apprentis, Négociants, et Marchands, tant en gros qu'en detail; II. Des Agens de Banque et courtiers; III. Des livres et Registres de Négocians, Marchands, et Banquiers; IV. Des Sociétés; V. Des Lettres et Ballets de change et promesses d'en fournir; VI. Des intérêts de change et du rechange; VII. De Contraintes par Corps; VIII. Des séparations de biens; IX. Des Défenses et Lettres de répit; X. Des Cessions de biens; XI. Des Faillites et Banqueroutes; XII. De la juridiction des Consuls (Isambert's *Recueil Général des Anciennes Lois Françaises*, vol. xix., pp. 93 to 107). [4] Tit. VI., *supra*.
[5] *Colbert, Promoteur des Grands Ordonnances de Louis XIV.*, by Alfred Aymé, p. 40; and see Tit. II. of the Ordinance.
[6] Tit. I. of the Ordinance; and see *Colbert, Promoteur des Grands Ordonnances de Louis XIV.*, *supra*, p. 40.
[7] See Tit. IV. of the Ordinance. [8] *Ibid.*
[9] See Tit. XI. of the Ordinance; *Colbert, Promoteur des Grands Ordonnances de Louis XIV.*, p. 40.

L'Ordonnance de Commerce was, in 1680, followed by the Salt Tax (Gatelle) Ordinance, to which no further reference need, however, be made.

It was in August, 1681, that the celebrated Ordonnance pour la Marine was issued, which was subsequently largely adopted by the English Admiralty.[1] The elaboration of this Ordinance was confided to special Commissioners, to aid whom in their task Colbert appointed a Maître des Requêtes to visit all the ports of the kingdom.[2] This Ordinance comprised, besides other matters too numerous to mention, all that concerns the duties of Admirals, the jurisdiction of Admiralty officials, the mode of procedure to be adopted in Admiralty cases, the prerogatives of Consuls in foreign countries, the organization of French merchants, and of the navigation of the ports of the Levant, "en assemblée ou Nation."[3] It also prescribed the conditions of capacity for employment of pilots and captains of ships, obliged ships making long voyages to carry chaplains and surgeons,[4] regulated the policing of the coasts and of the seashores, introduced measures for saving life at sea, and provided for the infliction of the death penalty on those who robbed shipwrecked persons.[5]

Two years after Colbert's death was issued the last Ordinance with which his name is associated, and which was prepared during his ministry—namely, L'Ordonnance Coloniale of 1685, which is best known by its nickname of the "Code Noir."[6]

The responsibility, and the honour and credit, for the production of this Ordinance, which regulated the government of the French West Indian colonies and the condition and treatment of negro slaves and freedmen,[7] have been ascribed to Colbert's eldest son, the Marquis de Seignelay, though it certainly was inspired by the great Colbert himself, whose spirit it breathes.[8]

This Ordinance regulated generally the treatment of negroes in all the French colonies,[9] and established the obligations of

[1] *Colbert, Promoteur des Grands Ordonnances de Louis XIV.*, supra, p. 42.
[2] *Colbert, Promoteur des Grands Ordonnances de Louis XIV.*, by Alfred Aymé, p. 42.　　[3] *Ibid.*　　[4] *Ibid.*　　[5] *Ibid.*
[6] Clement's *Histoire de Colbert*, vol. ii., chap. xxviii., pp. 323, 324; Martin's *History of France*, 4th ed., vol. xiii., p. 555.
[7] Latham's *Dictionary of Names*, etc., p. 62; and see *Colbert, Promoteur des Grands Ordonnances de Louis XIV.*, by Pierre Clement, pp. 43 et seq.
[8] Clement's *Histoire de Colbert*, vol. ii., chap. xxviii., p. 324. Colbert's eldest son only survived his father for seven years, dying November 3, 1690 (*Works* of Voltaire, xvii., p. 35; *Lettres de Madame de Sévigné*, annotated edition, 1862, vol. ix., pp. 582, 583).
[9] *Manuel de Droit Français*, 9th ed., by Judge Pailliet, p. xxiv.

masters towards their slaves, protecting the latter from oppression by exemplary punishments.[1] It provided that negro slaves should be suitably clothed and fed, and also taken care of in time of sickness; that the murder of a black slave by his master should be the subject of criminal prosecution;[2] that negroes could marry and have families; that the husband and wife and children, though slaves, should not be sold separately; that the child of a slave husband and a free mother should follow the condition of the latter; and that all slaves should be baptized and instructed in the Catholic religion.[3]

Having regard to the terms of this Ordinance, which was certainly an improvement on the existing law,[4] it scarcely seems to deserve the severe judgment passed upon it by Voltaire, who wrote that "le Code Noir n'a servi qu'a montrer que les gens de loi, consultés par Louis XIV., n'avaient aucune idée des droits de l'humanité."[5] That it remained operative until 1847, some months before the abolition of slavery in the French colonies, testifies to its intrinsic worth.[6]

In reviewing Colbert's work as a legislative reformer, it should always be remembered, to his credit, that he aimed at reducing the whole body of the ordinances of his country, by means of their codification, into as complete and uniform a system of jurisprudence as the Roman law itself became, in the time, and thanks to the labours, of Justininan.[7] Such being his ambition, Colbert naturally urged Louis XIV. not to be satisfied merely to reform the administration of justice, but to fulfil what is believed to have been the ambition of both Louis XI. and Henri IV.—namely, the bringing of the whole kingdom under the same law, "*même mesure et même poids.*"[8] To have achieved such a result would probably have required thirty years of continuous peace, which Colbert's ambitious sovereign would not concede.[9] Nevertheless, much was undoubtedly accomplished, in the right direction, by the great codifying ordinances already referred to, which, however, in point of fact, represent " quelques

---

[1] *Biographie, Universelle et Moderne*, tit. Colbert, p. 216.
[2] *Colbert, Promoteur des Grands Ordonnances de Louis XIV.*, *supra*, p. 44.
[3] Martin's *History of France*, 4th ed., xiii., p. 556.
[4] *Ibid.*
[5] Voltaire's collected *Works*, ed. of 1819, xviii., p. 197, note 1, where it is also stated, however, that "il y eut même une jurisprudence nouvelle établie en faveur des nègres de nos colonies, espèces d'homme qui n'avaient pas encore joui des droits de l'humanité."
[6] Martin's *History of France*, 4th ed., xiii., p. 556.
[7] *Ibid.*, p. 76.   [8] *Ibid.*, p. 77.   [9] *Ibid.*

fragments seulement de la pensée de Colbert sur l'unité des lois," though it is likewise true that "la France judiciaire à vécu de ses fragments jusqu'en 1789."[1]

After Colbert's death in 1683, several ordinances were issued besides that termed the "Code Noir." Of these, he does not seem to have had any hand in their preparation, and, most probably, they were not even thought of till after his death. Neither was he in any way responsible for the Edict of 1683, which repealed the Edicts of Nantes and Nimes.[2] This Edict, which is said to have been drawn up by the Chancellor le Tellier shortly before his own death,[3] seems to have been issued by the advice of Louvois, who, on Colbert's death, became the chief Minister of State.[4] Colbert himself was very tolerant, both to Huguenots and Jews,[5] and his eldest son, the Marquis de Seignelay, was also opposed to religious persecutions.[6]

In the reign of Louis XIV.. the great-grandson of the Grand Monarque, further codifying ordinances were, from time to time, registered. The credit for these has justly been ascribed to the Chancelier Aguesseau, reputed to have been the greatest lawyer of his age, just as, in the preceding reign, the great ordinances issued were largely due to the inspiring genius and influence of Colbert.[7]

The Ordinances of Louis XV. seem to have been prepared in much the same manner as those issued by his predecessor, and after consultation with persons possessing the necessary expert knowledge and skill.[8] By means of these ordinances, that part of the civil law governing donations, wills, and substitutions was codified.[9] The production of the Codes of the Consulate and Empire were also the result of most elaborate and laborious preparation.[10]

The French Civil Code (Code Napoleon), as it ultimately ap-

[1] Martin's *History of France*, 4th ed., xiii., p. 77.
[2] *Manuel de Droit Française*, 9th ed., by Judge Pailliet, p. xiv.
[3] Martin's *History of France*, 4th ed., xiv., p. 47.
[4] *Lectures on Modern History*, by Lord Acton, p. 244 ; Martin's *History of France*, 4th ed., xiv., pp. 39 et seq.
[5] *Lettres, Instructions, et Mémoires de Colbert*, by Pierre Clement, iii., pt. 2, p. xxii.
[6] Martin's *History of France*, 4th ed., xiv., p. 2.
[7] *Cours Elémentaire d'Histoire du Droit Français*, 2nd ed., by Adhémar Esmein, p. 785 ; *Le Code Civile, Livre du Centenaire*, p. 17.
[8] *Le Code Civile, Livre du Centenaire*, p. 17.   [9] *Ibid.*
[10] *Ibid.*; and see *Cours Elémentaire d'Histoire du Droit Français, supra*, p. 785.

peared, was not a new creation, and its compilers were disciples, and not prophets,[1] but the Code actually issued was totally different from what was contemplated and intended by the men of the Revolution.[2] It is based on the Roman law, and was the first successful effort to give complete unity to law in France.[3] A step so bold could hardly have been attempted by an autocrat, and on the morrow of a Revolution.[4]

Closing Years of Life.—The closing years of Colbert's life did not yield much happiness or contentment to the great statesman, whose colossal administration of wellnigh twenty-two years' duration had accomplished so much for the good of his country in all departments of the public service, and notably, as has been seen,[5] in that of finance, which needed the exercise of the utmost skill, and the possession of supreme gifts by Colbert, in order to avert national bankruptcy, which appeared to be the almost inevitable consequence of Fouquet's previous mismanagement, extravagance, and dishonesty. For some time before his death Colbert was the victim of intrigues and accusations, skilfully contrived by Michael le Tellier and his able but unscrupulous son François, or François-Michel, Marquis de Louvois,[6] whose sinister influence over Louis XIV. was at first counterbalanced by that of Colbert and Lionne.[7] No longer able to count upon the support and full confidence of the King, whom he had ever loved[8] and faithfully served, hated by the people, who wrongly attributed to his prodigality the heavy taxation, under which they groaned, and which was really due, amongst many other causes beyond ministerial control, to wars which Colbert opposed and Luvois advocated,[9] and despised by the old aristocracy, who sneered at his comparatively humble origin,[10] Colbert must indeed

---

[1] *Le Code Civile, Livre du Centenaire,* p. 5.   [2] *Ibid.*
[3] *Studies in History and Jurisprudence,* by James Bryce, pp. 376, 377.
[4] *Ibid.*   [5] *Ante,* p. 241.
[6] Martin's *History of France,* 4th ed., xiii., p. 633.
[7] *Lectures on Modern History,* by Lord Acton, p. 239.
[8] Martin's *History of France,* 4th ed., xiii., p. 633; *Colbert, Promoteur des Grands Ordonnances de Louis XIV.,* by Alfred Aymé, p. 10.
[9] " La lutte entre Colbert et Louvois était incessante ; pendant la guerre, Colbert avait poussait à la paix ; pendant la paix, Louvois poussait à la guerre " (Martin's *History of France,* 4th ed., vol. xiii., p. 545).
[10] According to a contemporary epigram on Colbert :

" Colbert serait un gros drapier
Si chacun faisait son métier."

(*Lettres, Instructions, et Mémoires de Colbert,* by Pierre Clement, i., pp. 467 *et seq.*).

have felt that he who had "once trod the ways of glory" was, at the close of his life, discredited, if not actually disgraced.¹

It was in Paris, at his residence in the Rue Neuve des Petitschamps, that Colbert breathed his last, on September 6, 1683, being then aged sixty-four.² The disease which proved fatal to him was stated to have been stone.³ In his last illness his spiritual wants were attended to by that great Jesuit preacher Bourdalone, assisted by the Curé of St. Eustache, as parish priest.⁴ When near his end a letter from the King to his dying Minister was handed to Colbert, who exclaimed : "Je ne veau plus entendre parler du roi ; qu'au moins il me laisse mourir tranquille. C'est au roi des rois que j'ai maintenant a répondre " ; likewise adding, "Si j'avais fait pour Dieu ce que j'ai fait pour cet homme—la, je serais sauvé dix fois, et maintenant je ne sais que je vais devenir "⁵—words which recall the noble language attributed to Cardinal Wolsey after his fall.⁶

Owing to the hostility of the people,⁷ whose ingratitude to Colbert was even greater than that of the King,⁸ who did show some signs of grief at his great Minister's death,⁹ it was deemed prudent to conduct the obsequies of Colbert with little or no

---

¹ Martin's *History of France, supra*, xiii., p. 633 ; *Colbert, Promoteur des Grands Ordonnances de Louis XIV.*, by Alfred Aymé, p. 10.
² Jal's *Dictionnaire de Biographie et d'Histoire*, p. 399 ; *Life of Famous John Baptist Colbert*, done into English in 1695, p. 233 ; *Biographie Universelle, Ancienne et Moderne*, ix., tit. Colbert, p. 224.
³ Chalmers' *General Biographical Dictionary*, vol. v., p. 19.
⁴ Martin's *History of France*, 4th ed., xiii., p. 634.
⁵ Martin's *History of France*, 4th ed., xiii., p. 634. To a Vicaire of St. Eustache, who told Colbert that the faithful would pray for his recovery, he replied, "No, not that; but let them pray God to have mercy on me" (Bachelet's *Les Grands Ministres Français*, tit. Colbert, p. 403). Probably the dying statesman felt then, like the great King Arthur, that

> "More things are wrought by prayer
> Than this world dreams of."

⁶ See *Henry VIII.*, Act iii., Scene 2. Wolsey's actual words are said to have been, "Had I but served my God as diligently as I have served my King, He would not have given me over in my grey hairs. But this is the just reward that I must receive for my diligent pains and study, not regarding my service to God, but only to my King."
⁷ It was feared that insult might be offered to Colbert's remains by the populace (Martin's *History of France, supra*, xiii., p. 634 ; *Eloge de Jean Bap'iste Colbert*, 1783, p. 60 ; *Encyc. Brit.*, 11th ed., vi., p. 659).
⁸ Martin's *History of France, supra*, xiii., p. 634 ; *Colbert, Promoteur des Grands Ordonnances de Louis XIV.*, by Alfred Aymé, p. 10.
⁹ *Life and Times of Louis XIV.*, by G. P. R. James, iv., p. 73.

publicity. He was accordingly, the day after his death, buried, at night,[1] in the Church of St. Eustache, his remains being consigned to a tomb in the Chapel of St. Louis de Gonzaque, which was the private property of the Colbert family.[2] His wife, who only survived her husband for four years, put up to Colbert's memory a monument, executed from a design by Le Brun, which represents the great statesman, on his knees, reading out of a book, held open by an angel, and arrayed in the robes of the Order of the Saint Esprit.[3] At the foot of the monument are figures of Religion by Tubi, and Abundance by Coysevox.[4] This was one of the monuments saved from destruction in 1792 by Lenoir, who had it removed to the Musée des Petits-Augustins, where it remained till 1801, when it was restored to St. Eustache.[5]

So eminent a statesman and patriot as Colbert proved himself to be needs no grand tomb or epitaph to perpetuate his memory. Though not free from faults, which were largely the product of the corrupt age in which he lived, he will ever be remembered as one who desired the good of his nation as a whole, and who did not sacrifice one national force to benefit another.[6] In the pages of history he is still "le grand Colbert," of whom it has been truly said that "he accomplished for his country, to which he was sincerely devoted, not indeed all that he would, but all that he could."[7]

[1] Martin's *History of France, supra*, p. 634.
[2] Jal's *Dictionnaire de Biographie et d'Histoire*, p. 399; *The Churches of Paris*, by S. S. Beale, p. 139.
[3] *The Churches of Paris*, by S. S. Beale, p. 139.   [4] *Ibid.*
[5] *Ibid.* It appears that Colbert had two chapels erected at his own cost in the Church of St. Eustache, Paris, namely, one for marriages and the other for baptisms. These, together with the west front, were afterwards destroyed by fire, which accounts for the great disproportion between length and height which the Church now presents (*The Churches of Paris*, by S. S. Beale, p. 125).
[6] Martin's *History of France*, 4th ed., xiii., p. 35.
[7] See *Biographie, Ancienne et Moderne*, ix., tit. Colbert, p. 224.

LEIBNITZ

LEIBNITZ

Leibnitz as a Jurist.[1]—It is only right that Leibnitz should be included among "The Great Jurists of the World." It was he who first suggested a series of lives of the chief jurists as one of the *desiderata* of legal literature; and for many reasons he is here fitly named. Leibnitz, who originated so much, who struck out more new paths than his own generation was aware of, who is one of the half-dozen great names in philosophy, who developed mathematics along new lines, and who was an innovator in logic, philology, history, and many other regions of science, may be considered one of the chief founders of modern jurisprudence. He was truly, if any one ever was, in Du Bois Reymond's phrase, the omniscient. He is now chiefly looked upon as a mathematician, a logician, and a metaphysician. His philosophical works receive increasing attention. Such is the trend of modern speculation that note is taken more and more of ideas which he first developed. Inquiries as to the ultimate constitution of matter and the nature of energy revolve round ideas which he struck out. It is possible that there will be, sooner or later, a revival of interest in his conceptions of jurisprudence and in his legal works. It may be doubted whether even in his own country full justice is done to his activity in jurisprudence, its extent and originality. He sat freely to all the ideas of his own time; he looked beyond its necessities; he had conceptions of law in many ways nearer to those of our age than those of his own. One cannot read his legal works—and the same is more impressively true of his letters—without marvelling at the richness, variety, and novelty of his suggestions, scattered with prodigality; suggestions often left incomplete and indefinite; but even, if mere hints or surmises, more valuable than the laboured performances of mediocre minds.

[1] His father signed himself "Leibnüz." On the title-page of his first work he described himself "Leibnuzius." He sometimes wrote "Leibnitz, sometimes "Leibniz." The date of his birth was 1646, that of his death 1716.

One point I would emphasize : he was no amateur or dilettante in law, no theoretical reformer knowing it only from books.[1] In his lifetime he published little on the subject of philosophy: *Les Nouveaux Essais sur l'Entendement Humain* did not see the light until some fifty years after his death; but he was well known to his contemporaries as a copious writer on law. When a mere youth he published his *Nova Methodus discendæ docendæque Jurisprudentiæ*—a tract full of comprehensive suggestions, but marked also by that sobriety of judgment which distinguished his legal writings. "I have been a jurist from my youth, and in more than one Court ; and jurisprudence forms part of practical philosophy." When still young he wrote a tract entitled *Specimen Difficultatis in jure, seu Quæstiones philosophicæ amœniores, ex Jure collectæ ;* and he was always turning aside to jurisprudence. He belonged to a family of lawyers. His grandfather on the mother's side was editor of a synopsis of canon and criminal law. Of himself he writes : " ad jus, ut ita dicam, necessitudine rapiebatur." He had studied it practically and theoretically, and at one time with almost feverish zeal. "When I had resolved upon the study of law, I put aside everything else for it." If there was one study to which his ubiquitous curiosity was constant, it was jurisprudence. It was, if any was, his *Berufswissenschaft*. Leibnitz, unlike Bacon, was not an advocate. Indeed he probably never thought of practising as such : "judicis munere delectabar ; advocatorum aversabar." At the age of twenty-four he was appointed a member of the Court of Appeal of Mainz. He had also, as Hofrath in Hanover, no small practical experience of legal work. For some seventeen years after his return from Jena he immersed himself in jurisprudence. He composed *Prozessakten*, and did this technical work with great skill.[2] Towards the end of his life, when he was in the service of the House of Brunswick, he was often called away from mathematical and philosophical studies to deal with legal questions of interest to his patrons.[3]

Whether he was successful as a Judge, I do not know. Cer-

---

[1] "La jurisprudence et l'histoire m'ont occupé de ma jeunesse" (Dutens, *Opera* I., 74).

[2] He was consulted about important matters by the Czar, Peter the Great, and the Emperor. He wrote at the instance of the latter several legal opinions ; *e.g.*, as to the succession to the Duchy of Tuscany.

[3] Kuno Fischer asserts that Leibnitz, in writing the *Prozessakten* in German, did much to perfect that language (ii. 66).

tainly he had a high idea of the duties of a Judge, as he states in his *Nova Methodus*. If I may surmise from his writings, he had the saving good sense which makes learning a help instead of an impediment to a right decision. His earliest writings are on law. His legal works altogether are of great extent; they occupy about two-thirds of the fourth volume of Dutens' edition of his works. Further fragments have been brought to light; and we are assured by those who have examined the Leibnitz manuscripts at Hanover that many treasures relating to law have still to be published.[1] For years inquirers have been digging in this quarry, and it is not exhausted.

Very often he has been reproached for scattering his energies over many fields. I am not able to judge how far this marred his work in mathematical and physical science, or in philosophy. But this diversity of occupations and interests, this dissipation of energies, brought compensations. He gained in the sense of unity; he saw things as a whole, their relations and interaction; he escaped the vices due to minute specializing which Comte deplored and which have not diminished; he used the light of one science to illuminate another; he found in one domain materials sorely needed elsewhere; the axioms recognized in one region proved useful imported novelties in another.[2] He is pleading for himself—he is protesting against a fallacy old and enduring, and unjust to versatile minds—when he says, "Les combinaisons des choses qui paraissent éloignées servent souvent à produire des effects extraordinaires, et c'est encore les raisons pourquoy ceux qui se bornent à une seule recherche manquent souvent de faire des découvertes qu'un esprit plus étendu, qui peut joindre d'autres sciences à celles dont il s'agit, découvre sans peine."

At all events, to jurisprudence he was constant. In many ways, and in some which need not here be adverted to, he recalls Bacon. In extent his legal writings probably equal those of the great Englishman; and, so far as I am able to judge, the discussion of legal points occupies far more of his letters than do similar topics in Bacon's.

The impression to be got from reading Leibnitz's legal tracts is

[1] See *Rechtsphilosophisches aus Leibnitzens ungedruckten Schriften von Dr. George Mollat* (1885). In some of his letters we get a glimpse of the prodigious variety of his labours (*e.g.*, Dutens, vi., 29); the range of reading disclosed in the correspondence is amazing. No wonder that he writes: "*Quam mirifice distractus sum, dici non potest.*" Couturat, *La Logique de Leibnitz*, p. 574.
[2] *Lettres et Opuscles Inédits*, par A. Foucher de Carel, 287.

all in favour of his practical sagacity. No pedant, or admirer of pedantry in an age when it was common, he had a passion for knowing things as they are, a contempt for lawyers who busied themselves with their formulæ without regard to the facts of life or history. He is all for that union of science and practice wherein lies the sound development of law. No one perhaps came nearer than he to his conception of the man of true learning—one who knows all that is worth knowing : " qui res maximas in orbe cognito gestas, quo usque hominum memoria pertingit, animo complexus est."[1] But he set little store on mere learning. Though widely read himself in every part of jurisprudence, he, a diplomatist and man of affairs, was always dilating on the value of experience ; he wished lawyers to keep a firm hold of the realities of life. Rarely severe in his strictures, carrying into all regions a spirit of serene tolerance and magnanimity, he censures those who will not use their eyes and note what is going on around them, but prefer to display useless learning. In a remarkable passage in which he speaks with a certain bitterness foreign to his nature, he says :—

"In explicando Suprematu difficilem me provinciam suscepisse fateor, et, quod quis miretur, in re tam vulgata prope intactam. Cujus rei ratio est, quod illi, qui ad scribendum plerumque animum appellunt, miserabili ingeniorum morbo non nisi vetera crepant, quorum nostris temporibus vix apparent vestigia, recentium incuriosi : de quibusdam jurisperitis vulgaribus hoc non miror ; illis enim omnis sapientia in uno Romani juris corpore conclusa videtur ; experientia autem rerum humanarum, si quam habent, forensis auditorii cancellos non egreditur ; unde non nunquam de publico et gentium jure misera sunt eorum judicia. Hos ergo Cæsarem pro domino mundi, principes nostros pro præsidibus provinciarum, licet perpetuis et hereditariis, habere, mirum non est ; neque ab his aliquid magnopere expectes illustrando publico jure, quod nunc viget. Sed illud semper miratus sum, illustres dignitate et rebus gestis et eruditione viros, cum ad scribendum accessere, maluisse eruditionis suæ documenta dare, quam xperientiæ atque judicii (Dutens, iv. (2) 355)."

Again and again he betrays his impatience with the *frigidam eruditionis affectionem* then much in favour ; he does not spare Grotius (whom he much admired) for not sufficiently dealing with facts of his day ; and he is constantly dwelling on the rarity of the combination of learning and invention. He censures those

[1] Letter to Huet, Gerhardt, iii., 14.

jurists who secretly delight in the uncertainty of the law.[1] The whole of the chapter in which he inculcates this is worth reading and demonstrates his practical wisdom. It is true that, unlike in this respect Bentham and some other legal reformers who do not appreciate sufficiently the difficulties which confront lawyers, he sees the good points of the existing legal system, its thoroughness and the honesty of many of its practitioners. He admired the Roman lawyers : " Dixi sæpius, post scripta geometrarum nihil extare, quod vi ac subtilitate cum Romanorum jurisconsultorum scriptis comparari possit :[2] tantum nervi inest, tantum profunditatis." In the recently published *Opuscula*,[3] edited by Professor Couturat, is a paper entitled " Ad Stateram Juris de Gradibus Probationuum," in which Leibnitz expresses somewhat reluctantly his admiration for the ingenuity and perseverance devoted by lawyers to comparatively small matters. Over a question as to a right of way, an easement for grazing for three goats, they will take as much pains as if it were the Roman Senate dealing with Asia or Egypt. Not that he does not see the drawbacks to this elaboration ; he fears that the substance is often sacrificed to the observance of solemn forms—" lassatis litigantibus exhaustisque inter judiciorum moras."

With his strong practical sense, he had no patience with the delays, costliness, and formalities of the Reichskammergericht, so admirable in promise, so feeble in performance, strong only against the weak ; a Court which often did not decide until all the parties had died or had changed their minds.[4]

Leibnitz's Legal Works.—His chief legal works or tracts (for many of them run only to a few pages) were these :—

(1) *Specimen Difficultatis in Jure, seu Quæstiones philosophicæ amœniores, ex Jure collectæ*, Leibnitz's thesis for the degree of Master of Philosophy in 1664 (Dutens iv., 68). He argues that a study of the relations of philosophy and law will help to remove the contempt of students of the latter for the former. He discusses such questions as these : Whether an indefinite proposition is equivalent to a universal proposition ; whether the maxim *affirmanti incumbit probatio* is reconcilable with the maxim *quod opponens teneatur ad probationem*. He gives mathematical and physical reasons for the rule attributed to Solon that he who

[1] Dutens iv., 356.
[2] Letter to Kestner, iv., 267. See also iv., 254.   [3] P. 210.
[4] Pfleiderer, 446. See also Goethe, *Wahrheit und Dichtung*, Werke xvii., p. 70. Goethe was a *praktikant* in the Imperial Court.

digs a trench or grave must leave a space from the land of his neighbour equal to the depth. He also discusses the question whether bees, pigeons, and peacocks are wild animals. Then comes a series of logical and metaphysical questions; *e.g.*, whether of two contradictions both may be false; whether a person who is asleep is present; what is the true nature of a part *pro diviso* and a part *pro indiviso*, etc. Of the seventeen questions some seem nowadays singularly trivial, but perhaps not more so than many of the questions which our Courts daily discuss. A generation which spends hundreds of pounds in determining what is "an accident," and which carries the question from Court to Court, cannot with any grace be censorious of the scholasticism of Leibnitz's age.

(2) One of the most luminous of his law tracts is that entitled *De Casibus Perplexis* (1666)—questions of great difficulty; questions as to which some thought no solution possible; others, that the matter should be determined by lot; others, by the decision of an arbitrator. He will have it that such expedients are unnecessary, that all cases can be determined *ex mero jure*; that no case arises for which jurisprudence has not an answer. "Casum igitur (proprie) perplexum definio (eum, qui realiter in jure dubius est ob) copulationem contingentem plurium in facto eum effectum juris habentium, qui nunc mutuo concursu impeditur. In Antinomia autem ipsarum immediate legum pugna est, quanquam et Perplexitas Antinomia quædam indirecta dici potest." He divides these "cases" into two classes: (*a*) *Dispositio perplexa*, cases in which it is clear who is to be plaintiff or defendant, and the point in controversy is whether there is a right of action, as we should say; and (*b*) *concursus perplexus*, cases in which, the right of action in certain persons being clear, the difficulty is as to priority. With much technical learning he illustrates these questions, particularly rights of preference.

(3) *De Nova Methodo discendæ docendæque Jurisprudentiæ*, composed about 1667; on the whole, the chief statement of Leibnitz's opinions as to jurisprudence. Of this book Leibnitz says: "Liber est effusus potius quam scriptus in itinere, sine libris, sine poliendi otio."[1] It is a work of magnificent promise rather than performance. Part I. is general, and deals with matters common to law and other faculties. The first chapter

[1] Dutens, vi. 4. See also 5, 378, where Leibnitz says that the book was composed in a Frankfort Inn.

is headed "De Ratione Studiorum in universum," *i.e.*, modus perveniendi ad statum (*i.e.*, habitum) actionum perfectarum (p. 1). He considers the causes of character, which are either supernatural (*infusio*, divine or diabolical) or natural (*assuefactio*). In short, the first part contains the elements of a theory of education. The second part relates to jurisprudence, which is divided into didactic, historical, exegetic, polemical; in other words, Leibnitz adopts the divisions of theology upon the analogy of which to jurisprudence he insists; a point, by the way, to which he often returns. Didactic or positive jurisprudence contains express enactments and the like. Historical jurisprudence is divided into two parts—internal and external jurisprudence; the latter is concerned with the sources of law; the former with the substance. Of exegetical jurisprudence there are two kinds —(*a*) *philologia ac philosophia juris*; (*b*) *interpretatio legum*. The latter is of two kinds—*alia ex textu, alia ad textum*. I cannot describe or do more than refer to the wealth of observations which he makes on the subject of the rules of construction, juridical logic, and grammar, or his suggestions as to the formation of a juridical lexicon. I pass to his remarks on "polemical jurisprudence."

The principles of decisions are reducible to *ratio ex jure naturæ*, analogy, and *ratio ex jure civili certo*. Of the *jus naturæ* there are three varieties—*jus strictum, æquitas*, and *pietas*. The first is not explained clearly; it is nothing else, he says, than the *jus belli ac pacis*; it is reducible to the maxims *suum cuique tribuere, honeste vivere, neminem lædere*. Equity he defines as consisting in a certain harmony or proportion; you are not, if you are injured, to declare internecine war; you are to seek restitution, consent to arbitration, etc. The third principle is the will of the ruler, not the crude will of the strong man, but the will of the Ruler of rulers, "Existentia igitur Entis alicujus sapientissimi et potentissimi seu Dei, est juris naturæ fundamentum ultimum." Leibnitz next considers the subject of legal reports, or collections of decisions; the great virtue in them which he desiderates is brevity. I am not sure that I exactly apprehend all that he suggests in this connection, for example, as to forming a collection of legal commonplaces (*de locis communibus juris instituendis*). It is to be the work of jurists, especially professors in universities. From these reports should be constructed pandects, which need not exceed two folio volumes; " quia in multa disciplina et facultate plus librorum, minus rerum, quam in jurisprudentia." He sketches a course of legal study to be divided into three periods—elementary, exegetical, and polemical. I may mention as to the last that Leibnitz insists upon the value of moots or arguments on cases conducted in the manner of a trial; they are in his view an admirable preparation for practical life.

(4) *Specimen Certitudinis seu Demonstrationum in Jure exhibitum in Doctrina Conditionum*, a treatise in which Leibnitz expounds the doctrine of conditions or hypothetical propositions as a part of juridical logic. It might also be defined as a treatise of construction of instruments containing hypothetical propositions. It sets forth a long list of theorems (seventy in all) useful in the construction of wills and other documents; *e.g.*, "existente conditione, jus conditionale retrotrahitur ad tempus dispositionis mero jure; si unum pluribus applicandum est, in singula ducitur, seu est omnium ab initio; si conditio defecit, dispositio vitiatur." I have not examined the treatise closely; but it is clear that it is drawn largely from the common source of many of the rules of pleading once in use in our Courts and of our rules of construction.

(5) *Specimen Demonstrationum politicarum pro eligendo Rege Polonorum;* composed about 1668, and designed to persuade the Polish nobility to elect as successor to John Casimir, Philip William Neuburg, Count Palatine. Under the name of Georgius Ulicovius Lithuanus, Leibnitz composed this treatise, which had a distinctly practical end: it was intended to support a particular candidature for the throne of Poland. The argument takes an immense sweep; almost every part of political philosophy is touched upon; the best polity for Europe and Christendom is discussed. Formally in some sixty propositions, and with immense accumulation of learning, he makes good his conclusion. Incidentally there are remarks unfavourable to Russia, which Leibnitz regarded as a menace to European civilization and as a possible second Turkey. The security of Germany was to be considered in the choice of a King of Poland. The treatise reveals the weakness and the strength of Leibnitz—his learning, his acuteness, his ingenuity, and at the same time a marked obsequiousness of character; a disposition to accommodate his arguments to the temper of those whom he addressed. "To please a prince, to refute a rival philosopher, or to escape the censures of a theologian, he would take any pains."[1]

---

[1] See *Philosophy of Leibnitz*, by Bertrand Russell, p. 1. *Interim cogimur accommodare nos humanæ imbecillitati et utilia jucundis condire*, Dutens, vi. 69.

(6) *Ratio Corporis Juris reconcinnandi,* composed, with the aid of Dr. Lasser of Mainz, about 1669. It is a tract consisting of about 156 brief paragraphs. It starts by assuming that Roman law will by a sort of spontaneous reception continue to be the common law of Europe. Its authority cannot be removed without a total subversion of law; but its vices may be, and ought to be, removed. And he proceeds to point out and illustrate such vices; which are chiefly *superfluitas, defectus, obscuritas, confusio.* He describes (s. 71 *et seq.*) the effects of these vices, among them being: " Ita jus infinitum, incertum, imperceptibile, arbitrarium, antiquum denique chaos reddi clamarunt plurimi " (s. 76). He passes to the remedies: this confusion is to be removed by *Corpore Juris Reconcinnato* (s. 83); and he proceeds to sketch the outlines of a modern code.

(7) *De Matrimoniorum Principum Protestantium in Gradibus solo canonico jure prohibitis contractorum validitate Dissertatio.* This was called forth by the protest of Duke Charles of Mecklenburg against the marriage of his brother, Duke Christian of Mecklenburg, with Madame de Chastillon. The question was whether this marriage was contracted at a time when a previous valid marriage existed; a question of interest to several German Princes; according as it was answered, they were legitimate or illegitimate. The book is a closely reasoned argument as to the marriage of Protestants *in gradu prohibito,* with a multitude of examples. The great principle established is that the complete power of legislating as to marriage is vested in the supreme authority of the country. Even now the dissertation is instructive as to mixed marriages.

(8) In the year 1678 Leibnitz composed, under a feigned name, *De Jure Suprematus ac Legationis Principum Germaniœ,* in which he discussed primarily the question whether at the Congress of Nymegen the representatives of the German electors and other princes should be treated as representatives of sovereign States. They were powerful princes with armies of their own and possessing many of the outward marks of sovereignty. But they had taken an oath of fealty to the Emperor; they had paid homage to him; they were in a sense his vassals; and they were subject to the Imperial Court. Mixed with profound reasoning as to sovereignty is a strain of flattery; Leibnitz here, as in so many other of his writings, shows a resemblance to Bacon in his servility to the great. After all that has been written on the subject of

sovereignty, this treatise is still remarkable for insight into the nature of government and for the desire which it reveals to bring political and legal theories into accordance with facts more complex and varied than mere bookmen are apt to suppose. "Multiply your categories; study present facts; be not the slaves of your books and your formulæ," is his advice.

(9) *Codex Juris Gentium Diplomaticus*, published in 1693; a collection of treatises and State papers, preceded by an introduction in which are unfolded Leibnitz's views on international law. Leibnitz foresaw its future development. It is true that he immersed it in a theory as to natural law; but he was almost unique in the attention which he gave to treatises and other instruments as evidence of the consent of nations, more trustworthy than quotations from poets, orators, and moralists.

(10) In 1700 appeared a supplement to the *Codex Diplomaticus*, entitled *Mantissa Codicis Juris Diplomatici*, in which he further developed his ideas as to some points of international law.

(11) In 1701 appeared *Cogitationes de iis quæ juxta præsens Jus Gentium requirumtur*, etc. He discusses under the headings "De titulis honorificis," "De titulis regiis," questions as to what States are sovereign, and the like.

(12) 1706. *Compendaria expositio juris, quo augustissimus Borussiæ pollet*.

(13) *Observationes de Principio Juris*. Leibnitz discusses such matters as the basis of the law of nature, positive law, the law of nations, the definition and rule of justice.

(14) *Monita quædam ad Samuelis Pufendorfii Principia*, a criticism of Pufendorf's work. He was no admirer of Pufendorf, whose treatise had in Leibnitz's time acquired authority. He refers to Pufendorf as *vir parum juris consultus et minime philosophus* only; the chief reproach being that Pufendorf derives law solely from the will of the superior. According to Leibnitz, there is a natural or, as he would prefer to say, divine basis for the rules which Pufendorf regards as arbitrary.

Law and Philosophy.—I have not named all Leibnitz's legal works, nor have I referred to the many passages in his letters and elsewhere in which he discusses legal problems. These were labours sufficient to fill the life of an ordinary man; they at least show that Leibnitz was a prolific writer on law.

A point to be insisted on is that Leibnitz was no pure theorist or admirer of pure theorists. He was always reiterating the advantages of uniting practice with theory. " Je tiens qu'il faut se défier de la raison toute seule, et qu'il est important d'avoir de l'expérience, ou de consulter ceux qui en ont."[1] He is constantly dwelling on the value of practical training. But in his legal writings he never ceases to be the philosopher. In his tract entitled *Specimen Difficultatis in Jure, seu Quæstiones philosophicæ amœniores, ex Jure collectæ*, he endeavour to cure jurists of their contempt of philosophy.[2] He proposed to show that philosophy was of assistance and to convince them " plurima sui juris loca sine hujus ductu, inextricabilem labyrinthum fore, et veteres suæ scientiæ auctores mystas quoque sapientiæ summos extitisse." The peculiarity of modern German legal writers, certainly those who treat of *Rechtsphilosophie*, is that they seek to deduce particular rules from a *Rechtsidee*, some *Begriff*, or conception of which special rules are the consequence. I do not question the reasonableness of this process; in fact, I do not see how jurisprudence in the largest sense can exist without these conceptions. I would go farther; the divorce between law and philosophy, which most English students of the former prize highly, is attended by serious disadvantages. It is scarcely conceivable, for example, that certain parts of criminal law now in a state of flux can be dealt with satisfactorily without a discussion of some fundamental philosophical questions. They cannot be cast out without violence, and they will return even if they are bidden begone out of sight. He who reasons of crime and punishment cannot ignore such questions as : Is the will free, or is free will a mere phantom ? Are men mere machines or automata ? If they are such, what is the meaning, what the reasonableness, of blame or censure ? What is the justification of responsibility ? If a theory of punishment is based on determinist lines, such theory

---

[1] Quoted by Couturat, *La Logique de Leibnitz*, p. 156 *n*. A favourite notion of Leibnitz was the improvement of legal procedure. In one of his proposals to the Czar, Leibnitz says : " J'ai songé principalement aux moyens d'établir la meilleure procédure possible afin d'atteindre le juste milieu entre les actes arbitraires de juges et les procès Européens interminables et funestes, etc."

[2] Here is a characteristic remark as to the relations between logic and legal procedure :—" Quid aliud processus judiciarius quam forma disputandi a scholis translata ad vitam, purgata ab inaniis, et auctoritate publica ita circumscripta, ut ne divagari impune liceat, aut tergiversari, neve omittatur quodcumque ad veritatis indagationem facere videri possit." Couturat, *Opuscules*, 211. See also Couturat, *La Logique de Leibnitz*, p. 566, as to the parallelism which Leibnitz establishes between Logic and Law.

will have important practical results.¹ It is difficult to work out a system of punishments without dealing with fundamental, ethical, and philosophical questions. It is in a sense true that, as Leibnitz said, "jurisprudentiam veram a religione et philosophia inseparabilem esse." To be sure, such discussions are apt to breed logomachies, and to bring about a faithful repetition of some of the worst failings of the schoolman. There must be constant contact with facts and practice if jurisprudence is not to become mere word-spinning. Leibnitz, who would not admit that philosophy and law lay far apart, always insisted upon viewing the latter as concerned with living affairs.

I hesitate to speak of the relations of Leibnitz to the jurisprudence of his own time; that could be done to much purpose and with accuracy only by one with knowledge which I do not possess. But some points are clear. Leibnitz found the jurisprudence of his time a collection of dry bones; the lawyers little better than soothsayers and medicine-men, proud of their useless learning. He was profoundly impressed by the faults of the law of the time—its chaotic condition, scattered through many volumes, the important and the trivial thrown together without sense of proportion, the same rule expressed in different terms, to the perplexity of the inquirer, absurd attention given to barren subtleties. He sought to purge it of scholastic barbarities, and bring about a renaissance of jurisprudence. To pass from Leibnitz to other contemporary writers, so far as I know them, with the exception of Bacon, to whom obviously he was much indebted, is to enter a land tenanted by shadows and hollow forms; to come upon endless discussion of texts; refinements on refinements; unwearied accumulations of quotations collected uncritically; acceptance of the loosest statements as if inspired. It was one of the great objects of his life to rationalize and simplify jurisprudence. "Multi anni sunt, quod promisi illustrare jurisprudentiam et amplissimum juris Oceanum ad paucos revocare fontes limpidos rectæ rationis."² There is no saying what he might have done had he devoted more time to giving effect to the ideas which he evolved.

We see the practical turn of his mind in his remarks on legal education. His dominant idea is that the student is preparing for action; and so he recommended the use of moots. The legal

¹ See Die deterministische Gegner der Zweckstrafe, Liszt, *Strafrechtliche Aufsätze*, ii. 25. ² Dutens, v. 118.

curriculum which he describes is intended to familiarize the student with the knowledge of affairs, and is to extend over two years. He dwells upon the necessity of a wide and thorough legal training as a preliminary to practice, and he insists also, with emphasis which the most enlightened modern advisers of youth could not surpass, on the expediency of supplementing technical study by general reading, travel, and acquaintance with the affairs of life. Having passed through this novitiate, the young student will be fit to deal with legal affairs. Possibly the *Nova Methodus* contemplates a plan of education too vast for intellects much less capacious than his own. But it does not err on the side of underrating the value of practical training. It is worth while quoting Leibnitz's remarks on the effect of the education of the perfect lawyer. We have not much advanced beyond his conceptions. "Hunc ego verum juris philosophum, hunc justitiæ sacerdotem, hunc juris gentium et quod ex eo pendet, publici atque divini consultum dixero; cui possit committi respublica, quem neque ineptæ status ratiunculæ ad novandum impellant, neque a promovenda publica salute inanis juridicarum quarandum spinarum metus deterreat; concident sponte sua Machellivistarum convicia (ipsi se politicos, et, si Diis placet, etiam statistas vocant) qui jurisconsultos rerum imperitos, cautelarum scientes, ineptos leguleios vocant," &c.

Leibnitz and Law Reform.—Before his time in regard to many things, he was far in advance of it as to law. He advocated reforms some of which have long ago been carried out, but others of which are still incomplete. In his eyes the cardinal virtues of any system of law are brevity and perspicuity; he goes so far as to say that it may be better to have unjust laws than laws uncertain and obscure. He admires the inimitable simplicity and *judicii color naturalis* of the early jurists. He who is usually moderate in speech writes with indignation of the legal chaos before him: "jus infinitum, incertum, arbitrarium." It is difficult for us to conceive the confusion and uncertainty before legislation became common—before there was a recognized organ for expressing the will of the community. What would be the state of things if, to take one branch of jurisprudence, there had been no Factory Acts, no Truck Acts, no Employers' Liability Act, no Workmen's Compensation Act, no Coal Mines Act; if, while great industrial changes were in progress and new conceptions of duties were arising, the Courts sought to modify the law by expending endless ingenuity in giving to old rules wholly new meanings? What, to pass to another region of law, would be the result if there had been no statutory company law, and there had been attempts so to expand the law as to partnership to meet the necessities and convenience of modern commerce? I have not read deeply in the literature of that time; but it is clear to me that there was a profound sense of inability to stretch the old rules so as to meet new circumstances; something like a deadlock; a conviction that the principles of Roman law were unsuited to the new and rising order of things. To put an end to the evils which Leibnitz deplored, he proposed large changes. Few of them, so far as I can make out, he lived to see. Most of them have since been carried out. One or two still remain dreams and hopes. Among his desiderata—some of them suggested by Bacon's *De Augmentis Scientiarum*—recommended in the *Nova Methodus* are:

Partitiones Juris; Sciagraphia Juris in Artem redigendi; Novum Juris Corpus; Elementa Juris; Reformatio Brocardicorum; Compendium Menochii et Mascardi de Probationibus et Præsumptionibus; Theatrum Legale; Historia Mutationum Juris; Historia Irenica; Philologia Juris; Philosophia Juris; Concordantiæ Juridicæ; Tropi, Formulæ, Adagia Juris; Arithmetica Juris; Antinomicus Minor; Institutiones Juris Universi; Institutiones Juris Cæsarei; Institutiones Juris Saxonici; Summa Titulorum; Leges Numeratæ; Versio Legum Germanica; Ars Hermeneutica; Juris Naturalis Elementa demonstrative tradita; Scientia Nomothetica; Breviarium Controversiarum Juridicarum; Tractatus Tractatuum Reformatus; Bibliotheca Juris; Loca Classica seu Sedes Materiarum; Vitæ Jurisconsultorum; Repertorium Juris; Pandectæ Juris Novi.

A few of these *desiderata* were anticipated by Bacon; some of them anticipated suggestions made by Bentham more than a century later; others were intended for passing needs; others could be accomplished only by those possessed of Leibnitz's genius. But the very titles of some of them are suggestive. They hint at possible developments of jurisprudence which more than two centuries have left unfulfilled.

His essentially modern spirit comes out in his remarks as to codification: he advocated the formation of a code stating in language as homely as possible the law as it is—a Codex Leopoldinus, as he termed it; a code not in the old sense, but a reasoned, orderly exposition of legal principles. It is interesting to compare his views with those of Bacon; the comparison is not to the disadvantage of Leibnitz. It is interesting also to note his proposed divisions of the code which he had in his mind. Though an admirer of Roman law, Leibnitz saw much to censure in it. He was one of the earliest critics of the division in the Institutes. His chief objections to the classical division were, as to actions, that actions were concerned with both persons and things: were brought by persons and related to things. His further objection was: *persona* and *res* are divisions of *fact; potestas* and *obligatio* divisions of law. If a division of fact is to be adopted, why not continue it? Why not divide the *persona* into deaf, dumb, rich, poor? Why not divide things into many kinds? Leibnitz's suggested division was as follows:—

(1) Generalia juris et actionum; (2) Personæ; (3) Judicia; (4) Jura realia; (5) Contractus; (6) Successiones; (7) Crimina; (8) Jus publicum; (9) Jus sacrum. These divisions are not unlike those which have been adopted in several modern codes.

He insisted that the principle of the law was worth a thousand commentaries.[1]

Among the many original ideas which he threw out is the idea (subsequently elaborated by Lassalle in his *System der Erworbenen Rechte*) as to the will (testamentary succession) being dependent on the belief in immortality—" testamenta vero mero jure nullius essent momenti, nisi anima esset immortalis." His reason, such as it is, is as follows: " Testamenta vero mero jure nullius essent momenti, nisi anima esset immortalis. Sed quia mortui revera adhuc vivunt, ideo manent domini rerum." Heirs are merely "procuratores in rem suam." This opinion or fantasy was adopted by Lassalle to prove his contention that rights apparently the creation of others are really the outcome of the will of the individual.[2] In Leibnitz it appears as a passing observation: one which illustrates his ability to give a reason for anything; the more absurd the proposition, one is tempted to say, the more brilliant and ingenious the justification.

[1] "Ratio autem legis est instar mille commentariorum, quia huic omnis ejus interpretatio pendet. Nam omnis interpretatio constat ampliatione (ut vocant) ad casus similes, et limitatione in ordine ad dissimiles" (Gerhardt, i. 162). See as to plan for shortening litigation by limiting the issues, Gerhardt, i. 60; and for reducing all law in use in Germany into two or three large tables, which might be hung upon walls, Gerhardt, i. 161.

[2] Oncken's Lassalle, 181.

He was all for unity; we may speak of him as a universal reconciler. He was always composing *irenica ;* always striving after universal schemes—a universal Church, a universal language, a universal method of writing, a universal coinage, a universal system of weights and measures—and among such schemes was a project for a rational and universal system of jurisprudence. In a letter to Hobbes he explains his plan to be based on Roman law, which in the main accorded with natural law, and which was in use in the greater part of Europe.[1]

Leibnitz and Jurisprudence.—What was Leibnitz's conception of the aim and object of jurisprudence? We have not arrived at so clear an agreement on this point as to make his answer unimportant. Is it a sort of grammar of law, a concise statement of certain rules? Is it the study of the forms of legal institutions and instruments, or is it something much more? Is it an attempt to discover order in these various forms, to arrive at the laws regulating all legal phenomena? Under the once common and fallacious assimilation of laws of nature and laws enacted by society was there a truth? Is jurisprudence wholly concerned *de lege lata?* or is it occupied *de lege ferenda?* His answer to these questions is not precise. He was not very particular as to drawing the boundaries of sciences. He travelled freely across their frontiers; he had, indeed, a predilection for questions lying partly in the regions of several sciences. It must be owned, too, that he is not very consistent and that, owing to his habit of pursuing different lines of study, abandoning them for a time and then resuming them without always taking up his investigations at the point at which they had stopped, his language is often fluctuating. A further circumstance is to be noted: in his desire to propitiate and convince he accommodated his language to his audience; he spoke to theologians very differently from the manner in which he addressed princes or scholars.[2]

Undoubtedly he does not distinguish sharply between jurisprudence and ethics. In his *Elementa Juris Naturalis,* Leibnitz defines justice as "habitus (seu status confirmatus) viri boni." "Vir bonus est quisquis amat omnes." "Amamus eum cujus felicitate delectamur." He expresses the same point thus: "Justitia habitus amandi alios." In the preface to the *Codex Diplomaticus*

---

[1] Gerhardt, *Philosoph. Schriften,* i. 82.
[2] See the preface to *Œuvres de Leibnitz,* par A. Foucher de Carel, ii., p. xi, as to Leibnitz assuming now the *rôle* of Protestant, now that of Catholic, in order to bring about a reconciliation.

he returns to this point of view. " Justitiam . . . definimus caritatem sapientis. . . . Caritas est benevolentia universalis, et benevolentia amandi sivi diligendi habitus. Amare autem sive diligere est felicitate alterius delectari, vel, quod eodem redit, felicitatem alienam adsciscere in suam." In his works such expressions as these are common : " La justice dans le fond n'est autre chose qu'une charité conformé à la sagesse." " Cum vero (nihil) aliud apud me justitia sit quam caritas ad normam sapientis."[1]

He divides the *Jus Naturæ* into three grades : *Jus strictum—justitia commutativa ; œquitas—justitia distributiva ; pietas (vel probitas)—justitia universalis*. To these are related three injunctions—*neminem lœdere, suum cuique tribuere, honeste vel potius pie vivere*.[2]

He mixes jurisprudence with theology. The latter is to him a special kind of jurisprudence. Both rest on the same foundation. In a letter to Conring (Gerhardt, i. 160) he insists as necessary foundations for justice a belief in God and in the immortality of the soul. Sometimes he draws no distinction between jurisprudence and ethics, as in such phrases as these : " Jurisprudentia est scientia justi seu scientia libertatis et officiorum seu scientia juris, proposito aliquo casu seu facto." " Jurisprudentia est scientia actionum, quatenus justæ et injustæ sunt." Sometimes he deviates from the ethical conceptions developed in certain of his books ; *e.g.*, " Justitia est virtus servans mediocritatem circa effectus hominis erga hominem "—the Aristotelian doctrine. Sometimes there is an approximation to the utilitarian theory : " Justam aliquis injustam est quicquid publico utile vel damnosum est."[3] More than one of his definitions come to saying that one thing is something else altogether different from it.

It is naturally objected to Leibnitz's notion of jurisprudence that it is much too large. In giving it a very wide province he

---

[1] It is worth while quoting his definition of Sapientia : " Sapientia est perfecta eorum rerum, qua homo novisse potest, quæ et vitæ ipsius regula sit et valetudini conservandæ artibus omnibus inveniendis inserviat." See also Gerhardt, vii. 90, *De Vita Beata*.

[2] See his letter to Nicaise (Gerhardt, ii. 581), where he defines justice as " charité reglée suivant la sagesse "; " charité " as " une bienveillance universelle," " bienveillance," " une habitude d'aimer," and concludes that " la félicité est le fondement de la justice," and that " ceux qui voudroient donner les véritables éléments de la jurisprudence, que je ne trouvé pas encore écrits comme il font, devroient commencer par l'établissement de la science de la félicité." As to *la félicité*, it consists of " un estat durable de la possession de ce qu'il font pour gouster du plaisir."

[3] iv. 185.

was not alone. In the sixteenth, seventeenth, and eighteenth centuries, three minds of the first order—Bacon, Leibnitz, and Vico—applied themselves to the study and practice of law. All three of these great thinkers conceived of jurisprudence in a very large sense; none of them understood it more comprehensively than Leibnitz. All three of them agreed in seeking a basis in the order of nature, in the constitution of society, for jurisprudence. Leibnitz does not treat law as a set of arbitrary rules, similar to those of a popular game. In his view it is not a mere external arrangement, the accidental expression of power. It arises necessarily out of the constitution of society. Austin has taught us to distinguish sharply between law in the legal sense and law as a term of science, expressive of the observed order of nature. But dwelling at great length upon this distinction and exposing a common fallacy, he has drawn away attention from important truths. He turned, so far as he could, jurisprudence into a narrow channel, and shut out lawyers from the larger views and fruitful inquiries which Leibnitz and Vico pursued. I do not propose to discuss here a question which I have elsewhere dealt with. But it may be pointed out that the study of comparative jurisprudence brings us nearer to Leibnitz's point of view. We now know that there exists at each stage of society a *Rechtsordnung* corresponding to the economical structure and ethical ideas of the time; that to the economic skeleton of society belongs a certain legal covering; and that the law and ethics of an age are of one piece. Modern sociology insists upon the close relationship of all parts of the social organization; the interplay of legal, ethical, and economic forces, and the harmony resulting therefrom. In his own language Leibnitz conveys the same idea. He too insists upon the harmony of which laws are the expression. As Höffding points out, "in Leibnitz's philosophy of law, as in his whole system, the fundamental thought of harmony existing between individual beings is prominent."

It is objected to Leibnitz's conception of jurisprudence that it mingles law and theology; a criticism applicable to almost all the writers of his age.[1] To them this fusion was as natural as is

---

[1] Of theology he says: "Quæ est quasi jurisprudentia specialis." "Theologia species quædam est jurisprudentiæ universim sumtæ." There are many similar sayings by Leibnitz. My friend the late Mr. Taylor Innes told me that in a conversation with Mr. Gladstone the statesman said to him with emphasis, "Believe me, sir, no one can be a perfect lawyer who is not a a theologian." See *De Arte Combinatoria*, s. 47; Pichler, i. 146; i. 202. Punishment was unintelligible, Leibnitz thought, without theology.

to our generation the consideration in one view of the facts of the physical and mental world. Leibnitz could not be content with a synthesis which did not include theology, ethics, and law—in his view parts of one whole. And there are advantages in this large treatment; advantages similar to those claimed to-day for sociology; particularly the advantage of co-ordinating legal phenomena with cognate facts.

Leibnitz and International Law.—Leibnitz is one of the founders of international law. He was one of the first to take steps to reduce to order the mass of treaties. His preface to the *Codex Juris Gentium Diplomaticus* is a review of the whole field of diplomatics, and contains a discussion of some of the chief questions of international law. He did much to give form and definiteness to international law. He appreciated the significance of Grotius, to whom he never refers without respect. But he was sensible of the uncritical character of Grotius's work, the confusion and disjointed state of the law expounded therein, the absence of an adequate philosophy of law. Leibnitz did his best to create what is still a desideratum, an accurate and stable terminology of international law. It is true that his ideas are coloured by his teaching as to natural law, and that in his hands it took a shape not unlike morality. But is there an end of the idea of natural law? May it not, revised in the light of psychology, history, and comparative jurisprudence, have a future before it? The notion of a law accepted by all persons is dead. But with its death has come the truth that the play of arbitrary legislation is small; that customary law is but another name for a group of rules determined by the ethical beliefs, the economical conditions, the structure of the society in which it prevails; and that law is the natural, that is the inevitable, outcome or concomitant of a particular social organization.

One thing must impress the readers of his tracts on international law—his unconsciousness of some of the difficulties which press upon modern students. They ask, Who is the law-giver? What is the authority or the sanction for these rules? Leibnitz asks nothing of the kind, or is at no loss as to the answer. In civilized states at some epochs these questions might be put with equal propriety as to their municipal laws; it would be hard to say who is the legislator or where the sovereign power resides. Certain jurists, private persons, members of no Court or legislature, have great authority. What they say is accepted as law, unless the counter-dictum of some one equally eminent can be cited. What was the authority of Baldus or Cujas or the many jurists whom Leibnitz quotes? Much the same as the authority of municipal law. The word of the civilian had a force in itself. It was opinion, but generally irresistible opinion. Leibnitz—who deprecated the eternal fruitless logomachies as to definitions of jurisprudence—in a letter to a correspondent, says on this subject: "Nec video, quod prohibeat consuetudines plurium gentium annotare, quas vim juris habere arbitror, non minus quam in civitate mores statuto æquantur. Atque hæc adeo vera puto, ut ea quoque, quæ recepta patent inter gentes circa publica cujusque populi jura seu communia jurium publicorum quæ sunt apud diversas gentes, ad jus gentium referam."

Leibnitz as an Historian.—No account of him would be just which did not refer to his work as an historian. Here, as in all that he did, he was original. His Annals of the Western Empire are models of precision, acuteness, and conciseness. Pertz, the best of judges, speaks of them in the highest terms;[1] a treatise amazing by the knowledge upon which it is based and the sagacity and foresight which it displays. One of Leibnitz's chief arguments is the capital importance of the Isthmus of Suez as the link between Europe and the East.[2]

Leibnitz as a Politician.—An account of his labours as a politician would require a volume. His connection with the House of Brunswick influenced him. His patron, the Duke Johann Friedrich, who was a warm admirer of Louis XIV., sought to exalt the position of the lesser Sovereigns of Germany. Leibnitz was their advocate. He claimed for them the right as Sovereigns to send ambassadors to Nymegen; it is the main object of his treatise, *Cæsarinii Fursternerii de Jure Suprematus ac legationum principium Germaniæ* (1677).

Leibnitz also was a supporter of the Empire, in the interest of which he wrote much. He was a warm advocate of the unity of

---

[1] After enumerating the merits of the Annals of the House of Brunswick, Perz observes: "Alles dieses sichert den Annalen einen Ehrenplatz neben den tübrigen Werken ihres Verfassers und unter den ausgezeichnesten Büchern neuerer Geschichtern, Baronius, Raynald und Muratori" (xxv).

[2] "C'est le lien, la barrière, la clef, la seule entrée de deux parties du monde, l'Asie et l'Afrique. Cest le point de contact, le marché commun de l'Inde d'une part, de l'Europe de l'autre. Je conviens que l'isthme de Panama, en Amérique, pourrait rivaliser avec lui, si cette partié du monde était aussi fertile et si les autres richesses étaient prodiguées avec la même abondance."

Germany. In support of this he wrote in 1670 his pamphlet, "Securitas publica, interna et externa," in which he pointed out the peculiar and unfortunate position of his country, which, divided as it was, had become the apple of discord. The weakness of Germany has been the opportunity of those who threatened the peace of Europe. The arena in which was disputed the supremacy, it will never cease to be the occasion of bloodshed until, strong in unity, it will be able to repel attacks.[1]

Most of his political writings—and he was a copious political pamphleteer—were directed against the aggressions of Louis XIV. (*e.g.*, "*Nouveaux Intérests des Princes de l'Europe, Remarques sur un Manifeste Français, Consultations sur les affaires générales*").

A large part of his many political writings are concerned with questions of law. Thus, in his pamphlet, "*Paix d'Utrecht Inexcusable*," and in his "*Manifeste pour le defense des Droits de Charles III.*," he argues, elaborately and on legal grounds, in favour of the validity of the renunciation of all rights to the Spanish throne by Anne of Austria, Marie-Térèse, and Marie-Antonia: "Rénunciations les plus solennelles que la prudence humaine puisse inventer, jurées sur les évangiles, confirmées par les sermons de leur époux et par les traitez publics les plus autorisez." Both pamphlets are masterly pieces of legal reasoning. They are marked, too, by felicity of expression and tactful touches which show that in an age of pamphleteers Leibnitz was one of the most effective.

Among his political writings should be classed his *Projet de Conquête de l'Égypte*, a treatise designed to prove the expediency of an expedition to Egypt and its conquest by France, not only in the interest of that country, but of all Christendom. It is one of the many proofs of his sagacity that he, who predicted in clear terms the coming of the French Revolution, pointed out the importance of the Isthmus of Suez as the link between the East and the West, and added that the only place in the world comparable to it was the Isthmus of Panama.

A word as to the character of the man. Knowing much, he tolerated and pardoned much; seeing the best in men and all that they did, and always disposed to dwell upon points in which he agreed with them rather than upon those as to which he differed. He had a certain serenity of temper, an unflagging

[1] See Pfleiderer, p. 53.

desire for peace and good-will, scarcely less remarkable than his intellectual greatness. He was in all things faithful to his favourite motto: *In Worten Klarheit, in Sachen den Nutzen.*

To bring these notes to a close: Leibnitz had book learning and its rare companion, a desire to keep in touch with facts. He sought to bring jurisprudence into line with other sciences. He was interested in its philosophy, versed in its history. He had always present the great object of law, to do justice between men; he rediscovered, it may be said, justice beneath the formalities and technicalities of his time; if he resembled Selden or Savigny, he also resembled Bentham. He anticipated more or less clearly many of the future developments of jurisprudence, and some even now dimly seen, and only by a few.

SAMUEL PUFENDORF

SAMUEL PUFENDORF

THE conception of modern law in general is based to a large extent on the assumption of a contractual foundation. The ubiquitous *consensus ad idem* is usually regarded as the predominating and determining principle. In the process of legislation " objective " methods alone are applied and insisted on ; so that to offer arguments savouring of abstract analysis is stigmatized as fantastic, as unpractical. In other words, only the *positive* construction of law is held to be valid, whilst the elaboration and coordination of doctrines derived from axiomatic principles of *natural* law is deemed untenable. And yet these two aspects, these two processes, cannot wholly be divorced from each other : one or the other may for this or that purpose be emphasized and considered apart, but both are inseparable concomitants of all intellectual, all juridical constructions. The " positivist " regards the immediate needs of a society of men or of a society of regularized communities or States as the indispensable criterion ; he looks to the outward manifestations of men's minds, and prescribes accordingly—he tacitly (or maybe openly) holds that man is the measure of all things. (One may well ask in what respects modern " pragmatism " makes an intellectual and moral advance on the oft-discredited sophistic doctrine of old Protagoras and his school). On the other hand, the " naturalist " investigates the fundamental attributes of human consciousness, invokes the conception of cosmic harmony and of man's relation thereto, and points out that certain conclusions drawn from such premises are inwardly approved and ought to be explicitly accepted by men and nations as unfailing guides of conduct. There is thus no real antagonism between the two, and the results of their respective methods are not necessarily incompatible. The votaries of natural law have no doubt often been led into extravagances through paying too little heed to actual conditions and going beyond the implications warranted by their data ; but in this respect the fault lies not in the method but in its users. However, natural law, in spite of its being frequently maligned and scoffed at, will continue to hold the minds of men as long as men remain psychologists and moralists. Indeed, the modern world that casts it aside as "stale and unprofitable" is actually enjoying the benefits of many rules and institutions whose establishment is due to the practices and principles of previous generations relying on and submitting to the guidance and sanction of natural law. A great deal of modern international law is the outcome of the customs and rules of earlier nations and sovereigns who constantly appealed to natural law, and partly also the result of the advocacy of jurists like Gentilis, Grotius, Pufendorf and others who, to a greater or lesser extent, based their contentions on the same notion. Of all writers Pufendorf is perhaps its most consistent, systematic, thorough-going exponent. An examination of his main work will show how the conception is interpreted and applied in the relationships between men as constituting the State, as well as in those between States as constituting the "civitas gentium."

Life.—Samuel Pufendorf, the son of a Lutheran pastor, was born at Chemnitz in January, 1632. The first elements of his education he received at Grimma. Originally intended for the ministry, he was sent to Leipzig to study theology. But there dogmatic doctrines and the prevailing spirit of intolerance turned him rather to the study of philology, philosophy, history, and jurisprudence. To Grotius and Hobbes he always acknowledged his great indebtedness. In 1656 he moved to Jena, where he met the mathematician Erhard Weigel, who introduced him to the philosophy of Descartes and its demonstrative methods of ratiocination, and taught him that Euclidean processes are as applicable to moral and juristic discourse as to mathematical inquiries.[1] Early in 1658 he became tutor in the house of P. J. Coyet, who was an ambassador of Charles Gustavus, King of Sweden, at Copenhagen. At this time the Swedish monarch who was pursuing his policy of aggrandizement in Denmark, extorted the treaty of Roeskild, but soon after recommenced hostilities. The Danes at once took retaliatory measures against the Swedish envoys; Coyet managed to escape, but the second minister, Steno Bjelke, and the whole suite, including Pufendorf, were arrested and thrown into prison. An eight months' captivity was spent by the latter in reflecting on the foundations and sanctions of

[1] It will be recalled, in this connection, that Spinoza's famous *Ethica* (*Ordine geometrico demonstrata*) was written between 1663 and 1665.

law; and after rejoining Coyet in Holland he published at The Hague, 1660, his *Elementorum iurisprudentiae universalis libri III.*, which was received in many quarters with great applause. The following year he was appointed by Charles Louis, the elector palatine (to whom the latter work had been dedicated), to the chair—expressly established for him—of Law of Nature and Nations in the university of Heidelberg.[1] This was the first public professorship of its kind, and consequently its foundation marks a memorable event in the history of political and legal science. In 1667 he published, with the consent of the elector, a tract entitled *De statu imperii germanici*, which exercised a profound influence on German political policy, and was translated into several European languages. Pufendorf had come, during his residence at Heidelberg, into contact with many prominent public men, as, for example, Boineburg, whom he esteemed one of the ablest of statesmen, and the elector himself, who also commanded his high regard. The latter was believed to have supplied the author with many data for the last-mentioned critical work. However, the bitter controversies that were aroused by its publication induced him to leave Heidelberg, and so the next year he went to Sweden and accepted a professorship at Lund. After issuing many "dissertationes academicae," he produced (1672) his most famous work, *Iuris naturae et gentium libri VIII*. This was followed (1673) by an abridgment, *De officiis hominis et civis*, which was translated into most of the languages of Europe, including Russian by order of Peter the Great. These works were violently attacked in Sweden by several professors and pastors, who were joined in Germany by many assailants, especially amongst theologians, including Alberti of Leipzig. The denunciations of the alleged mischievous character of Pufendorf's writings, on the ground of their divorcing natural law from theology, were vigorously answered by him in his *Eris Scandica* (1676). In 1677 he proceeded to Stockholm, where he was appointed royal historiographer at the death of Loccenius, and at the same time was made a Secretary of State and Privy Councillor. Some ten years later, following on historical writings dealing with the European States and the Swedish sovereigns, there appeared *De habitu christianae religionis ad vitam civilem*, and soon after its publication he was called to Berlin by the Grand Elector,

[1] It is particularly interesting to note that some dozen years later Spinoza was invited to the chair of Philosophy in the same university; but he refused it.

was appointed historiographer of Brandenburg, and was loaded with other honours. To this last period of his life belong many writings of a polemical character—historical, religious, political—as, for example, the posthumous publications *Ius feciale divinum sive de consensu et dissensu protestantium* and *De rebus gestis Frederici Wilhelmi magni electoris Brandenburgici commentarorium libri XIX*. A translation of the latter, which is perhaps his most important historical work, into German as well as French was ordered by Frederick III. In 1694 Charles XI. of Sweden created Pufendorf a baron ; and in October of the same year he died, and was buried in the church of St. Nicholas, in Berlin.

Chief Works.[1]—For the purpose of the present essay, attention will be directed mainly to the *De iure naturae ;* but it will be of advantage to add a brief note on one or two other works in order to indicate the author's wide activities, his interest in philosophy, in ethics, in religion, in jurisprudence, in economics, in politics, in all social phenomena. Indeed, questions relating to all these subjects occur again and again in the major treatise. It may be that in the case of Pufendorf devotion to such a large field dissipated his energies overmuch, and therefore diminished to some extent the value of his purely juristic work. But a jurist can scarcely attain consummate skill, deep penetration, and effective power in his own particular sphere if he does not also apply himself to the various branches of study directly bearing on human life, individual, social, and political.

The *De statu imperii germanici* was published under the pseudonym of "Severinus de Monzambano" (of Verona) at The Hague, though it bore Geneva on the title-page. By its form, its irony, its critical acumen it may be regarded as a worthy forerunner of Montesquieu's *Lettres Persanes*. The political condition of Germany is subjected to keen criticism. Full of enthusiasm and sincere love for his country,[2] he sets forth with biting wit the fundamental weakness of the organization of the Holy Roman

---

[1] *Cf.* P. Meyer, *Samuel Pufendorf : Ein Beitrag zur Geschichte seines Lebens* (Grimma, 1894), in which booklet, concerned mainly with Pufendorf's genealogy and early life, there is a list of thirty-four publications.

[2] *Cf. Allgemeine deutsche Biographie, s.v. Pufendorf* (by H. Bresslau), Bd. 26 (Leipzig, 1888), p. 703 : " Unbarmherzig, mit überlegener Ironie und kühler Nüchternheit, mit bitterem Spott, der aber doch überall von inniger Vaterlandsliebe zeugt, wird hier das trügerische und lügenhafte Gewölk von Phrasen, mit denen die damalige Reichpublicistik die deutschen Zustände zu verhüllen liebte, durchlöchert und zerrissen ; und in erschreckender Nacktheit treten die verkommenen und verrotteten Zustände aus Licht, in denen sich das officielle Leben der deutschen Nation bewegte."

Empire, the misconception as to its being a continuation of the Roman, he denies that it conferred great benefits on the German people, denounces the faults and misdeeds of the Austrian house, and impugns the politics of the ecclesiastical princes. Judged from actual practice, he declares, the government is hopelessly irregular, conducted as it is by a strange medley of prelates and princes of more or less doubtful title; judged from political theory, it is no less than a unique monstrosity. After dealing with the prevailing confusion and its causes, he suggests remedies. He does not go to the length of assenting to proposals that had been made as to calling in French or Swedish intervention, or excluding Austria; he insists rather that the only way to procure unity and harmony is to establish a confederation of German States with a standing authority at its head. Pufendorf was the first who ventured to deal so plainly and forcibly with the existing conditions. By his trenchant criticisms, political insight, and masterly analysis, he prepared the way for the measure which was to put an end to the multitude of pretty tyrants and mediatized princes; and he laid down more rational conceptions of polity and sovereignty in place of the narrow scholastic notions based on distorted interpretations of Aristotle and the Bible.[1]

De habitu religionis. This is, in certain respects, an elaboration of doctrines which had been briefly suggested in the preceding work. The limits of Church and State, of the ecclesiastical and the civil authority, are clearly defined; and the State is certainly to enjoy supremacy. The Church is regarded as a union, resting on voluntary agreement, with various rights and obligations relative to its particular sphere and its maintenance and security, so that in relation to the State it stands in the position of corporations in general. This "collegial" system, adequately set forth for the first time by Pufendorf, later played a noteworthy part in Germany—especially in Prussia—and was the means of promoting greater toleration, and of smoothing over difficulties in the relationships between the Catholic Church and the Protestant Governments.[2]

---

[1] Bluntschli bestows high praise on this work of Pufendorf. See *Geschichte des allegemeinen Staatsrechts* (München, 1864), p. 111: "Das Büchlein ist eine politische Schrift ersten Ranges"; p. 120: "Die Schrift Pufendorfs ist ein staatsmännisches Meisterstück. Sie est ebenso ausgezeichnet durch den klaren historischen Ueberblick über die Entwicklungsgeschichte des Reiches als durch die psychologische Erkenntniss seiner organischen Mängel...."

[2] On this part of Pufendorf's work, *cf.* F. Lezius, *Der Toleranzbegriff Lockes und Pufendorfs* (Leipzig, 1900).

The *De iure naturae et gentium*, a large work in eight books, presents an entire system of jurisprudence, private, public, and international, based on the conception of natural law. Book I. considers the fundamental principles of law and its various divisions, the meaning of the state of nature, persons as natural and as moral entities and as fictitious creations, society, right, obligation, sanction. The second book expounds further the notion of natural law, state of nature, the foundation and *raison d'être* of law, the validity of customs, the doctrines of necessity and innate human reason, the relationship between natural and positive law, the hypothesis of divine command. The next five books deal with numerous matters of private law, from the point of view of the principles and conclusions emphasized in the previous exposition. The last book discusses briefly the meaning of sovereignty, and, from the sixth chapter to the end, the law of war in its three main stages, viz. commencement, conduct, and conclusion, and, finally, the establishment of treaties, conventions, and alliances.

In his earlier legal work, *Elementa iurisprudentiae universalis*, which embodies, as it were, a "philosophy of law," Pufendorf adopts the Euclidean method, and professes to establish certain conclusions by the strict process of mathematical demonstration. He first defines a number of elementary legal notions, and then sets forth certain propositions, as being an analytical summary of natural law. Of these some are termed *axiomata*, on the ground that they flow necessarily from the reason of man ; others are designated *observationes*, as in them account is taken of experience also. From these the power of judgment and free will as well as self-love and the social instinct are inferred ; thence the deduction is made that every one must inevitably seek self-preservation, but must do so in such a way as not to injure or imperil the welfare of society. The various precepts " implicitly " contained in this formula are inferred, and finally the conclusion is drawn that natural law alone will not suffice in a State, but must be supplemented and fortified by positive legislation.

From the point of view of composition these works are at a disadvantage as compared with those of other great jurists. They possess none of the force, concision, and facility of the style of Grotius, nor the variety, flexibility, and personal element of that of Gentilis ; they are often monotonous, cumbrous, inanimate. Even the greater part of Pufendorf's historical work is somewhat dry, although its subject-matter is particularly susceptible of bright, vivid presentation. Mackintosh is not sparing in his praise of the *De iure naturae et gentium*, but none the less he deplores that the treatise may repel students because it is " so prolix, and so utterly devoid of all the attractions of composition."[1]

Natural Law—Course of Development.—In order to understand better the nature of Pufendorf's juristic work, its relation to that of his predecessors, and its influence on his contemporaries and successors, it will be well to consider briefly the conception of natural law which was prevalent before his time.[2]

The law of the modern world, whether municipal or international, is much indebted to natural law. Those who glorify the positive school of legal science are apt to overlook the concrete character of natural law, and to assign to it attributes of merely abstract, metaphysical significance. The exponents of the law of nature are not always at one in every particular, but their fundamental conception is that " Nature " represents the supreme, unifying, controlling power manifesting itself in the universe at large ; and that " Reason " is a special aspect of this principle as looked at from the point of view of man and the operation of his mental and moral faculties. In so far as men are men they possess common elements ; and in their political and social life these elements inevitably emerge and are recognizable in custom and law. Hence the substratum of this law is thought to be of necessity established by the universal guiding force, personified as Nature. Such natural law represents the permanent portion of human law in general, and it is prior and superior to positive legislation, which is only a supplement thereto demanded by changing circumstances in different localities. Conventional justice may well elaborate or extend its applications, but must not oppose its essential content or violate its spirit. In the field of international relations the law of nature was in early times repeatedly appealed to, because on the one hand of its unimpeachable sanction, and on the other because of the conflict of practices, and, where these were generally recognized, their apparent inadequacy.

[1] Sir James Mackintosh, *A Discourse on the Study of the Law of Nature and Nations* (London, 1828), p. 25.
[2] See Sir F. Pollock, " History of the Law of Nature," in *Journal of the Society of Comparative Legislation*, No. 1, 1900, pp. 418-33 ; J. Bryce, " The Law of Nature," in *Studies in History and Jurisprudence* (Oxford, 1901), vol. ii., pp. 112 *seq.* ; and the present writer's *International Law and Custom of Ancient Greece and Rome* (London, 1911), vol. i., pp. 78 *seq.* and *passim.*

Medieval writers, variously influenced by Aristotelian and Stoic doctrines, by Cicero as well as by the *Digest*, often spoke of divine law as forming another category, but the idea of natural law nevertheless remained the predominating factor in legal development. As Prof. Nys says : " Les théories de l'égalité naturelle et d'un état de nature ont rempli dans l'histoire de l'humanité un rôle bienfaisant, car c'est en leur nom que presque tous les anciens abus ont été dénoncés, attaqués, détruits."[1] Ecclesiastics like St. Chrysostom and Isidore of Seville considered that the law of nature was identical with divine law, and that human law was based merely upon the force of custom.[2] This view was adopted five centuries later in the *Decretum* of Gratian,[3] one of the oldest portions of the collected canon law, which accepted also Isidore's division into *ius naturale, ius civile*, and *ius gentium*.[4] St. Paul had already spoken of a law written by God on men's hearts ; St. Augustine had pointed to the eternal law which governs the City of God ; Dante conceived the all-pervading universal force to be divine love ; Aquinas distinguished between natural tendencies (self-preservation, protection and rearing of families, etc.) and the precepts of reason (*e.g.* in regard to man's relationship with God and with society), and held (with the Stoics) that natural law is the divine, eternal law as revealed to, as shared by the mind of a rational creature,[5] and is the source of human law (*i.e.* the positive laws of States). Thus " nature " is the criterion as to the validity of human law, and serves as a final appeal against injustice ; as Suarez says : " Lex iniusta non est lex."[6] This is not a new principle, but a return to the doctrine of the Greek sophists and cynics. In England the law of nature, outside the canon law, played a comparatively small part. Bracton looked upon the law of nations as a product of natural

---

[1] E. Nys, *Les origines du droit international* (Bruxelles, 1894), p. 8.

[2] *Decretum Gratiani, Dist. prima*, c. 1 : " Omnes leges aut divinae sunt aut humanae. Divinae natura, humanae moribus constant, ideoque hae discrepant, quoniam aliae aliis gentibus placent. Fas lex divina est, ius lex humana."

[3] To the same effect Gratian says, *ibid.* : " Humanum genus duobus regitur, naturali videlicet iure et moribus. Ius naturale est quod in lege et evangelio continetur, quo quisque iubetur alii facere quod sibi vult fieri et prohibetur alii inferre, quod sibi nolit fieri."

[4] On the ancient conception of the relation between *ius naturale* and *ius gentium*, see *International Law of Ancient Greece and Rome*, vol. i. pp. 52 *seq.*, 67 *seq.*

[5] *Summa Theologiae*, 1a, 2ae, qu. 91, art 2 : " Participatio legis aeternae in rationali creatura lex naturalis dicitur."

[6] *De legibus*, III. 19.

law, and William of Ockham, whilst discriminating various senses of *ius naturale*, regarded it as being due to God.[1] Again, from time to time sovereigns appealed to natural law as a ground for legislation, for fortifying their own claims against the Pope or monarchs, or for opposing the extravagant contentions of others ; and not infrequently the principle invoked was scarcely distinguishable from that of utility or expediency. In the Renaissance and in the Reformation controversies the *ius naturale* occupied a prominent place. The contractual theory of government was regarded as depending on the law of nature. Classical authority began to displace that of the schoolmen. The *ius gentium* of Roman law was sometimes identified with the natural law of the canonists ; and in England the Chancellor's equity was referred intrinsically to the *ius naturae*, and by historical kinship to the praetorian jurisdiction. In general, the fundamental conception was becoming gradually divested of theological significance ; and the Roman legal compilations acquired a preponderance over those of the canonists, so that a more secularized law of nature was often appealed to instead of the Church. Thus, the disintegration of the Romano-Germanic empire, the decay of papal authority, the decline of feudalism, the discrediting of religious sanctions through the religious conflicts, the various speculative constructions of publicists, the resuscitation of classical literature together with Roman jurisprudence conduced to the more general acceptance of systems of law and ethics on a philosophical instead of a theological basis,[2] and to the production of great works (to speak only of those in the legal sphere) like those of Gentilis and Grotius. And to Grotius the indebtedness of Pufendorf was incalculably great.

Gentilis set himself to show that a large body of international law could arise from natural law, compacts, and inveterate customs, and advised theologians to keep to their own sphere.[3] Grotius attempts to indicate that a political philosophy in general, and a juridical system in particular, can be validly constructed

---

[1] *Dialogus*, Pars III., tract ii., l. 3, c. 6 : " Omne autem ius naturale est a Deo qui est conditor naturae." (In the Lyons edition, 1494, at the British Museum, I. B. 41906 (1), at fol. cclxiii. v°, col. 2.—This is a work of which a modern edition is eminently desirable.)

[2] On this point, *cf.* W. Hasbach, *Die allgemeinen philosophischen Grundlagen der von François Quesnay und Adam Smith begründeten politischen Ökonomie* (Leipzig, 1890).

[3] See *supra*, p. 109.

without the aid of theology and its disputed doctrines. He begins with the internal and immutable law of nature as "dictatum rectae rationis," and implicit in the first principles of things. Though God is its author, He cannot change it. Hence it is distinguished from the *ius divinum voluntarium*, the more arbitrary laws of God,[1]—His revealed law. He elsewhere remarks that human nature may be said to be the mother of natural law, and, through contractual relationships due to the exigence of society, the great-grandmother of "civil" law.[2] Natural law does not necessarily demand the establishment of particular institutions, private or international, but it does enjoin on us certain conduct towards them when they have been created;[3] that is, it comprises such rules of justice as would govern men as moral and responsible beings, living in society independently of positive human institutions—in other words, in a "state of nature." Hobbes, on the other hand, whilst retaining the expressions *lex naturalis*, *ius naturale* and admitting the immutable and eternal character of natural law, gave them a different interpretation. Indeed, his doctrine was revolutionary, in that his *ius naturale* indicates not rules of supreme sanction, but the state of nature, wherein each man might use his power for his own advantage, and be solely concerned with his own preservation.[4] Thus in these circumstances men were inevitably in conflict with each other; and to remove or minimize their strife they agreed to renounce their natural rights, and place them in the hands of a monarch who could henceforth command their allegiance. As his right is due to the power conferred on him and not to any bilateral engagement, there is no restriction on the reasonable exercise of his sovereignty. Amongst opponents of Hobbes may be mentioned Cumberland, who insisted on the principle of utility and the general good.[5]

From the point of view of Pufendorf's work and its chronological

---

[1] *De iure belli et pacis*, Proleg. 9; I. 1. 4-5. Hooker (*Ecclesiastical Polity*, Bk. I.) had already considered natural law as the essential substratum of revealed religion.

[2] *Proleg.* 16: "Nam naturalis iuris mater est ipsa humana natura, quae nos, etiamsi re nulla indigeremus, ad societatem mutuam appetendam ferret: civilis vero iuris mater est ipsa ex consensu obligatio, quae cum ex naturali iure vim suam habeat, potest natura huius quoque iuris quasi proavia dici."

[3] Grotius, I. 1. 10, 7.   [4] *Leviathan*, c. 14.

[5] *Cf.* his definition of law of nature, *De legibus naturae*, v. 1: "Lex naturae est propositio a natura rerum ex voluntate primae causae menti satis aperte oblata vel impressa, quae actionem agentis rationalis possibilem communi bono maxime deservientem indicat, et integram singulorum felicitatem exinde solum obtineri posse."

position, there is no need to trace further the subsequent development of the theories of "nature" and the social contact, in the hands, for example, of thinkers like Locke, Montesquieu, Rousseau, and others. Pufendorf throughout acknowledged his debt to Grotius and Hobbes; he often criticized the latter, whom, however, he sometimes misinterpreted, and generally accepted with approbation the views of the former, as well as those of Cumberland. But to a thinker like Spinoza he manifested undisguised hostility; he was perhaps unable to appreciate this great philosopher's doctrines of pantheism and determinism, and his views as to the unity, infinity, and self-containedness of nature.

Pufendorf's Method.—Pufendorf composed his *De iure naturae et gentium* as a professor writing for students of law in general. Grotius launched forth his work as an ardent reformer addressing the nations of the world. The work of the later writer is from many points of view so closely connected with that of the earlier that it constitutes almost an appendix to it, offering here a commentary, a more detailed exposition of some matters, and there (though less frequently) a refutation of others. Perhaps it is not too much to say that had the *De iure belli et pacis* never been produced, the *De iure naturae et gentium* would never have appeared, at all events in its present form. Pufendorf is to Grotius what Wolf is to Leibnitz, Condillac to Locke, what, in fact, the systematizer is to the inventor; as a French writer says: "Ce que l'esprit d'organization est à l'esprit d'invention."[1] As has already been pointed out, Weigel, the Jena mathematical professor, exercised a great influence on Pufendorf, who soon became convinced that given certain fundamental principles appertaining to human life, it was possible to develop deductively—whether directly or mediately—an entire body of valid conclusions representing a code of conduct. This method likewise appealed to philosophers like Descartes, Spinoza, Wolf, and others who worked in more or less different fields. In the days of Pufendorf the boundaries of the spheres of philosophy and the regulative or normative sciences were seldom clearly differentiated and separately marked out. So that we find his work comprehending matters of metaphysics and ethics, politics and economics, as well as jurisprudence; but amongst modern writers he was perhaps the first to emphasize the distinction between duties of perfect obligation (the sphere of

[1] A. Franck, *Réformateurs et publicistes de l'Europe: Dix-septième Siècle* (Paris, 1881), p. 336.

law) and those of imperfect obligation (the sphere of ethics), though Kant's statement of the doctrine is clearer, profounder, and more acceptable. Likewise he separated natural law from theology, as Spinoza[1] had separated the latter from philosophy; and thereby both aroused the bitter hostility of the orthodox. Writers like Vico found fault with Pufendorf as well as with Grotius and Selden for not taking divine Providence as a true basis for natural law. Pufendorf felt that Grotius in his treatment of international relations had not sufficiently shown the necessary connection between ethical and legal principles; hence in his *De iure naturae et gentium* he attempted to construct on foundations derived from human nature not merely an international law, but an entire system of jurisprudence that would be universally and permanently applicable.

Throughout his argument proceeds logically; sometimes it is put in another form to exhibit its consistency and cogency. He manifests a constant and invincible tendency to analyze and classify; interminable divisions and subdivisions, endless distinctions and discriminations are made. He frequently makes cross-references to his work, a practice but little indulged in by early writers; this insures uniformity and minimizes self-contradiction. Writers of supreme genius can afford now and again to be inconsistent; not so those of lesser capacity, and those possessing chiefly systematizing aptitudes. He endeavours regularly to reinforce his generalizations by means of citations from both ancient and contemporary authors, and also by illustrations drawn from his knowledge of human psychology.

His Theory.—Grotius conceived that the intrinsic nature of things formed the foundation of law; Hobbes held that its source was the will of a sovereign of undefined power. Pufendorf effected a certain compromise between these views. The basis of legal obligation is for him the will of a superior, strong enough to punish resistance and disobedience, but at the same time consulting reason and justice so as not to interfere unduly and without cause with the liberty of subjects. The State and the power of the emperor may be said to be derived from contractual transactions, firstly between the constituent individuals of the State, and secondly between them and him; but in reality the institution was ordained by God, as peace is attainable only in

---

[1] *Cf.* his *Tractatus theologico-politicus* (1670). (This work, along with Hobbes's *Leviathan*, suffered synodic condemnation in 1671.)

organized social life. "Sociability" is the natural principle of rights and duties. Natural law regulates the external acts of mankind. The state of nature is not one of war, as Hobbes held, but a state of peace. This peace, however, being precarious, insecure, it must be insured by means of positive legislation, which will thus serve as a supplement to and extension of natural law, and will be in accord with it. Pufendorf is not content to see in this sociability a fact of universal experience; he claims for it a metaphysical significance, and traces it to more elemental causes.

The fundamental principles immanent in social phenomena he designates "moral beings," *entia moralia*, which were created by God—determined by the divine *impositio*[1]—in order to introduce order and harmony into human life. Indeed, the very existence of God is perfectly demonstrated (in Pufendorf's opinion), not so much by reference to the manifestations of the physical universe as to mankind's possession of reason, a moral consciousness, a moral nature, an innate power to discriminate between good and evil, between justice and injustice. These moral entities lie at the root of family relationships and civil obligations; and their totality constitutes the "state of nature." They act as guides and monitors; and their implicit behests—forming the law of nature—may be deductively applied to particular cases by human individuals or groups acting in the capacity of "moral persons." We see, therefore, that Pufendorf, unlike Grotius, repudiated the Thomist doctrine as to the independent existence of the good, and affirmed rather the Scotist principle that a thing is good simply because God has imposed it. Hence starting from the axiom that the divine will has enjoined on man a peaceful and social life, it follows on the one hand that all conduct antagonistic thereto is necessarily prohibited, and on the other that everything tending to its conservation is necessarily commanded. From this conclusion all human obligations may be derived specifically; as such they are divisible into duties towards oneself, and those towards one's fellow-creatures. And by the due fulfilment of these, one's duties to God are performed at the same time.[2] Then discrimination is made between the duties of men as men and the duties of men as citizens of a given State. (In the

---

[1] On this question Pufendorf is in opposition to Leibnitz, who accepted the Thomist doctrine.
[2] In the *De officiis*, Pufendorf placed the obligations towards God in a category by themselves, and before the two other classes.

treatment of the former he borrows much from Grotius, in that of the latter from Hobbes.) Non-fulfilment of these duties would mean the annihilation of society. As for the law of nations, Pufendorf, like Hobbes, considers it merely a fragment of natural law; for States are "moral persons," subject to the same principles of conduct as are applicable to individuals. Thus he holds, with certain qualifications, that there is no really positive international law; treaties cannot *per se* establish a law, they can only confirm what is already implicit in natural law.[1] All nations, including non-Christian and heathen, are governed by this universal law, and equally share its rights and obligations.

It is, no doubt, easy to find various defects in Pufendorf's theory. Sometimes it is vitiated by unjustifiable assumptions, at other times by the elimination of relevant matters, and again through his occasionally failing to discriminate between certain relative conceptions, in spite of the multiplicity of his distinctions. He does not recognize adequately the practical character of law, private or international. He misinterprets Grotius's use of the expression *ius voluntarium* in reference to the law of nations, as based on natural law, and denies that there can be " voluntary " and therefore mutable law. So that in view of his insistence on the immutable, invariable character of law, the demands of time, place, circumstance, necessity are disregarded. Again, he attaches himself too much to the external organization of natural law. He tends to confuse legal obligation with legal sanction, the intuitions of the moral consciousness with the commands, direct or indirect, of objective law. As to his doctrine that duty is founded on the will of a superior, he does not perceive whether the strength or the justice of that superior is the determining factor. Further, in trying to better Grotius's doctrine, which insists on human sociability, reason, and divine will as the threefold basis of natural law, he almost entirely eliminates the element of reason and associates the other two in such a way that the divine will exerts no perceptible influence on human sociability and therefore appears to be of little use. Leibnitz, in his *Monita quaedam ad Samuelis Pufendorfii principia* [2] examines the philosophical value of Pufendorf's doctrines. He urges that Pufendorf unduly restricts the sphere of natural law in referring it exclusively to man's life on earth, and neglects to exhibit the connection

---

[1] *Cf.* his *Elementa iurisprudentiae*, 24-6.
[2] *Opera*, 6 vols., ed. L. Dutens (Genevae, 1768); in vol. iv., pt. 3, pp. 276 *seq.*

between the idea of divinity and that of justice; that he makes law occupy itself solely with external actions;[1] that he does not distinguish clearly between right and law, between morality and legality; that his definition of law as the arbitrary will of a superior (namely God) is erroneous in that it negatives the spontaneous character of duty, and necessarily regards those without a superior as being exempt from obligations;[2] that justice does not depend on the arbitrary will of God, but has its source in His essential being in eternal and immutable truths ("Neque ipsa norma actionum aut natura iusti a libero eius decreto, sed ab aeternis veritatibus divino intellectui obiectis pendet").[3]

Analysis of "De iure naturae et gentium."[4]—This is a large work in eight books; and its matter may be conveniently presented in the order of Pufendorf's treatment but in accordance with the following modified classification: (1) Fundamental principles of law, and its divisions (Book I.), (2) State of nature, natural law (Book II.), (3) Elementary rights and duties of humanity: civil societies and sovereignty (Book III.—Book VIII. c. 5), (4) Law of war (Book VIII. c. 6.—Book VIII. c. 7), (5) Treaties of peace, leagues, and other conventions (Book VIII. c. 8—end). The third division is of a very comprehensive character, and occupies a large proportion of the entire work; but for the purposes of this essay its substance will be but briefly touched upon. It is important to bear in mind that Pufendorf's object was to set forth not merely the outlines of a code of law, but the principles of a philosophy of jurisprudence. Hence the lawyer must bear with seemingly superfluous metaphysical argu-

---

[1] *Cf. Opera*, 6 vols., ed. L. Dutens (Genevae, 1768); in vol. iv., pt. 3, p. 277: "Itaque neque aliud admittendum est, quod insinuat auctor, quae intra pectus latitant, nec foris prorumpunt, ad ius naturae non pertinere; qua ratione ex mutilato fine iuris naturae, etiam obiectum eius nimis contrahi manifestum est."

[2] *Ibid.*, p. 279: "Quae si admittimus, nemo sponte officium faciet; immo nullum erit officium, ubi nullus est superior qui necessitatem imponat; neque erunt officia in eos qui superiorem non habent. Et quum auctori officium et actus a iustitia praescriptus aeque late pateant, quia tota eius iurisprudentia naturalis in officii doctrina continetur, consequens erit omne ius a superiore decerni."

[3] *Ibid.*, p. 279: *Cf.* the subsequent observation: "Neque enim iustitia essentiale Dei attributum erit, si ipse ius et iustitiam arbitrio suo condidit. Et vero iustitia servat quasdam aequalitatis proportionalitatisque leges, non minus in rerum immutabilitate divinisque fundatas ideis, quam sunt principia arithmeticae et geometriae."

[4] The edition used here is that of Amsterdam, 1715.—There is an English translation by Kennett (London, 1729), which, however, appears to be based more on the French translation of Barbeyrac than on the Latin original.

ments and distinctions found in his work (*e.g.* those relating to entities, modes, space, time, etc.), and the metaphysician must be sparing in his condemnation if he perceives that they present no definite, coherent system of philosophy, and are constantly —perhaps indiscriminately—associated with matters lying outside the sphere of metaphysics. In the course of the following concise analysis critical observations will be largely avoided, as enough will perhaps have been said in other parts of the essay to indicate the jurist's merits and defects. To offer an elaborate critique of the entire work would demand an investigation into the fundamentals and relationships of many subjects, and would therefore need several volumes.

1. **Fundamental Principles of Law : its Divisions.**—Physical substances or beings are the creatures of God, and constitute the universe. All these have their particular attributes. Moral entities ("entia moralia") are certain modes or attributes superadded to natural things and motions by intelligent beings, chiefly for directing and tempering the freedom of man's voluntary actions and for procuring decent regularity in human life.[1] It is God's will that human actions be moderated by definite principles.[2] To be a man necessarily implies possession of rights and subjection to obligations. The state of man is either natural ("status naturalis") or adventitious ("status adventitius"), *i.e.* as modified by human institutions;[3] and the relationship it involves subsists both in time of peace and of war. Peace is common, when maintained through duties derived purely from the law of nature ; it is particular, when its force is due to express compacts binding the parties thereto. Moral beings considered as substances are called "moral persons";[4] they are either simple or compound. Simple persons are public (either political or ecclesiastical) or private (simply citizens). Pufendorf holds that Hobbes[5] unnecessarily erects legal fictions, as when a man is made to bear the *persona* of an inanimate object or place, such as a church, a hospital, and that it is better to say plainly that certain men are empowered by the community to collect the revenue settled for preserving such places or things and to bring or defend actions that may arise therefrom.[6] Compound moral persons

---

[1] I. 1. 3 : " Modi quidem, rebus aut motibus physicis superadditi ab entibus intelligentibus, ad dirigendam potissimum et temperandam libertatem actuum hominis voluntariorum, et ad ordinem aliquem ac decorem vitae humanae conciliandum."   [2] *Ibid.*   [3] I. 1. 7.
[4] I. 1. 12.   [5] *Leviathan*, c. 16.   [6] I. 1. 12.

(societies) consist of several individuals so united that what they will or do in virtue of that union is deemed a single will or a single act.[1] They are public (either civil or sacred) or private (families, colleges, or corporations). Examples of the sacred are the Catholic Church, councils, synods. The civil may be subdivided into general (*e.g.* a commonwealth) and particular (senate, parliament). Armies may be called military societies. Moral beings established by divine imposition can be destroyed only by the will of God; those due to human institution may be abolished by human will, without affecting the physical substance of the persons or things involved, *e.g.* the degradation of a man of rank means the loss of rights peculiar to that rank, and leaves intact all rights other than these. Further, moral entities may be considered as, or by analogy with, modes. Modes are either "affectivi" or "aestimativi," *i.e.* relate to quality or to quantity. Qualities are formal (simple attributes) or operative (which are divided into primitive and derivative).[2] Moral operative qualities of the primitive kind are either active or passive; and of the former the chief are power, right, and obligation.[3] Power with respect to its efficacy may be perfect (when it may be asserted by force, if need be, as by war or an action at law), or imperfect (when it may not be so asserted, though it would be "inhuman" to prevent one's enjoying it); with respect to its subject it is personal or transferable; with respect to its objects, power may be exercisable over our own persons and actions (liberty), over our own things or goods (property), over the persons of others (empire or command, which may be absolute or limited), over the things of others (servitude).[4] Pufendorf then points out the ambiguity of the Latin word *ius*, but fails to give a satisfactory definition of "right."[5] An obligation is that by which a man is bound under a moral necessity to perform, or admit, or undergo anything.[6] As to moral quantity, it is price in things, esteem in persons (though both of the latter may be included under value); in the case of actions, no name is suggested.

Next the author discourses on the certainty of moral science, which he defends against those who deny it,[7] on the human understanding, conscience, error,[8] on the freedom of the will,[9] on moral actions,[10] on the rule of moral actions, or law in general.[11]

[1] I. 1. 13.   [2] I. 1. 17.   [3] I. 1. 19.   [4] *Ibid.*   [5] I. 1. 20.
[6] *Cf.* I. 6. 5: "... qualitatem moralem operativam, qua quis praestare aut pati quid tenetur."
[7] I. 2.   [8] I. 3.   [9] I. 4.   [10] I. 5.   [11] I. 6.

He distinguishes law from counsel, compact or covenant, and right. Obedience to law arises not from its matter (as in counsel), but from the legislator's will,[1] as law is the command of a sovereign to his subjects,[2] who have no power to examine or reject it. Right denotes a liberty, but law includes a bond restraining our natural liberty. It is sufficient if the legislator's will is communicated to his subjects in any way whatever, even "by the internal suggestion of natural right." Hence it is a piece of "inutilis subtilitas" on the part of Hobbes to hold that the laws of nature have force only when promulgated by the word of God in Holy Scripture, and not when simply apprehended by reason. He also rejects Grotius' view,[3] which implies the existence of the just and right before that of any rule of law. Obligation involves moral consciousness, and self-censure, if the prescribed rule is not obeyed; compulsion merely shakes the will by an external force. He alone is obliged who has knowledge of the rule, and has a will intrinsically free, "able to steer contrary ways," but which perceives that it ought not to depart from that rule.[4] Neither mere force[5] nor any other natural pre-eminence is alone sufficient for imposing an obligation[6] (for nature and law are often contrary to each other); it is necessary that one who is to be subjected to another's will should have either received some considerable good from him or should have voluntarily submitted to his direction.[7] Thus the doctrine that law is the will of the stronger must be modified.

Further, the law-giver, as well as the law, ought to be known. The use of reason shows that the author of the universe is the author of natural law.[8] Civil laws are made known to subjects by formal promulgation; but natural laws are apprehended by

---

[1] Pufendorf refers to and adopts Hobbes's distinction between law and counsel (*De Cive*, XIV. 1).

[2] I. 6. 1: "Lex est eius, qui potestatem habet in eos quibus praecepit." I. 6. 4: "... decretum quo superior sibi subiectum obligit, ut ad istius praescriptum actiones suas componat."

[3] *De iure belli et pacis*, I. 1. 9-10.

[4] I. 6. 8: "Sequitur ergo, ut ille obligationis sit capax, qui et norma praescriptam potest cognoscere, et voluntatem habet intrinsece liberam, et in diversa flexilem; quae tamen, ubi norma per superiorem fuerit imposita, sentiat ab eadem sibi non esse discedendum."

[5] I. 6. 10. Here he criticizes Hobbes's view, *De Cive*, XV. 5.

[6] I. 6. 12.

[7] *Ibid.*: "Omnino agnoscendum est, non solas vires sufficere, ut mihi ex alterius voluntate obligatio nascatur: sed accedere insuper oportere, ut aut ab isto insignia quaedam bona sint in me profecta, aut ut ipse ultro in eiusdem directionem consenserim." [8] I. 6. 13.

reflecting on the intrinsic significance of human nature. The obligatory character of laws does not depend on the consent of the subjects—unless it be implicit consent, as when a man agreeing to the sovereignty of another is supposed to have agreed at the same time to all his future acts.[1] The sovereign must have understanding as to the fitness of his prescriptions, and sufficient strength to enforce them by penalties. Thus, every law consists of two parts, declaratory (defining what is to be performed or omitted) and " vindicative " (the penal sanction).[2] The sanction of law must consist rather in punishments than in rewards ; so that the view of Cumberland, in admitting the latter, is not sound.[3]

In respect of its origin, law is divine or human ; in reference to its matter, it is natural or positive.[4] Natural law is that which so necessarily relates to the rational and sociable nature of man that human society, honest and peaceful fellowship could not exist without it ;[5] that is, it has such virtue as makes for the good of mankind. Another reason for calling it so is that it is recognizable by the common intelligence of men contemplating universal human nature. On the other hand, positive law (called by some voluntary law) is that which emanates from the will of the law-giver, and varies according to the needs and circumstances of communities. Human law in the strict sense is only positive, and hence susceptible to abrogation ; natural law is immutable.

Pufendorf ends the first book with a discussion on the qualities of moral actions.[6] He examines in what the goodness or evil of actions consists,[7] the justice of actions,[8] universal and particular justice,[9] justice as distributive[10] and commutative.[11] Injury is an intentional unjust action ;[12] any harm ("laesiones") done inadvertently or unwillingly is not an " injury."[13] No injury is done to any man who wills it (" volenti non fit iniuria ").[14] The view of Hobbes, urges Pufendorf, that an injury can be inflicted only on one with whom a compact has been made is imperfect.[15]

2. **State of Nature ; Natural Law.**—The natural state of man is that in which we may conceive him to be placed " by birth itself," apart from all inventions and institutions either human

---

[1] I. 6. 13.   [2] I. 6. 14.   [3] *Ibid.*   [4] I. 6. 18.
[5] *Ibid.* : " Quae cum rationali et sociali natura hominis ita congruit, ut humano generi honesta et pacifica societas citra eandem constare nequeat."
[6] I. 7.   [7] I. 7. 3.   [8] I. 7. 6.   [9] I. 7. 8.   [10] I. 7. 9.
[11] I. 7. 10.   [12] I. 7. 15.   [13] I. 7. 16.   [14] I. 7. 17.   [15] I. 7. 15.

or inspired by God ;[1] that is, men would owe obedience neither to each other nor to a common lord.[2] In this state the rights of man relate to the instinct of self-preservation and independence; and he is bound to others simply in virtue of the tie resulting from natural resemblance. Pufendorf holds that Hobbes cannot have meant that each has unlimited licence; but that each has the liberty to provide for the preservation of his life, and has the right to act as he likes—if in accordance with the light of reason. Besides, the human race has never been and cannot be in a state of nature pure and simple. Against the state of nature Pufendorf sets "accessory states," of which the chief are marriage, relation of father and son, that of master and servant, the state of a citizen or member of a civil society. There cannot be any such natural liberty to man as shall exempt him from the obligations of natural law or of divine commands. To live without law is inconsistent with human nature.[3] Government, indeed, is natural; it is the design of nature that men shall constitute governments among themselves.[4] The establishment of societies and of positive law is inevitable. Further, the state of nature is one of peace and not of hostility; it is not opposed to a social life.[5] Pufendorf emphasizes that the question is the natural state not of animals governed by mere impulse and inclination, but of man endowed with reason (*ratio*)—the controller of all his other faculties—which even in a natural state has a common, steadfast, uniform measure to go by, viz. the nature of things.[6] Reason does not suggest to man that only his particular interest shall be the guide of his conduct. Indeed it dissuades him from making war, or adopting other violent measures, without provocation. It points out his fundamental obligations, such as to respect the liberty and possessions of others, to perform faithfully all engagements entered into, to promote spontaneously the interest and happiness of others when a superior obligation does not intervene. Thus peace depends solely on those obligations binding men as reason-

[1] II. 2. 1: "In qua homo per ipsam nativitatem constitutus concipitur, prout abstracta intelliguntur inventa, atque instituta humana, aut homini divinitus suggesta, quibus aliam velut faciem vita mortalium induit."

[2] II. 2. 5.   [3] II. 1.

[4] II. 2. 4: "Naturale est equidem imperium, *i.e.* naturae intentio fuit, ut homines imperia inter se constituerent."

[5] II. 2. 5: "Nam status naturalis et vita socialis sibi proprie non opponuntur."

[6] II. 2. 9: "Quae etiam in naturali statu communem, eamque firmam et uniformem habet mensuram, rerum nempe naturam...."

able creatures and does not owe its origin to agreements and conventions. The latter may well serve as solemn protestations to confirm explicitly the subsistence of mutual rights and duties, or even to establish closer unions, *e.g.* friendship, but they really superadd nothing substantial to the obligations of the law of nature.[1] Still it must be confessed that in practice reason does not always exercise perfect and exclusive sway; the prevailing passions of men have been potent enough to drive them to crimes and unjust wars in spite of divine teaching; so that as natural peace is uncertain it must be strengthened by special provisions.[2]

Natural law is universal, in that it is binding on the entire human race, *qua* human. It is perpetual, and not subject (like positive law) to the changing circumstances of time and place.[3] Pufendorf rejects Ulpian's definition, which was adopted in the *Digest* and *Institutes* of Justinian: "Ius naturale est, quod natura omnia animalia docuit." As reason is not common to man and beast, so law cannot be. We must suppose the Roman jurisconsults to have spoken figuratively.[4] Those who refer the law of nature to brutes, on the ground that they are seen acting, now and then, with some appearance of regularity and design; abuse the term law by an undue and unnecessary application;[5] for such acts of the lower creatures are far from corresponding to the totality of human action and obligation.

Prior to the imposition of law, actions are to be deemed indifferent; for the legitimacy of conduct depends on the existence of law. God in creating man intended that his actions should not all be indifferent, and therefore at the same time constituted a law for his nature. Those who hold (like Grotius[6]) that the virtue or turpitude of actions determines natural law are landed in a vicious circle.[7] [But this is not the position of Grotius; for he would say that the essential honesty or baseness of the acts commanded or forbidden by natural law comes from the harmony or disagreement, as the case may be, with a reasonable and social nature. And this necessity is not independent of divine will. Thus Pufendorf and his predecessor are on this point substantially at one.] It cannot be said that natural law is common to God and man. It would be impious to hold that it can contain any rule contrary to divine justice and sanctity; but there is no

---

[1] II. 2. 11.   [2] II. 2. 12.   [3] II. 3. 1.
[4] *Cf.* the explanation offered in the present writer's *International Law and Custom of Ancient Greece and Rome*, vol. i., pp. 83 *seq.*   [5] II. 3. 2.
[6] *Cf. De iure belli et pacis*, I. 1. 10. 1.   [7] II. 3. 4.

perfect resemblance between the rule of human actions and the order according to which God acts in regard to His creatures. For divine omnipotence is absolute, is necessarily independent of all law and obligation. God *cannot* but observe His promises, and men *ought* not but to observe theirs. Hence human promises involve obligations, but divine promises are made good only through grace. The intrinsic nature of things and the relationships between them depend on divine determination.[1]

Is natural law due to general consent ? Those who attribute the recognition of the rules of natural law to the consent of mankind argue *a posteriori*, and Hobbes[2] (as Pufendorf points out) has demonstrated the untenability of this doctrine ; for unanimity would in that case be indispensable, yet there are striking differences of opinion and custom,[3] and even amongst the most famous people on record diversity and contrariety of manners and institutions are observable.[4] Besides, to extract the law of nature from practice involves a further difficulty, as every nation has a large element of positive law ; also, inveterate custom often assumes the semblance of natural reason.[5] Nevertheless, we are not on this account to infer that natural law has no existence. Nor can we hold that convenience and profit alone are its foundation. Utility is of two kinds : that which appears such to the depraved judgment of ill-composed affections ("affectuum male compositorum pravo iudicio") which are so capricious and transitory, and that which is universally such, assuring constancy and permanence ("quod in universum tale est, et ad diuturnitatem facit"). Actions done in conformity with the law of nature have a double excellence : they conduce to the promotion of honour and good credit of men, and they contribute to their happiness by furthering their true interests and advantage. On the other hand, actions done contrary to the law of nature are always base and dishonest, and though they now and then bear some appearance of profit and pleasure, yet these charms soon vanish and are replaced by evils and misfortunes. If every man considered only his own private advantage regardless of others, confusion would ensue.[6] The adoption by States of different laws on the ground of utility does not negative the existence and efficacy of natural law.[7]

Does the law of nature appear from the end of creation ? It

[1] II. 3. 6.   [2] *De Cive*, II. 1.   [3] II. 3. 7.   [4] II. 3. 8.
[5] II. 3. 9.   [6] II. 3. 10.   [7] II. 3. 11.

cannot be held that divine and human justice have a common measure, that the order prescribed by God to man (namely, the observance of the law of nature) indicates the end which He proposed in creating the world.[1]

The principles of natural law are revealed by the light of unperverted reason implanted by God in man. Not that these are complete entities imprinted, as it were, on men's minds at birth, and expressible in distinct propositions as soon as the faculty of speech is acquired and without further instruction or meditation;[2] the observation of St. Paul[3] that natural law is written in the hearts of men is merely figurative. But the capacity to obtain a knowledge of it is imparted to men.[4] By contemplating the significance of human life they can discover a necessity of living agreeably to this law, and discern those principles by which its precepts may be effectively demonstrated, without fearing that any one may foist upon them for natural law "the ravings of his ill-purged brain or the disordered passions of his mind."[5] Thus the true and essential nature of man is the origin of natural law; but owing to the "summa imbecillitas atque naturalis indigentia" of man as an individual, he is compelled to associate with others and admit the common good to be his good.[6] Hence the fundamental principle of this law may be formulated thus: Every man ought, as far as in him lies, to promote and preserve a peaceful sociableness with others, in harmony with the essential disposition and purpose of the human race.[7] Sociableness does not imply a mere propensity to join in any society whatever, e.g. irregular or ill-constituted, but rather a disposition to effect a union based on benevolence, charity, peace, and involving, as it were, "a silent and secret obligation." Now the duty to seek a common end of necessity implies the duty to carry out the means leading thereto. Therefore all actions which conduce to the advancement of this mutual sociableness are commanded by the law of nature, and all those detrimental to it are forbidden.[8] Pufendorf points

[1] II. 3. 12.
[2] II. 3. 13: "Animis hominum ab ipsa nativitate congenita, et velut impressa esse iuris naturalis saltem generalia praecepta."
[3] Rom. ii. 15.   [4] Cf. Cumberland, De legibus naturae, Proleg. 5-7.
[5] II. 3. 13: "Ne quis cerebri sui male purgat deliria, aut incompositam animi cupidinem pro lege naturali venditare possit."   [6] II. 3. 14.
[7] II. 3. 15: "Cuilibet homini, quantum in se, colendam et conservandam esse pacificam adversos alios socialitatem, indoli et scopo generis humani in universum congruentem."
[8] Ibid.: "Omnia, quae ad istam socialitatem necessario faciunt, iure naturali praecepta quae enadem turbant aut abrumpunt, vetita intelligi."

out that this doctrine is in agreement with that of Cumberland,[1] and that Hobbes's view[2] has been by some writers too rigorously interpreted. But he cannot accept the observation of Grotius[3] that natural law would still obtain even if God did not exist; for the obligations arising therefrom are imposed by divine Providence.[4] The underlying sanction is referable to His will.[5]

Is there a law of nations distinct from the law of nature? Pufendorf says he accepts the view of Hobbes,[6] who holds that natural law is divided into the natural law of man and the natural law of States (*i.e.* law of nations). Both are made up of the same precepts; for States assume, as soon as they are formed, the personal properties of men. Consequently there is no positive law of nations proceeding from a superior. The provisions due to the needs of human nature necessarily relate to natural law. Most of the matters of the *ius gentium* (*e.g.* contracts, modes of acquisition, etc.) dealt with by the civilians belong rather to the law of nature or to municipal law. Indeed, the legal provisions of many nations are found to agree on various points which do not depend on the universal reason of mankind; but such similar laws, not arising from any fundamental universal obligation, are not to be erected into the category of positive law of nations, for they may be altered or cancelled at the discretion of each State quite independently of the others. And so, too, in the case of customs, *e.g.* as to relaxations in war; for a belligerent waging war in a just cause may disregard these and observe simply the law of nature, which alone imposes an indefeasible obligation. In restraints and mitigations dependent on tacit consent, it seems reasonable that either party should be free to absolve himself from them by making a declaration to that effect, which would *ipso facto* discharge the other side too. Thus time and prevalence of contrary customs tend to eliminate such observances as are due to the mere consent of peoples and not to natural law. Grotius regards some rights, *e.g.* those of embassy, burial, etc., as forming part of the voluntary or the special class of law of nations; but this division is not really necessary, as the essential rights of legation spring from the duty to promote peace, and those of burial from the duty to observe humanity; and both these duties are already imposed by natural law. International compacts infinite in number, diverse in character, and temporary in effect as they

---

[1] *Op. cit.*, I. 4.   [2] *De Cive*, I. 2.   [3] *Proleg.* 11.
[4] II. 3. 20.   [5] II. 3. 21.   [6] *De Cive*, xiv. 4, 5.

are, form the subject of history rather than the basis of law; though, of course, the observance of good faith in such transactions is commanded by the law of nature. Customs, in so far as they have universal applicability and involve definite legal obligations, are attributable directly or indirectly to the prescriptions of natural law; so that by referring customs to the latter as their veritable progenitor greater authority and a higher sanction are assigned to them, than by deriving them from mere conventions of peoples.[1]

This distinction leads to the division of duties, so far as they concern others, into absolute and conditional, or duties of perfect obligation and those of imperfect obligation. (Natural law governs also man's behaviour towards himself.) Absolute duties bind all men at all times and in all conditions, independently of human institutions. Conditional duties presuppose certain civil forms and methods to have been voluntarily constituted; for example, certain acts may be performed at pleasure, but when once performed a moral necessity or obligation supervenes by virtue of some precepts of the law of nature, or the manner and circumstances of the acts are thereby adjusted and determined. Thus there is a constant relationship between natural law and positive law; to violate the latter may well involve an infringement—mediate or indirect—of the former. But positive law does not form an intrinsic portion of natural law so as to amount to identity; natural law, indeed, commands obedience to the sovereign, but his dominion is exercised in virtue of his subjects' consent, *i.e.* through a binding engagement. There is this great difference ever to be considered: natural conditional laws are derived from the universal constitution of the human race, whilst civil positive laws depend only on the particular interests of community, or on the good pleasure of its legislator.[2]

3. **Certain Elementary Rights and Duties; Civil Societies and Sovereignty.**—After considering in general the duties of man towards himself, as to the care of his body and the improvement of his mind,[3] and in particular the primary duty of self-defence,[4] Pufendorf examines the doctrine of necessity.[5] Most laws, especially positive, are deemed to except circumstances of urgent necessity, *i.e.* to lose their binding force when their observance would obviously be attended by some evil "destructive of our nature, or exceeding the ordinary patience and constancy of

[1] II. 3. 23. [2] II. 3. 24. [3] II. 4. [4] II. 5. [5] II. 6.

human minds," unless, however, the case in question be expressly included in those laws. But apart from exceptional cases, the rule is that no one may arrogate to himself, on the ground of necessity, the liberty to violate a positive law. Similarly, a command of natural law may be disobeyed when one, through no neglect or default of his own, is placed under extreme necessity; but not so when the command is so absolute as to require its fulfilment even at the price of laying down one's life. In no case whatever can necessity make it permissible to offend against God.[1]

Next, Pufendorf sets forth various common rights and duties regarding both municipal relationships and international. All men are to be accounted by nature equal.[2] If any injury is done, due reparation must be made.[3] The troops of another State have the right of free passage over our territory; but if they are in large numbers, a guarantee (*e.g.* hostages) may be demanded by us to insure the safety of our subjects and their property. In the absence of special compacts or concessions, natural law does not give such right if the troops are proceeding against our friendly neighbour; hence it is our duty to prevent their passage if we have power enough to do so, unless our opposition would bring on us a disastrous war. In other words, necessity would excuse the non-performance of our duty.[4] Free access to our shores is to be allowed to strangers having no hostile intention and suffering no contagious diseases.[5] The admission of aliens and the kind reception of travellers, if their purpose be honest, are duties of natural law.[6] The settlement of exiles ought to be permitted if they submit to our government and conduct themselves peacefully.[7] Further, foreign citizens have the right of intermarriage (*ius connubii*)[8] and of commercial intercourse (*ius commercii*) with us, subject to such restrictions as State policy or economic reasons may demand.[9]

After examining the nature of promises and pacts, the consent required therein, their matter and conditions, and the doctrine of agency,[10] the author inquires into the obligations attending speech and its expression,[11] and discusses various moot problems arising therefrom, *e.g.* when untruths are not to be considered perfidious or criminal,[12] how far part of the truth may be legiti-

[1] II. 6. 2.   [2] III. 2.   [3] III. 1.
[4] III. 3. 5.   [5] III. 3. 8.   [6] III. 3. 9.
[7] III. 3. 10.   [8] III. 3. 13.   [9] III. 3 11.
[10] III. 5—III. 7. 9.   [11] IV. 1.   [12] IV. 1. 9.

mately concealed,[1] to what extent simulation and mental reservations are permissible,[2] in what circumstances governors of States may issue false reports,[3] whether it is lawful to send false communications to an enemy,[4] whether a guilty person may deny the charge, and what his advocate may do in such a case.[5] Then he deals with the legal significance of the oath, its interpretation and perjury,[6] with the origin and object of property or dominion.[7] As to ownership of the sea, Pufendorf observes that many of the writers engaged in the controversy were animated more by affection for their country than by regard for truth. The main ocean cannot be under anyone's dominion; its illimitability makes it impossible to defend its possession effectively, and, moreover, the use of it is inexhaustible and therefore sufficient for all. The world was given by God to the human race in general, and all men have by nature equal rights. Dominion, however, may be exercised over parts of the sea, *e.g.* territorial waters, and other particular regions when acquired in virtue of treaties with neighbouring and other States concerned.[8] Thus freedom of navigation is the right of all, for no one people may obtain such a power over the seas as will justify the exclusion of all others from the same benefit. Ordinary rights may be modified by compacts, but not if prejudicial to a third party.[9]

These questions lead to the exposition of such matters as modes of acquiring ownership, occupation, rights over another's property, transference of property, testaments, intestate succession, usucaption, prescription, obligations arising from the right of property.[10] Then follows an analysis of the conception of price[11] and of the nature of commercial transactions.[12] As regards international relationships, Pufendorf observes that there is an implied agreement in wars, at least after all terms of peace have been rejected, that whichever party conquers shall have the right to impose laws on the vanquished; so that a defeated belligerent cannot urge as a ground for the non-fulfilment of a treaty that he was forced to enter into it through fear—for he who takes the field when the dispute in question may be decided otherwise is deemed to commit its decision to the sword. There must be no subtle evasions in the interpretation of contracts. In a state of nature controversies cannot be settled by judges, but

[1] IV. 1. 11.　　[2] IV. 1. 12-14.　　[3] IV. 1. 1.
[4] IV. 1. 191.　　[5] IV. 1. 20-2.　　[6] IV. 2.
[7] IV. 4-5.　　[8] IV. 5. 5-9.　　[9] IV. 5. 10
[10] IV. 6-13.　　[11] V. 1.　　[12] V. 2.

by submission to mediators and arbitrators.¹ The sixth book deals with the institutions of marriage, paternal power, and master's authority.²

Finally, the author discusses the establishment of civil societies and sovereigns, and the rights and incidents of sovereignty. Men are induced to set up organized communities in order to protect themselves from injury.³ To secure lasting peace more is needed than the law of nature and the temporary intervention of conciliators and arbitrators. Besides, in a state of nature the arbitrator is not vested with authority to compel the contending parties to accept his judgment, and so to prevent the adoption of forcible measures.⁴ The greatest part of mankind have regard to the immediate present rather than to the future; they act not with rational motives but by wild impulse.⁵ Thus by a union of wills and strength, produced by intervening covenants, a civil State and a sovereign authority are erected. In the conception of a civil State, Pufendorf emphasizes the corporate existence, the *persona* as the essential. In a monarchy, the will of the prince is the will of the State; under other forms of regularized government, the will of the State is represented by that of the majority of the subjects; but both cases may admit of limitations.⁶ The author then inquires whether the majesty of princes is immediately derived from God;⁷ he points out that civil authority cannot be simply the effect of war as it must exist before war is made,⁸ and discusses the forms of government,⁹ the ways of acquiring sovereignty (especially monarchical),¹⁰ the parts of sovereignty and their natural connection (*e.g.* the legislative power, the judicial right of taxation, power to make war and peace and to enter into treaties and alliances, etc.),¹¹ the duty of the sovereign,¹² his power to direct the actions of his subjects and to dispose of their persons and property in behalf of the commonwealth and in criminal cases,¹³ to determine their rank,¹⁴ and his power over the kingdom as the "public patrimony."¹⁵ His authority is however, subject to various restrictions, *e.g.* he cannot alienate the kingdom or part of it or the sources of public revenue, he cannot make it a fief, or mortgage it without the consent of his people.¹⁶

4. **The Law of War.**—This part of Pufendorf's subject has by no means as great value as the corresponding portions of Gentilis

---

¹ V. 2. 13. ² VI. 1-3. ³ VII. 1. 7. ⁴ VII. 1. 9.
⁵ VII. 1. 11. ⁶ VII. 2. ⁷ VII. 3. 3. ⁸ VII. 3. 5.
⁹ VII. 5. ¹⁰ VII. 7. ¹¹ VII. 4. ¹² VII. 9.
¹³ VIII. 1-3. ¹⁴ VIII. 4. ¹⁵ VIII. 5. ¹⁶ *Ibid.*

or Grotius, the latter of whom he follows very frequently. Many important and interesting questions are passed over, and some others are presented in a somewhat superficial analysis. Nevertheless, taking all failings into account—his too great readiness to draw conclusions, insufficiently considered, from his hypothetical principles, his almost exclusive concern with abstract relationships and disregard of actual inevitable phenomena—it must be admitted that his exposition occupies no mean place in the history of the law of war.

Starting from a point of view different from that of Gentilis and Grotius, Pufendorf's definitions of peace and war are wider, less concise, and less definite than those of his great predecessors. Peace is that state in which men live quietly together, untroubled by violence, and voluntarily discharge their obligations.[1] War is the state of men engaged in offering and repelling injuries, or endeavouring forcibly to recover what is their due.[2] Peace is the normal state of mankind; the law of nature was given to men principally to establish and preserve peace. Only by an extraordinary indulgence does it permit them to make war, *i.e.* when natural law itself is wilfully violated, as by unjust aggression (defensive war) or refusal to restore what is naturally due to them (offensive war).[3] In any case peace is necessarily the price and reward of war.[4] But such alleged causes of war must be manifest, and free from doubt and uncertainty. Pacific settlement must be tried first by negotiation, or arbitration, or by lot.[5] Following Grotius, he mentions certain unjust causes of war, of which some are obviously unlawful (*e.g.* avarice, ambition, desire to extend dominion), and others have a mere colour of lawfulness (*e.g.* fear due to the increasing might of a neighbouring State). Mere suspicion is not enough; there must be certainty that designs are formed against us. To consider utility a ground for war is "impudens." The inhuman practices of barbarians (*e.g.* cannibalism, immolation) are not sufficient cause, unless directed against our subjects who had done them no injury.[6]

[1] I. 1. 8: "Pax . . . est status ille, quo homines inter se quiete, et citra iniuras violentas agunt, et quae invicem debent, velut ex obligatione et ultro praestant."
[2] *Ibid.*: "Bellum . . . est status iniurias violentas mutuo inferentium et propulsantium, aut quae sibi debentur vi extorquere nitentium."
[3] VIII. 6. 3.
[4] VIII. 6. 2: "Ita tamen natura permittit bellum, ut id gerens pro fine sibi constituere pacem debeat."
[5] VIII. 6. 4.   [6] VIII. 6. 5.

It is legitimate to use stratagem and fraud against the enemy, provided there be no treachery, or violation of a compact or good faith thereby.[1] But it is difficult to settle the limits of hostile conduct; for every war appears to involve an understanding of this kind: "Try your strength and we will try ours."[2] Retribution cannot (as in civil tribunals) always be measured by the offence. But the law of humanity not only prohibits the infliction of unnecessary excessive injury on the enemy, but demands generosity on the part of the victor;[3] hence natural law requires the observance of moderation, "temperamenta" (as Grotius had insisted).

In a state of nature all men have the right to conduct hostilities, but when States are constituted the right is transferred to the sovereign authority.[4] War may be divided into solemn (or formal) and less solemn.[5] The first is formally proclaimed, commenced, and directed by the supreme authority on both sides; in which case the belligerents are considered "iusti hostes." The second is not publicly declared, or is conducted by or against private subjects; in the former case it might be such an irregular proceeding as a depredatory incursion, in the latter intestine warfare.[6] No community, civil or other, is responsible for acts of particular members, unless there be some culpable act or omission of its own, *e.g.* connivance at or acquiescence in crimes committed by its subjects, or refusal to surrender fugitive offenders.[7] A foreign State refusing "to administer justice" is liable to reprisals at the hands of the injured party, who may seize the persons and property of the former's subjects.[8] War may be justly made on behalf of other peoples, if the auxiliary State is under some tie or obligation to them (*e.g.* as allies, or confederates), and the assisted State itself has just reasons for war. Otherwise, it is unlawful to aid one belligerent against another, as all men equally deserve favour; and it is contrary to the natural equality of mankind to force oneself upon the world as a judge and decider of controversies. To take up arms in defence of subjects of a foreign State against their sovereign's oppressions is lawful,

---

[1] VIII. 6. 6.
[2] VIII. 6. 7: "Tenta quid ipse valeas, ego itidem omnia experiar."
[3] VIII. 6. 7: "Ast vero lex humanitatis non id solum considerari vult, quid hostis citra iniuriam possit pati, sed et quid humanum, adde et generosum victorem facere deceat." [4] VIII. 6. 8.
[5] *Cf.* Grotius, I. 3. 4. 1. [6] VIII. 6. 9. [7] VIII. 6. 12.
[8] VIII. 6. 13: "Violentae executiones in cives aut bona civium alterius reip., quae iustitiam administrare detrectat."

provided they themselves may rightfully oppose the tyranny and cruelty of their governors.¹ As to declaration of war, Pufendorf accepts without qualification the doctrines laid down by Grotius.²

With regard to the treatment of the enemy and his property in general, Pufendorf says it is not possible to lay down rules to modify the law of nature and impose clearly defined limits to cruelty and outrage; it is safer to leave these matters to the conscience of the combatants. Besides, it is understood between them, "tacito quodam pacto," that they are at liberty to increase or abate the heat of the war.³ But there are various mitigations, as Grotius insisted.⁴ May assassins be employed against the enemy? Yes, in the case of rebels, pirates, highwaymen. Good faith is to be maintained between the belligerents; but it does not of necessity follow that the adversary's subjects may not be induced to desert.⁵ In a legitimate solemn war natural law confers on a belligerent the right to take possession of such property of the enemy as will amount to the original claim, together with an indemnity to cover damages and expenditure, and to exact other securities from the enemy. Moreover, according to universal practice a combatant becomes the absolute proprietor of everything taken from the enemy, even though it exceeds the original claim. But to give the victor a right of property, there must be a pacification and agreement; otherwise the right is deemed to continue in the old owner, who may justly regain it when he is strong enough to do so.⁶ The booty goes to the sovereign, who may share it amongst his soldiers, after restoring what was due to any one on whose behalf the war was begun. Mercenary soldiers have no right to anything but their pay; and private adventurers are not entitled to anything other than what the sovereign decides to allow them.⁷ Things incorporeal can only be acquired along with the subjects—persons or things—they inhere in. The capture of a person having rights over others does not, without their consent, effect a transference of those rights to the captor. Thus if a king is taken prisoner, the captor does not thereby acquire his kingdom. Similarly, taking a husband gives no right over his wife or children. A prisoner's rights in things are not acquired unless those things are taken along with him;⁸ nor are his actions and credits unless he

---

¹ VIII. 6. 14.   ² VIII. 6. 15.   *Cf. De iure belli et pacis,* III. 3.
³ VIII. 6. 16.   ⁴ *De iure belli et pacis,* III. 4. 5.   ⁵ VIII. 6. 18.
⁶ VIII. 6. 20.   ⁷ VIII. 6. 21.   ⁸ VIII. 6. 22.

consent to make them over—though such consent may be extorted by threats.¹ Dominion over the vanquished is obtained if they promise expressly or tacitly to acknowledge their conqueror as their lord, and he for his part undertakes not to treat them any longer as enemies.² Finally, prisoners of war recover their former status if, not being under any obligation of faith to the adversary, they escape and return to their country. If during the war captured things, whether movables or immovables, are retaken, they are to be restored to their former owners.³ And a whole nation regains its liberty when it shakes off the enemy's yoke, either by its own strength or by the aid of allies or friends. But should a third State by warlike proceedings made in its own name and for its own advantage wrest a subjugated and enslaved nation from its adversary, dominion over that nation is transferred to the new victor.⁴

The hostilities of the belligerents may be "confined," or suspended, or entirely terminated by means of compacts and conventions.⁵ But it is doubtful whether validity can be claimed for truces and armistices, or their violation regarded as an infringement of natural law. For the proper use of good faith is to advance peace; and such engagements may tend, on the contrary, to protract the war. Though active hostile proceedings are in abeyance the state of hostility continues, and in itself gives a combatant unlimited liberty to take all the advantages he can against his opponent.⁶ It seems absurd to employ faith without thoughts of restoring or preserving peace thereby; it is contradictory to a belligerent's actions to make a protestation not to use the liberty of an enemy whilst a state of war subsists. Thus, these compacts are to be measured simply by the use and advantage derived from them, "eadem utilitate aestimari." A belligerent is not bound to make use of the utmost rigours permitted by the law of war; it is generous and noble to spare an enemy when he may be quite legitimately dispatched. But if we do not obtain our rights by pacific measures, and war becomes necessary, then the shortest way to attain that end is the one most conformable to nature. Hence such conventions as tend only to moderate and qualify hostilities and prolong warlike relationships

---

[1] VIII. 6. 23.   [2] VIII. 6. 24. *Cf.* Grotius, III. 8.
[3] VIII. 6. 25.   [4] VIII. 6. 26.   [5] VIII. 7. 1.
[6] VIII. 7. 2: "Nam hostilis status utique in se dat licentiam nocendi alteri in infinitum."

are repugnant to nature.¹ In the more civilized parts of the world, however, custom has established the use of truces and armistices for various purposes. A truce being temporary in effect leaves undecided the dispute which caused the war.² Therefore when the engagement expires, there is no need to make a new proclamation of war ; nevertheless, if not obligatory, it is at least honourable to do so when the truce was of long date and has entirely put a stop to the progress, and transformed the complexion of war, or when there is an express stipulation that conferences be held to determine the difference in question.³ Of course, if one side commit a breach, it is by no means incumbent on the other to make any declaration before taking up arms again.⁴ Truces may be established either by explicit agreement, or impliedly by conduct—though merely to forbear from hostilities for a short time is not necessarily giving a truce.⁵ What liberties does a truce allow ? Acts purely of a defensive character are lawful, even though the truce was obtained for another purpose. For example, if a cessation of war be agreed upon in order to bury the slain, it is not on that account unlawful to retreat to a more secure position, or to repair or raise a fortification ; and so also if a besieged town request a truce for the purpose of deferring the assault, it may also receive fresh supplies of men and provisions.⁶ On the expiration of a truce subjects of a belligerent found on enemy territory may be made prisoners.⁷

In this part of the subject Pufendorf follows Grotius to a very large extent ; indeed, he very frequently mentions a heading and merely refers to his predecessor for argument and solution. When he differs, however, his opinions are generally less progressive than those of the great Dutch jurist, on account of his too stringent adhesion to *a priori* assumptions attributed to the exigence of natural law, and owing to his scanty consideration of the actual development of international relationships. In his advocacy of the lawful severities of war, as against the numerous relaxations proposed by Grotius and others, he supports his views—apart from insistent appeals to elementary principles which he considers incontrovertible, but which he sometimes applies too mechanically —almost entirely by the citation of ancient principles.

---

[1] VIII. 7. 2 : " Adeoque ubi per pacta illa, vim hostilem temperantia non nisi bellum alatur, naturae eadem repugnare manifestum est."
[2] VIII. 7. 5.   [3] VIII. 7. 6.   [4] VIII. 7. 12.   [5] VIII. 7. 7.
[6] VIII. 7. 10.   [7] VIII. 7. 11. *Cf.* Grotius, III. 21. 9.

5. **Treaties of Peace, Alliances, and Other Conventions.**—Are treaties of peace invalidated through fear? Grotius replies in the negative,[1] on the ground that according to the common practices of nations such compacts are not held to be vitiated; if they were, it would be impossible to put an end to wars, or even to moderate their severity. Pufendorf, however, contends that what is got through extortion and the ravages of an unjust war cannot conscientiously be retained; hence it is allowable "to plead an exception of fear" against an unjust conqueror, who forced his adversary to consent to rigorous demands and accept a hard peace. But it is otherwise if the combatants agreed to let the sword alone settle their difference.[2] Is a treaty of peace made by a sovereign with his rebel subjects binding?[3] Pufendorf maintains that to enter into a compact with them implies *ipso facto* that their offence is pardoned; and that they may well claim that their promised obedience is conditional on the sovereign's observance of the engagement.[4] Such a treaty may be of the nature of a charter or a fundamental law of the constitution. Further, private property may be ceded on pacification, in virtue of the prince's right of "dominium eminens," which may be exercised under stress of necessity and for the public interest. But the State is bound to make good as soon as it can such losses of its citizens. As to hostages given for insuring the ratification of peace, Pufendorf accepts what Grotius says,[5] and emphasizes that if the hostage is the prince's heir and successor another is to be substituted for him on that prince's demise.[6]

With regard to treaties and conventions ("foedera") entered into apart from war, they may be divided into two classes according to their subject-matter; firstly, those asserting rights and obligations which were already conferred or imposed by natural law; secondly, those superadding certain special provisions to the general duties of natural law, or modifying and restricting those general duties to specifically defined circumstances. The first are treaties of friendship, providing merely for the exercise of mutual civility and humanity. But now that nations are more civilized and "polished in their manners" than the ancient peoples who made pacts of this kind, such treaties are really redundant; for it is a disgrace to human nature that people

---

[1] *De iure belli et pacis*, II. 17. 19; III. 19. 11.
[2] VIII. 8. 1.
[3] *Cf.* Grotius, III. 19. 6.
[4] VIII. 8. 2.
[5] *Op. cit.*, III. 20, 52, etc.
[6] VIII. 8. 6.

outside barbarism should establish conventions whose purport does not go beyond what is incontestably demanded by natural law.[1] The second class comprises alliances which may be, from one point of view, either equal or unequal, and, from another, real or personal. A personal alliance is one made with a sovereign in his personal capacity, and hence expires with him. A real alliance is one made irrespectively of the life of the contracting sovereign, and therefore has permanent effect; *e.g.* when it is expressly mentioned that it is to be perpetual, or it is made for the prince and his successors, or when its duration is limited to a certain period. In case of doubt, a favourable compact (*e.g.* for the advancement of commerce) may be construed as real, an onerous one as personal. In these questions Pufendorf follows the Grotian doctrines, but he considers them inadequate, as it remains to be determined when a prince's successors are bound by the treaties entered into in the preceding reign. In general then, a successor is bound (1) in the case of a *peace* made by his predecessor, (2) in agreements by which the late sovereign transferred any right to a third party, (3) when either contracting party has performed his part and the other has failed in his through death, and (4) in engagements where nothing has been done on both sides, or where the performances have been equal. However, it has become a custom to renew, upon a new succession, the treaties and alliances—even though real—entered into by the late prince. But (as Pufendorf remarks in contradictory terms) a successor has the right to disregard a previous league which he thinks is now grown useless and unprofitable to the State.[2]

If a contracting prince is exiled or deposed, is he entitled to call on the other party for performance of the compact? Grotius[3] holds that he is entitled, if he has been unjustly deposed: for he has still a right to his kingdom though he has lost possession of it. But Pufendorf decides that if the treaty expressly provides for the protection of the prince's person and dynasty, he has a right to be aided to recover his position. On the other hand, if the object of the treaty is simply the advantage of the State, the case is doubtful; for aid that had been promised is presumed to have been promised against foreign enemies. Of course, a lawful sovereign may, in virtue of such a league, be

[1] VIII. 9. 1-2.   [2] VIII. 9. 6-8.
[3] *De iure belli et pacis*, II. 16. 17: "Sane cum rege initum foedus manet, etiamsi rex idem aut successor regno a subditis sit pulsus. Ius enim regni penes ipsum manet, utcunque possessionem amiserit."

assisted against a usurper.[1] Further, the author holds that the term "allies" includes not only those who were confederates at the time the league was made but also those subsequently taken into alliance;[2] that when compacts of limited duration expire, a tacit renewal is not necessarily to be supposed;[3] and then examines the nature of "sponsiones," and the results of their non-ratification by the sovereign authority.[4]

Next, the private engagements of princes are considered. A sovereign may repudiate a disadvantageous contract made with an alien;[5] but one made with his subjects he is bound in honour, though not in law, to observe. If he gives the latter liberty to bring an action against him in his own Courts the suit proceeds rather on natural equity than on the civil law of the State.[6] Can he transmit a contractual obligation to his successors? If the kingdom is his "patrimony," his successor inherits his goods and possessions together with his liabilities; but if it is held merely as a usufructuary right, the successor is not so bound,[7] inasmuch as he derives his right to the throne not from the preceding sovereign, but from the people. In general, however, contracts of the prince are binding on the State, unless they are obviously absurd or unjust;[8] in a doubtful case the presumption is in favour of the prince. The grants and donations of a ruler cannot be revoked by his successor, provided they were made on good and fair grounds.[9]

Finally, Pufendorf discusses in what circumstances civil subjection ceases, and what the effects are of a change of sovereignty and of a dissolution of the commonwealth. If a prince dies without a successor, the citizens of the country cease to be subjects as such, but remain united to one another by the original bond and compact of society.[10] Subjection also terminates in case of permanent settlement in foreign territory.[11] Grotius thinks that such removal, if in large companies, is unlawful, in that it is inconsistent with the nature of civil society, but Pufendorf sees no reason for this contention, as civil society among men in general is not destroyed, though this or that State may thereby

---

[1] VIII. 9. 9.
[2] VIII. 9. 10; following mainly the conclusions of Grotius, II. 16. 13; but the latter holds that future allies are not necessarily included.
[3] VIII. 9. 11.   [4] VIII. 9. 12.   [5] VIII. 10. 2.   [6] VIII. 10. 6.
[7] According to the view of Grotius, II. 14. 10-11.
[8] VIII. 10. 8: "Contractus regum obligabunt civitatem, qui non manifeste absurdi aut inqui sunt."   [9] *Cf.* Grotius, II. 14. 13.
[10] VIII. 11. 1.   [11] VIII. 11. 2. *Cf.* Grotius, II. 5. 24.

be dissolved. The decline of one State means the generation of another; what is lost in the one is gained in the other.¹ When men began to multiply, nature caused them to be divided into civil communities, but never ordained that this or that particular commonwealth should flourish and prosper for ever.² After examining the causes of loss of citizenship (*e.g.* banishment, surrender of subjects to an enemy),³ Pufendorf points out that changes of government (monarchy, oligarchy, republic) do not necessarily affect the status of the people, nor are debts of the State thereby extinguished.⁴ The acts of a usurper may be considered valid, so far as foreign relationships are concerned, for a foreign power need not question his title if the transactions are otherwise regular; but his unjust acts limited to the State may, on the expiration of his reign, be abrogated by a lawful authority.⁵ A sovereign reigns and passes away, but the commonwealth subsists. It is dissolved only when the people are destroyed, or when the moral tie which unites them is entirely broken. Grotius holds that if through some desolation only a few inhabitants are left, they are not entitled to assume sovereign power or any of the rights consequent thereon;⁶ but Pufendorf contends that if those few can effectively defend themselves against foreign invasion and possess sufficient resources for "growing up again" and remaining an independent nation, then they may legitimately claim and exercise the rights of the former people.⁷

Conclusion.—Pufendorf's juristic writings enjoyed immense success. They were frequently reprinted, and translated in several languages; extracts, commentaries, and abridgements were issued in large numbers. For nearly a century the majority of continental writers on the law of nature and of nations, especially in Germany, acknowledged the leadership of Pufendorf, and adopted the lines marked out by him. Among the numerous adherents may be mentioned : in Germany, Christian Thomasius, Cocceji, Wernher, Wagner, Griebner, Koehler, Heineccius; in France, Barbeyrac, Richer d'Aube; in Denmark, Holberg; in Switzerland, Vicat, Burmalaqui, De Felice (the latter two being

---

[1] VIII. 11. 4: "Sed unius corruptio alterius est generatio; unius decrementa alteri incremento cedunt."
[2] *Ibid.* : "Natura quippe civiles esse societates in genere humano iam multiplicato voluit; sed ut haec vel illa civitas perpetua, florensque subsisteret, nusquam iussit."
[3] VIII. 11. 6-9.   [4] VIII. 12. 1-2.   [5] VIII. 12. 3.
[6] *De iure belli et pacis*, II. 9. 4.   [7] VIII. 12. 8.

of Italian origin). As for Italy, Pierantoni observes that the theory of Pufendorf had no vogue in his country;[1] none the less, several later Italian writers produced works which unmistakably showed the influence partly of Pufendorf and partly of Wolf. On the other hand, there were not wanting resolute dissentients, even in Germany; among these were the powerful adversaries of natural law, Samuel Rachel and Wolfgang Textor.

Leibnitz's disparagement of Pufendorf's philosophical and juristic capacity was entirely unmerited, and sprang rather from personal hostility than from a well balanced appraisement of his work. The opposition between them first arose in connection with Pufendorf's well-nigh revolutionary pamphlet on the condition of the German Empire; the conservatism, the political timidity of Leibnitz ill harmonized with the progressive tendency, the aggressive spirit of Pufendorf; and the breach between them was aggravated by the triumph of the latter in the stirring controversy. The laconic dictum of Leibnitz: "Vir parum iurisconsultus et minime philosophus,"[2] recalls Ben Jonson's valuation of Shakespeare's classical scholarship, and comes from an overweening sense of superiority in regard to a particular sphere. But the aphorism is characterized more by concision than by truth. To Leibnitz's harsh and unfair judgment is largely due the under-estimation of Pufendorf by many of his successors. Locke's high opinion, however, may serve as a corrective of that of Leibnitz. Sir James Mackintosh, too, says: "His treatise is a mine in which all his successors must dig."[3] And in recent times the eminent economic historian, Professor Roscher, has expressed his emphatic dissent from the opinion of Leibnitz; indeed, he places Pufendorf also among the greatest political and economic writers.[4]

In his various writings, especially in his legal work, Pufendorf does not show the genius, the penetration, the profound erudition of a Grotius, nor the practical sagacity, the argumentative skill,

[1] A. Pierantoni, *Storia degli studi del diritto internazionale in Italia* (Modena, 1869), p. 49: "L' intelletto italiano non s'immedesimò in tale epoca con detta scuola."
[2] *Opera*, ed. Dutens, vol. iv., pt. 3, p. 261.
[3] *Op. cit.*, p. 25.
[4] W. Roscher, *Geschichte der National-Oekonomik in Deutschland* (München, 1874), p. 305: "Aber zwischen diesen Alternativen bleibt noch eine dritte Möglichkeit übrig: Pufendorff war ein, durch Philosophie, Jurisprudenz und Geschichte gründlichst vorgebildeter, Staatsgelehrter und National-ökonom von ausserordentlicher Bedeutung."

the power to grapple with actual conditions of a Gentilis. And in originality also he is certainly inferior to the first, and in some respects to the second. But none the less his treatises on jurisprudence occupy a high place, as they elaborate for the first time a systematic body of law, magnificent in its proportions, logically coherent, congruous, scientifically constructed, and based throughout on fundamental principles; although the adoption of these first principles is to be largely attributed to his study of, and attempt at reconciling, the doctrines of Hobbes and Grotius. He is at once the best representative and the head of the school of natural law. His works display a spirit of tolerance, an impatience with narrow sectarianism, a determination to separate law from theology, a desire to mete out justice to all mankind, whether Christian or heathen, whether high or low in the scale of civilization.

It has been held that the doctrines of natural law have at times had a retarding influence on the development of international law. But this was not due to any defect inherent in the former, but rather to the analogical and syllogistic inconsequences of over-enthusiastic devotees of natural law, to the careless vagaries of special pleaders advocating or opposing this or that particular provision or institution. The law of the present world—whether municipal or international — no doubt possesses above all a positive character. The modern age is inordinately given to glorifying the visible, the tangible. But there are signs of a spiritual awakening; there is now manifested in many quarters a desire to go beyond the veil of phenomena and to search for the ultimate principles of life, of thought, of human relationships. Science is now becoming strikingly transcendentalized; the study of comparative jurisprudence, so extensively grown of late, shows that men have become keenly anxious to learn not only how legal problems have been or are being solved in different places, but also how law has originated, and what are its essential foundations universally recognized as such. As in science metaphysical entities are being more and more imported, so in the sphere of law will those principles of natural law come to be more and more emphasized, through the ineradicable promptings of the intuitive consciousness of men and of States. Does not the recent Hague Convention—considered by many the very incarnation of the positive method in international law—speak of conscience and humanity ? And does it not thereby affirm the inadequacy of that positive method, and make a covert appeal to natural law, which is in its simplest form an expression of what is introspectively discerned in human conscience ? There are conceptions which retain a perennial potency in spite of their being openly disavowed at one time or another.

VICO (1668-1744)

THE golden age of Italian literature may be said to have passed away when, by the treaty of Castel Cambrésis, in 1559, the hegemony of the Austrian House of Spain was established over the peninsula, and the era of foreign domination had begun. The decrees of the Council of Trent completed the work of the counter-reformation, and before 1565 the old toleration of literary liberty had given place to a general policy of repression and obscurantism sufficient to chill all intellectual activity. Henceforth the main currents of European life were to be no longer essentially literary or artistic. The dynastic interests of France and Spain had become centres to which all that was best steadily gravitated.

The boundary mark between medieval and modern Italy lies somewhere about the middle of the eighteenth century. Metastasio and Goldoni, Alfieri and Monti, show us the old art in process of transformation into the new. But they are not representatively Italian. Metastasio's tragedy is inspired by Corneille; the comedy of Goldoni by Molière. Their world is an artistic mistake. False heroics and degenerate pastorals, sensual music and tinsel ornamentation, betray their unworthiness to represent their predecessors. In the domain of history and philosophy, however, things wore a new and fruitful aspect. The wonderful erudition of Muratori had helped to throw light upon the darkest recesses of the past, and before the eighteenth century had opened Naples produced her most illustrious citizen, Giambattista Vico, whose profound originality of mind was enough to place him in the forefront of European learning.

Although it may be said that the story of a man of letters is best studied in his works, it is generally necessary, in order to form some clear notion of his relative value and of the manner in which his thought was moulded, to inquire into the conditions in which he lived and into the influences which produced him.

Although Giambattista Vico was essentially a modern in spirit, he was born in an almost medieval atmosphere. Naples in 1668, the year of his birth, was under the domination of the House of Aragon. The Spanish viceroys, who, since the time of Ferdinand the Catholic, had wielded almost supreme power in the province, were careless of the conduct of affairs, and usually corrupt. Far from Madrid, and holding in their own control the means of communication with the central Government, they hindered commerce by vexatious restrictions, and practised nepotism in its most ruinous forms. Provided they extorted a sufficient tribute and sent it regularly to Spain, the only check they had to fear was the anger of the Neapolitan populace. Brigandage had, in the seventeenth century, assumed unprecedented proportions : the bandits were protected by the nobles and, in time of sedition, boldly entered Naples to support one or other of the rival factions. Assassins claimed sanctuary in almost every church, and if they were of sufficient social importance were graciously protected by the Viceroy, who would intervene in open court on their behalf. False coiners abounded, some of them renegade monks, who, in one instance, when condemned to the hulks, placidly continued their trade with the connivance of their gaolers. One of the Viceroys, Benavides, himself emulated the enterprise of his subjects in producing false coin. The professional thieves in Naples were reckoned at 30,000, or three among every sixty of the inhabitants. Despite the lawlessness that prevailed, the Church in Naples had attained immense power over the people. She was by far the greatest landowner, and her dignitaries were able to carry out unfettered their schemes for their own aggrandizement or for that of their community. There were 16,000 ecclesiastics in the city of Naples, and the religious foundations were entitled to a third of every intestacy ; the miracle of the liquefaction of the blood of San Gennaro—" miracolo da fare ogni Turco Cristiano "—was merely one of the host of similar prodigies in which the populace had an unswerving belief. In 1707, when the Spaniards had fled before the arrival of the victorious Austrians in Naples, it was by parading the image of San Gennaro that the more peace-loving citizens succeeded in averting a sanguinary tumult. The influence of the Church was all-pervasive, and it was often intolerantly exerted. When, in 1740, the Jews were allowed to enter Naples, the monks predicted innumerable evils to the king and his advisers. Astorino, a man remarkable for his intellectual capacity, was accused of having acquired his knowledge by witchcraft. Majello, who first introduced the Cartesian philosophy, was long the object of clerical persecution, and Giannone, the author of the *Storia Civile*, although a friend of the Church, was, after the publication of his book, disowned by his countrymen.

In such surroundings only three careers were open to the intelligent or enterprising citizen. The armies of the Emperor and of the King of Spain were largely recruited from the Neapolitan nobility; the cloister afforded a safe and often pleasant retreat for the meaner classes who were content to seek bodily and mental peace within its walls and in the pages of Suarez and Bellarmine. The law was the last profession wherein the unwarlike but more worldly-minded Neapolitan might find a livelihood.

Although the eleven systems of legislation which were simultaneously in vigour in the province of Naples must have afforded a rich pasture for its lawyers, it may be doubted if many of the four thousand *avvocati* who thronged the Courts can have had a substantial practice in a country where commerce was stagnant and political unrest had become endemic. The advocate was, however, often a person of influence and weight. He defended the noble whose privileges were infringed, and was often liberally rewarded by his distinguished patrons. The legal profession was, moreover, a means of attaining to high office and to literary distinction; many of the lawyers of the time have won a place on the roll of Italian literary celebrities. Naples had, however, little part in the early development of Italian literature. The communal life of Tuscany which had produced Petrarch and Boccaccio, was rendered impossible by the maintenance of feudal institutions, and the character of the people, blended out of Greek, Saracen and Norman blood, was, perhaps, unfavourable to the formation of those currents of thought which, in other places, have found expression in distinctive schools of art and science.

Vico's Life.—An autobiography is, in many respects, an unsatisfactory source of information, but it is from the *Vita di G. B. Vico, scritta da sè medesimo*, that we are obliged to take nearly all that is known of its author's personality. This autobiography was written, at the request of the Conte di Porcia, to form one of a series of literary lives, and selected as the most fitted to head the series, although Vico protested his unworthiness of the honour. In writing his own life, Vico adopted a method which renders it easy to trace the development of his mind and throws light on some of the obscurities of his other works. It affords a concrete example of the historical method which was to so great an extent the creation of Vico. His letters furnish further information, and are of assistance in the attempt to sketch the main occurrences of his life.

Antonio, the father of our philosopher, kept a small bookstall in one of the tortuous narrow streets that traverse the older parts of Naples. Though his parents were poor, Vico had a kindly recollection of them. "Lasciarono," he says, "assai buona fama di se." A fall from a ladder caused a fracture of the skull when he was seven years of age, and he was unable to work for three years. When he returned to school his disposition was melancholic but earnest, a fact which he attributed to his parentage; but his long illness and absence from youthful companions had, no doubt, helped to strengthen the natural bent of his character. Vico now set himself the task of making up for the time lost during his illness, and so rapid was his progress that he was soon permitted to enter the senior class. His father sent him to the Jesuits' school, where he competed successfully with the most brilliant of their pupils. He believed himself treated unjustly by his teachers, and left to pursue his studies alone. Becoming absorbed in his task, he no longer observed regular hours, and his mother, he tells us, more than once found him, at daybreak, still poring over his books. To assist his private studies Vico attended the lectures of a Jesuit named Del Balzo, and was by him recommended to read Pietro Ispano and Paolo Veneto, two decadent scholastic writers whose learned incomprehensibilities proved so unpalatable to his clear-thinking mind that he abandoned work for eighteen months. The meeting of a society known as the "Accademia degli Infuriati" recalled him to himself. As he quaintly expressed it, he had been like a charger after training, put to pasture for a time, and he now returned to the strife at the sound of the trumpet of learned discussion. The teaching of another Jesuit inspired in Vico an admiration for the greater scholastic writers, and he seems to have sought acquaintance with Greek philosophy in Scotus and similar writers. The fame of the philosophic Jesuit Suarez of Granada induced Vico to make a special study of him;

but it is a remarkable fact that not alone is no trace of the ideas expounded in the *Tractatus de Legibus* to be found in Vico, but he does not once refer to its author. The desultory course which Vico had hitherto pursued in the acquisition of learning might, perhaps, have led him far from the fields in which he was destined to take so brilliant a place. One day, visiting the royal university he happened to listen to a law lecture at the moment when the professor was commending Vulteius to his hearers as the best commentator of the *Institutes*. Vico, seized with the desire of studying this author, persuaded his father to obtain a copy from a well-known author. The latter saw the lad, and was so favourably impressed that he gave him the book as a present. It was thus, he tells us, that he was initiated into the study of jurisprudence. After he had mastered the principles of law, Vico at first thought of practising at the bar, and at the age of sixteen he successfully pleaded a case in defence of his father. His health was, however, precarious, and he was, by temperament, disinclined to take part in the noisy striving of the courts. He sought distraction in versification, and made little or no progress in the profession he had chosen.

A happy chance at length afforded Vico the opportunity of meeting Rocca, Bishop of Ischia. Struck by the ability with which he demonstrated the true method of teaching law, the bishop procured him the post of preceptor for his nephews, the sons of the Marchese di Vatolla. During the next nine years Vico lived in learned ease and retirement among congenial surroundings, with the use of an excellent library and leisure to pursue his studies. He devoted himself equally to the study of law and of literature. His interest in canon law led him to inquire into the Jansenist controversy, and he systematically read Dante and Virgil, Petrarch and Horace, noting the comparative merits of their languages and perusing each three times. It was during this period that Vico formed most of the conceptions of Platonism and Aristotelianism which afterwards had considerable influence in moulding his system of thought. These conceptions reached him at second hand, through the treatises of scholastic and renaissance writers, and they were consequently often misleading, if not entirely false. So little was he acquainted with Greek literature that he confounded Zeno the Eleatic with Zeno the founder of Stoicism.

When, in 1694, Vico returned to Naples he found himself out

of touch with the intellectual life of the time. The teaching of the
Italian renaissance had been supplanted by an influx of French
philosophy. The vogue which Cartesianism enjoyed had dulled
the fame of Ficino and Pico della Mirandola. Contempt for
classical learning and all authority had become almost universal,
and the recluse issuing from the woods of Vatolla found himself
a stranger in his own country. This estrangement must have
proved, at the outset of his more public life, a serious obstacle to
success. Staving off destitution by writing adulatory verses and
by composing funeral orations, Vico at one time contemplated
becoming a theatine monk, but the desire of serving his aged
parents deterred him, and he set about obtaining employment.
He was refused the post of secretary to the city of Naples, but
ultimately, in 1697, he obtained a professorship of rhetoric in
the university, with a salary only slightly exceeding 100 scudi.
He married, shortly afterwards, Teresa Destito, the daughter of
a scrivener, who was, however, herself unable to write even her
name. His children did not reach to any distinction—except
perhaps, Gennaro, who succeeded his father in the chair of eloquence, but whose principal claim to recollection is, undoubtedly,
his parentage.

The lectures delivered by Vico at the opening of seven academic
years, together form the earliest consecutive embodiment of his
views on education, a topic in which he always took particular
interest. The discourse delivered in 1708 was subsequently
published under the title *De Ratione Studiorum*. It is the earliest
of Vico's writings in which clear indications of the subsequent
progress of his mind are to be found. His aversion from the
critical method of Descartes, his confidence in the spontaneous
workings of the human mind, the cultivation of the memory and
of the imagination, the merits of the " topics " of the rhetoricians,
are points here touched upon with vigour, although not without
some of the bias which always remained characteristic of him.
Whilst teaching rhetoric, Vico still devoted his attention to legal
studies. He gave lessons in jurisprudence, and wrote several
brochures on the civil law. His assertion that the great Roman
lawyers had been exclusively Patrician in origin, was the occasion
of a controversy with the royal prefect of studies which ultimately resulted in the production of Vico's principal legal treatise,
the *De uno universi iuris principio*. When in the following year
(1721) the complimentary volume, *De constantia Jurisprudentis*,

had been published, Vico might not unreasonably have claimed to be one of the most distinguished jurists in Italy.

For some time previous to 1723 he had contemplated seeking a professorship of law, and on the death of Campanile, the principal morning reader in Civil Law, he presented himself as a candidate for the vacant chair. Besides the merit of his works, the fact that he was the senior member of the university, for which he had won considerable renown, led Vico to hope for success in the competition. Many forces militated, however, against his candidature. He was without personal or family influence, his political writings had, probably, created many enemies, and he was prevented, partly by his earnestness, from making a favourable impression on persons accustomed to cringing adulation. The competitors were given a day to compose a dissertation on one of several texts from the Digest, which were selected by drawing lots. The composition of Vico, which he distributed after it had been delivered, won the admiration of many distinguished men, but the professorship was awarded to Domenico Gentile, a person of whom nothing is now known. Vico henceforth lost all hope of recognition by his countrymen, and, although he lived to bless the adversities which had driven him back to his literary pursuits and thus enabled him, as he says in the autobiography, to wreak a noble vengeance on his detractors, his failure embittered his life and made his lot seem harder than before. But, however sad it may seem that none of the joys of worldly success should be his, we cannot regard the fact as unmitigated evil if we recollect that to it is probably due the production of the *Scienza Nuova*, Vico's most permanent contribution to the world's literature.

> " Sempre natura, se fortuna trova
> discorda a se, come ogni altra semente
> fuor di sua region, fa mala prova."

The preoccupations which the possession of the chair he coveted would necessarily have entailed, might in all probability have turned him from the paths of research, in which he found a glory denied to his puny competitors. The *New Science* appeared in 1725. It was the logical development of his earlier work, and, by boldly dedicating it to the universities of Europe, Vico appealed to the tribunal of all the learned to judge his claim to intellectual greatness. Scarcely any writer is so entirely without precursors: Michelet was exaggerating but slightly when he declared : " Avant Vico le premier nom n'était pas dit; après lui, la science était, sinon faite au moins fondée." The historical method, which, in most departments of human knowledge, is of immense importance, and to which some owe their very existence, was the discovery of Vico.

In the light of this achievement his minor merits must of necessity pall. With the intuition of genius the author of the *Scienza Nuova* felt the greatness of his work ; he had, as he expressed it, put on a new man. "Mi ha fermato," he says, "come sopra un' alta adamantina rocca, il guidizio di Dio, il quale fa giustizia alle opere d' ingegno con la stima dei saggi."

The remaining years of Vico's life were devoted to the revision of his great work and to the composition of some studies of minor importance. The second edition of the *Scienza Nuova* was dedicated to Clement XII. The Pope ordered his hearty approval to be conveyed to Vico, although he might reasonably have considered it far more subversive than the *De iure belli et pacis*, by which Vico had profited so greatly, but which had been placed upon the "Index expurgatorius." A third edition was published in 1744, but Vico was nearing the end of his life, and the notes and additions inserted by his son Gennaro rendered this edition obscure and worthless.

In 1735, at the instance of the principal chaplain of Charles of Bourbon, Vico was appointed royal historiographer. But favour had come too late. There is a deep melancholy in the closing scenes, which have been described for us by a devoted pupil named Solla. Although tortured by disease and far advanced in years, Vico continued to lecture on rhetoric and to give private instruction. "The throng of young men at his lectures was innumerable. He did not confine his teaching to mere precepts of rhetoric, but sought to broaden the minds of his hearers by apt illustration and instruction in general knowledge." "He taught," says his pupil, "tutto lo scibile." In his very dejection Vico preserved his greatness of character. His devotion to duty was complete, and the pupils whom he instructed at his house benefited by his great erudition and were carefully trained to think and to act worthily. On January 20, 1744, he passed away whilst attempting to repeat one of the psalms. His friends and all the learned, says Solla, deeply regretted him, enmity was put aside, and envy hushed in the recollection that Italy had lost a great citizen.

Vico was of medium height, his features clear cut and somewhat aquiline. To his hasty temper was due much of the animosity he excited, but the latent fire of his nature was also a force which urged his genius forward, with splendid perseverance, towards the accomplishment of his task. If, in his weaker moments, quick outbursts of indignation afforded his adversaries a pretext for vilification, they were but indications of a strength of will which made it possible for him to bear up against "outrageous fortune."

Like Buckle, like Rousseau and many distinguished men, Vico had not enjoyed the advantages to be derived from following a regular course of studies. The fact is apparent upon the face of his writings. Their profundity and originality are, no doubt, greater than they might have been, had his mind been trained to conform to recognized literary precepts; but much of the obscurity of his thought must be attributed to his not having passed through any organized curriculum, and it can hardly be doubted that the involved style which rendered many of his writings unpleasant to read, and hindered his being duly appreciated by his contemporaries, was largely due to the same cause. Vico has been accused of servility, and the charge cannot be said to be unfounded. His speeches, letters and biographies teem with overdrawn expressions of adulation. "Tam bonus erat laudator," says a contemporary, "ut immortalitatem donare posse putaretur." It is well, however, before passing judgment on him, to remember that to one of his lowly origin nobles and prelates must have appeared very great folk, and that it was only through their favour that he could hope to obtain a hearing at a time such as that in which he lived. His praise was often merely an ornate expression of gratitude, and to his countrymen cannot have sounded so excessive as to a less imaginative race. Let it be added, also, that no laudation was directed to the furtherance of a shameful end, nor to the stifling of what he believed to be true.

Although a tradition which is traced to Genovesi, a contemporary of Vico, ascribes the obscurity of his style to desire to conceal the heterodoxy of his opinions, the suggestion may be safely rejected in view of his manifestly religious spirit, and of the fact that he enjoyed the friendship of the ecclesiastical authorities, including even the censor himself. Vico's opinions contained much which the Church might fear, but, whether he was himself aware of their character or not, his good faith is unmistakable.

As has been said, Vigo was imbued with a reverent spirit, his mind turned around deep religious convictions. Nothing is more strange than the frankness with which he accepts the adage "Multa sunt vera secundum philosophiam sed non secundum theologiam." Affirming propositions which had been hitherto regarded as contradictory to Scripture, Vico brushes the difficulty aside with the remark that his opinions relate to Gentile and not to Jewish history. In one to whom the human aspect of the Bible was unknown, such language is not, perhaps, so strange as it may seem to a modern ear, but the inconsistency of this position is best accounted for by the reflection that Vico was entirely unconscious of the subversive tendency of his historical method.

Vico's Teaching.—The teaching of Vico did not result in the formation of a distinct school of philosophy, as did that of Descartes and Locke; but during his lifetime and for a short period after his death, his admirers in Naples and even in the Northern Italian cities were both numerous and zealous. In the *Biografia degli uomini illustri di Napoli*, Martuscelli relates that Vico's house was the rendezvous of all the literary men of the time; and Romano, a contemporary critic, states that he feared to publish his work controverting Vico's historical opinions because of the number of the latter's adherents and of their strongly partisan feeling. "A great part of our city would," he says, "have supported Vico against any opponent." The same critic tells us that the "Vichiano," or fanatical Vico scholar, quickly became a type in which devotion to the master was not always equalled by general intelligence. Some there were, of these scholars, who would read nothing which Vico had omitted to explain. Such elements as these, although they help to show the attraction exercised by an original mind, were hardly calculated to form the nucleus of a new system. A wider sphere of development presented itself in the North, and the interest which Vico excited at Venice, where the trammels of literature were less tightly drawn, made it seem for a while that his ideas had fallen on good ground. But the times were out of joint. Italy had ceased to take a prominent place among the thought-producing nations, and the hope of Vico to renovate her and win her a place beside Holland and Germany demanded the accomplishment of a task which was not to be completed before the lapse of more than a century. The greatness of Vico itself explains his failure. "He had," says Michelet, "forgotten the language of the past, and could speak only that of the future." When his speculations were at last made known to the nineteenth century their worth was, in many instances, no longer recognizable, because they had ceased to rank as discoveries. The first movement towards a better appreciation of Vico took place in Lombardy at the opening of the nineteenth century. A number of Neapolitan exiles published at Milan some critical essays on the system of their distinguished countryman, and there rapidly came into being a new growth of Vico literature which spread beyond the Alps when, in 1807, Wolf published a mongoraph in reply to the charge of having borrowed his Homeric theory from the *Scienza Nuova*. The publication of Niebuhr's *Römische Geschichte*, in 1811, brought Vico into still greater prominence, when it was pointed out that there was a remarkable resemblance between the view of early Roman history there propounded, and the almost forgotten hypotheses of the Neapolitan philosopher.

The final impulse, to which the complete recognition of Vico is undoubtedly due, was given by Michelet, who, in 1827, published a translation of the *Scienza Nuova* and of some of the minor works, accompanied by a very eulogistic introduction, in which the great historian's youthful zeal has, perhaps, led him to display too freely the enthusiasm of a discoverer. From thenceforward the attention of eminent men has in many countries been directed to the study and elucidation of Vico. Cousin, Mill and Mancini were acquainted with the theories of the *Scienza Nuova*. Special studies on Vico have at intervals appeared in French, German, and English, and although M. Penjon, writing in 1888,[1] declared " comme la mode était venue, elle a passé," if we judge from the fact that, in almost every succeeding year, new students of Vico have appeared, we may reasonably believe that his fame is not dead nor even diminished, but that the poor Neapolitan professor, whom a contemporary satirist pictured,

"Stralunato e smunto
colla ferola in mano,"

has survived failure and at last come by his own.

We have now described in their broad outlines the age in which Vico lived and the vicissitudes of his life and writings. It remains to give a brief account of his opinions, to point out their value, and so to place ourselves in a position from which we may judge of his comparative worth.

[1] *Revue Philosophique*, 1888, xxv.

The earliest of Vico's philosophical writings are, as has been said, his Academic speeches. He did not himself attach any permanent value to them, and even regretted having published the only one which was printed before the nineteenth century. They have, however, considerable interest both as furnishing the earliest indications of his mature opinions, and because they show the methods of study which he advocated and, to a considerable extent, himself followed. The Orations are six in number, and are composed in a clear style. The first deals with the importance of introspection. The Delphic inscription $\gamma\nu\omega\theta$ $\sigma\epsilon\alpha\upsilon\tau o\iota\nu$ is represented as the beginning of all wisdom. Self-knowledge leads to the knowledge of God. The dignity of human nature is shown by the fact that the heathen gods were personifications of human attributes. The proper study of mankind is man, and by developing his mind he fulfils the fundamental law of his being and attunes himself to the Divine purposes. The struggle between the dictates of wisdom and man's perverse tendencies is dwelt on in the second Oration. The Divine reason generates the world of realities, and by exercising his reason alone can man have knowledge of that world. Wisdom and virtue are in themselves identical.

In the third Oration the functions of literature are indicated and the enormity of their abuse insisted upon. The consciousness of ignorance is the mark of true learning. Vico teaches in the fourth and fifth Orations that an altruistic ideal should govern the pursuit of science, that the seeker after knowledge should emulate the Divine goodness in promoting the common welfare. He advances a remarkable argument to prove that war is connected with literary activity, and that both phenomena have, in fact, usually synchronized. This is the earliest of Vico's historical generalizations. The sixth and last Oration, published under the title *De ratione studiorum*, may be looked on as forming, in certain respects, an introduction to Vico's later works. As appears from the Autobiography, the attention of Vico was directed, on his return to Naples, to the Cartesian philosophy and to what he came to consider its fundamental error. Vico was unable to appreciate the causes which had brought the scholastic philosophy into disrepute. His education had kept him apart from the action of the forces that led the seventeenth century to embrace so readily the universal doubt of Descartes. To most of his contemporaries severance from the past and total rejection of its authority seemed the only rational means by which to emancipate the mind and initiate an acceptable system of thought: to Vico, steeped as he was in the wisdom of the ancients, and with his unqualified admiration for Roman Jurisprudence, Descartes' pretension seemed a mere madness, capable of causing, if accepted, irreparable loss. In the *De ratione studiorum*, therefore, he proposes to discuss this fundamental question of method, and to show cause why the principles of the *Discours sur la méthode* should be repudiated in any sound system of education. He was aware of the service Descartes had rendered by asserting the importance of individual judgment (*vide* Answer to a criticism of his *De antiquissima sapientia*), but the assertion that to know Latin was to know no more than Cicero's servant seemed to one of Vico's temperament to betray a total lack of the historical sense. The discovery of the application of algebra to geometry might ultimately lead to that of the differential calculus, but even were Descartes able to construct the world out of motion and extension he could not reconstruct its wisdom, the accumulated product of ages. The attempt to confine instruction to the mathematical and kindred sciences, to dispense with the study of subjects in which merely moral certitude is attainable, cannot be justified, for it fails to take into account man's proper nature. Vico perceived the truth of the rule governing all modern education, which was afterwards more clearly enunciated by Pestalozzi, that the method and order of instruction should be adapted to the natural course of intellectual development. The early study of abstract science is wrong because it fails to call into play the powers that are strongest in childhood. Although Vico must have disapproved Bacon's scant respect for Aristotle and his doctrines, he was at one with him in insisting on the reform of scientific method, on the importance of observation and experiment in natural science, and he desired this oration to be regarded as the complement of the *De augmentis scientiarum*. The analytical method of study Vico maintains to be logically out of place when the mind has not been already stored with an adequate knowledge. Topic must precede criticism. The hope that the secrets of nature might be unlocked by the mathematical reasoning of the Cartesians had led to the abandonment of practical research. Ethics and politics had ceased to be seriously taught. These are merely examples of the evils which result from the employment of defective method. The argument then proceeds to seek confirmation from the history of Roman law, and the discussion is ended by an apology for the vastness of the subject undertaken. Rhetoric, in the true sense, is concerned with all wisdom.

The point of view of the writer of this discourse is, as has been seen, essentially that of a teacher. The difficulties Vico had encountered in pursuing his own studies had, no doubt, impressed on his mind the practical rather than the philosophic view of the importance of method. His criticism of Descartes is necessarily crude, because he was but ill acquainted with that philosopher's opinions, and appreciation of the immense importance of Descartes' mathematics could hardly be expected in a publicist who declared that he had not succeeded in crossing the *pons asinorum*. The *De ratione* is, however, notwithstanding its obvious limitations, based on sound educational principles. The broad grounds on which Cartesian doubt is rejected are acceptable at the present day, and the necessity of providing an education before all things practical is one that has gained universal recognition. "Men must not be taught," said Vico, in one of his letters, "as if they were destined to enter a world composed of lines, numbers and algebraic symbols!" Such common-sense views were rare in the eighteenth century.

The prominence given in the *De ratione* to the study of jurisprudence is an indication of the importance Vico attached to it. The insight into the past which a knowledge of Roman law must bring with it, was, in his opinion, sure to create that sense of human solidarity which is of the essence of wisdom. Jurisprudence was, therefore, the most indispensable of studies; it was the foundation on which Vico subsequently reared the structure of historic criticism. Before dealing with Vico's works on jurisprudence it will be necessary to briefly refer to a book intended to form part of a philosophic treatise which Vico did not live to complete. The *De antiquissima Italorum sapientia*, more usually known as the *Liber metaphysicus*, led to a long controversy immediately after its publication, and it constitutes in many respects a strange anomaly in the development of its author's mind. The science of language may be said not to have existed before the foundation of the Asiatic Society of Calcutta. The systematic study of all languages, with a view to ascertaining the rules that govern their formation and development, has been undertaken in times comparatively recent: the task would have been fruitless until a knowledge of Sanskrit made it possible to see the underlying unity of European languages. The immense strides that the new branch of knowledge has made since Sanskrit became part of university curricula render it difficult for us to appreciate the attempts made in previous times to deal with the phenomena of language. Vico proposed, in writing the *Liber metaphysicus*, to discover the principles of a primeval philosophy by studying the origins of Latin words. The belief in prehistoric wisdom was not a new one. From the Hebrew story of the Fall down to the belated lucubrations of Mr. Gladstone, there has been a steady flow of contributions to this attractive subject. Vico's attention was first drawn to it by the *De sapientia veterum* of Bacon. But the end he had in view was different, as it was from that of the *Cratylus* of Plato, from which he professed to draw much of his inspiration. The importance of etymological studies may have been brought home to Vico by his acquaintance with Roman law. The theory clung to for a thousand years, that the letter of the law must remain unimpaired, that the quasi-sacred structure of the Twelve Tables contained the whole law—*finis æqui iuris*—cannot have failed to impress on a mind, already imbued with veneration for the past, a keen sense of the wisdom of the ancient world. Worship of the past is a common creed among scholars. In thus founding a philosophy on the study of the past, Vico, no doubt, also sought to find a solid ground on which to make a stand against the inroads of Cartesianism. To an adversary who could establish on an historical basis the whole of human knowledge, it were folly to oppose the all-sufficiency of individual experience. Although the entire fabric of the *De antiquissima sapientia* had to be definitely abandoned when Vico wrote the *New Science*, it may be useful to note a few of the main positions of the early work. The first and principal question which Vico proposed to solve was that of the origin and validity of knowledge. The Latins, according to Vico, held that that which is made is alone true. Complete truth resides only in the Divine mind. God has made all things, and contains them in Himself; hence His mind has entire knowledge of them. The mind of men, on the other hand, is outside created things, and is therefore unable to attain to any knowledge of them beyond what is purely superficial. Divine knowledge may be compared to a solid figure, human knowledge to a plane. Adopting the principle that nothing is knowable of which the cause is unknown, Vico denies reality to human knowledge which is not confined to the products of the mind. The *verum* must always be the *factum*, and nothing more. Reality is for us confined to abstract truth, the generation of our own mind. The logical outcome of this position is complete surrender to the Cartesians. Man is the god of his mental world of abstractions; beyond that world all is darkness and unreality. From the "*cogito, ergo sum*" to the complete certitude of mathematical truth, a universe of form and number, these are man's domain, but with them it ends. This test of truth was too artificial to bear examination. The fact that an idea is generated in the mind affords guarantee that it has its counterpart in the outer world. Yet Vico was led to use his criterium as an argument against scepticism, and to urge that the mere comprehension of causes was sufficient to establish the existence of Deity. By asserting the claim of metaphysical truth to rank before that of mathematics, Vico virtually ceased to maintain the validity of the text. Metaphysics is not a knowledge of causes as such, and it is only by abandoning the notion that *notitia rerum per causas* is the only reliable truth, and by relying like Fichte and Hegel, on an instinctive belief in the absolute, that the science of Being can be placed at the top of the scale of certitude.

The inconsequence of Vico's metaphysics was in great part due to the desultory character of his training, and to the fact that he was lacking in the clearness of mental analysis, without which metaphysics become a mere logomachy. His mind had not assimilated the store of notions he derived from Greek philosophy and from his immediate predecessors. To one not naturally moulded for such studies, confusion was the inevitable result. The doctrine of metaphysical points, erroneously attributed by Vico to Zeno of Citium, is treated in the *De Sapientia* in a characteristically confused and unsatisfactory manner. Against the Pythagorean view that everything must be reduced to a sum of points, Zeno the Eleatic had, by the argument from dichotomy, established the mathematical view that a point is merely position wihout magnitude. If a line be composed of points we must be able to say how many points it contains, but we can always divide a line into halves so that if it be made up of points there will always be more than any given number. The argument was one of many advanced by Zeno to prove the unreality of matter and motion and the falsity of the pluralist theories of the Pythagoreans, and was intended to accredit the pure monism of Parmenides. It served the same end as the celebrated puzzle of Achilles and the tortoise. The metaphysical point was, therefore, according to Zeno, a mere figment of the mind, and Vico's belief that he had propounded the doctrine of points betrayed grave ignorance of Greek philosophy. The fact that the Scholastics had represented Zeno of Citium as teaching that matter was ultimately composed of points no doubt led to the belief of Vico that the Zeno of his imagination had solved the problem of "the one and the many" by means of the doctrine of points. The great question as to how the absolute is related to the relative, or in other words how God has produced nature, had tormented the Greek mind, and it was now to receive its final solution by aid of an old conception applied in the light of revelation. The points are, according to Vico, unmaterial—they belong to the intelligible world, they are without material attributes, they, like the monads of Leibnitz, produce extension without being themselves extended, they are the essences or *virtutes* from which all things proceed. These points emanating from the Divinity are the *materia prima* of created things, the "form" of which is impressed on them by the Divine mind. Although Vico sometimes appears to regard the points as, like the substance of Spinoza, *ens per se existens*, he does not consistently do so, for he attempts to distinguish the Divine substance from that of which the points are composed; whilst, in other passages, he appears to suggest that the points are in reality one and indivisible, and he even boldly lays down in his *Risposta* propositions which, literally read, involve complete pantheism. The evident dangers of heterodox views led Vico to make a declaration of his adherence to the tenets of the Church, but the natural trend of his metaphysical speculations was undoubtedly towards pantheism, and the tardy insertion of a saving clause merely serves to accentuate the difficulty. Some of the positions taken in the *De sapientia* are purely Cartesian—*e.g.*, that nature abhors a vacuum; whilst, as we have seen, his metaphysics are strikingly similar to those of Leibnitz. The whole work teems with contradictions and confusions into which it is useless to enter, and nowhere has Vico attempted to furnish satisfactory evidence of his theories. So useless is his theory of points to serve as an explanation of the problem which he set himself, that he unconsciously drifts from it (as we have seen) towards pantheism. The *De sapientia* is undoubtedly the least original and the worst thought out of all the compositions of Vico. A striking testimony to this opinion is afforded by the fact that Mamiani claimed Vico as a sensationalist, Rosmini held him to be an idealist, and in the opinion of Gioberti his doctrine tended towards realism.

Vico and Jurisprudence.—We have now given a sufficient sketch of the earlier writings of Vico, and may proceed to a short exposition of his juristic and moral philosophy. Besides the fact that the legal side of the philosopher is of more direct interest, it should not be forgotten that his fame in wider fields of speculation is largely due to a profound study of Roman law, and to the broad grasp of the principles of historical development which a thorough acquaintance with both civil and canon law could alone enable him to attain to. The experience of Vico as a teacher and his ambition to obtain a chair of jurisprudence had probably some influence in determining the direction of his thought. In what appears to have been a purely fortuitous way, he came to read the *De iure belli et pacis* of Hugo Grotius. The book had been published in 1625, and had exercised a very profound influence in Europe. Gustavus Adolphus carried a copy with him in his campaigns, and so rapidly did the science created by Grotius assume importance that the Elector Palatine founded a professorship of International Law at Heidelberg within the lifetime of the Dutch jurist. Although the *De iure* was mainly practical in its aims, the fact that it presented a very broad and entirely novel view of a department of law unknown to the Roman world rendered it antecedently probable that the work would impress a speculative mind such as Vico's. It must undoubtedly have led him to enlarge his previous notions of the domain of law, and sharpened his perception of the principles which originate and govern the legislation of mankind. The conception that human nature is the mother of rights, *naturalis iuris mater quæ nos etiamsi re nulla indigeremus ad societatem mutuam appetendam ferret*—the belief in a common human nature governed by a social instinct, the οἰκείωσις of the Stoics—became a principle on which Vico built his philosophy of law and, eventually, his philosophy of history. True it is that, whilst expressing his indebtedness to Grotius, Vico thought he saw serious ground for criticizing him. As his own mind began to perceive the true nature of the historical method, the accumulation of authorities and the display of erudition in the *De iure* seemed less and less philosophic. It became apparent to Vico that the natural development of law must be dealt with in a fundamentally different manner. It is of course true that much of the criticism directed by Vico against the great work of Grotius is beside the point. The supreme importance which Vico attached to the primary source of legal principles may explain, but cannot justify, the reproach that Grotius, by severing theology from law, cut the latter adrift from its vital principle and deprived it of the power of fructification. In the eyes of modern science, and even in those of later eighteenth-century writers, the treatment of law as a self-contained subject marked a distinct advance in that department, and might be regarded as a manifestation and necessary consequence of the new spirit which, in wider fields of knowledge, had, since the seventeenth century, been substituting the idea of a natural order of things for the medieval conception of Divine intervention. It seems equally futile to detract from the merits of Grotius on the ground that he was insufficiently acquainted with municipal law and its historical basis. The statement, were it true, would not seriously compromise the theses which Grotius intended to establish. The work of Grotius is undoubtedly open to censure, both in point of style and of the absolutist character of polity which he approved. The strange view of natural law which, distinguishing *ius naturale simpliciter* from that *pro certo rerum statu*, led to the admission of slavery and the savage usages of warfare such as that of poisoned weapons, as sanctioned by natural law, may well be considered a more solid ground for unfavourable comment. The confusion into which Grotius seems to have fallen in affiliating positive law to laws of nature from which at the same time it derives its legitimacy and with which it may nevertheless be in contradiction, leaves, also, ample room for objection. The explanation of the unsatisfactory character of Vico's criticism of Grotius may, perhaps, be found in the fact that the aims of the two writers had little in common, and that whilst the jural speculations of the one were directed towards the elaboration of a philosophico-historical theory, those of the other tended towards an end primarily practical, and probably gained in force in direct proportion to their severance from speculative topics.

The influence of Pufendorf and Gravina on Vico seems scarcely traceable, although the former is frequently cited by him in a somewhat vague way, as are also Hobbes and Selden. But if there be a direct precursor of Vico in the department of law, it is clearly to Grotius that the honour is due. He was, for Vico, *iurisconsultus generis humani*. Professor Flint has ingeniously attempted to show that the historical method applied by Vico to the study of law and, in the *Scienza Nuova*, to that of the social cosmos, were derived, although illogically, yet by a natural sequence, from the arbitrary criterion of certitude laid down in the *Liber metaphysicus*. The restriction of knowledge to the truths which the mind has itself produced, and the consequent necessity, if an almost entire scepticism was to be avoided, of admitting a further field of mental activity, to which he gave the name of consciousness, resulted in confusion; but it also led, in the view taken by Professor Flint, to the great idea of a development of human thought and of the evolution of the moral world. The wide regions of belief, in which the arbitrary rule of *verum* and *factum* had no application, were, by a great rational process, contemporaneous and conterminous with the advance of science, gradually to be incorporated in the dominions of real knowledge, where they would be subject to no shadow of doubt. This notion, propounded by Vico at the expense of strict logic, may well have been the nucleus from which his later speculations derived their earliest origin.

Vico's principal work on law is entitled *De uno universi Iuris principio et fine uno*. A glance at its plan is sufficient to show that, in form at least, it is dominated by distinctly theological notions. Accepting the definition of the *Institutes*, "*iurisprudentia est divinarum atque humanarum rerum notitia*," Vico divides his subject into three parts: *i.e.*, the study (1) of the origin, (2) of the course, (3) of the subsistence of jurisprudence, and undertakes to establish the three propositions:

Origine, omnes a Deo provenire;
Circulo, ad Deum redire omnes;
Constantia, in Deo omnes constare.

He appears to have believed that this distribution of the subject-matter by reference to a theological conception was an integral part of the system he taught, but it may safely be assumed that such is not the case, and that the scheme is but an instance of the author's tendency to subdivide in an arbitrary and needless manner. The clearness of the work is also marred by the enunciation of principles or disjointed lemmata, the presence of which renders the legal and moral principles treated of unnecessarily obscure. If these peculiarities be overlooked, the doctrine of Vico in the *De uno* may be more readily explained. The fundamental position may be expressed in the proposition that the science of law is based both on reason and on authority, or, in other words, on philosophy and history. Philosophy brings to light the laws to which human nature is subject, and accounts for the causes of events. History bears witness to events, teaches the order in which they succeed, and the circumstances in which they may be expected to recur. Universal jurisprudence is thus formed of three parts—" *coalescit expartibus tribus, philosophia, historia et quadam propria arte iuris ad facta accommodandi.*" A proof of the proposition is sought by Vico in the history of law in Greece and Rome. The principles of law had, among the Greeks, been of considerable importance in philosophical discussions. The branch of philosophy which politics treat of grew out of legal studies. It was intimately connected with ethics, and this again finds its principles in metaphysics, the fountain-head of pure wisdom—*hominis consummatrix*. Besides these teachers of law as an abstract science, there were, at Athens, a body of practitioners ($\pi\rho\alpha\gamma\mu\alpha\tau\iota\kappa o\iota$) who, confining their attention to pure practice, were acquainted only with recorded law and decided cases. The whole body of Attic law was familiar to them, but their knowledge was unreasoned and contemptible. The inevitable result of this separation of theory from practice was that law as an art, *iuris ars*, did not exist in Greece. The rational application of broad legal principles to the facts of particular cases was impossible alike both to the pure theorist and to the pragmatist. When the question at issue was mainly one of fact, it was argued according to the precepts of rhetoric; where one of law, the pleader, without regard to the righteousness of the cause, invoked indiscriminately the written law or the precepts of philosophy.

The Romans show us an entirely different state of things. The free spirit of the people had engendered broad views and a love of their country which placed the public welfare before private interest. For the Roman, experience in a succession of responsible offices took the place of theoretical training; the worship of the gods that of metaphysic. The Patrician magistrate was, at once, legislator and jurisconsult. Schooled in civic wisdom, acquainted with the underlying reason for the law and accustomed to determine its application, the early citizen of the metropolis of law combined in himself the philosopher, the pragmatist and the Greek rhetorician. This state of things did not long endure. Before the first Punic war Tiberius Coruncanius began to give systematic legal instruction to the Patrician youth. His teaching marked the inception of Roman jurisprudence *doctrina propria Romanorum*. This early form of instruction, intended as a preparation for service in the magistrature, dealt with law from the political point of view (*ratio civilis*). It was not till the Empire had spread civilization over the world, that law, tinged with humanitarianism, and by adopting the principles of equity, became truly *iusti atque iniusti scientia*. A third source of law, independent of history and pure philosophy, is to be found in the etymological study of legal terminology. The jurisconsult was, in Rome, the eminently wise man, familiar with all things, Divine and human. For us, however, in the opinion of Vico, Roman law is not final—we are furnished with another guide in Reason. The idea of our power, our knowledge and our wishes (*Nosse, velle, posse*), guided by the light of revelation, affords us the principal means of attaining to universal justice. It is the human conscience reflecting Divine light, that is represented in all legislation which really embodies the rules of immutable justice. In order to attain perfection the true jurisconsult must, therefore, keep before him the principles of philosophy as well as the positive law which they underlie, and he must, above all, strive, by a study of events and monuments, to discover the origin of legal principles and the manner in which the various ages have regarded them. This combined method is the true key to jurisprudence; it avoids the endless contradictions to which all other methods have led, and it alone affords a means of reconciling Christian precept with the systems of antiquity. Man is a fallen creature, he possesses in his degraded condition vestiges of the perfection which was his before the Fall. By striving to win back some of the good he has lost and overcoming mere animal instincts, much may still be retrieved with the Divine assistance.

These semi-theological conceptions do not greatly influence the subsequent argument of the *De uno*, which proceeds in a singularly modern spirit.

The problem of the origin of society and social polity is to us less attractive than it was to the writers of the seventeenth and eighteenth centuries. It was a prevalent belief among them that, should they succeed in discovering the origin of society, its formative influences and earliest tendencies, that knowledge would be of the very greatest value, since it would enable them to lay down the rules of the science of government, and perhaps to predict the ultimate end to which mankind may aspire. Although we no longer believe that results so far-reaching can be thus obtained, and therefore attach far less importance to these studies, yet when we reflect that, with all our modern progress, our ideas on the origin of society are as dim and may turn out to possess no more finality than the theories of Hobbes or of Rousseau, it is natural that we should examine the earlier speculations and compare them, with interest, to our own.

The modern question as to whether society was first formed by voluntary aggregation of many families or by the natural expansion of one, may be said to be the political aspect of the problem as to what were the motives which actuated its members. To the latter Vico attempted to give the answer. Man in a state of isolation and ignorance suffers from a twofold need. On the one hand his feeble mind requires the support of those of his fellow-creatures in order to arrive by intercourse at some modicum of truth. On the other his fragile body cannot, alone, hope to struggle successfully against the blind forces of nature. The first of these requirements supplies the spiritual basis of society; the second its material foundation. If this supposition be sound, society may be defined as an exchange of utilities—*utilitatum communio*—mental and material, and the function of law will be to secure justice in such exchange. To the Roman precept *Bona fide agito* we may add as a necessary corollary *Ex vero vivito*. Society, aided by the legislator, aims thus at our perfection, moral and material, and it is necessarily governed in its aim by these two precepts. They are inseparably correlated; for who can be honest in his dealings if he be morally depraved, or morally honest if his acts be unjust? That reason alone bears out these principles is shown by their expression in the *præcepta iuris* of the *Institutes*. To attain to a complete justice, it is necessary, however, according to Vico, to superimpose on these purely rational rules the Christian law of charity—*in omnes hominis præ Deo charitatem*. To injure no one is not complete justice; its natural complement is service of our neighbour, in act and thought. To give our neighbour his due is but a partial fulfilment of the law, if that due does not comprise all things necessary for the perfection of his existence. These principles led Vico to enunciate two rules which may at first sight seem inadmissible. The first—*Lex summæ necessitatis*—sanctions in case of urgent necessity an inherent right in every man to preserve his life by taking the property of another even against the will of the owner. By the second—*Lex innocuæ utilitatis*—every man has the right to use and even to abuse the property of another, if he profits by so doing and the owner thereby suffer no loss. As rules of everyday conduct these rights might no doubt be open to serious question. M. Franck[1] has pointed out that the second rule is inconsistent with the current definition of ownership, and would in many cases imply the right to do violence to an owner's wishes. With regard to the first he objects that such a right would destroy the virtue of charitable acts, which would no longer be voluntary, and that no limit can be assigned to the necessity which would justify spoliation. Such objections lose force when it is remembered that Vico's object is to determine the conditions of a pure distributive justice, putting aside, for the purposes of his argument, all considerations of mere expediency or practicability. The conception of ownership we have formed is the result of a vast historical experience, and is, like all positive law, moulded by the exigencies of social life. It may not, therefore, perhaps be theoretically perfect. The Christian obligation of charity, again, is not dependent on charitable acts being unsanctioned by the law of the land, nor is it any ground against necessity as a justification for despoiling another of his property, to point out that the necessity may be hard to establish, as might be alleged against the justifiability of self-defence. From the eloquent judgment of Lord Coleridge in *R.* v. *Dudley* (L.R., 14 Q.B.D., 273), it appears that even the question whether necessity may justify the taking of another's life—his most precious possession—is one (at least morally speaking) not entirely removed from discussion.

Since the end of society is an exchange of utilities in a just proportion, and the function of law is to secure that this proportion be maintained, two broad divisions of legislation may be naturally distinguished. Equalizing justice (*iustitia æquatrix*), comprising the law intended to maintain equality of rights between persons subject to the same duties, embraces the whole civil law. Distributive justice (*in distributionibus regnat*) deter-

[1] *Journal des Savants*, Mars et Avril, 1861.

mines the apportionment of rewards and punishments. It is grouped together as penal law, and its principles stated as follows. The sanction provided by nature for the safeguard of rights lies in the moral conscience and the pangs of remorse to which she has subjected their violator. Habitual depravity lessens, however, the acuteness of these pangs, and it is for the purpose of inflicting on the wrong-doer the necessary supplement of suffering that the legislator subjects him to bodily pain (*ipsis est ferme peccandi necessitas*). Other motives for punishment would degenerate to mere vengeance or tyranny. Keeping the basis of penalty before us, it becomes clear that the legislator would be unjustified in punishing acts which are harmful to the wrong-doer alone, the " reflective offences " of Bentham. Conscience is here a sufficient deterrent. He must likewise make his aim coincide with that of conscience, which is the amendment of the culprit, and where that amendment is hopeless his duty is confined to safeguarding society ; he cannot gratify its desires of vengeance. "The least excess," says Bentham, "consecrated to the sole object of vengeance would be pure evil." The doctrine is as old as the *Gorgias* of Plato.

Civil law is, according to Vico, comprised in three divisions : "Dominium," or the right of dealing with things ; "Libertas," that of living unimpeded ; "Tutela," that of protecting oneself or one's interests. Of these rights the civil personality is composed, and they are each of them an essential part of it. If our existence be hindered we cannot enjoy ownership ; if we be deprived of our property our liberty is useless. If we be unable to protect our liberty and our property they are both of them equally illusory. The liberty of man is part of his constitution. The natural exercise of his faculties, his will and intelligence, or the moral instinct which tells him *recta agere est necesse, vivere non est necesse*, demands that he shall be free to act. The admission of liberty as an innate prerogative of man logically entails the recognition of property. The body is meant to obey the mind, for it cannot act alone ; and in the same way material things fall naturally under the dominion of reason, the supreme arbiter of things created. "Tutela," the right of protection, is equally well founded. The senses protect the body, reason protects the rashness of instinct, and the self-conscious soul guards her own sanctuary. The duty of positive civil law is to protect these three rights and to obviate their abuse. When we turn from theory to the world of history, we, in fact, find that the principles thus rationally deduced have been slowly evolved from age to age, and, under the pressure of outward circumstance, found expression in the existing social order. Where these principles have been misunderstood and a false growth has consequently taken place, the institutions evolved contain in themselves the germ of dissolution; they must inevitably pass away.

It will be seen from the foregoing sketch of Vico's system of origins that the theory of the Social Compact is left entirely out of account. That theory, which, although its ultimate development in Spinoza and Rousseau was due largely to the desire to supply a theoretical apology for resistance to the abuse of power, was based in its origin on a political truism which Vico would doubtless not have hesitated to admit. That Society implies the consent of at least a majority of its members cannot be reasonably gainsaid. Aristotle's notion of the State as a κοινωνία implies his recognition of the fact, and it is equally involved in the transition from the *status ex lege* of the *De Uno* or the *stato ferino* of the *Scienza Nuova* to the most rudimentary form of a common life. Vico, however, was not led astray, as were so many authors of the age, by the attractive simplicity of a theory which remained plausible only if all but one of the integrating influences to which primitive man was subject were overlooked. Whilst recognizing the fact that the wish to form a community must be supposed present in the minds of its founders, however barbarous, he did not admit that such wish and consequent consent were the determining influences.

Man in his primeval condition was, according to Vico, far lower than the angels; he bore a far closer likeness to the post-simian species of Darwin. The whole picture presented to us in the *De Uno* and in the *Scienza Nuova* bears, in fact, a striking resemblance to that drawn by Huxley and the evolutionist school. The primitive family of Vico is, broadly speaking, the cyclopean family of modern sociology.

The substance of the *De Constantia Jurisprudentiæ*, the sequel to the *De Uno*, is incorporated in the *Scienza nuova*. It will therefore be sufficient and convenient to refer to it incidentally in speaking of the latter work. Our remarks will be confined to a succinct statement of the general scope of Vico's principal treatise and of some of the more important questions arising out of it.

The *New Science* is an extremely difficult book to analyze.

Encumbered with strange and often grotesque illustrations of historical doctrines, uncouth in language, eccentric in turns of thought, and, in most editions, badly printed, the *magnum opus* of Vico presents an aspect so forbidding that nothing less than originality of the highest order can explain its survival and frequent republication. Its formal defects are attributable, in part, to the speed with which Vico wrote—he prepared the second edition in four months—and in part also to his disregard for purity of language. In many letters are found expressions of his contempt for lexicons and current works of reference. His method seems to have been to meditate long and carefully and then to hurriedly commit the result to paper, under the pressure of an intellectual fervour which a contemporary describes as akin to the *furor poeticus*. Corrections, when he made them, related invariably to the substance of his work, and rendered it more obscure than before.

Vico and History.—In spite of the scholastic stamp of Vico's philosophy, some of his modern admirers have claimed him to be a positivist. Professor de Luca, in his *Dinamica delle Forze sociali*, has a chapter entitled " Vico e Comte," and an introduction to a recent reprint of the *Scienza nuova* is devoted to showing its persistent positivism. The points in which our author is supposed to betray his positivist tendencies might be more aptly indicated as proof of the modernity of his temper. Prominent among them is his historical scepticism, which raised a storm of protest among his contemporaries. Although Vico had found the methodic doubt of Descartes repugnant, and had devoted a considerable part of his dialectical skill to showing its absurdity in philosophy, in his historical studies the preliminary rejection of traditional beliefs is so absolute that he might be thought a disciple of the French philosopher. No writer prior to Vico had attempted to question the general credibility of early history and tradition to an extent at all comparable with that to which he went in the *Scienza nuova*. There had, of course, been critical treatises on special documents or dealing with the traditions of particular nations.

The *Declamatio* of Lorenzo Valla successfully exposed the forgery of Constantine's donation. The efforts of Gerard Jan Vossius and Pico della Mirandola to unite in a harmonious design Christianity and the fables of classical antiquity may, perhaps, imply an intelligent distrust in the surface meaning of history.

Later, Heinrich Loriti began a series of attacks on the accepted accounts of early Rome which the Dutch historians of the seventeenth century vigorously continued. But the radical criticism of Vico went much farther. The result of his views was to sweep away the entire body of traditions which had been accepted as the true account of human affairs anterior to the Peloponnesian and the second Punic Wars. "Thucydides," he says, "informs us that, up to his father's time, the Greeks knew nothing about their own past. What, then, could they know of the past of the Barbarians, they who, alone, have made it known to us, and what shall we think of the past of the Romans, a people wholly preoccupied with agriculture and war, when Thucydides makes us this confession in the name of the Greeks who so early became philosophers?"

"Livy," he adds, declares that after the second Punic War, "he will write Roman history with greater certainty," but even then that historian is in doubt as to many important matters. "All that has come down to us concerning Pagan antiquity previous to the times we have indicated is uncertainty and obscurity. We do not therefore hesitate to boldly enter into it as into an unowned field which belongs to the first occupier (*res nullius quæ occupanti conceduntur*). We shall not fear to infringe the rights of anyone when, in treating of these matters, we shall not agree with or shall even be opposed to, the opinions hitherto accepted as to the origins of civilization." These bold declarations forcibly recall the proposal of Descartes to empty the mental "apple-basket." It is, of course, true that the critical attitude of Vico towards the Bible was in marked contrast with the freedom he displayed in dealing with profane writings. Most of his apologists, and especially his countrymen, have attributed this singular conservatism to political or other ulterior motives. Signor Pio Viazzi, for instance, writes that Vico's profession of orthodoxy "ha quasi sempre tutta la forma di un voler parere più che altro." Passages in this *Scienza nuova* have been pointed out in which Vico appears to recognize the artificial character of the hard-and-fast distinction he professed to see between the history of the Hebrews and that of other peoples. When he says that "poetry was the earliest method of expression among all peoples, including the Jews," or when he seems to entertain a doubt as to whether the Jews of the age of Abraham practised human sacrifice, these apologists see the half-suppressed wish of a free-thinker to submit the Bible to the rules of literary criticism. A simpler, and surely sounder, explanation of Vico's peculiar attitude may be found in the *milieu* in which he wrote. When the Pentateuch was still regarded as the oldest book in the world, when the spade of the excavator and the patience of the decipherer had not yet revealed the fact that the prophets and even Abraham lived in a world permeated with literary culture, when nothing was known of the progress in art and mechanical science made by the ancient empires of the East, the high literary development, the philosophic conceptions, and the moral enlightenment embodied in the Old Testament were sufficient, apart from the sanctions of ecclesiastical authority, to cause the history of the Jews to be looked upon as entirely *sui generis*, having nothing in common with that of the Gentile world. The eighteenth century had, of course, its Bayles and its Voltaires who were prepared to gibe at the inconsistencies of Scripture and to attack with ironical reverence the "respectable prejudices" of their times. But the object of such writers was political rather than literary. Like Candide, they felt that, primarily, they must cultivate their garden and help to pluck out the weeds with which society was overgrown rather than confine their efforts to the humble objects of mere scholarship. When they attacked the accepted historical interpretation of the Bible, it was because they, however mistakenly, regarded religion as the enemy of social reform, and not from any desire to furnish, in the light of advanced historical knowledge, a more acceptable exegesis. Hence the crudeness of Voltaire and the Deistic writers. Their criticism had no permanent value. It was not intended and could not therefore assist to form the essentially modern conception of the Scriptures with which we now are so familiar that it is hard to realize the standpoint of an age which was ignorant of their composite character, and which held it little short of blasphemous to admit that they had undergone change and revision.

The position of Vico towards the Bible was natural and almost unavoidable, because no rational view of it had as yet been suggested which a Christian might be expected to adopt. The very fact that Vico "shelved" the questions of Biblical interpretation, and did not attempt to furnish any explanation of Hebrew tradition, may, perhaps, indicate some suspicion on his part that the current method of dealing with the Bible was unsatisfactory.

He might readily have attempted an explanation on the teleological lines of the *Discours sur l'Histoire universelle,* or at least have proposed a method by which his philosophy of history might be "reconciled" with the coexistence of a separate Hebrew dispensation. This he did not do. His attention was absorbed by the vast fields of speculation in which he traced the story of the savage races which had not yet learnt to distinguish good from evil, and who were outside the process of Divine selection described in the Book of Genesis. It is not unreasonable to attribute to a man of his extraordinary historical intuition some glimmering of the true scope of the Bible and its historical value. The passages which are quoted to show that Vico did not really believe in the special character of the Bible ought more correctly to be regarded as manifestations of the independence of his thought and of the genius which, in many respects, made him so superior to the prejudices of his time. If the exclusion of sacred history from his plan led to contradiction, he was, we may believe, unconscious of the fact. His scientific instinct, if the expression be allowable, enabled him to put aside when necessary assumptions and prejudices which might have hindered his general conclusions.

" Der Mensch in seinem dunkeln Drange.
Ist sich des rechten Weges wohl bewusst."

The historical scepticism of Vico, like the methodic doubt of Descartes, was merely a clearing of the ground for the construction of his positive system. The conviction underlying the *New Science* was, in the words of Dr. Klemm, the most recent expositor of Vico, that " it is possible to represent the life of peoples in accordance with scientific principles, or to establish a general science of peoples " (*Völkerwissenschaft*). To create this science Vico thought, however, that the Cartesian contempt for erudition and its endeavours to build all knowledge on the facts presented by consciousness were quite inadequate. The science of peoples must avail itself of two distinct lines of investigation. It must rely on philosophy for absolute rational knowledge, for all truths which can be deduced from pure reason, but it cannot make fruitful use of the results of speculation unless at the same time it is acquainted with philology. By the latter term Vico understood all knowledge other than that derived from philosophy. History, literature, general experience, "la cognizione delle lingue e dei fatti dei popoli," compose philology, and are material for systematic study. By them the data of deductive reasoning are to be checked, and they in turn are to receive a new interpretation in the light of rational principles. Too great reliance on abstract ideas on the one hand, and the lack of a co-ordinating power on the other, were dangers which Vico believed could be obviated by his combined method of study. It is probable that the conception of this method was derived from his doctrine that history is the unfolding of the eternal idea of God. All external events lie, he believed, inevitably determined, in the Divine mind, and might be equally well known by us without observing their occurrence in time and space were we sure that our intelligence did not deceive us by allowing us to mistake figments of our own brains for a revelation of the designs of Providence.

It would be useless and difficult to describe the peculiarities and inconsistencies of this semi-Platonic doctrine. Suffice it to say that the notion of human development being an inevitable outcome of human nature—one of Vico's most fruitful ideas—and the metaphysical doctrine of the pre-existent Divine plan are constantly clashing in the *Scienza nuova*, so that the author is often driven to speak of Providence as if he meant merely the conception of Providence present in the thought of individual men. In other words, he sacrifices unconsciously the idea he adapted from the schoolmen in favour of his own original theory. Providence, instead of remaining outside the laws of social growth and imposing itself on the world of fact, became part of a human process influencing mankind from within. The variations in Vico's view of Providence afford good proof that, although he wore so many of philosophy's cast-off garments, he had begun in reality to think in a modern way.

In a note entitled *Tavola delle discoverte generali*, Vico summed up the main points which he claimed to have established in the *Scienza nuova*. One of them was "Una storia ideale eterna commune a tutte le nazioni." This idea of a "storia ideale" as understood by Vico was that on which sociology is based. Sociology, it may be said, is, in a sense, an attempt to write history briefly—more briefly than any record of events would permit. In analyzing recorded facts, in observing existent social phenomena, in classifying the results and attempting to state the conditions of social stability and social progress, sociology is but applying the method common to all the sciences, and, in proportion as the general formulas it lays down are found to cover facts hitherto unobserved, approaches more nearly to the condition of an exact science. To know that historical phenomena are never of a casual character, that general propositions may be deduced from them when rightly understood, is of fundamental importance for establishing a theory of human action. If sociology is possible—a supposition denied by many—if the gap in the scientific *Weltbild* where man stands, with his complex motives and actions, is to be filled up, it must be admitted that the conception of the succession of historical events as governed by fixed laws was one of the greatest thoughts which man has ever had. Vico was the first who gave clear expression to this thought. By "storia eterna" he meant an explanation of history by reference to universal historical laws. This was the central purpose of his great work, and he was justified in calling his science "new" as fully as any discoverer was ever justified in claiming originality. Darwin's theories were none the less new because the work of Lamarck and Saint Hilaire had helped towards their formation, nor is Lavoisier denied the merit of his chemical discoveries because Priestley had contributed to them. We may similarly recognize that Plato's *Republic*, the *De Civitate Dei* of Augustine, the *Discorsi* of Machiavelli, and possibly, Bodin and Campanella, helped in various ways towards the formation of Vico's conception of social law. The city depicted in the *Republic*, of which "perhaps in heaven there is laid up a pattern for him who wishes to behold it," Vico did not seek for, because he recognized that it was confined to the region of speculation, but with the thought of such a city in his mind, he was not improbably led by his belief in a Providence inherent in the earthly order of things to suppose that the apparent confusion and incoherence of history might in reality conceal the outline of an unknown Divine scheme. The frequent reference to Augustine found in the *Scienza nuova* renders it likely that the *De Civitate* had a considerable influence on Vico's historical speculations. No doubt the Providence of Vico was far removed from that which "rules and governs all earthly events, but of which we are not to question the justice, though we may not see its motives." The narrow dualism of the *gloriosissima civitas* and the *civitas terrena* was implicitly rejected by Vico when, as we have seen, he refused to enter into the conventional distinction between Jewish and Gentile history ; the attempt to fit preconceived theological notions into historical generalizations did not attract him. But these facts do not render it less sure that Vico's theory was helped by Augustine's conception of the Divine direction of human destiny and by his arguments against the Greek necessity and fortune as explanations of history. Machiavelli's doctrine of the essential depravity of human nature left no trace in Vico's speculations; the local bias everywhere traceable in *The Prince*, the advocacy which contributed so largely to the œcumenical fame of the Florentine politicist, have no reflection in the scientific detachment of the *New Science*. But when Machiavelli writes, "All things in the world, at all periods, have an essential correspondence with past times," when he systematically employs historical parallelism in the arguments of the *Discorsi*, he approaches appreciably to Vico's conception of historical law, and, in attempting to base his investigation on the common congenital character of man, seems to have partly seen the necessity insisted on by Vico, of establishing the psychological foundation of historical science.

It is interesting, in noticing writers whose influence on the *Scienza nuova* is apparent, to refer to a predecessor in the scientific study of history who, although he cannot have been known to Vico, seems to have anticipated him to a remarkable extent by more than three centuries. Ibn Khaldoun, whose ancestors had taken part in the Moorish conquest of Spain, died at Cairo in 1406. His passion for political intrigue made his life one of vicissitude. Sent on a diplomatic mission by the ruler of Tilimsaan, he tarried for years on the road in order to write his Prolegomena, the general part of *The Book of Examples* (Kitab-el-Ibar). The prose of this work is of the kind Matthew Arnold called *Asiatic*, and it is marred by lack of balance, but it contains a philosophy of the history of the Moslem peoples far in advance of anything in European literature prior to Vico.

"History," says Ibn Khaldoun, "has for its object to treat of the formation of social groups, of the conditions to which mankind is exposed, of the refinement of customs, of family and tribal feelings, of the idea of national superiority which leads to the founding of empire, and, finally, of the changes which the very nature of things impresses on the character of society. It is a self-contained science having for object civilization.... The part in which we deal with this topic contains a new science remarkable alike for originality and utility." These passages and such headings as " Of the differences of races, and of the countries which they inhabit "; " Of the forms of government of the Khalifate and *of such forms as are essential in every state,*" are sufficient to show how advanced were the tenets of the Arab writer.

With his conception of social law clearly in view, Vico proceeded to deal with problems which may be divided into two groups. In the first he attempted a critique of historical materials and an inquiry into the causes, the laws, and the ends of social development. In the second, he inquired into the psychic factors which are discoverable in all communities and have everywhere a common value—*e.g.*, language, myth, and custom. Few modern writers would approve of the importance Vico gives to the study of language and myth for the purposes of social science. They are too concerned with that aspect of change which Giddings characteristically described in the dictum, " Progress is at bottom an economic phenomenon," to give prominence to a philosophy of mental development. The modern ethical school of sociology is, nevertheless, following the example of Vico in its attempt to work out a theory of evolution from egoism to altruism, and it is, moreover, a fairly common proceeding in modern social science to try to explain a phenomenon— *e.g.*, interest—by the history of the word by which it is signified.

" Man," says Vico in the *Scienza nuova*, " has certainly made the civil world." Providence, immanent, as it were, in the human race, co-operated in the making, but, as has been seen, the " Provvedenza " of Vico bore little resemblance to the Providence of Bossuet's *Discours*. It is, in the *Scienza nuova*, a deduction and not a postulate, a generalization from the ideas found, by Vico, to underlie the whole of human history. When man emerged out of the darkness into which he was plunged after the flood, he bore upon him all the traces of the brutishness which his sins had developed in him. Without family, without form of speech—*mutum et turpe pecus*—a prey to wild impulse and illusion, the shaggy forest-dweller was led towards better things under the influence of two main factors—Force and Reason. At first the only right was that of the strong. The physically superior compelled the weak to labour for them, to hew wood and draw water. Physical superiority it was, too, which led to the suppression of promiscuous sexual intercourse; the strong man selected his mate and jealously guarded her from his weaker fellows. This was the earliest form of marriage, and with marriage the family came into existence, children of sure parentage to whom their father naturally hoped to transmit the fruits of his labour, his slaves and his lands. For Vico, as for Maine, " the power of the strong man was the principal formative cause of social progress." Inheritance implied division of land and the absolute power of its owner, *dominium*. But mere force, although so potent an agent, could not achieve the rudiments of civilization. Man's mind is moved to some sort of supernatural belief in all times and places. Vico is not consistent in explaining the origin of this belief. At times it arises, he says, from mere fear of natural forces; in terror of the thunder—"fu fantasticata una divinata in cielo che fulminasse." At others, the conception arises from man's realization of his own littleness or from conscience, "coscienza del' malfatto." But whatever its cause, the belief became a means by which man was civilized. Even when his perversity had led him to adore false gods, he, in his ignorance, attributed human passions to them, sought to know their will by auguries and to pacify them by prayer and sacrifice. His whole life became associated with the supernatural; marriage became a sacrament; wills were placed under the protection of the gods; the priest and the legislator were identified. It was because, in the beginning, the family, legal rights, and virtue itself were thus founded on religion that Vico called his system "una teologia civile ragionata." The persons who resorted to the practices of religion were, naturally enough, those who had profited by the exercise of superior strength and skill. He who already possessed a dwelling, a wife and a family, was the first to build an altar or a sacred grove where the unseen power might be propitiated, where the firstlings of his flock were brought as an offering. "I Padri come più sperimentati dovettero essere i Sapienti : come più degni i Sacerdoti : come posti in una somma potesta . . . i Re delle loro famiglie." Worldly wisdom, supernatural relations, and absolute temporal authority were the rightful prerogatives of the paterfamilias ; his despotic power was beneficent in its results. The savage passions of the group he held in subjection were curbed and mollified. After death his services were recognized, and he became the hero and the demigod. The medieval view of pagan mythology, according to which its gods were baseless myths, or, at best, incarnations of evil spirits, was false and shallow. The whole world of ancient fable is imbued with meaning and filled with real men. "We have in it the civil history of the earliest peoples," material from which to fashion a true conception of the mind and history of primitive man, whose mythopœic faculty is everywhere evident. The method by which he proposed to utilize mythology is, to a great extent, approved and followed by recent writers, but the fantastic interpretation of specific myths which we find in the *Scienza nuova* is liable to hide its substantial soundness. His attempts to show that the twelve great gods of Greece represent as many epochs of history, or that Juno, for instance, symbolized the history of marriage, are to us, of course, absurd, and we are surprised, when we have read it, to find him, nevertheless, as fully aware as any modern writer of the "automorphism" of primitive races : " L'uomo ignorante, cio che non sa, estima della sua propria natura."

Early languages were, Vico believed, to a great extent imitative in origin. Their subsequent development was brought about by an unconscious process, and their diversity he accounted for as follows : "Come certamente i popoli per la diversità dei climi, han sortio varie diverse nature onde son usciti tanti costumi ; cosi dalle loro diverse nature et costumi sono nate altrettante diverse lingue ; talche per la medesima diversità delle loro nature, siccome han guardato le stesse utilità o necessità delle vita umana con aspetti diversi, cosi son uscite tante lingue diverse." The same terrors which had led to the formation of the earliest religious belief caused man to give vent to his feelings by simple monosyllabic sounds. These, his first words, produced by a simple reflex action, gradually came to express all the simple feelings—grief, joy, expectation—by an unconscious process. "Spiegavano le loro passioni urlando brontolando fremendo : spinti da violentissime passione." On this basis of pure interjection was begun the building of ever-increasing verbal complexities. Proper names passed into common nouns and these into adjectives signifying abstract qualities : " Una nazione di mente cortissima non sa appellare una proprietà astratta, ossia in genere, ... ed ove vogliano dire diverse proprietà di due corpi di specie diverse, eglino uniranno in una idea essi corpi." The onomatopoetic character of great part of early speech was recognized by Aristotle. An objection to the doctrine is raised by Max Müller and other modern philologists. Before man can form any notion of an external thing he must perceive the impression it makes upon him, and this impression it is which he seeks to express by a mere cry and not by any sort of imitative sound. But it is argued, on the other hand, that since impression must reflect some quality inherent in the object that causes it, the word expressing the impression must also, to some extent, represent the external cause. Hence Vico was not perhaps wrong in giving the importance he did to onomatopœia. Poetry and song preceded prose. "Men, at first, feel without remarking the things felt; then they remark them but in the confused manner of a wild and primitive soul; in the end, enlightened by pure reason, they begin to reflect." Poetry, the mental vehicle of feeling, is earliest everywhere. When the new languages of Europe were forming, the poets were, once more, the earliest to make use of them. The early poets were creatures of such high imagination that they believed their own fancies, "Fingunt simul creduntque." This is the reason why so much of the earliest poetry conveys a strong impression to us. These views of Vico are sufficient to show the direction which his thoughts on language took. Although, as we have pointed out, it was impossible for him to arrive at any but very rudimentary notions as to the origin of language, he succeeded, here as elsewhere, in divining many truths only recently verified. His greatest merit consists in his having seen the importance of language as the earliest available storehouse of human history and in the way in which he approached its problems.

Herodotus attributed to the Egyptians the division of universal history into three periods: "la prima degli Dei, la seconda degli Eroi, la terza degli Uomini." Vico accepted this division, and to prove that the periods were contemporaneous in all countries he constructed a very arbitrary chronological table. The divine age, that of the primitive family, is described, as we have noticed, in the *Scienza nuova* with the assistance of the conceptions of Roman family law. The twelve tables merely registered a *de facto* despotism when they edicted: "Patrifamilias ius vitæ necisque in liberos esto." The name "family" would have been a misnomer in its origin unless we suppose it derived from *famuli* or the servants of the first *patres familias*. The transition to the second or heroic age was begun when the weak and the persecuted began to repair to the *aræ* of the strong, and were taken under their protection. The virtues developed in these *famuli*—docility and submission—were just those most needed for the future state in the governed classes. In process of time these *famuli* increased in numbers and began to acquire confidence in themselves. They forgot the old dread in which their masters had been formerly held, and no longer entertained feelings of gratitude for protection from dangers which they had not personally experienced. Finally, resentment against their enslavement reached the point of revolt, and they boldly claimed recognition of their rights and guarantees of future good treatment. But resistance, again, reacting on the masters, compelled them to combine and to select a chief under whom they might successfully oppose their rebellious dependants. This is the broad outline of the earliest inception of the state. In it are no longer found only family groups, but also opposing parties, class interest and, when a *modus vivendi* was established, also a rudimentary constitution whereby the striving classes secured the observance of the conditions of peace. In the forces which militated to create this new social unit, not by the action of any external agency, but, as he said, "ipsis dictantibus rebus," Vico saw the working of that Providence which is, at the same time, present in the human spirit, and, in a sense, identified with it, securing the conformity of social development to the basal laws of humanity. Its agency is manifest in what he called the "common sense of nations," the spontaneous expression of their common nature, "formed without reflection, felt by all the members of a class or of a people, or by all the human race." The importance of the "senso commune" appears also in the *De Uno*, where it is said to be "communem tuæ civitatis . . . prudentiam, qua id sequaris aut fugias, quod omnes tui cives . . . sentiunt sequendum vel fugiendum." The notion of a common human nature is of capital importance in the *Scienza nuova*. It was, of course, in itself by no means novel, but what had formerly been a mere expression of sentiment became imbued by Vico with a new significance when he used it to explain national growth and decay. Vico's "Völkerpsychologische Betrachtungen," says Dr. Klemm, "sind uns demnach zunächst ein eigenartiger Zug seiner Geschichtsphilosophie." It is, none the less, a fact that our author was the founder of *Völkerpsychologie* in the sense that he was the first to see the basis which it presupposes and to attempt the generalizations which it hopes to establish. Some of the *elementi* or general truth of mental history enunciated by Vico may be mentioned incidentally as examples of his sagacity and because they pervade the *New Science* throughout :

"Men first heed what is necessary, then what is useful; they afterwards seek successively comfort, pleasure, and luxury. In the end they abuse their riches."

"The character of peoples is first cruel, then severe, and, in turn, gentle, good-natured, inquisitive, and finally dissolute."

"Governments should be suited to the nature of the governed, hence knowledge of the people is the best acquirement of princes."

"Customs are more natural and, therefore, more powerful than laws." This opinion he explains more fully in the *De Uno*, where we are told: "Both customs and laws (*leges*) are the interpretation of the law (*jus*) of nature; but customs are the more secure interpretation since they are approved by existent circumstances, and, in the course of time, they disappear therewith: laws, even when better than customs, are always less secure, since they emanate from the changeable will of a legislator."

The early state, of the formation of which we have seen Vico's account, was of an aristocratic type. The king was merely *primus inter pares*, and the supreme power was in the hands of the assembly of chiefs, who had, as it were, delegated to it their separate family authority, their rights of private vengeance, and, at the same time, recognized the sovereign prerogative of the public power to deal with and, if necessary, dispose of their family patrimonies when the interest of the State required. This view is still, in general outline, that of modern writers. The earliest state of which we have any knowledge is, according to Freeman, "that of the single king ... ruling not by his own arbitrary will, but with the advice of a council of chiefs." The diversity of land tenure in the Middle Ages had its counterpart, according to Vico, in the commonwealth thus constituted. The lands granted by the chiefs to the revolted plebeians were held by a base or bonitary tenure similar to the *feuda rustica*; those of the chiefs themselves by quiritary or noble tenure, whilst over all lands there was the immanent right of the sovereign assembly of chiefs equivalent to that of the feudal king. The policy of the aristocracy was conservative because their interests were all opposed to change. Class privileges, religious rights, family authority, and legislation were reserved to the chiefs. Such a condition of things could not endure. The plebeian class, compelled to pay a tribute to the patricians, unable to transmit their land to their children because deprived of the *connubium* and without political power, at length once more revolted and extorted from their oppressors equality before the law. This marked the end of the heroic age. The system of law and custom which grew out of this establishment of a community of equals was better adapted to the practical needs of life, but the popular form of government inaugurated was soon transformed into monarchy, the inevitable latest type of constitution in the recurring cycle of history. It will be convenient here to mention the celebrated theory of the "corsi e recorsi." From the nature of its subject-matter, social science must have a theory to explain a shifting series of phenomena. Modern writers usually represent the course of political change as one of progress; Vico preferred the astronomical conception of movement in an orbit. Not content to apply his theory of the three ages to the history of antiquity, and persuaded of its universal validity, he asserted that it must also apply to the course of events subsequent to the fall of the Roman Empire. The attempt to establish this thesis was unfortunate, for although he did not assert absolutely complete repetition of events to have taken place—"identita in sostanza" but "diversita nei modi lor' di spiegarsi"—yet the difficulties of the argument drove him to evident sophisms and to historically baseless assertions.

The poets of the first cycle of history were, he said, represented in the second by the chroniclers; there was among the barbarians who peopled Europe a similar growth of languages, the same system of private justice and family religion. The heroic age was repeated in the feudal organization where the vassal held the place of the plebeian and did homage to his lord, whom he served in peace and war. When kingship had absorbed the feudal system and the Roman law of Justinian had spread through Europe, we had a second "human age," which Vico asserted to be most highly developed in the countries of his time where absolute monarchy was established. So strong was his desire to generalize this idea that he sought to apply it to countries of which he had practically no knowledge, and even asserted Japan and other Eastern countries to be in a state of development similar to that of Rome at the time of the wars against Carthage. All this may seem fanciful, but although, as we have said, the cyclical theory of history is generally abandoned, there are not wanting authors who, even at the present day, assert the existence of a law not unlike that of the *recorsi* whereby the substantial identity of certain social transformations with those of former time is inevitably determined. Gomplowicz is notably one of them. Although there are passages in the *De Uno* in which Vico appears to imply that monarchy is essentially better than other forms of government—" maxime naturæ conveniens "—it may be assumed that this was not his mature opinion. " Where," he says in the *Scienza nuova*, " there is doubt as to the character of a people they will be best governed in accordance with the nature of their surroundings (in conformità della natura dei siti) . . . in hot and stimulating climates after a manner different from that suitable to cold and slow-blooded peoples (di ottuso ingegno)." Such an opinion reminds us less of Aristotle's academic order of merit among constitutions than of the vigorous sentence of Macaulay : " A man who, upon abstract principles, pronounces a constitution to be good without an exact knowledge of the people who are to be governed by it, judges as absurdly as a tailor who should measure the Belvidere Apollo for the clothes of all his customers."

Monarchy, aristocracy, and democracy are, for Vico, all of them natural forms of government : each belongs to one or more stages of civilization, and works better than either of the others when a nation is in need of a particular set of advantages, or when its mood turns in certain directions.

The justifiableness of all governments is to be measured by the continuance of the cause to which they owe their existence. So long as the best and wisest men are secured in authority the government is legitimate and its transformation wrongful, however more symmetrical or more plausible its substance may appear. When the patricians alone possessed knowledge, capability, and organization, their rule was reasonable. When the lower classes had advanced in culture and their rulers no longer had any real superiority, but relied, for their political preponderance, on inherited privileges, the time had come when it was right and proper to depose them from power. Absolute monarchy is equally suitable in countries like those of the East, where a degenerate people without self-control, weakened by sloth and riches, bows the more readily before a despot because he arrogates to himself a discretion they are too dull to desire or too effete to exercise. When an energetic race has become self-conscious and developed the faculties of collective action, its need for a more popular form of constitution, in which its best elements may find room to expand, is as real as the physical requirements of the individuals who compose it. The trend of the transformation of nations is, however, in its essence decadent. The accumulation of riches, the refinement of social life, and class discord lead to the weakening of the body politic. At times the shattered machinery of state is put right by the iron hand of a Cæsar. But if the machinery is past repairing nothing can save from dissolution and anarchy but the rude repression of a foreign conqueror. The subjection of one people by another is justified and beneficial when it supplies a means for bringing back to the vanquished renewed power of political life; "he who cannot govern himself must allow himself to be governed by another..., the world will always be governed by those whose nature is superior."

The sound sense of these opinions is mingled with the despondent note of the "corsi e ricorsi," but, as may be seen, the idea of the recurrence of political history is not in reality essential to the spirit of the *Scienza nuova*, nor does it preclude the possibility of real and permanent progress. The strain of pessimism in the social speculations of Vico is due to a variety of causes. The degradation of the prehistoric past he had discovered, the disruption and downfall of the great institutions of Rome and of Greece which he had studied, the lawlessness of the Italy in which he lived, had all contributed to distemper his outlook on the future and to prevent him from duly appreciating the signs of serious improvement. When he expresses faith in the intentions of Providence, he does not seem to base it on the lessons his science had taught him, nor to realize that the instinctive belief in progress is, in his own phraseology, part of the *senso commune* of mankind, or, as we might put it, one of the best guarantees of its attainment.

A French critic has disparaged the political studies of Vico, as compared with those of Montesquieu, on the ground that he confined himself so exclusively to the examination of the institutions of Rome. It is true that the author of *L'Esprit des Lois* surveyed a larger field, but his attention to medieval history is due rather to his desire to indicate the right means of reforming the absolute monarchy of France than to his having a wider grasp of his subject than Vico.

Just as, in the region of ideas, the study of politics is still influenced by the speculations of Plato, Isocrates, and Aristotle, political facts are still taken by modern authors very largely from the records of Roman history. "If we were compelled to set aside the study of Roman law, our inquiry into the origin of law and of society would," says Maine, "be at once reduced, in great part, to vague conjecture." .The best proof that Vico did not commit an error in relying too much on Roman history is that he arrived at many of the best established conclusions of Montesquieu and later writers. He might, himself, have attempted to justify his method on the ground of the essential sameness of political evolution in all nations, a result of the "commune natura della nazioni." It was, of course, impossible for him to have any exact knowledge of the primitive indigenous races of Italy, deprived, as he was, of the assistance which his successors have derived from philological and archæological discoveries, but he made excellent use of the materials at his disposal. The importance of clearing up the origin and phases of the struggle between plebeians and patricians seems to have been as evident to him as to Niebuhr and Mommsen. In his account of the primitive nature of the *gentes*, in his opinion that the clients were, at first, identical with the plebeians, he is in agreement with Mommsen, although Niebuhr had differed from him. Later writers have not, it is true, agreed to the complete dismissal of the kings as pure myths. For them there is more reality in the Tarquins than in Romulus and Numa, but distinction is a characteristic of matured thought, and ought not to be expected in a pioneer.

One of the most remarkable and most successful of Vico's Roman researches was that into the origin of the "Twelve Tables." His conclusion that the statements of Livy, Pliny, and other classical writers were not to be relied upon, that the "Tables" were derived from the customary laws of the peoples of Latium, and not from Greek legislators, is now generally accepted. Vico gave all the strongest reasons that have been advanced to disprove the existence of a mission to Greece. He showed the contradictions in the story and pointed out that the similarities between Attic and Roman law are traceable to general causes and are insufficient to warrant belief that the one system borrowed from the other. But these conclusions, remarkable as they may be, are less important than the opening of new fields of discussion to which the controversies which arose out of them immediately led. Throughout Italy opponents and partisans of Vico quickly began to discuss his breach with tradition, and inquiry into early Roman law received a new impetus and began to take the direction which it has since followed. Freedom of debate was thus introduced by Vico into yet another branch of study.

In the second edition of the *Scienza nuova,* Vico devoted the third book to "the discovery of the true Homer." His inquiry into the origin of the Homeric poems has importance because he regarded it as a model of the proper treatment of early myths, and from the fact that many of his opinions are derived from the results with which it furnished him. Although so many Greek scholars readily accept Arnold's advice to the translator "not to go into the vexed question of Homer's identity," it is still a debated point whether the poems were written, or rather "edited," by a single author. For Vico, the true Homer was the Greek people itself. No one genius, but the spirit of the race groping in the secular struggle for national light and life, expressed its pains and its ideals in the *Iliad* and the *Odyssey.* The youthful exuberance of earliest Hellas appears in the *Iliad* with its Achilles, the demigod of Force and virile aggressiveness. Odysseus reveals no longer the same temper. In him is seen another order of virtues. Worldly wisdom and stratagem are more important than bodily strength, Calypso and Circe are less resistible. The second poem is unmistakably the product of a later age. Both are the work of many poets, but their fundamental difference in sentiment and style shows that the pieces united in the *Iliad* belong to a more remote age. The "true Homer" is thus the founder of Hellenic civilization, he is its first philosopher and historian, for early history was necessarily poetical, and poetry was but an idealized history.

Friedrich August Wolf refused to acknowledge that his Homeric theory had been anticipated by Vico. "Alles hat eher das Ansehen von Visionen" was hardly a fair verdict on the third book. It is, in fact, on Vico, and not on the German critic, that we should look as the originator of the modern view of Homer and of the true method of kindred *Quellenkunde.*

The preceding sketch of the principal contents of the *Scienza nuova* may help to show that it was one of the most remarkable books of the eighteenth century. In many respects, besides the points to which we have adverted, Vico foreshadowed the methods of modern writers. He saw, for instance, that valuable assistance might be derived from biology for the purposes of social studies, and illustrated some of his theories by reference to what was then known of savage races. But so much in his great work was novel, so many discoveries had to be made before his ideas could be tested and arranged, that it was impossible for him to do justice to his powers. Tradition has it that Vico sent a copy of the *Scienza nuova* to Newton. He wished, perhaps, that the author of the *Mathematical Principles* might know that, while the principle of universal gravitation had been discovered by an Englishman, an Italian had found that man in society, no less than matter, was subject to the action of ascertainable laws. Although Newton could not admit that Vico's "laws" were clear or unexceptionable in the same sense as the uniformities of nature, he may, nevertheless, have recognized that the attempt of Vico, abortive though it might be, was worthy of high praise. The progress of all knowledge is slow, and the saying of Wilhelm von Humboldt is especially true of social science : "Between the conception and the realization of an idea extend vast intervals of space and time."

A complete list of "Vico literature" may be seen in the *Bibliografia Vichiana*, by Signor B. Croce (Naples, 1904). The best and latest critique of Vico's ideas on social science is that of Dr. Otto Klemm in his *G. B. Vico als Geschichtsphilosoph und Völkerpsycholog* (Leipzig, 1906). An excellent general view of Vico is given by Professor Flint in the volume on Vico in Blackwood's *Philosophical Classics*.

CORNELIUS VAN BYNKERSHOEK

CORNELIUS VAN BYNKERSHOEK, the son of a merchant, was born at Middleburg in Zealand, May 29, 1673. He was educated at the University of Franeker, in Friesland, where he first studied the humanities and then the Roman law. His university career was a distinguished one; and he received the highest eulogy from the celebrated professor Huberus. Afterwards he settled at The Hague, became an advocate, began the preparation of a work on Dutch municipal law, *Corpus juris Hollandici et Zelandici*, and published various dissertations on Roman law. In 1702 appeared a study on the *L. ἀξίωσις* ix. *ff. de L. Rhodia de jactu*, immediately followed by his well-known *De Dominio Maris*, a work on the sovereignty of the sea, dealing with many important matters which had during the two preceding centuries aroused great controversy. Like Grotius, he did not remain at the bar. In 1703 he was appointed a judge of the Supreme Court of Holland, Zealand, and West Friesland, which sat at The Hague, and in 1724 became the President of that Court. His duties gave him an insight into the nature and customs of interstatal diplomatic relationships and a thorough knowledge of the usages and practical details of maritime international law. In 1720 he published his work on the rights and duties of ambassadors, *De foro legatorum*, and in 1737 *Quæstiones juris publici*, of which the first part, *De rebus bellicis*, considers the most vital questions relating to the international laws and customs of war. He died April 16, 1743.

An unfinished work, *Quæstiones juris privati*, appeared after his death. His various writings, which had attracted a good deal of attention, and had already begun to exercise much influence on the legal and political thought of the time, were collected by Vicat, the Professor of Jurisprudence at Lausanne, and published in 1761 at Geneva, in two folio volumes. The contents of these are as follows: Vol. i.—(1) *Observationes juris Romani*, in eight books, matters of Roman law, some considered from a novel standpoint; (2) *Opuscula varii argumenti*, six dissertations on

CORNELIUS VAN BYNKERSHOEK

Roman jurisprudence —*e.g.*, on *de origine juris*, on *patria potestas*, etc.; (3) Reply to certain criticisms of the preceding. Vol. ii.—
(1) *Opera minora*, six dissertations, of which the fifth is *De Dominio Maris* and the sixth *De foro legatorum*; (2) *Quæstiones juris publici*: (a) *De rebus bellicis* (b) *De rebus varii argumenti*, considering a variety of subjects relative to the law of nations and to Dutch law—*e.g.*, c. iii. to c. xii. on legal position of ambassadors, c. xxi. salute to ships of war at sea; (3) *Quæstiones juris privati*, in forty-eight chapters, divided into four books—questions of civil law, and Dutch municipal law, and also of insurance and other matters of maritime and commercial law.

In addition to these published treatises, he wrote also two other works, the *Corpus juris Hollandici et Zelandici*, and *Observationes tumultuariæ*, notes on the cases which had come before him in the course of his judicial work; but, in accordance with his will, these writings were never published.

The work of Bynkershoek entitles him to a very high place among international jurists. Indeed, Hall[1] says he "was the earliest writer of real importance, and few of his successors have equalled him in sense or in sight." His range of subjects was not so wide as that of Grotius, Pufendorf, Wolf, or Vattel, for his intention was not to produce a systematic work on the law of nations. But the matters he took up for examination are treated more fully, more thoroughly, with stricter logic, and with more practical wisdom than had ever been done before. By his long professional life he had acquired a habit of concise statement, terse expression, exact analysis of complex problems, clearness of explanation, mastery over details, and, generally, an attitude of impartiality in the consideration of conflicting claims. On more than one occasion he gives a deliberate opinion, directly opposed to the practice of his own country; in dealing, for example, with the question of neutral goods on an enemy's vessel, he is against the Dutch diplomacy and ordinances by means of which Holland had been enriching herself: and this attitude is the more remarkable as he occupied a prominent judicial position in his country's service. His reasoning is constantly emphasized by apt historical and legal allusions, though he carefully avoids that superfluous display of learning[2] which frequently interferes

---

[1] *International Law* (Oxford, 1904), p. 583.
[2] Barbeyrac, in the preface to his translation of *De foro legatorum*, says: "Quand on est si riche de son propre fonds, on fait très bien de laisser à d'autres le soin d'emprunter ce qui a été déjà fait."

with the argument and obscures the principles laid down by his predecessors. His argument is characterized by the practical readiness and directness of a prudent and just man of affairs, rather than by the circuitous abstractions of academic subtlety. His convictions are supported not by metaphysical ingenuity, but by appealing to reason and common sense and the actual practice of his time. He is not partial to visionary theories, and yet does not apotheosise mere precedent. He takes a middle course, supplementing actual practice by the corrective criterion of reason, and interpreting the philosophical demands of reason in the light of actual facts, the necessities of daily life, the inevitable human limitations, and the allowances to be made for the maintenance of harmonious international relationships. One may say that general utility is his determining principle, and the positive method his constant guide, the application of which is marked by a sound judgment, an active intellect, and wide learning.[1] Many of his decisions in difficult controverted questions—*e.g.*, limits of territorial sea—have always been referred to as possessing high authority.[2] His writings throughout reflect a certain geniality and buoyancy of temperament; at times a dry vein of humour is introduced, as, for example, when he refers to the many disputes arising out of the classification of tobacco as contraband of war: nothing substantial, he says, really resulted from the controversy—it went off in smoke ("in fumum abierat"). It is, of course, possible to discover certain faults in Bynkershoek's work, such as a certain disposition to arrive at solutions, by his rigorous logic, of diverse matters which were already generally accepted, and a tendency to disregard the growing humanness in the attitude of the time towards some of the incidents of warfare.[3]

To gain a better understanding of his doctrine, it is well to

---

[1] Heineccius, in his edition of the first four books of *Observationes juris Romani* (Leipsic, 1723), says of him: "Admiratus præcipue viri eruditissimi judicium acre, ingenium solers, juris scientiam inusitatam ac denique incredibilem." *Cf.* also the opinion of Rivier of Bynkershoek's position as a civilian: "Auch als Civilist muss sein Name unter den ersten der grossen Niederländischen Schule genannt werden, neben Huber, J. Voet und Noodt" (F. von Holtzendorff, *Handbuch des Völkerrechts*, Berlin, 1885, Bd. i., p. 459).

[2] "Lord Mansfield spoke extremely well of Bynkershoek, and recommended especially as well worth reading his book of prizes, *Quæstiones juris publici*" (2 Bur. 690, in margin).

[3] "Des théories plus douces, plus humaines, ont définitivement prévalu quand le magistrat hollandais s'attache encore à prôner et à justifier de dures et cruelles maximes" (E. Nys, *Le Droit International*, Bruxelles, 1904, I., p. 252).

realize his position relative to the different juristic schools which had already been established before he began to write. In the thirteenth century we find "l'école canonico-internationaliste"[1] expounding a canonical theory of the law of war. In the next two centuries civilians take a wider range of subjects : questions of alliances and other international relationships, questions relating to war, and the ambassador. Writings increase in the sixteenth century, showing substantial progress in the conception of interstatal regulations ; the scope is further widened, maritime matters and the rank of States receive more systematic treatment. The two most important writers of this time, the Spanish Jesuit Francis Suarez[2] and Albericus Gentilis,[3] have been termed[4] the precursors of Grotius. The *De jure belli ac pacis* (1625) of Grotius is really the first complete and methodical treatise, which soon began to exercise a profound influence on Europe. It attempted to reconcile to some extent the conception of ethical transcendentalism with that of the practical necessity and utility of national and international policy—that is, a harmonizing of the *jus naturale* with *jus voluntarium*, of which the former element is considered predominant as being " dictatum rectæ rationis,"[5] and which is "adeo immutabile, ut ne a Deo quidem mutari queat."[6] The positive or voluntary element is the result of the manifestation of the will of nations, which necessarily varies according to time and circumstances, but yet recognizes the principle of utility.[7] Such consent is only to be considered as tacit like the "jus non scriptum quod consensus facit " of the Roman jurisconsults. This attitude of Grotius compels him to have constant recourse to ancient examples, and deliberately to avoid modern illustrations.[8]

Soon afterwards, the work of Zouche introduced an important modification of Grotius' doctrine. His book,[9] which has been called the first manual of the *positive* law of nations, lays the first foundation of the English School, though similar tendencies are already found in Selden.[10] With Zouche, the voluntary element, based on actual usage, is the more important ; and again, unlike

---

[1] P. Leseur, *Introd. à un cours de droit inter. pub.* (Paris, 1893), p. 74.
[2] *De Legibus.*
[3] *De Legationibus* (1583) ; *De jure belli* (1589).
[4] Rivier, in Holtzendorff's *Handbuch, op. cit.,* I. § 85.
[5] Bk. I., c. 1, § 10. [6] *Ibid.* [7] Proleg., § 17.
[8] *Cf.* his own avowal, Proleg., § 58.
[9] *Juris et judicii fecialis, sive juris inter gentes,* etc. (1650).
[10] *Mare Clausum* (1635) ; *De jure naturali et gentium,* etc. (1640).

Grotius, he adduces examples and facts from more modern times. The *jus gentium* of Grotius becomes with Zouche the *jus inter gentes*, an expression which prepared the way for Bentham's *inter*national law.

In the seventeenth century the law of nations begins to be more widely and seriously studied—*e.g.*, in the universities of England, Holland, Germany, and Sweden. Philosophical writers add a new note, urging a philosophical rather than a juridical basis for interstatal relationships. Conflicting tendencies are manifested; there is a wavering between the "naturalism" of Grotius and the "positivism" of Zouche, or a desire to effect a reconciliation. Thus, three schools had evolved—the "naturalists," the "positivists," and the "Grotians." Pufendorf is[1] at the head of the first. He starts from Hobbes's assertion,[2] the germ of which is found in Grotius, that the so-called law of nations is only an application of natural law to State relationships, maintains that the positive element has not the character of real law apart from the natural law, which alone possesses the legal sanction—"quod quidem legis proprie dictæ vim habeat, quæ gentes tamquam a superiore profecta stringat."[3] The positivists at first held that the positive element in the law of nations is distinct from the natural, and that the principles underlying usages and treaties possess legal force. This is the point of view of Textor and Rachel,[4] who emphasize the positive character of "jus plurium liberarum gentium, pacto sive placito expressim aut tacite initum, quo utilitatis gratia sibi invicem obligantur," and urge that the rules arising from custom constitute a *jus gentium commune*, obligatory on States in general, whilst those arising from treaties form a *jus gentium proprium*, obligatory only on the contracting parties. The Grotians occupy an intermediate position; they retain the distinction between the *jus naturale* and the *jus voluntarium*, but, unlike Grotius, they consider the two of equal importance. This position was taken up in the seventeenth and eighteenth centuries by a large number of writers, of whom Wolf[5] and Vattel[6] are the most important.

The course of events in Europe after the Thirty Years' War tended, in many respects, to emphasize the positive aspect of

[1] *De jure naturæ et gentium* (1672).
[2] *De cive* (ed. 1669), c. xiv., § 4, p. 234.
[3] *Op. cit.*, II., c. iii., § 22.   [4] *De jure naturæ et gentium* (1676).
[5] *Institutiones juris naturæ et gentium* (1750).
[6] *Droit des gens.* (Neuchâtel, 1758).

international law. The principle of consent acquired greater influence than ever. The Peace of Westphalia (1648) was itself the first great act of European diplomacy, the first great international settlement by treaty. The meeting of the Protestant Powers at Osnaburg and that of the Catholic Powers at Münster are noteworthy events in the development of international relationships; the conception of European equilibrium became prominent, and the independence of States was recognized. The family of nations began to acquire somewhat more than a chimerical existence. The extension of maritime intercourse gave rise to usages and customs which gradually assumed the force of law, and diplomatic methods became more uniform and systematized. Congresses were held more frequently, and the rise of newspapers helped to spread the conclusions arrived at. Memoirs were published, and collections of diplomatic documents made. In France, England, and Germany collections of treaties were issued. Daniel von Nessel in 1690, and Leibnitz in 1693, were then led to bring together the treaties and diplomatic documents of every age and country.[1] Writers having now the actual facts before them, were not so ready to indulge in metaphysical abstractions, but were more disposed to draw generalizations from the mass of data furnished by the arranged catalogues of historical events. Thus it became clear that the development of the law of nations would be more fully understood and facilitated if time, place, and circumstance be taken into account, and the force of treaties and usage with their express or implied consent recognized. Grotius and Leibnitz[2] had already suggested the principle of utility, Cumberland[3] had emphasized it, it was admitted by nearly all subsequent writers, and later it became the basis of an entire political philosophy, such as that of Bentham. Now the modern school of jurists recognizes, as is pointed out by Leseur,[4] the positive value and juridical nature of rules involved in treaties and customs, the possibility of a rational regulation of interstatal relationships, the self-sufficiency of positive law, which cannot be superseded, but only guided, by natural law (the modern meaning of which is, however, different from that of Grotius), and attaches importance to systematic exposition and codification. And of this modern school it may with much truth be said that Bynkershoek is the

---

[1] *Codex juris gentium diplomaticus* (1693); and a supplement, *Mantissa codicis juris gentium diplomatici* (1700).
[2] *De usu actorum publicorum*, § 13.
[3] *De legibus naturæ*, c. v., § 1.   [4] *Op. cit.*, p. 125.

precursor. "On peut dire de Bynkershoek et de G. F. de Martens, qu'ils sont les deux précurseurs de l'école moderne, qu'ils lui ont donné son orientation."[1]

Bynkershoek not merely lays stress on the positive element, but makes it almost exclusively the basis of his work. The will of nations, express or implied, is more important than elaborate theories of natural law, though there is in every system a place for reasoned criticism (*ratio*) serving as a corrective. He emphasizes the avowal of Grotius: "Rationes, quæ pro se quisque afferunt, nihil definite concludunt, quia jus hoc, non ut jus naturale, ex certis rationibus certo oritur, sed ex voluntate gentium modum accipit."[2] The law of nations is derived from usages (*usus*) traditions and customs (*mores*), and the express consent of States (*consensus gentium*) as manifested in treaties. Usage is also based on the evidence of agreements and ordinances (*pacta et edicta*). In the absence of written law, the existence of long-established universal customs and practices is a presumption of their legal character, and of their binding force upon all men "si . . . ratione utantur"; and in this manner rights are acquired by nations and obligations imposed on them, without which peace and war, commerce, embassies and alliances are meaningless.[3] Express consent always overrides the presumption of tacit consent.[4] Certain practices of other States may sometimes be contrary to our own advantage, but we should regard these in the light of reason and not from personal advantage or otherwise; "utilitas equidem nostra non admittit, sed de ratione, non de utilitate, omnis disputatio est."[5] The rules laid down by our laws and treaties are not alone sufficient to establish the law of nations; in order to be just and valid they must be consonant with reason. "Nulla ullorum hominum auctoritas ibi valet, si ratio repugnet."[6] Bynkershoek tries to obtain a harmonized combination of reason and custom as the whole basis of international law. This is, indeed, the truest ideal; but the difficulty is to determine precisely what is the real significance

---

[1] Leseur, *op. cit.*, p. 125.
[2] *De foro legatorum*, c. xvii., p. 147 (ed. Vicat, *Opera omnia*, 2 vols., folio. Coloniæ, Allobrogum, 1761).
[3] ". . . Sine quo jure nec bellum nec pax nec fœdera nec legationes nec commercia intelliguntur" (*De foro leg.*, c. iii., Vicat, II., 125-6).
[4] "Voluntas expressa tacitam excludit" (II., 150).
[5] *De rebus bellicis*, c. ix., p. 179. *Cf.* also c. xii., p. 186, as to "ratio, juris gentium magistra."
[6] Ad lectorem, ii., p. 161.

of reason. Sometimes *ratio*[1] is used in the earlier writers as it is used by the Roman jurisconsults, and in reference to the Roman law; at other times it is used in the sense of intuition, or of moral consciousness, or of common sense. As employed by Bynkershoek, it may be adequately interpreted as signifying the logical exercise of common sense. He recognizes that the Roman law, though the most admirable system of ancient jurisprudence, has been too much resorted to for the extraction of analogies; old codes, no matter how systematically and with what *elegantia* they have been constructed, do not necessarily fit new times and circumstances. The consent of modern States is far more important than the decisions enshrined in the Digest. Modern practice displaces ancient decrees. Bynkershoek quotes Wicquefort: "Les règles du droit public ne se tirent point du code, ni des digestes, et encore moins des décrets et des décrétales,"[2] and again and again urges that the modern law of nations depends on usage and custom, guided by reason.[3] He is one of the very few writers of the time who largely confine themselves to the most recent historical events,[4] diplomatic incidents, decisions of Courts or congresses, and declarations in the latest treaties. Of all writers, he is the first to make extensive use of the materials furnished by treaties, and the evidence of custom offered by them.[5] The decrees of the States-General are constantly referred to; indeed, his chapter on blockade[6] consists largely of a consideration of and commentary on the Dutch proclamation relative thereto. In this respect his treatment is analogous to that of such English writers as Selden and Zouche, who had directly applied the doctrines of the English Admiralty to controverted maritime questions of European importance—*e.g.*, the sovereignty of the narrow seas, and the legal position of neutral commerce. New rules embodied in two or three treaties do not necessarily become

---

[1] See the criticism, by Prof. Westlake, of the use of this term by writers generally (*Chapters on the Principles of International Law*, Cambridge, 1894 pp. 66-7).
[2] *De foro legatorum*, c. vii., II., 132.
[3] *Cf.* the emphatic passage, *ibid.*, II., 132.
[4] "Hanc (auctoritatem) malim arcessere ab exemplis hic illic frequentatis quam a testimonio veteris alicujus poetæ vel rhetoris" (Ad lectorem, *Quæst. jur. pub.*). This passage contains also a sly reference to the practice of Grotius, from whom he deliberately differs.
[5] "Usus intelligitur ex perpetua quodammodo paciscendi edicendique consuetudine. ... Dixi, ex perpetua quodammodo consuetudine, quia unum forte alterumve pactum, quod a consuetudine recedit, jus gentium non mutat" (*De rebus bellicis*, c. x., II., 181; *cf.* also *De foro legatorum*, c. iii., p. 126).
[6] I., c. xi.

law, for they may formulate special exceptions : "... non satis constare an, quod illi pacti sunt, sit habendum pro jure publico, an pro exceptione, qua a jure publico diversi abeunt."[1] In examining the question of neutral goods on an enemy's vessel, he refers to the interpretation of treaties, which should always be understood *subjecta materia*, having due regard to the circumstances determining the true intention of the parties. Accordingly he denies a general scope to the treaties concluded in 1650, 1662, 1674, 1678, 1679, 1697, and 1713 between the States-General and Spain, France, England, and Sweden. It is interesting to note that Bynkershoek advises a reference to arbitrators in case of dispute arising from the interpretation of treaties ; for treaties have often been concluded and subsequently repudiated owing to lack of agreement as to their construction, and so nothing has remained of them but an empty name—"inane nomen."

So much, then, for Bynkershoek's general attitude to international law, his conception of its sources, his doctrine as to its growth, his theory in relation to the standpoint of his predecessors and contemporaries, his position in, and affinities with, the modern school ; and more particularly his repeated insistence on the importance of custom and usage, the evidence of treaties, diplomatic documents, public ordinances and proclamations, and on the guidance of reason and logic impartially exercised. It will be well to consider now his more detailed treatment of several important questions concerning the sovereignty of the sea, the rights and duties of ambassadors, neutrality, contraband, neutral commerce, and certain special problems in the law of war.

The Sovereignty of the Sea.—The *De Dominio Maris* deals in a candid and unbiassed manner with the much-disputed question of the sixteenth and seventeenth centuries. The writer dispassionately examines in what cases the sea is capable of becoming the subject of sovereignty or exclusive jurisdiction ; he discusses the pretensions to dominion that have from time to time been made by States ; he strenuously opposes the doctrines of Gentilis and Selden, and adopts the views of Grotius and Pufendorf as to the common right of nations to liberty of navigation, of commerce, and of fishing in the open sea.

Grotius[2] accepted the principle of the Roman law,[3] and the

[1] C. xv., p. 190 ; *cf.* Zouche, *De jure feciali*, Part II., s. 8, Quest. 2.
[2] II., c. ii., § 12.
[3] "Et quidem naturali jure communia sunt omnium hæc ; aer et aqua profluens et mare et per hoc litora maris " (Just. *Inst.* II., tit. 1, § 1).

distinction that seas were *res communes*, and navigable rivers *res publicæ*. But from the Middle Ages claims to dominion over various territorial and narrow seas were asserted,[1] monopoly of fishing was hence demanded, salute and other maritime honours were expected, and the power to exclude belligerent operations of other States was exercised.[2] Sovereignty was soon extended to wider zones, and the attempts to put down pirates and to police the seas assisted this expansion. Tolls and dues were exacted from foreign vessels in return for the security afforded to them; and such exercise of limited jurisdiction developed into an attitude of exclusive dominion. In this way arose the claims of Genoa to the Ligurian Sea, of Venice to the Adriatic, of France to an indefinite maritime zone round her shores, of England, likewise of Denmark, to seas of Norway, and, with Sweden, to joint-ownership with the Baltic.[3] The still more extraordinary claims of Spain and Portugal, in their work of discovery, aroused the protests of excluded nations, and soon the entire principle of maritime sovereignty began to be repudiated. Queen Elizabeth strenuously opposed the Spanish claims to the waters of the Indies.[4] Some writers like Ange de Ubaldis and Nicholas Everardi denied in general the right of ownership, if unsupported by long occupation; others like Alphonse de Castro combated more particularly the specific claims of Portugal, Genoa, Venice. The difficulties arising in the struggle between the United Provinces and Philip II. of Spain called forth further writings, such as the *Advocatio hispanica* (1613), of Gentilis, the *Abridgement of all Sea-Lawes* (1613), and *De Dominio Maris* (1615) of William Wellwood, the *Sovereignty of the British Sea* (1653) of John Boroughs; but of all such contributions, Grotius' *Mare Liberum* (1609) and Selden's *Mare Clausum* (1635) were the most important and exerted the greatest influence.[5] Grotius insisted on the necessity of effective occupation opposed the establishment of permanent boundaries, distinguished between absolute property and sovereignty, and between the *oceanus apertus* and the *maria*

[1] *Cf.* Lapradelle, "Le droit de l'État sur la mer territoriale" (*Rev. gén. de dr. int. pub.*, t. v., 1898, p. 268); also E. Nys, *Etudes de dr. int. et de dr. politique* (Bruxelles, 1901), p. 181.
[2] *De Dominio Maris*, c. v., II., 107.
[3] Selden, *Mare Clausum*, II., cc. xxx.-ii.; Daru, *Histoire de Venise*, v., § 21; Loccenius, *De jure Marit.*, I., c. iv.
[4] Camden, *History of Elizabeth*, year 1580.
[5] *Cf.* Nys, *Origines du dr. int.*, etc. (Brux., 1894), p. 380 *et seq.*; Cauchy, *Le droit marit. int.* (Paris, 1862), ii., p. 95; Ortolan, *Diplomatie de la mer* (1864), p. 128; Hautefeuille (1869), p. 18 *et seq.*

interiora.[1] Selden did not clearly discriminate between territorial seas and the open sea; he asserted the sovereignty of England over the surrounding seas, and denied the claims of the Dutch to fish off the coasts.[2]

By the middle of the seventeenth century such wide claims were becoming rarer. The renewed pretensions of Charles I. and of Cromwell, and also of Genoa, were energetically denied by Pontanus and Graswinckel, whose arguments are often referred to by Bynkershoek.[3] The latter, following Grotius, adopts the Roman doctrine as to acquiring property. Continuous possession is essential, and this is not possible here. He points out the invalidity of Selden's argument (his "ambitiosa eruditio" notwithstanding), through confusing the *mare proximum* with the *mare exterum*, ridicules the traditional marriage of the Venetian doges to the Adriatic,[4] denies the English claims to maritime superiority, and does not consider that the conceding of naval honours to the English flag by his country necessarily implied any acknowledgment of the former's sovereignty,[5] and further objects to Selden's pretension[6] that a taking possession of the neighbouring waters of a shore involves, *ipso facto*, a right, or even a definite anticipation, of further extending such authority to more distant portions of the ocean.[7] He admits, however, that certain portions of the sea are capable of exclusive dominion —in the first place, the *mare terræ proximum*, and secondly, such seas as are entirely surrounded by the neighbouring territory of any particular state, with an outlet into the ocean, of which both shores are exclusively occupied by it—*e.g.*, the Mediterranean to the Roman Empire, and, in his own time, the Black Sea to Turkey. He recognizes, further, that in certain cases it is legitimate for a maritime Power to claim special rights over certain parts of the high sea; but these rights are distinct from complete sovereignty, inasmuch as they are to be exercised in the general interests of commerce and navigation, and to consist in privileges of police and superintendence.

As to the limits of the territorial sea, Bodin,[8] relying on a dictum of Baldus, had asserted that sovereigns of maritime nations had

---

[1] *Mare Liberum*, c. v.; *De Jure B. ac P.*, II., c. ii., §§ 2, 3; I., c. iii., § 13; also Bodin, *La République* (Paris, 1577), I., c. xi., p. 215.
[2] *Cf.* conclusion of *Mare Clausum;* Walker, *Hist. of Law of Nations* (1899), vol. i., § 92, p. 164.
[3] *De Dom. Maris*, c. vi., II., p. 109; *cf.* Nys, *op. cit.*, p. 388.
[4] *De Dom. Maris*, c. vi. [5] *Ibid.*, c. v. [6] *Mare Clausum*, II., c. 30.
[7] *De Dom. Maris*, c. iii., II., 104. [8] *La République*, I., c. x., p. 170.

a right to an extent of at least sixty miles from the shore. Bynkershoek was the first to solve the problem, or at least to offer an acceptable definition of marginal waters. Effective protection, depending on the force of arms, is made the criterion of territorial sovereignty; ... "potestatem terræ extendi quousque tormenta exploduntur, eatenus quippe cum imperare, tum possidere videmur; ... alioquin generaliter dicendum esset, potestatem terræ finiri, ubi finitur armorum vis."[1] The marine league, as being originally the distance from the shore measured by a cannon-shot, was thenceforth accepted as the limit of territorial waters; and Bynkershoek's proposal has been adopted not only in private legislation, but also in great international documents, such as the North Sea Fisheries Convention of 1882.[2] Some attempts have been made[3] in recent times to extend this limit, but there is no doubt that the rule of the three-mile limit remains part of modern international law.

The Legal Position of Ambassadors.—At the time Bynkershoek wrote his *De foro legatorum*, opinion on the legal status of ambassadors was far from unanimous. The two chief points considered are their inviolability and independence. The former principle was universally admitted in theory, and generally followed in practice, even in the case of an enemy's envoy in the Saracen wars; but in the thirteenth century it rested rather on the promise made, and on the moral obligation to remain faithful to it, than on any recognition of its legal significance.[4] The independence of ambassadors was not so readily admitted. Some writers had denied their immunity by invoking the authority of the Roman jurisconsults in reference to the *legati;* but Bynkershoek pointed out[5] that the analogy was untenable, owing to their different functions. Afterwards, the fiction of exterritoriality was conceived, as a device to guard public ministers representing their sovereigns against local caprice or disturbance,[6] but this did not extend to their suite or servants till much later.[7] In 1576 Pierre

---

[1] *De Dom. Maris*, c. ii., II., 103-4.
[2] Hertslet, *Collection of Treaties*, XV., p. 795.
[3] See *Brit. State Papers, North America, United States* (1864), LXII., pp. 19-29; and also Wharton, *International Law of the United States*, §§ 32, 327.
[4] *Cf.* Joinville, *Histoire de Saint Louis*, c. lxxi., as to the practice which then prevailed.
[5] *De foro legatorum*, c. i.
[6] Pradier-Fodéré, *Cours de droit diplom.*, I., 272; Rolin-Jacquemyns, *Consultation dans l'affaire Arnim*, p. 123.
[7] *Rev. gén. de droit int. pub.*, t. viii. (1901), p. 493; Pillet, *Le droit int. pub., ses éléments constitutifs* ... (Paris, 1894), p. 13.

Ayrault[1] urged the criminal exemption of ambassadors from the local jurisdiction for reasons of law as well as of fact. Albericus Gentilis and François Hotman dealt more fully with the question of an envoy's conspiracy against the sovereign to whom he is accredited. These two jurists were consulted by the English authorities in the famous case of Mendoza, the Spanish ambassador, who had conspired against Elizabeth. He was ordered to leave the country, and a commissioner was sent to Spain to prefer a complaint against him.[2] Grotius held that the ambassador and his suite are free from local jurisdiction by the tacit consent of nations. But in the case of Don Pantaleon Sa (brother of the Portuguese ambassador in England), who was tried for murder in 1653, found guilty, and executed, the claim of exemption on the ground of belonging to the ambassador's suite was rejected by the Court. Zouche, who was one of the judges, concurred in this decision.[3] Wicquefort's work[4] (1679) is merely a collection of examples. The systematic development of doctrine and formulation of principles from given data was reserved to Bynkershoek, who at once grasps the fundamental distinction between law and politics—" quod iterum prudentiæ politicæ est, cujus causam a jure gentium semper distinguendum esse reor."[5] He holds that all public ministers, irrespective of title or grade, have an equal right to protection, as well as their families, servants, and suite, and criticizes his own government for not always acting on this principle. The competence of the civil tribunal depends on domicile as to the person, and on the *lex rei sitæ* as to property. He agrees with Hilligerus that in respect to property a king is on the same footing as an ordinary subject : it may be seized to satisfy just claims ; but only such goods of an ambassador are attachable as are not necessary to him in his official capacity except household goods for his or his family's personal use.[6] An ambassador who takes part in commercial transactions becomes liable for resulting debts, just as an ordinary merchant,[7] though even here diplomatic proceedings are perhaps more advisable. Unlike Wicquefort, Bynkershoek maintains that a subject of the State to which he is accredited minister by another State is not

---

[1] *L'ordre, formalité et instruction judiciaire* . . .; Bk. I., Pt. IV., s. 12.
[2] Walker, *op. cit.*, I., § 98.
[3] *Cf.* his dissertation on the subject : *Solutio quæstionis veteris et novæ de legati delinquentis judice competente* (Oxon, 1657).
[4] *L'Ambassadeur et ses fonctions* (Cologne, 1679).
[5] *De foro leg.*, II., 156.   [6] *Op. cit.*, c. xvi.
[7] *Op. cit.*, c. xiv., II., 141.

entitled to any immunities—which is but the logical sequence of his fundamental principle.

As to criminal jurisdiction, a distinction is made between crimes against the individual and those against the State. He considers the case of Don Pantaleon Sa,[1] and says contradictory precedents are insufficient, only general practice being reliable. Ambassadors cannot be tried and punished by the local tribunal, though in crimes against the State they may, in accordance with the customs of the seventeenth and eighteenth centuries, be arrested, examined, and, if found guilty, expelled.[2] On the principle that consent renders competent an otherwise incompetent tribunal,[3] an ambassador may renounce his privilege of *renvoi*, or any other exemption, and submit to the local jurisdiction, if his sovereign consent. The house of an ambassador is inviolable to the same extent as his person;[4] but it may not offer refuge to criminals.[5] Finally, third Powers are forbidden all measures of reprisal or retorsion against ministers; though a State is permitted to avenge any injury inflicted on its own ambassadors.

In the seventh chapter of *De rebus varii argumenti*, the question is examined whether an ambassador's acts, which are contrary to his secret instructions, are binding on his sovereign. Apart from the fact that there is no strict analogy between international conventions and private contracts, the possibility of involving great issues brought about the practice, general in Bynkershoek's time, of requiring ratification by the sovereign, except when the entire instructions are contained in the patent full power. But if the minister goes beyond these instructions, or in any other way manifestly exceeds his authority, the sovereign is not bound; though he is bound if the acts are within the limits of his known authority, and he has exceeded only secret instructions. This doctrine has received the support of various recent writers.[6]

The Law of War.—The *De rebus bellicis* does not present a comprehensive treatment of the laws of war, but deals thoroughly

---

[1] CC. xvii., xviii., and xix.
[2] C. xvii., II., 147. *Cf.* the cases of a Spanish ambassador's secretary, implicated in a plot (1605) to deliver up Marseilles to the Spanish (Walker, *op. cit.*, I., 179); 1716, Gyllenberg, a Swedish minister, accused of conspiracy (Mahon, *Hist. of England* . . ., I., 389); 1718, Cellamare, Spanish ambassador in France, of conspiracy against the Regent (De Martens, *Causes célèbres*, I., 139).
[3] Dig. V., tit. i.
[4] See Politis, *Rev. gén. de droit int. pub.*, III., 694.
[5] C. xxi., II., 152.
[6] *E.g.*, Klüber, § 142; Phillimore, II., lii.; Heffter, § 87.

and practically with certain matters of prime importance. Bynkershock's aim is not to compile a code, after the fashion of Grotius and Pufendorf, but to suggest solutions to urgent problems. It is not too much to say that his treatment of commercial and maritime questions, and especially the relationships between neutrals and belligerents, is more thorough, more searching, more related to actual practice, more pervaded with sound sense, with legal and statesmanlike skill, than that of any other work on the subject before his time.

The tendency of the philosophical writers of the eighteenth century was to lay greater obligations on belligerents and to impose certain restrictions on their rights in warfare. The actual practice of the century was otherwise; and Bynkershoek was inclined to the sterner attitude. Fighting for a just cause sanctions the use of every means to attain the desired aim speedily and effectively. Justice is the essential of war; generosity is only an accident. "Justitia in bello omnino necessaria est, animi vero magnitudo a mera voluntate proficiscitur."[1] Humanity, clemency, piety, and other magnanimous virtues are certainly noble, but cannot be insisted on by law.[2] Reason (by which he often means the logical rigour and impartiality of nature) permits the use of all means except perfidy against an enemy.[3] Hence his definition: "Bellum est eorum, qui suæ potestatis sunt, juris sui persequendi ergo, concertatio per vim vel dolum,"[4] the main defect of which is the omission to emphasize, as Grotius had already done,[5] that war is a state or condition; the inclusion also of *dolus* is superfluous.

Grotius held that custom requires a declaration of war, but Bynkershoek cites many examples to refute him; unless there is a special convention to the contrary, it is not necessary. As a rule the opening of hostilities implies a cessation of commercial relations; but commerce is, in the interests of the subjects, sometimes permitted, either generally or as to certain merchandise only.[6] Hence peace and war may coexist. "Pro parte sic bellum, pro parte pax erit inter subditos utriusque principis."[7] This is a strange position in view of his rigorous general doctrine.

[1] C. i., II., 164.   [2] C. iii., II., 167.
[3] C. i., II., 163.   [4] *Ibid.*
[5] "Status per vim certantium qua tales sunt" (I. 1, 2, 1).
[6] In the time of Bynkershoek, however, the practice of "licences de commerce" was rare. See Kleen, *Lois et usages de la neutralité* (Paris, 1900), II., 227.
[7] C. iii., p. 168.

There are at times certain contradictions in Bynkershoek's writings, due to his reasoning, on the one hand, inductively from usages and customs, and on the other, deductively from "reason"; and occasionally the conclusions reached are different, and are not compromised or reconciled. His recognition of the possibility to maintain warlike and commercial relations simultaneously has been claimed as the secret which explains so many apparent contradictions in our modern law of nations.[1]

We may exercise the rights of war only in our own territory, in the enemy's, or in a territory which belongs to no one.[2] To commit hostilities on neutral territory is to make war on its sovereign, who is obliged to use every means to prevent belligerent operations, and to compel a restoration of any property there captured. A combatant's necessity, in this respect, is no sufficient justification. Retaliation is to be exercised directly against the enemy and never through the injury of a neutral. The decree of the States-General, October 10, 1652, rightly prohibited violence in a neutral's port, because of the danger to the neutral. Hence, it is unlawful to commence an attack in neutral territorial waters, within cannon-shot, but if the attack has already begun elsewhere, it is perhaps permissible—"dum fervet opus"—to pursue the enemy to jurisdictional waters, provided the neutral's interests are not injured.[3] This opinion, however, is given conditionally, and Bynkershoek admits that it is by no means universally accepted by his contemporaries.

As to private property in war, he lays down the general rule—
"Quæcumque hostium sunt, recte capimus, ex autem bona pars sunt imperii hostilis, quæque ita hosti, prodesse, nobis nocere possunt." Neutrals on enemy's territory may be considered as enemies; and their goods, if previously taken by the enemy, may be lawfully captured by us. Little attention is given to the immunities of private persons or property during a state of war; but the conditions under which an enemy may acquire property in captured movables or immovables, or the conditions under which they return to the former owners, are considered more fully. Capture does not, *ipso facto*, confer rights of property;

[1] "C'est ici qu'une remarque profonde de cet habile publiciste vient éclairer la question d'un jour nouveau, et nous révéler, pour ainsi dire, le secret qui explique tant de contradictions apparentes de notre droit des gens modernes" (E. Cauchy, *Le droit marit. inter.*, Paris, 1862, p. 60).

[2] "Jure belli adversus hostem duntaxat utimur in nostro, hostis, aut nullius territorio (c. viii., p. 177).

[3] C. viii., I., 178.

apart from any title, it merely operates as a conditional transfer. Grotius' criterion of twenty-four hours' just possession[1] does not always hold good.[2] Firm possession follows on conveyance of the price *intra præsidia*, so that it may effectively be defended— *i.e.*, the question is one of real possession and not one of arbitrary limitation of time,[3] though twenty-four hours' possession *intra præsidia* is a presumption of just possession. The same rule is also given by Loccenius,[4] and, in later times, followed by Sir William Scott, who refers to the principles laid down in the *Consolato del Mare*,[5] and in the work of Bynkershoek. The general rule may be modified by special circumstances in any particular case; but the fundamental point is an ability to defend the prize.

The rights of postliminium, consequent on recapture, do not apply if the enemy obtained possession in any other manner than by force. The case of immovable property differs from that of movable. The former when recaptured returns to the original owner by postliminium; but the latter, retaken from the enemy, vests in the recaptors, since recapture effects as valid a transference as capture. A belligerent may condemn enemy's property whilst lying under capture in a neutral port. The same opinion was expressed in 1789 by Sir William Scott and the whole Court of King's Bench, though later this great judge advanced a different doctrine.[6] In the United States, decisions were given in several cases[7] in conformity with Bynkershoek's view, which, indeed, accorded with long-established European practice. A reward must be given to the recaptors by the original owners for their sacrifice and risk, to be estimated by impartial assessors. He approves the rule, in this respect, of the *Consolato del Mare*, which, however, he believes to be largely a "farrago of nautical laws."[8] If a portion of a country be occupied, the whole is considered in occupation and possession, if such has been the inten-

---

[1] " . . . Recentiori jure gentium inter Europæos populos introductum videmus, ut talia capta censeantur, ubi per horas vigintiquatuor in potestate hostium fuerint " (*De Jure B. ac P.*, Bk. III., c. 6, § 3, n. 2).

[2] *Cf.* case of the *Santa Cruz*, 1 C. Rob., 58.

[3] C. iv., p. 169.

[4] *De Jure Marit.*, Bk. II., c. iv., s. 4.

[5] *The Ceylon* (1811), 1 Dod. Adm. Rep., 105.

[6] *Smart* v. *Wolff*, 3 Term Rep., 329.

[7] *Cf. Rose* v. *Himely*, and *Hudson* v. *Guestier*, 4 Cranch's Rep., 241, 293; see also Lampredi, *Del Commercio*, etc., Pt. I., § 14.

[8] " Dando a quelli che a i detti nimici tolta haveranno, beveraggio conveniente, secondo la fatica che ne haveranno avuta, e secondo il danno che ne haveranno sofferto " (c. 287, § 1136).

tion of the captor, and if the vanquished enemy has retained no other part of it.

It is permissible to confiscate an enemy's actions and credits (*actiones, nomina*), but not if war is so mildly carried on that commerce continues between the combatants. Though an enemy, as such, forfeits his *persona standi in judicio*, as it is expressed in the decrees of the States-General of October 2 and 29, 1590, and so held in subsequent cases, yet there is an exception when commercial intercourse is allowed on both sides.[1] Vattel acknowledges the legality of such confiscation, but points out that in more recent times a more liberal practice was generally adopted.[2] If, however, credits and actions have not actually been handed over to the sovereign, the former right of creditors revives at the conclusion of peace, by an application of the principle of postliminium. "Si exegerit, recte solutum est, si non exegerit pace facta reviviscit jus pristinum creditoris. . . . Nomina igitur, non exacta, tempore belli quodammodo intermori videntur, sed per pacem, genere quodam postliminii, ad priorem dominum reverti."[3]

If before the war we owned in the enemy's country any property which, during the war, had been concealed and therefore not confiscated, it returns to the former owners and does not become the property of the recaptors, in case it is retaken by our subjects.[4]

As to the right of postliminium on an ally's territory, Bynkershoek says: "He who returns to his sovereign's ally is entitled to the right of postliminy because he is deemed to have returned to his own country; for allies are considered as constituting one State with ourselves" ("Qui revertitur ad fœderatos, jus postliminii habet, qui ad suam civitatem videtur reversus, fœderati enim nobiscum unam quodammodo civitatem constituunt").[5] Similarly, if our property, captured by enemies, eventually comes into the territory of our ally, it is regarded as having been restored to us.[6] The propositions laid down regarding postliminium on neutral territory will be misleading, unless due attention be given to the distinction between military rights, accruing to the belligerent through capture or conquest, and civil rights, acquired apart from war by contract or otherwise. Actual possession is

---

[1] C. vii., p. 176.
[2] "Mais aujourd'hui, l'avantage et la sûreté du commerce ont engagé tous les souverains de l'Europe à se relâcher de cette rigueur" (Bk. III., c. 5, § 77).
[3] C. vii., p. 177. [4] *Ibid.*
[5] C. xv., p 190. [6] C. xv., p. 191.

the criterion of military rights, ordinary proof of title being that of civil rights. Hence a prize taken by captors or their agents into neutral territory does not return to its former owner: for to the neutral State possession is evidence of the military right, and in such a case, as Hertius says, the fact must be taken for the law.[1] From this it follows that if after having been captured a vessel escape, or be taken into a neutral territory by others than the original captor, or his agents, the civil right of the former owner revives, and the property returns to him. It does not, of course, apply to cases of regular condemnation by the captor's tribunal, which would turn the military into a civil right. Further, as Bynkershoek says, this is true only of captures made in regular warfare: capture by pirates in no way transfers the property. Respecting the right of postliminium as applied to cities and States, he approves the rule of Grotius that "the right of postliminy is applicable to a whole people, as well as to an individual, and that a political body, which was free before, recovers its liberty when its allies, by force of arms, deliver it from the power of the enemy."[2]

Neutrality.—The conception of neutrality was not unknown in ancient times—*e.g.*, among the Greeks—but there was never systematic practice. Rome regarded another State either as an ally or an enemy: "Romanos aut socios aut hostes habeatis oportet, media nulla via est."[3] In the Middle Ages feudalism favoured a similar view. With the increase of maritime commerce and other State relationships, and the founding of colonies, the notion of neutrality became more clearly defined. The objects of war became changed, and peace was promoted by the Church. "Mais le grand facteur de la neutralité a été surtout un sentiment de solidarité intéressé et d'ordre économique."[4] Treaties and conventions began to play a prominent part. Early in the seventeenth century practice was unsettled and capricious, and the doctrine of Grotius was inadequate and incoherent, being one of the most unsatisfactory portions of his work. By the eighteenth century the duty of impartiality and respect of neutral territory began to be more seriously recognized. Later, Bynkershoek and Vattel formulate more thorough principles of neutrality; and, in some respects, the doctrines of the former,

[1] *Adnot. ad Puffend. De Jure Nat.*; see also Grotius, Bk. VIII, c. 6, n. 25.
[2] *De Jure Belli ac Pacis*, Bk. III., c. 9, § 9, n. 1.
[3] Livy, xxxii.
[4] A. Thonier, *Contrebande de Guerre* (Bordeaux, 1904), p. 9

though he wrote earlier, are more advanced than the latter's, in spite of the fact that Bynkershoek uses the negative expression *non hostes*, and Vattel adopts the more significant *neutralité* and *neutres*. Greek writers[1] had used the phrases ἡσυχίαν ἄγειν (to keep silent), ἐκ τοῦ μέσου καθῆσθαι, and ὁ διά μέσου (expressing the idea of an intermediate position); Roman writers spoke of *medii, amici, pacati*, words used also in the Middle Ages. In a proclamation of the King of France, 1408, *neutralitas* is used in reference to the popes of Rome and Avignon; and a little later, in the German and Swiss wars, the terms *stille sitzen* and *Unpartyschung* are found. In a convention between England and Denmark, 1465, *guerrarum abstinentiæ* appears, and at the end of the century *neutralité* is common in treaties, conventions, and edicts. In the Thirty Years' War, we get the Germanized *Neutralität;* and again Machiavelli and Guicciardini make use of *neutralità*, and Bodin uses *neutralité* and *neutre*. Grotius reverts to the Roman form *medii in bello*, and Bynkershoek calls neutrals *non hostes*, defining them as those "qui neutrarum partium sunt."

Bynkershoek occupies a high place in the discussion of neutrality,[2] though not all his propositions are now accepted. Grotius' treatment is vague and meagre; Zouche relies more on State policy than on law: Pufendorf denies to neutrals the right of undisturbed commerce, apart from special conventions. Unlike Grotius and Vattel, Bynkershoek does not allow a neutral to judge as to the just or unjust cause of belligerents and offer help accordingly, except when the two combatants are both allies of the neutral, and there is no treaty otherwise regulating the relationships. The general principle is "belli justitia vel injustitia nihil quicquam pertinet ad communem amicum,"[3] subject to the rare exception suggested, which, of course, applies only to treaties concluded before the war,—"bello jam exorto . . . neutri amico auxilia recte vel promittuntur vel mittuntur."[4] Our tributary or protected States may assist their immediate sovereign against us, but not with arms and men.[5]

[1] E. Nys, *Études de dr. int. et de dr. pol.*, 2ᵐᵉ série (Brux., 1901), p. 57.
[2] "Dans l'histoire de la doctrine de la neutralité, Bynkershoek occupe un rang distingué" (E. Nys, *op. cit.*, p. 86).
[3] C. ix., p. 179.
[4] C. ix., p. 180. (As to allies and neutrality, see the opinion of Lord Hawkesbury, afterwards Earl of Liverpool, in his *Discourse on the Conduct of the Government of Great Britain in respect to Neutral Nations*, London, 1794, p. 68).
[5] P. 181.

Bynkershoek clearly recognizes the claims of neutral commerce, and the necessity to effect a reconciliation, legally rather than diplomatically, and of the conflicting interests of neutrals and belligerents. Reason, and not personal advantage, is to be the guide—"de ratione, non de utilitate, omnis disputatio est." The main guiding principles, presenting a substantial advance on the ideas and practice of the time, are an obligation on the neutral not to assist one belligerent in any way which would be detrimental to the other—"si medius sim, alteri non possum prodesse, ut alteri noceam"—and a corresponding right not to be injured by the belligerents in its pacific commerce—"qui injuriam non fecit non recte patitur." With Bynkershoek it is mainly a question of supplying subsidies and materials; the enlistment of troops on neutral territory is not prohibited, if there is no law or declaration to the contrary. In this respect he is at one with Grotius, Wolf, Galiani, and other publicists of the time, and with the practice then prevailing. The right of recruiting was frequently allowed in treaties—*e.g.*, in 1656 between England and Sweden.[1]

Contraband.—The Roman emperors prohibited commerce with the barbarians in certain articles—*e.g.*, arms, iron, etc.—and later the popes forbade trade with the infidels in weapons and munitions of war—*merces banno interdictæ*. Sovereigns assumed the right to draw up lists of contraband goods, and vary them at pleasure. The growth of commerce fostered clearer notions; and treaties were concluded in favour of the pacific trade of neutrals. The Treaty of the Pyrenees (1659), in Art. 12, specifies goods which are contraband—*e.g.*, objects directly connected with war, also saltpetre, horses, and saddles; and in Art. 13 declares provisions and other necessities of life to be free. In the Treaty of Utrecht (1713) contraband goods are enumerated (Art. 19)—horses, harness, warlike arms and instruments. As to provisions, they are declared contraband in the treaties of 1303 between France and England, of 1613 between Sweden and the Hanseatic towns, of 1625 between England and the same, of 1654 between England and the United Provinces; but excluded in the treaties of 1655 between Louis XIV. and the Hanseatic towns, in the treaties of the Pyrenees and Utrecht, and in the Treaty of Versailles, 1786. The writers of the eighteenth century were as inconsistent in their theories as the age was in its practice.

---

[1] Dumont, *Corps universel diplomatique*, etc., VI., ii. 3., and VI., ii. 125.

Thus Heineccius,[1] writing in 1721, regarded as contraband not only arms and munitions, saltpetre, and horses, but also cordage, sails, and other naval stores, and further included provisions.

Bynkershoek refers to Grotius' threefold classification of objects—(1) those useful for purposes of war ; (2) those not so useful ; (3) those which may be used either in war or peace ; and says that there is no doubt as to (1) and (2). As to (3) Grotius permits the intercepting of *res ancipitis vel promiscui usus*, but only in case of necessity, and then under the obligation of subsequent restitution. But Bynkershoek points out that the difficulty is in determining who is to be judge of that necessity— ". . . Quis arbiter erit ejus necessitatis, nam facillimum est eam prætexere "—that it is against law to sit as judges in our own cause, and further that Grotius' distinction is not supported by the usage of nations. His own definition is : " Contraband articles are such as are proper for war, and it is of no consequence whether or not they are of any use out of war."[2] Are the materials themselves contraband, out of which contraband articles are made ? Zouche[3] inclines to this opinion ; but, says Bynkershoek, reason and usage point to the contrary—" ego non essem, quia ratio et exempla me moveant in contrarium."[4] If all such materials are prohibited, the catalogue of contraband goods will be enormous, amounting to a total prohibition of commerce.[5] However, certain articles may be decreed contraband, not from their intrinsic nature, but from other special circumstances—*e.g.*, from the large quantity required, such as saddles, holsters, belts ; or in anticipation that prohibiting certain articles will quickly bring the war to an end—*e.g.*, provisions, when the enemy is besieged ;[6] or generally those articles without which the enemy could not possibly continue the war. He states that the last two exceptions accord with the decrees of the States-General of December 5, 1652, against the English, and of December 31, 1657, against the Portuguese. As to the decree of May 6, 1667, against Sweden, there was a special reason—viz., the right of retaliation,

---

[1] *De Nav. ob Vect. Merc. Vetit.*, xiv.
[2] " Contrabanda dici, quæ uti sunt, bello apta esse possunt, nec quicquam interesse, an et extra bellum usum præbeant " (c. x.).
[3] *Op. cit.*, Part 2, § 8, Quest. 8.
[4] C. x., p. 182.
[5] " Si omnem materiam prohibeas, ex qua quid bello aptari possit, ingens esset catalogus rerum prohibitarum, quia nullo fere materia, ex qua non saltem aliquid, bello aptum, facile fabricemus. Hæc interdicta, tantum non omni commercio interdicimus, quod valde esset inutile " (c. x., II., 182).
[6] C. ix., p. 180.

as therein expressed—for prohibiting even materials not themselves fit for purposes of war, but which might be so adapted. Zouche relates that there was a dispute between England and Spain regarding tobacco, which, Spain contended, might be used for preserving provisions; but Bynkershoek repudiates the action of Spain, as tobacco cannot be of any use in destroying the enemy. The tendency of Bynkershoek is clearly to lay down a definite rule restricting contraband, but finding that it would be opposed to the practice of his own country, and, indeed, of the European countries in general, he seeks to extract from such usage and from the circumstantial dispositions of treaties certain exceptional rules, which all but destroy the force of his fundamental principle. But great difficulties in connection with contraband were met with in later times, and there is by no means unanimity of opinion at present. The First and Second Armed Neutrality of 1780 and .1800 endeavoured to limit the kinds of articles that could be regarded as contraband, but they failed; and the Declaration of Paris of 1856 makes use of the term "contraband" without any attempt to define it.

Respecting the treatment of vessels carrying contraband, Bynkershoek is opposed to the declarations in the various Dutch decrees and treaties between the Peace of Westphalia and the Treaty of Utrecht, according to which only the contraband goods were to be confiscated and the vessels carrying them allowed to go free. His doctrine, an application of the Roman law[2] and followed by many eminent jurists amongst his successors, was that though the owner or master was unaware of the illegal nature of the cargo, the vessel also could be justly seized. Further, if the cargo consist of a mixture of lawful goods and contraband, and both belong to the same owner, the whole may be condemned; if they belong to different owners, then the illegal act of one ought not to affect the legal act of the other. This is in full agreement with the rule laid down by Zouche.[3] By a French ordinance of July 26, 1778, only contraband goods were to be confiscated, unless they amounted to three-quarters of the entire cargo, in which case the whole merchandise would be condemned, as well as the ship. Art. 17 of the treaty between Great Britain and the United States, November 19, 1794, stipulated "that in all cases where vessels should be captured or detained on just sus-

---

[1] Cf. Leseur, op. cit., p. 104.   [2] Dig. III., tit. iv.
[3] Op. cit., Part II., § 8, Quest. 13.

picion of having on board enemy's property, or of carrying to the enemy any of the articles which are contraband of war, the said vessel should be brought to the nearest and most convenient port ; and if any property of an enemy should be found on board such a vessel, that part only which belonged to the enemy should be made prize, and the vessel should be at liberty to proceed with the remainder without any impediment."

Blockade.—Bynkershoek holds that everything carried to a blockaded or besieged place, contrary to law or treaty, is to be considered as contraband and treated accordingly ; and usage sanctions the infliction of the capital penalty on offenders, or a milder punishment according to the circumstances of the case. In the time of Vattel, however, a milder policy prevailed ; such offenders could be regarded as enemies, but usually only their goods were confiscated. Earlier in the work, Bynkershoek says that retaliation is to be exercised only on the offending party— " retorsio non est nisi adversus eum qui ipse damni quid dedit, ac deinde patitur, non vero adversus communem amicum " ;[1] but here he maintains that an injury inflicted on a neutral is justifiable on the principle of retaliation upon the enemy—a view adopted in consequence of the edicts of the States-General against the Spaniards. The rules as to what vessels may be captured he derives from an examination of the famous Dutch decree of 1630, which presents the first systematic State legislation governing the question of blockade. "Le décret hollandais du 26 juin 1630 promulgué déjà avant l'indépendance, dans le but de régler un blocus des ports de Flandre relevant de la domination espagnole, est considéré comme la première législation nationale du blocus moderne. En effet, on y trouvé ses premières règles définies."[2] Thus the following vessels may be captured and confiscated : (1) Those found so near to the blockaded ports as to show clearly an intention to enter therein, unless it appears that they were driven there by stress of weather; (2) those found at a distance from the ports, but whose papers indicate an intention to enter, unless before the offence is committed they alter their course of their own accord ;[3] (3) those vessels issuing from such ports, not having been forced thither by stress of weather, even though taken at distance : unless after leaving the ports they had performed a

[1] C. iv.
[2] R. Kleen, *Lois et usages de la neutralité* (2 vols., Paris, 1898-1900), I., 543.
[3] In his case Bynkershoek is not fully determined ; for the matter is to be decided according to conjectures and circumstances.

voyage to a port of their own country, or to some other neutral port; but liable to confiscation if on issuing from the blockaded port they are pursued to their own or to any other port, and afterwards found on the high sea coming out of the latter port.

Bynkershoek admits the rigorous character of these rules, but he says the severity may be relaxed, if thought fit, and, indeed, has often been relaxed. "Sed mutatis hominibus sententias mutari quid obstat ?"[1] He states further that the above decree was put into effect by the application of a sufficient force to maintain the blockade; and does not make any suggestion that a blockade by proclamation, or a "paper blockade," could lawfully impose any restriction on neutral commerce. Actual practice in the seventeenth century was very changeable, and was often adapted to the demands of self-interest; and Bynkershoek repudiates the inconsistency in the conduct of his own country.

Neutral Goods on Enemy's Vessels.—The two cases of neutral goods on an enemy's vessel, and an enemy's goods on a neutral vessel, are considered in a more liberal manner than had been done before, and often in antagonism to Dutch policy. At the time he wrote three systems[2] had been developed: (1) the doctrine of "hostile infection," represented by the French ordinances of the sixteenth century, of 1681, and of 1704, by which ships and goods connected in any way with enemy's goods or vessels were condemned; (2) the rule of the *Consolato del Mare* (*suum cuique*), by which only the enemy's property, vessel or cargo, was seizable, and a neutral vessel was not necessarily regarded in the light of neutral territory; (3) the rule of Utrecht, the principle of which is free vessel free goods, enemy vessel enemy goods—that is, liberty or condemnation depends only on the nationality of the carrying vessel.

Bynkershoek does not accept the rule of Utrecht; one or two special treaties, he insists, are not necessarily evidence of international law. The rule that neutral goods found on an enemy's vessel may be condemned is contrary to reason; at most it is only a presumption that they belong to the enemy, as Grotius also thinks. They cannot be confiscated even if the shipper knew it was the enemy's vessel. The essential criterion is—Have I, in shipping the goods, intended to do you an injury? The various questions as to whether the owner of the merchandise

---

[1] C. xi., p. 185.
[2] See J. Delpech, *Bynkershoek*, in *Les fondateurs du droit international* (Paris, 1904), pp. 385-446; and Thonier, *op. cit.*, p. 77.

on the enemy's vessel knew of the war or not, and whether, knowing this, he knew his conduct to be legal or not—all these finespun niceties may indicate legal ingenuity, but will not satisfy unsophisticated common sense. "Sed hæ sunt pragmaticorum lautitiæ, quibus indoctum vulgus excipiunt."[1] He is largely in agreement with the *Consolato del Mare*, by which the enemy's vessel is seizable, but the neutral goods on board must be returned to their owners; he differs in not allowing freight should the vessel be carried into the captor's port.[2]

In the case of enemy's goods found on a neutral vessel, he is against the principle of hostile infection, and agrees with that of the *Consolato del Mare*. The enemy's goods may be seized, but the neutral vessel must go free, unless, of course, the owner was aware that the cargo was contraband. The right of visitation and search is allowed. It is lawful to detain the vessel, and to ascertain, not merely by the flag, which may be fraudulently assumed, but by the documents on board, whether she is really neutral, and whether enemy's property is concealed therein.[3] In a word, a neutral commits no offence against the laws of nations in carrying enemy's goods, which are seizable *ex re*, the neutral vessel going free; but to carry contraband is an offence *ex delicto*, and hence both the contraband goods and the vessel are liable to confiscation.

As to privateering, Bynkershoek is severer than Gentilis or Grotius; though he deprecates the defence of necessity which is often put forward in the subordination of neutral rights to those of belligerents. If a privateer makes an illegal capture, the captain is liable for the damage suffered, should he have exceeded his authority; but if he has acted according to his authority then the owners of the vessel are liable for all damage, whether the captain is dishonest or unskilful. The owners of the vessel are not liable if they have not appointed the master for the purpose of making captures. If a vessel is not a privateer—*i.e.*, has no commission—and makes captures by order of the owners,

---

[1] C. xiii., p. 187.

[2] *Ibid.*, p. 188. (*Cf.* the opinions of Heineccius, *De nav. ob vect. vetit*, etc., c. ii., § ix.) In *The Fortuna*, the captor of an enemy's vessel was held not entitled to freight on neutral goods unless he took them to the port of destination; in *The Diana*, freight was allowed in certain cases, where the cargo was taken to the claimant's own country.

[3] "Eatenus utique licitum esse amicam navem sistere, ut non ex fallaci forte aplustri, sed ex ipsis instrumentis, in navi repertis, constet navem amicam esse . . . et inde discere, an quæ hostium bona in nave lateant" (c. xiv., pp. 188-9).

the same rules apply as though she were a regular privateer. Should a non-commissioned vessel, attacked by an enemy, capture the enemy's vessel, the prize belongs to the master as captor—". . . constat prædam quicunque ceperit, solius capientis esse, nisi ex præpositione et mandato aliorum ceperit";[1] this is an application of the general doctrine of principal and agent. When a prize is taken by one or more armed private ships, others being present but not assisting, the prize belongs only to him who has fought and conquered the enemy's vessel; but in case vessels of war are present, it is permissible to enact a different law.[2]

A few other questions are considered, such as piracy, the insurance of vessels liable to capture,[3] the authority of prize courts, whose judgment if manifestly unjust cannot be enforced, and the remedy by letters of reprisal;[4] and finally, the *De rebus bellicis*, a remarkable work of permanent value, the work of a sound legally-disposed mind, concludes with a wise reflection on war, and the frequently alleged "reason of State," that "monstrum horrendum, informe, ingens, cui lumen ademptum": "If governments will yield to that monster and indulge themselves by following its dictates and consider the property of other nations as their own, it is idle to investigate further the law of nations and discuss its principles."[5]

[1] C. xx., p. 199.
[2] Sir W. Scott held—the same principles being adopted in the French ordinances of January 27, 1706, and June 15, 1757—that mere presence in the case of a privateer is not sufficient to raise the presumption of co-operation in order to be entitled to a share of the prize (*L'Amitié*, 6 Rob., 261), but in the case of a vessel of war it was sufficient to support the *animus capiendi* (*The Flore*, 5 Rob., 270).
[3] C. xxi.
[4] C. xxiv. (*cf.* Treaty of Rhyswick, Art. 9, and Treaty of Utrecht, Art. 16).
[5] C. xxv., p. 209.

MONTESQUIEU

MONTESQUIEU [1]

WHEN Sainte-Beuve sat down, in the year 1852, to write a *causerie* about Montesquieu, he gave as a reason for not having dealt with the subject before that Montesquieu belonged to the class of men whom one approaches with apprehension on account of the respect which they inspire, and of the kind of religious halo which has gathered round their names.

This was written more than fifty years ago, and the language reflects the glamour which still attached to Montesquieu's name during the first half of the nineteenth century. That glamour has now passed away. Not that Montesquieu has died, or is likely to die. But he is no longer the oracle of statesmen; his *Spirit of Laws* is no longer treated by framers of constitutions as a Bible of political philosophy, bearing with it the same kind of authority as that which Aristotle bore among the schoolmen. That authority ended when the greater part of the civilized world had been endowed with parliamentary and representative institutions framed more or less on the model which Montesquieu had described and had held up for imitation. The interest which attaches to him now is of a different order. It is literary and historical. He lives as one of the greatest of French writers, and his *Considerations on the Greatness and Decay of the Romans* are still read as a school classic by French boys and girls, much as the masterpieces of Burke are, or ought to be, read in English schools. To the student of political history he is known as the source of ideas which exercised an influence of incomparable importance in the framing of constitutions both for the old and for the new continent. And for the student of political science, his work marks a new departure in methods of observation and treatment. The *Spirit of Laws* has been called the greatest book of the eighteenth century: its publication was certainly one of the greatest events of that century.

If it were necessary for me to offer an apology for taking

[1] Delivered as The Romanes Lecture at Oxford, 1904.

Montesquieu as my subject to-day I might plead, first, that no student of history or of political or legal science can afford to disregard one who has been claimed, on strong grounds, as a founder of the comparative method in its application to the study of Politics and of Law; next, that some recent publications[1] have thrown new and interesting light both on his character and on his methods of work; and lastly that one cannot return too often to the consideration of a really great man. Moreover, it may be suspected that, in this country at least, and at the present day, Montesquieu belongs to the numerous class of authors whom everybody is supposed to know but whom very few have read. It will, of course, be impossible for me to do more than touch on a few of the aspects of such a many-sided man.

Let me begin by reminding you of the leading dates and facts in Montesquieu's life, so far only as is necessary for the purpose of "placing" him historically.[2] Charles Louis de Secondat was born in 1689, a year after the Revolution which ended the Stuart dynasty, five years before the birth of Voltaire, 100 years before the outbreak of the French Revolution. He died in 1755, four years after the publication of the first volume of the French *Encyclopedia*, the year before the Seven Years' War, five years before George III. came to the throne, and seven years before Rousseau preached to the world, in the first chapter of his *Social Contract*, that man is born free and is everywhere in chains.

---

[1] The Collection Bordelaise referred to in note 2.

[2] The fullest life of Montesquieu is that by L. Vian, *Histoire de Montesquieu*, Paris, 1878. But it is inaccurate and uncritical, and has been severely criticized by M. Brunetière (*Revue des deux Mondes*, 1879). The best contemporary appreciation of Montesquieu is by the Marquis d'Argenson (*Mémoires*, p. 428, edition of 1825). The standard edition of Montesquieu is that by Laboulaye in 7 vols., Paris, 1873-9. This must now be supplemented by the "Collection Bordelaise," which contains further materials supplied by the Montesquieu family, and which includes *Deux opuscules de Montesquieu*, 1891; *Mélanges inédits de Montesquieu*, 1892; *Voyages de Montesquieu*, 2 vols., 1894; *Pensées et fragments inédits*, 2 vols., 1899, 1901. The literature on Montesquieu is very extensive. A list of books, articles, and *éloges* relating to him will be found in an appendix to Vian's *Histoire*. Among subsequent works the first place is taken by M. Sorel's *Montesquieu* in the series called *Les grands écrivains français*, a little book of which I can only speak with the most respectful admiration. Reference may also be made to Oncken, *Zeitalter Friedrichs des Grossen*, i. 80, 457; Taine, *Ancien Régime*, pp. 264, 278, 339; Janet, *Histoire de la science politique*, vol. ii.; Faguet, *Dix-huitième siècle*; Faguet, *La politique comparée de Montesquieu, Rousseau et Voltaire*; Brunetière, *Études critiques sur l'histoire de la littérature française*, 4ᵐᵉ série; Flint, *The Philosophy of History*, 262-79; Sir Leslie Stephen, *English Thought in the Eighteenth Century*, i. 186; Henry Sidgwick, *The Development of European Polity*; Sir F. Pollock, *History of the Science of Politics*.

His birth-place was the Chateau of La Brède, a thirteenth-century castle some ten miles from Bordeaux.[1] Thus he was a countryman of Montaigne, with whom he had many affinities. His family was noble, and belonged to that more modern branch of the nobility which had acquired its fortunes from the exercise of judicial or financial functions, and which was known as the *noblesse de la robe*. Therefore he was a member of one of the two privileged classes which under the old régime owned between them some two-fifths of the soil of France, and were practically exempt from all the burdens of the State.

On his mother's death he was sent as a boy of seven to the Oratorian College at Juilly near Meaux, and remained there eleven years. He then studied law, and in 1714, at the age of twenty-five, was made counsellor of the Parlement of Bordeaux, that is to say member of the Supreme Court of the province of Guienne. In the next year he married a Protestant lady. The following year, 1716, made a great difference in his fortunes. His uncle died, and he succeeded to the barony of Montesquieu, to a considerable landed property, and, above all, to the dignified and lucrative post of *Président à Mortier*, or Vice-President, of the Parlement of Bordeaux, a post which the uncle had acquired by purchase, and which the nephew retained until he parted with it to another purchaser in 1726. His judicial duties were such as to leave him a good deal of leisure. After the fashion of his time he dabbled in physical science. The papers which he read before the newly established Academy of Bordeaux were of no scientific value, but they influenced his subsequent political speculations, and supplied a sufficient excuse for his election during his English visit to a fellowship in our Royal Society.[2]

[1] Sixteen and a half miles by railway.
[2] He was elected February 12, 1729 (old style). Proposed by Dr. Teissier and recommended by M. Ste-Hyacynthe and the President (Sir Hans Sloane). He refers to his reception in a letter to Père Cerati, dated London, March 1, 1730 (new style). Among the documents of the Royal Society is the copy of a letter from Montesquieu to Sir Hans Sloane, dated Paris, August 4, 1734, and enclosing copies of his book on the *Grandeur et décadence des Romains*. The M. Ste-Hyacynthe, who figures as Montesquieu's backer, must have been the " Thémiseul de Ste-Hyacinthe, the half-starved author of the *Chef-d'œuvre d'un inconnu*, who, after having served, if we may believe Voltaire, as a dragoon during the persecution of the French Protestants, had crossed over to England, there had been converted, had translated *Robinson Crusoe*, and though always a destitute wanderer, had been nominated a member of the Royal Society of London " (Texte, *Jean-Jacques Rousseau, and the Cosmopolitan Spirit in Literature*, translated by J. W. Matthews, p. 18). The English translation of this book embodies additions to, and corrections of, the original work.

His real interests lay neither in law nor in physics, but in the study of human nature. His first book, the *Persian Letters*, appeared in 1721. He resigned his judicial office in 1726, and became a member of the *Académie française* at the beginning of 1728. The next three years were spent in travel, and his travels ended with a stay of nearly two years in England. The *Grandeur et décadence des Romains* appeared in 1734, and the *Esprit des lois* in 1748. He died, as I have said, in 1755.

His personal appearance is known to us from the excellent medallion portrait by Dassier, executed in 1752. Aquiline features, an expression subtle, kindly, humorous. He was always short-sighted, and toward the end of his life became almost entirely blind. "You tell me that you are blind," he writes to his old friend Madame du Deffand, in 1752: "Don't you see we were both once upon a time, you and I, rebellious spirits, now condemned to darkness? Let us console ourselves by the thought that those who see clearly are not for that reason luminous."[1]

The three books to which Montesquieu owes his fame are the *Persian Letters*, the *Considerations on the Greatness and Decay of the Romans*, and the *Spirit of Laws*. Of these the first appeared during the Regency, that period of mad revel which followed the gloomy close of Louis XIV.'s reign. The second was published under the ministry of that aged and suspicious despot, Cardinal Fleury, when it was safer to speculate about ancient history than about contemporary politics or society. The last appeared under the rule of Madame de Pompadour, when the Encyclopædists had begun that solvent work of theirs which prepared the way for the French Revolution. It should be added that all the three books were published anonymously, and printed in foreign countries, the first two at Amsterdam, the last at Geneva.

In order to trace the origin and development of Montesquieu's conceptions, and the course and tendency of his thoughts, the three books must be read consecutively, and must be supple-

[1] The Earl of Charlemont, who, as a young man, made a tour through the South of France, either in 1755, or in the latter part of 1754 (the dates are not quite clear), has left a delightful description of a visit which he and a friend paid to Montesquieu at La Brède. He found, instead of a "grave, austere philosopher," a "gay, polite, sprightly Frenchman," who took his visitors for a walk through his grounds, and being unable to find the key of a padlocked three-foot bar, solved the difficulty by taking a run and jumping over it.—Hardy, *Memoirs of Earl of Charlemont*, i. 60-73.

mented by what we know of his studies and experiences during their preparation. For this knowledge very interesting additional materials have been supplied by the recent publication of the manuscripts which had for many years been preserved in the family archives of the Montesquieu family. They include the journals of travel which Sainte-Beuve said he would sooner have than the *Spirit of Laws*, and the three quarto volumes of *Pensées* in which Montesquieu stored materials for his published works.

The *Persian Letters* supply a clue to the plan of the *Spirit of Laws*, and contain the germs of many of the ideas which were subsequently developed in that book. They are the work of a young man. They profess to be written, and were probably composed or sketched, at different dates between 1711 and 1720,[1] that is to say, during the last four years of Louis XIV.'s reign, and the first five years of the Regency, and they describe the impressions of three Persians who are supposed to be travelling in Europe at that time. There is an elder, Usbek, who is grave and sedate, a younger, Rica, who is gay and frivolous, and a third, Rhédi, who does not appear to have got further westward than Venice.

[1] The view that the composition of the Letters extended over several years is confirmed by internal evidence. The correspondence changes in character as it goes on. Compare for instance the apologue of the Troglodytes in Letters xii. to xiv. with the speculations as to the origin of republics in Letter cxxxi., or with the comparative view of the political development and characteristic features of different European states in Letters cxxxiii. to cxxxvii. The Troglodytes are a community that perished through disregard of the rules of equity, but was restored to prosperity by two wise survivors who preached that justice to others is charity to ourselves. After the lapse of some generations their descendants, finding the yoke of republican virtue too hard, ask for a king, and are reproved for doing so. The apologue is interesting because it contains phrases which recur and ideas which are developed in the *Spirit of Laws*. But it is very youthful and abstract. Between the date of the Troglodyte letters and that of the later letters the writer had read much, observed much, and reflected much. Or compare again the story of the travellers and the rabbit with the later observations on the advantage of having more than one religion in a state and on the duty of respecting and tolerating each. The lively personal sketches become more rare: more space is devoted to the discussion of serious problems such as the causes and effects of the decrease of population in Europe since the flourishing days of the Roman Empire. The writer is no longer content with noting and criticizing: he begins to draw conclusions. In short, the feuilletonist is ripening into the philosophical historian and the political philosopher. But at this stage his political philosophy has perhaps not advanced beyond the point indicated by a passage in Letter lxxxi.: "I have often set myself to think which of all the different forms of government is the most conformable to reason, and it seems to me that the most perfect government is that which guides men in the manner most in accordance with their own natural tendencies and inclinations."

The device was not new, but it had never been employed with such brilliancy of style, with such fine irony, with such audacity, with such fertility of suggestion, with such subtlety of observation, with such profundity of thought. And it was admirably adapted for a writer who wished to let his mind play freely on men and manners, to compare and contrast the religious, political and social codes of different countries, to look at his manifold subject from different points of view, to suggest inferences and reflections, and to do all this without committing himself to or making himself responsible for any definite proposition. Any dangerous comment could be easily qualified by a note which explained that it merely represented the Mahommedan or the Persian point of view.

There were a great many dangerous passages, There was the famous letter about the Two Magicians, which nearly cost Montesquieu his election to the Academy.

"The king of France is the most powerful prince in Europe. He has no gold mines, like his neighbour the king of Spain, but he has greater riches, because he draws them from an inexhaustible mine—the vanity of his subjects. He has undertaken and carried on great wars without funds except titles of honour to sell, and, through a prodigy of human pride, his troops have found themselves feared, his fortresses built, his fleets equipped. Moreover he is a great magician. His empire extends to the minds of his subjects : he makes them think as he wishes. If he has only one million crowns in his treasure-chest and he wants two, he has merely to tell them that one crown is equal to two, and they believe it. If he has a difficult war to carry on and has no money, he has merely to put it into their heads that a piece of paper is money, and they are convinced at once. But this is no such marvel, for there is another still greater magician, who is called the Pope, and the things which he makes people believe are even more extraordinary."

Then there was the description of the old king, with his minister of eighteen, and his mistress of eighty,[1] surrounded by a swarm, of invisible enemies, whom, in spite of his confidential dervishes he could never discover. There were many references to religion, mostly irreverent, though not with the fierce and bitter irreverence of Voltaire. Usbek finds imperfect and tentative approxi-

[1] The references, of course exaggerated, were to Barbézieux and Mme. de Maintenon.

mations to Mahommedanism in many of the Christian dogmas and rites, and ascribes to the finger of Providence the way in which the world is being thus prepared for general conversion to the creed of Islam. About diversities of ceremonial belief he has naturally much to say. " The other day I was eating a rabbit at an inn. Three men who were near me made me tremble, for they all declared that I had committed a grievous sin, one because the animal was impure, and the second because it had been strangled, and the third because it was not a fish. I appealed to a Brahmin, who happened to be there, and he said, " They are all wrong, for doubtless you did not kill the animal yourself." " But I did." " Then your action is damnable and unpardonable. How did you know that your father's soul has not passed into that poor beast ?" '

Neither the burning question of the Bull Unigenitus,[1] or Law and his scheme, is left untouched.

He pursues a somewhat less dangerous path, though still a path paved with treacherous cinders, when he sketches, after La Bruyère's manner, contemporary social types, the "grand seigneur" with his offensive manner of taking snuff and caressing his lap-dog, the man "of good fortunes," the dogmatist, the director of consciences who distinguishes between grades of sin, and whose clients are not ambitious of front seats in Paradise, but wish to know just how to squeeze in. There are also national types, such as the Spaniard, whose gravity of character is manifested by his spectacles and his moustache, and who has little forms of politeness which would appear out of place in France. The captain never beats a soldier without asking his permission; the inquisitor makes his apology before burning a Jew. In a more serious vein is the description, so often quoted, of the ruin and desolation caused by the trampling of the Ottoman hoof. No law, no security of life or property: arts, learning, navigation, commerce, all in decay. "In all this vast extent of territory which I have traversed," says the Persian after his journey through Asia Minor, "I have found but one city which has any wealth, and it is to the presence of Europeans that the wealth of Smyrna is due."

The success of the *Persian Letters* was brilliant and instanta-

---

[1] Horace Walpole complained once that he found life in England so dull that he must go to Paris and try and amuse himself with the Bull Unigenitus.

neous,[1] and Montesquieu at once became a leading personage in Parisian society. He took lodgings in the most fashionable quarter,[2] paid his devotions to Mlle. de Clermont at Chantilly, was a favourite guest at the salon of the Marquise de Lambert, and through these influences obtained, though not without a struggle, a seat in the Academy. But he was dissatisfied with his reception there, and made up his mind to travel.

In the year 1728, when Montesquieu set out on his travels, the international politics of Europe were in a singularly confused and tangled position. Congress after congress, treaty after treaty, succeeded each other with bewildering rapidity and with little permanent effect. In Germany, Charles VI., the last male descendant of the Hapsburgs, had recently published his Pragmatic Sanction, was straining every nerve to secure the succession for his daughter Maria Theresa, and was wrangling with the "Termagant of Spain" for the reversion of the Duchies of Modena and Parma. Frederick William of Prussia was recruiting his grenadiers, holding his tobacco parliaments, and negotiating his double marriage project. In Italy, the commercial republics of Venice and Genoa were sinking into decay, Piedmont was emerging as a military power, Florence was under the last of the Medici Grand Dukes. In England, Walpole had secured the confidence of the new king through the influence of his capable queen, and was doing his best, with the help of Cardinal Fleury, to maintain the peace of Europe.

Montesquieu started from Paris in April in the company of Lord Waldegrave, Marshal Berwick's nephew, who had recently been appointed ambassador to the imperial court at Vienna. He travelled through Austria and Hungary, thence went to Venice,[3] visited in turn all the petty states into which Italy

---

[1] "Les *Lettres Persanes* eurent d'abord un débit si prodigieux que les libraires de Hollande mirent tout en usage pour en avoir des suites. Ils alloient tirer par la manche tous ceux qu'ils rencontroient ; Monsieur, disoient-ils, faites-moi des *Lettres Persanes*."—*Pensées*, Collection Bordelaise, i. 46.

[2] Vians talks about his having joined the well-known Entresol Club. But d'Argenson's list of its members (*Mémoires*, p. 248, edition of 1825 ; i. 93, edition of 1859) does not contain his name.

[3] The well-known story, repeated by Vian, of the trick played by Lord Chesterfield on Montesquieu at Venice seems to be a fable (see the remarks in the preface to Montesquieu's *Voyages* in the Collection Bordelaise, i., p. xxiv). It may perhaps be traced to a gossipy letter written by Diderot to Mlle. Voland on Sept. 5, 1762 (Diderot, *Œuvres*, xix., p. 127). We know from the *Chesterfield Letters* that when Montesquieu was at Venice (Aug. 16, Sep. 14, 1728) Chesterfield was writing to Mrs. Howard and Lord Townshend from the Hague.

was then divided, spent several months at Florence, where he devoted himself mainly to art, and made even a longer stay at Rome, to which he returned after Naples. Of his last interview with the Pope a story is told, for which one could wish there were better evidence.[1] The Pope expressed a wish to do something for his distinguished visitor, and at last offered him for himself and his family a perpetual dispensation from fasting. The next day a papal official called with a bull of dispensation made out in due form, and an account of the customary fees. But the thrifty Gascon waved away the parchment. "The Pope is an honest man," he said; "his word is enough for me, and I hope it will be enough for my Maker."

After leaving Italy he visited Munich and Augsburg, travelled by Würtemberg and the Rhine countries to Bonn, the residence of the Elector and Archbishop of Cologne, had an interview with our king George II. at Hanover, explored the Hartz country (on whose mines he wrote a paper), and thence went to the Low Countries. At the Hague he met Lord Chesterfield, who was then British Ambassador, and was on the point of taking leave for England, where he hoped to be made Secretary of State. Montesquieu sailed with him in his yacht on the last day of October, 1729, and remained in England until some time in 1731.

A distinguished German historian,[2] who takes a rather depreciatory view of Montesquieu, says that he travelled rather as a tourist than as a student. The journals of travels and copious notes which have been recently given to the world by the Montesquieu family do not bear out this statement. Probably no man ever started on his travels better equipped by reading and observation, or with a more definite notion of what he wanted to see, hear, and know, or had better opportunities for finding out what was most worth knowing.

Montesquieu had already travelled in imagination through the countries which he was to visit in the flesh. In one of the earlier Persian Letters, written long before Montesquieu left France, Rhédi describes his sojourn at Venice. "My mind is forming itself every day. I am instructing myself about the

---

[1] The story is told by Vian, but is doubted by the Editors of the *Voyages* (Pref., p. xxviii). Vian is responsible for much apocrypha. But apocryphal stories are of historical value as illustrating Montesquieu's reputation among his contemporaries.

[2] Oncken, *Zeitalter Friedrichs des Grossen*, i. 463.

secrets of commerce, the interests of princes, the forms of government. I do not neglect even European superstitions. I apply myself to medicine, physics, astronomy. I am studying the arts. In fact I am emerging from the clouds that covered my eyes in the country of my birth."

That was the programme sketched out in advance, and he had excellent opportunities for carrying it out. At Vienna he spent "delightful moments"[1] with that great captain, Prince Eugene of Savoy. At Venice he had long conversations with two famous adventurers, the Comte de Bonneval, and the Scotchman, Law. At Rome he made the acquaintance of Cardinal Alberoni and the exiled Stuarts. At Modena he conversed with the great antiquarian, Muratori. In England Lord Chesterfield's introduction brought him at once into the best political and social circles. His English journals, if they ever existed, are lost, and for our knowledge of his English experiences we are mainly dependent on the scanty but witty *Notes on England*, which were first published in 1818, and on the numerous references to English books, persons and things which are scattered up and down his recently published *Pensées*. But we know that he attended some exciting debates in Parliament, and we know also how profoundly his study of English institutions influenced the *Spirit of Laws*.

On the preparation for that great work Montesquieu was engaged for the next seventeen years of his life. In 1734 appeared the *Considerations on the Greatness and Decay of the Romans*, which might be treated as the first instalment of its contents. Machiavelli had treated Roman history from the point of view of a practical statesman, and had used it as a storehouse of warnings and examples for the guidance of an Italian prince. "Chance," he said, "leaves great room for prudence in shaping the course of events." Bossuet wrote as a theologian, and sought for evidence of "the secret judgements of God on the Roman empire." Montesquieu wrote as a political philosopher, and tried to find in the history of a particular state the application of certain broad general principles. "It is not fortune that rules the world. There are general causes, moral or physical, on which the rise, the stability, the fall of governments depend. If a state is ruined by the chance of a single battle, that is to say, by a particular event, the possibility of its being so ruined arises from some general cause, and it is for these causes that the

[1] Letter to Abbé de Guasco of Oct. 4, 1752.

historian should seek." In this short treatise Montesquieu's style perhaps reaches its highest level. He is not distracted by a multiplicity of topics; the greatness, dignity and unity of his subject gives force, character, and continuity to his style. His sentences march like a Roman legion.

"The work of twenty years." So Montesquieu describes the *Spirit of Laws*, counting in his three years of travel. And he describes also how the scheme of the book originated, and how it was developed. "I began by observing men, and I believed that in their infinite diversity of laws and manners they were not exclusively led by their fancies. I laid down general principles, and I saw particular cases yield to them naturally. I saw the histories of all nations appear as the consequence of these principles, and each particular law bound with another law, or proceed from one more general. . . . I often began and often dropped the work: I followed my object without forming a plan. I was conscious of neither rule nor exceptions: but when I had discovered my principles, everything that I sought came to me. In the course of twenty years I saw my work begin, grow, advance, and finish."

What, then, are the principles which after so long and painful a search, Montesquieu ultimately found? In brief, they are these. The world is governed, not by chance, nor by blind fate, but by reason. Of this reason, the laws and institutions of different countries are the particular expressions. Each law, each institution, is conditioned by the form of government under which it exists, and which it helps to constitute, and by its relations to such facts as the physical peculiarities of the country, its climate, its soil, its situation, its size; the occupations and mode of life of the inhabitants, and the degree of liberty which the constitution can endure; the religion of the people, their inclinations, number, wealth, trade, manners and customs; and finally by its relations to other laws and institutions, to the object of the legislator, to the order of things in which it is established. It is the sum total of these relations that constitutes the spirit of a law. The relativity of laws—that is Montesquieu's central doctrine. There is no one best form of state or constitution: no law is good or bad in the abstract. Every law, civil and political, must be considered in its relations to the environment, and by the adaptation to that environment its excellence must be judged. If you wish to know and understand the spirit of a law, its essence, its true and inner meaning, that on which its vitality and efficiency depend, you must examine it in its relations to all its antecedents and to all its surroundings. This is the theme which Montesquieu tries to develop and illustrate in the course of his book.

He begins with the relations of laws to different forms of government. There are three kinds of government—republics, with their two varieties of democracy and aristocracy, monarchies, and despotisms. The threefold division is, of course, as old as Plato and Aristotle, but the mode of distribution is new, and is not easily to be defended on scientific grounds. But the historical explanation of the distribution is quite simple. Montesquieu was thinking of the three main types of government with which he was familiar through study or observation. By a republic he meant the city states of the Greek and Roman world, and also such modern city states as Venice and Genoa. Monarchy was the limited monarchy of the West, which still preserved traditions of constitutional checks, but which was, in most countries, tending to become absolute. Despotism was the unbridled, capricious rule of the eastern world.

Each form of Government has its peculiar principle or mainspring. The principle or mainspring of democracy is virtue (by which he practically meant "public spirit"), of aristocracy moderation, of monarchy honour, of despotism fear. These are the principles which must be borne in mind in framing laws for each state. Having exhausted this branch of the subject, he goes on to consider laws in their relation to the military force, political liberty, taxation, church, soil, manners and customs, commerce, finance, religion. It is under the heading of political liberty that are to be found the first of the two famous chapters on the English constitution, and the famous arguments on the necessity for separating the three powers, legislative, executive and judicial.

Nothing is further from my purpose than to enter on a detailed analysis of the *Spirit of Laws*. Indeed, there are few books which it is less profitable to analyze. The spirit evaporates in the process. The value of the book consists, not in the general scheme of arrangement and argument, which is open to much criticism, but in the subtle observations and suggestions, the profound and brilliant reflections, with which it abounds. And the questions which are of most interest to us are, first, What was the cause of the rapid and enormous influence which the book exercised on political thought in all parts of the civilized world ? and, secondly, What was the nature and what were the main effects of that influence ?

But before passing to these questions I should like to touch on one or two points which must be borne in mind by all who read Montesquieu.

In the first place he was an aristocrat, a member of a privileged, exclusive, and fastidious class. He was no upstart of genius like Voltaire, who could be insulted with impunity by a sprig of nobility. He belonged to a good family and moved habitually in the best society.

His *milieu* and his point of view were different from those of typical bourgeois, such as Marais and Barbier. He was a country gentleman, and was fond of strolling about his vineyards, and talking to his tenants and labourers. "I like talking to peasants," he said; "they are not learned enough to reason perversely." But his attitude towards them was that of a great Whig nobleman or squire. Of their feelings and points of view he could know nothing. The third estate, which was nothing and was to be everything, was to him, for most purposes, an unknown world.[1] But, though he was not wholly free from the faults of his class and his time, he was a great gentleman, with a genuine public spirit, a genuine love of liberty, a genuine hatred of oppression, cruelty, intolerance, and injustice. Among the three great political thinkers of the day, Montesquieu stands for liberty, as Voltaire stands for efficiency, and Rousseau for equality.[1] If Lord Acton's projected History of Liberty had ever seen the light, Montesquieu would doubtless have been among its greatest heroes.

In the next place Montesquieu belonged to a hereditary caste— the caste which supplied the staff of judges and magistrates for France. Not that he wrote as a lawyer. For some fourteen years he was a member of the judicial bench known as the Parlement of Guienne, and in that capacity administered Roman

[1] " On turning from Montesquieu to Rousseau we may fancy that we have been present at some Parisian salon, where an elegant philosopher has been presenting to fashionable hearers conclusions daintily arranged in sparkling epigrams and suited for embodiment in a thousand brilliant essays. Suddenly, there has entered a man stained with the filth of the streets, his utterance choked with passion, a savage menace lurking in every phrase, and announcing himself as the herald of a furious multitude, ready to tear to pieces all the beautiful theories and formulas which stand between them and their wants."—Leslie Stephen, *English Thought in the Eighteenth Century*, p. 191.

law, such of the Royal Ordinances as extended to his province, and no less than ten different local customs. But he did not take much interest in the technical side of his professional work, and it may be doubted whether his judgments, if reported, would have carried more weight with his professional brethren than those of his distinguished predecessor on the same bench—Montaigne. Nor did he take any active part in the scientific work in which the great French lawyers of the eighteenth century were engaged. That work was digesting, expressing, and systematically arranging the principles of the customary law and the modernized Roman law, and thus collecting the materials and preparing the framework for the codes of the revolutionary and Napoleonic eras. The leaders in this work were the great Chancellor d'Aguesseau and Pothier. But Montesquieu does not, so far as I am aware, make any reference to Pothier or his school at Orleans, and his relations to d'Aguesseau were scanty and formal. Indeed, between the lively President and the grave Chancellor[1] there was little in common. If Montesquieu had lived in the latter half of the nineteenth century, he would not, we may feel sure, have got on with Lord Cairns. It was Voltaire, and not Montesquieu, that preached the duty of unifying French law, and Montesquieu's personal preference would probably have been for diversity rather than for uniformity. But Montesquieu was a great " Parliamentarian " in the French sense of the word. He attached great political importance to the existence of a "dépôt of law," entrusted to the custody of an organized independent body, and he scandalized Voltaire by defending the system of purchasing judicial offices as the best practical security for judicial independence.

And lastly Montesquieu wrote with the Censor and the Index always before his eyes. Hence the allusive and hypothetical style, which in some of his imitators became a mannerism. This characteristic is nowhere better illustrated than in the chapter on the English constitution. It is headed " Of the constitution of England," but the text of the chapter consists of a number of "ifs " and "oughts." Such and such an arrangement ought to exist. If such an arrangement were made it would lead to political liberty. It is not until the concluding paragraphs that the English are specifically mentioned, and then only in a guarded

[1] See d'Argenson's sketch of d'Aguesseau: *Mémoires* (edition of 1825), p. 152.

manner. "It is not for me to examine whether the English actually enjoy this liberty or not. It is sufficient to say that it is established by their laws, and I seek no more." In Montesquieu's time it was not always safe to dot your "*i's*." And that his nervousness was not unfounded is shown by the fact that, notwithstanding his precautions, his book found its way on to the Index, and remained for two years under the ban of the civil censor.

And now to come back to the main problem. How was it that a book with such obvious and glaring defects exercised an influence so enormous? The leading definitions are loose and vague; the treatment is unmethodical and uncritical; half the statements of facts are inaccurate; half the inferences are mere guesses. And yet it changed the thought of the world. What is the explanation of this paradox?

Much, no doubt, was due to charm of style. If you want to be read, still more if you want to be widely read, you must be readable. In Montesquieu's time, books on political and legal science were, as a rule, unreadable. But the *Spirit of Laws* was, and still is, an eminently readable book. No one before Montesquieu had dealt in so lively and brilliant a manner with the dry subject of laws and political institutions. The book reflects the personality of the writer. His personality is not obtruded in the foreground, like that of Montaigne, but it is always present in the background, and its presence gives a human interest to an abstract topic. You see the two sides of the author; the favourite guest of Parisian *salons*, and the solitary student, the desultory and omnivorous reader. He lived, we must remember, in an age when conversation was cultivated as a fine art. That untranslatable word "esprit," which was in the mouth of every eighteenth-century Frenchman, meant, in its narrowest and most special sense, the essence of good conversation.[1] Montesquieu had, like other Frenchmen of his time, thought much about the art of conversation, and had practised it in the best *salons*—where, however, he had the reputation of being more of a listener than a talker—and the rules that he

[1] "L'esprit de conversation est ce qu'on appelle de l'esprit parmi les Français. Il consiste à (*sic*) un dialogue ordinairement gai, dans lequel chacun, sans s'écouter beaucoup, parle et répond, et où tout se traite d'une manière coupée, prompte et vive. . . . Ce qu'on appelle esprit chez les Français n'est donc pas de l'esprit mais un genre particulier de l'esprit."—Montesquieu, *Pensées* (Collection Bordelaise), ii. 302, 303.

laid down for good writing are practically the rules for good conversation. "To write well," he says somewhere, "you must, skip the connecting links, enough not to be a bore, not so much as to be unintelligible.'[1] Hence his book is not so much a dissertation as a *causerie*. It rambles pleasantly unmethodically from point to point, welcomes digressions, and often goes off at a tangent. You feel yourself in the presence of a learned, witty, and urbane talker, who does not wish to monopolize the talk, but desires to elicit that free, responsive play of thought which is essential to good conversation. "I don't want to exhaust the subject," he says, "for who can say everything without being a deadly bore."[2] And again, "My object is not to make you read; but to make you think."[3]

But Montesquieu is also a man of the closet, a man who spent long, solitary hours in his library at La Brède,[4] filling note-books with copious extracts, and condensing his thoughts in maxims and reflections. And he is too often unable to resist the temptation of utilizing the contents of his note-books without considering sufficiently whether they are relevant to or assist the progress of his argument. Indeed, he is essentially a "fragmentary" thinker, sententious rather than continuous, and constitutionally reluctant, perhaps unable, to follow out persistently long trains of thought. But these peculiarities, though they detract from the scientific merit of his book, make it more readable. So also do the little asides by which he takes his readers into his confidence, as when he reminds himself that if he dwells too much on the absence of any need for virtue in a monarchy, he may be suspected of irony, or when he gives expression to the feelings of lassitude and discouragement which overtake him towards the end of his task.

Charm of style, then, counts for much in explaining Montesquieu's influence. But freshness and originality count for much more. The orthodox way of dealing with a subject of political or legal science was to start from general propositions laid down authoritatively, and derived either from Aristotle, or, more often from the Roman jurists, and to deduce from them certain general conclusions. Bodin's great treatise on the Republic, to which Montesquieu was much indbeted, especially for his theory on the

---

[1] *Pensées*, ii. 14.   [2] *Esprit des lois*, Preface.   [3] *Ibid.*, book xi., ch. xx.
[4] A description of the contents of Montesquieu's library is given by Brunet in the Collection Migne : *Troisième encyclopédie théologique*, tome 43, col. 344.

influence of climate, was framed on these lines. But Montesquieu broke away from the old lines. His starting-point was different. He began at the other end. He started from the particular institutions, not from the general principles.

I have dwelt at length, perhaps at undue length, on the *Persian Letters*, not because, as has been inaccurately said, the *Spirit of Laws* is merely a continuation of the earlier work, but because the Montesquieu of the *Spirit of Laws* is still the Montesquieu of the *Persian Letters*, matured and ripened by twenty-seven years of study and experience, but in essentials still the same.

He began his literary career with no preoccupied theory or object, but as a detached and irresponsible critic and observer of man in his infinite diversity, the man *ondoyant et divers* of Montaigne. And he retained much of this irresponsibility and detachment to the last. It is true that after much search he found, or believed that he found, certain general laws, or principles, to which his observations could be attached, under which they could be grouped. But one often feels, in reading his opening chapters, that they are a sham façade, giving a deceptive appearance of unity to a complicated and irregular set of buildings, richly stored with miscellaneous objects of interest. His doctrine of the relativity of laws, which is the foundation of enlightened conservatism, and has been used in defence of much conservatism which is not enlightened, is not a sufficient foundation for a constructive system, but was an admirable starting-point for a man whose primary interest lay in observing and comparing different institutions and drawing inferences from their similarities and diversities. "Any one who has eyes to see," he wrote in his subsequent *Defence of the Spirit of Laws*, "must see at a glance that the object of the work was the different laws, customs and usages of the peoples of the world." A vast, an overwhelming subject, which the author failed to succeed in mastering and controlling, or bringing within a synthetic grasp. And owing to this failure the *Spirit of Laws* has been not unfairly described as being, not a great book, but the fragments of a great book.[1]

[1] Brunetière, *Études critiques*, 4ᵐᵉ série, p. 258. The Marquis d'Argenson, one of the most sagacious and prescient observers that the eighteenth century produced, was shown some portions of the *Esprit des lois* before the book was published, and his forecast of its character proved to be singularly accurate:—" On prétend qu'il (Montesquieu) se prépare enfin à publier son grand ouvrage sur les lois. J'en connais déjà quelques morceaux, qui, soutenus par la réputation de l'auteur, ne peuvent que l'augmenter. Mais je crains bien que l'ensemble n'y manque, et qu'il n'y ait plus de chapitres

What he did succeed in doing was in indicating the path by which alone effective and fruitful progress could be made either in jurisprudence or in the science of politics, the path through diversity to uniformity, through facts to principles. He refashioned political science and made it a science of observation, and by so doing he made the same new departure in political and legal science as Bacon had made before him in physical science. He closed the period of the schoolmen. He was not content to mumble the dry bones of Roman law. He turned men away from abstract and barren speculations to the study and comparison of concrete institutions. And it is in this sense that he may be claimed as one of the founders of the comparative method as applied to the moral and political sciences.

He began at the other end. This may seem a little thing. In reality it was a very great thing. The human mind is intensely conservative. For generations men go on working at the old subjects in the old ways. Then comes a man who, by some new thought, it may be by some new phrase, which becomes a catchword, like "evolution," takes his fellow-men out of the old ruts, and opens up to them new regions of speculation and discovery. These are the men that change the world. And Montesquieu was one of these men.

He has been claimed on high authority,[1] but with less accuracy, as the founder of the historical method, which is at least as old as Thucydides. That he appreciated the importance of this

---

agréables à lire, plus d'idées ingénieuses et séduisantes, que de véritables et utiles instructions sur la façon dont on devrait rédiger les lois et les entendre. C'est pourtant là le livre qu'il nous faudrait, et qui nous manque encore, quoiqu'on ait déjà tant écrit sur cette matière.

"Nous avons de bons instituts de droit civil romain, nous en avons de passables de droit français; mais nous n'en avons absolument point de droit public général et universel. Nous n'avons point l'*esprit des lois*, et je doute fort que mon ami, le président de Montesquieu, nous en donne un qui puisse servir de guide et de boussole à tous les législateurs du monde. Je lui connais tout l'esprit possible. Il a acquis les connaissances les plus pastes, tant dans ses voyages que dans ses retraites à la campagne. Mais je prédis encore une fois qu'il ne nous donnera pas le livre qui nous manque, quoique l'on doive trouver dans celui qu'il prépare beaucoup d'idées profondes, de pensées neuves, d'images frappantes, de saillies d'esprit et de génie, et une multitude de faits curieux, dont l'application suppose encore plus de goût que d'étude."
—*Mémoires du Marquis d'Argenson* (ed. 1825), pp. 430, 431. It is to be hoped that this passage has not, like others in the edition of 1825, been recast by the editor. As to the defects of this edition, see Sainte-Beuve, *Causeries du Lundi*, vol. xii. And as to the later editions of d'Argenson, see Aubertin, *L'esprit public au xviiie siècle*, p. 194.

[1] By Sir Henry Maine, Sir Leslie Stephen, and others.

method is true. "I could wish," he says in one of his fragments,[1] "that there were better works on the laws of each country. To know modern times, one must know antiquity: each law must be followed in the spirit of all the ages." But for its application he had neither the requisite knowledge nor the requisite capacity. Like his predecessors, he speculated about the state of nature. But for any knowledge of savage or uncivilized man, without which all speculations and theories as to the origin of society are idle, he was dependent on books of travel and accounts of missionaries, with no means of checking their accuracy. Of the Iroquois who stood for the typical savage in the early eighteenth century, he had doubtless read in *Lahortan* and in *The Relations of the Jesuits*, but one is sometimes tempted to think that he knows no more about him than might have been picked up from some stray Bordeaux mariner who had navigated Canadian waters. In his account of early Roman history he follows implicitly Livy and Florus, and of Beaufort's critical investigation he does not seem to have heard. Nor is there any evidence of his having read or having been influenced by Vico, that solitary, mystical, suggestive Neapolitan thinker, who seemed to live out of due time, and whose significance was not appreciated until the following century. He had heard of the *Scienza nuova* at Venice, where the first edition was much in demand, and made a note of it as a book to be purchased at Naples, but there is nothing to show that the purchase was made.[2] And in the main his method of procedure is unhistorical. He takes more account of the surroundings of laws than of their antecedents. He sees laws of different periods all in the same plane. He conceives of the State as a condition of equilibrium which is to be maintained. He realizes the possibility of its decay, but the notions of progress and development, which are to figure so largely in Turgot and Condorcet, are foreign to his mind.

On the influence exercised by Montesquieu's great book, a substantial volume could be written. It was far-reaching and

[1] *Pensées*, i. 195.
[2] See *Voyages de Montesquieu*, i. 65. The first edition of the *Scienza nuova* was published in 1725. Vico tells us in his autobiography that the Venetian ambassador at Naples had orders to buy up all available copies from the Neapolitan publisher, Felice Mosca. See " Vita di G. B. Vico " in *Opere di Vico*, iv., p. 456 (ed. by G. Ferrari, Milan, 1876). It may be that when Montesquieu reached Naples he found that the edition had been sold out. The relations of Vico to Montesquieu are discussed by Professor Flint in his little book on Vico.

profound. It was felt in the course of political thought; it was felt in the methods of political science. It is almost true that Montesquieu invented the theory of the British constitution. At all events he was the chief contributor to what may be called the authorized version of the British constitution, the version to which currency was given by Blackstone[1] and Delolme, which was used by the framers of constitutions on the continent of America and on the continent of Europe, and which held the field until it was displaced by the Cabinet theory of Walter Bagehot. The question has often been asked how far Montesquieu really knew and understood the institutions which he described.[2] On this there are two things to be said. In the first place the British constitution which grew up out of the Revolution of 1688 was, when Montesquieu wrote, still in the making. The lines on which it was developed were not yet fixed; whether it would give preponderance to the King or to Parliament was still uncertain. In the next place Montesquieu wrote with a purpose. England was to him what Germany had been to Tacitus. It was a neighbouring country in which he found, or thought that he found, principles of liberty which had vanished from his own country, and for the restoration of which he hoped. And he sketched those principles like a great artist, with a bold and free sweep of the brush. He sought to render the spirit and characteristic features: for minute accuracies of topographical detail he cared as little as Turner cared in painting a landscape.

That a book thus conceived should be read with delight and admiration by Englishmen was not surprising.[3] Its practical

[1] M. Sorel goes too far in saying that Blackstone "procède de" Montesquieu. But the *Spirit of Laws* is expressly quoted in ch. ii., book i., of the *Commentaries*, and its influence is clearly apparent throughout that chapter.

[2] How much was known in France of English institutions when Montesquieu published his *Esprit des lois?* Rapin's *History of England*, published at the Hague in 1724, was probably the principal available authority. "No book did more to make Europe acquainted with Great Britain" (Texte, *J.-J Rousseau*, etc. (trans. by J. W. Matthews), p. 21). Much knowledge was disseminated by Huguenot refugees in England, and much could have been learnt from English political refugees, like Bolingbroke, in France. But the amount of information available in a literary form for French readers was probably not great. Voltaire's *Lettres anglaises*, based on his visit of 1726-9, were published in France in 1734.

[3] Nugent's English translation of the *Spirit of Laws* appears to have been published in 1750. See Montesquieu's letter to the translator of Oct. 18, 1750. A second edition, of which there is a copy in the British Museum, appeared in 1752, and several other editions followed.

"My delight," says Gibbon in his autobiography, "was in the frequent influence was first exercised in English lands, not indeed in Old England, but in the New England which was growing up beyond the seas. When Washington talked about the Lycian republic, we may be sure he was quoting directly, or indirectly, from the *Spirit of Laws*. From the same book Hamilton and Madison in the *Federalist* drew arguments for federation and for the division between legislative, executive, and judicial powers.[1] And later on, Thomas Jefferson, a statesman bred in a widely different school of thought, had a curious commentary on the *Spirit of Laws* prepared for him by a peer of France, who was a member of the French Institute and of the Philosophical Society of Philadelphia.[2]

In England the spirit of Montesquieu found its fullest and most glorious expression in Burke, both when in his earlier years he was protesting against monarchical infringements of the British constitution, and when in his later years he was denouncing the tyranny of the French Convention.

From the language used by Sir Henry Maine in the famous fourth chapter of his *Ancient Law* one might infer that in his own country Montesquieu's influence was at once eclipsed by that of Rousseau. But such an inference would be erroneous. Montesquieu, Voltaire, and Rousseau, different as were their methods

---

perusal of Montesquieu, whose energy of style and boldness of hypothesis were powerful to awaken and stimulate the genius of the age."

There is a curious and characteristic rhapsody on Montesquieu in Bentham's *Commonplace Book* (Works by Bowring, x., p. 143). "When the truths in a man's book, though many and important, are fewer than the errors; when his ideas, though the means of producing clear ones in other men, are found to be themselves not clear, that book must die: Montesquieu must therefore die: he must die, as his great countryman, Descartes, had died before him: he must wither as the blade withers, when the corn is ripe: he must die, but let tears of gratitude and admiration bedew his grave. O Montesquieu! the British constitution, whose death thou prophesiedst, will live longer than thy work, yet not longer than thy fame. Not even the incense of [the illustrious Catherine] can preserve thee.

"Locke—dry, cold, languid, wearisome, will live for ever. Montesquieu—rapid, brilliant, glorious, enchanting—will not outlive his century.

"I know—I feel—I pity—and blush at the enjoyment of a liberty which the birthplace of that great writer (great with all his faults) [forbade him to enjoy].

"I could make an immense book upon the defects of Montesquieu—I could make not a small one upon his excellences. It might be worth while to make both, if Montesquieu could live."

[1] See Letters 9 (A. Hamilton) and 47 (Madison), and Bryce's *American Commonwealth*, part i., ch. xxv.

[2] Destutt de Tracy. His curious commentary is really an attempt to rewrite the *Spirit of Laws* from the commentator's point of view.

and their aims, were all factors of the first importance in the French Revolution. "Every enlightened Frenchman," says M. Sorel, "had in his library at the end of the eighteenth century a Montesquieu, a Voltaire, a Rousseau, and a Buffon."[1] The *Spirit of Laws* was a storehouse of argument for the publicists of 1789, and French writers of repute have maintained that the influence of Montesquieu counted for as much in the Declaration of Rights as the influence of Rousseau. It must be remembered that, though Montesquieu wrote as a monarchist, his heart was in the little republics of the Græco-Roman world, and he is responsible for much of the pseudo-classicism which characterized political thought at the end of the eighteenth century. It is true that during the interval between 1789 and 1793 the influence of Montesquieu waned as that of Rousseau waxed. He was identified with the aristocrats and Anglophiles[2]: the Girondists were charged with studying him overmuch ; and if Robespierre quoted him for his purpose, he quoted him with a significant difference. "In times of Revolution," said Robespierre, "the principle of popular government is both virtue and terror : virtue without which terror is fatal; terror without which virtue is powerless."[3] Napoleon had studied the *Spirit of Laws*, but a system which aimed at the preservation of political liberty by the separation of political powers did not commend itself to his mind.[4] Dormant under the Consulate and the Empire, the influence of Montesquieu arose to renewed and more powerful life at the Restoration, and was, during the first half of the nineteenth century, the inspiration of all constitutional monarchists, both in France and in other European countries.

The influence of Montesquieu on methods of study was as important, though not as immediate,[5] as his influence on the

[1] Sorel, *Montesquieu*, p. 149.
[2] Under the Terror Montesquieu's son was thrown into prison as a suspect and his property was sequestrated. He died in 1795. Montesquieu's grandson, who had served under Washington in the United States, became an *émigré*, married an Irish lady and settled down in Kent, where he died without issue in 1825. He left his MSS. and his French property to a cousin, descended from a daughter of the great Montesquieu.
[3] Sorel, p. 155.
[4] See the interesting letter of Sept. 19, 1797, written by Napoleon from Italy to Talleyrand, with a request that it might be shown to Sieyès. Napoleon, *Correspondance*, vol. iii., p. 313 (No. 2223).
[5] "Un seul écrivain, Montesquieu, le mieux instruit, le plus sagace et le plus équilibré de tous les esprits du siècle, démêlait ces vérités, parce qu'il était à la fois érudit, observateur, historien et jurisconsulte. Mais il parlait comme un oracle, par sentences et en énigmes ; il courait, comme sur des

course of political thought. Of the historical and comparative method, in their application to Law and Politics, he was, as has been justly remarked,[1] rather a precursor than a founder. His appreciation of the historical method was imperfect, and his application of it defective. It was not until the expiration of a century after his death that the importance and significance of either the historical or the comparative method was fully realized. But in the meantime his central doctrine, that the true spirit and meaning of a law or constitution cannot be grasped without careful study of all its surroundings and all its antecedents, had sunk deeply into the minds of students, and prepared the way for and gave an enormous stimulus to those methods of study which are now recognized as indispensable to any scientific treatment either of Law or of Politics.

Within the last half-century societies for the study of Comparative Law and Comparative Legislation have come into existence in France, England, Germany and elsewhere,[2] and have done, and are doing, work of the greatest interest and utility. Some of them approach their subject mainly from the point of view of the lawyer or the jurist, and devote their attention primarily to those branches and aspects of the subject which fall within the domain either of private or of criminal law. Others look primarily at the constitutional and administrative experiments which are being tried by the legislatures of different countries, and thus deal with their subject as a branch of political science. Their areas of study overlap each other, and the point of view is not quite the same. Within each area they have collected and compared a vast quantity of facts which form an indispensable preliminary to, and constitute the raw material for, a scientific treatment of the studies with which they are concerned. The task that remains for the scientific jurist and for the political philosopher is to elicit, in the spirit of Montesquieu,

---

charbons ardents, toutes les fois qu'il touchait aux choses de son pays et de son temps. C'est pourquoi il demeurait respecté, mais isolé, et sa célébrité n'était point influence."—Taine, *Ancien Régime*, p. 278. This statement of Taine must be read as applying to Montesquieu's influence on method, not to his influence on political thought.

[1] By Sir F. Pollock in his farewell lecture on the "History of Comparative Jurisprudence" (*Journal of the Society of Comparative Legislation*, August, 1903).

[2] Société de Législation Comparée, founded 1869; Gesellschaft für vergleichende Rechts- und Staatswissenschaft, founded 1893; Internationale Vereinigung für vergleichende Rechtswissenschaft und Volkswirthschaft, founded 1894; (English) Society of Comparative Legislation, founded 1894.

but with fuller knowledge, and with better critical methods, the inner meaning of the laws and institutions of different countries, and to trace the general lines on which they have developed in the past, and may be expected to develop in the future.

One might amuse oneself by speculating on the differences which Montesquieu would have observed, and on the general reflections which he might have made, if he had been called upon to pass in review the governments and legislation of the present day. He would have found in almost every part of the civilized world governments with representative legislatures and parliamentary institutions, all more or less on the English lines which he had admired and described, and all recognizing, though in greater or less degree, and in different forms, his principle of the separation between the three functions of government, legislative, executive, and judicial. And he would have found all these legislatures actively and continuously engaged in the work of legislation, and producing new laws with prodigious fertility and in bewildering variety.

Besides the legislatures of European and South American States, there are within the British Empire between sixty and seventy different legislatures, and in the United States forty-eight local legislatures, in addition to the central legislature consisting of Senate and Congress. And in the year 1901 these forty-eight United States legislatures enacted no less than 14,190 new laws. When Montesquieu wrote, the British Parliament was practically the only representative legislature in the world, and the only legislature which was continuously at work. And its output of legislation was comparatively modest. Let us take the record of the session of 1730, when Montesquieu was attending debates at St. Stephen's. There was no reference to legislation in the King's Speech. The Acts of the session were forty-eight, and of these twenty were local and four fiscal. There was an Act, which gave rise to some debate, for placing restrictions on loans by British subjects to foreign States, a measure which, as Sir Robert Walpole explained, arose out of a projected loan for the assistance of the Emperor Charles VI., whose diplomatic relations with George the Second were strained. The care of Parliament for trade and industry was minutely paternal. There was an Act for regulating the methods of burning bricks, and another for better regulating the coal trade. There was an Act for granting liberty to carry rice from His Majesty's Province of Carolina in America directly to any part of Europe southward of Cape Finisterre in ships built in and belonging to Great Britain and navigated according to law, and another Act for the importing of salt from Europe into the colony of New York with the view to the better curing of fish, "whereby the trade of Great Britain and the inhabitants of the said colony would reap considerable benefit which would enable the said inhabitants to purchase more of the British manufacturers for their use than at present they are able." And there was one of the numerous "omnibus" Acts then allowed by Parliamentary procedure, dealing, within its four corners, with the price of bread, the relief of bankrupts, deeds and wills executed by Papists, and the settlement of paupers. And this is nearly all. The eighteenth-century statutes, except so far as they are purely local, consist chiefly of detailed regulations made by landowners sitting at Westminster for their own guidance as justices of the peace in the country. And the executive functions of the central government were at that time very limited. "The Prince," says Montesquieu, "in his exercise of executive functions, makes peace or war, sends or receives embassies, keeps the peace, prevents invasions." It was in fact to the maintenance of the internal peace that, apart from foreign relations and war, the duties of the central government were mainly confined. There was no Local Government Board, no Board of Education, no Board of Agriculture, and the duties of the Board of Trade were almost nominal. Nor, on the other hand, were there county councils, district councils, or parish councils. The municipalities were close, corrupt, irresponsible corporations, existing for the benefit of their members and not of the local public. There were no railways, and no limited companies. Gas and electricity had not been utilized. Parliament did not concern itself with educational or sanitary questions, and factory legislation was a thing of the distant future.[1] Thus almost all the materials for modern Parliamentary legislation were absent.

This, then, would have been one of the differences that Montesquieu would have noted—the prodigious increase in the extent and variety of legislation. And on investigating the causes of the difference he would have found the main cause to be this—that the world has, since his time been absolutely transformed

[1] I have ventured to repeat some expressions used in chapter x. of my book on *Legislative Methods and Forms*.

by the operation of physical science. What has physical science done for the world ? It has done three things. It has increased the ease and speed of production. It has increased the ease and speed of locomotion. It has increased the ease and speed of communicating information and opinion.[1] And by so doing it has made for democracy, it has made for plutocracy, it has made for great States. It has made for democracy, both by enabling the popular will to act more speedily and effectively, and by the creation of wealth which levels distinctions based on social position. But it has also increased, to an extent unimaginable even in the days of Law's system and the South Sea Bubble, that power of great finance which manufactures through its press what is called public opinion, pulls the strings of political puppets, and is the most subtle, ubiquitous and potent of modern political forces.

Physical science has made great democratic States possible, and great States, or agglomerations of States, necessary. For Montesquieu, as for Aristotle, a democracy meant a body of citizens who could meet together in one place for political discussion. The body must not be too large, for as Aristotle says, if it were, what herald could address them, unless he were a Stentor ? But the modern statesman, to say nothing of the modern reporter who heralds a cricket match, can, without being a Stentor, speak to the Antipodes. And science has made great States necessary by increasing both the effectiveness and the cost of munitions of war. States agglomerate both for economy and for self-defence, and small isolated States exist only by sufferance.

Since Montesquieu's time both the area and the population of the civilized world have enormously increased. And yet for political purposes it has become a much smaller world, smaller, more compact, more accessible. And this has tended to greater uniformity of legislation and institutions.

The greater uniformity has been brought about mainly in three ways. First, by direct imitation. Man, as M. Tarde has reminded us, is an imitative animal. He imitates his forefathers : that is custom. He imitates his neighbours : that is fashion. He imitates himself : that is habit. And direct imitation plays a large part in institutions and legislation. English Parliamentary procedure has made the tour of the world. Guizot

---

[1] See Faguet's interesting essay, *Que sera le xxme siècle*, in *Questions politiques* (Paris, 1899).

reminded a Committee of the House of Commons in 1848 that Mirabeau had based the rules of the National Assembly on a sketch of the proceedings of the House of Commons furnished to him by Étienne Dumont,[1] and that when the Charter was granted by Louis XVIII. in 1814, the same rules were adopted with some changes. Thomas Jefferson, when President of the United States, drew up for the use of Congress a manual consisting largely of extracts from English Parliamentary precedents, and Jefferson's Manual is still an authoritative work. Every colonial legislature conforms to the rules, forms, usages, and practices of the Commons House of Parliament of Great Britain and Ireland, except so far as they have been locally modified. A very large proportion of Colonial enactments are directly copied from the English Statute-book, with minor local variations. And the practice of looking for and copying precedents supplied by other legislatures is steadily on the increase, not only within the British Empire, but in all parts of the civilized world. This, then, is one cause of uniformity.

In the next place the facility of intercourse, and especially the closeness of commercial relations between different countries, tends to a general assimilation of commercial usages. The diversity of laws which was found intolerable in France at the end of the eighteenth century, and in Germany at the end of the nineteenth century, has long made itself felt as a serious and as a remediable nuisance in matters of commerce throughout the world, and in many parts of the domain of commercial law we have either attained to or are within measurable distance of that common code of laws which is the dream of comparative jurists.

And lastly, in a world compacted and refashioned by science, those causes of difference to which Montesquieu attached importance, and in some cases exaggerated importance—causes such as climate, race, geographical conditions, difference in forms and degrees of civilization—tend to become of less importance. Not that they have disappeared, or can be left out of account. Montesquieu took much interest in questions of political economy,

[1] Evidence before Select Committee on Public Business, Q. 309. Dumont's own account (*Souvenirs sur Mirabeau*, p. 164) does not quite bear out Guizot's statement. According to Dumont, Romilly had made a sketch of English Parliamentary procedure, which Dumont translated for Mirabeau. Mirabeau laid this translation on the table by way of a proposal, but the Assembly declined to consider it: " Nous ne sommes pas Anglais, et nous n'avons pas besoin des Anglais." Romilly's own account of his sketch, and of its fate, s to the same effect. *Memoirs*, i. 101.

and he would certainly have pointed out that fiscal arrangements which are well adapted to a State whose territories are continuous, are presumably less well adapted to a State whose component parts are sundered by oceans. The question of race is always with us, and the jealousies and antipathies of white, brown, yellow and black races present an insoluble problem to the legislator in almost every part of the globe. Nor are the legislative problems which, apart from race, arise from the contrast between different degrees and stages of civilization, less numerous, less difficult, or less interesting. Within the British Empire we have to legislate for the hill-tribes of India, for the fetish-worshippers of Western Africa, and for the savages of New Guinea ; and a museum full of instructions and suggestions to the statesman and the jurist is to be found in the Regulations made by the Government of British India for its less advanced regions and in the Ordinances which have been passed for the West African Protectorates. Thus the causes of difference remain and are of importance. But on the whole the importance of the causes which make for difference tends to decrease, and the importance of the causes which make for uniformity tends to increase. Take up one of the annual summaries of the world's legislation which are published by the French and English Societies of Comparative Legislation. Your first impression will be one of bewilderment at the multiplicity and variety of the subjects dealt with. But if you read on, and still more if you extend your studies over a series of years, you will be struck with the large number of important subjects which recur with unfailing regularity in the legislation of each State in each year. Education, factory laws, mining laws, liquor traffic—everywhere you will find the same problems being dealt with on lines of increasing similarity, though with a due recognition of the differences arising from diversities of race, character and local conditions. In the year 1902 the legislature of the Straits Settlements was imposing on little Malay children the duty of compulsory attendance at school, and the legislature of Sierra Leone was regulating Mohammedan education on Western lines, whatever that may mean. It is perhaps in the field of industrial legislation that this similarity of treatment and of trend is most remarkable. A quarter of a century ago the liability of employers for injuries to their workmen was in every civilized country regulated by rules derived directly or indirectly from the old Roman law. Since that time almost every legislature has been altering those rules, and has been altering them in the same direction. It has been recognized everywhere that the principle of basing liability on personal negligence is inadequate to meet the modern conditions of corporate employment, of employment by great companies, and the universal tendency has been towards placing the employer in the position of an insurer against accidents to his workmen, and of thus imposing on him a risk which he again meets by modern methods of insurance. Similar tendencies may be observed in other departments of industrial legislation, such as the further recognition of the right of workmen to combine, the regulation of the conditions of employment, especially in such organized employments as mines and factories, the restrictions on the employment of women and children, the requirement of precautions against risk to health and life, the formation of Government pension funds against sickness and old age, and provisions for the settlement of labour disputes. In all these branches of legislation there is a general move in the same direction, though with differences of detail and at different rates of progress. In short, the whole civilized world appears to be advancing towards a common industrial code, as it is advancing towards a common commercial code.

Some hundred years after Montesquieu's death another brilliant book was written on the Spirit of Law.[1] Savigny had laid down the dogma that the law of each nation is the natural and necessary outgrowth of the national consciousness. Ihering reminded his readers that Rome had thrice conquered the world, first by arms, secondly by religion, and lastly by law; and that the general reception of Roman law, of which Savigny was the historian, was inconsistent with the dogma of the exclusively national character of law, of which Savigny was the prophet. As nations live commercially by the free interchange of commodities, so they live intellectually by the free interchange of ideas, and they are not the worse, but the better, for borrowing from each other such laws and institutions as are suitable to their needs. It is true, as Savigny taught, and as Montesquieu had indicated before him, that the laws of a nation can only be understood if they are studied as part of the national life and character. But it is also true that the object of the jurist is to discover the

[1] The first edition of Ihering's *Geist des römischen Rechts* began to appear in 1852.

general principles which underlie different systems of law. Only he has now realized that those principles cannot be discovered except by a profound and scientific study of the legal institutions and the legal history of different nations, and by comparing with each other the laws of different countries and the different stages of legal development. It was in order to discover the true meaning of the legal rules derived from ancient Rome, as the main factor of European law, that Ihering undertook his inquiry into the Spirit of Roman Law. He who would measure the advance in the breadth and depth of comparative jurisprudence between the middle of the eighteenth and the middle of the nineteenth century could not do better than compare Montesquieu's *Spirit of Laws* with Ihering's *Spirit of Roman Law*.

Montesquieu left two great legacies to the world. He formulated the theory of the British constitution which held the field for a century, and was the foundation of every constitutional government established during that period; and he gave a new direction to the study of legal and political science.

Montesquieu was one of the greatest of the apostles of liberty in modern times. Socially and politically, he belongs to the old régime, to the régime which in France passed away in 1789, which in England, where changes are less catastrophic, began to pass away in 1832. Scientifically also he belongs to a bygone age. His new ideas, his new methods, once so fresh, so attractive, so stimulating, have passed into and been merged in the common heritage of Western thought. But in his generation he succeeded, with a success beyond his most sanguine hopes, in doing what he tried to do—he made men think.

ROBERT JOSEPH POTHIER

ROBERT JOSEPH POTHIER AND FRENCH LAW

ROBERT JOSEPH POTHIER was born in the town of Orleans on January 9, 1699, and he died there on March 2, 1772. He came of an Orleans family of good position that had for generations exercised magisterial functions in the town. His father was Robert Pothier, his mother Marie Madeleine Jacquet. Robert Pothier held the magisterial office of Conseiller au Présidial d'Orléans, an office that his son was destined to hold, and which his father, Florent Pothier, had held. He was descended from the Florent Pothier who was Mayor of Orleans in 1603. Robert Pothier died when his son was only five years old, but the influence of the future jurist's mother determined that his career should follow the hereditary legal bias. The child was educated in the Jesuit College at Orleans, and there, despite his feeble health and poor instruction, he made rapid progress in Latin literature, the humanities, and ancient philosophy. His fine memory, his ease of acquisition, and his application, made him, indeed, at an early age a master of the classical studies of his age. When he passed from the Jesuit College, he hesitated for a moment as to his course. He was naturally attracted to the study of mathematics and pure thought; on the other hand, the legal tradition was in his blood, and he was strongly urged by his mother and by his father's friend, Prévost de la Jannès Jauné, to follow the family tradition. In fact, as we shall see, he both followed that tradition and indulged to the full his capacity for pure thought. He joined the law school of the University of Orleans, at that date, according to M. le Trosne,[1] in a deplorable state. "Les Professeurs qui occupoient alors

[1] M. le Trosne was the Avocat du Roi au Présidial d'Orléans at the date of Pothier's death in 1772. His *Éloge Historique de M. Pothier* is prefixed to the edition of Pothier's works issued jointly at Paris and Orléans in 1773-4 in four volumes which was followed by a second revised edition in 1781. Three volumes (Paris, 1777, 1777, 1778) contain the posthumous works, and with the other four, supply the authentic text of all the works.

les Chaires de l'Université, absolument indifférens aux progrès des jeunes gens, se contentoient de leur dicter quelques leçons unintelligibles, et qu'ils ne daignoient pas mettre à leur portée." The King's advocate goes on to describe the method in which law was taught at the beginning of the eighteenth century by the professors :

> "Ce n'étoit pas proprement la science du Droit qu'ils enseignoient : ils ne présentoient de cette science si belle et si lumineuse par elle-même, que ces épines et ces contrariétés qui lui sont étrangères, et qui n'y ont été introduites que par l'incapacité et la mauvaise foi des Rédacteurs des Pandectes. Au lieu d'expliquer les textes d'une manière propre à instruire, ils ne remplissoient leur leçons que de ces questions subtiles, inventées et multipliées par les Controversistes.
> "À cette manière d'enseigner, on auroit pu croire qu'ils n'avoient d'autre objet que de fermer pour toujours le sanctuaire des Loix aux Etudians, par le dégoût qu'ils sçavoient leur inspirer ; semblables à ces anciens Patriciens, qui, pour tenir le peuple dans leur dépendance, lui cachoient avec un si grand soin les formules des actions, et s'étoient approprié la connoissance des Loix, qu'ils avoient soin de voiler sous une écorce mystérieuse. Un enseignement si peu instructif et si défectueux, ne pouvoit satisfaire un esprit aussi solide et aussi juste que celui de M. Pothier : heureusement il ne fut pascapable de le rebuter ; il en sentit les défauts, et suppléa, par son travail, aux secours qui lui manquoient. Dans toutes les sciences, ce sont les premiers pas qui sont les plus difficiles ; il les franchit seul par l'étude sérieuse des Institutes, dans laquelle il s'aida du Commentaire de Vinnius,[1] et se prépara à aller puiser à la source même du Droit, par l'étude la plus profonde et la plus suivie des Pandectes."

He passed brilliantly through the various stages then necessary in the University to qualify for the Bar and the Magistracy. The difficulty of the material with which he had to deal, and the poverty of the teaching, served but to stimulate his great powers while his close study of the Institutes of Justinian in the pages of Arnoldus Vinnius inspired him with a profound interest in the law and history of a people with whose literature he was already intimately familiar. Yet when all the examinations were passed, he was faced, according to M. le Trosne,[2] once more by the parting of the ways. His profoundly religious mind and his un-

---

[1] *Commentary on the Institutes* in Four books. A further edition of this work was issued in 1755 in two volumes, by Gottlieb Heineccius.

[2] The fact is not mentioned in the admirable article on Pothier in La Rousse's *Grand Dictionnaire du XIXe Siècle*. There the only crisis mentioned occurred before he entered the University.

worldly nature were greatly attracted by the religious life, and at this time (about 1720) he almost decided to enter the Order of Regular Canons, and was only deterred from this step by his close attachment to his mother. He then at last determined to adopt the law as his profession, and his immense knowledge justified the local Ordinance by which, at the age of twenty-one, he was nominated to the same magisterial position that had been occupied by his father and grandfather, Conseiller au Présidial d'Orléans. His position determined finally not only his avocation, but his course of work. To the study of the theory and history of law he turned all his powers, while at the same time, in the chambers of Mᵉ Perche, the most learned and brilliant advocate in Orleans, he obtained a close knowledge of actual practice. It is important to dwell on these early stages of Pothier's career. The fact that with him (as with Savigny at the end of the century) ceaseless toil at the history and theory of law was coupled with assiduous attention to law in actual practice (he sat on the bench at Orleans for over fifty years) gave a value to Pothier's work on French law and on the principles of law that will never be lost.

In the ten or twelve years following his appointment, he combined with the study and the practice of law a close consideration of the basis of theology. His favourite author was St. Augustine, but he joined the Port Royalist school of thought, and found in Pierre Nicole (1625-1695) that combination of vast learning in philosophy and theology with profound reverence that exactly fitted his own mind. Nicole closely approached the Jansenist position, and in this particular Pothier went past his master, and became a Jansenist, a fact never forgiven by the Roman Catholic Communion in Orleans, who even refused him burial room in the Cathedral of the city that he had adorned.[1] The study of theology Pothier maintained all his life, and the fact has to be kept in mind in considering his whole position, since his attitude towards theology was really his attitude towards law. The right to think and the duty to think clearly on all subjects was the claim that made him one with the great Post Royalists, and a symptom of the change that was passing over France.

[1] The remains were translated to the cathedral in 1823 with much pomp, but in 1843 they were removed to an obscure part of the building, where the school-children sat. But Pothier, the teacher, would not have complained.

It will be convenient here to sketch as briefly as may be the juridical and judicial system into which Robert Joseph Pothier was born, for it was from his practical experience of this system that he drew that knowledge of affairs which gives such a profound value to his work. The long story of the reduction to writing and revision of French customary law, a work that began with the ordinance of Charles VII. in 1453, and had been for the most part achieved after titanic labour by the end of the century—though some districts lingered on under unwritten customary law until the middle of the eighteenth century—cannot be dealt with here. It is sufficient to say that the Custom of Orleans was revised and reduced to writing by Achille du Harley and his school in 1583. M. D. Dalloz and M. H. Thiercelin, in their *Essai sur l'Histoire Générale du Droit Français*, dwell enthusiastically on the marvellous work that was accomplished when the teeming customs of France were in effect codified. "Car c'est peut-être le plus grand travail législatif qui ait jamais été accompli. On ne peut mettre en parallèle ni la composition des compilations justiniennes, ni même le travail bien supérieur de la rédaction de nos codes. Bien plus, la rédaction des coutumes n'est même pas mise parmi les titres de gloire de l'esprit juriste français, et cependant c'est peut-être le premier."[1]

The codification was opposed by the magistrates of the local courts, the bailliage, and the *sénéchaussée*, but it was carried through exhaustively, and both actual practice and all the customary books containing recorded cases—*Le livre Coutumier du Greffe*—were examined with detailed care.

First we must obtain some general notion of the customary law of France after the sixteenth century. The law of persons is full of interest. All persons dwelling in France had been, from the date of the ordinance of Louis X., of July 3, 1315, free persons, though, until the eve of the Revolution, this rule of law did not apply to black persons imported from the Colonies. But two years before our *Somersett's case* the law in this respect was changed in France.[2] Free men were classified into Frenchmen, naturalized aliens, non-naturalized strangers. Naturalization was a state act under the great seal, and persons naturalized had the same rights as Frenchmen. Non-naturalized aliens could neither

[1] *Essai sur l'Histoire Générale du Droit Français*, p. 135.
[2] *Cf. Édits*, October 25, 1706, art. 5, et December 15, 1738: *L'Arrêt Roch, rendu sur la plaidoirie d'Henrion de Pansey en 1770, fut le premier qui décida le contraire.*

succeed to property or make a will. For a long time their heir was the King, but it was eventually held that their children, if resident in France, could succeed to their estate. All subjects were nobles or roturiers, while all roturiers were bourgeois or villein.[1] Both these latter classes were subject to seignorial authority, and held their property subject to charges; but the bourgeois formed a definite community, enjoying privileges accorded to their commune, and governed by their own magistrates. There were serfs, but they were continuously diminished in number by formal enfranchisements up to the end of the *ancien régime*; while, in fact, the servile, apart from the taxable, condition of those who remained unenfranchised had become in some measure, perhaps largely, nominal. Nobility was acquired by birth, by marriage, or by the gift of the Prince. In most customs nobility only descended through the father, though some districts recognized uterine nobility, the descent through the mother. About the fifteenth century the idea of the holding of office conferring nobility was entertained, and a little later an ordinance of 1470 declared that in Normandy the fact of holding a fief involved nobility; and when the right to hold fiefs was extended to all, the nobility was open to all. And thus there grew up a nobility of place and land in addition to a nobility of race, and at the time of the fall of the Monarchy there were many Marquesses and Counts who were, in fact, not of noble blood. The nobles possessed various privileges of jurisdiction and exemption from *la taille*. The roturiers who held land had to pay to the Crown a fine, called the "franc fief," but various provinces and towns were exempt from this, Paris having been exempt since 1371.

The age when majority was attained differed for nobles and roturiers; indeed, it varied even in the case of the nobility, for the minor possessor of a fief had two minorities, one feudal, the other customary. By the feudal law the vassal came into possession of his fief at from eighteen to twenty years for males, fourteen to eighteen years for females. Up to this age the minor was in the power of his or her guardian. We must not confuse this period of majority, which only referred to feudal rights and services, with the customary majority, which related to non-feudal matters. This was ordinarily fixed at twenty-five, in

---

[1] Roturier, "a plebeian;" *lit.*, a peasant who holds a *roture—i.e.*, villein-land: from *Ruptura*, the act of breaking (clods) and hence of cultivating fields. Thus *Rupturarius* becomes *Roturier* (see A. Brachet's *Etymological Dictionary of the French Language*).

imitation of the Roman law. The noble guardian acted in feudal matters, the bourgeois guardian in other matters. Some customary areas refused to recognize the bourgeois guardianship; others, such as Paris, limited it to certain districts. It could only be held by parents; it ended at fourteen for males and twelve years for females; it ceased when the guardian remarried—a rule revived in the Civil Code of to-day. It was a profitable office, and the noble guardianship was certainly not less valuable.

In addition to these guardians, there was the tutor, and we find him from the thirteenth century both in the districts of written law and the districts of customary law. This creature of Roman law appeared in the districts possessing a written law in the various varieties of the Roman law—Testamentary, Legitimate, Dative; while in the districts governed by customary law only dative tutors were appointed. The customs recognized the gatherings of relations, called *Conseils de familles*. Tutors were nominated at these gatherings.

The question of marriage is important. Customary law did not deal with it as a contract, this being left to the Canon law; but custom regulated the position of the wife, and the civil duties imposed on both spouses. The wife was in the power (*manus*) of the husband. She could not sell his goods, or bind herself by contract, nor suffer judgment, without his authorization, unless she was separate from him or was a public trader. He administered his wife's goods; he held her lands, though he could not alienate them without her consent. In some provinces (Artois and Auvergne) simple betrothal put the daughter into the power of her future husband. Under most customs marriage emancipated the spouses from parental power, but by many customs (Normandy, Auvergne, Burgundy) the wife alone was emancipated; in other provinces the roturier (plebeian) only became emancipated a year and a day after marriage in a separate home. In Bourbonnais (confiscated to the Crown by Francis I. in 1531, the modern Department of Allier) the father, when consenting to the marriage of a minor son, could stipulate that he remained in his father's power. In the districts governed by customary law the wife did not bring, and in the districts governed by the written law she did bring, to her husband a *dot* in the Roman sense (*dos*). In fact, in some cases in the customary districts the *dot* consisted of two sums, half contributed by each family, the husband's contribution being called *un augment de dot*. In the districts under the written law there was, of course, the *donatio propter nuptias* given by the husband. The wife's dower varied according to the custom. In some provinces the widow had the usufruct of one-half of the immovables that her husband possessed at her marriage, or which had descended to him since the marriage. Brittany, Normandy, Maine, Anjou, Poitou, fixed the dower at one-third, without distinction between nobles and roturiers. In Artois the dower was half of the lands and half the plebeian goods. In some districts dower depended on marriage, in others on consummated marriage; in some districts the dowager had the seisin of the land, in others she had to demand it of the heirs. But it became due only on the death of the husband, though on his civil death and in various other cases the wife obtained a charge on his goods, called *mi-douaire*. Very often the property of the goods, the use of which formed the dower of their mother, was in the children. In this case the children had to choose between the succession of their father and the dowry of their mother. They could not succeed to both. The dower passed equally among the children. It is the fulfilment of a contract, so to speak, that the father had entered into with his wife and future children by her.

Dower has not passed into modern French law. The sole vestige of dower custom in the Code is in Article 1465, which accords to a wife accepting or renouncing community of goods, her costs of living during the three months and forty days which follow the dissolution of community of goods. The doctrine of community of goods obtained throughout France, with the exception of Normandy, Auvergne, and the Haute-Marche. The spouses jointly owned from the day of marriage all the movable property, all the immovable property acquired during the period of community, and all the proceeds of the joint property, and they were jointly responsible for the debts of either. In some districts community of goods began with the betrothal. The doctrine of community could be excluded by mutual agreement before the marriage, or an unequal division of the property at the end of the marriage could be arranged. This variation of the original strict custom was apparently introduced with marriage settlements in the fourteenth century. In the districts governed by customary law it often happened that the principle of community was incorporated in the marriage settlement, but where the principle of community was forbidden (as it was by the custom of Normandy) this could not be done. This was in some cases avoided by a declaration by the parties that they were bound by the custom of Paris, which in a sense was the common law of France ; but the practice was held to be ineffective in Normandy. By the custom of Normandy the wife had certain rights of succession to her husband ; thus she had a right to one-half of immovables acquired *en bourgage* during the marriage, and she had also a right to half the movables. The husband had a right to his wife's movables, but half could be used solely in the purchase of immovables. The *dot* was inalienable, and passed to the wife or her heirs on the husband's death, as well as the above right of succession, or, in the alternative, her husband's *paraphernalia*. If the husband survived, he had a life estate (usufruct) whilst unmarried (if there had been a child born alive) in the income of his wife's property. If he remarried, his life estate was reduced to one-third. The law of Normandy, M. Laferrière suggests, was an amalgam of Scandinavian, English, and Neustrian (Norman or Frankish) law.

In the case of the common law of community the husband could dispose of all the common property *inter vivos ;* he could by his will only deal with his share. On the dissolution of the marriage the wife could accept or renounce the community. If it was not renounced, it continued with the infant children, provided that this was for their benefit. On remarriage each party took a third part of the community property, and the children of the first marriage the remaining third. The thirds became fourths if the new spouse had already got children ; while the thirds became sixths if both parties had children by both marriages. The *jus accrescendi* applied as between brothers and sisters. But the details of the law of community varied very greatly, and often only applied to the *roturier* class.

When we consider the general doctrine of rights of property under the feudal law in France, we find in the age when the customs were reduced into writing that the great principle of division into movables and immovables still subsisted. Land (or immovable property) consisted of fiefs, of lands subject to seignorial rights, of lands free of lord (*alleux*). The last were rare in the customary districts, where the maxim ran, "No land without a lord," but lordless land might be *noble* or might be *roturier*. These types of land-holding gave rise to a most complicated land law and an almost inexplicable system of land charges, that in some cases ran with the land. The French law of land has not yet received the attention of a school of jurists at all comparable with the school created by Pollock and Maitland in England. The French doctrine of seisin or possession was originally of extraordinary elaboration, and throws much light on the analogous doctrine in England.[1] The doctrine had certain applications to movables that are of interest if considered in connection with the earliest doctrine of seisin in England. It is not possible here to trace in detail the French law of seisin or the law that regulated property in its relation to the family, a phase of law that scarcely passed the Channel. One may, perhaps, however, say one word as to the feudal doctrine of *amortissement*—the freeing of land from feudal burdens. In every case this required under the customary law the consent of the successive overlords up to the King himself. Hence it became a doctrine (despite the resistance of lower lords) that the King alone had *le droit d'amortir*. As this doctrine had special application to persons, the enfranchisement of serfs was a royal prerogative, though the lords had a right to claim an indemnity from the freed men.

When we turn to the law of succession we find that in the districts governed by the written law succession was governed by the law of Justinian (*Novellæ*, 118, 127), while in the places subject to customary law there were endless customs as to succession. The main distinction in the customary law was between succession to fiefs and lordless land of noble origin on the one hand, and all other property of any origin on the other. With respect to the fiefs, the principle of primogeniture applied though not always the primogeniture of males, as is seen from the customs of Anjou, Poitou, and Touraine. Throughout the North of France this principle is attached to the land itself. Thus, if non-nobles acquired land which gave them a title without ennobling them, the "nobility" of the land, so to speak, set the principle of primogeniture at work; while, on the other hand, if land were possessed by a noble which nevertheless was not "noble land," the principle did not apply. The full elaboration of the customary laws of succession can be gathered from *Dalloz*. One may note that the customary law recognized wills; but the power was limited under different customs differently:

[1] The French lawyers used the technical words "vest" and "devest" to indicate the process by which, on a transfer of property, the old possessor had to suffer disseisin, and the new possessor had to prove the process by which he became seised.

it might be a third or a fourth, or even the whole, that came under the will of the testator. The property that could not be disposed of by will passed to the customary heirs. Again, the persons to whom the property could be left were limited; the will was subject to *la légitime*. Thus, under the custom of Paris, a child had a right to the one-half it would have had if the parent had died intestate.

Something must be said as to the customary and written law of obligations, a subject that owes so much to Pothier. The customary law of France adopted during the thirteenth century the Roman law on the subject of obligations. The jurists of the sixteenth century developed the modern theory of contracts, as it is set forth in the French code. We should note that many customary codes recognized communities as property holders subject to the law of obligations. Quite early it was recognized that a sale by legal authority gave a good title to the property sold. The laws of the Church condemned the whole notion of interest on money, but this doctrine, which obtained until the law of October 2, 1789, was evaded in various ways. The mortgage, though repeatedly condemned, came into general use in the early Middle Ages, and held its ground. The enfranchisement of the serfs threw much labour on the market, and gave a larger activity to the contract of service.

When we enter the sixteenth century we find the King all-powerful; the dangerous vassals as well as the practically independent republics known as "communes" have disappeared. We have towns under local government; we have trading companies, such as the Merchants of Paris, gaining great influence; we have the Universities and other great Corporations—all forces changing the face of society. We see a reigning house controlled by the hereditary principle, and ruling over lands inalienable by the Crown but taxable. In this society individual liberty, despite the sittings of the States-General, had no guarantee; the *lettre de cachet* was in active use to the end. On the other hand, property was adequately protected by the King, despite the weight of occasional taxation. From the sixteenth century onward the King was supreme as legislator and administrator, and the written and the customary laws were supplemented by Crown Ordinances.

The ordinances of Villers-Cotterets (1539), of Orleans (1561), of Roussillon (1563), of Moulins (1566), of Blois (1579), really formed a supplementary code dealing with (1539) the administration of justice and forms of procedure, (1561) the clergy, with general administration, (1563) commercial law and judicial administration, (1566) the abolition of communal judges, judicial efficiency, the Crown right to create dignitaries, (1579) religion, education, the administration of justice, Crown servants, Crown lands, taxation. The same age saw many ordinances dealing with religion. In the sphere of law we have seen that customary law had already become fixed. The ordinances of the sixteenth century amended legal machinery with great elaboration, but it did not deal with the status of persons or the rights of property, though it dealt in some measure with property in connection with the family regarded as an entity.

But the ordinances had the effect of unifying the whole system of customary law, of stamping upon it the specific national character which, despite its indebtedness to Roman and Germanic influences, was and is a unique thing—personality. So we see a judicial and administrative system arise capable of moulding customary law into its final form, while the law as to family life was rounded off and made complete. Thus, in February, 1556, Henry II. forbade clandestine marriages, and introduced the famous rule which still persists that a person under paternal power cannot contract marriage without the consent of his relatives. It was not possible in that age for such a marriage to be declared null, but it was possible to deprive the spouses of all the advantages of their family system, to disinherit the child, to revoke all premarital gifts, to cancel all rights of succession. Many other provisions as to the form of marriage date from this time. The rights of second husbands in the fortune of their wife was strictly limited by ordinance (1560, 1579), and these provisions are repeated in the code of to-day (Art. 1098).

The ordinance of Moulins (1566) introduced a profound change into the law of evidence, by the substitution of written for personal evidence in all classes of evidence where strict proof (as of birth, marriage, death) is necessary. It was this period, too, that gave to the legal system adequate officers to carry the law into effect. Thus there existed in the sixteenth century (*a*) notaries of the Crown, (*b*) notaries of the Seigneur, and (*c*) Apostolic notaries to deal with questions of the Canon law. The ordinances regulated the form of notarial acts. The notary or the parish priest had to take a part in the formality of will-making. Again, we see by 1579 a regular class of counsel (*les avocats généraux*), and a regular class of solicitor (*les procureurs généraux*), undertaking argument and the preparation of cases. There was also by this date the class of counsel exactly equivalent to our King's Counsel (*les avocats du roi*).

The idea of codifying the entire French law was in the mind of Henry III., and, in fact, Barnabé Brisson in 1587 issued his draft *Code de Henri III.*; but this, though revised in the reign of Henry IV., never acquired the force of law.[1]

The period of the great ordinances (1539-1579) was the begetter of an age of great jurists. The French Renaissance school of law may be said to begin with the Roman lawyers, Alciati (1492-1550), who taught at Avignon and Bourges, and his pupil, Cujas (1520-1590), and Doneau (1527-1591), the first of the purely philosophical jurists; Jacques Godefroy (1587-1652), who edited the Theodosian Code; and Denys Godefroy, who annnotated Justinian, Douaren, Govean, Hotman, Brisson, and Pierre Pithou (pupil of Cujas). The work of these Roman lawyers laid a basis for the study of French law. The first scientific student of French jurisprudence was the indefatigable Charles Dumoulin (1500[?]-December 28, 1566).

"L'ardeur au travail de Dumoulin était extrême; on le sait par des témoignages irrécusables d'ailleurs, et le caractère et l'immensité de ses productions l'attesteraient suffisamment. Elle eut pour objet toutes les parties du droit : le droit coutumier, le droit féodal, le droit romain, le droit canonique et l'histoire ; mais c'est surtout vers le droit coutumier, le droit féodal et la matière des obligations que se dirigèrent ses efforts.[2]

He taught law chiefly at Dôle, but his impetuosity in public affairs drove him into exile, and much of his work was done abroad. His greatest work was his commentary on the customs of Paris.[3] The first title in this great work is *de Feudis*, comprising seventy-two sections, and occupying 1305 columns in the small type great double-column quarto pages

---

[1] In 1615 L. Charondas le Caron, a Parisian jurist, issued in a vast volume the Code "de puis augmenté des Edictes du Roy Henry IV. et Louis XIII., à present regnaut, avec la Conference des Ordinances, et rapporté aux anciens Codes de Theodose et de Justinian, et aux Basiliques."

[2] *Essai sur l'Histoire du Droit Français* (Dalloz), p. 215, on which this historical sketch is based.

[3] See the collected edition of his works in four volumes, *Caroli Molinaei Franciae et Germaniae celeberrimi jurisconsulti . . . Opera quæ extant omnia*, Paris, 1658, with a life of the author prefixed to the first tome.

of this edition. The second title is *De censu et juribus Dominicalibus*, dealing with the obscure law of seignorial rights. This contains twenty-three sections, and takes us to column 1619 of the first volume. The remaining titles dealing with the customs of Paris were published after Dumoulin's death: (3) *De complainte en cas de saisine et de nouvelleté ;* (4) *De præscriptionibus ;* (5) *De personalibus et Hypothecariis actionibus ;* (6) *de servitutibus realibus, urbanis et rusticis ;* (7) *De testamentis, donationibus, legatis, executoribus testamentorum ;* (8) *De custodia nobili ;* (9) *De custodia paganica ;* (10) *De communione bonorum ;* (11) *De successionibus in linea directa ;* (12) *De Doariis ;* (13) *De successione in linea collaterali ;* (14) *De donatione mutua inter conjugis ;* (15) *De pignorationibus, sequestrationibus, et executione sententiarium et instrumentorum ;* (16) *De retractu jure proximitatis ;* (17) *De subhastationibus ;* (18) *De cœteris articulis consuedinariis*. With this last title the first *tome* ends at column 1795. The second *tome* gives us a lengthy treatise on the French law of contracts and rents and loans. The third *tome* still deals with French law, and includes a tract, *De l'origine, progrez, et excellence du Royaume et Monarchie des François*. The fourth *tome* is largely filled with tracts on Roman law, but also deals with various French customary areas: La Prevosté et Vicomté de Paris, Meaux, Melun, Sens, Estampes, Montfort, Mantes, Senlis, Clermont, Valois, Troyes, Chaumont, Vitri, Vermandois, Chalons, Rheims, Amiens, Beauvoisis, Monstrueil, S. Omer, Chauny, Boullenois, Estappes, Comté d'Artois, Bourgongne, Auxerre, Nivernais, Ville de L'Isle, Chartres, Mons, Lorris, Orléans, Touraine, Anjou, Maine, Blois, Dunois, Berry, Bourbonnois, Auvergne, La Marche, Lodunois, Poictou, Augoulemois, La Rochelle, Bordeaux, Bretagne, as well as the ordinance of 1539. The volume of work is enormous, and it forms a magnificent storehouse for research in late Medieval French law. The study of Charles Dumoulin necessarily lies behind any adequate conception of the work of later French jurists or of the evolution of French law. It is the first trumpet note of revolt against feudalism. Moreover, the sidelights on English law are, we must believe, of profound importance.

Two treatises in the fourth *tome* are of great importance from the point of view of modern law: the treatise *De Verborum obligatio* (col. 128), and the treatise *Extricatio labyrinthi Dividui et Individui* (col. 188). Of this later treatise the essay above referred to says :

> "Dans son traité *de Dividuo et Individuo,* Dumoulin crée, on peut dire, la théorie française de l'indivisibilité des obligations, et Pothier a pu se borner à analyser et à co-ordonner les doctrines de Dumoulin pour en faire sortir la doctrine qu'il expose dans son Traité des obligations, et qui devait venir se condenser dans deux articles du Code Napoléon."

The other jurists of this great juridical period were the Breton feudalist, D'Argentré (1519-1590); Guy-Coquille (1523-1603), Charondas (1536-1617), the authority on French customary law ; René Choppin (1537-1606), who specialized on the custom of Anjou, Chassaneux (1480-1541), an authority on Burgundian customs ; Loysel (1536-1617), an authority on customary law ; and Loyseau (1566-1627), the latest and perhaps the clearest exponent of the French juridical system.

A word must be said as to the royal ordinances of the seventeenth century, for they show the royal authority at its height unhampered by powerful feudal lords or by religious turmoil. Under Henry IV. the whole country, its finances, its industries, its agriculture, and its defences, were reorganized, and the manifestations of constitutional life that came into being at his death were less a sign of the decay of kingship than of the growing sense of national unity and efficiency. Richelieu (in 1641) forbade the Parlements and other courts of justice to interfere in public affairs. Mazarin was not slow to adopt the same policy, and it was rather by strength of policy than anything else that the code of constitutional liberty set forth in that significant year 1648 did not become law. Louis XIV. was strong enough to reduce the Parlements to their judicial functions, and his reign gave to Frenchmen the glory that sometimes is an apt substitute for liberty. In 1692 the Crown announced the existence of a right of eminent domain with respect to all land in the kingdom. There were to be no more allodial lands ; the English doctrine that there is no absolute right to land in any subject was adopted. The King thus resumed his strictly feudal position as *le seigneur suzerain.* During the century the distinction between *les biens nobles ou roturiers* was maintained, and the latter only were subject to the *taille.* The domain rights were maintained, though they were often confused with the seigneurial rights.

This is not the place in which to discuss the legal position secured by the Church in this age, though it should be noticed that the declaration of the clergy of 1682 laid the basis of the whole system of *concordats* between Church and State. The civil ordinances of the century left the customary law standing, but the law of obligation was largely affected; whilst in 1667 French civil procedure was codified, and in 1673 the commercial law of France received complete treatment. In the essay on the history of French law, to which reference has repeatedly been made, we have a careful account of the legislation as to obligations. In 1606 the application of the Velleian *Senatus Consultum* to French law was forbidden by the Parlement of Paris, and this position was largely adopted in the districts subject to customary law. The general reform of procedure was attempted by the code or ordinance of 1629, in itself ineffective, and the last of the many attempts at codification that distinguished the sixteenth century. A new codification movement with respect to procedure began with the ordinance of 1667 on civil procedure, which was the basis of the code of 1806. It also dealt with the question of proof. In 1670 the code of criminal procedure was issued, to be followed in 1673 by the commercial code, drafted by the jurist Savary. The last thirty years of the reign saw little more legislation. In twenty years Louis Quatorze had done enough to earn, if not to secure, the title of the French Justinian. In this age the practical jurist came to give effect to practical codes: the labours of Brodeau and Lebrun largely lay behind the work of Pothier, while legal philosophy and speculation were kept alive by Grotius and Domat.

The most important legal event in the earlier years of Louis XV. (apart from the growing constitutional power of the Parlement de Paris) was the Edict of 1738, which formulated the procedure that governs even to-day the appellate jurisdiction of the Cour de Cassation. A right of appeal in error against the decision of a Parlement was recognized as early as 1302; *la proposition d'erreur* could from that date be brought against a decision of a Parlement. The principle was confirmed by a series of sixteenth-century ordinances, but the right of appeal was abolished by the procedure reforms of 1667, though the Crown reserved the right to declare all judgments contrary to its ordinances null. Thus the Crown (*le conseil privé* or *conseil du roi*) became the Court of Appeal by virtue of its inherent jurisdiction. The principle was enforced by D'Aguesseau in the Règlement de

Conseil of June 28, 1738 : an appeal to the Cour de Cassation was only to be allowed where there had been a plain breach of a precise law. It was frankly stated that the object of the appeal was rather to maintain the authority of the ordinances as against the Parlements than to further the cause of justice. The struggle with the Parlements was the notable fact of the last days of the *ancien régime*. They represented and kept alive through the centuries the constitutional idea. It was a function worthy of a juridical assembly ; but we must remember that the establishment of an appellate jurisdiction emanating from the Crown in check of Parliament was likewise a constitutional development that also made for liberty and justice.

But if the constitutional idea was germinating rapidly during the reign of Louis XV., this period was fruitful in amendments of the civil law. In 1729 the rights of succession of a mother to property of her children under certain circumstances (which had been destroyed by the edict of Saint Maur of 1567) were restored. The *ordinance sur les donations* of 1731 was a step towards the unification of the written and the customary law at which the great French jurists from Dumoulin onward had aimed. D'Aguesseau felt acutely the necessity for uniformity of law, independent of places or persons. This doctrine is laid down with great precision in the preamble to the ordinance of 1736. The ordinance as to *donationes inter vivos* and *donationes mortis causa* is a step in this direction. The new law laid down that all non-onerous donations were revoked by the birth of issue. D'Aguesseau next turned to the law of wills, with the difficult problem before him of reconciling the Roman and the customary law. His solution appeared in the ordinance of August, 1735, dealing with the form of wills and the witnesses to wills, with the principle of heirships and its relation to the *locus* of the property affected. The nuncupative will (in the presence of seven witnesses) was preserved when sanctioned by custom. It became *le testament authentique* of the *Code Napoléon*. The principle of the institution of heirs was retained in the districts where it was in force. The Roman law (*e.g.*, the *lex Falcidia*) was carefully applied to the modern case. Thus the old cleavage was still recognized between the countries of written and unwritten law, but the ordinance found where possible a common ground for the two systems of law, and prepared the way for codification. In 1747 came the ordinance as to the law of substitutions, which clearly laid down the limitations of that branch of Roman law in its relations to gifts *inter vivos* or by will. The last ordinance of great importance to the civil law under the *ancien régime* was issued in 1771, the year before the death of Pothier : the protection of mortgagees, who could be defrauded, since the sixteenth century, by the simple expedient of a sale of the land under an order of Court. Thenceforward the place of a decree of the Court was taken by a document issued by the *Conservateur des hypothèques* in each district. The letters (of ratification of sale) could only be issued after public notice had been given that the land was for sale. If the mortgagees did not come in and make their claim within two months after public notice, the purchaser acquired a good title free from incumbrances.

The reign of Louis XV. almost coincided with the working life of Pothier. We are now in a position to consider his work in the light of the legal system, the intricacies of which have been barely indicated here. In the above-mentioned *Éssai sur l'Historie Générale du Droit Français*, Pothier is written of in the following fashion :

"Que dirons-nous de Pothier que ne sachent tous deux qui s'intéressent à la Science du droit ? les traités seront toujours les meilleurs commentaires du Code, dont les rédacteurs lui ont tant emprunté. Par la clarté de son exposition, la lucidité de ses aperçus, la sûreté de sa doctrine, qui toutefois ne sonde pas au delà des profondeurs nécessaires pour établir les fondations d'une jurisprudence applicable et pratique, plûtot que philosophique et élevée, par tout cela, Pothier est le jurisconsulte par excellence ; mais il manque à ces qualités éminemment françaises celle de la vivacité du tour et de l'expression comme écrivain. Il est vieux par la manière, l'étant par l'esprit en dehors des matières du droit. Les grands jurisconsultes du xvie siècle étaient de leur temps. Dumoulin, Duaren, les Hotman, etc., étaient mêlés au mouvement politique et au mouvement religieux de leur époque. Ceux du xviiie siècle semblent avoir vécu en claustration, au millieu d'une société dont l'état moral se transformait. Pothier était contemporain de Rousseau et de Voltaire, et, à la lecture de ses traités, nul ne le croirait. Mais le bon sens, la raison claire et simple, ne perd jamais son autorité ; il est de tous les temps ; et malgré ce qu'il est permis de penser sur ce que les livres de Pothier laissent à désirer, ils ne vivront pas moins par l'autorité du bons sens, qui jamais ne faiblit chez lui."

We must now return to the life of Pothier, and trace out the order of the publication of his treatises, and the relation of his work to the legal systems described above. The work which underlay all else was his prolonged study of Roman law. For years he devoted his leisure to the problem of the order of the text of the Pandects, and in 1736 he communicated some essays on the subject to M. Prévôt de la Jannès, who at once laid the work before the Chancellor d'Aguesseau. D'Aguesseau saw the great importance of Pothier's scheme of reconstruction of the text of the Pandects, and gave him every encouragement by letter, comparing his work to that of Vigelius. In September, 1736, Pothier went to Paris and saw the Chancellor on the subject, and from time to time he sent to the Chancellor specimens of the work. In the second edition of Pothier's work (published in 1781) we have printed letters from the illustrious Chancellor to Pothier on the subject of this work written between 1736 and 1745. The work, the result of a quarter of a century of incessant labour, was published in 1748 under the title *Pandectæ Justinianæ in novum ordinem digestæ* (Paris: three volumes in folio). It was a work that had become essential. The labours of many jurists had not cleared up the order of the text, and till that problem was solved Roman law could not come into its own. Pothier performed, wrote M. Dupin in 1825, what the sixty jurists appointed by Justinian failed to do for the laws of their own country. The need for such a work is trenchantly expressed by a modern French writer on Pothier:

> "L'étude de cette science était hérissée d'obstacles presque insurmontable, à cause du désordre et de la confusion qui régnaient dans le *Digeste* justinien, où les fragments précieux des anciens jurisconsultes, les décisions, les textes, les extraits, les interprétations, les commentaires, tous les matériaux de l'édifice immense du droit romain étaient entassés pêle-mêle, sans liaison, sans suite, sans critique, sans méthode et dans un désordre rendu plus inextricable encore par les modifications postérieures et par les erreurs des copistes. Pothier entreprit de porter la lumière au millieu de ces ténèbres, de rétablir l'ordre au millieu de ce chaos, d'accomplir enfin l'œuvre devant laquelle avaient reculé les jurisconsultes les plus célèbres, que Cujas lui-même n'avait qu'incomplètement essayée et que le vaste génie du Chancelier de l'Hospital avait rêvée. Pendant vingt ans, il interrogea les anciens, étudia les modernes, dévora tous les commentateurs, poursuivant l'accomplissement de son plan avec une persévérance plus forte que les obstacles et en terminant enfin l'exécution après des prodiges de travail, de sagacité et de scrupuleuse érudition."[1]

[1] Art. "Pothier," La Rousse's *Grand Dictionnaire de XIXᵉ Siècle*, pp. 1517-18.

Pothier based his work on the current text of the Pandects and the Code, supplemented by the work of Cujas and Dumoulin. The great treatise opens with a Prolegomena dealing first with the sources of Roman law, with the *plebiscita* and the *senatus consulta*, with the Pretorian law, with the interpretation of the Roman jurists. A second part of the Prolegomena gives us an account of the great jurisconsults, whom he classifies as follows : (1) Those before the time of Cicero ; (2) the Ciceronian jurists to the age of Christ ; (3) the jurists from the Christian era to the age of Hadrian ; (4) from Hadrian to Gordianus (A.D. 117-240) ; (5) jurists of uncertain date. Ninety-two classical jurists are enumerated, with some account of the work of each. Some juridical writings immediately after the classical period are next mentioned. A note follows on the Roman schools of legal thought, Proculian and Sabinian. A third part discusses the labours of Justinian. The work then opens with a considerable treatise, giving and discussing the fragmentary text of the twelve tables, followed by the extant fragments of the Perpetual Edict, and these lead us up to the Digest or Pandects of Justinian. These 208 folio pages of introduction are a miracle of unassuming, unsuspected learning. Pothier, in dealing with the Digest, preserved the old arrangement of the titles, which was the order of the Perpetual Edict, but under these main headings—each title having a full introduction—the texts are arranged in methodical order, and the true place of every text is found. The labour of recreating the correct order of the text was immense. It represented years of work by one of the fastest and most methodical workers who ever lived. It is impossible to turn to the five-volume edition, published in Paris in 1825, of this work without reflecting not only on the achievement itself and all that that achievement meant for subsequent workers in the field of Roman law, but also on the immense range of legal knowledge that the very production of such a work must have involved and reinforced. When Pothier finally issued his edition of the Pandects, his must have been the best-stored mind, in the matter of the principles of law, in the world. And we have to remember that Pothier was not working at Roman law as a sole subject : all the while he was pursuing the practice of the law of his own country, he was in contact with the finest jurists of his day, and was, in fact, working hard at the legal historical problems of his own country.[1]

[1] It should be noted that Pothier was assisted in the work by M. de Guienne, an *avocat du parlement*, who was responsible for the literary com-

The conclusion of his work was marked by a complete breakdown in health, the result not only of fever, but of prolonged labours, from which recovery was only slowly achieved. In October, 1649, his old friend and helper, M. de la Jannès, died, and the Chancellor D'Aguesseau appointed Pothier to the vacant Professorship of French Law in the University of Orleans. The other candidate for the post was M. Guyot, and each sought to yield the chair to the other; and Pothier was not satisfied till M. Guyot[1] was associated with him in the work. Pothier seems to have been an ideal teacher. M. le Trosne tells us:

"Il sçavoit tellement cacher la supériorité du Maître, que les Étudians croyoient converser avec un ami. Ses leçons étoient des conférences dans lesquelles il soutenoit l'attention par des interrogation qui mettoient les jeunes gens à portée de faire valoir leurs études particulières. La question s'addressoit à un seul, et tous s'empressoient d'en chercher la réponse. Tous étoient en haleine, parce que la question suivante pouvoit s'addresser à eux. La réponse étoit-elle difficile ? la tournure même de la question servoit à y conduire, et l'indiquoit aux esprit attentifs, en leur laissant tout le plaisir de la recherche, et l'honneur de la solution. L'objection la moins solide, celle même qui annonçoit ou le peu d'avancement, ou l'oubli du principe, étoit écoutée et répondue avec bonté."

It is very interesting to note that Pothier, in the testing of his scholars, revived the medieval method of public disputations, a method that had only then recently died out in England, but which in France had long given place to the modern system of formal examinations. The method of disputation, in which the victor was awarded a gold medal, aroused every faculty in the students (for questions as well as answers were considered by the judges), and, as M. le Trosne says, "None would enter the lists if not assured, if not of victory, at least of honour." Moreover, it created public interest in the University and in the law school of the University. Pothier took up this work from the sheer love of teaching. His emoluments he divided between the poor and his pupils during the five-and-twenty years that he held the professorship. Alongside of his professorial and his judicial work Pothier, on the completion of his work on Roman

---

position of the Prolegomena (the material was supplied by Pothier), who had a large share in the commentary on the law of the twelve tables, and revised, with critical exactitude, the entire work. Pothier was also a good deal influenced by Rousseau, the professor of law at Paris and his intimate friend.

[1] Guyot edited Pothier's posthumous works in 1777.

law, turned with all the zest of a lover to that object of a true lawyer's passion—the law of his own country. For years he had prepared from time to time for his own use treatises or handbooks of French law. He needed such works in the daily round of his life. But now that the great foundation was laid, now that Roman law had yielded up to his capacious mind principles and equities, he turned to the law of his own land with the determination to do what had never yet been attempted. As long before as 1740 he had published conjointly with M. de la Jannès and M. Jouffe, an edition of the *Coutume d'Orléans*, and now, on a demand for a second edition, he produced a work of a singularly valuable kind; for at the head of each custom he added a little treatise on the subject of the custom, thus drafting schemes or designs for the series of treatises that he subsequently produced. This treatise completed, he turned to the work for which he is most famous—his famous *Traité des Obligations*, which he published in 1761 in two volumes, as the foundation of other projected treatises, and which was, in fact, the first fruit of his unique knowledge of Roman law. Of the classical treatise it will be necessary to give some summary, but before doing so it is desirable to refer to the series of works that sprang, so to speak, out of it. In 1762 he issued his *Traité du Contrat de Vente* and his *Traité des Retraits*. This was followed in 1763 by *Le Traité du Contrat de Constitution de Rente* and *Le Traité du Contrat de Change;* in 1764 by *Le Traité du Contrat de Louage* and *Le Traité du Contrat de Bail à Rente*. In 1765 Pothier supplemented his *Traité du Contrat de Louage* with a treatise on Maritime Hire (*Louage Maritime*), chiefly on charter parties, damage (*avaries*), and the hire of seamen, and also issued his *Traité du Contrat de Société* and his *Traité des Cheptels* (the leasing of cattle). In 1676 and 1767 he published the treatises on the contracts de Bienfaisance—i.e., *Le Traité du Prêt à Usage et du Précaire* (forming one treatise); *du contrat de Prêt de Consomption* (a second treatise); *du contrat de Dépôt* (a third treatise); *du contrat de Mandat*, with the quasi-contract *Negotiorum Gestorum* (a fourth treatise). The same years saw the treatises *Du Contrat de Nantissement* (pledge), *Des Contrats Aléatoires* (contingent contracts), *Des Contrats d'Assurance, du Prêt à la grosse Aventure* (bottomry bonds), *Du Jeu* (gaming contracts). In 1768 Pothier issued his *Traité du Contrat de Mariage;* in 1769 *Le Traité de la Commumauté*. These two great treatises on the marriage contract and the law of property and marriage together come to about 800 folio pages—the work of a lifetime in itself. With these treatises Pothier concludes his labours on the law of obligations. He has, he tells us, reserved the good wine to the last.

> "Nous avons crû ne pouvoir mieux terminer notre Traité des Obligations, et des différens contrats et quasi-contrats d'où elles naissent, que par un Traité du Contrat de Mariage, ce contrat étant le plus excellent et le plus ancien de tous les contrats. Il est le plus excellent, à ne le considérer même que dans l'ordre civil, parce que c'est celui qui intéresse le plus la société civile. Il est le plus ancien, car c'est le premier contrat qui ait été fait entre les hommes. Aussitôt que Dieu eut formé Ève d'une des côtes d'Adam, et qu'il la lui eut présentée, nos deux premiers parens firent ensemble un contrat de mariage; Adam prit Eve pour son épouse, en lui disant : *Hoc nunc, os ex ossibus meis, et caro de carne mea . . . et erunt duo in carne una* : et Eve prit réciproquement Adam pour son époux."

This is indeed a characteristic passage, setting forth Pothier's profound respect for the institution that underlies all civilized society, coupled with his entirely reverent acceptance of the text of the Old Testament (for the Post-Royalists were not modernists in our limited textual sense), and his passion for detecting the binding operation of law even in the spontaneous utterances of love.

In 1770 he issued the treatise *Du Douaire* (dower), followed in 1771 by its appendix *Du Droit d'Habitation* (the right of the widow to occupy the former marital residence for life or widowhood), and *Le Traité des Donations entre Mari et Femme*, with an appendix discussing Article 68 of the Custom of Orleans, by which either spouse could leave to the other by a mutual gift, confirmed by a mutual will, practically a complete interest in the other spouse's entire estate (subject to debts and maintenance of infants). The discussion is full of interest. These essays complete the monumental treatises on marriage and the law of property arising out of marriage.

In 1771 and 1772 came the last treatises, those which reconsider the whole Law of Possession : *Le Traité du Droit de Domaine de Propriété ; Le Traité de la Possession ; Le Traité de la Prescription qui résulte de la Possession.*

The *Traité du Droit de Domaine de Propriété* sets forth two kinds of rights, the *jus in re* and the *jus ad rem*, the first being the rights that we have in the thing itself, the second being the rights we have against the person who has contracted with us an obligation to give us the thing. The *jus ad rem* is the subject of the law of obligations ; the *jus in re* is the subject of the law of possession, and of feudal and censual rights, and rights of mortgage. Pothier supplements this elaborate treatise with a treatise on Possession—and this, his last published work, should be compared with Savigny's first published work, which is so famous, dealing with the same theme. Possession, Pothier tells us, is one of the ways of acquiring dominion : a treatise of possession necessarily follows on a treatise as to dominion over property. Pothier deals first with the nature of possession, and then discusses the different kinds of possession, the things susceptible of possession, and of quasi-possession, the manner of acquiring (and of losing) possession, and finally the rights of action springing from possession. Possession itself is "la détention d'une chose corporelle que nous tenons en notre puissance, ou par nous-mêmes, ou par quelqu'un qui la tient pour nous et en notre nom." It is a fact rather than a right, but it gives rise to rights in the things possessed—namely, a reputation as owner (*propriétaire*) till the true owner appears, and the right of action to obtain possession and recover possession. This is the case whether the title be just or unjust ; but if the title be just and of good faith, dominion also follows after a lapse of time by virtue of prescription.

There are two kinds of possession, civil and natural—the former springing from a good title, the latter from no title, or a bad title, or a nul title, or a good title that has not inherent in it any right of transfer. This doctrine should be compared with that of Savigny. It will be remembered that Savigny dwelt on the fact that modern law had extended the doctrine of possession from property and *jura in re* to every possible right, including rights of personal status and obligations. The comparison between the two works cannot be carried out here.

Pothier died on March 2, 1772, after a brief illness from fever. The brief summary given above of his works must suffice to supply some idea of his labours, but the four great volumes in which they are contained in no sense exhausts his legacy to the world of law. In 1777 his posthumous works were issued in three volumes, and these are further tribute to the enormous industry of the great jurist. The work was edited by his colleague, M. Guyot, the well-known lawyer and jurist of Orleans. That an authorized edition was necessary, was shown by the fact that a clandestine or pirated and imperfect edition of *Traité des Fiefs* was issued at Orleans (apparently from a student's copy of the manuscript) before the official edition appeared. There was a real demand for any works from the pen, to quote M. Guyot's prefatory letters to Monseigneur de Miromesnil (Garde des Sceaux de France): "D'un Jurisconsulte qui a honoré notre Province, autant par ses Ecrits immortels, que par ses travaux assidus dans l'exercice des fonctions de la Magistrature et l'enseignement public du Droit."

The first volume contained the *Traité des Fiefs*, an elaborate treatise of great historical value, that gave the exact legal position as to ownership of land on the eve of the French Revolution. Pothier tells us that "Les biens immeubles se divisent, par rapport à la manière dont de font tenus, en Féodaux, Censuels, et Allodiaux." He goes on to distinguish those classes of land with a clearness not to be found in the best modern French dictionary: "Les immeubles féodaux ou Fiefs, sont ceux qui sont tenus à la charge de la foi et hommage. Les Censuels sont ceux qui sont tenus à la charge d'une redevance pécunaire, en reconnoissance de la Seigneurie du Seigneur de qui ils font tenus. Les Biens allodiaux ou franc-alleux sont ceux qui ne sont d'aucun Seigneur."

This work discusses fiefs. The *Traité des Cens*, which follows it, deals with a certain class of charges on land:

> "Le contrat de bail à cens est un contrat par lequel le propriétaire d'un héritage ou d'un autre droit immobilier l'aliene, sous la réserve qu'il fait de la seigneurie directe, et d'une redevance annuelle en argent ou en fruits, qui doit lui être payée par le preneur ou ses successeurs en reconnoissance de ladite seigneurie. Cette redevance annuelle s'appelle *cens*. L'héritage chargé de cette redevance, à la charge de laquelle il a été concédé, est ce qu'on appelle un héritage *censuel*. Le possesseur de cet héritage s'appelle *censitaire*. Celui à qui est due cette redevance récognitive de la seigneurie directe qui est par-devers lui, est ce qu'on appelle le *Seigneur de Censive*."

The distinction between the *Cens* and the *Rente foncière* is carefully brought out; and here we see the cleavage between the old law and the new. The *Rente foncière* is never seigneurial, and is therefore subject to the law of prescription; while the *Cens* is subject to no such law. Indeed, the *Cens* really enabled the owners of free or lordless land to grasp a lordship, for when they granted the *Cens* they reserved the lordship. The next treatise deals with the feudal or seigneurial right or rent known as *Le Droit de Champart*. This is followed by *Le Traité de la Gardenoble et Bourgeoise*; *Le Traité du Préciput* (preferential legacy) *légal des Nobles* (relating to a special aspect of the law of property in marriage in the case of the noble class); *Le Traité de l'Hypothèque*; *Le Traité des Substitutions*, a derivative of the Roman law of wills. The second volume (which, as does the third, again warns the reader against imperfect pirate editions of works by Pothier, such as the 1774 edition of the *Procédure Civile*) opens with the lengthy *Traité des Successions*, and passes on to the *Traité des Propres* ("l'esprit de notre Droit Coutumier est que chacun conserve a sa famille les biens qui lui en sont venus. De là est venue la distinction entre les Acquêts et Propres "), *Traité des Donations testamentaires*, *Traité des Donations entre Vifs*, *Traité des Personnes et des Choses*. This last work opens with an invaluable analysis of the classes that made up French society immediately before the Revolution. He summarizes the privileges of the *noblesse* under eleven heads. The third head is the most notable : " Ils sont exempts de taille, et de plusieurs autres cottisations, connues sous le nom de *Taillons, de Crues d'Aides, et de Subsides*, auxquels les roturiers sont sujets ; ils ont même le droit de faire valoir quatre charrues, sans pouvoir y être imposés." In return they are destined for the military service, and have some small special burdens. When Pothier deals with serfs he is careful to point out that they are not slaves : a negro permanently resident in France becomes free. The serfs of the Royal Provinces, such as Burgundy, have a civil status, are citizens : " Ils ne font pas *in dominio* du Seigneur auquel ils appartiennent et ne sont appellés Serfs qu'a cause de certains devoirs très-onéreux, dont ils sont tenus envers lui." There were three classes of serfs : the serf born, who must remain a serf ; the serf in respect of a heritage, who can become free by abandoning the heritage ; and *les serfs de meubles*, who can only achieve their freedom at the cost of all their personal estate. *Les serfs de corps* cannot escape from their burdens " tels que la taille que leur Seigneur a droit d'exiger, le droit qu'a leur Seigneur de recueillir après leur décès tours les biens qu'ils délaisseront." The *taille*, the *corvée*, the inability to marry out of the serf class, and the limitation on testamentary disposition, were certainly negative forces moving towards revolution. The last volume contains *Traité de la Procédure civile* and *Traité de la Procédure criminelle*, the value of which in tracing the history of French law can hardly be overestimated. This brief sketch of the contents of these volumes give some slight idea of the vast volume of Pothier's work. It is desirable, however, to make some fuller reference to the famous *Traité des Obligations*, since that work is in one sense Pothier's chief contribution to the science of law in general —a work that stands out as something different in kind to, and scarcely less monumental than, his presentation of the entire Corpus of French law as conceived and practised in his age. The work falls into four parts, as follows :

I. *Première Partie :* De ce qui appartient à l'essence des obligations ; et de leurs effets.

II. *Seconde Partie :* Des différentes espèces d'obligations.

III. *Troisième Partie :* Des manières dont s'éteignent les obligations, et des différentes fins de non-recevoir, ou préscriptions contre les créances.

IV. *Quatrième Partie :* De la preuve tant des obligations que de leurs paiemens.

The work runs to 459 folio pages, and is, of course, of great elaboration.

Part I. falls into two chapters. In the first chapter Pothier discusses what belongs to the essence of obligations, and in the second chapter the effect of obligations. It is, he says, of the essence of an obligation that there should be a cause from which the obligation springs ; that there should be persons between the obligation is contracted ; that there should be a thing that is the object of the obligation. The causes of obligations are contracts, quasi-contracts, delicts, and quasi-delicts, and sometimes the mere operation of law or equity. It is of profound interest to see Pothier fall back on Natural Law as the cause of obligations. He says : " 123. La Loi naturelle est la cause au moins médiate de toutes les obligations : car si les contrats, délits et quasi-délits, produisent des obligations, c'est primitivement, parce que le Loi naturelle ordonne que chacun tienne ce qu'il a promis, et qu'il répare le tort qu'il a commis par sa faute." Pothier first deals with contracts : a contract is a pact or convention to form an engagement. He refuses to adopt the Roman basis of contracts, "n'étant pas fondés sur le droit naturel." He proceeds to define a contract as " une convention par laquelle les deux parties réciproquement, ou seulement l'une des deux, promettent et s'engagent envers l'autre à lui donner quelque chose, ou à faire ou à ne pas faire quelque chose." The parties must promise *and* engage : for a promise may be merely " une obligation imparfaite " (a famous phrase). This is not the place in which to contrast the various views as to the nature of contract held by various famous jurists, but it is perhaps worth noticing that both Savigny and Austin (with his distinction between a contract and a pollicitation taken apparently direct from Pothier) owe much to Pothier's analysis. The English doctrine of Consideration is no doubt implied in Pothier's definition, for in the absence of what we should call consideration, Pothier would find that the obligation was imperfect, and that therefore there was no contract. But in English law as late as 1765 (see Sir William Anson on *Contract*, twelfth edition, p. 90 ; *Pillans* v. *Van Mierop*, 3 Burr. 1663) the doctrine of consideration was in the balance, and it was not until 1778, after Pothier's death, that in the case of *Rann* v. *Hughes* (7 T.R., 350 [*n*]) it was finally laid down that an agreement without sufficient consideration was *nudum pactum*. Without this specific doctrine Pothier apparently drew from the law of Nature a doctrine of contract that rejects as non-contractual agreements that in fact do not exhibit what English lawyers call consideration. But Pothier says that each contract must be considered by itself in order to determine the elements that are the essence of the contract. Pothier next passes to the other causes of obligation, to the persons between whom obligations can arise, to the things that can be the object and subject-matter of obligations. Lastly, in this first part, he discusses the effects of obligations.

In the Second Part he opens with an analysis of the different classes of obligations, and in the second chapter distinguishes between *obligations civiles* and *obligations naturelles*. He says that French law, refusing to follow Roman law in its distinction between contracts and simple pacts, "ces obligations naturelles du Droit Romain sont, dans notre Droit, de véritables obligations civiles." But these simple pacts, which are unenforceable because the law denies the right of action, or one of the parties incapable of contracting, must not be confounded with the "imperfect obligations" which he has already excluded from the realm of true obligations—obligations which create no manner of right. In other words, if the consideration exists, the obligation exists, even if for some technical reason the obligation cannot be enforced in the courts. In the next chapter Pothier discusses the different ways in which obligations can be contracted. In the fourth chapter he considers particular kinds of obligations with reference to the subject-matter of the obligation. In the fifth chapter he discusses penal obligations; in the sixth accessory obligations, such as the obligation of a guarantor.

The Third Part deals with the extinction of obligations (and the running of prescription against debt) in eight important chapters. A creditor must bring his action within thirty years. This doctrine, he says, springs from the presumption that the debt would be paid within that time, and also to relieve debtors from the duty of keeping receipts for ever. The prescriptive period in some Customs (*cf.* Orleans) in the case of a debtor bound by notarial act was (following the Roman law) forty years. On the other hand, small shopkeepers had to demand payment of their accounts within six months, and merchants within a year; but these rules did not apply where the debt could be proved by evidence in writing. The last part deals with the question of the proof of the existence of obligations. The creditor has to prove the debt, and then it lies on the debtor to prove, if he can, that it is already discharged. There are, Pothier says, two kinds of proof: literal proof, arising from acts or written words; and proof arising from evidence. The place of admissions, presumptions, and oaths in the realm of proof are also considered at length.

To those who are interested in the personality of Pothier we may recommend a perusal of the general observations that conclude this great work. He uses this chapter very largely for the purpose of discussing the views of a certain M. le Brun (Avocat au Parlement de Paris) as to acts of default in relation to contracts. Pothier adopted the views of all the interpreters of Roman law and the jurists up to his time—the views of Accursus, Alciati; Cujas, Duaren, d'Avezan, Vinnius, Heineccius—that there are three degrees of default: *lata culpa* (namely, not applying to the affairs of others the degree of care that the most careless and stupid person would devote to his own affairs); *levis culpa* (not using the care which an ordinary man would devote to his own affairs); and *levissima culpa* (not using the care which the most attentive person would devote to his own affairs). Pothier proceeds to ascertain the principles that determine when one or other of these degrees of carefulness is necessary. The first only is necessary (save in certain cases) if the debt is solely for the benefit of the creditor; where the interests of the parties to the contract or quasi-contract are reciprocal, the second class of carefulness is necessary; the third class is necessary in contracts when the act done is for the sole benefit of the party in possession the thing which is the object of the contract—as in the contract of *commodatum*. M. Le Brun roundly denied the doctrine of three degrees of carefulness. There are only two kinds of diligence: the diligence which a man of business is accustomed to show; the diligence that a man usually shows in his own affairs. It depends on the contract which kind of diligence is necessary. Pothier quietly joins issue with M. Le Brun ("Je suis demeuré attaché à l'ancienne doctrine"), and is full of apologies for disagreeing with his junior, and ends up with this charming sentence: "Au reste, quoique l'Auteur n'ait pu me persuader d'embrasser son système (ce qu'il doit pardonner à un vieillard à qui il n'est pas facile de se départir de ses anciennes idées), je dois cette justice à sa Dissertation, qu'elle est tres ingenieuse et très savante, et qu'elle mérite d'être lue par tous ceux qui ont quelque goût pour la jurisprudence."

Space is not available here for dealing in any way with the series of treatises on special contracts that supplement the treatise on obligations or the vast group of treatises on the contract of marriage. This latter work has a peculiar value, as it deals at length with the question of marriage and divorce in the age when the new law was becoming effective. Pothier points out that no divorce can take place in France, but he adds that "Dans les États Protestans, le divorce est encore permis pour de certaines causes, et en observant certaines formalités," and refers the reader to the Code of Frederick of Prussia. The treatises give us a detailed picture of social life in France in the mid-eighteenth century, laying bare as Pothier does, with the pen of a practical lawyer, the whole of the marital régime that was reflected in every detail by the elaborate law governing the contract of marriage and the multitudinous swarms of property rights springing out of that contract or out of the preliminary contract of betrothal.

One word of summary. In Pothier we listen to a lawyer who saw that there were three aspects of law that must enter the legal mind: the great bases which he found in Roman law partly, but also largely in the Law of Nature ; the great realm of practice ; the great and varying systems of customary law. He laboured like a Titan to bring together into one perfect whole these aspects of law, and performed a task of inconceivable labour and difficulty when he produced what was practically a code of French substantive and procedural law. No one but a great thinker and great jurist and a great practical lawyer could have done this : and he was all these things. But he was something more than this : he was a great man in whom character shone forth not only in his work, but in his life. His life was one of complete orderliness, entirely pervaded by faith, hope, and charity. He saw that the law which must govern society must also govern the individual, and he found, as Milton found, that the inner law of spiritual liberty was the necessary supplement of the outer law that governs the interaction of men and nations.

ÉMERICH DE VATTEL

THE late Mr. Joseph Chitty in 1834, after his relinquishment of an enormous practice at the Bar, employed part of his unfamiliar leisure in re-editing for a world that was fast forgetting the terribleness of war the English anonymous edition of Vattel's *Le Droit des Gens*, issued in 1760 and amply revised in 1797, possibly by William Cobbett, who in 1795 had translated Marten's *Law of Nations*.[1] Mr. Chitty's object was the object of every self-respecting lawyer: he desired to bring Vattel's work up to date, with special reference to the legal decisions that had sprung out of the Napoleonic and American wars. But this eminent lawyer in his retirement did not only look upon Vattel's honoured work as a book to be "noted up." The moral aspect of his labours particularly appealed to the most technical pleader that the English Bar has produced. He affirms in his preface, "without the hazard of contradiction, that every one who has attentively read this work, will admit that he has acquired a knowledge of superior sentiments, and more important information than he ever derived from any other work." Mr. Chitty indeed regarded Vattel's work not only as a book for sovereigns and statesmen but as a moral guide for every educated person. He says:

"It has been generally supposed that it is only adapted for the study of sovereigns and statesmen, and in that view certainly the author's excellent preface points out its pre-eminent importance. But it is of *infinitely more extended utility*. It con-

---

[1] Mr. Chitty had already in 1812 published a work (dedicated to Lord Erskine) entitled *A Practical Treatise on the Law of Nations, relative to the Legal Effect of War on the Commerce of Belligerents and Neutrals, and on Orders in Council and Licenses*. It is a work of importance in the history of international law. Mr. Chitty's edition of Vattel is not included in the list of his works published in the *Dictionary of National Biography*. I may add here that I have used the copy of the 1760 English version of *Le Droit des Gens* in the Cambridge University Library. Lincoln's Inn Library possesses a copy (which I have also used for the purposes of this paper) of the *Questions de Droit Naturel, et Observations sur le Traité du Droit de la Natur de M. le Baron de Wolf* of 1762. The work is rare.

tains a practical collection of ethics, principles, and rules of conduct to be observed and pursued, as well by *private individuals* as by *states*, and these of the utmost practical importance to the well-being, happiness, and ultimate and permanent advantage and benefit of all mankind ; and therefore ought to be studied by *every gentleman of liberal education*, and by *youth*, in whom the best moral principles should be inculcated. The work should be familiar in the *Universities* and in every class above the inferior ranks of society."

I have quoted Mr. Chitty's enthusiastic and profusely italicized dedication of the work as this, in a sense, prepares the way for an analysis of it. It is true that this eminent lawyer's desires failed. Vattel is not perused with eagerness by every gentleman of liberal education or even by youth, while it is to be doubted if his masterpiece is familiar in any English University or in any English grade of population. It may well be that women and the inferior ranks of society, the classes so thoughtfully excused by Mr. Chitty, know as much about the genial disciple of Christian von Wolff as is known by other general or special readers. Let us see what a new dedication, a new recommendation at large, can do for this famous and suave Swiss publicist.

Vattel's Life.—Émerich de Vattel was the son of David de Vattel, a minister of the Reformed Church, and his wife Marie de Montmollin, daughter of a Prussian Treasury official. He was born at Couvet in the principality of Neufchâtel on April 25, 1714. He early showed a taste for philosophic subjects, which, in common with general scholarship, he pursued at the University of Bâle. He passed on to the University of Geneva, where he finally specialized upon moral philosophy. He became an ardent student of Leibnitz and Wolff and published against Crousaz a luminous summary and defence of the Leibnitz position. This he dedicated to King Frederic II., and in 1742 he followed his book to Berlin in order to offer his services to the King whose subject he was by birth. He was rebuffed by the bluff monarch and passed on to Dresden, where his great abilities were at once recognized by the Prime Minister of Saxony, Comte de Brühl. The future jurist was placed in the diplomatic service, where his unique knowledge of the law of nations and of the history of treaties enabled him to perform services of considerable moment. It was, however, possible for him to spend some years at Neufchâtel, but in 1746 he returned to Dresden, when the King, Augustus III., appointed him adviser to the Embassy and sent him the next year to Berne as minister-plenipotentiary. He had long been composing his famous treatise *Le Droit des Gens*, and it was at Berne, amidst pleasing and congenial diplomatic duties, that he finished this work. He also during this period wrote widely on philosophy and literature, closely investigated the whole theory of natural rights and, as a relaxation, published some poems.[1]

In 1758 he returned to Dresden, was made a Privy Councillor, and became the chief adviser of the Government on foreign affairs. During the same year *Le Droit des Gens* was printed at Neufchâtel and issued with the name London on the title-page. A second edition appeared in the same year bearing the impress of Leyden. In 1762 he issued his last work: *Questions de Droit Naturel, et Observations sur le Traité du Droit de la Natur de M. le Baron de Wolf*.[2] This book, a volume of great importance, was written some years before publication and consists of material collected during the composition of *Le Droit des Gens*. We have, almost beyond doubt, further examples of Vattel's work in three volumes (of quite the first importance as historical sources) published at Frankfort and Leipsic simultaneously in 1757 and 1758. These are volumes of essays par "un observateur Hollandois." The first volume (1757) is entitled " *Mémoires pour servir à l'Histoire de notre tems*, par l'Observateur Hollandois, Rédigez et Augmentez par M. D. V." The Lord Acton Library Catalogue suggests that M. D. V. is "Monsieur de Vattel," and a careful consideration of the Preface and the Notes makes this certain. Following the preface is a "Dissertation sur la Raison de la Guerre," by the jurist Strube, which was almost certainly selected for insertion by Vattel. Vattel's preface is a wonderful piece of writing in which he advocates the formation of a United States of Europe, in which no single state is to be allowed to have a predominating power. This volume consists of twenty essays. The second volume (bound up, in Lord Acton's collection, with the first) is entitled " *Mémoires pour servir à l'Histoire de notre tems, par rapport à la Guerre Anglo-Gallicane*, par l'Obser-

[1] In his *Observations* he included a chapter on Tragedy and Comedy.
[2] A Berne, chez la Société Typographique MDCCLXII. I think that the first edition of *Le Droit des Gens* is clearly the "London" edition, for it has at the end of the second volume a list of *Errata* which in the "Leyden" edition have been duly corrected. Through the kindness of Dr. T. A. Walker, of Peterhouse, Cambridge, I have been able to compare the "London" edition in the Peterhouse Library with the "Leyden" edition (two volumes in one) in Dr. Walker's fine collection of works on the Law of Nations. He also lent me Mr. Chitty's work of 1812.

vateur Hollandois, Rédigez et Augmentez par M. D. V." (1757). The third volume is entitled " *Mémoires pour servir à l'Histoire de notre tems, où l'on deduit historiquement le Droit et le Fait de la Guerre Sanglante qui trouble actuellement toute l'Europe*, par l'Observateur Hollandois, Rédigez et Augmentez par M. D. V." (1758). From 1762 onwards his official position in the Court of Saxony and the new interests of his home life rendered further juridical work impossible.

It was not until late in life that he married, on January 27, 1764, at Dresden, Mademoiselle Marianne de Chesne, a member of a noble French family which had settled in Saxony. A son was born on January 31, 1765, who died in the year 1827. Vattel only lived for about four years after his marriage. The strain of his official work proved very great, and in 1766 he broke down and retired for rest to his native district, Neufchâtel. In the autumn, with characteristic energy, he returned to Dresden and resumed his duties. In the following year he broke down again and once more sought relief at Neufchâtel. But it was too late, and he died on December 28, 1767, in his sixty-fourth year. Vattel left behind him an annotated copy of the first edition of *Le Droit des Gens*, and an edition crudely incorporating these notes was issued from Neufchâtel in 1773. The volume, in the hands of a critic, is invaluable as reflecting the jurist's latest views, but it was issued in a form that would have revolted his fine sense of style and order. The editor of the edition of 1775 indeed comments in terms of great severity on this edition, and declares that it " devrait être abandonné à l'épicier comme vraie maculature."

Vattel's Works.—In considering Vattel's works it will probably be found convenient to make some detailed examination of the *Questions de Droit Naturel, et Observations sur le Traité du Droit de la Natur de M. le Baron de Wolf*, since this remarkable volume contains most of the material on which *Le Droit des Gens* was based and reveals the jurist at work collecting his materials, sorting his ideas, and criticizing the intellectual position of his great master Wolff. The work shows us the shrewd utilitarianism that was the salient intellectual characteristic of Vattel. There never was a shrewder mind. He has all the logical clearness and hardness of Bentham, and is as inelastic as that eminent thinker. He is in point of time and thought the predecessor of Bentham, whose doctrine of utility appears largely written throughout these *Observations*. Vattel indeed enunciates the aphorism of the "greatest good of the greatest number," in almost similar words. Yet, reading Vattel, there seems a great gulf fixed between him and the English utilitarians. His doctrine is so wrapped up in elegant writing and precious sentimentalism that the bitter pill is swallowed before the victim has any knowledge of the fact. That was not Bentham's way. Bentham had to be translated into French by Dumont, and re-translated into English before the great British public would have anything to do with his philosophic nostrums. Vattel at once found his audience, and an English edition appeared, as we have seen, in 1760, within two years of the publication of the original work. A German edition (from the pen of J. P. Schulin) also appeared in 1760,[1] simultaneously at Frankfort and Leipsic, thus recalling the "Acton" volumes referred to above. He, moreover, appealed directly to the religious sense, deliberately limiting his utilitarianism to the natural interrelations of men. He recognized, as standing out above and enveloping these relations, the love of God to which men could turn, and in the glow of which they could transform the pure selfishness of natural law into the pure altruism of supernatural law. The passage in which he describes this transition shows the idealism that underlay the utilitarianism of his philosophy. This idealism is continually in sight, and adds a vivid interest to almost every proposition that he advances. When we have a utilitarianism that is the necessary but not the last resort of the human soul, humanity feels that it can adopt it without a sense of shame. Indeed, as we have seen, Mr. Chitty adopted it with a sense of enthusiasm.

In considering the *Observations* we may dismiss Vattel's profuse apologies for venturing to criticize his great master, Wolff, without further comment than the remark that local anæsthetics of this type are very characteristic of our author. He does not spare the scalpel, but skilfully manages to convey the impression that it hurts the surgeon more than the patient. Indeed such was his respect for Wolff that probably this was true. The work opens with the end and aim of Being. Our first and most general obligation, the foundation of all other obligations, is to work for

[1] The English editions of 1760, 1797, and 1834 are not, it would seem, included in Klüber's Bibliography (*Dans le Droit des Gens Moderne de l'Europe*, édit. Guillaumin, 1861, p. 446). See M. P. Padier-Fodérér's edition of *Le Droit des Gens* (Paris, 1683), vol. i., p. xiii (n.). This edition is probably the best and is largely followed here so far as the text and the facts of Vattel's life are concerned. But see also Hoffmann's edition of 1835, containing Sir James Macintosh's Essay on the Law of Nature and Nations.

our individual happiness and well-being. Now perfection alone can secure perfect happiness. Therefore, each must work for his own perfection, and this can only be done by acquiring and practising virtue. How near, he asks, does this natural ideal approach the Christian ideal? Have we, for instance, a natural duty to love our enemies? This is discussed in a remarkable passage:

"Nous nous aimons premièrement nous-mêmes, et nous nous devons, préférablement à tous, le soin de notre conservation et celui d'avancer notre perfection. Mais l'homme ne pouvant se suffire à soi-même, se conserver et se perfectionner seul et sans le secours de ses semblables, la nature et l'essence des hommes les obligeant à s'aider réciproquement, et il faut qu'ils y soient sincèrement et constamment disposés : d'où il suit, qu'ils doivent s'aimer les uns les autres. Mais l'amour que je dois aux autres ne dérivant que de celui que je me dois à moi-même, il cède à celui-ci et ne peut jamais lui nuire. Si un homme rompt les liens qui doivent nous unir, et se déclare mon ennemi, cherchant à me nuire, bien loin de m'aider, il m'est permis de faire contre lui tout ce qui est nécessaire à ma défense et à ma sûreté. Mais comme cette division est un mal dans la société humaine, et un mal pour moi-même, je dois faire mon possible pour empêcher qu'elle ne s'aigrisse, et pour la finir entièrement ; et rien n'y contribuera davantage que ma modération dans ma juste défense, et la générosité avec laquelle je rendrai, dans l'occasion, à mon ennemi même les devoirs de l'humanité, et lui ferai tous les biens qui ne contribueront pas à le mettre mieux en état de me nuire, ou à lui donner, et à ses pareils, plus de hardiesse à m'attaquer" (pp. 35-6).

We cannot go farther than that if we base our actions on the simple nature and essence of men in their mutual relations. If you desire more than this you must turn to the love of God. If the heart, Vattel adds, is actually inflamed with that love, then it is really possible to love your enemies. Morality can only be carried to its highest point of perfection by the aid of a just conception of the supernatural. Vattel then elaborates an utilitarian system of psychology based on the relations of men. The system is empirical, and Vattel entirely declines to adopt Wolff's great attempt to apply mathematical thought to the moral sciences. The basis of his system of humanitarianism is that the "right" of demanding help from other men is a "perfect right," inasmuch as there is joined to it the right of constraining those who refuse to allow a man to exercise this right.

The First Part of the book concludes with a discussion of the measure of damages caused by a wrongful act. There must be a certain proportion between the punishment and the crime. This proportion must be maintained even if the punishment will not prevent the wrongdoing. If capital punishment only will prevent apple-stealing from an orchard, the loss must be tolerated. A man has a duty to preserve and protect, not only himself but others, and if the loss in question is of less importance to a man's perfection than kindly conduct, then the loss must be suffered. If, however, it is found that certain offences become common it may be necessary to inflict penalties out of proportion to the offences in order to preserve society.

The Second Part deals with certain elementary propositions. Vattel discusses the difference in a primitive community between the gifts of nature and the fruits of industry. The first are held in common by the whole community, but each man has "un droit de préférence sur les fruits de son industrie et de son travail." The result, in the end, is the dissolution of primitive conditions. A man cultivates a piece of land ; discovers that he has a special right to the fruits of the field, and appropriates them ; insensibly he acquires a right to the field itself, and his successors continue to hold it. In this demonstration we see clearly enough the peculiar vice of eighteenth-century speculation. Had Vattel not been content to reason from the necessarily sophisticated outlook of his own age and class, but had turned to the examination of the village communities within his reach, he would have seen that, in fact, his theory was absolutely untrue ; that the appropriation of the fruits of the soil had gone on for untold centuries without individual appropriation of the soil. Vattel attacks Wolff's theory of the origin of property and ownership as a result of the exercise of natural liberty and apparent needs, but his own generalization is far less convincing. It is as follows : As the race multiplied the simple products of the earth ceased to be sufficient ; industry and art became necessary ; foreseeing men began to provide against the future, and to cultivate fields instead of roaming at large. A general right to everything existed, so these men could not be restrained from taking a particular portion of land and renouncing the rest. They thereupon acquired the right to the produce of this soil. Others followed their example : " voilà la *proprieté* et le *domaine* établis." In the light of modern investigations it is probable that Wolff's speculations are nearer the truth than those of Vattel. But the subject is not one for speculation at all. It is a question of fact to be ascertained in accordance with correct laws of evidence.

The Third Part discusses some interesting questions of contract and lays down two propositions of natural law : first, that no one can be presumed to have abandoned property ; and secondly, that a holder in good faith must be protected.

The Fourth Part continues the discussion of contracts, raising questions of curious interest such as, can a man accept an offer by silence ? must a seller point out the patent faults of his goods ? In the latter case Vattel is apparently guided by the maxim *caveat emptor*. The discussion as to accidental injury to a workman is interesting. The employer is responsible, in the case of a hired workman, but not where the work is done by a contractor.

The Fifth Part continues the discussion of special cases. Are lotteries allowable by the law of nature ? Vattel, in opposition to Wolff, declares that they are allowable. Again Vattel upholds in principle contracts of insurance made in good faith after the event. He agrees that it is illegal to agree to terminate a difference by a duel. He declares that a vendor of land can reserve a right of passage over it for the use of a neighbour. Problems of these various types are, of course, familiar to English lawyers.

In the Sixth Part, after a discussion of certain questions relating to land (such as the right to the surface) Vattel proceeds to discuss the law of necessity. He is surprisingly and admirably uncompromising as to the limits of lawful action in cases of necessity. He lays down the definite principle : " qu'il ne nous est jamais permis de faire tort à quelqu'un, d'aller contre son droit bien établi." There is a right to do all things that are not illegal in themselves or contrary to the absolute right of another person. For instance, you may *kill* an aggressor because he began the evil, and has not an exclusive right to preserve his own life. But you must not kill a defenceless person for the purposes of food in a case of desperate necessity, unless he voluntarily consents to sacrifice himself for others.

Wolff denies this last position (s. 587) on the ground that a man has no right over his own life and therefore cannot consent to give it up. This, as Vattel points out, is illogical since the same argument would forbid a man to sacrifice his life for his country. Wolff, while declaring that a boatful of men ought rather to die of hunger than feed upon each other, yet allows a party to make a hopeless sally to save a town. Vattel will have none of this. " Je ne voudrois donc pas dire qu'un homme n'est point le maître de sa propre vie ; mais je dirois, qu'il est obligé de la conserver précieusement, à moins qu'il n'ait des raisons très-fortes et très importantes de l'exposer, ou même de la sacrifier." The general rule of necessity is stated as follows : " Il faut choisir le plus grand bien, ou le moindre mal ; mais en considérant la chose dans toute son étendue, avec toutes les liaisons et toutes ses conséquences et dépendances. Car la décision ne doit pas se fonder seulement sur le cas présent, considérée en lui-même et indépendamment de ses conséquences dans le monde." Vattel proceeds to exemplify this doctrine by a protest against the use of poisoned weapons—a use that had been justified by Wolff. If the use established itself, " la guerre deviendroit atroce, ses maux n'auroient plus de bornes, et elle seroit capable de détruire le genre-humain " (p. 213). But does not this argument destroy itself and re-establish Wolff's position ? The more terrible war is made, the less likely it is to be waged. The argument against poisoned weapons applies, if it applies at all, with renewed force to the use of airships from which explosives can be poured upon defenceless towns, involving combatants and non-combatants in irretrievable destruction. The whole tendency of war is to become more terrible and, in fact, less frequent and less destructive. War was far more bloody when it resolved itself into a vast number of single duels fought *à outrance* according to highly artificial rules. According to Vattel's own principles, the more terrible war is made the more likely is it to fulfil the laws of nature and secure peace.

The Seventh Part opens with an interesting discussion of the manner of counting votes. Here Vattel follows Grotius and not Wolff. The principle laid down is that those who have *any* opinion in common must be ranged together for the purpose of arriving at a decision. Thus if four judges condemn a man to death, two to banishment, two to a thousand crown fine, two to a hundred crown fine, and three are for an acquittal, we have *nine* in favour of life against *four* in favour of death ; but *ten* are in favour of some form of punishment, while only *three* are in favour of freedom. So the man must live, but must be punished. *Six* are in favour of death or banishment, and *seven* in favour of something else. Therefore the punishment must be a fine, and the higher fine, since eight are in favour of that *at least*—for the greater includes the less. So the man is fined a thousand crowns.

It is an interesting discussion, but it leaves out of account the fundamental problem, why should a majority carry the day ? Counting by heads is surely not the result of the law of nature, for, in fact, in nature it is always one head that dominates the rest. The rule is presumably a rule of convenience which in fact gives the law of intellectual dominance full play while it creates that illusory atmosphere of equality which is so dear to the human heart. But it is necessary to lay stress on the fact that there is no natural law which gives a special sanction to the decision of majorities, though possibly there are signs of conventions on the subject in the earliest stages of tribal life. The elemental man had no respect for liberty, equality, or fraternity outside his clan or kinship bond or hunting troop ; while inside that fundamental unit *ex hypothesi* none of these things existed. In their place was chieftainship, the *Manus*, the system of slavery.[1] The idea of equality was entirely remote from tribal life, and consequently the democratic idea of government by majorities was non-existent. But there was, as there is to-day, a primary force or passion (the existence of which is acutely recognized by Vattel) which tended to create a conventional recognition of human equality. I refer to the passion of jealousy. A force so disruptive had to be met by definite structural variations in social life. Consciously or unconsciously the fiction of equality was introduced to combat this universal force or passion. If men could be led to believe that they were equal, society could maintain stable equilibrium. Out of this transparent fiction an ideal of real equality emerged, and human society through long ages has made from age to age desperate efforts to realize on earth the platonic pattern of a divine society laid up in Heaven. To-day the fiction is as transparent as ever, but the ideal has at last descended from a transcendental Heaven into the heart of man, and to-day efforts, unprecedented in the history of mankind, are in progress to secure a real equality among the sons of men.

Vattel is full of interest when he turns from the doctrine of human equality to the subject of women. He sees here, at any rate, no equality, nor has he, despite his suavity, any illusions.

[1] It is to be noticed that while Wolff denies that slavery existed in primitive communities, Vattel declares that the slave could come into existence as soon as other sorts of property. The right to kill involves the lesser right to enslave. Vattel's assertion that parents have no natural right over the lives and liberty of their children must be met by the answer that for untold years they, in fact, exercised such rights. No doubt this was wrong, but was it more unnatural than the right to die which is supported by Vattel ?

He sees nothing fundamental in the doctrine of monogamy. He denies that the laws of nature forbid plurality of wives, though he admits the inexpediency, in most cases, of polygamy. In certain cases, however, he admits its use and possibly its necessity, while he thinks that concubinage can quite well be legalized. He claims that a man should be allowed a divorce for sterility, and asserts that marriage is never indissoluble in itself but that natural law imposes on us the obligation never to break it without strong and just reasons, especially if there are children. His treatment of this subject is a striking instance of the luminous way in which he applies the principle of utilitarianism to human problems. It is from the utilitarian standpoint that he goes on to inquire as to the person to whom authority belongs in marriage. It is curious that a question which is creating such unpleasant interest in the present day should have been discussed with such gusto more than a century and a half ago. M. de Vattel would not have been popular with the army of women who are demanding the franchise to-day. His cold reasoning and his uncompromising views on the superiority of the male sex would have caused pain in many sensitive hearts. Far otherwise would it be were M. Christian de Wolff suddenly to glide once more on to the platform of life with his thrilling declaration: "Le Droit Naturel établit une parfaite égalité entre le mari et la femme" and his emphatic repudiation of the predominance of the male sex. The text of Vattel's disagreement with his great master deserves to be reprinted: He asserts that men are "plus capables des affaires importantes, plus fermes, plus forts et plus courageux. Il paroît donc que la nature a destiné la femme à vivre sous la protection du mari, et cette protection donne déjà une supériorité." Some one, says this jurist, even then trembling on the verge of matrimony, must lead and that one must be the stronger. "Dans une pareille société, dis-je, celui qui est le plus capable ait le droit de décider, en cas de partage dans les sentimens." Then follows the touch of sentiment that is intended to sweeten the bitter draught. The husband must use his superiority "avec douceur, avec sagesse et avec équité, pour l'avantage commun." Vattel is not as wise as usual here; some things in life should be taken for granted. But he adds, to cure all, "outre l'amour et les soins que le mari lui doit, elle a ses droits, qu'il est obligé de respecter."[1] Wolff's answer, of

---

[1] It should be noticed that in the Eighth Part he asserts (against Wolff) that women are far less capable of public government than men (p. 355).

course, would have been that Vattel was begging the question, that he was constructing a universal argument from his own very imperfect knowledge of the past, when in fact the law of nature depends as much on the potentiality of women as on their actual achievement. You cannot, for instance, argue that there is a law of nature asserting that the negro is necessarily inferior to the Aryan. Wolff in asserting the equality of the sexes no doubt wrote as a theorist, while Vattel in denying the equality wrote as a practical utilitarian. But the weakness of the utilitarian position is that while it necessarily depends on the appeal to experience, it invariably appeals to a very limited experience. If experience were exhaustive, the idealist and the utilitarian would be at one. But as it is, there can be no finality about the utilitarian position, which shifts in the direction of idealism as the ages pass and knowledge increases.

It is very difficult to ascertain how Vattel formulated his laws of nature. We have seen that he holds it to be unnatural for a parent to enslave or kill his child. On the other hand, he holds that though the giving of a bad example by a parent is a great fault, it is not such an infringement of a natural law as to constitute a natural injury. Now no doubt this distinction does exist in municipal law. Until the year 1908 a drunken mother could carry her children with her to any tavern in the land, and they not infrequently shared her libations from their tenderest infancy. Moreover it was decided as long ago as February 25, 1796, in the deservedly immortal case of *Hodges* v. *Hodges*,[1] that the common law of England imposed upon parents no duty to educate their children. Lord Kenyon stated the legal position in the words, " A father was bound by every social tie to give the children an education suitable to their rank, but it was a duty of imperfect obligation, and could not be enforced in a court of law." It was not until August 15, 1876, that the legislature turned this " duty of imperfect obligation " into a duty enforceable in a court of law by declaring that " it shall be the duty of the parent of every child to cause such child to receive efficient elementary instruction in reading, writing, and arithmetic, and if such parent fail to perform such duty, he shall be liable to such orders and penalties as are provided by the Act."[2] The tendency of municipal law to-day is in the direction of enlarging the imperfect obligations of natural

---

[1] Peake's *Reports of Cases at Nisi Prius*, vol. ii., p. 79.
[2] The Elementary Education Act, 1876 (39 & 40 Vict., c. 79), s. 4.

law; but still, of course, the distinction between the two is very marked. Yet how natural law can regard as not naturally injurious conduct on the part of a parent that leads a child directly into the very mischiefs aimed at by the imperfect obligations of natural law as well as by municipal law it is not easy to see, especially if we adopt as the basis of all natural law the dogma that the ultimate obligation of man is so to acquire and practise virtue as to secure that personal perfection which is essential to complete personal happiness. The truth is that Vattel only develops the premisses on which he bases his theory of natural law so far as that development does not interfere with his own preconceived notions of what is likely to be useful in the evolution of society. If his absolutely artificial utilitarian standard does not square with the logical results of the premises from which he starts in reconstructing the evolution of society, those results are abandoned. This is the necessary and the vicious consequence of the *a priori* method. It is all very well to have a Theory of Evolution and check it and correct by historical tests, but it is quite another thing to have a Theory of Evolution and a Theory of Social Life and to attempt to check and correct one theory by the other. The appeal to experience is the only test, and this applies in the realm of natural juridical conceptions as truly as in the realm of material energy and force.

It is interesting to see how Vattel is faced with these difficulties when he tries to explain why marriages between ascendants and descendants are contrary to natural law. He flings aside Wolff's theory that such marriages are forbidden by respect and reverence, and says that they are inexpedient, against the law of perfection, likely to be barren and occasion natural horror. His own theory is not in the least convincing. He begins by saying that they are contrary to the law or theory of utility; he goes on to say that they infringe the law of perfection on which his social scheme is based—thus attempting by mere assertion to bring his two theories into accord; he then makes a desperate appeal to experience, without any knowledge that justifies the appeal; and finally really falls back on Wolff's theory, on the theory elaborated in *Œdipus the King*. Now what Vattel failed to recognize was that mere utilitarianism—natural utilitarianism—is incapable of solving problems that involve the spiritual depths of human nature. A transcendental element is involved which is not explained by a reference to " natural horror." This element was no doubt evolved from some utilitarian basis; but once in existence it regulates the behaviour of the whole scale of creation that possesses it in a way that does not apply to a lower scale. Love itself has its roots on earth though its flowers and fruits belong to a region of self-sacrifice that can only be called transcendental. The relation of human parent and child is regulated by this transcendental love; physical relations are in fact replaced by metaphysical relations, and any tendency to reverse the process long since became so impossible as to be unnatural even in the case of an adopted child. Vattel's attempt to create a great gulf between the physical and the metaphysical has made it impossible for him to supply a metaphysic of social life. Wolff refused to cut himself off from this means of analysis, with the result that he finds the true solution.

Each of these jurists might well have based their discussion of the right of inheritance on the same ground—that the relationship of parent and child is such as to involve perfect continuity of possession. This is evidently in Wolff's mind when he asserts that the right of inheritance is a complete right. Vattel, with singular lack of historical knowledge, denies this on the ground that such a theory destroys the natural right of will-making. He therefore compromises with his master by asserting that a child has a "perfect right" to succeed to a portion of the estate of his parent, a portion determined by circumstances; and that a parent has an equal right to the heritage of his childless child (p. 295). Here we have arbitrary utilitarianism running havoc among all analyses and all history. There is nothing elemental in the power of will-making. Primitive races know nothing of it. There is something primitive in the notion of transmission to children, and the practice of the earliest races coincides with what we might expect to be the case from the transcendental relationship of human parent and child or even adoptive child. Vattel's law of perfection would indeed seem to involve this transmission of property from parent to child which Wolff asserts to be a "perfect right."

In the Eighth Part Vattel turns to the question of sovereignty. He does not accept the divine right of kings. The only sovereign is the community itself, which is capable of delegating its power but not of finally parting with that power. The people, he asserts, always hold the reversion of power even if that reversion is not nominally reserved, and can resume, for just cause, their rights. No man can possess a patrimonial kingdom. "Le peuple seul, j'entens le peuple entier et unanime, possède l'empire comme véritablement patrimonial" (p. 343). The patrimony is not in a majority of the people but in the whole people.[1] The rights of a majority are merely rights of expediency, he in effect says. It is therefore necessary to submit to the majority in a state even if the fact involves some injustice. But this is not so if the majority becomes oppressive and destructive. It is curious to see how Vattel's mind is continually wavering between his theories of utilitarianism and perfection. Having made his doctrine of sovereignty clear, he goes on to state that if a people unanimously elect a despot, the contract will bind them but will not bind the children of the original electors. This, of course, is a compromise, but it is quite inconsistent with the original proposition that a reversion of power is always sleeping *in gremio populi*. That this latter proposition is the one that he finally holds is shown by his subsequent statement that the people have the right to decide between two pretenders to the crown. He has much that is very significant on the question of state religions. The priesthood must not be independent: "Mais si vous les rendez indépendantes de la puissance Civile, vous ouvrez la porte à mille désordres, à des troubles dangereux ; et les Rois ne font pas fermes sur leur Trône" (p. 319). But while the State must control the priesthood it must not lend itself to acts of uniformity : "La Société, ou le souverain qui la représente, n'a donc aucun droit de gêner la conscience des citoyens" (p. 370). There we must leave Vattel's *Observations*, a work of originality and insight that deserves to be reprinted, for it contains the seeds of most of the thought that dominated Europe and England from 1789 to 1830.

The above analysis of Vattel's fundamental ideas will enable us to treat with brevity his great work *Le Droit des Gens*. It is not difficult to see how, from the premises set out above, he would apply the laws of nature to the interrelations of sovereign peoples. His preface opens with the magnificent untruth which the Institutes of the Emperor Justinian enunciated for all time : *jure enim naturali ab initio omnes homines liberi nascebantur ;*[2] a legal fiction which in the evolution of things will at last become a natural

[1] It should be noticed that here Vattel appreciates the fundamental difficulty discussed above of the question of natural rights residing in a majority.
[2] *Institutionum Libri Quattuor*, lib. i., tit. 2.

truth. He refers to Thomas Hobbes as being the first to give a distinct though imperfect notion of the rights of nations. But Wolff and Vattel differ from Grotius, Hobbes, Pufendorf and Barbeyrac in seeing that the law of nature dealing with individuals must be modified if it is to be applied to political societies. Such societies are moral persons, but they differ in their nature from the moral man. Closely as Vattel follows Wolff he is careful to point out the many fundamental differences between them. Wolff asserted the existence of patrimonial kingdoms ; Vattel will have none of them ; Wolff justified the use of poisoned weapons ; Vattel will have none of them either. But a deeper difference exists. Wolff derives the idea of a voluntary society from a kind of mighty republic founded by nature herself, a universal society of which all the nations of the world are members. Consequently the civil law of the natural republic of men would be the law of all its members. "Cette idée," writes Vattel, "ne me satisfait point, et je ne trouvé la fiction d'une pareille république ni bien juste, ni assez solide pour en déduire les règles d'un droit des gens universel et nécessairement admis entre les États souverains."[1] He can recognize no other natural society among nations than nature has established among all men. It is the essence of all civil society that each member has ceded a part of his rights to the whole body which possesses authority over all the members. "On ne peut rien concevoir ni rien supposer de semblable entre les nations. Chaque État souverain se prétend, et est effectivement indépendant de tous les autres." The laws that apply to nations differ from those that apply to men, since a nation is a different type of moral being from a man. But it has, nevertheless, fundamental and necessary laws which are purely natural in their origin, and these are supplemented by voluntary laws of convenience. Vattel elaborates this position as follows (I use Mr. Chitty's revised version) :

"The necessary and the voluntary laws of nations are therefore both established by nature, but each in a different manner : the former, as a sacred law which nations and sovereigns are bound to respect and follow in all their actions ; the latter as a rule which the general welfare and safety oblige them to admit in their transactions with each other. The necessary law immediately proceeds from nature ; and that common mother of mankind recommends the observance of the voluntary law of

[1] But it was his goal (see p. 19 above).

nations, in consideration of the state in which nations stand with respect to each other, and for the advantage of their affairs. This double law, founded on certain and invariable principles, is susceptible of demonstration, and will constitute the principal object of this work."

It is necessary before going on to deal with this demonstration to draw attention once more to the fact that Vattel's mind fails to appreciate the profundity of Wolff's intellect. Vattel, in his elegant, apologetic way which perhaps recalls the critical manner of Sainte-Beuve, spurns Wolff's fundamental assumption of a universal republic instituted by Nature herself of which all nations of the world are members. Far be it from me to assert, or to deny, the validity of such an assumption. I am certainly not prepared to deny the assumption, for it is, in fact, merely the traditional medieval form of asserting the universal brotherhood of man—an assertion which appeals with singular attraction to the modern mind. Vattel, however, repudiates the assumption, and he is undoubtedly at liberty to do so; but he proceeds to make a new assumption which involves every intellectual difficulty presented by Wolff's assumption and new difficulties as well. He assumes that a nation is a moral being, one and indivisible. I do not desire to challenge this assumption—if we are to be in the land of assumptions at all. It is certainly desirable that nations should be moral beings, and probably the best way to make them so is to assume that they are so. But Wolff's assumption is likely in the long run to prove nearer truth. The world is probably drifting or gliding in glacier-fashion towards the universal republic of which nations are the members, that the great German philosopher evolved from his inner consciousness. "M. D. V." in fact advocated the creation of such a Republic. And we must remember that those juridical thinkers who enunciated from the days of Augustine onwards the laws of nature in society were, in fact, looking towards the end and not the beginning, were looking for what should be when they thought that they were looking for what had been; that they were platonic idealists without knowing it; that the pattern laid up in the heaven of their high imaginings was what they saw, and that our modern investigations into actual primitive conditions had and could have no meaning or attraction for them. When they wrote of the law of nature they meant, each according to their respective spiritual insight and intellectual gifts, what Plato, what Augustine, what Dante, what Sir Thomas More meant. No doubt they thought they were dealing with reality; but so, for the matter of that, did Euclid. If, then, Wolff and Vattel were dealing not with reality but with ideals that each desired to bring down into the realm of actualities, Wolff was incomparably the greater thinker. A universal republic is a higher ideal than a family of nations whose morality is exhibited in bloody feuds, in inextinguishable hatreds, in malice, jealousy and lust for power : in every possible telescopic magnification of the vices of petty tribal life. It is not unjust to make this criticism of Vattel's position, for that position is a persistent criticism of a nobler ideal than his own, a criticism adopted for the purpose of creating a purely utilitarian system of international relations, a system that to this hour has hampered a larger outlook on the relations of organized communities. Limited utilitarian ideals, that is to say, the hand-to-mouth wisdom of practical politicians, are the ideals that Vattel, a rather shame-faced follower of a much greater thinker of the same type, Machiavelli, crystallized for the use of the Foreign Offices of Europe for a century and a half after his death. Vattel was essentially a diplomat, and he chose, as his fundamental assumption, the highest ideals consistent with practical political life. Having done that, he plunges into current political problems and shapes his course in accordance with the apparent needs of the times. He takes a new and most useful attitude towards these problems. He is above all a practical man, and therefore he abandons the stale precedents of the classical ages and uses modern instances of the clearest kind. "I have quoted the chief part of my examples from modern history, as well because these are more interesting, as to avoid a repetition of those which have already been accumulated by Grotius, Pufendorf, and their commentators." But it cannot be said that his examples encourage reliance on his fundamental propositions.

Let me now briefly refer to Vattel's definitions in the realm of the law of nations. "Nations or states are bodies politic, societies of men united together for the purpose of promoting their mutual safety and advantage by the joint efforts of their combined strength." Such a society, we are told, is a moral person susceptible of obligations and rights. The law of nations is a science which teaches the rights subsisting between nations and the obligations corresponding to those rights. Nations are to be considered as so many free persons living together in the state of nature. The entire nation (whose common will is but the result of the united will of the citizens) remains subject to the laws of nature : consequently the law of nations is originally no other than the law of nature applied to nations. This application gives us the necessary Law of Nations called by Grotius " the internal law of nations " and by other jurists "the natural law of nations." Every treaty and every custom which contravenes the injunctions or prohibitions of the *necessary* law of nations is unlawful and condemned by the law of conscience even if validated by the external law. A nation is obliged to live on the same terms with other nations as an individual man was obliged, before the establishment of nations, to live with other men. A man when he joins a nation is still bound by his duties to the rest of mankind. Men, adds Vattel, are naturally equal, and a perfect equality prevails in their rights and obligations, as equally proceeding from nature.

It would answer no purpose here further to dwell on the unscientific nature of these various assumptions. I pass at once to the general laws that Vattel derives from his definitions. He tells us that each individual nation is bound to contribute everything in her power to the happiness and perfection of all other nations. But each nation should be left in the peaceable enjoyment of that liberty which she inherits from Nature. It follows also from the natural equality of all men that nations, being composed of free persons living together in a state of nature, are naturally equal and inherit from Nature the same obligations and rights. It also follows that a nation is mistress of her own actions so long as they do not affect the progress and perfect rights of any other nation. These and their derivatives are the Natural Law of Nations. It is a necessary, a natural, an internal law binding the national moral conscience. The external law corresponding to this internal law is the Voluntary Law deliberately adopted by nations, which as supplemented by Conventional Law (that is to say, the law contained in treaties) and Customary Law, constitutes the Positive Law of Nations. This argument concludes with a characteristic passage : " As the *Necessary* law is always obligatory on the *conscience*, a nation ought never to lose sight of it in deliberating on the line of conduct she is to pursue in order to fulfil her duty ; but when there is a question of examining what she may demand of other States, she must consult the *Voluntary* law whose maxims are devoted to the safety and advantage of the universal society of mankind." This passage exhibits clearly enough the real difficulty that Vattel (and indeed his predecessors in thought) had not the courage to face. Vattel is in reality searching for a sanction to his law. He felt as strongly as Austin felt that a law involves a law-giver, and in fact he invents a sanction for the Positive Law of Nations by creating behind it the Interior Law of Nations. We see at once why he has to postulate a moral consciousness in a nation. It is necessary to find a sanction, and so in Kantian fashion, though in pre-Kantian days, he evolves his necessary laws that bind the consciousness of the moral beings that he has created. Unlike Frankenstein, he was not doomed to see these beings hurling aside their moral consciousness and their internal laws in the very name of the Natural Code that he, scarcely less than Rousseau, helped to frame: Napoleon Buonaparte was not yet rocking in his Corsican cradle when Émerich de Vattel was so complacently pondering on these things.

Sovereignty.—Having established what seemed to him the unimpugnable basis of the family of nations, Vattel with serene logic unfolded the necessary scheme of things. A nation, as he defines it, involves a Public Authority to order and direct what is to be done by each man in relation to the end of this association of men. "The political authority is the sovereignty; and he or they who are invested with it are the sovereign." There are three kinds of sovereignty—a Democracy or Popular Government, an Aristocratic Republic represented by a Senate, and a Monarchy represented by a single person. Since, "to preserve and to perfect his own nature" is the sum of all the duties of a moral being to himself, so it must be with a nation. "The preservation of a nation consists in the duration of the political association by which it is formed," and the perfection of a nation is found when everything in it must conspire "to procure for the citizens whatever they stand in need of for the necessities, the conveniences, the accommodation of life, and, in general, whatever constitutes happiness—with the peaceful possession of property, a method of obtaining justice with security, and, finally, a mutual defence against all external violence." A nation is under an obligation to preserve itself and its members, and it has a right to everything necessary to its preservation and is not unjust in itself or absolutely forbidden by the law of nature. "The second general duty of a nation towards itself is to labour at its own perfection and that of its state." The individual citizen must also strive towards the end. Vattel points to England as the nation that has realized his ideals, and there is not a flicker of his diplomatic eye as he does so. Indeed England, England in her eighteenth-century deadness and corruption, is to him a standard nation. "Heureuse constitution ! à laquelle on n'a pu parvenir tout d'un coup ; qui a coûté, il est vrai, des ruisseaux de sang, mais que l'on n'a point achetée trop cher." And he adds with a touch, one is tempted to think, of irony but more probably in sheer earnestness, "Puisse le luxe, cette peste fatale aux vertus mâles et patriotiques, ce ministre de corruption si funeste à la liberté, ne renverser jamais un monument honorable à l'humanité, monument capable d'apprendre aux rois combien il est glorieux de commander à un peuple libre." The praise of one's friends is sometimes hard to bear. The second chapter of the First Book ends with a sentiment that goes deep indeed into the heart of national life : "Une nation doit se connaître elle-même. Sans cette connaissance, elle ne peut travailler avec succès à sa perfection." How few nations can answer to this test ! Yet it is this self-knowledge that has kept the Jewish nation intact through two millennia of national misfortunes.

The sovereign represents the nation. "When . . . a people confer the sovereignty on any one person, they invest him with their understanding and will, and make over to him their obligations and rights, so far as relates to the administration of the State, and the exercise of public authority. The sovereign, or conductor of the State, thus becoming the depositary of the obligations and rights relative to government, in him is found the moral person, who, without absolutely ceasing to exist in the nation, acts thenceforwards only in him and by him." Such is the origin of the representative character attributed to the sovereign. He represents the nation in all the affairs in which he may happen to be engaged as sovereign. The Prince derives his authority from the nation ; he possesses just so much of it as they have thought proper to entrust him with. He must respect and support the fundamental laws. "As soon as a Prince attacks the constitution of the State, he breaks the contract which bound the people to him ; the people become free by the act of the sovereign, and can no longer view him but as an usurper who would load them with oppression." Here Vattel adopts the views of Grotius, who had declared that "France, Spain herself,

England, Sweden, Denmark, furnish instances of kings deposed by their people; so that there are at present few sovereigns in Europe whose right to the crown rests on any other foundation than the right which the people possesses of divesting their sovereign of his power when he makes an ill use of it."

It is very difficult, at any rate to the present writer, to follow in the light of history this class of reasoning. It is difficult to say more in the light of instances than that people always get rid of sovereigns that they (with good or bad reason) dislike if they have an organization capable of securing this result. If the sovereign is an able man he usually retains his seat. And conversely, if a man is sufficiently able he will attain the sovereign power in fact, if not in name, in the community to which he belongs. Vattel's theory of the origin of representative kingship leaves out of account men like Cæsar, Cromwell, and Napoleon. And the doctrine of representation is scarcely more real when it is applied to Parliamentary Government, though of course the swing of the pendulum to some extent secures to every man in the course of a long life some rough representation of his political notions What in fact happens is that sovereignty tends to accommodate itself to a line of government that encounters the least resistance in the bulk of the people and secures the most stable equilibrium in the State. In practice rights and representation have little meaning. In England a Government could be in power for years after having been elected by a minority of the persons who actually voted.

However, sovereignty is and must be a fact however it is attained and retained. We approach a more practical matter when Vattel proceeds to discuss the business of a sovereign. It is his (or their) business to procure for the land a happy plenty of necessities. For this there must be a sufficient number of workmen. Emigration should therefore be forbidden.[1] "L'état doit encourager le travail, animer l'industrie, exciter les talents, proposer des récompenses, des honneurs, des priviléges, faire en sorte que chacun trouvé à vivre de son travail." The sovereign ought to neglect no means of rendering the land under his jurisdiction as well cultivated as possible. The labours of agriculture should be held in honour. Who " osent mépriser une profession qui trouvait la genre-humaine, la vocation naturelle de l'homme ?"

---

[1] It may be noticed here that this view has been from time to time favoured by the English Courts, which has never repudiated the argument that emigration is against public policy. See *Hingeston* v. *Sidney* [1908], 1 Ch., 126, 488.

Vattel even advocates the establishment of granaries as an excellent regulation for preventing scarcity, as an automatic regulation of prices. From agriculture he turns to commerce, by which—

"Les particuliers et les Nations peuvent se procurer les choses dont ils ont besoin et qu'ils ne trouvent pas chez eux. . . . Le commerce intérieur est d'une grande utilité ; il fournit à tous les citoyens le moyen de se procurer les choses dont ils ont besoin, le nécessaire, l'utile et l'agréable ; il fait circuler l'argent, excite l'industrie, anime le travail, et, donnant la subsistence à un très-grand nombre de sujets, il contribue à rendre le pays plus peuplé et l'État plus puissant."

Foreign trade has two additional advantages: it gives a country things she cannot herself produce and it may augment the wealth of a nation, and Vattel adds with respect to England, "Aujourd'hui c'est principalement le commerce qui met en sa main la balance de l'Europe."

The laws of nature with respect to commerce are based on the duty to assist and make others perfect. Every one has an imperfect right to purchase what he wants at a reasonable price from those who do not need the goods in question. But there is no such right to compel persons to buy, since everyone is at liberty to buy or not to buy. This clumsy analysis is an early statement of the law of supply and demand, obscured of course by the curious doctrine of imperfect obligation by which Vattel attempted to clarify his juridical ideas. Everyone is willing to sell what he does not want to keep, and is unwilling to sell what he does want to keep ; while everyone is willing to buy what he needs and is unwilling to buy what he does not need. That is really Vattel's position, and it is clearly a statement of the law of supply and demand. But Vattel goes on to justify the then current doctrine of protection on the ground that there is no duty to buy, though there may be to sell : "Tout état, par conséquent, est en droit de défendre l'entrée des marchandises étrangères ; et les peuples que cette défense intéresse n'ont aucun droit de s'en plaindre, pas même comme si on leur eût refusé un office d'humanité." We may seriously doubt if Vattel's premises will stand the strain of this argument. His earlier argument of equal and reciprocal rights and duties seems inconsistent with a policy that tends to shut a nation out from its family obligations. However, the jurist feels no doubt on the subject :

"Comme donc il appartient à chaque nation de voir si elle veut exercer le commerce avec une autre, ou si elle ne le veut pas, et à quelles conditions elle le veut, si une Nation a souffert pendant quelques temps qu'une autre vînt commercer dans son pays, elle demeure libre d'interdire quand il lui plaira ce commerce, de le restreindre, de l'assujettir à certaines règles, et le peuple qui l'exerçait ne peut se plaindre qu'on lui fasse une injustice."

This no doubt is an excellent statement of the condition of things with which Vattel the diplomatist had to deal, but to derive or attempt to derive such a condition from the laws of nature as they obtain among moral beings seems more interesting than convincing. Few persons can doubt that protection is an interference, possibly a heaven-sent interference, with the laws of nature, with the law of supply and demand. However, Vattel was desirous of discussing commercial treaties, and it was perhaps natural to justify their existence. As soon as a Government has provided for national necessities and insured plenty, the second purpose of its being, that of procuring the true happiness of the nation, comes into sight. To secure national happiness the sovereign must instruct and enlighten the people. The education of youth is one of the most important matters for the attention of the Government. Vattel's foresight in this question is very remarkable. He foresaw, indeed, in his shrewd, kindly way the whole social struggle of the nineteenth century. He was not to be blinded by the talk of the sacredness of preserving intact the sense of parental duty. If parents are unable by their circumstances to fulfil their duties, the State must intervene in the interest of the State. "Il ne doit point s'en reposer entièrement sur les pères." But the Government ought not to stop at the education of the individual. It ought directly to encourage arts and sciences and freedom of philosophical discussion. It ought to make every effort to inspire the people with the love of virtue and the abhorrence of vice by direct example, by the distribution of favours, by the banishment of whatever is corrupt. Moreover it should inspire the people with patriotism. State railways even are foreshadowed by the statement that the maintenance of highways and canals is the business of the sovereign power. Vattel carries his socialism, as some people would call it, even into the realm of Religion: "Une Nation doit donc être pieuse." Religion, in so far as it is an external matter, is an affair of the State. He would, of course, constrain no one in the matter of religion. Liberty of conscience, he tells us, is a natural and inviolable right. But a citizen must not *openly* do what he pleases without regard to the consequences that this may produce in society. It belongs to the nation at large to determine what religion she would follow and what public worship she thinks proper to establish. If necessary she can establish more than one religion ; but if a particular sect is too small to demand a separate establishment, the dissenters may depart. There should, however, be " a universal toleration of all religions which contain no tenets that are dangerous either to morality or the State." The religion of the Prince himself does not matter so long as he carries out the behest of the community. Did not Joan of Hochberg remain ruler of Neufchâtel after that principality adopted the Protestant faith ; and did she not, though still a Catholic, sign and sanction the ecclesiastical laws and constitutions ? Here we have State control indeed ; a State with rulers who are mere conduit-pipes of the popular will. Vattel is determined that the State shall be absolute master in its own house. He will have no Papal interference; no appeals to Rome; nothing that can limit in any fashion whatever the perfect freedom of the community. He amply justifies his position with elaborate instances.

Vattel turns from Religion to Justice, which he defines as the force which supports the laws with vigour and justly applies them to every case that presents itself. He carries justice farther than the Courts. He insists on the uses of distributive justice—the treatment in society of everyone according to his deserts. This principle ought to regulate the distribution of public employment and public rewards. His discussion of the right of punishment is full of interest. It is founded on the right of personal safety, the right to provide for security against any and every attack. When men unite in a society or nation, that society is charged with the duty of providing for the safety of its members. In this way the right of private war is merged in this public duty of protection. The nation, being a moral person, has also a right to provide for its own safety by punishing those who trespass against its laws. Thence arose both civil and criminal jurisdiction ; the avenging both of private and public offences. The right of public war also exists, for the nation must protect itself against other nations as well as against individuals.

This leads us to the Third Object of Government, the duty to fortify the nation against external attacks. The strength of a nation consists in the number of its citizens, their military capacity and their riches. It is the business of a Government to increase these three sources of strength, always remembering that "la puissance d'une nation est relative ; on doit la mesurer sur celle de ses voisins, ou de tous les peuples dont elle peut avoir quelque chose à craindre."

The principle that lies behind all modern discussions of what is known as the two-power standard of naval strength has not often been stated with such lucidity. The remaining propositions of the book hardly call for notice here, though much might be written on the right of separation from a nation, on the doctrine of effective occupation, and on the right of Eminent Domain, the right on the part of the State in case of necessity to all the wealth within the State. This doctrine is of course a natural corollary of the duty of self-protection, but it is also a convenient instrument in the hands of a doctrinaire socialist or a Finance Minister.

I do not propose to do more than touch upon that portion of Vattel's great work which is restricted to what we call to-day International Law. The field in one sense is too vast, in another too restricted. I have indicated at some length the general principles that inspire Vattel's treatment of international relationships, and that is sufficient for my general purpose since I was chiefly anxious to consider this author as a jurist without reference to any special branch of law. But some additional reference must be made to his first principles as set forth in his Second Book, which treats " of a nation considered in its relation to others."

Whatever duties each man owes to other men, the same does each nation in its way owe to other nations. Therefore one State owes to another State whatever it owes to itself, so far as that other stands in real need of its assistance, and the former can grant it without neglecting the duties that it owes to itself : "Telle est la loi éternelle et immuable de la Nature." Thus, he points out, the calamities of Portugal arising from the Lisbon earthquake gave England an opportunity of fulfilling the duties of humanity with that noble generosity which characterizes a great nation. But one nation must not force its good offices on another. Grotius asserted the general right to punish infamous behaviour by other nations, but Vattel denies this unless the behaviour directly affects the nation desiring to intervene. And again, you have no right to compel another nation to help you. But the law of love applies. It is the duty of nations to love one another. In all this there is much that is interesting. The earthquake at Messina and the misconduct of the Government responsible for the Congo horrors, make Vattel's remarks as modern as may be.

Again he asserts the general obligation of nations to trade with each other and he advocates the utmost freedom of trade, though he adds, with his usual caution, that each nation must decide if the commerce in question is likely to be useful to it. He then lays down the rule that every nation is entitled to security—namely, to preserve herself from all injury and to prevent all intervention or interference in her private affairs. He is careful, however, to point out that the occupation of a nation does not exclude absolutely all rights of other nations in the territory. Everyone retains the right to obtain, if necessary, not only food and ships and other goods at a fair price, but also the right of intermarriage in order to secure the continuity of the nation. Women for this purpose, he adds, may be carried off. It is in this book that the subject of treaties, on which Vattel was the greatest living exponent in his age, is treated at length. It is not possible to deal with his special branch of law here, but Vattel's treatment of it is not likely to be forgotten. His advocacy of Arbitration is likewise of very real importance, and may be of more value in the future than during the last century and a half.

The Third Book deals with War, which Vattel defines as "cet état dans lequel on poursuit son droit par la force." Public war is carried on between nations; private war between individuals. Private war comes within the law of nature. Nature gives men a right to employ force when it is necessary for their defence, and for the preservation of their rights. But as we have seen, society takes upon itself this duty and so has, for the time being, extinguished the right of private war. Thus the sovereign power alone has the right to make war. For this purpose he has the right to raise troops, and every citizen is bound to serve and defend the State so far as he is capable. No person is naturally exempt from taking up arms in defence of the State. But war must be just. The right of making war belongs to nations only as a remedy against injustice. Here once more Vattel gives us the ideal for the real. He knew well enough that wars on behalf of right and justice have been rare enough. He tells us of no remedy against unjust war. The only remedy is that great Republic of which Wolff dreamed and which to-day is again in the minds of men. But so insistent is Vattel on the necessity of maintaining peace that he insists on the necessity of a formal declaration of war—a *Res Pœnitentiæ,* so to speak.

It is noticeable that this jurist gives us no lengthy discussion of the vexed problems of neutrality. His definition of contraband is, however, of real value: "les choses qui sont d'un usage particulier pour la guerre, et dont on empêche le transport chez l'ennemi, s'appellent marchandises de contrebande." He goes on to deal with the rights of nations in war forbidding assassination and the use of poison; with faith between enemies, acquisition by war, the right of postliminium, the rights of private persons in war; and, lastly, convention in war.

The Fourth and last book deals with the Restoration of Peace and Embassies. The question of the asylum offered by an ambassador's house is discussed with care.

Le Droit des Gens is certainly a work of the first magnitude. It modernized the whole theory and business of International Law, brought it out of the study into the field, the mart, the council chamber, and the palace. The law of nations was no longer a mystery. One of its most brilliant practical exponents became its popularizer. He did, indeed, much for nations, for he imposed upon them theories of moral rational development up to which it became, in a sense, necessary for them to live. I have ventured here and there in this paper to criticize Vattel's premises, methods, and conclusions, and even to say that the ideals which he placed before the nations of the world, high though they are, might possibly have been higher. Certainly it appears to me that Wolff was by far the greater thinker of the two, and no doubt Vattel himself would have admitted this. But, on the other hand, Vattel was a practical man, and he brought Wolff's doctrines, with certain modifications, into the domain of practical life. To have done this was in itself an achievement that will immortalize his name. But Vattel was far more than a practical man. He was a thinker of great distinction and of great honesty, and he possessed what few thinkers of that age possessed, a profound religious faith. If he has no other lesson for our age he has this: that the limits of human speculation are narrow while the range of faith is infinite, and that man may choose the range of faith with perfect reasonableness for the purpose of determining his conduct. The logical structure of human society stands within a larger and nobler house. But Vattel had, as we know, much else to teach, and the amity of nations to-day owes many things to the Diplomatist of Neufchâtel.

CÆSAR BONESANA, MARQUIS DI BECCARIA

CÆSAR BONESANA, MARQUIS DI BECCARIA

THIS eminent Italian Jurist, descended from an ancient family, was born, 1735, at Milan, and died in that city, 1794. Educated by the Jesuits of Parma, he was one of the first members of a literary society which was formed in Milan on the model of that of Helvétius, his elder by twenty years.

Beccaria published a journal *Il Caffè*, or *Le Café*, about 1763, after the manner of *The Spectator*, by Addison, jointly with the distinguished brothers Peter Verri, statesman and author, and Count Alexander Verri, barrister and historian, both Milanese of the same perod.

The object of this Journal was to spread new ideas in Italy. The writing of these ideas led Beccaria to see the iniquities of the criminal justice of his day, and by the advice of the brothers Verri, he was persuaded to write his famous treatise *Dei Delitti e delle Pene*. This book was commenced 1763 and was published 1764. It was translated into several languages and universally admired—into French (1766) under the name of *Des Délits et des Peines*, with a commentary attributed to Voltaire, and into English (1676) under the title of *An Essay on Crimes and Punishments*.

The author of this celebrated work was not at the time quite twenty-seven years of age. Many times he nearly abandoned his undertaking, for he was easily discouraged, being of a lethargic and nervous temperament. "I owe all," he said, "to French books; they have developed in my soul the feeling for humanity previously filled with eight years of fanatical education." He frequently quoted those authors which were to him the most familiar, D'Alembert, Diderot, Buffon, Hume, Condillac, Montesquieu, Helvétius. "Their immortal works were my continual reading, the object of my preoccupation during the day and of my meditation during the night." The work of Helvétius, *L'Esprit*, or *The Mind* (wherein it was suggested that virtue and vice chiefly depended on climate), awoke his attention to all the blindness and misery of humanity.

After the completion of his writings he feared to publish them. Notwithstanding the protection he had under the administration of Comte Firmiani, he secretly published them in Livourne. In 1764 he wrote to Pierre Verri: "If our friendship had not sustained me, I should have abandoned my project, for by inclination I prefer obscurity." He feared persecution, and often veiled his thoughts in vague, uncertain expressions.

His reply to L'Abbé Morellet, who reproached him for obscurity in some of his passages, was: "I ought to tell you that I have had before me whilst writing the example of Machiavel, of Galileo, and Giannone. I have heard the clank of the chains of superstition and fanaticism stifling the cry of truth, and the sight of this startling spectacle determined me to envelop the light in cloud. I wish to defend the cause of humanity without being a martyr."

The Essay on Crimes and Punishments appeared as the outcome of his study of French philosophy, of French rationalism, as bearing on existing penal legislation. It invoked juridical tradition, reason, and sentiment. It eloquently interpreted the protestations of the public conscience against secret procedure; against the oath imposed on the accused; against confiscation, infamous punishments: their inequality, and the atrocity of torture. It separated clearly divine justice from human justice, crimes from sins, repudiated the right of vengeance, assigned rightly the basis of punishment for general use, declared the punishment of death useless, demanded the proper proportion of punishments to crimes and the separation of judicial power from that of legislative power. Never did a book appear at a more opportune time. It had an extraordinary success; it was an event; in eighteen months from publication it passed through six editions; in a few years through thirty-two Italian editions; four editions of the English translation were issued, and it was translated into most European languages. The French philosophers welcomed it with enthusiasm, as the result and to the honour of their doctrines. L'Abbé Morellet translated it; Diderot annotated it; Voltaire commentated it. It was applauded by D'Alembert, Buffon, Helvétius, Baron d'Holbach and all the *âmes sensibles*. Perhaps no book of the kind was ever received with more avidity, more generally read, or more universally applauded. There was also published a commentary, attributed to Voltaire. There is no evidence of this being Voltaire's except that of public opinion.

In 1766 Beccaria went to Paris and was received everywhere with the most lively admiration and sympathies, *con adorazione*, says Alexander Verri, who accompanied him. The visit lasted only a few weeks. Happily married to a wife he adored, and whom he left at Milan, he could not live away from her, constantly writing to her, expressing his sorrow at not seeing her, and inconsolable at leaving her. "*Souviens-toi*," he wrote to her, "whom I prefer to all Paris, the most attractive place in the world. My wife, my children, and my friends fill, without ceasing, my thoughts. Imagination, the despot of my life, leaves me to enjoy neither the spectacles of nature nor those of art, which are not wanting in this journey and in this beautiful city."

Returning to Milan, he never again left that city. His life flowed on, as he said, peacefully and in solitude. ("Io meno una vita tranquilla e solitaria.") Some passages in his book which touched on religion disturbed him, but no denunciation followed. "Le Comte Firmiani," he wrote to L'Abbé Morellet, "protected my book, and it is to him that I owe my tranquillity." He was far from being insensible to glory; he recognized that a literary reputation, liberty for himself, and a compassion for the misfortunes of mankind, were in him three sentiments equally alive, but he wished for a glory which would not disturb him or require him to sacrifice the repose and the happiness of his private life. His enthusiasm for reform fell short before this peril, and he wisely conciliated the established power.

In 1768 the Austrian Government, hearing that Beccaria had refused the offer of Catherine II. to live in St. Petersburg, created in his favour, at Milan, a chair of political economy. He was induced by this honour conferred on him to publish some work upon this subject. He had the satisfaction in seeing during his life the introduction into legislation of the principles that he had proclaimed. He took part in 1791 in the Milanese Commission instituted for the reform of civil and criminal procedure.

L'Abbé Morellet, the translator of Beccaria's great work, said that its author was actuated by true sentiment, love of literary fame, love of liberty, and compassion for the unhappy condition of mankind enslaved by so many errors. "Beccaria," said M. Villemain, "had a sensible and generous heart, rather than a far-seeing mind; a man full of ideas. One owes to the author of *The Essay on Crimes and Punishments* an everlasting recognition, though his work could not be considered as that of a genius."

"Beccaria," said M. Mougin (*Encyclopédie Nouvelle*), "was never a thinker. He was confused by an equal admiration for two different men, Helvétius and Montesquieu. Between these two different men, he himself (their pupil) said he could see no distinction—to him they were both philosophers. In these two lives he only saw their feeling for humanity and a tenderness for every one. He could not fathom their assertions, often diverse and contradictory, either in the germ or developing. His work was not one of original thought, of learned and profound thought, which one expects to find in Beccaria."

"The age in which Beccaria wrote," said M. Leminier, "was one in which the rights of humanity (before ignored and violated) were suddenly and quickly sought to be established. The science of criminal law was without scientific character, and met with general opposition. It was a period when, in the pursuit of such a reform, talent was genius, and courage was talent—one who took the lead was certain to receive the esteem and admiration of his contemporaries. Beccaria published his *Essay on Crimes and Punishments* not as a scientific work, but as a zealous pamphlet, which showed the enthusiasm of his opinions."

Another writer says: "These appreciations do not seem to render sufficient justice to Beccaria. All the world now recognizes that Beccaria took up the reform of penal legislation, which he pleaded with a luminous reason, an eloquent passion, and won almost immediately an honour no one could share with him. The rapidity of his success seemed to diminish his merit. It was at the same time his good-fortune to formulate the sentence pronounced at a later period, by the public opinion of all Europe against existing judicial institutions." Is that the idea we ought to have of Beccaria? Has his book only been negative, or destructive, or revolutionary? Ought one to consider his *Essay* as a mere pamphlet, that is to say, a mere incident? It is a work in all the acceptance of the word. For Beccaria was not born to destroy the ancient edifice of a legislation previously so odious. He dug the foundations of a new edifice, he fashioned the material, he traced the plan. *The Essay on Crimes and Punishments* is one of the books of the eighteenth century from which one can even at this day draw some lessons. One must not forget that Beccaria was the first publicist to question the law as to the punishments of death. His name will ever be associated with the idea of the suppression of the scaffold. Whatever objection there may be to this idea, one must always recognize that Beccaria was brave and original enough to proclaim—in the face of legislators who maintained a vigorous belief to the contrary, and of philosophers who justified it, and of all history, which proved that the punishment of death was applied everywhere and at all times—that this punishment exceeded the right of the legislator and the Judge ; in one word, he denied their right, in the name of the human heart—that source of all great thoughts (according to Vauvenargues) of the past, of the present, and until cold reason appears to repress it, also of the future.

After this is it true to say that societies for the promotion of that principle and the social philosophy of the eighteenth century owe nothing to Beccaria ? Was he not, as he said of himself, in the track of the French philosophers ? He did not work his thoughts in new ways, he worked upon the lines of the old masters. He accepted without dispute the " contrat social " of Rousseau. He supposed, like Rousseau (and by so doing followed in the same stream of ideas where Rousseau and Helvétius had given him the lead), that this contract was founded on social grounds, derived from a common want, a common interest. Like Voltaire, Beccaria saw in the religious institutions of humanity nothing but the politics of legislators, the work of daring men, which deceived others, who, like themselves, trained the ignorant to follow in their steps."

Another writer says : " When the *Essay* appeared, Beccaria was stamped with that immortality which belongs only to geniuses, born to be benefactors of their times. *Quique sui memores alios fecere merendo.* Never before did so small a book produce so great an effect. Never were truths so consoling and sacred compressed into so small a space. Innocence and justice, human liberty and social peace were shown to the world welded into one indissoluble link. The origin, the basis, and the limits of the right to punish were presented in such a manner impossible to be ignored. The legislator knew that he should not pronounce judgment, and the Judge that he should only interpret the laws."

Dumont wrote in 1811 : " Beccaria first examined the efficacy of punishments by considering their effect upon the human heart; by calculating the force of the motives by which individuals are impelled to the commission of crimes, and of those opposite motives which the law ought to present. This species of analytical merit was, however, less the cause of his great success than the courage with which he attacked established errors, and that eloquent humanity which spreads so lively an interest over his work"; after this, says M. Lunefont, "I scruple to say that he is destitute of method, that he is not directed by any general principle, that he only glances at the most important questions, that he carefully shows all practical discussions in which it would have been evident that he was acquainted with the science of jurisprudence. He announces two distinct objects: Crimes and Punishments; he adds to these occasionally Procedure; and these three vast subjects with difficulty furnish matter for one little volume."

The editions of this work, not more than two hundred pages, including the commentary attributed to Voltaire, multiplied rapidly. In Italy three editions were sold in the first six months, and three more the following year. It was translated into French (1766) at the instance of Malesherbes, by L'Abbé Morellet, who brought into this work his passionate interest for human misery, and arranged the different parts of this fine work in an order he judged suitable, and approved by Beccaria.

M. Challon de Lisy published a second translation, and in 1797 a second edition of Morellet's translation appeared with notes by Diderot, together with St. Aubin's translation of Bentham's *Theory of Penal Law*. In Prussia, in Russia, and in Tuscany, the sovereign and the people honoured the man who was at the time the defender of the safety of subjects and of the stability of Governments. Catherine II. of Russia had the *Essay* translated and inserted among her new Code of laws, abolished torture in her dominions, and accompanied the abolition by an edict of toleration. Frederick of Prussia and Duke Leopold of Tuscany took the same step. The movement that destroyed torture was an emotional one rather than an intellectual one. Joseph II. of Austria soon after abolished, with few exceptions, the punishment of death throughout his dominions. The administration of Berne ordered a medal to be coined in Beccaria's honour. Coray translated the *Essay* into Greek and published it in 1802. Lord Mansfield, it is said, never pronounced the name of Beccaria without a visible sign of respect. So great a success, even though it was in the interests of humanity, was not exempt from attacks of envy and fanaticism. These attacks were brought against him in Milan, accusations of impiety and sedition. The powerful influence of Count Firmiani alone protected him, declaring that the author and his work were under his protection, he had created for him in Milan the chair of political economy, and when it was established Beccaria endeavoured to teach those who had formerly planned his ruin. Beccaria's other important works were: *On the Disorder of Money in the State of Milan and the Means of Remedying it* (1792), *Researches upon the Nature of Style* (1765), an ingenious reflection upon the formation of languages—where the author alluded to two principles—the *expression* of pleasure and of sorrow and the imitation of objects. It was printed in his Journal *Le Café* and translated (1771) by L'Abbé Morellet; *Discourse upon Commerce and Public Administration* (1769), translated by Antoine Comparet; *Report upon a Project of Uniformity of Weights and Measures* (1781).

A hundred years after the publication of the *Essay on Crimes and Punishment*, Cæsar Cantù, a learned Milanese historian, published a work called *An Essay on Beccaria and the Penal Law*. This work appeared in Italian in Florence in 1862. In this long and complete monograph Cantù first examined the earlier state of penal legislation before the time of Beccaria—the prisoner, his punishments in Italy, and especially among the Milanese at that period—and of torture previous to and since the Christian era. He cited the most important Roman authorities upon penal law and torture, and mentioned the most ancient works which he had read on the applications of that punishment. He cited the work of Martin Bernard, which reverted to the early times of Christianity, *La Tortura ex foris Christianorum proscribenda*, and a jurisconsult Grœvius who, before Beccaria, had shown their iniquity. The authors he cited in this work are innumerable. There is not a criminologist of the least distinction whom he did not bring to light. Cantù, after he had written the history of Beccaria's great work, demonstrated the doctrines of the Encyclopédistes, the social contract, the system which gave society the right to defend itself, which forms the basis of law, and the foundation of punishment.

Passing from the theoretical to the practical, Cantù reviewed and criticized the reforms which were accomplished under the influence of Beccaria's book, and, approaching the theories and modern application of the criminal law, he appreciated with a profound suggestion the juridical strength and philosophy of Beccaria's work. In his appreciations of the law of punishment, Cantù was inspired by some clearer principle, and criticized the theories of Beccaria founded upon the system of the origin of society, such as were conceived by the philosophers of that period. He reproached Beccaria for resisting the interpretation of the law, enumerating the cases where this interpretation was perhaps useful and necessary, noting at the same time the economical errors of Beccaria. He nevertheless assigned him his true place in the reform of criminal jurisprudence, and concluded that if Beccaria was not quite the first to demand reform, the glory of accomplishment was at least his alone. In a word, Cantù admires and criticizes at the same time.

Beccaria's work was not intended to be a complete system of penal law; it was mainly directed against the most flagrant errors and abuses of contemporaneous legislation, particularly against torture and the punishment of death. These two forms of punishment previous to the days of Beccaria were the chief and largely the only forms of punishment. Two of his objections to the punishment of death were—that as a deterring example execution lasts so short a time, whereas perpetual slavery (his mode of punishment for the greatest crime) affords a more lasting example, and that capital punishment is too great an example of barbarity. "If," he wrote, "the passions or necessity of wars have taught men to shed the blood of their fellow-creatures, the laws which are intended to moderate the ferocity of mankind should not increase it by the example of barbarity, the more horrible, as this punishment is usually attended with formal pageantry." It was to his impressive style, his lively eloquence, that the author of the famous *Essay* owed his success, and the diffusion of his principles to the animated style in which he appealed to the feelings of mankind.

Bentham, writes Mr. C. M. Atkinson, followed Beccaria, and denounced, as a false principle that had long reigned a tyrant throughout the best province of penal law, this "reasoning by antipathy," as he phrased it; for it is but an irrational subjection to the blind impulses of anger and revenge which have in all ages obscured the vision of judges and legislators.

Bentham (1747-1832) was a contemporary of Beccaria, who is

said to have stated during different periods of his life that he took the "Greatest Happiness" principle from Hume, Montesquieu, Barrington, Beccaria, and Helvétius. Bentham had noted in his commonplace book that Priestley was the first (unless it was Beccaria) who taught his lips to pronounce the sacred truth that " the greatest happiness of the greatest number is the founda- of morals and legislation."[1]

According to M. Halévy, Beccaria sketched the ideas in outline, but did not approach Bentham either in vigorous definition of the principles or in the systematic development of their far-reaching consequences. Bentham, says Professor Montague, grasped with astonishing firmness axioms which Beccaria had merely indicated with the light touch of an essayist.

W. E. H. Lecky, reviewing the effect of Beccaria's work upon torture, says :[2] "In Italy, the great opponent of torture was Beccaria. The movement that destroyed torture was much less an intellectual than an emotional movement. It represented much less a discovery of the reason than an increased intensity of sympathy. There is perhaps one exception to this. Beccaria grounded much of his reasoning on the doctrine of the Social Compact. I cannot, however, think that this argument had much influence in producing the change." Reviewing its effect on the Penal Code he says :[3] "The reform in England, as over the rest of Europe, may be ultimately traced to that Voltairian School of which Beccaria was the representative, for the impulse created by the treatise *On Crimes and Punishments* was universal, and it was the first great effort to infuse a spirit of philanthropy into the Penal Code, making it a main object of legislation to inflict the smallest possible amount of suffering. Beccaria is especially identified with the cause of the abolition of capital punishment, which is slowly but steadily advancing towards its inevitable triumph. In England the philosophic element of the movement was nobly represented by Bentham, who, in genius, was certainly superior to Beccaria, and whose influence, though perhaps not so great, was also European."

Howard the philanthropist (1726-1790), also a contemporary of Beccaria and Bentham, advocated the abolition of capital punishment. Howard's pilgrimages to improve the prisons of Europe

---

[1] *Bentham, his Life and Work*, by C. M. Atkinson, pp. 30, 31, 36, 160, 161.
[2] *Rationalism in Europe*, vol. i., p. 331.
[3] *Ibid.*, p. 349.

and Bentham's writings added to and aided the great objective principle laid down by Beccaria.

Before concluding this article it may be interesting shortly to review as far as possible the effect of Beccaria's small but far-reaching literary work relating to the two great principles he laid down. As regards torture, as meant and understood by Beccaria, it may be said to have entirely disappeared, so far as Occidental countries are concerned. Capital punishment still remains, but in a greatly modified degree since the days of Beccaria.

Filangieri (1752-1788), a Neapolitan barrister, also a contemporary of Beccaria, published in 1782 his great theoretical work the *Scienza della Legislazione*, and carried into effect a general reform in the legislation of his country. This work went through many editions, translated and published in Germany, France, Spain, and America. Filangieri does not advocate the total abolition of capital punishment, but limits the infliction of death to a few crimes, viz., murder with intent after cold-blooded deliberation (*a sangue freddo*), treason, and high treason. The immediate effect of Beccaria's teaching was first to be found in his own country. The first Government to be impressed with Beccaria's views was that of Tuscany.

The Grand Duke Leopold abolished the punishment of death (1786). The preamble of his Act asserts that it had not been inflicted in Tuscany for fourteen years before (1772), Beccaria's essay having been published (1764). In Germany—the Germany of the eighteenth century—the first example was set in Austria. The death sentence could not be passed without the special mandate of the Emperor Joseph II. (1781). It was actually abolished (1787). It was limited in Prussia (1788). In Bavaria, Feuerbach, the author of its Code, following his own penal theory, considered that the temptation to the grossest crime ought to be checked by a death penalty.

In France Beccaria's ideas were received with approval before the Revolution (1790), and it was moved in the National Assembly that except in political subjects the death penalty should be abolished. Robespierre spoke in favour of its abolition. Condorcet, after the execution of Louis XVI., moved (1793) that the death penalty should be abolished for all crimes. Both these measures were lost.

In America the Quakers specially endeavoured to make capital punishment unlawful, and in the Pennsylvanian legislature (1794) the death penalty was limited to cases of murder. The above merely shows the effect of Beccaria upon the century which produced Beccaria.

The effect on the nineteenth century it would be too long now to follow. We must always recognize in the last century the great work of Sir Samuel Romilly, who drew his inspiration from Beccaria, and induced Parliament to mitigate the extreme severity of the English Penal Code. With his name and exertions in the past century there will ever be remembered the names of other illustrious penal reformers from Sir James Mackintosh to Charles Hopwood. In concluding this article, and for the purpose of comparative legislation, we enumerate some of the European countries which have now abolished, or partially abolished, capital punishment as a record of the law existing at the opening of the twentieth century.

Italy.—It was abolished by the Penal Code of 1889, previous to which date for a long period it was commuted to penal servitude for life. It has been retained in the Army and Navy Penal Law.

England, India, and the Colonies.—Punishment by death abolished in a great number of cases (1824-29). Abolished, except in certain cases such as wilful murder and treason, and chiefly commuted to penal servitude for life by the Criminal Law Consolidation Acts, 1861. Commission on Capital Punishment recommended penal servitude in cases of unpremeditated murder and that executions be private (1865).

United States.—Entirely abolished in some States: Maine, Rhode Island, Wisconsin.

Germany.—Practically abolished in Prussia and Bavaria; abolished in Saxony (1868).

Belgium.—Save in one exception in 1866, during the late King's reign, begun in 1865, no capital punishment took place, though the law existed. Sentence is commuted into penal servitude for life.

Denmark.—It exists against premeditated homicide and crimes against the safety or independence of the State or Constitution. It is, as a rule, commuted.

France.—Rarely enforced; four executions in 126 convictions in one year.

Netherlands.—It has been abolished since 1870.

Norway.—No capital punishment since 1876. It is decreed by the Code.

Portugal.—No capital punishment exists except for criminal and military offences since 1867.

Russia.—There is capital punishment only for attempts against the life of the Chief of the State or for treason or sedition against the State.

Sweden.—During ten years, 1891-1900, four persons were executed.

Switzerland.— Abolished in seventeen out of twenty-one cantons.

Well may it be said of the Marquis di Beccaria, looking at these results of his *Essay*, that it is indeed one of the most important Works that has ever been written, and that he has contributed towards the enduring happiness of nations.

NOTE.—Two statues are erected to Beccaria in Milan—a sitting one on the staircase to the Museum (Palazzo di Brera); a standing one in front of the Palace of Justice, in the Piazza Beccaria, leading from the Via Cesare Beccaria. On the pedestal of each are recorded the virtues of Beccaria, as the first scientific opponent of the death-penalty, with quotations from his "Essay." Beccaria's daughter became the mother of Alessandro Manzoni (poet and novelist), who left a daughter, the wife of Massimo d'Azeglio (statesman and author). Cesare Lombroso (the greatest modern criminologist) lived and died (1911) in Milan.

LORD STOWELL

LORD STOWELL

In the annals of English law there is no other instance of two brothers attaining such a high place as did William Scott and John Scott, who came to be known as Lord Stowell and Lord Eldon. Their excellences were different : the elder was pre-eminent in counsel, the younger in advocacy ; the one was supreme as jurist, the other as statesman. Each of them occupied a most distinguished position on the Bench, the one as head of the Chancery Courts, the other as judge of the Court where the Civil Law and Law of Nations was administered ; and if Lord Eldon figured more prominently in the life of his own time, his brother left a greater name in the record of jurisprudence. Before his day England had not perhaps produced any supreme jurist who by his writings marked a new development of the Law of Nations, unless we place in that class Richard Zouche ; and it was fitting that the great contribution to International Law in a country which has always excelled in practice rather than in theory should be made by a practical and not by a theoretical exponent. Lord Stowell made the law of prize in administering it, as Mansfield and Holt had made the law merchant on the Bench. He did, in fact, for the law of commerce in war what they had done for it in peace—established its rules on a clear and broad basis. But while Holt and Mansfield's work had validity only for the people of their country, much of Lord Stowell's obtained the respect of the community of nations. The judgments that he gave were the "living voice" of the *jus gentium*.

Lord Stowell's Life.—William Scott and John Scott were the sons of a Newcastle shipper. William, who was six years the elder, was born in 1745, and by a lucky accident his mother had removed shortly before his birth to a house on the Durham side of the Tyne, in order to escape the turmoil caused by the invasion of the Young Pretender. The accident was lucky in that it enabled William Scott, when he had passed through the Grammar School at Newcastle, to be elected in 1761 to a Durham Scholarship at Corpus Christi College, Oxford. Three years later, profiting further by the lucky accident of his birthplace, he was elected to a Durham Fellowship at University College. Though he had entered as a student at the Middle Temple in 1762, and was already bent on a career at the Bar, his own caution and his father's wish led him to remain at Oxford as tutor of the college. He lectured in ancient history, and in his academic period he acquired a large knowledge of the Roman jurisprudence and of the whole classical culture, to which he owed the grasp of the Civil Law and the dignity and lucidity of expression which marked him as a judge. In 1774 he was appointed Camden Professor of Ancient History; and in that office he delivered courses of lectures, of which one of his biographers says that "the fame of them rendered his classic youth the rival of his judicial age." Gibbon's remark that he was "assured that were they given to the public they would form a most valuable treatise" is less eloquent but more convincing. Throughout his life Stowell retained a close association with literary pursuits and literary society; he was an intimate friend of Dr. Johnson, and was elected a member of the famous literary Club of which the doctor was dictator, and he lived to be its doyen. He did not write a book in the ordinary sense of the term, but the stamp of literature and liberal culture is upon his judgments. The turning-point of his life was the death in 1776 of his father, who left a fortune of not less than £20,000 and made his eldest son residuary legatee. Cautious as he was about risking a loss of income, his circumstances were now such that he could with an easy mind forgo some of his offices at the University, and turn to that career to which he had looked forward from his youth. He resumed his suspended studies at the Middle Temple, and in 1777 he writes: "I have got a room in the Temple, and keep Term with a view of being called to the Bar as soon as possible, which will be in about two years."

His brother John was already making his way at the Common Law Bar, but William elected to practise in the Ecclesiastical and Admiralty Courts, which were then combined in the precincts of Doctors' Commons. He took the degree of Doctor of Civil Law at Oxford—a necessary qualification—and was admitted into the faculty of advocates of those Courts, and at the same time called to the Bar in 1780, when he was thirty-five years of age.

While the Common Law prevailed almost exclusively in the Court of King's Bench, and in the Courts of Chancery an original system of English equity was being evolved, in the Ecclesiastical and Admiralty Courts, which had jurisdiction over testaments, marriages, and shipping, or as a wag put it, over "bad wills, bad wives, and bad wessels," the Civil Law continued to form the basis of jurisprudence. From the beginning of the sixteenth century the barristers practising before those Courts had formed themselves into a college, of which each member was a Doctor in the Civil Law. The register dates from 1511, and the college's first habitation was in a block of houses in Knightrider Street which belonged to St. Paul's Church. After the fire of London in 1666, which destroyed their property, the doctors were for a time lodged in Exeter House in the Strand—since put to different uses—but in 1672, by an Order-in-Council, they were authorized to retake possession of their old site, and they erected a new building which henceforth bore the name of Doctors' Commons. This college, which received a charter of incorporation, consisted of a number of fellows all of whom had to be doctors, practising in the Court of the Arches or the Archbishop's Court; and the judges of the tribunals before which they pleaded were regularly chosen from among the members. The number of advocates was narrowly limited and seldom exceeded twenty-five, so that once a man of ability was admitted, he was well-nigh certain to secure a large practice.

William Scott was peculiarly fitted for success in the branch of law to which he attached himself. He brought to it not only a splendid intellect, an unrivalled lucidity of expression, an intimate acquaintance with the Civil Law and a wide knowledge of the history of the ages in which it grew, but also some personal experience of shipping affairs. For a year after his father's death he carried on the shipping business preparatory to winding it up; and a privateering enterprise on which a younger brother embarked led him to direct his attention to the Law of Prize. The only quality he lacked was fluency in public speaking. At first he wrote out his speeches, but as the Ecclesiastical and Admiralty Courts knew no jury and relied more on written than on oral testimony, readiness of speech was less requisite than knowledge of law and clearness of argument. In those respects he was pre-eminent. A year of silence was imposed upon all the newly elected members of the college, during which they were expected to attend the Courts, but as soon as the enforced probation was over, Scott leapt to the front. His brother wrote of him in 1783 : "His success has been wonderful, and he has been fortunate beyond example." In that year he obtained a sinecure, being appointed the Registrar of the Court of Faculties, and in 1788 he became at once judge of the Consistory Court of the Bishop of London, Vicar-General of the Archbishop of Canterbury, and Advocate-General—a position which had the same rank at Doctors' Commons as that of the Attorney-General at Westminster. The post was exceptionally lucrative at the time he held it, because of the war which broke out between England and France in 1793. Privateering, as Franklin said, was the passion of England ; the spoils were large, and Scott gathered in large fees. It was his duty to appear for the Crown in all cases of disputed prize, and as between 1793 and 1815 the English Admiralty granted 10,000 letters of marque, the number of captures which were brought in for decision was immense. In 1798, having obtained a commanding position as advocate, he was appointed judge of the High Court of Admiralty, while a few months later his brother became Solicitor-General. He had entered the House of Commons in 1790 as member for the borough of Downton, after having been unseated on petition for the same borough six years earlier, and in 1801 he was elected as member for the University of Oxford. He kept his seat till he was raised to the peerage as Lord Stowell in 1821. But he did not take a prominent part in the political sphere : he spoke but seldom in debate and, strangely enough, without distinction. His whole energy was given to, and his fame was entirely gained in, his judicial work, whereby " he stamped the image of his own mind upon the international jurisprudence of the world." As proof of his industry and of the volume of cases he was called upon to decide in that epoch of incessant war, it may be mentioned that in the year 1806 he gave 2,206 decrees and judgments. In addition to this, he was continually advising the Lords of the Admiralty, and was at the same time presiding over ecclesiastical causes. In 1821, he resigned his Consistory judgeship, but he retained his position as judge of the Admiralty Court till 1827. Then, at the age of eighty-three, but while his vigour was still unimpaired, he vacated that office. He gradually declined, and died in 1836, leaving a vast property of nearly a quarter of a million in personalty and considerable real estate. Though a bon vivant, he had been saving to the point of meanness throughout his life, and he loved, as he put it, "the elegant simplicity of the three per cents." "Scott will take any *given* quantity of wine," was remarked of him by a clerical wit who noted that he drank more when dining out than when at home. But his little failings of personal character fade away before his immense services to English law, and indeed to the whole science of law, which raised the fame of our international jurisprudence to a height to which it had never risen before.

It was the good-fortune of Stowell that all his chief judgments were well reported and have been preserved to illuminate posterity; or rather it was the happy fortune of Dr. Christopher Robinson that on taking his seat in the Admiralty Court in 1798 he determined to add to the collection of reports in the other Courts of Justice a set recording the decisions in Admiralty, which had not hitherto been so served. At the same time it was happy for the judge that he was not fettered in his application of broad principles and the usage of nations by the findings of predecessors in his office. "With the exception of a few notes by Sir J. Simpson and some scattered memoranda . . . and occasional references to tradition there was no precedent for the guidance of Scott," and, one may add, no obstacle in his path. In the field of Ecclesiastical Law he was not so unhampered: here the Canon Law text-books and precedents hedged him about; and his decisions preserved in the reports of Haggard and Phillimore, do not possess the same permanent value and originality. Nevertheless, there are several cases in which his judgment has marked an important step in the development of the law. His place among the world's jurists depends, of course, upon the other part of his work, which is preserved in the volumes of Drs. Christopher Robinson, Dodson, and Edwards. As the Napoleonic struggle brought forth a Pitt to direct our politics, a Nelson to carry our navy to triumph, and a Wellington to lead our army to victory, so too it brought forth a Scott to erect our Prize Law upon a new and firm foundation, and to establish justice in our hegemony of the sea. The judge fitly realized the unique opportunity which lay before him, and he lavished an infinite care upon the preparation and edition of his judgments. By their clear adherence to the principles of justice, strict, perhaps, but seldom strained, as much as by their "inimitable felicity of language," they have commanded since the death of their author the assent not only of the English but also of the American Courts, and, more than that, many of the rules which he laid down in adjudicating upon the cases before him have passed into the law of nations. Coleridge in his *Table-Talk* recommended to all statesmen with the perusal of Grotius, Bynkershoek, Pufendorf, Wolf and Vattel the reports of Dr. Robinson; and the verdict of later generations has confirmed for Lord Stowell the place which the contemporary poet and philosopher assigned to him, as the finest exponent in practice of the law regulating the rights of belligerents and neutrals in war upon the high seas. Amid all the violence and unwarrantable pretensions of the time, advanced by his own country as well as by Napoleon, he held aloft the standard of fairness towards neutrals, enforcing the established law with exactitude and severity, but cutting at the roots of innovation; never countenancing sham evasions of the law, but never, on the other hand, countenancing oppressive fictions. In the stress of war his judgments were impugned by some American judges, but his vindication came upon maturer consideration: as one of them wrote to him later: "On a calm review of your decisions after a lapse of years, I am bound to confess my entire conviction both of their accuracy and equity."

Lord Stowell's Judgments.—The distinguishing characteristic of Lord Stowell's judgments is his unerring faculty for seizing on the true bearing of every problem presented to him, and his equally unerring powers of applying broad propositions of law to every combination of circumstances. Perhaps it is due to his early career that he brought to the Bench a philosophic grasp such as few English judges have exhibited. Certain it is that he scorned all chicanery and fiction, and that the distinctions which he drew between different cases of capture and prize are always based upon clear principles.

To deal, however, first with the minor part of his work which affected only English jurisprudence. Several of his decisions when sitting in the Episcopal Courts have become leading cases. What characterizes them all is the thoroughness and symmetry of their form. First he lays down the broad principles to be applied in the class of case before him, with apt reference to the Civil or Canon Law applicable: then with mastery of learning he deals with the text-writers or judicial precedents, and distinguishes or adopts their remarks : and finally he dissects with singular acumen and lucidity the facts and the evidence in the case before him and applies the law which he has already enunciated. Typical is his judgment in the case of *Dalrymple* v. *Dalrymple*, reported in Haggard (vol. ii., p. 54). In that case he was called upon to decide whether a marriage entered upon by civil contract without a religious celebration according to the law of Scotland was valid, one of the parties being an English officer on service, quartered in Scotland. Of the objection raised on this score he makes short work :

"Being entertained in an English court, the case must be adjudicated according to the principles of English law applicable to such a case. But the only principle applicable to such a case by the law of England is that the validity of Miss G.'s marriage rights must be tried by reference to the law of the country where, if they emit at all, they had their origin. Having furnished this principle, the law of England withdraws altogether, and leaves the legal question to the exclusive judgment of the law of Scotland." He passes on to an elaborate analysis of the general Roman and Canon Law of marriage, and then to a consideration of the marriage law of Scotland, in order to see in what instances it has " resiled " from the general law. He reviews first the opinions of all the authoritative Scottish jurists, and next the judicial decisions of the Scottish Courts, and finally enunciates the rule that by the law of Scotland " the *marriage contract de præsenti* does not require consummation in order to become very matrimony ; that it does *ipso facto et ipso jure* constitute the relation of man and wife."

Similar in its general framework is the judgment in *Lindo* v. *Belisario* (1 Haggard, 216), where he has to determine the validity not of a Scottish but of a Jewish marriage—a new point in the English Courts. Here, in the same thorough fashion, he examines and weighs the opinions of the various Rabbinic authorities upon the question whether a betrothal carried out with certain ceremonies ranks as a binding marriage contract, and in the end, feeling himself, as he says, to be on novel ground, " on which doubts ought to be entertained and questions sifted with great caution," he frames a few particular questions which he addresses to the Jewish authorities ; and upon the answers to these questions he later gives his judgment. " If," he remarks, " I were to determine the question of marriage on principles different from the established authorities amongst the Jews as now certified, I should be unhinging every institution, and taking upon myself the responsibility as Ecclesiastical Judge, in opposition to those who possess a more natural right to determine on questions of this kind."

The principle here laid down that domicile does not involve an unlimited subjection to the ordinary laws of the country, he affirms again in one of the last decisions he gave as judge of the Consistory Court—*Reading* v. *Smith*, 1821 (2 Haggard, 371), when the question was as to the validity of a marriage celebrated in South Africa between two British subjects which would have been void by the local law. He held that the marriage was good, because of the circumstances that the husband was an officer in the British forces occupying the country, the parties had been married by the English chaplain, and the marriage had stood for twenty-five years. He was free to apply equitable principles, because "while the English decisions have established the rule that a foreign marriage, valid according to the law of the place where celebrated, is good everywhere else, they have not *e converso* established that marriages of British subjects, not good according to the general law of the place where celebrated, are universally to be regarded as invalid in England."

Though willing to apply equitable justice wherever he felt it open to him, Sir William Scott never allowed himself to be moved from the strict administration of the established law by vague considerations of humanity. At the outset of his judgment in *Evans* v. *Evans* (1 Haggard, 35), where he defined the conditions of "legal cruelty" as a ground of divorce in a way which has never been excelled, he states his maxim concisely : "Humanity is the second virtue of the Courts, but undoubtedly the first is justice." It was the same outlook which led him to hold in the trial of *The Slave Grace*—which came to him on appeal from the Vice-Admiralty Court of Antigua—that the temporary residence in England of a negro slave without manumission suspends, but does not extinguish, the status of slavery of a person who after such residence voluntarily returns to a country where slavery is legal. The decision aroused great opposition at the time and is of only academic interest to-day; but though the last of Stowell's reported judgments, it is impregnated with the same mastery of principle and unswerving respect for the law as his Admiralty decisions in prize law. It is significant that in a letter to Mr. Justice Story he expressed his personal disgust at the continuance of slavery in the West Indies, and that the American jurist in reply declared his complete agreement with his reasoning in this judgment.

As he did not allow personal feeling to influence his judgment in times of peace, so in times of war he was not swayed by national antipathies in considerations of national interest. Foreign critics have indeed accused him of undue severity; but the complaint is rather that the law which he administered was oppressive upon neutrals than that he administered it with partiality or national bias in favour of captors. And in defence of his attitude towards neutrals, it should be pointed out that he was judge of the Admiralty Court when England was fighting for her national existence, and when Napoleon sought to make neutrals his instruments in the war against English commerce. The supreme justification of Stowell's decrees is that the United States, whose merchants had been hardest hit by them, came afterwards to recognize their equity and to follow them when they became belligerent.

Prize Law.—To turn now to these decisions, it is unnecessary to summarize the Prize Law of England as it was established by Stowell. All one can do is to notice a few points which illustrate his general outlook, and some of the rules which he laid down. His judgment delivered during the first year of his office (1798), in the case of *The Maria* (1 C. Rob., 350), one of a fleet of Swedish merchantmen which was sailing under convoy of a ship of war, and in pursuance of the principles of the Armed Neutrality resisted visitation and search by a British cruiser, has become a classic of International Law. He enunciates in two sentences the proper character of the Prize Court as a tribunal where the law of nations is administered. "The seat of judicial authority is locally here in the belligerent country, according to the known law and practice of nations, but the law itself has no locality. It is the duty of the judge sitting in an Admiralty Court not to deliver occasional and shifting opinions to serve present purposes and particular national interests, but to administer with indifference that justice which the law of nations holds out without distinction to independent States, some happening to be neutral and some belligerent." And upon the merits of the case before him he insists that the usages and practice of nations have recognized the right of the belligerent to protect himself through search of suspected ships against assistance being given to his enemy by neutrals, and he sweeps away the loose arguments urged in support of the rules of the Armed Neutrality that convoyed ships should be free from search. " Upon such unauthorized speculations it is not necessary for me to descant; the law and practice of nations (I include particularly the practice of Sweden when it happens to be belligerent) give them no sort of countenance, and until that law and practice are newly modelled in such a way as may surrender the honour and ancient rights of some nations to the present conveniences of other nations (which nations may perhaps remember to forget them when they happen to be themselves belligerent), no reverence is due to them : they are the elements of that system which, if it is consistent, has for its real purpose an entire abolition of capture in war, that is, in other words, to change the nature of hostility as it has ever existed among mankind, and to introduce a state of things not yet seen in the world—that of a military war and a commercial peace." The Declaration of London of 1908 proposes indeed the renunciation of the right of search of convoyed neutral vessels, so that the exact point decided in the case may be obsolete ; but the principles which are laid down in this judgment as to the bindingness of international practice, till by the consent of nations it is changed, remain of abiding validity.

Lord Stowell conceived the position of a Prize Court in its full dignity and responsibility as an international Court, administering not the national judge's theories, but the acknowledged practice of nations, and he defined this conception most eloquently in a case where he had to determine whether a belligerent could set up a Prize Court in neutral territory (*The Flad Oyen*, 1 C. Rob., 135). A French privateer had carried an English prize vessel into Bergen, and there procured its condemnation by the French Consul. In repudiating the condemnation he declares : " It is my duty not to admit that because one nation has thought proper to depart from the common usage of the world and to treat the notice of mankind in a new and unprecedented manner, that I am on that account under the necessity of acknowledging the efficacy of such a novel institution, merely because general theory might give it a degree of countenance independent of all practice from the earliest history of mankind. The institution must conform to the text-law and likewise to the constant usage upon the matter." He neither introduced new doctrines himself, nor could he respect their introduction by foreign powers. His function, as he understood it, was where a clear practice did not exist, to define exactly, by application to particular and varying cases, the general principles that were to be found in the works of the great publicists ; where it did exist, to follow it and if necessary amplify its scope.

Among the doctrines hitherto attended with doubt, which Lord Stowell placed upon a certain foundation, was the illegality of trading with the enemy during war. In the case of *The Hoop* (1799, 1 C. Rob., 196) he reviewed the large number of cases decided by the English Lords of Appeal during the eighteenth century, and, bringing to their support the statements of Bynkershoek, he enunciated the clear principle that " all trading with the public enemy unless with the permission of the Sovereign is interdicted." The disability of an alien enemy to sue in the Courts is the reason for the prohibition ; since " a state in which contracts cannot be enforced cannot be a state of legal commerce." The excellence of this, as of so many of Stowell's judgments, is not that it introduces a new rule, but that it elucidates the existing doctrine and confirms it with reason. His statement of the rule is an illustration of Pope's words, " What oft was held, but ne'er so well expressed."

The doctrine of " trade domicil in war " is another to which he gave definiteness and stability. In his day the requirements of domicil for the purposes of the personal law had not been thoroughly investigated ; but sitting as a Prize Court judge he was concerned with a different kind of domicil—viz., the quality of residence in, or association with, a foreign country which was necessary to clothe a man with enemy or neutral character.

The object of the prohibition of trade with the enemy and the confiscation of enemy ships and cargoes being to prevent the increase of wealth which commerce brings, the belligerent attached enemy character to a merchant not according to his nationality, but according to his place of residence or his place of business. If a British or an enemy subject, either before or during the war, removed to a neutral country and *bona fide* took up his residence there, then his innocent trading did not offend against the belligerent ; if, on the other hand, a neutral subject took up his residence or established a business house in England or in an enemy country, his ship or his cargo received the national character of its origin. Under the influence indeed of the ideas of the French Revolution which emphasized the principle of nationality, the French Prize Courts adopted another criterion of enemy character, and made it depend upon the political allegiance of the subject. Thus it was held in the case of *Le Hardy*, 1802, that a neutral merchant domiciled in a belligerent country did not acquire a belligerent character, and his property at sea was neutral property.

The new doctrine, however, found no favour with Stowell. Every person domiciled in an enemy state, whether a born subject of that state or not, he regarded as an enemy, and he condemned his ship or cargo if captured (*cf. The Indian Chief*, 1801, 3 C. Rob., 12). Conversely, every person domiciled in a neutral country, whether a British or a neutral or an enemy subject, he regarded for purposes of maritime capture as a neutral (*cf. The Danous*, 1802, 4 C. Rob., 255). This was the general rule, but with his strict application of the law in favour of captors Stowell further laid down in *The Jonge Klassine* (1804, 5 C. Rob., 302) that a merchant may have mercantile concerns in two countries, and if he acts as a merchant of both must be liable to be considered as a subject of both. Hence the cargo derived from the business house of a neutral owner in the enemy country might be condemned. On the other hand, he pointed out in *The Herman* (1802, 4 C. Rob., 228) that "when a person has a house of trade in the neutral country, and one in Great Britain secondary to his house in the neutral country, that he may carry on trade with the enemy from his first house cannot be denied, provided it does not originate from his house in London, nor vest an interest in that house." And while the intention of permanent residence in a country was necessary in his day to fix domicil for civil purposes, he held, as the nature of the case required, that a trade domicil for the purpose of establishing enemy or neutral character might be more easily acquired. Any residence or establishment in the country for commercial purposes such as made a person's trade or business contribute to and form part of the resources of such country was sufficient, whether or not there was an intention to make the country a permanent home. The trade domicil, again, might be lost as easily as it was gained. Stowell formulated the two main rules which still govern the subject of commercial domicil in the cases of *The Harmony* (1800, 2 C. Rob., 322) and *The Indian Chief* (1801, 3 C. Rob., 12). In the former he pointed out that " time is the grand ingredient in constituting domicil . . . be the occupation what it may, it cannot happen but with few exceptions that a mere length of time shall not constitute a domicil," while in the latter he declared : " The character that is gained by residence ceases by residence ; it is an adventitious character which no longer adheres to him (the merchant) from the moment that he puts himself in motion *bona fide* to quit the country *sine animo revertendi*."

Some modern writers have denied that there should be any difference between trade domicil in time of war and personal domicil in time of peace, but the distinction is reasonably based on the different purpose and consequences of the two statutes, and it has been regarded by both English and American Courts for a century ; and Stowell's standard of domicil for prize purposes has been throughout adopted.

It would be tedious to mention the decisions in which Lord Stowell defined the English rule as regards contraband, absolute and conditional, and the penalty for its carriage, the conditions of a blockade by notice and *de facto*, and the varying penalties for its breach, unneutral service by carriage of despatches or military officers of the enemy, and the legal consequences attaching to it, the effect of recapture of a prize, and of the transfer of a cargo *in transitu* by a belligerent to a neutral owner, and the engagement by a neutral in the colonial and coasting trade of the enemy. Suffice it to say that he settled our Prize Law upon all these points, and, though circumstances have changed, and international agreements have largely cut down the rights of maritime capture, his judgments still remain the surest guide upon Prize Law, and mark out with scarcely an exception the proper limit of interference with neutral trade.

The Doctrine of Continuous Voyage.—On one point, indeed, modern practice has countenanced an extension of a rule which he formulated, beyond the point to which he applied it. In order to evade the prohibition against carrying merchandise from the French and Dutch Colonies during the Napoleonic wars, the shippers of the United States were in the habit of consigning the goods in the first place to some neutral port in the United States or elsewhere, and then transhipping them on another vessel which brought them to Europe as colourable American merchandise. Lord Stowell, however, crushed this evasion in condemning *The Maria*, No. 3 (5 C. Rob., 365), and *The William*, No. 2 (*ibid.*, p. 585). The Court, he insisted, did not regard the fiction, but the fact, and if the cargo were in fact destined for the enemy's country, or in fact derived from the enemy's colony, then it was confiscated whether it was nominally consigned to, or had been nominally transhipped from, a neutral port. "The truth may not always be discernible, but when it is discovered, it is according to the truth and not according to the fiction that we are to give to the transaction its character and denomination. If the voyage from the place of lading be not really ended, it matters not by what acts the party may have evinced his desire of making it appear to have ended."

But in the case of ordinary contraband trading he did not apply the so-called doctrine of continuous voyage. A ship, he said, could only be condemned out of her own mouth, and the articles to be confiscated must be taken *in delicto*, in the actual prosecution of the voyage to an enemy's port (*The Imina*, 3 C. Rob., 167). Though there might be the strongest reason to suspect the ultimate hostile destination of her cargo, yet, if her own port of delivery were neutral, the cargo was immune. The growth of railways and the desire of belligerents to compensate themselves for the loss of offensive rights which the Declaration of Paris has entailed, by pressing those that remain, have led to the application of the rule of continuous voyage to any cargo of contraband goods which is ultimately destined for the enemy's forces. Long disputed, the usage has received the sanction of the Declaration of London as regards goods which are absolute contraband, though not as regards those which are only conditional contraband. To another innovation of latter-day belligerents which has not yet received, and it may be hoped will never receive, international sanction, Lord Stowell lent no countenance, viz., the destruction of neutral prizes before proper condemnation in a Prize Court, without making compensation to the neutral owner, if in the end the guilt of the vessel were not proved. His opinions upon the proper treatment of prizes by the captor are set out in his last recorded prize judgment, *The Felicity* (1819, 2 Dodson, 381).

In all cases of capture, he says, it is the captor's first duty to bring in the prize to port for adjudication. "If impossible to bring in, the next duty is to destroy enemy's property. Where doubtful whether enemy's property and impossible to bring in, no such obligation arises, and the safe and proper course is to dismiss. When it is neutral, the act of destruction cannot be justified to the neutral owner by the gravest importance of such an act to the public service of the captor's own state; to the neutral it can only be justified under any such circumstances by a full restitution in value. These are rules so clear in principle and established in practice, that they require neither reasoning nor precedent to illustrate or support them."

It has been said of sermons that, while dealing with eternal subjects, they tend to be the most ephemeral literature; and so it might be said of prize judgments, that though concerned with International Law, they tend to be the most national expressions of judicial opinion. But at the beginning of the nineteenth century Stowell in England, and to a smaller degree Marshall in the United States, bringing to their national Prize Courts two of the greatest intellects of the time, realized the ideal character of the jurisdiction entrusted to them, and established an Anglo-Saxon law of prize which may truly be described as "a light to the nations." It is one of the surest testimonies of the stability of Stowell's work that the Declaration of London, which was recently drawn up by representatives of the great Powers to serve as a code of maritime law in war, embodies many of the rules which he formulated when sitting as judge of the British Prize Court. And the International Convention for the establishment of an International Prize Court, which was promoted by the British Government and signed by the delegates of all the Powers at The Hague Peace Conference, 1907, gives reality at last to that ideal of the Prize Court which he upheld, as a tribunal administering the law of nations, by providing for the constitution of an appeal court in matters of prize, which shall be as well in fact as in theory, and both in its membership and the law it applies, international.

BENTHAM

THE accepted tradition calls Jeremy Bentham a jurist. But there is nothing paradoxical in the statement that in any true and proper sense of the term he is not a jurist at all. It may be conceded that upon English legislation in the domain of the penal law, and in the sphere of the procedure, both civil and criminal, and in the great revolution, whereby the fusion of law and equity was accomplished, his influence was paramount. It is not doubted that he had a very extended knowledge of the English law of his day, but he knew little, if anything, of the history of that system for the study of which the materials were so abundant. He gravely records "a curious fact, that in Henry the VI.'s time the judges had laid a plot for getting all the land in the Kingdom (like the priests), by outlawing all whom they liked—with great formalities always, but no grounds. The abuse was got rid of by somebody declaring that this should not be done." A writer who can make such an assertion has, of course, no pretension to legal scholarship. Bentham had but to look into the Year Books of that reign, or to read the *De Laudibus* of Fortescue, then a Chief Justice, to ascertain that what he took for history was as absurd as the statements of Horn's *Mirror*. Bentham knew not his Year Books nor his Coke, much less his Bracton, and even when criticizing Blackstone, he would have been much better occupied in acquiring an historical knowledge of the development of the common law. The fact is that Bentham knew English law simply as an articled attorney's clerk would have known it, in the base, mechanical fashion of the empiricist; he knew it as an existing body of arbitrary rules, but the antecedent conditions that made the law what it was, the marvellous phenomena of its development, never occurred to him as a subject of research.

Even on the subject of the rules of evidence, where his views have attained such a distinct triumph in legislation,

JEREMY BENTHAM

Bentham was profoundly ignorant of the reasonable basis for those rules. The slow and careful outgrowth of the experience of centuries of acute practical and enlightened men, striving to make a jury of twelve men chosen at haphazard an adequate instrument for the intelligent decision of legal controversies, was to him a closed book. The influence of the jury system in the orderly development of English political liberty, whereby the citizen was welded to the existing government as an integral part of it, never occurred to him as an extraordinary political device. He treated the whole subject of judicial evidence as if the rules had been enacted in his own day, to suit merely that small part of the contemporaneous life of his country, which he appreciated, and that small part of the population which he understood. His advocacy of the abolishment of the rule that interested parties should not testify in courts of law took little account of the vivid realization by religious men that he who had taken an oath to speak truly with the help of God had taken the name of his Lord in vain, if he committed perjury; and that it conduced more to "the greatest happiness of the greatest number," that parties in interest should not testify at all, rather than that courts should lead them into the temptation of imperilling their immortal souls.

While Bentham was little versed in the history of English law, he was profoundly ignorant of Roman and Continental law. His view of the Roman law was so inadequate as to cause him to pronounce it "a parcel of dissertations badly drawn up." Although Bauer and Weiss and their great pupil Savigny had created during Bentham's life the critical study of Roman law and medieval jurisprudence, although the greatest legal phenomenon in history—the survival of Roman law through the ruin of the Empire and through the Dark Ages—was fully demonstrated, although Savigny in his famous pamphlet had saved Germany from the evils of such a raw codification as Bentham proposed for all countries, although Savigny had demonstrated that an historical study of the existing law was a condition precedent to any science of law, without which codification is *brutum fulmen*, Bentham never seems to have discovered that such men were living and writing. His fundamental idea was that the legislator must first arrange a proper code of laws upon a philosophy of human nature borrowed from Helvétius, which considered a balancing of so-called pleasure and pain that ignored the higher attributes of the human spirit; then this code so arranged should be settled so that no body of decision in regard to the meaning of its provisions could ever grow up around it; then this result should be made certain by never permitting any lawyer to become a judge, and that code so settled would be good and workable for any nation regardless of its existing law, or its past history, or its racial or social characteristics. This is the secret of Bentham's offers to make the same code for Turkey, for Egypt, for France, for Spain, for Portugal, for Russia, for Switzerland, for Morocco, for the States of our Union, and for the new South American Republics.

These facts make it apparent that Bentham has no claim to the title of jurist. A school of English jurists was to arise, but Bentham missed the opportunity of creating it. His leisure, his ample means, his long life, would have furnished an ideal setting for a great jurisconsult. But Bentham had no taste for that kind of labour. The mass of material which later generations were to use with such brilliant effect he passed by, although he knew its value, for he himself has told us: "Traverse the whole continent of Europe, ransack all the libraries belonging to all the jurisprudential systems of the several political States, add the contents together, you would not be able to compose a collection of cases equal in variety, in amplitude, in clearness of statement —in a word, all points taken together, in constructiveness—to that which may be seen to be afforded in the collection of English reports of adjudged cases." Knowing all this, Bentham deliberately turned to the easier task of constructing a general political philosophy. Although his application of his greatest happiness principal was really based upon a low view of human nature, and although, as his letters show, like most reformers, he had the lowest possible view of the men with whom he came in contact, although he had little confidence or trust in his fellow-men in private life, he based his theory of a proper form of government upon the idea which all history disproves, but which was then so fashionable, that the individual human being is something divine, that all history and all the past have been a conspiracy against him, that, if permitted, he will do what is right without exertion, without self-conquest, because it agrees with his nature to do so. This conception finds no small part of its support in the naïve belief that conscience actually teaches us what is right, not merely to do what we may happen to think is right. Given this fundamental concept, the remainder of Bentham's political arrangements, including his form of government, universal suffrage, one code for all peoples, the secret ballot, the abolition of the legal profession and elective judges is an easy deduction. It is apparent that there is nothing novel in any of his suggestions. Most of them somewhere had been tried with conspicuous lack of success. Yet at the same time, with a system based upon collectivism as his was, he was no less an ardent believer in pure individualism, and like all his school, until his greatest disciple John Stuart Mill, in his *Essay on Liberty*, demolished the whole Benthamite theory of government, he failed to perceive that collectivism is bound to destroy individualism, because it substitutes, instead of the domination of a ruler or of a ruling class, the far more destructive domination of a generally unfit majority.

In England itself Bentham was never in touch with the spirit of his time or of his race. He once spoke to his disciple Bowring of the only time that he had met Edmund Burke. "I met Burke once at Phil Metcalf's," said Bentham; "he gave me great disgust." This is the sole impression that the greatest English political philosopher, a man far more entitled to the appellation of jurist than Bentham, made on the man who is considered our foremost writer on jurisprudence. But the occurrence is characteristic of Bentham. He could have no sympathy with Burke's cast of thought, he had none of that historical sense, that sense for institutions, that vast historic imagination, which saw the political problems of each country as a concrete thing modified by all the conditions of time, place, and race, of existing institutions and the influence of the past in molding existing sentiments and beliefs. Burke "saw life steadily, and saw it whole." Bentham never comprehended the lesson that Burke was continually teaching, that the whole fabric of national life is an actual organism which acts upon individuals as they react upon it, that a nation's law is simply a part and parcel of the national life and is as it is because that particular nation could have no other; an idea never better expressed than by the old Roman poet: "Moribus antiquis res stet Romana, virisque." But such conceptions were alien to Bentham. He once said that Pope's famous line on government, "Whate'er is best administered is best," was the most foolish thing ever penned. Yet Hooker's no less famous saying on forms of government, "The kinds thereof many being, nature tieth not to any one, but leaveth the choice as a thing arbitrary," is probably the wisest thing ever said on the subject.

With Bentham's influence in England we are not here concerned. What has been said will indicate that his influence out of England is due rather to his political ideas than to his legal writings. Such ascertainable facts as the evolution of the secret ballot are easy to follow. The present-day ballot in certain districts where the names of hundreds of candidates are printed upon it, and where a large and cumbrous volume of proposed laws is submitted to the voter, would be a development grotesque enough, if it were not so melancholy.

The cardinal reforms of the abolition of the distinction between law and equity, the simplification of legal pleadings and procedure, the creation of tribunals which act with celerity, the registration of conveyances of real estate, the cheapening of legal processes, the substitution of fixed salaries for public officials instead of fees, the abolition of imprisonment for debt, the creation of public prosecutors, the abolition of most of the exclusionary rules of evidence, and to a limited extent his ideas on codification, have found a ready acceptance in countries which have the English law. But Bentham knew only the English system, and all his views were coloured by a refraction through that medium. Even his codes were possible to him, only because he could copy his principles out of that mass of "judge-made" law which he affected to despise.

In the Germanic countries Bentham has never exerted any appreciable influence. The school of historical jurists which has ruled there has nothing in common with him. Its jurists have searched out English law for themselves. On what they desired to know his works had nothing to tell them. Their codes are constructed, not on Benthamite principles, but according to the views of their own jurisconsults. But in certain of the Latin countries Bentham has had an apparently powerful influence.

The first writing of Bentham appeared in 1776. It was an assault upon the complacent optimism of Blackstone's *Commentaries*. It has no real importance. But his next work, published in 1789, was his *Introduction to the Principles of Morals and Legislation*. Practically all the main doctrines of Bentham are contained in it. Just before this time Bentham had met Etienne Dumont, a Genevese, who became vastly interested in Bentham's ideas, and as an earnest disciple spent years on Bentham's voluminous manuscripts, beating them into coherence and intelligibility, cutting out their purely local matter and giving them a finished French form.

Through Dumont, Bentham's ideas became known to Mirabeau. Later he became somewhat intimate with Talleyrand. The fair and peaceful beginning of the French Revolution offered Bentham an opportunity. He sent to Abbé Moullet his treatise on the *Tactics of Deliberative Assemblies*, and in March, 1790, he sent a report for the organization of the French judiciary. Then, in 1791, he offered to establish in France a model prison after the style of his "Panopticon." His scheme was printed by the Assembly, and his ardent "love of humanity" was recognized. In 1792 the title of French citizen was conferred upon him. But a legislative body that was about to burst into the atrocities of the Terror had little use for parliamentary tactics or model prisons or schemes of penal reform. Bentham himself learned something from the horrors of the French Revolution. He was no longer so radical, and he records that he voted in 1800 to make Bonaparte First Consul.

In the meantime Dumont had been working on his French *rédactions* of Bentham's manuscripts. In 1802 he published under Bentham's name three volumes entitled *Traités de Legislation civile et penale*. Volume one contained the General Principles of Legislation and Principles of a Civil Code; volume two, Principles of a Penal Code; and volume three, the proposals for a model prison. These writings created a great stir in Europe, especially in Spain. In 1811 Dumont published Bentham's *Theory of Punishments and Rewards*, the valuable part of which was due to Beccaria. Still later, in 1816, was published by the indefatigable Dumont the *Tactics of Deliberative Assemblies* and the *Treatise on Political Fallacies*. Finally, in 1813, came the *Treatise on Judicial Proofs* and the *Judicial Organization and Codification*. Practically all of Bentham's European reputation was based upon Dumont's publications, and Englishmen discovered Bentham by way of the Continent.

Dumont had striven in 1802 in his Preface to soften Bentham's radicalism and render his views acceptable to moderate people. He had expressly disclaimed for Bentham any preference for any particular form of government, had claimed that Bentham was antagonistic to those political theories which begin by attacking existing institutions, and had asserted that Bentham believed that legal reforms can be accomplished only when government has stability, and that Bentham's sole aim was to prevent the overturning of authority and revolutions in property and power. It may be that this Preface is what caused Bentham long afterwards to declare that Dumont understood not a word of his meaning. Be that as it may, it is doubtless true that Dumont obtained a hearing for Bentham's doctrines.

By 1810 Bentham was persuaded that his fame was extended over the civilized world. He thought that codes on his principles were being proposed in France and Germany. His hope was preposterous as to Germany; as to France, he had wholly misconceived the situation. France—unlike England—had no single and coherent body of law applicable throughout the whole country. As Voltaire said, a man travelling in France changed laws as often as he changed horses. In such a condition it is apparent that a code is the only remedy, and the Napoleonic Code was designed by French lawyers to meet that condition; but it merely adapted for the whole country what was found to be best in the various local jurisdictions. Bentham never conceived of codification for such reasons as existed in France. He had England in his eye. His scheme was to abolish the legal profession, to wipe out the law reports, and to reach the Utopia where every man could be his own lawyer. His theory of judicial proofs had no effect upon French law, for the reason that France had not the English law of evidence. It may be said that so far as the actual law of France is concerned, Bentham had no effect whatever; for in legislation the greatest good of the greatest number, as a workable principle, comes in the end to mean simply that the majority ought to have what it wants.

But in the meantime Bentham had found a number of disciples in Spain. Jovellanos, a member of the Spanish Junta, had written treatises upon legislation in Bentham's vein. Nunez, the Librarian at the University of Salamanca, applied Bentham's ideas to a plan for national education in a manner quaint enough; and in 1820 he published a volume on *The Spirit of Bentham*, which has been characterized as the "best existing exposition of Benthamism." Nunez had the cruelty to say of the faithful Dumont: "Sir Bentham (*sic*) handed to Mr. Dumont (*sic*) original MSS. of his theories, from which the latter composed those undigested French treatises that till now have kept under eclipse that light of Bentham's which glimmered through them." The book on Prisons was translated into Spanish as early as 1819, and translations of his other works continued to appear, so that, to quote Señor Silvela, between 1820 and 1845 "no other foreign author exercised in Spain so great an authority as Bentham." Borrow relates that in 1842, while travelling in Spain, he was welcomed by an Alcalde on Cape Finisterre, who had upon his shelves all the works of the "grand Baintham," and compared him to Solon, Plato, and even Lope de Vega. The latter comparison seemed to Borrow somewhat overstrained.

In the period between 1808 and 1812, while Spain was in revolt against Joseph Bonaparte, some attention was paid to legislation, but it was not until the outbreak against Ferdinand in 1820 that Bentham's influence became apparent. The Constitution was restored. Bentham sent to the Cortes a present of his collected writings. He wrote pamphlets on Spanish affairs. Then he turned to Portugal, which had just adopted the Spanish Constitution, freely criticizing what he considered its defects. The Cortes of Portugal received a present of his works, which was gratefully accepted. He wrote another letter to Spain strongly opposing a second chamber for the Cortes, but as usual he had England in his eye, for he argued against a House of Peers, while the Spanish and Portuguese had in mind a second representative chamber.

In August, 1820, the Spanish Cortes entered upon the work of drafting a penal code, and Count Toreno, the President of the Cortes, addressing Bentham as the "Light of Legislation and Benefactor of Man," sent to Bentham a draft of the proposed code for suggestions. Bentham's answer was a querulous criticism of the Cortes for not having applied to him. Bentham suggested to the dignified Spanish aristocrat that he was a functionary who had points of his own to further, and that he would be likely to use the suggestions to give support to his own views. The stately note of cold politeness, says Mr. Kenny, in which Toreno acknowledged Bentham's answer, "affords a fine picture of Castilian dignity; wounded, yet still courteous." Bentham continued to pour out letters to Toreno against the existing legislation of Spain, with an utter disregard for existing conditions. But the political revolution in Spain, enforced by French bayonets, soon put an end to Constitution and Cortes.

In the Spanish possessions in America Bentham from the first took a deep interest. He seriously considered going to Mexico in the company of Aaron Burr, who was to become emperor, while Bentham was to play the Tribonian to Burr's Justinian. Certainly Bentham would have fitted the rôle, for he was a closer approach to Tribonian than he was to great philosophical jurists like Ulpian or Papinian. Miranda, the Spanish revolutionist in South America, had known Bentham in London, and Bentham would have been glad to follow him to Venezuela, for he was convinced that his laws would be received there with glad acclaim, but Miranda died in a Spanish prison.

Bolivar and Santander were ardent Benthamites, and sedulously cultivated the Benthamite plant of reform in that most congenial soil. It is computed that in 1830 forty thousand volumes of Bentham's works in French were sold in Spanish America alone. Among those races every educated man studied his writings as those of another Lycurgus or Solon. Rivadavia, the legislator of Buenos Ayres, was his pupil; José del Valle, the President of Guatemala, was another pupil. They, as well as Andrade, the Brazilian Minister, corresponded with the sage regarding the legislation of their States. The constitutions and all of the laws of the new republics show traces of Bentham's influence. His works were used as textbooks in the schools; though, sad to relate, his earnest disciple, Bolivar, when he turned Dictator in 1826, forbade the use of his master's works in the public schools. The remarkable instability of these Benthamite governments is probably the best commentary upon the value of Bentham's political theories.

In the department of the penal law his influence has been of great and constantly increasing value. The amelioration of punishments and the adaptation of penalties to offences, through the work of Bentham re-enforcing Beccaria, can be traced in the legislation of every civilized country. But this change a careful student of social conditions would be more likely to ascribe to the increasing density of the population and to the greater efficiency of the police, acting in connection with a greater and oftentimes mistaken regard for human life. It has been claimed that once his Panopticon prison scheme was put into successful operation in Russia. The ideas which it embodied—solitary confinement, constant surveillance, physical health for prisoners, and their application to laborious pursuits are now commonplaces in all prison discipline. But those ideas belong not so much to Bentham as to Howard.

One proposal of Bentham, that of reducing and fixing the armed force of nations, now seems to have some chance of realization. He proposed it in the closing years of the eighteenth century, a singularly inopportune time. Bismarck in 1877 sneered at its utter impracticability; yet the impending danger of national bankruptcies may bring it about. In the kindred realm of "international law," a phrase which Bentham invented, he has been a living force. It is apparent that a Benthamic code is the only solution for a law of nations, and as early as 1789 Bentham had worked out a theory of international law, which Wheaton has published in his *History*. All subsequent attempts at codification of the law of nations are largely based on Bentham's proposals.

Bentham's advice to France in 1793 to emancipate her colonies as a sedative for her evil condition has been answered by the vast colonial development, not only of France, but of Germany and England. He was not any more successful in his advocacy of the abolition of the jury, whose value in reconciling the citizen to a system of law he never seems to have understood. His proposal to abolish banking and bankers as "always hurtful to every State" shows that he never understood what has been the most potent engine in the development of modern industrialism. Dumont had a saying of anything that seemed to him good, "C'est convainquant, c'est la vérité même, c'est presque Benthamique," yet nothing could be more wholly absurd than Bentham's proposal to Mehemet Ali in 1828 to give to Egypt a Constitution minted on a Benthamite die. One of the humorous applications of Bentham's teachings is that Stanhope carried with him to Greece the *Table of the Springs of Action*, with which he tried to indoctrinate Byron, then fighting for the Greeks; but (as Leslie Stephen dryly remarks) "the poet, however, thought with some plausibility that he was a better judge of human passions than the philosopher." Bentham's impassioned address to the Greeks was no doubt of no little influence in foisting upon them their unfortunate career as a pitiable republic. Bentham's admirers would gladly forget that in 1830 he advocated putting the public offices up for sale to the highest bidder. In these United States under our newly devised system of primary balloting, that particular one of the Benthamite dreams will probably become a reality.

It is painful to be compelled to admit that he is exercising so little influence. But the reasons are not far to seek. The ultimate dogmas of Bentham are mere words without meaning. The greatest good to the greatest number means absolutely nothing. It is one thing to-day in any given country, it is another thing to-morrow. For one race it produces a particular result, for another race it leads to a wholly different result. In legislation it is as barren and *jejune* as in morals. In morals it means that a man should do what is right, while in legislation it means nothing more than that legislation should be good. The argument in its last analysis becomes one that whatever is right from a moral standpoint, or whatever is good from a legislative standpoint, decides what makes for the greatest happiness of the greatest number. It is no more definite or satisfying than to say that a legislator should strive for the good of his country. On such a principle everything that Bentham attacked can be defended, just as he had no difficulty in defending duelling as furnishing a remedy for a wrong that the law did not redress. The difficulty is never in being ready to enact laws that are good; the real trouble is to settle what laws are good.

Then, too, Bentham's balancing of pains and pleasures, his various sanctions for a law as satisfying his test, by conducing to physical, social, political, or religious pleasure rather than detriment, have not proved of any particular value, except that in their application to the penal law they have some sort of surface validity. But upon analysis they will be found to be resolvable into the proposition, so far as penalties are concerned, that the punishment of an offender should go no farther than the interest of the offender and the general interest of society demand. To reconcile those considerations is the real difficulty, although by Bentham's formulæ it can very plausibly be maintained that a criminal who has such a congenital physical organization as to be at all dangerous to society should be put to death. Those Russian enthusiasts who saw so much to admire in Bentham's writings found it sufficiently painful to make the wholly useless attempt to reconcile Bentham's political theories with the maintenance of the Czar's autocracy. Men are more easily satisfied with words than with facts. The difficulty in legislation has always been that many are called to the task, but few are chosen. Average men find a Cleon or a Bentham far more convincing than an Aristotle or a Burke.

But although Bentham died consoling himself with the thought that his efforts to uplift the world had been thwarted by a base conspiracy of George III., he yet had his happy moments. In 1823 he visited Paris, where the venerable sage, with his long white hair and snuff-coloured garments, excited among the lively and impressionable Gauls the greatest enthusiasm. One day during his stay, casually and unannounced, he visited one of the higher courts. The whole body of advocates, that legal profession whom he had never ceased to denounce, generously rose and paid to him the highest marks of respect. The judges upon the bench, whose function and authority he had done so much to undermine, invited him to the seat of honour ; and there we shall leave him.

MITTERMAIER[1]

CARL JOSEPH ANTON MITTERMAIER was born at Munich on August 5, 1787. His father was an apothecary, a man of excellent training in natural science, with a quick intelligence and a disposition benevolent almost to eccentricity. His mother is depicted to us as a busy woman, with a clear, calm, and shrewd understanding. His father's brother-in-law, Zimmermann, was a seafaring man, and had been helmsman to Captain Cook, the celebrated circumnavigator of the world. The sailor's stirring description of distant lands found the boy a receptive hearer, and served to awaken that yearning for foreign travel which Mittermaier kept to his last days.

Mittermaier's Life.—His father died at an early age; and upon the second marriage of his mother the youth was sent to a school kept by a clergyman, a man of stern and narrow mind, whose wide acquaintance, however, with ancient and modern tongues served to instil into his pupil the liking and knowledge of foreign languages. His later linguistic accomplishments, the product of the seed thus sown, were unusual in a German scholar, and secured for him the friendship and admiration of many foreigners whose acquaintance he made on his numerous journeys and in his varied correspondence.

On entering the Munich Lyceum, he applied himself with zest to natural science; this he never forsook in later years, endeavour-

---

[1] The author of this biographical sketch was a colleague of Mittermaier at Heidelberg. Dr. Goldschmidt himself became the most famous German jurist of his day in commercial law, and at his death, twenty years ago, was one of Europe's greatest legal scientists. The article here translated was published first in the *Archiv für civilistische Praxis*, 1867, vol. vii., p. 417, and afterwards in the author's *Vermischte Schriften*, 1901, vol. i., p. 653.

A few lines have been inserted from the Notice of Mittermaier's life given in the Preface to the French translation (1868) of Mittermaier's *Criminal Procedure in England, Scotland, and the United States;* that translation was made by A. Chauffard, Judge at Albi.

The present translation is by Dr. Victor von Borosini, of Hull House, Chicago.

CARL JOSEPH ANTON MITTERMAIER

ing always to turn it to account in his legal studies. His plan then was to become a mining engineer, and he took the preliminary examination for this when he was thirteen. But on account of his apparently weak constitution his stepfather refused him permission to follow either this occupation or that of a physician, which he next preferred. At sixteen he entered the law course of the University of Landshut, but he attended the lectures on anatomy and medicine as well as those on law and philosophy. His scanty resources obliged him to earn money by giving private lessons; but amidst all these tasks he showed even at this stage the indefatigable nature of his industry by producing while yet a student a treatise (never printed) on Natural Law. As a private tutor he came into close relations with Von Zentner (then minister of State, formerly professor at Heidelberg) who took a kindly interest in his welfare. On completing his course at the University he practised at Munich, mostly in criminal cases, before the provincial court of the Au suburb. His thorough knowledge of foreign tongues attracted the attention of the great criminalist of the time, Anselm von Feuerbach, who had come from the University of Landshut to draft the criminal code for the Bavarian government. Feuerbach made him his secretary, with the special work of making excerpts from the French and Italian codes and draft-codes.

Mittermaier had in view an academic career, and planned therefore to train himself thoroughly by pursuing studies at some other university. The government allotted him a travelling scholarship of 600 florins; not so much indeed with a view to seeing any productive results, as merely to recognize his merits, and to gladden his brief remaining span of life; for at this time the fragile youth of twenty-one (as he himself, grey with years, afterwards recounted with much zest on the occasion of the fiftieth anniversary of his doctorate) was regarded by all, himself included, as doomed by an incurable tuberculosis; and a year longer at the most was allotted to him on earth.

At Zentner's suggestion, he went to Heidelberg, and there studied under such masters as Martin, Heise, Thibaut, Zachariae, and Klüber. To enlarge his income, he continued to do private tutoring; and the consequence of this overwork was a dangerous attack of fever. While still convalescent, he received an appointment from the Bavarian government as professor of the newly-founded University of Innsbruck. He accordingly applied for his doctorate at Heidelberg, which was awarded on March 29, 1809. His thesis was entitled *Void Judgments in Criminal Cases*.[1] His first large treatise, likewise in the field of criminal procedure, dates in the same year—*Theory of Proof in Criminal Procedure*,[2] But through the publishers' bankruptcy it did not appear until 1821, when Heyer of Darmstadt published it under the same title.

Before Mittermaier entered on his duties at Innsbruck, the Tyrol had been freed from Bavarian rule by a popular uprising; so that the young jurist was left without an appointment. After practising for a while with a barrister at Munich, he became *privat-docent* at Landshut. After refusing a call to Kiel, he received the Landshut professorate, which had been promised him. In the ensuing year he made his choice of a life companion by marrying the sister of a friend and colleague, the famous surgeon, Ph. F. von Walther; and the union proved to be one of unbroken happiness. The marriage was blessed with seven children.

For ten years he pursued at Landshut an academic career of the most productive activity. Young as he was, the University honoured him by electing him rector three times in succession. Moreover, the administration of the large properties of the University, hitherto managed by the government, was through his earnest efforts restored to the University and confided to his care. The scope of his courses was extensive. The course on Roman Legal History, which he had begun at the instigation of Savigny (his colleague at Landshut) he soon gave up, for he realized that it interfered with the necessary concentration of his efforts. But he gave courses in Criminal Procedure, in German Private Law and Legal History (one of the earliest courses on this subject), and also (after von Goenner had been appointed in 1810 on the Legislative Committee in Munich) in Civil Procedure. His already numerous writings of this period dealt with these three subjects.

In the first group fall: *Handbook of Criminal Procedure*,[3]

[1] *De nullitatibus in causis criminalibus observat. spec.*, Heidelberg, 1809.

[2] *Theorie des Beweises im peinlichen Prozess, nach den gemeinen positiven Gesetzen und den Bestimmungen der Franzoesischen Civilgesetzgebung*, 2 parts, Mannheim, 1809.

[3] *Handbuch des peinlichen Prozesses, mit vergleichender Darstellung des gemeinen deutschen Rechts und der Bestimmungen der Französischen, Oesterreichischen, Bayrischen und Preussischen Kriminalgesetzgebung*, Bd. I., Abth. i. and ii., Heidelberg, 1810; Bd. ii., Heidelberg, 1812.

Introduction to the Art of Defensive Advocacy in Criminal Cases,[1] and *Public and Oral Procedure and the Jury System*.[2] Here belongs also his editorship of the *Archiv für Kriminalrecht*, which in 1816 he took over with Konopak and Kleinschrod; this journal, founded in 1798, was now called *Neues Archiv für Kriminalrecht* (16 vols., 1816-1833), and afterwards *Archiv des Kriminalrechts, Neue Folge* (24 vols., 1834-1857). Mittermaier remained throughout at its head. In the second group belong his *Introduction to the Study of German Legal History*[3] and *Sketch of a Scientific Treatment of German Private Law*.[4] In the third group, Civil Procedure, no elaborate book was published in this period, but in 1818 he founded with Gensler and Schweitzer the *Archiv für Civilistische Praxis*, whose chief editor he was, after his removal to Heidelberg, until his death. The first volumes contain from his pen numerous abstracts of trials, reviews of the literature on procedure, and of codes and draft codes on procedure and on mortgages.

He accepted in 1819 a chair in the newly established University of Bonn, after he had refused a call to Halle; thus finishing his career in Landshut. He was the first dean of the faculty of law in Bonn. During his two years in the Rhenish city, he began to work on two of his most important books: *Textbook of German Private Law*[5] and *German Common Civil Procedure*.[6]

At Bonn he lectured on German Private and Criminal Law and Procedure, laying stress on practical exercises, including legal rhetoric; and as the Code Napoléon was there in force, he thoroughly studied the French law and its procedure. As provisional proctor of the university, he was forced to take an official part in the lamentable prosecutions for sedition, which during those years were very actively carried on in Bonn; and he disliked his position for this reason. He refused a call to the Supreme Court

---

[1] *Anleitung zur Vertheidigungskunst im Kriminalprozess*, Landshut, 1814; 2 Auflage, 1820.

[2] *Ueber die offentliche und mündliche Rechtspflege und das Geschworenengericht in Vergleichung mit dem Deutschen Strafverfahren*, Landshut, 1819.

[3] *Einleitung in das Studium der Geschichte des germanischen Rechts*, Landshut, 1812.

[4] *Versuch einer wissenschaftlichen Behandlung des Deutschen Privatrechts, mit einem Grundriss zu Vorlesungen*, Landshut, 1815.

[5] *Lehrbuch des Deutschen Privatrechts*, Landshut, 1821.

[6] *Der gemeine deutsche bürgerliche Prozess in Vergleichung mit dem französischen Civilverfahren und mit den neuesten Fortschritten der Prozessgesetzgebung*, 1 Beitrag, Bonn, 1820; 2 Beitrag, 1821.

of the four Free Cities in Lübeck; but accepted in 1821 a call to the University of Heidelberg.

Here he taught for forty-six years, interrupted only by a short parliamentary activity. In the winter of 1847 he lectured only for a few months, on account of the initial sessions of the Diet of Baden; in the following summer, and in the winter of 1848-49, he did not teach at all, on account of his attendance at the German Parliament. In spite of the distance, and the poor communications between Karlsruhe and Heidelberg, he lectured regularly while a member of the Diet of Baden. His yearly course of lectures covered German Private Law, Criminal Law and Procedure, Civil Law; he also held seminars in Civil and Criminal Procedure. On arriving at the age of sixty-four he gradually restricted this immense activity. German Private Law was lectured upon for a last time in the summer of 1850, Civil Procedure in the winter of 1855-56, the Methods of a Trial Judge in the summer of 1854. His seminar of Criminal Procedure met for the last time during the winter of 1854-55. From 1856 until his death he lectured during the summer on Criminal Procedure; during the winter on Criminal Law, besides giving public courses on the Jury System, English Procedure, Curious Criminal Cases, and some important doctrines of Criminal Law (murder, political and property crimes). He was from 1821 until his death at the head of the formerly much consulted *Spruchkollegium*.

His literary activity was prodigious. The following works begun in Landshut and in Bonn, were either continued, or brought out in enlarged and thoroughly revised editions: *Principles of German Common Private Law, including Commercial Law, Bills of Exchange, and Maritime Law* ;[1] *The German Common Law of Civil Procedure* ;[2] *German Criminal Procedure* ;[3] *Doctrine of Proof in German Criminal Procedure* ;[4] *An Introduction of the*

[1] *Grundsätze des gemeinen deutschen Privatrechts mit Einschluss des Handels-, Wechsel-, und Secrechts*, Landshut, 1824, 7th ed., 1847.

[2] *Der gemeine deutsche bürgerliche Prozess*, Erster Beitrag, 2 Auflage, 1822; 3 Auflage, 1838; Zweiter Beitrag, 2 Aufl., 1827; 3 Aufl., 1838; Dritter Beitrag, Bonn, 1823; 2 Aufl., 1832; Vierter Beitrag, Bonn, 1826; 2 Aufl., 1840.

[3] *Das Deutsche Strafverfahren in seiner Fortbildung durch Gerichtsgebrauch und Partikulargesetzbücher und in genauer Vergleichung mit dem englischen und französischen Strafverfahren*, 2 Abth., Heidelberg, 1827; 2 Aufl., 1832-33; 3 Aufl., 1839-40; 4 Aufl., 1845-46.

[4] *Die Lehre vom Beweise in deutschen Strafprozess nach dessen Fortbildung durch Gerichtsgebrauch und deutsche Gesetzbücher in Vergleich mit den Ansichten*

Art of Defensive Advocacy.[1] Besides numerous contributions to periodicals, we must note the following publications, of varying size, all of which, with one exception, pertain to Criminal Law, and mostly to Criminal Procedure: *Mental Alienation ;*[2] *The present Condition of Criminal Legislation in Germany ;*[3] *The Principle of Mental Alienation in Criminal Law ;*[4] *The Progress of Criminal Legislation ;*[5] *Conditions in Italy ;*[6] *Oral Procedure, the Theory of Accusation, Publicity, and the Jury System ;*[7] *Essays on Criminal Law ;*[8] *The Present System of Prisons in England ;*[9] *Legislation and Practice in Criminal Cases ;*[10] *Improvement of Prisons ;*[11] *The Present State of the Prison Question ;*[12] *Capital*

---

des englischen und französischen Strafverfahrens, Darmstadt, 1834. Among the numerous translations of this are: *Traité de la preuve en matière criminelle,* by Alexandre, Paris, 1848 ; *Teoria della prova nel processo penale,* by F. Ambrosoli, Milano, 1858 ; *Tratado de la prueva materia criminal,* Madrid, 1851.

[1] *Anleitung zur Verteidigungskunst,* 3 Aufl., 1828 ; 4 Aufl., 1845. Italian translation: *Guida all'arte della difesa criminale,* by C. F. Gabba, Milano 1858.

[2] *Disquisitio de alienationibus mentis quatenus ad jus criminale spectant,* Heidelberg, 1825. (Rectoral address.)

[3] *Ueber den neuesten Stand der Kriminalgesetzgebung in Deutschland.*

[4] *De principio imputationis alienationum mentis in jure criminali recte constituendo,* Heidelberg, 1837. (Rectoral address.)

[5] *Die Strafgesetzgebung in ihrer Fortbildung geprüft, nach den Forderungen der Wissenschaft und nach den Erfahrungen ueber den Werthneuer Gesetzgebungen, und über die Schwierigkeiten der Kodifikation mit vorzüglicher Rücksicht auf den Gang der Beratungen von Entwürfen der Strafgesetzgebung in konstitutionellen Staaten,* Erster Beitrag, Heidelberg, 1841 ; Zweiter Beitrag, 1843.

[6] *Italienische Zustände,* Heidelberg, 1844. Italian translation: *Delle condizioni d'Italia,* by P. Mugna, Milano, 1845.

[7] *Die Mündlichkeit, das Anklageprinzip, die Oeffentlichkeit und das Geschworenengericht, in ihrer Durchführbarkeit in den verschiedenen Gestzgebungen dargestellt und nach den Forderungen des Rechts und der Zweckmässigkeit mit Rücksicht auf die Erfahrungen der verschiedenen Länder geprüft,* Stuttgart, 1845. Italian translation: *Il processo orale, accusatorio publico e per giurati,* Modena, 1848.

[8] *Vier Abhandlungen aus dem Strafrecht. Als Einleitung zur neuesten Ausgabe von Feuerbach's Strafrechtsfälle,* Frankfurt a/M., 1849.

[9] *Der neueste Zustand der Gefängniseinrichtungen in England und Englische Erfahrungen über Einzelhaft,* Heidelberg, 1850.

[10] *Die Gesetzebung und Rechtsübung über Strafverfahren, nach ihrer neuesten Fortbildung dargestellt und geprüeft,* Erlangen, 1856.

[11] *Die Gefängnisverbesserung, insbesondere die Bedeutung und Durchführung der Einzelhaft im Zusammenhang mit dem Besserungsprinzip, nach den Erfahrungen der verschiedenen Strafanstalten,* Erlangen, 1858.

[12] *Der gegenwärtige Zustand der Gefängnisfrage, mit Rücksicht auf die neuesten Leistungen der Gesetzgebung und Erfahrungen ueber Gefängniseinrichtung mit besonderer Beziehung auf Einzelhaft,* Erlangen, 1860. Italian translation: *Stato attuale della questione sulle carceri,* by F. Benelli, Florence, 1861.

Punishment ;[1] *Experience Relating to the Efficiency of Juries in Europe and in America ;*[2] *English, Scotch, and American Criminal Procedure.*[3]

Mittermaier attached great importance to this last-named book, which is full of personal observations made during his sojourn in England, and embodies the results of his correspondence with jurists in the United States. Besides giving a vivid and true picture of English judicial customs and of the administration of law, he analyzes in an exceedingly lucid way the origin, development, and actual state of the English legal system, especially with regard to the jury. Every chapter of the book proves that it was written after a thorough personal examination of the most important institutions.

Systems of Procedure.—Mittermaier's remarkable preface gives us in concise form his extremely comprehensive statement of the fundamental principles of English, Scotch, and American Criminal Procedure, combined with a discussion as to the possible adoption of some of the principles by France and the German States. As an example of his lucid style, judicial attitude of mind, and shrewd penetration in practical affairs, we subjoin a translation of this Preface (from the French edition) :

" In order to carry out efficiently the administration of criminal justice, criminal procedure should be based on the principles of responsible accusation, oral trial, and publicity. A judicial organization in accord with these principles is needed ; by which speediness of trials, independence of judges, a carefully worked out system of jurisdiction, and uniformity of procedure and decisions are guaranteed. These problems may be solved in different ways. Legal history shows us two entirely different solutions.

" In the first system we find a judicial organization in which the administration of justice in a given territory is subjected to the jurisdiction of a superior court as a centre, on which all other courts depend. It presupposes the most active co-operation of the people at large in following up criminals, and necessitates in the preliminary proceedings the principles of responsible accusation and of publicity.

---

[1] *Die Todesstrafe, nach dem Ergebniss der wissenschaftlichen Forschung, der Fortschritte der Gesetzgebung und der Erfahrungen,* Heidelberg, 1862. Many translations, including : *De doodstraf,* by J. B. Vos, Leiden, 1863 ; *La pena di morte,* by Carrara, Lucca, 1864 ; *Capital Punishment,* by T. M. Moir, London, 1865 ; *La peine de mort,* by Leven, Paris, 1865.

[2] *Erfahrungen über die Wirksamkeit der Schwurgerichte in Europa und in Amerika, über ihre Vorzüge, Mängel und Abhülfe,* 3 Hefte, Erlangen, 1864-65. Russian translation by Nestor Lamansky, St. Petersburg, 1866.

[3] *Das Englische, Schottische und Amerikanische Strafverfahren im zusammenhang mit den politischen, sittlichen und sozialen Zuständen und die in den Einzelheiten der Rechtsübung dargestellt,* Erlangen, 1851.

It regards as indispensable a formal trial, oral examination, and responsible accusation. The presiding judge, who questions neither the accused nor the witnesses, directs the trial; the jury's findings are not confined to answers to specific interrogatories, but after receiving from the presiding judge an instruction upon all the important legal points in the case, they give a general verdict on the guilt of the accused, after an examination of the facts according to the rules of evidence.

"The second system is based on a logical division of jurisdiction between different courts, organically linked together, and on the assistance of a large staff of court officers, including a representative of the State, with sufficient powers for the discovery of crimes. It requires a secret preparatory investigation, which therefore is more of an inquisitorial character, and furnishes reports to be used for what they are worth at the trial. The oral and public trial is based on a charge emanating from a magistrate, and is directed by the presiding Judge of the trial court, who gives the final instruction to the jury. The latter's jurisdiction is limited to the most serious criminal offences. Not restricted by legal proofs, they render their verdict freely upon what is generally called 'intimate conviction,' and in the form of replies to the president's interrogatories.

"The first system, corresponding to Roman law principles, is adopted in England, Scotland, and the United States. The second is the basis of French and German codes.

"The first mentioned system appears in three different varieties.

"The first of those (adopted in England) is a product of ancient institutions, which in course of time have been improved; it is based on the principle of responsible accusation by private individuals, and the logical consequences of the latter's application. It gives much discretionary power to the judge in applying the law. It guarantees the justice of verdicts by submitting the charge to the approval of a grand jury, and by requiring that the verdict of guilt be only binding in case the petty jury is unanimous.

"The second variety (adopted in Scotland) requires the action of a superior court officer, who first determines whether the information gained through a secret preparatory investigation warrants an accusation or not. The prosecution depends therefore not upon a grand jury, but upon this officer alone. At the trial itself, counsel for the defence and public prosecutor enjoy the same privileges; the interests of the defence are protected in the most adequate way. A majority of the jury renders a valid verdict.

"The third system (as found in the United States) is on the lines of the English law; it is marked, however, by a different and simpler system of judicial organization, by the use of public prosecutors, and by great solicitude for the rights of the defence. It regulates by law what is left in England to judicial discretion, and rejects several antiquated distinctions preserved in English procedure.

"Every one interested in the progress of criminal legislation must study the English procedure. German lawgivers are accustomed to take French laws as models. Satisfied with imitating these, they never study English law, whose importance was not appreciated in France. French lawgivers failed to grasp the national spirit of the law in England and its intimate relation with the moral development and the political and social customs of the country. If we study the provisions of French criminal procedure, we find undoubtedly many of the improvements which the English law presents; for instance, a very good judicial organization, with a wise co-ordination of jurisdiction. But, when we look at the spirit of French and English criminal procedure, and then compare its application in the two countries, we notice many discrepancies. Frequently rules of the French code are in flagrant contradiction with principles which underlie the corresponding rules in England and guarantee their efficiency. In France, many of these rules have not a natural basis; in other words, institutions are lacking which are the necessary correlative to the same rules in England; the efficiency of the French rules is often handicapped by the lack of those principles which alone would justify them. Nowhere has criminal procedure such deep roots in the moral and social customs as in England; nowhere has its evolution more closely corresponded to the development of the nation and its destinies. In no other country can it look back on as many centuries of existence and experience; and an enlightened lawgiver cannot overlook such an advantage. Nowhere is criminal procedure better protected by sane guarantees, nor contributes as efficiently and generally in maintaining public order; while, by its method of guaranteeing absolute personal liberty, it is in great favour with the whole nation.

"The study of English, Scotch, and American law presents, however, some difficulties. Both theoretical and practical textbooks leave much to be desired in the way of stating fundamental principles and details. The authors, writing practical handbooks for their compatriots, in referring to the national law, assume that the reader is thoroughly acquainted with social and legal customs of which a foreigner is most likely totally ignorant. In order to get a thorough insight into English procedure, one must examine specific cases in their details, and see how fundamental principles are applied in their decision. It is imperative to know the course of judicial decision, and the historical development of institutions from time immemorial. The legal views of judges, as shown in the final instructions to the jury or in the introductory part of the judgments, must be analyzed, and the reasons ascertained on which rest the legal decision in each case. It is necessary, finally, to study public opinion and national feeling, as is expressed and interpreted by judges and lawyers, by citizens on jury duty, and by lawgivers.

"The present work aims at meeting the demand for an historical examination of each institution from its origin until the present day. It attempts to show how these institutions are connected with social and political customs and the stage of civilization of the people. The fundamental principles of the English system, and their application in numerous criminal cases, will be discussed, with citations from particular cases and instructions by judges. To succeed in such an undertaking is only possible by personal investigation, by consultations with jurists and other citizens, and by perusal of statistics and parliamentary reports. By such a method an exact picture can be secured of the judicial system, of its operation, and of reform measures proposed in different details. More than fifteen hundred criminal cases tried during the last three years were studied by the author, either by personally taking notes during the proceedings, or by perusing the shorthand reports and the journals, as well as the reports in the extremely valuable collection of Arkley (for Scotland). For the description of the actual conditions of criminal practice in the United States, the assistance of several leading legal scientists was secured.

"No impartial student of English criminal procedure could commend its complete imitation by other nations. This would do injustice to the improvements that have been introduced into French criminal procedure, and particularly to the many reforms made in German States since 1848, which were received with such favour by the public. It is undoubtedly true that whoever has watched trials of criminal cases in England is very strongly impressed with the efficiency of that system. While thoroughly recognizing the rights of the accused, and allowing him every liberty of defence, it insures the innocent person's acquittal and the guilty one's condemnation. And a system of criminal procedure, which shall conform to ideas of justice, and while inspiring the fullest confidence in each citizen, shall guarantee public order and security, must in the opinion of all intelligent men be of the greatest importance. They must consider how far it is feasible to establish a system of criminal procedure which will satisfy every requirement while avoiding the shortcomings observable in France, England, Scotland, the United States, and Germany. After a thorough study one will concede that English law can contribute a great deal to a theoretically and practically perfect system, and will yet be able to maintain that certain methods, whose efficient application in England, Scotland, and the United States is made possible by institutions peculiar to these countries and certain characteristics of their social life, would be impracticable in Germany.

"The present work is intended to prepare the reader for a more elaborate one, in which the shortcomings and defects of criminal procedure of different countries will be discussed more thoroughly, by analyzing the fundamental principles and their logical consequences. It is hoped to show in this work how a system of criminal procedure may be established, which shall safeguard in equal degree the interests of society and the liberty of the individual citizen, inspiring confidence in all worthy citizens and wholesome terror in all enemies of public order."

Mittermaier never wrote a handbook of Criminal Law, though he repeatedly declared that it was to be his life's work. Instead, he brought out the 12th (1836), the 13th (1840), and the 14th

(1847) edition of Feuerbach's *Handbook* ; to this he added numerous footnotes, in which he expressed his own ideas and embodied also the views of other authors, which were frequently opposed to Feuerbach's.

Besides all this, he wrote countless reviews and reports, covering the whole field of legal science, which were published partly in German and foreign journals, partly in the periodicals which he edited himself. Two of the latter, the oldest and most influential publications of German legal science, have been mentioned above—the *Archiv für civilistische Praxis* and the *Archiv für Kriminalrecht*. For fifty years, from its foundation, he was chief editor of the first-named journal. Every number contains contributions by Mittermaier, either under the form of discussions of specific questions or of reviews of codes, draft-codes, and the literature of the Law of Procedure. It is like a running commentary for fifty years on all publications on this subject. Some of his most frequent topics were: the legal profession, relations between justice and administration, statistics of civil cases, marital property rights ; we also find essays on the law of guardianship, railroad law, and other subjects. For forty-two years, until its publication ceased, he was chief editor of the *Archiv für Kriminalrecht*. He contributed to it regularly articles on criminal law and procedure, and reviewed codes, draft-codes, and literature.

Mittermaier would discuss the theoretical side of a question only so far as it served an immediately attainable end. He always avoided sacrificing practical advantages to an excessive aspiration for ideal perfection. Wise circumspection and broad experience always guided his deeply philosophical mind towards the real goal—the final application of principles to practice. With this object constantly in view, while advising German legal scientists to take up the study of foreign legislation and works of foreign authors, Mittermaier insisted on their keeping up the thorough method and scientific synthesis peculiar to German science. Though he was heart and soul in this great work of progress on universal lines (made possible by his industry and his linguistic knowledge), he took extreme care not to fall into the error (too common in our own days) of failing to appreciate enough the laws and institutions of one's own country, while praising to the skies those of foreign lands. He carefully avoided advocating dangerous innovations—an advocacy often due to an exaggerated admiration of foreign institutions insufficiently known. A clear-cut, judicial instinct protected him against consenting to sacrifice time-honoured institutions of his own country to those of foreign lands, the introduction and adoption of which would frequently be impracticable.

A third publication, founded by Mittermaier and C. S. Zachariae (later edited in co-operation with R. v. Mohl and for a time with Warnkoenig), attained great influence; this was the *Critical Review of Legal Science in Foreign Countries*.[1] Here Mittermaier published also many articles on foreign legal institutions, codes, and literature. Most of the more prominent jurists of foreign countries became its contributors, and thus the comparative study of law assumed international importance. After the *Archiv für Kriminalrecht* ceased to be published in 1857. Mittermaier (beginning with vol. x., 1858) joined the staff of the *Gerichtssaal* (first number in 1849), which was primarily devoted to Criminal Law. Many of his criminalistic essays appeared in this journal, as well as in Goltdammer's *Archiv für preussisches Strafrecht*, and in *Der Allgemeinen Deutschen Strafrechtszeitung* (v. Holtzendorff), to which he was a contributor.[2]

Mittermaier's active part in public life began in 1827, when he was elected a member of the legislative body of Baden, to which he belonged until its dissolution. The city of Bruchsal was represented by him in the Lower House of Baden from 1831 to 1840. In that year he resigned, crushed with grief by the death of his eldest son, Dr. Martin Mittermaier (whose graduating treatise, *Ueber die Gründe der Verpflichtung zur Edition von Urkunden*, (Heidelberg, 1835), is still considered a valuable contribution to science). He accepted a seat again from 1845 to 1849. With the exception of the first two years of his parliamentary activity, he was the presiding officer of the Lower House during the sessions of 1833, 1835, 1837, 1839, and 1845. Many legal and administrative reforms of far-reaching importance were secured by Mittermaier's active co-operation: a law regulating municipal self-government, relief for the peasantry, codes of civil and criminal procedure and of criminal law, laws introducing the jury system, and many others. He strongly favoured oral procedure, publicity, a public prosecuting attorney in civil procedure,

[1] *Kritische Zeitschrift für Rechtswissenschaft des Auslandes*, 28 vols., Heidelberg, 1828-1856.
[2] Many of the above contributions were translated into English and French, in books or periodicals.

and later the jury system. In criminal procedure he advocated thorough investigation of facts, humane penalties, and prison reform. The question of the jury system required an especially tactful treatment. At a time when it was of the utmost importance to convince the authorities and the lawyers of the advantages of oral and public procedure, in order to enlist their sympathy for this reform measure, Mittermaier refrained from publicly discussing the question of the jury. But as soon as both measures had been adopted by the legislature, he took up the question of the jury, which he had carefully investigated in France and other countries, and advocated its introduction. His numerous essays and articles on prison reform, life sentences, deportation, and capital punishment, had a decisive influence in making criminal law more humane. One who compares the principles advocated by Feuerbach and Grolmann at the beginning of the nineteenth century with the present state of criminal science and law in Germany will realize what invaluable services Mittermaier rendered.

Mittermaier's admirable services as president of the Lower House of Baden led to his election, on March 31, 1848, at Frankfurt, president of the first German parliament. After the failure of this German struggle for a constitution, he retired from politics, refusing for years the invitation from many districts to become their representative in the Lower House of Baden. In the civic life of Heidelberg, whose honorary freedom was conferred upon him in 1838, he was vitally interested. He was a member of the city council, the school board, and numerous benevolent societies, being one of the founders and directors of the relief society and the orphanage. In a memorial address, State Councillor Lamey has drawn us a picture of Mittermaier in the following appreciative terms: "Mittermaier was absolutely free from selfishness and prejudice. He undertook as his life's task to promote the welfare of the State and all its citizens. The misery of the poor, the appeal of the oppressed, and the affliction of prisoners touched his heart. All could rely upon his help, without being questioned as to their responsibility for the misfortune. Schools, orphan asylums, and other charitable institutions always secured his active co-operation. He tried unceasingly to lessen all forms of unnecessary distress and suffering, caused by human selfishness, superstition, and unkindness." By his teaching and writing, and by his varied social activity he did more than his share for the improvement of laws and for the raising of the standard of civilization.

His desire for knowledge induced him to spend his vacations travelling about in search of additional information on foreign countries, their inhabitants and institutions, instead of seeking a rest from his fatiguing professional activity. Besides collecting literature during these trips, he met the best-known German and foreign legal scientists, lawyers, and statesmen. His first Italian trip, for instance, yielded a rich harvest of rare books of medieval legal literature, which he carried home in his knapsack. Italy, suffering in her political and spiritual development from foreign oppression, attracted his special interest. Eight times he crossed the Alps, and in his *Conditions in Italy* he expressed his deep sympathy with that country. France and Belgium were frequently visited; he there came in contact not only with native, but also with Spanish and Portuguese statesmen and legal scientists. In 1850, when already sixty-three years old, he went to England and Scotland, thoroughly prepared by careful studies of their institutions and language. By personal contact with statesmen, lawyers, and prison officials, he was able to fill in the gaps in his knowledge of English legal and penal institutions. A much cherished project to visit the United States was never realized, but he gathered an unusually vast fund of information on legal conditions in that country by personal correspondence with statesmen and legal scientists in many States of the Union. In later years his vacations were specially devoted to visits to prisons and insane asylums. He attended the two international congresses of charities and correction in Brussels and Frankfurt; at the latter he was made temporary presiding officer. In 1846 and 1847 he went to the Congresses in Lübeck and Frankfurt. In Lübeck he was asked to prepare a report on the jury system for the next meeting in Frankfurt; and this report was there adopted. This led to the general introduction of the jury system after 1848.

His professional success and the honours bestowed on him in steadily increasing numbers as his age advanced never affected in the least his simple and modest character. Neither university titles, nor the tributes of thousands of scholars from every corner of the globe, nor the many German and foreign orders of merit nor his membership in the most important academies and scientific societies of the world, produced the slightest change in his character or manners. A helping hand was always extended to the most humble, as well as to the most prominent. He enjoyed the dedication of a work by an unknown author quite as much as one by a writer of repute. He lent freely the books which stocked his extensive library. He would answer any question from any part of the world. Mittermaier had become so famous an authority, not only on civil procedure, but also on general foreign law and its literature, that courts of law and legal scientists often saved themselves the trouble of investigating on their own account by simply referring the question to him.

His fiftieth jubilee as a doctor, in 1859, brought visits from deputations of the Universities of Heidelberg, Freiburg, and Basel, of primary and secondary schools, of representatives of the government, the municipality, and the clergy, and of many societies. The president of the Supreme Court offered congratulations in the name of the courts of law of Baden, eulogizing especially his merits as a legislator and legal scientist. The legal and philosophical faculties of nearly all German Universities commemorated the event by sending letters of congratulation. His doctor's diploma was renewed (according to custom) by the faculty of law, and the philosophical faculty of the University of Heidelberg conferred upon him the honorary title of doctor of philosophy. Numerous scientific works were dedicated to him on this occasion.

After 1859 Mittermaier began to restrict his academic, though not his literary, activity. We have mentioned before that he became greatly interested, during the later years of his life, in prison reform, the jury system, and the abolition of capital punishment. Most of the works written after 1858 related to these topics. His book on Capital Punishment,[1] published in 1862, the embodiment of fifty years of work and experience, astonished German and foreign legal scientists with its exhibition of indefatigable energy on the part of a man of seventy-six, and forced many to reconsider their ideas on this grave problem.

When repeated attacks of sickness began to undermine his seemingly robust health, he spoke often to his intimate friends of his intention of giving up his academic work. He suspended his lecture course in May, 1867, under an attack of pleurisy.

On his eightieth birthday he gave to the University of Heidelberg his library of 15,000 volumes, a royal gift, which will immortalize his name in the University.

He died of heart disease on August 28, 1867, a painless and beautiful death.

Characteristics.—The most appropriate epithet for Mittermaier is humanitarian; for this describes most adequately both the strength and the weakness of his talents. His chief aim throughout his life was to turn to practical use the abundant material which had been contributed to legal science. He was enabled by his astonishing receptivity and his learning to use these resources to the utmost. Legal science in his opinion embodied the principles which rule human society. As they continually change, he favoured a constant re-examination of the law and of social phenomena and social needs. He put on record even the minutest details of progress. The Historical School of Law had had proclaimed as its chief purpose the critical study of the existing laws and their historical evolution. But Mittermaier, aiming far beyond this, set as the task of his life the rational examination and improvement of existing laws. He advocated at the outset of his career improvements in procedure, especially in the antiquated criminal procedure, though the necessity of the introduction of the jury system dawned only slowly upon him. In his teaching and writing he tried to familiarize the people thoroughly with a subject, showing its evolution and the practical working out of fundamental principles. He was never content to advance only one argument for the support of a theory, but generally discussed it from many points of view. He relied, for instance, upon psychiatry and legal medicine to support his views on the needed changes of criminal law and procedure. Taking the point of view of comparative legal history, he showed how the almost hitherto unknown Italian law had influenced the evolution of Roman-German civil and criminal law and procedure; he likewise drew attention to the part played by Germanic and later sources of law. He was the first author to become thoroughly acquainted with the foreign literature on German legal science and on the evolution of German law. Until Mittermaier's indefatigable industry increased the scope of German knowledge in such astonishing degree, only the few most important foreign codes were considered by German jurists.

He was one of the founders and most influential representatives of the science of comparative law, which aims to collect all available material on the law of every people in all periods, and thus to prepare a basis for more uniform legislation in all civilized countries. Though much here remains still to be accomplished, Mittermaier has pointed out, in his more important works, the general legal principles and their relation and efficiency in the whole domain of social institutions of many countries. His method was to asecrtain how far they differed or were identical in theory and in practice, and how expedient would be the adoption of foreign principles in German law. Thus Mittermaier must be deemed the most important mediator between German and foreign legal science. Of all German legal scientists, even Savigny not excepted, his name is internationally best known and most esteemed.

Though his activity covered so much ground that even a detailed survey is difficult enough, he used to tell his friends that only by force of circumstances had he taken up so many different subjects; and he strongly advised younger men to concentrate their efforts and to specialize; for this alone guarantees progress in science. Mittermaier, as a jurist, was of prodigious fertility; he never allowed his political and public activities to interfere with his indefatigable industry along scientific lines. He was one of the most influential popularizers of legal science, of which he thoroughly knew every branch.

In the history of penal law his name is immortal; and he has here earned the title of the foremost legal scientist of his century. Posterity will for ever hold in memory how much progress was achieved through Mittermaier's efforts, and how many projects of reform still awaiting fruition were proposed and made possible by his enlightened toil.

FRIEDRICH CARL VON SAVIGNY

FRIEDRICH CARL VON SAVIGNY

THE ancient family to which Friedrich Carl von Savigny belonged was of Lorraine origin, deriving its name from the Castle of Savigny, near Charmes, in the valley of the Moselle, and Paul de Savigny, an ancestor of the jurist, was born at Metz in 1622. The family were Calvinists, and retained their German allegiance on the transfer of Lorraine to France. Paul entered the Swedish army, and settled in a military capacity in Germany, dying at Kirchheim in 1685. His son Louis-Jean became a lawyer, and served the Prince of Nassau. In 1692 he published a work attacking the ambitious wars of Louis XIV. He died in 1701. His son Louis, who was born in 1684 and died in 1740, also held a political office. Chrétien-Charles-Louis, the son of Louis, was born in 1726 at Trabens on the Moselle, and attained to a considerable position in diplomatic and political circles. He was a member of the assembly which met at Frankfort to represent one of the ten Circles of the Empire, the Circle of the Upper Rhine. On this body he was a representative of various princes. Friedrich Carl von Savigny (to adopt the German form of the name) was born at Frankfort on February 21, 1779. The father of the jurist was a Lutheran, the mother a Calvinist. In those days the Calvinists were not allowed to worship in Frankfort, though the ministers were very gifted men. The town was dominated by the Lutherans, who made up for the inefficiency of their clergy by the sufficiency of their police. The Calvinists were obliged to worship out of the town at the village of Bockenheim, and thither, Sunday by Sunday, the little fellow was taken by his mother, despite the father's adherence to the popular faith.

His mother watched over the child's early education with exemplary care. M. Charles Guenoux tells us that "she taught him French with the tragedies of Racine and *Les Veillées du Château* of Madame de Genlis. He had hardly reached the age of three years when she was already reading the Bible to him, and perhaps we ought to attribute to her lessons and to her example that truly religious spirit which formed one of the salient traits in the character of her son." Her life had many sorrows to foster her natural piety. All her children except Frédéric died young, and in 1791 her husband died. In 1792 she herself passed away, and at the age of thirteen Friedrich Carl von Savigny was left an orphan without sisters or brothers. His father's best friend, a famous lawyer, M. de Neurath, the Assessor of the Imperial Chamber at Wetzlar, became another father to the boy, and personally superintended the education of his son and Friedrich von Savigny. When they reached the age of fifteen he plunged them into a terrible course, comprising the science of law, natural law, international law, Roman law, German law, and so forth. The principles were driven into the boys' minds by the system of question and answer, and finally they were induced to commit to memory a vast volume of speculative thought. It was an extraordinary training, recalling to some extent the aridity of Mill's early life, but it was modified by the abiding influence of his mother and the personal tenderness of M. de Neurath. We are told that Savigny revolted against the unreality of this shadow-land of thought. Indeed his whole after-life of work was in a sense a protest against the unhistoric school of thought which robed in unreality his earliest period of intellectual effort. Neurath's lessons must, however, have been extraordinarily effective, for they turned the entire interests of the youth into the direction of the theory and history of law. At the age of seventeen (Easter, 1795) he joined Marburg University, and attended successive courses by Erxleben and Weiss on the Pandects.

Weiss was a dramatic and effective teacher, and he placed his fine library at the disposal of Savigny, who became one of his private pupils. Indeed, though not a lawyer of great fame, he really turned the mind of Savigny in the direction of the change of method that was then in the air. Weiss was a bitter opponent of Wolff and other standard authors, and though he did not accept the entire views of Hugo and Naubold, he felt that a sense of history or evolution was a necessary element in the study of law. Savigny, who had suffered as a boy many things from what we may call the *a priori* school of law, drank in the new doctrine with avidity, and, passing in October, 1796, to the University of Göttingen, his historical leanings were confirmed by the brilliant lecturing of Spittler on universal history. Göttingen had nothing else worth having to give this student, but it did, in fact, give him the one thing needful at the moment. An illness in the spring of 1797 interrupted work, and in October Savigny returned to Marburg for further study. From 1799 to 1800 he travelled through Germany, visiting various universities, including Leipzig and Jena, and devoting his entire time to study. In the year 1800 he received the degree of doctor at Marburg, his dissertation on the occasion being entitled *De concursu Delictorum formali* (*Vermischte Schriften*, iv. 74). The same year he became an authorized teacher (*Privatdocent*) at Marburg, and lectured on criminal law. He also lectured (as an additional or extraordinary professor) on the ten last books of the Pandects Ulpian, the Law of Succession, Obligations, the Methodology of Law, and the History of Roman Law. In these courses we indeed see laid out the ground-plan of his life's work. M. Guenoux (from whose work this life of Savigny is largely derived[1]) tells us of the growth of his attitude towards history. He says:

"L'Histoire du droit romain de Hugo avait excité vivement l'intérêt de Savigny, et par ses formes souvent énigmatiques, plutôt éveillé que satisfait sa curiosité. Les améliorations de onze éditions successives ont plus que décuplé l'ouvrage original sans faire disparaître entièrement ce caractère. Au reste, Savigny a toujours professé une respectueuse reconnaissance pour les travaux de Hugo, et quoiqu'il n'ait jamais suivi ses cours, c'est peut-être le seul jurisconsulte moderne qui ait eu de l'influence sur son développement."

No doubt this is largely true, but in fact Savigny came upon the scene at a moment when there was a struggle in progress between the supporters of the school of traditional learning and thinkers of the Hegelian type who desired to demonstrate and share in the processes of evolution or history. It must be remembered that Savigny represents a stage in a movement that is really a Renaissance movement, and that the eighteenth-century theories of law as put forward by Wolff and Vattel and many of their followers was rather an intellectual interlude than a

[1] *Histoire du Droit Romain au Moyen-Âge*, par M. de Savigny, traduite de l'Allemand sur la dernière édition et précédée d'une notice sur la vie et les écrits de l'auteur par M. Charles Guenoux (four volumes, one and two in one, Paris, 1839). But see also for the life and works of the jurist, *Friedrich Carl von Savigny : sein Wesen und Wirken*, by Professor Rudorff (Weimar, 1862), and a paper by Mr. William Guthrie in the *Law Magazine and Review* for May, 1863; Ihering, *Gesammelte Aufsätge;* Mignet, *Nouveaux Éloges Historiques*, 1877.

definite disturbance of the Renaissance movement. The pre-Renaissance jurisconsults from the twelfth to the fifteenth century, the Glossators[1] as they are called, had been engaged in the practical work of deriving from Roman law a working code that should destroy and replace the rapidly forming feudal law. With the Renaissance came Italian and French thinkers destined to do more than this—Andrea Alciati (1492-1550) and Jacobus Cujacius (Jacques Cujas) of Toulouse (1522-1590). Joseph Scaliger said of these two men, "Ce qu'Alciat a commencé, Cujas l'a accompli." Alciati gave new life, new literary form, to the study of jurisprudence; but Cujas did more than this, he penetrated into the very spirit of Roman law. M. Lerminier, in his *Introduction générale à l'Histoire du Droit* (1829, cap. v., pp. 43-46), says of Cujas:

"Ne craignons pas de le dire, il a aimé le droit romain en poëte, il a nourri le sentiment le plus profond de sa réalité, et, pa l'énergie qu'il a déployée dans cette voie, il s'est fait le véritable fondateur de l'école historique du droit : c'est de lui que procède l'école historique allemande en ce qui touche le droit romain. . . . Son génie : c'est un esprit d'historien, c'est une imagination d'artiste ; sous sa plume, tout est historique, individuel ; aussi dans la volumineuse collection de ses œuvres vous ne trouverez pas un ouvrage qui ne soit un commentaire, une explication, une note sur les vestiges de l'antiquité. Cujas est le modèle de l'exégèse."

The learned writer (M. Rapetti) of the article on Cujas in the *Nouvelle Biographie Générale*, after quoting the opinion of M. Lerminier, adds this important reflection :

"L'œuvre de Cujas ne fut pas seulement une explication plus habile de la loi romaine, un modèle d'exégèse, une révélation du vrai génie de la législation latine : en étudiant la loi romaine comme un objet de restauration historique, Cujas a obtenu un autre avantage ; le premier, il a suscité cette idée, à savoir qu'il est pour chaque civilisation une loi propre, et par là il a contribué à reléguer la loi romaine dans son antiquité vénérable ; il a émancipé de l'empire trop absolu de cette loi l'autonomie des nouvelles sociétés."

Cujas in the immense output of his work foreshadows the industry of Savigny. The six great folios of his collected

[1] The jurisconsults of the school of Bologna, Accurse, Bartole, Vinerius, etc. (see *Nouvelle Biographie Générale*, tome xii., art. de *Cujas*, col. 592).

works[1] overwhelm the mind. The first folio deals fully with four books of the Institutes of Justinian, twenty-nine titles from Ulpian, and with Julius Paulus. The second folio contains the brilliantly restored works of Papinian. The third gives us Paratitla in nine books of the Codicis Justiniani and a commentary on the three last books (x., xi., xii.) of the Codex, an exposition of the Novels and of the five books relating to Feuds, together with twenty-eight books of observations and emendations. The fourth folio gives us Paulus on the Edict and his books of Questions, and also the Responsa of Paulus, Neratius, Marcellus, Ulpian, Modestinus, and Scævola ; Notes on Modestinus and the works of Salvius Julianus. Folios v. and vi. contain the post-mortem publications (edited by T. Guerinus and C. Colombet), comprising Commentaries on no less than seventy-six titles of the Digest and innumerable notes on the Codex of Justinian and on Books ii., iii., and iv. of the Decretals of Gregory IX. Cujas was rightly called Jurisconsultus, for he placed Roman law on a new footing and brought it into line with the laws that it was destined to affect. This sturdy and genial scholar[2] and his bitter but brilliant opponent Hugues Doneau (Donellus) (1527-1591) were (in the matter of the study of law) the forerunners of Leibnitz (1646-1716), whose juridical works mark a definite stage in the study of the law, works such as *Nova methodus discendæ docendæque*[2] *jurisprudentiæ* (Frankfort, 1667) and *Codex juris gentium diplomaticus* (1693) with its supplement *Mantissa Codicis Juris diplomatici* (1700) ; of the universal-minded Jean-Etienne Pütter (1725-1807), who at Marburg, Halle, and Jena became deeply proficient in classics, mathematics, philosophy, Roman, feudal, and public law, who lectured on law (1746) at Göttingen, who produced between 1776 and 1783 his *Bibliographica du droit public allemand*, who wrote his *Manuel de l'histoire d'Allemagne* in 1772 and his *Développement historique de la constitution de l'empire d'allemagne* in 1786. In Pütter we see the exact spirit of the historical school. A descendant of these men was Gustave Hugo (1764-1844), who deliberately based his methods on Leibnitz and

[1] Jacobi Cuiacii, *IC. Operum quæ de jure fecit*, Paris, Apud Hervetum de Mesnil, 1637. Four volumes in six, prefaced by a life of, and many epitaphs on Cujas.

[2] "Vir quadrato corpore, firmoque ac bene constituto, adeo ut ex eo manans sudor non insuavis esset odoris (quod ille naturæ beneficium cum Alexandro Macedone commune se habere ludens nonnumquam inter amicos jactavit), statura brevi, barba tum longa et cana, sed in juventate nigerrima, capillitio simili, colore candido, voce firma et clara ". (*Vita*).

Pütter. He devoted much time to the historical documents and legislation connected with Roman law, and in 1788 published *Les Fragments d'Ulpien*, and was at once called to a professorship at Göttingen. Hugo classified law into persons (their state, their relations to the family and the city, their nature, character, and the method of acquiring and losing property) and the actions necessary for establishing or defending rights. This classification was adopted in the Civil Code. This was a philosophical classification. But Hugo did not neglect history. He divided Roman law into three periods : the period up to the xii. Tables, the Prætorian, and the Imperial periods. In 1790 he issued a History of Roman Law, in 1812 a Manual of Roman Law since the Time of Justinian, and between 1818 and 1829 he published his Elements of the History of Roman Law up to the Time of Justinian.[1] Through Hugo the whole historic school from the days of the Renaissance concentrated on Savigny.

At Marburg Savigny instantly made his mark as a teacher. We have the testimony of Jacob and Wilhelm Grimm (who both were pupils of his in 1802 and 1803) as to his capacity. Wilhelm Grimm wrote in his autobiography (pp. 170-1) as follows :

"Il me semble que ce qui attirait et captivait si puissamment ses auditeurs, c'était la facilité et la vivacité de sa parole jointes à tant de calme et de mesure. Les talents oratoires peuvent éblouir quelque temps, mais ils n'attachent pas. Savigny parlait d'abondance et ne consultait que rarement ses notes. Sa parole toujours claire, sa conviction profonde et en même temps une sorte de retenue et de modération dans son langage faisaient une impression que n'aurait pas produite l'éloquence la plus abondante, et tout en lui concourait à l'effet de sa parole. . . .

"Il nous fit comprendre la valeur des études historiques et l'importance de la méthode. Ce sont là des obligations que je ne saurais trop reconnaître, car sans lui je n'aurais peut-être jamais donné à mes études une bonne direction. Pour combien de choses n'a-t-il pas éveillé notre intérêt ! Combien de livres n'avons-nous pas empruntés à sa bibliothèque ! Avec quel charme ne nous a-t-il pas lu quelque-fois des passages de Wilhelm Meister, des poésies de Goethe ! L'impression que j'en ai conservée m'est encore si présente qu'il me semble l'avoir entendu hier."

It is a charming picture, bringing out not only the learning

[1] The influence of Haubold (1766—1824) on Savigny must also be kept in mind.

and the clarity of the man, but his humanity and charity. One impression conveyed by the lectures is the impression that all great lecturers indelibly impress on the minds of their pupils. Who that heard Maitland lecture can think of it as having been farther away than yesterday ? But Savigny was only twenty-three when he so impressed the great Grimm brethren !

Thirty years later he made a similar impression on M. Charles Guenoux. He wrote in 1839:

"Ce qui m'a surtout frappé, c'est la vivacité et la chaleur d'un cours qu'il répétait alors pour la vingt-cinquième fois. Son enseignement offre chaque année un intérêt nouveau, parce que chaque année on y retrouve le fruit de nouvelles études, les découvertes les plus récentes et le dernier état de la science. Aussi Savigny n'est-il pas insensible à l'intérêt qu'il excite dans son nombreux auditoire, et c'est ce qui lui fait continuer ses leçons quand des travaux plus importants peut-être sembleraient demander tout son temps. Sa parole abondante et précise éclaire si bien les matières les plus obscures que ses élèves n'en soupçonnent la difficulté, que si plus tard ils ont besoin de chercher une solution qui leur est échappée. Sa méthode est surtout remarquable lorsqu'à propos de matières controversées, il a occasion d'exposer des doctrines nouvelles. Sa parole, alors plus simple et plus grave, exprime une conviction profonde jointe à une modestie sincère ; bien différent de ces professeurs qui, pour persuader leur auditoire, recourent à tous les artifices de l'avocat comme s'il s'agissait d'un plaidoyer, et font d'une question scientifique une question d'amour-propre et de personnes."

Savigny's success as a teacher did not check, nay, rather encouraged, his efforts as a student. His business as yet was not to write books, but to study texts, and so to make possible a real revival in the scientific study of law. His master Hugo had already done much in this direction. M. Guenoux points out, as I have ventured to point out above, the value of Hugo's work. He found a lifeless and arbitrary school of Roman lawyers at work, men who never recognized the heredity, so to speak, of Roman law, men who had forgotten the lessons of the Renaissance.

"Mais en 1788, Hugo appela l'attention sur Ulpien et commença une réforme semblable à celle que Cujas avait accomplie au seizième siècle. Animé du même esprit que ce grand homme, il replaça la science du droit sur ses véritables bases en lui restituant le secours de la philosophie et de l'histoire. Haubold et Cramer partagent avec Hugo la gloire de cette régénération de la science."

M. Guenoux goes on to protest against the belief in his time (1839) that German jurists fell into two schools, the historical school and the philosophical school. The distinction was merely one of *pace*; all followed the Cujacian School and refused to isolate jurisprudence from either philosophy or history. That may have been the case in 1839, but it certainly was not the case in the mid-eighteenth century, when eminent jurists, men such as Wolff and Vattel, did in fact base new jurisprudence on *a priori* theories. The great triumph of the school of which Savigny is the shining and immortal light was the absolute destruction of the *a priori* method and the establishment on an impregnable basis of the vital and vitalising principles of the Renaissance.

In 1803 appeared Savigny's famous work on the Right of Possession, *Das Recht des Besitzes*. It is not possible (from considerations of space) here to supply an analysis of this treatise, but something must be said as to the scope and value of a work which Austin in his *Province of Jurisprudence Determined* (ed. 1832, App., p. xxxviii) declared to be "of all books upon law, the most consummate and masterly." It is divided into six books. The first deals at length with the notion of Possession. Savigny says that "by the possession of a thing, we always conceive the condition, in which not only one's own dealing with the thing is physically possible, but every other person's dealing with it is capable of being excluded." The exercise of property takes place by virtue of this condition of detention. Savigny's object was to consider the rights of possession (*jus possessionis*), and not the right to possess (*jus possedendi*), and in the first book he defines the notion in form and in substance: "in *form* by describing the rights which require possession for their foundation, thus giving the meaning which the non-juridical notion of Detention acquires in jurisprudence so as to allow it to be understood as a legal entity, as Possession; in *substance* by enumerating the conditions which the Roman law itself prescribes for the existence of Possession, and thus pointing out the precise modifications under which Detention operates as Possession." The second book deals with the acquisition of possession, the third with its loss; the fourth treats of the interdicts that act as remedies for the protection of possession; the fifth deals with possession in relation to legal rights that are separated from actual property (*juris quasi possessio*), such as personal and real easements and superficies (buildings). The last book deals with a subject which was necessary from Savigny's point of view to complete anything like exhaustive treatment of so important a branch of law as the doctrine of Possession. He says: "The theory of Possession has been discussed in the first five books of this work without any reference whatever to anything that may have been incorporated into the Roman law in modern times; and this method of inquiry is always necessary when we do not desire, by confounding the old law with the new, to misunderstand both together." It is important not to pass over the historical question, for "of all the important errors which are commonly entertained as to the Roman view of Possession, there is perhaps not one which has not also been raised in the Canon and German law." He goes on to point out as to the notion of Possession that, while in Roman law it referred only to property and *jura in re*, subsequently and especially by the Canon law it was extended to every possible right, including rights of personal status and obligations.[1] Thus the Roman law has been expanded to meet new objects. The forms by which Possession is protected were also modified in post-Roman times. The Spoliatory Suits in so far as they applied to prædial servitudes were a legitimate extension of the Roman law to meet cases that had not arisen when that law was in its prime. Savigny agrees with Mühlenbruch that these suits in so far as they were legitimate were an extension of the interdict *de Vi* to a third *mala fide* possessor.

It is in this final passage of his work that Savigny turns on the opponents of the new jurisprudence, and gladly cites in his favour Mühlenbruch, the author of the *Doctrina Pandectarum*. "An empty cry is often raised against the endeavours of what is called the historical school, to clothe every right exclusively with Roman forms, and thereby to do injustice to the original inventions of practice, and to the development of modern scientific intelligence." This attack from first to last irritated, by its obvious injustice, Savigny, and it is with a cry of delight that he shows how Mühlenbruch shares his views as to Spoliatory Suits: "Could this author have been a prophetic disciple of the German historical school?" Savigny goes on to show that the "absurd and vexatious" possessory suit used in Germany, Italy, Spain, and France from the thirteenth century down to his own day,

[1] I may note here that an analysis and summary of Savigny's latest work—that on *Obligations in Roman Law* (1851-3)—was published by Mr. Archibald Brown in 1872.

a suit called *Possessorium summarium* or *summariissimum* (a suit in which he once acted as a judge), could not be fitted into any scientific evolution of Roman law. He adds: "In modern times undoubtedly legal rules have been adopted which were unknown to the Roman law; but the whole Roman theory is so far from being broken in upon by the above rules, that on the contrary they cannot be understood except by treating them as additions to the above theory [of possession], the validity of which is thereby clearly recognised." To-day in dealing with Savigny's work on Possession it would be wise to preface the study of it by a close perusal of Dr. Roby's lengthy treatment of the doctrine of Possession as understood in the times of the Antonines. Savigny would have appreciated the need for a full study of this elaborate portion of Dr. Roby's work.

It is valuable to read what Savigny's pupil Guenoux said of his treatise on Possession in 1839:

"On sait que dans ce traité, après avoir passé en revue les quarante-quatre ouvrages qui composent la littérature de cette partie du droit, l'auteur s'est livré à une étude profonde et originale des textes, et qu'à l'aide de la philologie et de l'histoire, il a établi sur cette matière si difficile des doctrines entièrement nouvelles, ou plutôt a retrouvé les doctrines des anciens jurisconsultes romains; mais ce qu'on ne sait pas, c'est qu'un travail aussi immense a été achevé en cinq mois. Cette heureuse fécondité prouve que malgré sa jeunesse Savigny ne s'était pas trop hâté de produire; et cette fécondité ne s'est pas tarie, parce que, semblable aux grands fleuves, il avait attendu pour couler que sa source fût pleine.

"L'histoire et la science du droit ont certains problèmes qui sont éternellement livrés aux disputes des hommes, et dont il paraît impossible de donner une solution définitive. Dans la polémique à laquelle ces questions ont donné lieu, Savigny n'a pas montré moins de sagacité que de candeur et de bonne foi, en rétractant ses opinions dès qu'un de ses adversaires en avançait une plus probable. Mais il est une foule de points où Savigny a eu la gloire de réunir tous les suffrages, et son livre, quoique purement théorique, a déjà eu la plus heureuse influence sur la pratique du droit en Allemagne, influence destinée à s'accroître, car pour la possession comme pour tant d'autres, le droit romain est souvent la raison écrite, la loi véritable, c'est à dire l'expression *des rapports nécessaires qui dérivent de la nature et des choses*."

This remarkable testimony to the gifts, the serious nature, and the abiding influence of Savigny written in 1839 might have been written to-day, for the greatness of Savigny increases with the passing years. The vigour of his patriotism, and his efforts on the behalf of the poor (as in the cholera outbreak of 1831) were scarcely less noticeable than his efforts as a teacher.

In 1804 Savigny married Fräulein Kunigunde Brentano, daughter of a Frankfort banker, a member of a family well known in German literature from the correspondence between her brother and sister, Clemens Brentano and Bettina von Arnim, with the poet Goethe. This marriage was an ideal union, since the wife, herself an orphan, had every thought in common with her husband. There were six children of the marriage. Two of them died in infancy. The only daughter married M. Constantin de Schinas, Minister of Education at Athens, where she died in 1835. She was full of brilliant promise, and her early death was the abiding grief of Savigny's life. It is said that the enormous work known as the *System of Modern Roman Law* was undertaken to help him to pass through this sorrow.

Shortly before his marriage Savigny had severed his connection with the University of Marburg, and, refusing tempting offers from the Universities of Heidelberg and Greifswald, he set out with his wife on a tour of research to certain famous libraries, to the libraries of Heidelberg, Stuttgart, Tubingen, Strasbourg, and Paris. In Paris he had the misfortune to lose (by robbery) all the material that he had collected through Germany. He called his old pupil Joseph Grimm to his aid, and with his help and the help of his wife and one of her sisters they conquered the abundant French manuscript material, including the unpublished and almost indecipherable letters of the great Cujas. In 1808 he took up for a year and a half professorial work at the University of Landshut. When he left for Berlin the grief of the students was unaffected. His sister-in-law Madame von Arnim, who was staying with him at the time of the change, wrote to Goethe:

"Que Savigny soit savant tant qu'il voudra, la bonté de son caractère surpasse encore ses qualités les plus brillantes. Les étudiants l'adorent, ils sentent qu'ils perdent en lui un bienfaiteur. Les professeurs le chérissent également, surtout les théologiens. . . . Savigny avait donné une vie nouvelle à l'université, qu'il avait su réconcilier les professeurs ou du moins calmer leurs inimitiés, mais que son influence bienfaisante s'était fait surtout sentir aux étudiants dont il avait augmenté la liberté et l'indépendance.

Je ne saurais vous exprimer le talent de Savigny à traiter avec la jeunesse. Les efforts, les progrès de ses élèves lui inspirent un véritable enthousiasme ;il se sent heureux s'ils réussissent à traiter les sujets qu'il leur propose ; il voudrait leur ouvrir le fond de son cœur ; il s'occupe de leur sort, il pense à leur avenir, et leur trace la route qu'éclaire son zèle bienveillant. On peut dire de Savigny que l'innocence de sa jeunesse est devenue l'ange gardien de sa vie. Le fond de son caractère est d'aimer ceux auxquels il consacre toutes les forces de son esprit et de son âme, et n'est-ce pas là ce qui met le sceau à la véritable grandeur ? La simplicité naïve avec laquelle sa science descend au niveau de chacun le rend doublement grand."[1]

On the foundation of the University of Berlin in 1810, one of the first-fruits of the great educational campaign that sprang out of the disastrous field of Jena, Wilhelm von Humboldt, the head of the new Prussian educational system, offered Savigny the chair of law, which, chiefly from patriotic motives, he accepted. The jurist held this chair until 1842. It was his practice to lecture on the Pandects (excluding the law of succession) in the winter Semester and the Institutes in the summer Semester. He also lectured on Ulpian, Gaius, and the Prussian Landrecht. Among his pupils at Berlin were Hollweg, Klenze, Göschen, the editor of Gaius, Blume, Rudorff, Keller, Dirksen, Barkow, Böcking, and Puchta. He also sat on the University Appellate Tribunal, known as the Spruch-Collegium, to which questions of law were referred for decision by other tribunals. At Berlin Savigny became an intimate friend and pupil of the great Niebuhr, whose mind and character so closely coincided with his own, and who pays him a just tribute in the preface to his History of Rome.

In 1811, Savigny was elected a member of the Berlin Academy, a precedent followed by most of the Academies of Europe in later years, and to this body he read papers on the Roman written contract, on the Voconian law, on the lawsuit relating to the loan of money by Marcus Brutus to the town of Salamina, on the Protection of Infants and the lex Plætoria, on the Rights of Creditors under the old Roman law, on the History of the Nobility in Modern Europe.

In 1814 the jurist (who was then acting as law tutor to the Prince Royal of Prussia) issued a brief work entitled *De la Vocation de notre siècle pour la législation et la science du droit,* in which he closely and brilliantly criticized the proposed Civil Code as

[1] Goethe's *Briefwechsel mit einem Kinde,* vol. ii., pp. 171-188 (2nd ed.).

not in fact adopting, as it proposed to adopt, the principles of the Roman law at all. In 1817 he was given the honorary title of Geheimer Justiz-Rath in recognition of his work on the Council of State.

In 1819 he was appointed Counsellor to the Court of Revision and Cassation at Berlin which had been formed to take the place of the Courts at Düsseldorf and Coblentz. This practical work was of the greatest benefit to his juridical studies. A little later a nervous breakdown, the result probably of years of close work, became imminent, and in fact from 1822 to 1828 he was subject to a form of nervous illness that rendered at times all work impossible. M. Guenoux attributes to this illness the delay in the publication of the History of Roman Law in the Middle Ages.[1] The first volume appeared in 1815, but the sixth was not issued until 1831.

Savigny laid the greatest stress on the necessity of tracing the course of Roman law through the Middle Ages. He writes to M. Guenoux: "Ignorer ce que les siècles intermédiaires ont ajouté au droit romain primitif est absolument impossible, tout ce que nous apprennent nos professeurs et les livres modernes en est imbu." No student of, let us say, Bracton could doubt this, and Maitland in his brilliant papers on "The Beatitude of Seisin" (*Law Quarterly Review*, vol. iv.) has shown how the doctrine of possession in English law completely changed as the pressure, so to speak, of the Roman lawyers died away. Consequently Savigny determined to deal exhaustively with the history of Roman law in the Middle Ages. His great work falls into two parts: the period before and the period after the foundation of the School of Bologna about the year 1100. In the first two volumes he deals with the earlier period, first in general and then in detailed form. He begins with the sources of law and judicial organization in Rome and the provinces in the fifth century. He follows this by treating the same themes in relation to the states that arose on the ruins of the Western Empire. In the second volume he deals with Roman law in the kingdoms of Burgundy, of the Visigoths, in the German Empire, in Saxon England, in the kingdom of the Ostrogoths, in Italy under the Greek domination and under the Pope and the Emperor in Lom-

---

[1] *Geschichte des römischen Rechts im Mittelalter* (6 vols., 8vo., Heidelberg, 1815-31). A second edition began to be issued from Heidelberg in 1834. The last and *seventh* volume appeared in 1851, with a preface dated in May of that year.

bardy. He finally shows the part played by the Church in preserving the Roman law. In the third volume he collects much material on the literature of Roman law after the foundation of the School of Bologna, and has an important chapter on the history of the European Universities. Indeed this general volume dealing with the history of Roman law from the twelfth century to the end of the Middle Ages is professedly a literary history of law, since Savigny found that such a history was indispensable for the comprehension of the evolution of the law. He says on this point :

"Le but de toute composition historique est d'offrir une représentation complète et vivante du passé. Plus ce passé est éloigné, moins on a de moyens d'arriver à ce but. Ainsi l'on découvre un détail, mais on ne sait comment le rattacher à l'ensemble, ou il lui manque cette lumière qui éclaire un fait historique comme un fait contemporain. Si le but de l'histoire ne peut-être atteint complètement, on ne doit rien négliger de ce qui nous en rapproche ; l'on ne doit donc rejeter aucun détail comme peu important en lui-même, ou comme étranger à l'objet direct de notre étude."

So, having given us the means of studying the legal literary history of the period, a bibliography of the subject (with full reference to the work of, amongst others, Johannes Andreæ of Bologna, Pastrengo the friend of Petrarch, Severinas, Trithemius, Diplovataccius, Johann Fichard, Benavidius, Pancirolus, Taisand : we miss in this place the name of Aymarus Rivallius, whose important history of the Civil Law in five books was published at Mainz in 1539[1]), and treated of the Universities, he passes on to the legal sources possessed by the Glossators and considers at length their work. In the fourth volume we get the elaborate detail foreshadowed in the previous volume. Here we can read at large in more than five hundred closely printed pages of Irnerius, of the four famous jurisconsults of Bologna (Bulgarus, Martinus, Jacobus, and Hugo), of Rogerius, the pupil of Bulgarus, Placentinus, Johannes Bassianus, Pillius, and many other Glossators, including the famous Vacarius and scarcely less famous Azo. In the middle of the thirteenth century a new and dismal

[1] There is a copy of this work in the fine civil law section of Lincoln's Inn Library. Savigny gives a brief note on Rivallius in his fourth volume (pp. 256-7) and declares this work to be "remarquable, malgré ses défauts, comme le premier qui ait été fait sur l'histoire du droit."

era opened for the study of law : the text was swallowed up in detailed comment and the true treatise disappeared. Indeed the School of the Glossators was dead. In the fourteenth century fortunately a partial revival of scientific method came which carried the science of law on to the time of the Renaissance, when it was able to assert its place in the thought of the world. Savigny traces in detail this long movement, and illustrates each step with ample reference to the works of the jurisconsults of the fourteenth and fifteenth centuries. In this work he threw open a field of research that will occupy jurists for centuries to come. Maitland's work in England is but a sample of what has to be done throughout Europe.

Savigny's work on *The Vocation of our Age for Legislation and Jurisprudence*, issued in 1814 and passing to a second edition in 1828, was a notable publication. It was neither more nor less than an attack on the system of the Code imposed upon Europe. Napoleon's Code he declares "served him as a bond the more to fetter nations : and for that reason it would be an object of terror and abomination to us, even had it possessed all the intrinsic excellence which it wants." He attacks the Code, however, chiefly from the point of view of a juridical thinker, since at the overthrow of Napoleon in 1814 his Code, which had been in force "in parts of Bavaria, Hesse Darmstadt, the Rhenish provinces of Prussia, the kingdom of Westphalia, Baden, the Hanseatic towns, and some other ultra-Rhenish provinces," was discarded by all Germany with the exception of the Rhenish provinces. The danger from a foreign Code no longer existed ; but there still existed the danger of a Code at all. The eminent lawyer Thibaut of Heidelberg advocated the establishment of a German Code, and Savigny determined to throw his great weight in the other scale and restore a natural evolution of law. He attacked the demand for a Code first on the ground that the times being as they were, and the preparation for a Code (thanks to the paucity of great German jurists in the eighteenth century) inadequate and the language juridically undeveloped, it was not then practicable to construct a Code ; and secondly on the ground that the three great existing Codes—the Code Napoléon, the Prussian Landrecht, and the Austrian Gesetzbuch—proved that in practice Codes were not successful. Savigny's attack on the Code Napoléon was just, though he admits that its form was embittered by patriotic feelings. He says :

"The Revolution, then, had annihilated, together with the old constitution, a great part of the law; both, rather from a blind impulse against everything established, and with extravagant senseless expectation of an undefined future, than in the hope of any definite improvement. As soon as Napoleon had subjected everything to a military despotism, he greedily held fast that part of the revolution which answered his purpose and prevented the return of the ancient constitution—the rest, which all were now sick of, and which might have proved an obstacle to himself, was to disappear; only this was not altogether practicable, as the effects of the years that had elapsed upon the modes of thought, manners and feelings of the people, were not to be effaced. This half-return to the former state of tranquillity was certainly beneficial, and gave the Code, which was founded about this time, its principal tendency. But this return was the result of lassitude and satiety, not the victory of nobler thoughts and feelings; nor, indeed, would there have been any opening for such in that condition of public affairs which, to the plague of Europe, was preparing. This want of a sound basis is discernible in the discussions of the *Conseil d'État*, and must impress every attentive reader with a feeling of despondency. To this was now added the immediate influence of the political constitution. This, when the Code was framed, was, in theory, republican in the revolutionary sense; but all, in reality, inclined to the recently developed despotism. The elements of uncertainty and change were consequently mixed up with its fundamental principles. Thus, for example, in 1803, Napoleon himself, in the Council of State, pronounced those same Substitutions to be injurious, of a bad moral tendency and unreasonable, which were re-established in 1806, and, in 1807, adopted into the Code. But as regards the state of public feeling, a far worse consequence of this quick succession was, that the last, so often sworn to, object of belief and veneration was in its turn, annihilated, and that expressions and forms came more and more frequently into collision with ideas, whereby, in the greater number, even the last remains of truth and moral consistency were necessarily extinguished. It would be difficult to imagine a state of public affairs more unfavourable for legislation than this." [1]

Turning to the technical side of the Code, Savigny argues that the Conseil d'État could have, from its ignorance of general juridical doctrines, little influence on the Code. It was, as a matter of fact, the work of jurists who, so far as Roman law

---

[1] I use the translation made from the 1828 edition by Mr. Abraham Hayward in 1831. (London: printed but not for sale.) A copy, here used, is in the Acton Library at Cambridge (C. 48, 929). There is another copy in the Middle Temple Library.

was concerned, necessarily based their work upon Pothier. Dupin declared that three-fourths of the Civil Code was literally extracted from his treatises. "A juridical literature in which he stands alone, and is almost revered and studied as the source, must, notwithstanding [the real value of Pothier], be pitiable." Savigny proceeds to eviscerate the framers of the Code, Bigot Preameneu, Portalis, and Maleville. Certainly they were not supremely intelligent jurists. The results of their work were bad in the extreme. In the selection of subjects "the most palpable defects are to be found by wholesale." But worse was to follow. "Far more important in this respect, and much more difficult in itself, is the selection of rules on the subjects actually treated of; consequently the finding of rules, by which particular cases are to be governed in future. Here the object was to master the leading principles, on which all certainty and efficacy in juridical matters depend, and of which the Romans afford us so striking an example. In this point of view, however, the French work presents a melancholy spectacle." The fundamental and precise notions—the rights of things and of obligations—upon which the Roman law of Property depends are in the Code vague and ill understood, and this leads to a confusion of ideas which in the form of a Code is dangerous to the public. Last, Savigny attacks the provisions in the Code for dealing with cases that are not in fact covered by a precise section of the Code. It was not possible to regard the rules dealing with such cases as organic developments out of the Code—with which we may compare, though Savigny does not give the parallel, the growth of the English common law to meet new cases—since the Code itself had no organic unity. The Code is only a mechanical mixture of the Revolution and pre-Revolution laws, and the mixture is not even a logical whole, a formal unity that might be logically developed to meet new cases. Consequently the supplemental rules had to be supplied from outside sources, such as (that vague thing) the law of nature, the Roman law and local pre-existing laws, and the general theory of law. This introduction of an abrogated law into the Cour de Cassation is a real evil. A practice of the Courts could grow up, but no real juridical growth. The rules could indeed be applied at the tyrannical discretion of the judges. This indictment of the French Code, if we except the political note at the beginning, is effective in the extreme, and should be considered in every step towards codification. Before considering his general notion of legal reform it will be well to say something of Savigny's criticism of the German and Austrian Codes.

Savigny's criticism of the Prussian Landrecht designed by Frederick II. in 1746 is not less penetrating though his natural if somewhat unjudicial hatred of France and all her works induces him to attribute to the Prussian jurists a far nobler outlook than that which inspired Napoleon and the unhappy framers of the Code. We may doubt if Suarez was a greater man than Pothier, or Volkmar (or Pachaly) than Portalis, but in any event Savigny declares that if "we regard the composition of the Landrecht, it confirms my opinion that no Code should be undertaken at the present time." Frederick II. designed a Code that should abolish judge-made law altogether; but, in fact, the Landrecht in its latest form gave the judge full powers of interpretation. But still this was, after all, only for particular cases. "With the Romans all depends on the jurist, by his thorough mastery of the system, being placed in a condition to find the law for every case that may arise. This is effected by the precise individual perception of particular legal relations, as well as by the thorough knowledge of the leading principles, their connection and subordination; and where, with them, we find law cases in the most restricted application, they, notwithstanding, constantly serve as the embodied expression of the general principle." This was not the case with the Landrecht, the provisions of which "neither reach the height of universal leading principles, nor the distinctness of individuality, but hang wavering between the two, whilst the Romans possess both in their natural connection." Savigny goes on to criticize the German language, "which generally speaking, is not juridically formed, and least of all for legislation." The French language, he adds, has a great advantage in this respect: that it had not been better used "is accounted for by the low state of knowledge" in France. The Austrian Gesetzbuch was begun in 1753; by 1765 the groundwork of the Code, "a manuscript work of eight large folios, mostly extracted from the commentators on the Roman law," was complete. This was abstracted by Horten, digested into code form by Martini, published, submitted to the provincial authorities and the Universities, and, slightly revised, issued as the Gesetzbuch in three parts, covering 561 widely printed pages. The Empress Maria Theresa directed the draughtsmen to employ "natural equity" as well as Roman law. In fact, there was no attempt to cover all particular cases. The notions of legal relations were defined, and the most general rules laid down. Savigny considered these notions as too general and undefined, and often based on an imperfect appreciation of the Roman authorities. The Roman clarity of definition is absent. Moreover, the practical rules of the Gesetzbuch are as incapable as the rules of the Code Napoléon of meeting particular cases. The Gesetzbuch falls back for the solution of particular cases on cases analogous to those provided for, and on "natural law"; the principle carries one but a short way, and the use of "natural law" is "fraught with danger to the administration of justice." The Gesetzbuch, like the Code and the Landrecht, therefore confirms Savigny's argument "that the present time has no aptitude for the undertaking of a Code." The unsuccess of three such efforts shows that "there must be some unsurmountable obstacles in the juridical state of the whole age."

What then, asks Savigny, are we to do when there are no Codes ? He would hold to the "same mixed system of common law and provincial law, which formerly prevailed throughout the whole of Germany . . . provided [that] jurisprudence does what it ought to do, and what can only be done by means of it." We have inherited "an immense mass of juridical notions and theories. . . . At present, we do not possess and master this matter, but are controlled and mastered by it, whether we will or not. This is the ground of all the complaints of the present state of our law, which I admit to be well founded : this, also, is the sole cause of the demand for Codes." Savigny adopts the Hegelian position : " It is impossible to annihilate the impressions and modes of thought of the jurists now living—impossible to change completely the nature of existing legal relations ; and on this twofold impossibility rests the indissoluble organic connection of generations and ages ; between which, development only, not absolute end and absolute beginning, is conceivable." Savigny with a brilliant flash of juridical insight turns the indestructibleness of legal notions to permanent gain. He says : " There is consequently no mode of avoiding this overruling influence of the existing matter ; it will be injurious to us so long as we ignorantly submit to it ; but beneficial if we oppose to it a vivid creative energy—obtain the mastery over it by a thorough grounding in history, and thus appropriate to ourselves the whole intellectual wealth of preceding generations." In any other process the law may lose its consciousness of nationality, and only through history " can a lively connection with the primitive state of the people be kept up ; and the loss of this connection must take away from every people the best part of its spiritual life." Savigny goes on to say that the object of the strict historical method of jurisprudence "is to trace every established system to its root, and thus discover an organic principle, whereby that which still has life may be separated from that which is lifeless and only belongs to history." The importance of Roman law is that " by reason of its high state of cultivation " it serves as a pattern for the labours of the modern jurist. The importance of the local or customary law is that " it is directly and popularly connected with us." The modifications of these two primitive systems are important as showing how both Roman law and local law have varied under the stress of actual needs and the application of legal theory. Roman law must be grappled with at the root ; we must enter into the minds of the Roman jurists if we are to appreciate it and apply it to modern uses. Do not be afraid because the textbooks are as yet imperfect : " Everything which Thibaut here says of the uncertainty of our textbooks is equally applicable to the Scriptures. In these, also, the critic will never find an end ; but he who, on the whole, is able to find nourishment and joy in them, will certainly not be troubled upon that account." Savigny's appreciation of the spiritual weakness of the Higher Criticism of the Bible then growing into a force of negation is an important phase of his high and spiritual nature.

Savigny, with his habitually long vision, insisted that "this diffusion of legal science ought to take place, not only amongst the jurists of the learned class, the teachers and writers, but even amongst the practical lawyers." He demands the approximation of theory and practice, and applauds a proposal for free communication between the Faculties of Law and the Courts. Mr. Hayward in a note (p. 149) points out that "from the time of Maximilian, the immediate predecessor of Charles V., the Law Faculties, consisting of the Professors of the German Universities, have constituted Courts of Appeal in the last resort. The appellants, I believe, may select any University they please ; for instance, a case decided in Hanover may be sent to a Prussian University." It will be remembered that Savigny's father sat on one of these University Courts. But Savigny says that in his time these University Courts had become even more mechanical than the regular Courts.

Savigny having shown how the texts or legal authorities can be based "on a profound and comprehensive science," and how the judges may be made efficient, proceeds to deal with the third necessity of an efficient legal system, good procedure. To reform procedure, he says, we must have recourse to the legislature. The legal system so established would moreover derive great assistance from the legislature, which would settle disputed points of law (acting through Orders of Court) and record old customs that have received validity in practice. Then at last the historical matter of law will be transformed into national wealth, and the nation will possess a national system of its own and not "a feeble imitation of the Roman system." Savigny goes on to ask what is to be done under these circumstances with the Landrecht and the Gesetzbuch. It seemed clear that no "real, living jurisprudence" could be founded upon any one of the three Codes or upon the then proposed new German Code. The study of law must go on as if the Codes did not exist; the study, that is, of both the common law and the provincial laws; it must go on in the Universities, and there must be intimate intercourse between all the German Universities.

No one can read Savigny's attack on the Code movement of his age without feeling the immense weight that is due to his opinions. Step by step he urges an unanswerable argument and lays the foundation of the only true system of practical jurisprudence. To-day this work is of peculiar value and interest, for on the one hand we have England, a country that has in fact followed, unconsciously enough but in most exact detail, the lines of development suggested by Savigny, and on the other hand we have the rest of Europe under the dominance of that very system of Codes denounced by the greatest jurist that Europe has produced. Who is right? Savigny, England, and the Anglo-Saxon nations throughout the world, *or* Napoleon and his Europe?

Savigny's Preface, written in September, 1839, to his great work *System des heutigen römischen Rechts* (in eight volumes, five published in 1840-1 and the rest in 1847-9) amplifies with even a broader outlook the views expressed in the first edition of *The Vocation of our Age for Legislation and Jurisprudence* (1814), and repeated in the second edition (1828) of that finely critical essay. The material for the work on *Modern Roman Law* had been "gradually collected and worked up in the courses of instruction" delivered by Savigny for a period of forty years, and the work itself is his ripe and incomparable judgment on the subject. Pleading as he does for "the continuous cultivation" of the science of law, he feels the danger of the accumulation of material.

"To prevent this danger we must desire that from time to time the whole mass of that, which has been handed down to us, should be newly examined, brought into doubt, questioned as to its origin. This will be done by placing ourselves artificially in the position of having to impart the material transmitted, to one unskilled, doubting, controverting. The fitting spirit for such a testing work is one of intellectual freedom, independence of all authority; in order, however, that this sense of freedom may not degenerate into arrogance, there must step in, the natural fruit of an unprejudiced consideration of the narrowness of our own powers, that wholesome feeling of humility which can alone render that freedom of view fruitful of performances of our own. From two wholly opposite standpoints, we are thus directed to one and the same need in our science. It may be described as a periodically recurring examination of the work accomplished by our predecessors, for the purpose of removing the spurious, but of appropriating to ourselves the true as a lasting possession, which will place us in the condition, according to the measure of our powers in the solution of the common problem, of coming nearer to the final aim. To institute such an examination for the point of time, in which we actually are, is the object of the present work."

He goes on to defend "the historical school" (of which he was certainly the most distinguished representative) from the unjust criticism to which it had been subjected. The aim of that school was not (and one may add is not, for to-day the historical school is one of the most important agents of thought in Europe) to "subject the present to the government of the past." The historical view of legal science (and we may say of any science) "consists in the uniform recognition of the value and the independence of each age, and it merely ascribes the greatest weight to the recognition of the living connection which knits the present to the past, and without the recognition of which we recognize merely the external appearance, but do not grasp the inner nature, of the legal condition of the present."

Savigny's object was certainly not to assign an "immoderate mastery" to Roman law, but he claims that a thorough knowledge of that law is indispensable for a comprehension of existing legal conditions. The natural unity between the theory and the practice of law finds its expression in the Roman law, and the study of that law can do much to avoid the disastrous divergence of the practical and the theoretical. But to make the Roman law produce this result we must turn, not to summaries or general principles, but to the writings of the Roman jurists. Such a study will eliminate from law subjective and arbitrary aberrations, and give to law new life even where it exists in the form of a Code. "This is markedly shown by the example of the modern French jurists who, often in a very judicious manner, illustrate and complete their Code from the Roman law." Even in the case of the Prussian Code, if there could be at least a partial re-establishment of "the dissolved connection with the literature of the common law, the result now could be nothing but the arising of a beneficial influence upon practice, and the mischiefs, so sensibly felt at an earlier time, would certainly not recur." The effort to employ Roman law "constantly as a means of culture for our own legal condition" is no depreciation of "our time and our nation," for in view of the enormous accumulation of material we have a greater task than lay before the Roman jurists and we may rightly use their methods. "When we shall have been taught to handle the matter of the law presented to us with the same freedom and mastery as astonishes us in the Romans, then we may dispense with them as models and hand them over to the grateful commemoration of history." Till then we must use a means of culture that we are incapable at present of creating.

With such views in mind, Savigny proceeds to his critical and systematic treatment of Roman private law as it existed in his time. He searches out and rules out all that is dead in Roman law, and then he proceeds to demonstrate the great and living unity of what remains. "In the richness of living reality, all jural relations form a systematic whole." His business is to demonstrate this deep and fundamental relationship, which is apt to disappear when particular fields of law are momentarily in view. The fact of this relationship causes him to give in 1839 an "entirely different shape" to the doctrine of Possession from that presented by him in 1803. For this we must get back to the old jurists. From them we may secure "a vitalizing and enriching of our own juristic thought obtainable in no other way." Savigny says that the work he here performs he would have performed more thoroughly had he begun it in his earlier years. He would have checked his system by exegesis beginning from the Glossators and on through the French school, and by practical examples also derived from the authors of the numerous *Consilia responsa*, etc., also beginning from the Glossators. In this way his system would be checked in detail, and he suggests that some successors of his might undertake this work and give it literary completeness. With some pathos he suggests that it might be done piece by piece. He does not anticipate the coming of giants, of Cujas or another. So he gives his work to the world. The first volume deals with the problem before him, with the nature of law sources in general, with the sources of the modern Roman law, with the interpretation of written laws. The second book deals entirely with jural relations, and the first chapter treats of the nature and kinds of the jural relations. Up to this point we have a translation by Mr. William Holloway, formerly a judge of the Madras High Court. This was issued at Madras in 1807. The eighth volume of the work, a complete treatise on the conflict of laws and private international law, was translated by Mr. William Guthrie of the Scots Bar and published in 1869 (2nd ed. 1880) by Messrs. Clark of Edinburgh. In 1884 Sir William (then Mr.) Rattigan published a translation of the residue of the second book, in which are elaborately discussed "persons as subjects of jural relations." This translation exhibits the thoroughness of Savigny's investigations and his power of systematic grouping of material. For the purposes of this article it is not possible or desirable to discuss the details of a work such as this, with its close investigation into the facts and doctrine of legal capacity, of *Capitis Diminutio* and juristical persons, or as we should say artificial persons (such as corporations) possessing jural relations.

The pressure of public judicial and diplomatic work had long burdened the jurist. Dr. Reddie, in his very admirable volume entitled *Historical Notices of the Roman Law and of the Recent Progress of its Study in Germany*, published at Edinburgh in 1826, a work that traces in valuable detail, based on personal knowledge, the universal activity of the study of law throughout Central Europe at this date, says of Savigny: "A man of genius, he is not only a celebrated professor and judge, but a profound statesman.... Unfortunately for the study and the science in general, the time of von Savigny is too much occupied with the discussion of petty disputes in a kingdom, the attention of whose government is almost entirely directed towards military affairs, and where his labours, however highly valued, can be of little service to mankind at large " (pp. 111-114). It is certain that Savigny did not look at his judicial work in this light. He was descended from a family of soldiers, diplomatists, and lawyers, his son was an eminent diplomatist, and he continually dwells on the need for the closest touch between the theory and the practice of law. As a judge he certainly gave practical law something, but as a jurist there can be little doubt that he gained immense power from it. It kept his theory of law alive, and made the jurist feel in the most vivid sense the reality and the personal importance of his speculations. So important did he regard this class of work that in 1842 he resigned his chair at the University of Berlin and became the Prussian Minister of Justice, a post which he filled with rare ability until the year 1848, when the wave of revolution passed across Europe. In that year he retired and set to work to revise his publications and papers. Fortunately he was allowed long leisure in which to fulfil this important work of revision. Many of his papers are to be found in the *Zeitschrift für geschichtlichen Rechtswissenschaft*, the journal for historical jurisprudence which he founded with the help of Eichhorn and Göschen in 1815, and superintended for many years.[1] Before the great jurist died at Berlin on October 25, 1861, in his eighty-third year (his devoted wife his helper to the last), he could look back over a long vista of accomplished work, and could believe that the future of his beloved science was assured.

It is not possible even yet, half a century after the death of Savigny, to indicate fully his work in the history of the evolution of law, his place among the great jurists of the world. The depository, so to speak, of so many centuries of juristic activity, the forerunner of detailed juristic investigation of so manifold

---

[1] In October, 1850, on the occasion of the universal congratulations upon the completion of the fiftieth year of his doctorate, he issued as a thank-offering and memorial a collection of all the detached papers he had written in that period. The volume was entitled *Vermischte Schriften*. The only omission from it was a review of Glück's *Intestaterbfolge* which appeared in 1804 in the *Jenaische Literaturzeitung*. (See *Law Magazine and Review*, May, 1863, and biographies by Rüdorff and Bethmann-Kollweg.)

a character, it is perhaps as easy to undervalue as to overvalue his services to a science that mysteriously superintends the health and welfare of the social world. For my own part (but I write with hesitation, as one who dares not claim to have entered in any real sense into even a minute portion of the fruits of his cheerfully titanic labours), for my own part I should be tempted to call him the Newton or the Darwin of the science of law. His achievements resemble the achievements of both of these mighty men. He found, as Newton found, a world of phenomena, in his case of juristic phenomena, and he wrestled with it in the true hardihood of the Renaissance through the dark night until the Spirit of the Law cried out, "Let me go, for the day breaketh." It was reserved for Savigny to bring the daylight of the Renaissance to the science of law. He showed us that law itself is subject to law, that it is no arbitrary expression of the will of a law-giver, but is itself a thing obedient to a cosmic process. To show that law is itself the expression of a juristic process that runs through the ages was in itself an achievement of the highest order; but to go on to trace, as Savigny traced, what we may call the natural history of law, to trace its organic growth as a living thing, evolving with the evolutions of races and kingdoms and tongues, was a still greater triumph. When we think of the apparently chaotic mass of material into which Savigny introduced an evolutionary law, or, rather, indicated the processes by which, operating through and in this material, juristic forces adjusted themselves to the needs of successive ages, it is difficult to resist the decision that he stands in the forefront of European thinkers. It is true that his guiding star in his investigations and reductions was the Roman law, but he himself fully realized the importance of other systems of law, the common laws of general and particular customs of European nations, in arriving at general results. But while individual nations had their respective systems of common law, it must be remembered that, down to the Renaissance at any rate, Roman law was the common law of all Europe, a general system of law upon which local systems were more or less successfully grafted. To trace the natural history of Roman law in Europe was the only possible method of arriving at the secret that underlay the whole evolution of law. When once the secret was disclosed, then it was time enough for Savigny himself and his successors to retrace the ground, to reinvestigate sources, to turn the newly discovered processes on those sources, and so to bring into the field of juristic science material of every kind that, until then, had seemed beyond the control or operation of any general law of evolution.

There is no need to claim too much for Savigny. As we have seen, he was not the inventor of the historic method, nor can he claim to have carried that method to its scientific height. Newton and Darwin entered into the ideas and labours of their predecessors, and their supreme conceptions have certainly been applied with a thoroughness that would possibly have astonished the masters themselves. So it was and has been with Savigny. Of his forerunners we have seen something; and even while he was toiling, Semester by Semester, in the congenial work of teaching and judging at Berlin, his fellow-workers and pupils were applying his methods and were methodizing material to his hand. And his and their successors in Germany and England and France have gone far. His friend Niebuhr in 1816 discovered in the chapter library at Verona the priceless palimpsest manuscript of the Institutes of Gaius, the work on which the Institutes of Justinian were based. In 1820 Savigny's pupil Göschen published the first edition of this manuscript. Another pupil, Blume, obtained some further readings from this almost indecipherable palimpsest in 1822-3, and these were included in Göschen's second edition of 1824. The study of this manuscript has gone on until quite recently. Dr. Roby tells us that "Wilhelm Studemund in 1866-68 made a fresh copy of the MS., containing much that had not been previously read, and he published a kind of *facsimile* in 1874, and in conjunction with Paul Krüger a very careful and convenient edition in 1877. In 1878 and 1883 Studemund re-examined the MS., and thus obtained additions and corrections of some importance, which were published in subsequent editions of his and P. Krüger's book." Here, then, was one line of investigation worked out that must have been after the very heart of the master. Another investigation, of perhaps even greater importance from the point of view of the history of evolution of law, has been the work, one might almost say the life-work, of that eminent English scholar Dr. H. J. Roby in reconstructing, with an infinitude of labour that recalls the toil of Cujas and of Savigny, Roman Private Law as it existed in the times of Cicero and of the Antonines. It is a marvellous piece of work, and gives us substantially, if not actually clear of "Byzantine modifications," Roman Private Law as it stood at the time of its highest development (say A.D. 161 to 228). Savigny would have been the first to recognize the supreme importance of establishing this basis from which to trace the long centuries of modification, down even to the law of Holland or Scotland, Ceylon, Egypt or the Cape to-day; and he, too, would have been glad to know of the substantial assistance afforded to Dr. Roby by German scholars, and probably would have enjoyed some of Dr. Roby's not unkindly criticism of certain modern German critical methods. Beside Roby's work must be placed the tireless labours of the immortal Mommsen and his school in unravelling the texts of "law-books, authors, and inscriptions." No doubt vast fields lie open for future scholars in the period behind the Antonines, though much work has already been done in those dark ages. And, again, the field of Roman law in the Middle Ages calls for workers. Maitland's brilliant treatment of Bracton shows how much remains to be done to bring into cultivation the immense field over which Savigny cast his measuring-rod. This is not the place in which even to indicate the area of work, or to mention the work now in progress. But that work and the appreciation of its intensity and its range by great modern scholars show how thorough and how sound were the principles that Savigny laid down. His actual work was titanic, but it is plain enough (now that he has given us the guiding principle) that he but threw open an almost illimitable domain of investigation. As it was with Newton and Darwin, so was it with Savigny.

Sometimes it has caused wonder that a man of such vast intellectual powers should have devoted to law, and Roman law, gifts that might have seemed intended for mankind; for mankind, that is, in some practical and immediate way. The answer, however, is surely not far to seek. Man cannot live by bread alone; and even breadwinners cast their bread upon the waters that it may return after many days. A lawyer, even a jurist, does not appeal to the popular mind. To be a Napoleon does so appeal. Yet probably Napoleon's greatest work was one that brought Savigny, so far as intellect clashes with intellect, into direct conflict with the victor of Jena. The Code Napoléon was attacked by Savigny with a vigour, a swiftness, and a certitude worthy of the great captain himself. And Savigny's pungent criticism stands to this day. In so far as Napoleon's Code has survived and permeated Europe it has tended to diminish the efficiency of law as a thing that grows with a people's growth and reacts on their efficiency. Napoleon's successful enemy, England, strenuously maintained that identical system of legal development advocated by Savigny, with the result that we are approaching an age when codification slowly becomes possible in the sense anticipated by the jurist of Berlin. This illustration of the relation of a jurist to daily life is not without its value. The jurist is greater than the legislator. His function is so to lay down general laws of juridical development that nations in the course of remedial legislation may have a guide which will show them how to adapt that legislation to the needs of the people; how to evolve it from a living legal system; and how to make it stage by stage an expression of the life of the people, and at the same time a guiding force that will lead not only individual peoples but all nations to adopt ever higher standards of conduct, ever closer and closer approximations to the divine laws of righteousness and equity that stand like Platonic patterns towards which the nations turn their eyes. If this is the function of the jurist, then he stands among the great benefactors of the world, and few will doubt that Savigny, whose soul was a very pattern of clarity and charity, will remain a bright particular star as we move farther away from the great nineteenth century and watch through Time's impartial glass the fixed stars that brood over it and by which we guide our fate. The motto of Savigny's family, *Non mihi, sed aliis*, had had a real meaning in the lives of his ancestors. In the case of Savigny himself the words reveal his character, his ideals and his daily task. One of the very greatest of the jurists, he saw underlying all law the law of love.

RUDOLPH VON IHERING

RUDOLPH VON IHERING has often been described as the last of the Romanists. Misleading in some respects, this epithet has much truth in it. His works were so much concerned with Roman law,[1] he propounded so many new ideas as to it, gave so many answers of his own to problems in Roman law, that I wish that the task of describing his labours and estimating their value had fallen to one more conversant than I am with his special subject.

In reading his books, I have felt again and again the need of that close acquaintance with the civil law which comes only with long study. All that I can do is to state certain facts as to his life and a few general conclusions formed in studying with some care Ihering's writings.

There is little to be said about the events of his life; they were few and simple. His was the ordinary life of German professors in days when they were not politicians, and the pursuit of science was an end in itself. Ihering was born August 22, 1818, at Aurich in East Friesland. He was the son of a lawyer, and came of a legal stock. He was educated at Heidelberg, Munich, Göttingen, and Berlin. In 1843 he became a *Privatdocent* at Berlin, the subject upon which he lectured being Roman law. In 1845 he was called to Basle, in 1846 to Rostock, in 1849 to Kiel, and in 1852 to Giessen, where he spent some sixteen years of fruitful activity. He was called in 1868 to Vienna in circumstances honourable to him. It was characteristic of the man that he left Vienna, with its gaieties and distractions, to return to the quiet of Göttingen in 1872, and there he remained, declining to accept invitations to go to Leipsic and Heidelberg. At Göttingen he was very successful as a teacher. His classes were large. As a lecturer he had rare gifts. His own enthusiasm for law he communicated to others.

[1] Puchta died in 1846; Bruns, in 1880; Windscheid, in 1892.

RUDOLPH VON IHERING

He once stood as a candidate for the North German Parliament, but was not elected. He spent the rest of his days at Göttingen, leading the life of a scholar, but not of a recluse. He was an excellent musician, a true lover of art, an enthusiastic gardener. He was a shrewd judge of men, as well as of the best way of laying down wine. An ardent admirer—one might even say an idolater—of Bismarck, he watched with interest and delight the unification of Germany. He was of fiery and energetic temperament, enjoying life, decided in his gestures and demeanour and expressions, and in defence of what he believed right passionate and combative.

Strongly convinced of the need of making jurisprudence practical, he himself had little experience of the work of a lawyer. But when Professor at Basle, he was in close contact with practising lawyers and judges, and he was consulted upon important matters. He had an attractive personality. His influence on men was great. One characteristic must be mentioned at the outset. In all he did, or said, or wrote, there was vitality. He wrote much about the past, but not a page is dead matter.[1] One of his pupils and admirers—and all his pupils were admirers —says of him : "He lives and thinks in the present, and with the present and his surroundings. His intellectual character has the features of his own time as had none of his contemporaries or scarcely anyone since Ulpian and Papinian." The same writer adds : "Er ist der Jurist seines Jahrhunderts und der Zukunft." The man and his works, as his friend Merkel remarks, were of a piece.[2]

He has been called the last of the Romanists, but Roman law was to him a means to an end. His motto was "Through Roman law, but above and beyond it." He insisted that there was no understanding law in the past without comprehending the present.[3] In his eagerness to vivify dead matter he often, it seems to me, found more in Roman law than

---

[1] " Sie lehrten das Recht als die aus praktischen Zweckgedanken geborene Lebensordnung betrachten, welche dem Ideal der Gerechtigkeit nach dem Masse der Einsicht und Kraft jedes Volkes und jeder Zeit zustrebt, zugleich aber als das feine Kunstwerk, welches durch Formenschönheit und sinnvolles Ineinandergreifen der Theile anzieht " (Preface to *Kieler Festgabe*).

[2] In his preface to the *Jahrbücher* (Gesammelte Aufsätze, 1. 26) he says : " Die Aufgabe der Gegenwart gegenüber dem römischen Recht besteht aber nicht bloss im construiren, wovon bisher allein die Rede war, sondern im destruiren." Matters which have outlived their day can have no significance for us.

[3] *Scherz und Ernst*, fourth edition, p. 365.

was there.[1] In many pages he appears to be pouring new wine into old bottles.

His influence was great—great as a teacher, still greater through his writings, which had a circulation larger than that of any other German author writing upon law. He was endowed with a charm of style rarely possessed by lawyers. It has vivacity and dramatic qualities, though, let me add, it is rhetorical and diffuse, and he carries to excess the orator's proclivity to repetition. Gifted with great energy and force of character, he has exercised a profound influence in the face of much opposition from jurists of his own country. He was a scholar and a jurist; but he aspired also to be a philosopher, and he is best known in this country by his works which deal with some of the fundamental questions of jurisprudence—for example, by his *Kampf ums Recht*. He was not an historian in one sense of the term—that is, he was not a systematic investigator of the facts of any one period. He does not conform to the canons which a modern historian as a rule observes. "The real interest of the present counts with me much more than the investigation of the past"; the mood of the reformer rather than that of the unbiassed student of remote times. He is ingenious and prolific in brilliant conjectures; but he is also fantastic, putting little restraint on his ingenuity. Writing much and swiftly, he naturally fell into errors of which his critics made the most. For example, he ascribed to Antoninus Pius a rescript of Caracalla. But he had rare gifts of insight, and divination exemplified in all his works, and not least in his *Schuldmoment im römischen Recht*, in which he seeks to show that criminal law is the kernel of law, and that the history of law shows the continuous *Verdrängung* or expulsion of criminal law. Jurist, historian, ethnologist, philosopher—perhaps I ought to add humorist—he had a singularly wide range of interests and activity.

The following are some of his chief works:

1842. *Dissertatio de hereditate possidenda*.

1844. *Abhandlungen aus dem römischen Rechts*.

1847. *Civilrechtsfälle ohne Entscheidungen*.

1857. *Jahrbucher für die dogmatik des heutigen römischen und deutschen Privatrechts*—a publication which he founded and edited, and to which he contributed much.

1852-1858. *Geist des römischen Rechts*.—This is probably the most valuable and original of his works. It abounds in *esprit*.

---

[1] See *Scherz und Ernst*, p. 108.

It is written with immense knowledge. It is full of original ideas. It vivifies the whole subject. I know no book upon jurisprudence more stimulating or suggestive. It was not well received by the majority of professors of Roman law, who thought it was much too daring and fantastic.[1] In a letter to a friend he says : " It is now more than clear to me that the book finds no favour with all or most people who have got a position."

The book appeared almost contemporaneously with Maine's *Ancient Law*, and it does not suffer from the comparison. But it is diffuse ; there is much repetition ; there is no clear order of exposition. There are many incursions into subjects somewhat remote from law. Thus, in the second book, title 2, s. 39, Ihering treats of the participation of the State in the property of the individual and the social effects of slavery. He writes often in the spirit of the advocate. One side is presented with vividness and even passion ; the other is almost ignored. I might refer as an example to his eulogy of the Roman family and the working of the *patria potestas*, and his blindness to its defects. With all its imperfections, this is a singularly original work. The second book, title 3, dealing with *jus strictum* and the formalism of ancient law, is a storehouse of new ideas. So, too, are the remarks on fictions and their use.

1867. *Das Schuldmoment im römischen Privatrecht*.—A singularly brilliant study, which brings out the fact that the history of punishment is one of gradual decay, and that progress consists in a restriction of its province. The two main results of the author's investigations are—first, as to the power of ideas silently to affect, mould, and revivify law ; secondly, displacement of punishment as an element in law—" wenn die Idee des Rechts wächst sterben die Strafen ab, der Aufwand von Strafmitteln steht im ungekehrten Verhältniss zu der Vollkommenheit der Rechtsordnung und der Reife der Völker " (p. 67).[2]

1868. *Ueber den Grund des Besitzesschutzes*.

1870. *Die Jurisprudenz des täglichen Lebens*.—A collection of

---

[1] " Ueberfluss an Phantasie," " Mangel an Methode," were some of the criticisms of his contemporaries.

[2] " Die Geschichte der Strafe ist ein fortwährendes Absterben derselben. Der Anfang des Rechts ist die Uebermacht des Strafbegriffs, das Strafelement durchdringt das ganze Recht, alle Verhältnisse desselben sind mit ihm mehr oder weniger versetzt ; der Fortschritt des Rechts besteht in einer fortgesetzten Einengang des Gebiets und einer fortgesetzten Reinigung des Begriffs der Strafe " (p. 4). It is a short history of the principle " Ohne Schuld keine Verantwortlichkeit " (p. 20).

questions or cases for discussion, which has been translated into English by Professor Goudy.

1872. *Kampf ums Recht.*—To many Ihering is known only by this brochure—a work which has been translated into several languages, and has passed through many editions. It seeks to prove that it is the duty of the citizen to assert his rights, and that law triumphs by such assertion.[1] In fighting for his rights, every man is a champion of the law in the interests of society. This clever pamphlet is an exaggeration—and, as such, characteristic of the author—of one side of morality and law. It cannot be regarded as a scientific study of great value.

1877-1883. *Der Zweck im Recht.*—This is the most ambitious of Ihering's works—the one by which he would have desired to be judged—and intended by him to embody the substance of his teaching. He had closed his *Geist des römischen Rechts* by a refutation of the Hegelian doctrine that the essence of law was the expression of the general will. Utility, not will, was its essence. Ulpian had said as much : " Jus privatum quod ad singulorum utilitatem spectat." In other words, rights are interests judicially protected—an idea which Ihering proceeds to develop. It is impossible to describe adequately the varied contents of the two volumes, which, full of ideas, have the defect of all Ihering's works—great diffuseness—and which range over many subjects akin to, but outside, law. The motto of the book —" the *telos* or purpose is the creator of all law "—indicates the main argument of the book.[2] At the outset he draws a distinction between cause (*causa efficiens, Ursache*) operating in the physical world and object or purpose (*causa finalis, Zweck*) operating on the will. In the former there is no action without a cause (*Ursache*) ; in the latter no *Wollen*, or, what is the same, no act without a purpose (*Zweck*) (i. 5) ; or, as he expresses it, conduct is determined not by a " because," but by a " for." Without a purpose the will does not act. Then come a study of human aims or motives (*Systematik der menschlichen Zwecke*), which fall into two great groups—the individual and the social (*die des Individuums und die der Gemeinschaft*). The egoistic motives for social action are two—reward (*Lohn*) in its large sense and force (*Zwang*). The social motives are

---

[1] " Das Ziel des Rechts ist der Friede, das Mittel dazu, der Kampf." " Das Leben des Rechts ist Kampf, ein Kampf der Völker, der Staatwalt, der Stände, der Individuen." " In Kampfe sollst Du dein Recht finden."

[2] " Der Zweck ist der Schöpfer des ganzen Rechts."

two also—the sense of duty and love. Each of these motives is analyzed. For example, in c. 5 is an analysis of the different forms of force (*Zwang*). What is the object of law? Ihering's answer is not unlike that of Austin; its essence is force. "Ich das Recht inhaltlich definire als die Form der durch die Zwangsgewalt des Staates beschafften Sicherung des Lebensbedingungen der Gesellschaft." In other words, law is the securing by the State of the essential conditions of soci.ty. The means of attaining such conditions are extra-legal (*ausserer rechtliche*), the mixed legal (*gemischtrechtliche*), and the purely legal. The necessary conditions are the preservation of life, its continuance, work, and intercourse of mankind[1] (i. 453).

The second volume deals with morals, including teleology (ii. 135) and the theory of morals (ii. 243). The last chapters are devoted to a study of courtesy or *Höflichkeit* (ii. 480)—chapters rich in acute observations respecting manners, dress, symbolism, and speech. As illustrative of the wide range of the inquiry, it may be mentioned that the last chapter deals with the syntax of *Höflichkeit* (i. 701)—for example, the use of "thou" and "du"—and is full of discriminating and original observations. In the field of philosophy Ihering was, as he admits, somewhat of a dilettante. Contrasting his exposition with those of the best writers on psychology who treat of the will, one sees the imperfections of Ihering's analysis.[2] He greatly exaggerates the part of the conscious causes of action. He forgets the large part which is determined by accumulated energy, or by the blind natural impulses, such as sexual love, fear of death, etc.[3] For Ihering, law is the protection by force of "interests." It is left somewhat uncertain what are "interests" or what species of "interests" are protected. Obviously, some "interests," and among those some of the most important—*e.g.*, scientific truth—are not so protected.

1879. *Vermischte Schriften juristischen Inhalts*.

1881. *Gesammelte Aufsätze*.—The three volumes, consisting of reproductions of Ihering's articles in the *Jahrbücher des heutigen und römischen und deutschen Privatrechts*,[4] contain an interesting preface to the periodical in which he pleads for "a receptive

---

[1] "Selbsterhaltungstrieb, Geschlechtstrieb, Erwerbstrieb, sind die drei mächtigen Bundesgonessen der Gesellschaft," etc. (i. 453).
[2] *E.g.*, Bain's *Emotions and the Will*, fourth edition, p. 333 *et seq.*
[3] See Wundt, *Philosophische Studies*, vi. 585; also Wundt, *Logik*, iii. 588 n
[4] A periodical which he and Von Gerber started in 1857.

and productive jurisprudence," and in which he distinguishes between higher and lower jurisprudence, the former concerned with legal conceptions instead of legal rules, the latter constructive as well as critical. "Die höhere Jurizprudenz ist nicht bloss Bildnerin des Stoffs, sondern auch Schöpferin" (i. 12). The collection also includes articles on risk in sale contracts ("Gefahr beim Kaufcontract"), "culpa in contrahendo oder Schadenersatz bei nichtigen oder nicht zur Perfection gelangten Verträgen," the limitation on property in land in the interest of adjoining proprietors ("zur Lehre von den Beschränkungen des Grundeigenthümers in Interesse der Nachbarn").

Das Trinkgeld is a juridical and economic study of what Ihering describes as a form of begging—"eine durch die Sitte organisirte Art des Bettelei" (p. 50)—a habit which everyone who has at heart the public welfare should do his best to stop (p. 52).

1885. *Scherz und Ernst in der Jurisprudenz.*—A collection of essays and articles, or, according to the subtitle, "Confidential Letters upon Jurisprudence of the Day by an Unknown." Ihering's conception of humour may not be to the taste of all, but the letters are full of excellent sense. They enforce with emphasis and ingenuity the need of close relation between law and practice and of improvements in legal education. The chapter entitled "Im juristischen Begriffshimmel: Ein Phantasiebild," is a satire or humorous sketch which Jean Paul Richter might have penned.

1889. *Der Besitzwille, or Possessory Intention.*—One of the many contributions to a controversy which has engaged German jurists from the time of **Niebuhr** and **Savigny**, and later Bruno, Pernice, Kuntze, and many others.

Ihering published in 1868 in the *Jahrbücher für Dogmatik* an article, "Ueber den Grund des Besitzschutzes." In 1889 appeared his mature work, *Der Besitzwille, zugleich eine Kritik der herrschenden juristischen Methode*. It was one of the many attempts to find unity in the rules of Roman law on the subject and an explanation of the difference between *possessio* and *detentio;* of the fact that possession, as distinguished from property, was protected by actions. The Roman jurists had said: "Any kind of possessor, by the very fact that he is possessor, has more right than one who does not possess." Why is this ? Why is protection given not only in the case of the owner, but also of one who is not so, and who knows he is not so ? A generally accepted answer was that of Savigny:

the possession which is protected depends on the *animus domini*. The violation of possession is a violation of the person. For Ihering possession is the outwork of the fortress of property. In his later (1889) treatment of the subject, Ihering combats the " will theory " of possession in its many forms. He set up an objective theory, and he concludes that possession is not a mere fact, but a species of right.[1] Of Ihering's treatment of this subject it may at least be said that he recognizes more clearly than most writers the historical and, so to speak, accidental elements and origin of some of the distinctions in Roman law between those who had and those who had not possessory remedies;[2] that the subject was not discussed in a purely abstract fashion ; and that he had always in view the practical effect of the rules which he discusses. He did not attempt to devise a " Monstrum Begriff " (to quote Feuerbach's phrase) which would fit all uses of the term possession.

1894. His posthumous works, *Vorgeschichte der Indo-Europäer und Entwickelungsgeschichte des römischen Rechts.*—His *Vorgeschichte der Indo-Europäer* grew out of a plan for the history of the development of Roman law. The first book was to deal with the early times, which led him to a consideration of the condition of the early Aryan people and their law. "My profession—that of Roman law—caused me to study the ancient history of the European nations. I desired to discover clearly how the Romans treated their legal institutions, which they had derived from the original nation—what they kept and what they altered . . ."; and so, with the aid of philology, he endeavoured to spell out the laws, customs, and organization of the primitive people, the ancestors of the Indo-Europeans. The *Entwickelungsgeschichte* was unfinished. The draft of his work, edited by Ehrenberg, contains an introduction as to the task and method of legal history, together with an unfinished part relating to the Roman family. The *Einleitung* also contains a strong protest against the theory of the unconscious growth of law (p. 14) as "reines Phantasiegebilde " (p. 27).

To understand Ihering's teaching, we must know his time and the circumstances in which he wrote. He came after the influ-

---

[1] For a clear account of the various theories, see Girard's *Manuel Élémentaire de Droit Romain*, 3rd ed., p. 266.

[2] The theory of the canon law as to possession was different from that of the Roman law. See Pollock and Maitland, II. 41, and as to modern treatment of the subject, the *Swiss Civil Code*, Articles 919 to 941.

ence of Hegelianism upon law had reached its height, and at the close of a period when (to quote his own words) everyone who dared to question Hegel's decrees was looked down upon with supreme contempt. He desired to lay a philosophical basis for jurisprudence; he found it neither in Hegel nor in Krause. The purely speculative works on law were repugnant to him, and he covered them with ridicule.[1] Ihering followed a succession of eminent jurists. Puchta, his teacher, had died in 1846. Savigny, who influenced him profoundly, lived on until 1861; but his work had been completed long before. In some respects a continuer of Savigny, he was also in others an opponent. He always spoke with admiration of Savigny's services to jurisprudence, not so much on account of his historical researches as by reason of his reaction against the conception of a "natural" immutable law and of his having drawn together science and life (*Annäherung der Wissenschaft und des Lebens*). Ihering parted company with the historical school at many points. It tended to beget a kind of fatalism, to estrange law from present life, to exaggerate the national element and ignore the universal. He did not believe that law was merely the outcome of unconscious forces,[2] in which the efforts of individuals counted for little. He said, no doubt truly, that "the law of Nature" of the "Aufklärung" period was only an idealization of existing conditions; but he also maintained that it is the idea of universality which gives the character and the key to the present phase of law. "It was with a correct instinct for this trend and drift of modern law that the natural law school proclaimed its doctrine of the universality of law elevated above time and place" (*Geist des römischen Rechts*, i. 15). He had no liking for a purely territorial or national development of law. "The life of a nation is no isolated existence side by side, but, like that of individuals in a State, a common life, a system of reciprocal contact and influence, peaceful and hostile, a giving and taking, borrowing and bestowing—in short, a vast business of exchange that embraces every side of human existence."[3]

[1] See his essay in *Scherz und Ernst* on "Die spekulative Methode in der Jurisprudenz—Huschke, Lassalle," p. 17.
[2] "Das Recht ist kein Ausfluss des naiv im dunklem Drang schaffenden Rechtsgefühls, jenes mystischen Vorgangs, welcher dem Rechtshistoriker jeder weitere Untersuchung abschneiden und ersparen würde, sondern es ist das Werk menschlicher Absicht und Berechnung," etc. (Preface to *Jahrbücher*, p. 28).
[3] See *Scherz und Ernst*, fourth edition, p. 341.

Not less averse was he to the "fanaticism of juristic construction," which "infers that whatever does not suit it is impossible, and whatever does is necessary." He is constantly protesting against the excessive importance given to mere logical expressions of law and the absurdity of treating jurisprudence as if it were a sort of legal mathematics. He had a craving for actuality; he could not abide phantasies severed from facts. It was characteristic of him that he dismissed the brilliant theories in Lassalle's *System der Erworbenen Rechte* with the remark: "Speculation begins where human understanding ceases. To qualify for it one must never have had any intelligence or have lost it."[1]

Ihering had obvious defects. We miss in him the precision or conciseness of Dernburg. He had not the rare combination of gifts as an investigator of Mommsen. He was widely read in some directions, but, as one of his biographers remarks, his erudition was one-sided. Some of his original ideas do not bear the test of calm examination; they seem the effusions of a brilliant improviser rather than the results of a careful balancing of evidence. For example, he mentions the circumstance that there was no legal profession at Rome as with us, and he launches into a diatribe against *honoraria* as the curse of modern jurisprudence. *Honoraria* are the sources of frivolous and interminable lawsuits, the cause of the existence of jurists devoid of taste, without love of their art, without talents or intelligence. Money soils and debases their profession. The veteran jurist writes in the same strain as Ruskin or Tolstoy, and yet he admits that *honoraria* are necessary.[2] I might refer as an example of the many novel ideas which he threw out, often without due consideration, to his theory as to certain rights not belonging to or residing in any person. It was characteristic of this impulsive and discursive writer that he never completed his two chief works.[3]

Since the passing of the Civil Code there is a great gulf between jurists such as Ihering, whose writings were, for the most part, based upon or suggested by Roman law, and the present generation; but he who would dig deep and know the foundations of law must still turn to Ihering.

[1] *Scherz und Ernst*, fourth edition, p. 34.
[2] *Geist des römischen Rechts*, II., Part 1, title 3, c. ii.
[3] His theory as to mistakes in contracts is embodied in the German Code, Articles 119, 120.

INDEX

ALARIC II., makes use of institutes of Gaius, 10
Albericus Gentilis, 109–143
    acquaintance with Sir Philip Sidney and the Earl of Leicester, 110
    father of modern International Law, 109, 114
    his conception of the Law of Nations, 118–121
    latter-day appreciations of, 111, 112
    life of, 109–112
    position of, as a jurist, 114–118
    value of the work of, 142, 143
    views of, as to International relations, 121 *et seq.*
    works of, 112–114
Alciati, Andrea, 58–82
    as a reformer, 78–82
    founder of the Comparative Method of Jurisprudence, 58, 80–82
    life of, 69–76
    writings of, and their character, 76–78
Alexander Severus, friendship with Ulpian, 36, 37
    judicial work of, 37
America, influence of Montesquieu in, 437
American opinion of Lord Stowell, 522
Augustine, influence of the *De Civitate Dei* of, on the Social Theory of Vico, 376, 377
Augustus, Emperor, and licensed Prudentes, 23, 24

Austin, opinion of, in regard to Ulpian, 42
    opinion of, in regard to Savigny's *Das Recht des Besitzes*, 568
Authority of the *Responsa Prudentium*, 24, 25, 27, 28

Bacon, Francis, 144–168
    and the law of nature, 165, 166
    and the Sale of Judicial Offices, 148–151
    appreciation of, as a jurist, 155
    argument of, in Calvin's Case, 163–165
    argument of, in Chudleigh's case, 161–163
    career of, at the Bar, 147, 148
    his work in the Court of Chancery, 167, 168
    influence of, as a constitutional lawyer, 166, 167
    intimacy with Hobbes, 195
    legal works of, 156–158
    Maxims and Digest of, 151–153, 159–161
Bacon, Sir Nicholas, 144, 145
Bartolus, 45–57
    and the Glossators, 47, 48
    authority of, 50, 51
    compared with Ulpian, 45
    influence of, on the theory of Statutes, 52–55
    lucerna juris, xxiii
    personal history, 48–50
    the teaching of, 51–55
    works of, 55, 56

602 INDEX

Bartolus, works of, the influence of, at the present day, 56, 57
Beccaria, Cæsar Bonesana, Marquis di, 505–516
    appreciations of, 507–510
    his essay on Crimes and Punishments, 506, 507
    influence of, 510, 514–516
Ben Jonson, friendship with Selden, 186, 187
    his lines on Selden, 188
Bentham, Jeremy, 532–543
    his conception of justice, 200
    his debt to Beccaria, 513
    his ignorance of legal history, 532, 533
    his ignorance of Roman and Continental Law, 533, 534
    his influence, 542, 543
    his influence on criminal law, 540, 541
    on law of evidence, 533
    on Montesquieu, 437 *note*
    on reported cases of English law, 534
Brown, Mr. Jethro, on Hobbes, 217
Burke, Edmund, Bentham's meeting with, 535
Bynkershoek, xxii, 390–416
    his method of treatment, 391, 392
    his views as to what is the basis of International Law, 396–398
    outline of life, 390
    relation of, to his predecessors, 392–396
    summary of views on various subjects connected with International Law, 398–416
    works of, 390, 391

Calvin's Case, 153, 163–165
Cantù, Cæsar, on Beccaria, 511, 512
Caracalla and Geta, struggle between, 33
Caracalla and Geta, Civitas Romana conferred on freeborn subjects of Rome by, 21
    murder of Papinian by, 20
Chitty, Mr. Joseph, on Vattel, 477
Chudleigh's Case, 161–163
Code Napoléon, Savigny on the, 575–578
Codification of English law, Bacon's plea, 158–160
    of French law by Colbert, 260–280
    of German law advocated by Thibaut, 575
    Savigny on, 579 *et seq.*
    views of Leibnitz, 296, 297
Coke, Hobbes' criticism of, 204, 211, 212, 215, 216
Colbert, Jean Baptiste, 248–282
    life of, 252–259
    work of, 259–280
Commentators of the Middle Ages, 48, 65–67
Consolato del Mare, 414, 415
Court of Chancery and its corruption, 148–151
Crown ordinances in France, 456, 457
Cujas, Jacques, 83–108, 564, 565
    and the Renaissance, 85–89
    accomplishments and methods as a lecturer, 94
    contemporaries of, 102–106
    life of, 89–94
    method of, 98–102
    study of law in France before, 83–85
    works of, and their character, 95
    works of, and their result, 107, 108
Customary law of France after the sixteenth century, 450–456

Desiderata of Leibnitz, xxi, 296
Doctor and Student passage on the law of nature cited, 209, 210
Dumoulin, Charles, 105, 106, 458, 459

English law, development of, xxii
Evolution of law, xxiv

Gaius, 1–16
  conjectures as to his identity, 2–5
  conjectures as to his nationality and vocation, 5, 6
  discovery of Institutes by Niebuhr, 12, 13.
  evidence as to date of, 4, 5
  legal works of, 8, 9
  present-day estimate as to the value of, 14–16
  testimony of, as to the nature and effect of the *Responsa Prudentium*, 25, 26
  works obtain the force of law, 8, 9
Gentilis, Albericus. See Albericus Gentilis
Gibbon, opinion of Montesquieu, 436, 437 *note*
Glossators, the, 11, 47, 48, 62–65
Grimm, Wilhelm, on Savigny as a teacher, 566
Grotius, Hugo, 169–184
  character of, 177, 178
  death of, 176, 177
  De Jure Belli et Pacis of, 178–182, 393
  influence of *De Jure Belli et Pacis* of, on Vico, 362, 363
  early precocity, 170, 171
  exile and residence in France, 174–176
  religious tendencies, 172–174
  school of, 394
  works of, 182–184
Guenoux, M. Charles, on Savigny as a teacher, 567
  on Savigny's *Das Recht des Besitzes*, 570

Hadrian, Rescript of, concerning the *Responsa Prudentium*, 24, 25
Hegel, 594, 597, 598

Heliogabalus, Emperor of Rome, and Ulpian, 35
Hobbes, Thomas, 195–219
  and the construction of written law, 214, 215
  and the law, 212–217
  as a jurist, 217–219
  criticism of Coke, 204, 211, 212, 215, 216
  intimacy with Bacon, 195
  obligations to Selden and Christopher St. German, 208
  outline of life, 195, 196
  Social Philosophy of, 195, 196
  the lawyer, 203, 204
Homeric Poems, Vico on their origin, 388
Hugo, Gustave, 565–567
Huschke, Eduard, theory of, concerning Gaius, 6, 7
Hypothetical Cases of the *prudentes*, 22, 23

Ibn Khaldoun, his view of history, 377, 378
Ihering, 590–599
  and Gaius, 15, 16
  his *Geist des Römischen Rechts*, 445, 446
  influence of, 592
  on the Theory of Possession, 596, 597
  the last of the Romanists, 591, 592
  works of, 592–597
Imperial Rescripts, Papinian drafts, 18
Institutes of Gaius, 8, 9
  character and nature of, 13, 14
International Law, Bentham on, 541
  summary of Albericus Gentilis's views on, 118–142
  summary of Bynkershoek's views on, 398–416
  summary of Zouche's views on, 230–245

Jefferson, Thomas, President of the United States, 437, 443
Jerome, epistles of, written over the text of the Institutes of Gaius, 12
Judicial Offices, Sale of, in the sixteenth century, 148-151
Jurisprudence, decline of Roman, after Ulpian's death, 40, 41
    Leibnitz's conception of, 298-301
    Mittermaier and the comparative school of, 560
    Montesquieu and the historical school of, 434, 435
    psychology and, xxiii
    Savigny on the object of the historical school of, 580, 582
    sociology and, xxiii
    the comparative school of, 439, 440, 444
    Vico on the value of, 358
Justinian, Digest of, 42, 43
    incorporation of works of Ulpian in the Institutes of, 40

Kant, and the laws of Nature, 202, 203

Law and religion, xxiv
Law of Nature, course of development of, 289-293
    Doctor and Student and, 209, 210
    explained and expounded in Plowden's Reports, 205-207
    Francis Bacon and, 165, 166
    Grotius and, 180, 181
    Hobbes and, 197-202
    Kant and, 202, 203
    Pufendorf and, 294-307
    Selden and, 208
    Ulpian and, 41, 42
    Vattel and, 488-490, 494-496
    religious origin of, xxiii
Lecky, W. E. H., on Beccaria, 513
Leges Barbarorum, 10, 59, 60

Legis actiones, 26, 27
Leibnitz, 283-304, xxiii
    as an historian, 302
    as an international lawyer, 301, 302, 395
    as a jurist, 298-301
    as a politician, 302, 303
    a "universal reconciler," 298
    character of, 303, 304
    criticism of Pufendorf, 292
    aesiderata, catalogue of, xxi, 298
    Law and Philosophy of, 292
    legal works of, 287-292
Leminier, M., on Beccaria, 508
    on Cujas, 564
Lesley Stephen, Sir, on Hobbes, 195, 196, 197
    on Rousseau, 429 *note*
Lex Citationum of Theodosius and the *Responsa Prudentium*, 28, 29
Livy, Vico on, 372

Mackintosh, Sir James, opinion of Grotius's *De Jure Belli et Pacis*, 181
Maine, Henry, on Montesquieu, 437
    on the value of Roman law, 386, 387
Mittermaier, 544-560
    outline of life of, 544-548, 555-559
    remarks of, on English, Scotch, and American Criminal Procedure, 550-553
    teaching of, 559
    works of, 548-550
Mommsen, Theodor, 588
    theory of, concerning Gaius, 5, 6
Montesquieu, 417-446
    Bentham on, 437 *note*
    chief works of, 420
    foreign travel, 424-426
    his description of the origin and development of his *Spirit of Laws*, 427
    influence of, at present day, 417
    influence of his *Spirit of Laws*, 435-438
    outline of his life, 418-420

Montesquieu, speculations as to views of, regarding present-day conditions, 440–445
theories of, 427, 428

Napoleon and Montesquieu's *Spirit of Laws*, 438
Nationality and Domicile, Zouche on, 233, 234
Niebuhr, discovery of Institutes of Gaius by, 12, 13

Papinian, 17–31
   excellence of, as a jurist, 21
   honours conferred on, 18
   Imperial Rescripts and, 18
   Quæstiones and *Responsa* of, 19
   relationship to Septimius Severus, 17
   the Feast of, 30
Persian letters of Montesquieu, 421–424
Plowden, Edmund, 204, 205
Pollock, Sir Frederick, and the *Doctor and Student*, 210
Pothier, 447–476
   and the Code Napoléon, 576, 577
   his reconstruction of the Pandects, 464, 465
   method of teaching, 466
   outline of life of, 447, 449
   summary of his works, 467–469
   Traité des Obligations of, 472–475
Prudentes, the, and their hypothetical cases, 22, 23
   and the licence of Emperor Augustus, 23, 24
   both teachers and counsel, 27
   conflicts of opinion between, 28, 29
   Rescript of Hadrian as to, 24, 25
   testimony of Gaius as to, 25, 26
   Theodosius and, 28, 29
   the value of the work of, 30, 31
Prussian Landrecht, Savigny's criticism of, 578, 579, 581
Pufendorf, 305–344
   chief works of, 308–311

Pufendorf, his *De Jure Naturæ et Gentium*, 310
   his theory of natural law, 311 et seq.
   Leibnitz's criticism of, 292
   life of, 305–347
   on treaties of peace, alliances, and other conventions, 338–340
   opinion of, and his works, 341–343

Quæstiones and *Responsa* of Papinian 19

Reddie, Dr., on Savigny, 584, 585
Robespierre and Montesquieu's *Spirit of Laws*, 438
Robinson, Dr., reports of Lord Stowell's decisions, 521, 522
Roby, Dr., 587, 588
Roman jurisprudence and its decline after Ulpian, 40, 41
   development of, by the jurists, 22
   in the East after the death of Justinian, 10, 11, 58, 59
   in the West after the death of Justinian, 11, 12, 59–62
   Renaissance of, 67–69
   revival of, in second half of the eleventh century, 61, 62
   study of, in Middle Ages, 47
Romilly, Sir Samuel, 515

Savigny, Frederick Carl von, 445, 561–589
   accepts Chair of Law at the University of Berlin, 572
   and Ulpian's theory of *Ius Naturale*, 41, 42
   early education, 562
   his capacity as a teacher, 566, 567
   his place as a jurist, 585–589

Savigny, his work on the Right of Possession, 568–570
　on the Code Napoléon, 575–578
　on the history of Roman law in the Middle Ages, 573–575
　treatment of Roman private law, 583, 584
Selden, John, 185–194
　birthplace and early years, 185, 186
　his chosen motto, 189
　living laborious days, 187, 188
　monograph on the Judicial Combat, 187, 188
　on the Law of Nature, 208
　opinion of, concerning marriage, 191
　political life of, 189
　sketch of, by Lord Clarendon, 189
　the Society of Antiquaries, 186, 187
　wit and wisdom of, 192, 193
　works of, 188, 189
Septimius Severus and Papinian, 17
Social Contract, the, 197, 199, 200, 370
Sociology, 375, 376
　and jurisprudence, xxiii
Spirit of Laws of Montesquieu, 427
　reasons for its great influence, 431–434
Stowell, Lord, 517–531
　life, 517–521
　on freedom from search of convoyed ships, 525, 526
　on illegality of trading with enemy during war, 527
　on slavery, 524, 525
　on the Jewish law of marriage, 523, 524
　on the Scottish law of marriage, 523
　on trade domicile in war, 527–529

Theodosius, Emperor, publishes his *Lex Citationum*, 28, 29
Theory of Statutes, the, as propounded by the Post-Glossators, 53–55
　the influence of Bartolus on, 52–55
Thibaut, 575, 580
Thirty Years' War, the, 227, 394, 395
Thucydides, Vico on, 372
Twelve Tables, the, Vico on their origin, 387

Ulpian, 32–44
　banished by Heliogabalus, 35
　compared with Bartolus, 45
　decline of Roman jurisprudence after the death of, 40, 41
　friendship with Alexander Severus, 36, 37
　literary activity of, 33, 34
　political conditions of his age, 32, 33
　publishes his treatise *Ad Edictum* and *Libri ad Sabinum*, 33, 34
　qualities as a jurist, 38, 39
　style of the works of, 39, 40
　theory of, as to *Ius Naturale*, 41–43

Valentinian III. and Gaius, 8, 9
Vattel, 477–504
　examination of the *Observations* of, 480–491
　on sovereignty, 496–502
　on the end and aim of Being, 482
　outline of life of, 478–480
　views on international law, 502–504
　views on the law of Nature, 488–490, 494–496
Vico, 345–389
　academic speeches of, 356–362
　his juristic and moral philosophy, 362

Vico, his social theory, 367, 368, 376, 378
   life of, 348–352
   on civil law, 369, 370
   on history, 371–374, 381
   on the origin of languages, 380, 381
   state of Naples at birth of, 346, 347
   the religion of, 353, 354
   the teaching of, 354, 355

Wolff, M. le Baron de, criticism of, by Vattel, 481–486

Zeitgeist, the, xxi
Zouche, 220–247
   and Roman law, 225, 226
   method and general treatment, 227–229
   outline of his life, 220
   relation of, to his age, 226, 227, 393, 394
   relation of, to his English predecessors, 222–224
   value of his work, 245–247
   views on International Law, 230–245
   writings of, 221, 222

www.ingramcontent.com/pod-product-compliance
Lightning Source LLC
Chambersburg PA
CBHW032011230426

43671CB00005B/50